ENLIGHTENMENT AND RELIGION IN GERMAN AND AUSTRIAN LITERATURE

LEGENDA

LEGENDA is the Modern Humanities Research Association's book imprint for new research in the Humanities. Founded in 1995 by Malcolm Bowie and others within the University of Oxford, Legenda has always been a collaborative publishing enterprise, directly governed by scholars. The Modern Humanities Research Association (MHRA) joined this collaboration in 1998, became half-owner in 2004, in partnership with Maney Publishing and then Routledge, and has since 2016 been sole owner. Titles range from medieval texts to contemporary cinema and form a widely comparative view of the modern humanities, including works on Arabic, Catalan, English, French, German, Greek, Italian, Portuguese, Russian, Spanish, and Yiddish literature. Editorial boards and committees of more than 60 leading academic specialists work in collaboration with bodies such as the Society for French Studies, the British Comparative Literature Association and the Association of Hispanists of Great Britain & Ireland.

The MHRA encourages and promotes advanced study and research in the field of the modern humanities, especially modern European languages and literature, including English, and also cinema. It aims to break down the barriers between scholars working in different disciplines and to maintain the unity of humanistic scholarship. The Association fulfils this purpose through the publication of journals, bibliographies, monographs, critical editions, and the MHRA Style Guide, and by making grants in support of research. Membership is open to all who work in the Humanities, whether independent or in a University post, and the participation of younger colleagues entering the field is especially welcomed.

SELECTED ESSAYS

Each title in *Selected Essays* presents influential, but often scattered, papers by a major scholar in the Humanities. While these essays will, we hope, offer a model of scholarly writing, and chart the development of an important thinker in the field, the aim is not retrospective but to gather a coherent body of work as a tool for future research. Each volume contains a new introduction, framing the debate and reflecting on the methods used.

Selected Essays is curated by Professor Susan Harrow (University of Bristol).

Managing Editor
Dr Graham Nelson, 41 Wellington Square, Oxford OX1 2JF, UK

www.legendabooks.com

Enlightenment and Religion in German and Austrian Literature

RITCHIE ROBERTSON

LEGENDA
Selected Essays 1
Modern Humanities Research Association
2017

Published by Legenda
an imprint of the Modern Humanities Research Association
Salisbury House, Station Road, Cambridge CB1 2LA

ISBN 978-1-781884-65-2

First published 2017

Copy-Editor: Richard Correll

CONTENTS

TO KATHARINE

LIST OF SOURCES

The essays presented here originally appeared as follows, and are reprinted with the kind permission of the publishers.

'Freedom and Pragmatism: Aspects of Religious Toleration in Eighteenth-Century Germany', *Patterns of Prejudice*, 32.3 (1998), 69–80. Published by Taylor & Francis.

'Virtue versus "Schwärmerei" in Lessing's *Emilia Galotti*', *German Life and Letters*, 62 (2009), 39–52. Published by Blackwell.

'Literary Techniques and Aesthetic Texture in *Faust*', in *Goethe's Faust I and II: A Companion*, ed. by Paul Bishop (Rochester, NY: Camden House, 2001), pp. 1–27

'Schiller and the Jesuits', in *Schiller: National Poet, Poet of Nations*, ed. by Nicholas Martin (Amsterdam: Rodopi, 2006), pp. 179–200

'*Wallenstein*', in *Friedrich Schiller: Playwright, Poet, Philosopher, Historian*, ed. by Paul Kerry (Bern: Peter Lang, 2007), pp. 251–72

'Women Warriors and the Origin of the State: Werner's *Wanda* and Kleist's *Penthesilea*', in *Women and Death: Warlike Women in the German Literary and Cultural Imagination since 1500*, ed. by Sarah Colvin and Helen Watanabe-O'Kelly (Rochester, NY: Camden House, 2009), pp. 61–85

'Joseph II in Cultural Memory', in *Cultural Memory and Historical Consciousness in the German-Speaking World since 1500*, ed. by David Midgley and Christian Emden (Bern: Peter Lang, 2004), pp. 209–28

'Curiosity in the Austrian Enlightenment', *Oxford German Studies*, 38 (2009), 129–42. Maney Publishing.

'Johann Pezzl (1756–1823): Enlightenment in the Satirical Mode', in *Enlightenment and Catholicism in Europe: A Transnational History*, ed. by Jeffrey D. Burson and Ulrich L. Lehner (Notre Dame, IN: University of Notre Dame Press, 2014), pp. 227–45

'Joseph Rohrer and the Bureaucratic Enlightenment', in *The Austrian Enlightenment and its Aftermath* (*Austrian Studies*, 2), ed. by Ritchie Robertson and Edward Timms (Edinburgh: Edinburgh University Press, 1991), pp. 22–42

'Poetry and Scepticism in the Wake of the Austrian Enlightenment: Blumauer, Grillparzer, Lenau', in *The Austrian Lyric* (*Austrian Studies*, 12), ed. by Judith Beniston and Robert Vilain (London: Maney Publishing for the Modern Humanities Research Association, 2004), pp. 17–43

'Cosmopolitanism, Patriotism and Nationalism in the German and Austrian Enlightenment', in *Enlightenment Cosmopolitanism*, ed. by David Adams and Galin Tihanov (London: Legenda, 2011), pp. 12–30

'Hoffmann's *Die Elixiere des Teufels* and the Lasting Appeal of Conspiracy Theories', *Limbus: Australian Yearbook of German Literary and Cultural Studies*, 5 (2012), 11–31. Published by Rombach Verlag

'Faith and Fossils: Annette von Droste-Hülshoff's poem "Die Mergelgrube"', in *Das schwierige 19. Jahrhundert: Germanistische Tagung zum 65. Geburtstag von Eda Sagarra im August 1998*, ed. by Jürgen Barkhoff, Gilbert J. Carr and Roger Paulin (Tübingen: Niemeyer, 2000), pp. 345–54

'Mörike and the Higher Criticism', *Oxford German Studies*, 36 (2007), 47–59. Maney Publishing

'"Conversations with Jehovah": Heine's Return to God', in *Denkbilder: Festschrift für Eoin Bourke*, ed. by Hermann Rasche and Christiane Schönfeld (Würzburg: Königshausen & Neumann, 2004), pp. 126–37

'The Limits of Metaphor in Nietzsche's *Genealogy of Morals*', *Nineteenth-Century Prose*, 32 (2005), 75–96. Permission granted by Barry Tharaud

'Jesuits, Jews, and Thugs: Myths of Conspiracy and Infiltration from Dickens to Thomas Mann', in *In the Embrace of the Swan: Anglo-German Mythologies in Literature, the Visual Arts and Cultural Theory*, ed. by Rüdiger Görner and Angus Nicholls (Berlin: de Gruyter, 2010), pp. 126–46

'Schnitzler's Honesty', in *Order from Confusion: Essays presented to Edward McInnes on the Occasion of his Sixtieth Birthday*, ed. by Alan Deighton (Hull: New German Studies, 1995), pp. 162–85

'Savonarola in Munich: A Reappraisal of Thomas Mann's *Fiorenza*', *Publications of the English Goethe Society*, 74 (2005), 51–66

'Sacrifice and Sacrament in *Der Zauberberg*', *Oxford German Studies*, 35 (2006), 55–65. Maney Publishing

'Kafka as Anti-Christian: "Das Urteil", "Die Verwandlung" and the Aphorisms', in *A Companion to the Works of Franz Kafka*, ed. by James Rolleston (Rochester, NY: Camden House, 2002), pp. 101–22

'Alfred Döblin's Feeling for Snow: The Poetry of Fact in *Berge Meere und Giganten*', in *Alfred Döblin: Paradigms of Modernism*, ed. by Steffan Davies and Ernest Schonfield (Berlin: de Gruyter, 2009), pp. 215–28

'"My true enemy": Freud and the Catholic Church, 1927–1939', in *Austria in the Thirties: Culture and Politics*, ed. by Kenneth Segar and John Warren (Riverside, CA: Ariadne Press, 1991), pp. 328–44

INTRODUCTION

My essays collected here have appeared previously, some in readily accessible journals, others in books with small print runs available only in a few libraries. I wanted to bring them together in order to give them a better chance of being read, and also because they collectively represent, I hope, something more than the sum of their parts. The title is rather cumbersome. 'Religion and Enlightenment' covers the main themes running through the book, but several essays are on different topics. I wanted to reprint the essay on Nestroy simply because I am particularly fond of it, and the one on Döblin to draw attention to a still underrated author on the wilder shores of modernism. The addition 'and Austria' was unavoidable, since this part of the German-speaking world is too easily overlooked by literary histories focusing on Weimar or Berlin, even though it produced a large part of modern German-language literature. Besides, a whole section deals with the Austrian Enlightenment. Here and elsewhere, readers may discern fragments of unwritten books.

In the series to which this book belongs, authors are asked to reflect on their critical methods and approaches to literature. I want also to go a little further by indicating something of the personal motives behind some of my work. Reflecting on my critical methods is not something I find easy, for several reasons. I have no gift for philosophical analysis; my inclination is to focus on concrete particulars. I find that practice precedes theory: that is, when I read an exciting piece of literary analysis, I want to do something similar, and that means, not the instantiation of a theory, but applying the method, as I see it in practice, to different subject matter. Thus, in the essay on Goethe's *Faust*, the passage about 'complex words' signals a debt to William Empson's analyses of 'honest' in *Othello* and 'dog' in *Timon of Athens*, while the essay on *Moses and Monotheism* as Freud's covert reply to the views of Father Schmidt owes something to R. G. Collingwood's argument (since refined by Quentin Skinner) that texts are implicit engagements with prior texts.[1]

As these examples show, my intellectual debts are more often to anglophone than to German writers, not confined to the recent past, and eclectic. So I should say something about my education. My first degree was in English Literature at the University of Edinburgh. (Thanks to the structure of Scottish university courses, it is — or was, at least — possible to do two complete and separate Honours degree — not joint honours — over six years, so I graduated in English in 1974, and in German in 1976. In 1974–75, my year abroad, I earned my living by teaching in

1 R. G. Collingwood, *An Autobiography* (Oxford: Oxford University Press, 1939); Quentin Skinner, 'Meaning and Understanding in the History of Ideas', in *Meaning and Context: Quentin Skinner and his Critics*, ed. by James Tully (Cambridge: Polity, 1988), pp. 29–67.

a school under the British Council's Assistants programme, and in 1975–76 my parents generously supported me.) The English Literature course was serious and challenging. After the preparatory first two years, we were taken through English literature from *The Owl and the Nightingale* to *The Prime of Miss Jean Brodie* in chronological order. It was an old-fashioned kind of course which made excessive demands on students and teaching staff, but it was just what I wanted. There was no theoretical framework. Close reading was inculcated; the ghost of F. R. Leavis was close by. The underlying assumption was that literature is about important human experiences and that the practice of literary criticism is informed by humanist values — not a bad assumption, but nowadays it sounds rather too innocent, and needs to be held up for scrutiny. Looking back, there was surprisingly little attention to historical context. I read Leavis avidly, enjoying the critical insights less, I'm afraid, than the polemical fury. But I don't think Leavis was a good influence. His narrow and dogmatic criticism promotes less a love of literature than a censorious and even superior attitude towards it. Late in his life he became less a critic than a preacher, though oddly inarticulate about his message. I still much prefer the generous approach of C. S. Lewis, whose *Allegory of Love* is among my favourite studies of literature. And when Lewis preached, at least he did so in church.

In addition to the chronological course, one could either take a special subject, or learn another medieval language (in addition to the Old and Middle English which also fitted into the course). I was the only student in my year to take the latter option, and I chose to study Old Norse, which was taught by the eminent Icelandic scholar Hermann Pálsson. By this time, my third year, when I was nineteen going on twenty, I was feeling the need to locate my experience of literature within a larger intellectual framework, and Hermann provided me with one by advising me to read Northrop Frye's *Anatomy of Criticism*. The part I found most rewarding was the 'Theory of Modes', where Frye traces the transformation of literary themes and figures from myth through the high and low mimetic modes down to satire. This scheme obviously helped Hermann in moving between the myths of the *Edda* and realistic saga narratives. Nowadays I don't get much out of *Anatomy of Criticism*. Its scheme of seasonal *mythoi*, in which spring corresponds to spring, summer to romance, and so forth, feels attractively neat but strangely arbitrary, and also dated and parochial in its reliance on James Frazer's *Golden Bough*. I have, however, benefited greatly from some of the essays in Frye's collection *Figures of Identity*. His description of the spatial structure of romance in Spenser's *Faerie Queene* gave me, quite recently, a model for analysing Wieland's verse-narrative *Idris und Zenide*. Longer ago, I found in his essay on Wallace Stevens, and also in his little book on T. S. Eliot, a model of how to characterize a poet's work as a whole by identifying an implicit narrative and illustrating it with deftly chosen quotations. I applied this method when Cairns Craig asked me to write a short article on Edwin Muir for the *History of Scottish Literature* which he helped to edit. I am not, however, sympathetic to the large body of twentieth-century criticism which looks for mythic archetypes in literature. The results generally seem either unconvincing or vacuous, and often also reliant on a confused understanding of 'myth'.

From Edinburgh I went, on the advice of my final-year tutor, Wallace Robson, to Oxford, where I wrote a doctoral thesis in the English Faculty on 'Edwin Muir's Knowledge of German Literature and its Influence on his Thought and Writings'. If I had been more career-minded, or been shrewdly advised, I would have written about a recognized canonical author and produced something that could have been turned into a book. But one doesn't make important choices on the basis of rational calculation. Edwin Muir's poetry still speaks to me on a level 'too deep for daily tongues to say'.[2]

Although not exactly a masterstroke of career planning, my thesis, which is not just *Quellenforschung* but contains a thorough interpretation of Muir's poetry, including some difficult and obscure poems, was worth doing. I used occasionally to order up the copy in the Bodleian Library to see if anyone had read it (a few had). I gave a copy to the National Library of Scotland so that it could be added to the Edwin Muir archive and thus have the best chance of finding interested readers. Parts were published as journal articles, and I am still occasionally asked to speak about Muir at conferences on modern Scottish literature.

Meanwhile, however, criticism whose practitioners considered themselves humanistic was being challenged by the tidal wave of what is called, in shorthand, 'literary theory'. I won't enlarge on this, since everyone who remembers those 'sad, unhappy, far-off things, and battles long ago' will know what I am talking about. I read some way into this body of writing, enjoying Barthes's *S/Z* and temporarily fascinated by Roman Jakobson's analyses of lyric poetry — though the latter couldn't survive the demolition job done by Jonathan Culler in *Structuralist Poetics*. I was deterred from exploring far in poststructuralism, however. Some of its best-known exhibits put me off by their air of showmanship. And although the style favoured was superficially difficult and abstruse, I formed the impression that if one laboured to extract the substance, one would end up with a rather simple result, sometimes with a banal one, sometimes with one that was clearly untrue. Above all, I was repelled by the uncritical deference paid to the leaders of this movement. Certain names were repeated reverentially. One seldom saw attempts to criticize the masters constructively, to argue with them, to develop their ideas in different ways. It seemed to me that this movement, which often claimed to be challenging millennium-old assumptions, was actually inimical to critical thought.

There have of course been many arguments against post-structuralism, notably those advanced by John M. Ellis in *Against Deconstruction* and *Literature Lost*. Yet, although well-argued and invigorating, such books make little difference, because they don't address the reasons why so many people have been drawn to post-structuralism. It claimed to offer access to a wider intellectual world, especially to philosophy, without being intimidated by disciplinary boundaries. Thus it responded to a real and serious need, but not in the best way. Disciplines, and therefore disciplinary boundaries, exist for a reason. Disciplines are habits of thought and practices of analysis which take a long time to learn. I am, for better or worse, a literary scholar, and when I talk with historians or philosophers, I realize

---

2 'Day and Night', in Edwin Muir, *Collected Poems* (London: Faber, 1984), p. 240.

that we have different mental habits — which of course is a good reason for entering into dialogue with them.

This is a roundabout way of answering a question I am often asked: why, given my education, I pursued a career in German rather than in English. It was clear to me that competition in English was very severe, and that I would be hampered by a lack of dexterity in handling literary theory, whereas German studies in this country provided some refuge from the tsunami. That is the negative reason. The positive reason is that I was drawn to the study especially of modernist German authors — Kafka, Rilke, Trakl — whose very difficulty and obscurity was inviting. At an earlier stage, when I was about seventeen, I acquired Leonard Forster's *Penguin Book of German Verse*, which is certainly among the books that have done most to shape my life — though at that time, my taste being far from mature, the poem that first captivated me was Uhland's ballad 'Das Glück von Edenhall'.

Didn't my knowledge of German lead me to any German critical approaches? This question brings to mind two sharply contrasting books that I encountered during my year abroad. I spent 1974–75 as a teaching assistant in a large technical school in Mödling, outside Vienna, and also attended classes at the University of Vienna. To learn how things were done in the German-speaking world, I bought a paperback entitled *Grundzüge: Literaturwissenschaft*, in which I found various theoretical approaches to literature set out in an entirely theoretical manner and never applied to any actual texts. Even 'New Criticism', a body of work developed through the minute analysis of poems, as in Cleanth Brooks's *The Well Wrought Urn*, was explained in wholly abstract terms. No road was offered from the theory to what critics actually do. I infinitely preferred a sharply contrasting book, *Das sprachliche Kunstwerk* by Wolfgang Kayser, in which all the concepts discussed were illustrated through excellent textual analyses, and which was written in clear and accessible prose. I attended a course on Romantic poetry given by Werner M. Bauer (whom I got to know as a colleague many years later, and whose writings on eighteenth- and nineteenth-century Austrian literature I value highly), for which I wrote a term paper on two poems by Clemens Brentano. Although I was very ignorant about the poems' wider context, I analysed them, with the help of Kayser's book, well enough for Bauer to give my paper the highest available mark. It is of course true that the text-based approach practised by Kayser, known as 'werkimmanente Interpretation', soon became suspect in Germany because it seemed like an attempt to avoid confronting history, and in the 1960s the critical pendulum swung violently in the other direction. But I am not a German and that was not my problem. I continue to find *Das sprachliche Kunstwerk* an immensely rewarding book.

What about Marx and Freud? I have never seriously engaged with Marxism, sharing Northrop Frye's scepticism about the Marxist ambition 'to lift the whole of reality with a dialectical crowbar' (I quote from memory), but I have read a great deal of Freud and even done research on him. Psychoanalysis now has little scientific status; it is more likely to be taught in departments of French than in departments of psychology. When it succeeds as a practice, I am sure that the success results from the human skills and empathy of the analyst; that would certainly apply to the psychoanalysts I know personally. It would not apply to Freud himself. In making close studies of *The Interpretation of Dreams* and the *Fragment of an Analysis of a Case of Hysteria* (better known as 'the Dora case'), I was horrified by his authoritarian way of forcing interpretations on his patients, and amused by the fanciful illogic in his explanations of both neuroses and dreams. But psychoanalysis can't be dismissed. Elements from it have become part of the common sense of our culture. When it is applied to literature, however, full-dress psychoanalytic studies, whether guided by Freud himself or by later revisionists, always seem disappointing. That applies both to early reductive studies, like the interpretation of Goethe's poem 'Der Zauberlehrling' ('The Sorcerer's Apprentice') which concludes that it is 'really' about masturbation, and to serious and sophisticated studies such as Frederick Crews's book on Hawthorne.[3] One ends up asking: 'Is that all?' As for *Hamlet*, the showpiece of the Oedipus complex, I have pointed out (in a review of a very naïve exposition of Freudian criticism) that there is no need to invoke psychoanalysis to explain why a man should hesitate to kill his uncle on the basis of information provided by a ghost.[4] So there is not much psychoanalysis in the essays here, apart from such speculations as my oedipal interpretation of Schnitzler's tinnitus.

At some time around 1980 I explored hermeneutics as practised by E. D. Hirsch, whom I had heard give an inspiring lecture in Oxford. *Validity in Interpretation*, which argues in part that the interpretation of a text depends on a prior decision about its genre, still strikes me as a broadly persuasive book and, beyond that, a fine exercise in careful thinking and lucid exposition. His arguments were radicalized by Peter D. Juhl, who argues in *Interpretation* (1980) that the interpreter does not aim at one of several possible interpretations, but at the single right interpretation. But if Juhl challenged Hirsch, Hirsch was himself challenging Hans-Georg Gadamer's classic book *Wahrheit und Methode*, at which I eventually arrived. Schopenhauer allegedly said 'Let no one *tell* you what is in the *Critique of Pure Reason*'.[5] I would say 'Let nobody *tell* you what is in *Wahrheit und Methode*'. Read it for yourself, in the original if at all possible (it is not that hard), and learn why prejudice is not only unavoidable but positive, why to understand a past text is always to understand it differently, and why this enables one to recapture, not the author's intention, but the author's point of view. Although I seldom have occasion to cite it, I have found in *Wahrheit und Methode* the best guide to my practice as a historically minded critic. I also think that the relationship among Gadamer, Hirsch, and Juhl, in which each criticizes and refines the other's thesis, is exemplary as a relationship among thinkers, and infinitely preferable to deferential discipleship.

By 1981, when I submitted my thesis, I was fortunate enough to be in a temporary teaching post at Lincoln College, Oxford. I realized that I would have to publish or perish. Teaching, which has always been of great value to me in provoking

---

3 Frederick Crews, *The Sins of the Fathers: Hawthorne's Psychological Themes* (New York: Oxford University Press, 1966).

4 In *American Imago*, 60 (2003), 246–52. G. K. Chesterton made this point in 'Hamlet and the Psych-Analyst' in his *Fancies versus Fads* (London: Methuen, 1923), pp. 20–34.

5 Quoted in C. S. Lewis, *The Allegory of Love* (Oxford: Oxford University Press, 1936), p. 137.

questions and forcing me to clarify my thoughts, threw up some puzzles about Kafka in particular. No two Kafka commentators agreed, yet it was customary to say 'X says this about Kafka' and 'Y says the other', without asking how they arrived at their convictions or how the conflict between them might be settled. I was annoyed by this reliance on unexamined authority. I believed, and still do, that interpretations of literature should rest on the authority of fact and reason, and should be falsifiable by these criteria. This led me to what I now recognize as a naïve persuasion that philological and historical research might be able to resolve the problems of interpreting even an opaque author such as Kafka, and in this conviction I researched and wrote my book *Kafka: Judaism, Politics, and Literature* in three years, assisted by research leave which enabled me to spend substantial periods in Marbach and Vienna. I remember writing at least one chapter on an old typewriter whose roller would only turn forwards, not backwards, so that each sentence had to be perfectly formulated because I couldn't go back and correct it.

My book was an attempt to integrate close reading with historical contextualization. The concept of 'context' was a naïve one. It was less clear to me than it is now that the context of a literary text is not just given, but has to be chosen. I don't think there is any formula for choosing a relevant context: you move back and forth between your understanding of the text and your knowledge of the biographical, historical, intellectual backgrounds, till you find a relationship between text and context which is productive. This is more or less Gadamer's account of the hermeneutic circle.

The context I particularly chose was Kafka's relation to Judaism, meaning both the Judaic religion and Jewish ethnicity and culture. These matters were sometimes alluded to in studies of Kafka, but seldom with more than vague hints about how they might be relevant to the understanding of his texts. A rare exception was Anne Oppenheimer's Oxford thesis, 'Franz Kafka's Relation to Judaism' (1977). I set myself to find out as much as possible about Kafka's contact with various versions of Judaism and tried to read all the books from which he might have learnt something. I became fascinated with the lost world of Eastern European Jewry, and learnt Yiddish, though I was an extremely bad pupil because I kept mixing up Yiddish with German. However, I got as far as reading some short stories by Israel Joshua Singer in the original. My book probably owed its impact, not to any substantive discoveries, but to showing that Kafka's works, rather than inhabiting some rarefied textual sphere, did owe something to Kafka's interaction with the world around him. The core of the book, however, had nothing to do with historical context. It sprang from my lasting fascination with the aphorisms that Kafka wrote in Zürau in the winter of 1917–18, a selection from which he later arranged under the title 'Reflections on Sin, Suffering, Hope and the True Way'. Some of these aphorisms have been very important to me at crucial stages of my life, and have expressed my experience as nothing else could. 'From a certain point onward there is no longer any turning back. That is the point that must be reached.'[6]

6 Franz Kafka, *The Great Wall of China and Other Pieces*, trans. by Willa and Edwin Muir (London: Secker, 1933), p. 254.

Meanwhile, my reading was taking me in new directions. I had moved from a temporary job at Oxford to a temporary job at Downing College, Cambridge. Not being employed by the University, I was on very few committees, and had what now seems an extraordinary amount of leisure for reading. By reading (and eventually meeting) Peter Burke, in particular, my eyes were opened to a new world of cultural history. I had already been fascinated by Keith Thomas's *Religion and the Decline of Magic* and Robert Evans's studies on Habsburg intellectual history. I went on to Foucault, Marc Bloch, Philippe Ariès, Carlo Ginzburg, Robert Darnton, Roy Porter, and Simon Schama. I admired what historians could say about not only texts and contexts, but about actual experience in the past. John McManners's *Death and the Enlightenment* (1981) made a particularly strong impression, as did two books by Michael MacDonald: *Mystical Bedlam: Madness, Anxiety, and Healing in Seventeenth-Century England* (1981) and (co-written with Terence R. Murphy) *Sleepless Souls: Suicide in Early Modern England* (1990). What fascinated me, especially in *Mystical Bedlam*, was the process of starting with difficult, barely legible archival materials and ending with a coherent combination of narrative and analysis. That seemed to involve an intellectual energy and dexterity with hardly any equivalent in literary studies. You will notice that I was particularly drawn to morbid subjects. I was not very happy in myself at that time, and no doubt reading about madness, death and suicide (none of which, I hasten to add, I was remotely near experiencing myself) was an indirect way of acknowledging my own feelings, and also of encountering vicariously areas of experience that can't be ignored but that were outside my own sheltered life. (Though in the 1980s two people fairly close to me did attempt suicide, in one case successfully.)

What did all this mean for my own studies of literature? Rather little, I'm sorry to say. I am not a historian and could not become one; I lack the requisite palaeographical and archival skills. The nearest I came to practising cultural history was my study of the mental world of a Habsburg bureaucrat, Joseph Rohrer, included in the present selection. I discovered Rohrer through reading in the British Library an antisemitic tract of the 1810s, mentioned by Heine, which contained a reference to Rohrer's book on the Jews of the Habsburg Empire. When I ordered up Rohrer's book, I found that he had also written a whole series of ethnographic studies, in which the text was severely factual but the extensive footnotes were full of information about his reading and his opinions. Yet these fascinating books were almost completely unknown to modern scholarship.

In the outer world, meanwhile, scholarly agendas were changing. Post-structuralism was being displaced by a new interest in gender and race, itself the product of obvious social imperatives. This subject could not be accused of triviality. And it was ideally suited to treatment by a combination of the new cultural history and the critical close reading which — let me be fair — post-structuralism encouraged. My mentor here was the charismatic figure of Sander Gilman, whom I first met when he visited Cambridge. His book *Difference and Pathology: Stereotypes of Sexuality, Race and Madness* (1985) especially fascinated me. I must also acknowledge Sander's kindness in inviting me to give a 'brown bag' lunchtime talk at Cornell, where I attended a Heine conference in 1988, and in involving me later in a collective volume entitled *Reading Freud's Reading* (1994).

Questions of identity naturally came into the little book on Heine which Peter Halban asked me to write for his new series 'Jewish Thinkers'. I have not yet mentioned the towering figure of Siegbert Prawer, whose graduate seminars I attended at Oxford. Siegbert at first thought me a bit of a plodder — I remember him saying 'Mr Robertson, you are good at bibliography' — but he was visibly impressed by a seminar paper I gave on Freud's *Moses and Monotheism*. During his seminars, being an enthusiastic draughtsman, he would appear to be taking notes but in fact draw the speaker, as was apparent from his way of looking quickly up and down; you could tell that he was impressed when he stopped drawing. Anyway, though I never asked Peter Halban (with whom I am happily still in touch), I am pretty sure that he first asked Siegbert to write the Heine volume, and that Siegbert, having already written four books on Heine, declined and suggested me instead. If so, he did me a very great favour (by no means the only one). Writing about Heine was something of a relief after writing about Kafka. Kafka's imaginative world is intensely centripetal. Heine's is centrifugal. He was interested in everything, and to understand him on the most basic level you have to learn a great deal about the early nineteenth century, especially about German-Jewish history and culture.

I have often been asked why I spent so much time researching German-Jewish culture, and been at a loss to answer. So far as I know, I have no family connections with Jews or Judaism. I suspect that the answer has to do with the feeling I have always had of being an outsider. That in turn has to do with the fact that I was adopted at birth and have never known who my biological parents were (so I cannot speak about family connections with any confidence). My fascination led to the book *The 'Jewish Question' in German Literature, 1749–1929* (1999). The chronological bookends are the dates of Lessing's anti-antisemitic comedy *Die Juden* and Freud's *Moses and Monotheism*. I stopped short of the Holocaust, and have never wanted to write about that event. A visit to Auschwitz in about 1995 was the single most shocking experience of my life. The focus of the book was on the age of emancipation and assimilation, and its aim was to counter the common view, held most famously by Gershom Scholem, that assimilation was for German Jews a tragic folly or a hopeful illusion. On the contrary, it was an understandable endeavour which should not be criticized with the benefit of hindsight. Unfortunately antisemitism is protean: when religious antisemitism faded, antisemites found economic and racial justifications, with the results we know. My book was an attempt, not to recapture the past — Gadamer has shown that we can never quite do that — but to come close to understanding the past on its own terms.

A by-product of this project was *The German-Jewish Dialogue: An Anthology of Literary Texts, 1749–1993* (1999), for which I translated two-thirds of the texts myself. The translation that gave me most pleasure was the final act of Richard Beer-Hofmann's biblical drama *Jaákobs Traum* (*Jacob's Dream*), an exercise in theodicy, in which I did at times convey the force of the original; for example, when the fallen angel Samael describes himself to the archangels as

>   still at one
> With Him, your Master — not the servile choirs
> Who sing His praise with tedious jubilation!
> God cast me out because He needs a shadow
> To loom across the brightness of creation!

The hardest task was translating an extract from Karl Kraus's great anti-Nazi polemic *Dritte Walpurgisnacht* (*Third Walpurgis Night*). Anyone who knows Kraus's dense, knotty, allusive prose style will not be surprised. The anthology, though no longer in print, still seems to me one of the most worthwhile things I have done.

I must at this point express my gratitude to Judith Luna, for many years the editor of the series, Oxford World's Classics, in which the anthology appeared. I first contributed to the series by translating E. T. A. Hoffmann's *The Golden Pot and Other Tales* (1992), and was subsequently asked to provide introductions and notes to translations of works by Schnitzler, Musil, Fontane, Freud, and the five-volume series of new Kafka translations. Judith, now retired, was an editor's dream: enthusiastic, thorough, meticulous, and supportive. I believe, though I don't know this from personal experience, that she was strict with dilatory authors: stories are told of letters beginning 'I am very disappointed ...'

The importance for me of the Oxford World's Classics — and of the Penguin Classics, for which I translated two volumes — was the opportunity to address a wider than merely academic audience, as I had already done with my little book on Heine. I feel some missionary zeal to propagate interest in my subject, and to correct the many false ideas about German literature that are still in circulation (for example, that it is lacking in realistic novels, or in humorous works). I believe that even difficult matters can be explained clearly and in simple language, without talking down to one's audience. There need be no difference between academic and non-academic writing, beyond the fact that in academic writing one often goes into matters in an amount of detail that can interest only specialists. The criteria of good expository prose are the same in both forms of writing. Similarly in teaching: my constant endeavour is to work out what I want to say, and to say it simply and pithily; and — since the teacher should always talk less than the student — to encourage students to articulate clearly what they mean. I say 'endeavour', because only my students and ex-students can say whether this has worked in practice. I also set great store by reviewing books for the *Times Literary Supplement*. What used to be occasional requests have now become frequent, and I have also, though rarely, proposed subjects for reviews. The indulgent editors even allowed me to write a 3000-word essay on Daniel Casper von Lohenstein, a Baroque dramatist for whose blood-boltered tragedies I developed an enthusiasm, and who is unknown even to most Germans.

I should say something about my most recent large book, *Mock-Epic Poetry from Pope to Heine* (2009), which I was encouraged to write by the then head of Literature at Oxford University Press, Andrew McNeillie. I am not very satisfied with this book. It lacks a strong thesis, other than the claim that the mock-epic genre existed in the eighteenth and nineteenth centuries and that various well-known and some less-known works can be grouped in it. It has, I feel, too little of a personal voice. But I did try in it to do some new things. In contrast to the morbid themes mentioned earlier, this book is about satire and humour — about literature as fun. My enthusiasm for Austrian literature has a lot to do with its predilection for humour, from the Enlightenment mock epics that are discussed in my book, via Nestroy and Schnitzler, down to the massive post-war novels of Heimito von Doderer (whom, alas, I have never written about more than briefly). I had a lot of fun writing the book, largely during a single sabbatical year. The book poured out so easily that it seemed to have already been inside me, waiting to be written. *Mock-Epic Poetry* marks an attempt to extend my range by writing about English and French literature (and a little about Italian) as well as German. Writing about Pope and Byron was easy, but writing on Voltaire and Parny was a salutary excursion outside my comfort zone. Beyond that, presumptuous as it sounds, the book was an attempt to get a purchase on European literature as a whole by exploring literary relationships that extended from Homer and Virgil down to *Ulysses*.

Much of the work reprinted here was done during my tenure of a tutorial fellowship at St John's College, Oxford, between 1989 and 2010. My membership of that liberal and generous society, always hospitable to research, was both a great privilege and a very great piece of good fortune. Not the least benefit for me was becoming a colleague and friend of Terence Cave, whose academic distinction is equalled only by his modesty, and Elizabeth Fallaize, whose painfully premature death is still mourned.

Now to the present volume. The words in the title, 'Religion and Enlightenment', obviously imply a tension. Such a tension exists in my own life. Brought up, in a very lukewarm and relaxed way, in the Church of Scotland, I have twice formally joined churches, for reasons which at the time seemed obscure but compelling. What was really happening? Something to do, I suspect, with the feeling of being an outsider that I mentioned earlier (and which has only really been diminished by marriage and stepfatherhood). Now, although I am a member of the Church of England, I cannot assent to any of the propositions in the Nicene Creed. If I were asked the *Gretchenfrage*, 'Do you believe in God?', I would have to answer, not 'yes' or 'no', but 'I don't know what you mean'. Yet I enjoy church services (except the sermons, which usually annoy me), and value my parish church for making a neighbourhood more of a community. This is an uneasy situation. Religion, however, seldom consists in intellectual assent to propositions. It was the Protestant Reformers, as Peter Harrison has recently shown, who turned religion from a way of life into an intellectual programme, expressed in creeds and taught through catechisms.[7] Earlier, creeds like the Nicene Creed had a subordinate role in helping believers to lead a Christian life. But once Christianity was expressed in propositional form, it was easy for the Enlightenment to show that most or all of its propositions were false, thereby forcing the Churches into a continual retreat. Both sides, however, were thereby missing the point.

To put it differently: the Gospels invite us, often beautifully, to adopt a new way

---

7   Peter Harrison, *The Territories of Science and Religion* (Cambridge: Cambridge University Press, 2015).

of life, to become new persons. We cannot do this by the mere exercise of the will. We have to admit what Schleiermacher called 'the feeling of absolute dependence' and rely on a reality that we feel to be other than ourselves. But then the difficulties start. The reality on which we depend easily becomes reified into a God with all sorts of logically incompatible attributes. To preserve the Christian life, it is thought necessary to set up a Church with some degree of authority and hierarchy, and to turn 'belief in' into 'belief that' by formulating propositions as articles of faith. Authority is very easy to abuse, especially when those who wield it are convinced of their own righteousness. Articles of faith transform the spirit into the letter, suppress discussion and argument, and open the gate to orthodoxy, heresy, persecutions, and inquisitions. And yet Churches and creeds are not indispensable. The Quakers (I am fortunate enough to be married to one) have neither, and are exemplary in tolerance, humanity, and social commitment.

The authority arrogated by religious institutions cannot ultimately resist the Enlightenment imperative famously formulated by Kant: 'Sapere aude! Have courage to use your *own* understanding!'[8] When people undertook the philological and historical study of the Bible, they found that many important Christian doctrines are not in it, or present only as later interpolations. The Higher Criticism cast doubt on much that in the Gospels is presented as historical narrative. An essay in this volume, 'Mörike and the Higher Criticism', may convey my own mixed feelings. Much in the Gospels has to be discarded, except as poetry. But the sense of loss was counterbalanced, for me, by the exhilarating experience of reading David Strauss's *Leben Jesu*, a superb book which, since Strauss was a remarkable stylist, really has to be read in the original. But all this intellectual and historical inquiry is in conflict with a sense of reverence. One should not examine the object of one's reverence too closely, but surround it with discreet and decent silence. The story goes that when a phrenologist examined Bernard Shaw's head, looking for the 'bump of reverence', he found a hole instead. I hope I am not quite like that, but although I respect the reverence which forbids believers to look too far into the mysteries of their religion, I resist having my intellect bridled in that way.

In the end the conflict between religion and enlightenment may well be insoluble. I share Isaiah Berlin's conviction that human beings seek goals which are equally valuable, yet incompatible. For example, liberty and equality are both valuable, yet complete equality would be incompatible with complete liberty. Heine, having read Gracchus Babeuf's drastic *Manifeste des égaux*, satirically imagined a Babouvian future in which all authors would be compelled to write equally badly. Religion and enlightenment — devout reverence and free inquiry — may be another set of valuable yet irreconcilable goals.

In the foregoing, I have concentrated on myself and have not even tried to list the numerous colleagues and friends who have (often unwittingly) helped me clarify ideas through conversation and discussion, nor the people with whom I

---

8 An Answer to the Question: "What is Enlightenment?"', in *Kant: Political Writings*, ed. by Hans Reiss, trans. by H. B. Nisbet, 2nd edn (Cambridge: Cambridge University Press, 1991), pp. 54–60 (p. 54).

have collaborated, always rewardingly, on academic publications. I must however express deep gratitude to Edward Timms, whom I helped to found the yearbook *Austrian Studies* which we co-edited for ten years. Edward taught me not only how to edit, but also, again (mostly) unwittingly, a great deal about human relations, and remains an exemplary figure for me in many ways.

I should apologize for the lack of uniformity among the essays. In some, the German quotations are translated; in others, they are given only in the original. Some of the essays were written for books or journals that required all quotations to be in English. Others were intended for a readership that would not need translations. When I began assembling them, I intended to translate all the quotations, but I found it extremely laborious at best, and in some cases impossible without completely recasting the essay. That applies especially to the essays on Goethe's *Faust* and Schiller's *Wallenstein* which focus on the authors' use of certain key words and therefore require very many short quotations from the text. Rather than make the reader keep jumping from one language to the other, I have left the quotations untranslated. The long essay on 'Theophanies in German Classicism', however, which I wrote specially for this volume, was composed in such a way as to avoid much alternation between languages.

Apart from introducing translations in a few cases, I have reprinted the essays largely in the original form. I was tempted to alter the over-confident statement at the beginning of 'Jesuits, Jews and Thugs' that the age of nationalism is nearing its end: I wrote that before the recent sharp resurgence of Scottish nationalism, a development that I find distressing. But then I thought there was no point in trying to conceal my past errors of judgement. I have not tried to bring the references up to date, but I have in a few places added important recent publications (not all scholarly) in square brackets.

My thanks go to Colin Davis, the general editor of Legenda, for encouraging me to compile this volume; to Graham Nelson, the managing editor, for much detailed help and advice; and to those who invited me to produce the original versions, whether as conference papers or contributions to Festschriften and the like, notably Judith Beniston, Paul Bishop, Steffan Davies, Franz-Josef Deiters, Carolin Duttlinger, Paul Kerry, Ulrich Lehner, Nick Martin, David Midgley, Julian Preece, James Rolleston, Ernest Schonfield, Barry Tharaud, Galin Tihanov, Robert Vilain, and Helen Watanabe-O'Kelly.

Ritchie Robertson
September 2015

PART I

The German Classical Period

CHAPTER 1

Aspects of Religious Toleration in Eighteenth-Century Germany

By the early eighteenth century, Europe, and especially Germany, had seen two centuries of almost continuous warfare, much of it religious in motivation. The rulers, politicians and philosophers of the early Enlightenment increasingly agreed on the necessity for religious toleration. The basic argument for toleration was pragmatic: religious warfare was too destructive. But the moral and theological arguments for toleration were also being advanced. And in the course of the century it became widely accepted that religious toleration was good for a nation's economy. The purpose of this article is to sketch not only the growth of toleration but also the problems it entails, concluding with a brief study of a famous plea for toleration, Gotthold Ephraim Lessing's drama *Nathan der Weise* (*Nathan the Wise*, 1779). Above all, toleration represents a challenge for the rationality professed by the Enlightenment. For while reason may recommend the toleration of other religions, Lessing's play shows that people become tolerant not through rational precepts but through personal example.

Although the unity of Christendom had been decisively broken by the Reformation, many rulers wanted religious uniformity at least in their own territories. The Peace of Augsburg (1555) acknowledged this aspiration by the principle of *cuius regio eius religio*, which allowed princes to dictate the religion of their subjects and enforce conformity to the state religion. Those not content with the official religion were permitted to emigrate. The Treaty of Westphalia, which concluded the Thirty Years' War, was based on the same principle. It distinguished public worship, including baptism, marriage and funeral services, from private worship by congregations, and that in turn from domestic devotion, i.e. the holding of religious ceremonies in one's own home.

Despite the damage caused by religious conflicts, the homogeneity of public worship was an important integrative force, along with the semi-sacred figure of the prince, in territories where the state was not yet conceived of as an abstract entity separate from the person of the monarch. Sometimes the prince was also head of the Church: thus the Elector of Brandenburg was *summus episcopus* of the Lutheran Church in Prussia. It was doubted whether members of a different religion could be loyal subjects. In England, John Locke's *Letter on Toleration* (1689) argued that toleration should not extend to Catholics, because their first allegiance was to the

Pope.[1] And even if toleration were common among Catholics, Lutherans, and Calvinists, what was to be done with the many sects, for which the Treaty of Westphalia did not provide? Or with atheists, who were thought to dissent from the very basis of social morality?

Another problem was presented by members of minorities who threatened civil peace by trying to convert others. In the case for toleration made in 1669 by the lawyer Theophil Lessing (1647–1735), grandfather of G. E. Lessing, the horrors of religious strife are feelingly evoked, but complete freedom of religion is opposed as incompatible with civil peace; toleration should extend to those who hold false beliefs (*errones*), but be denied to trouble-makers (*turbones*).[2] In eighteenth-century Hamburg, Catholics were subject to more restrictions than any other minority, because, according to the Lutheran authorities, they regarded their Church as the only guarantor of salvation and would not desist from propagating their religion and requiring the children of mixed marriages to be brought up as Catholics; in addition, they enjoyed powerful external protection from the Emperor in Vienna, and until 1773 had a proselytizing organization in the Jesuits.[3]

While these problems remained unsolved, mass expulsions still occurred. The best-known followed Louis XIV's revocation of the Edict of Nantes in 1685. After subjecting the Huguenot minority to years of harassment, culminating in brutality from dragoons quartered in their homes, Louis thus drove some two hundred thousand of them into exile. In 1670, in response to Jesuit pressure and popular unease at the Turkish peril, the Emperor Leopold I expelled all Jews from Vienna, a late reprise of the expulsions from Western European cities which the Jews had suffered throughout the century of the Reformation.[4] In 1731 all Protestants were summarily expelled from the territory of Salzburg by the ducal archbishop Firmian: non-residents were ordered to leave within eight days, residents within three months.

In Catholic Austria, Maria Theresia, who became Empress in 1740, still upheld the ideal of religious uniformity. She organized missions to convert the Protestants of Carinthia and Upper Austria, and obliged the obstinate to move to Siebenbürgen in Transylvania. In 1777 she was alarmed to learn that more than 10,000 Protestants were conducting their own worship in a remote part of Moravia.[5] She remonstrated with her son Joseph II, fearing that the toleration he professed would lead to indifference towards religion: 'While you are thinking about keeping cultivators, or even in attracting them, you will be ruining your state, you will be the cause of so many souls being lost. What is the point of your possessing the true religion if you value and love it so little that you care little about maintaining and strengthening

1 John Locke, *Epistola de Tolerantia / A Letter on Toleration*, ed. by Raymond Klibansky, trans. by J. W. Gough (Oxford: Clarendon Press, 1968), p. 133.

2 Theophil Lessing, *De religionum tolerantia*, ed. by Günter Gawlick and Wolfgang Milde (Göttingen: Wallstein, 1991), Part IV, thesis 5; German text, pp. 61–62.

3 Joachim Whaley, *Religious Toleration and Social Change in Hamburg, 1529–1819* (Cambridge: Cambridge University Press, 1985), pp. 46–47.

4 See Jonathan I. Israel, *European Jewry in the Age of Mercantilism, 1550–1750* (Oxford: Clarendon Press, 1985), pp. 5–15 (sixteenth-century expulsions), pp. 146–48 (expulsion from Vienna).

5 On this episode, see Derek Beales, *Joseph II*, vol. 1: *In the Shadow of Maria Theresa, 1741–1780* (Cambridge: Cambridge University Press, 1987), pp. 466–73.

it? I do not see this indifference among any of the Protestants; on the contrary, I should wish them to be imitated, with no state permitting indifference in its own territories.'[6]

In reply, Joseph argued for toleration on grounds which were partly pragmatic, partly moral. He reassured her of his wish that as many people as possible should embrace the Catholic faith. 'God preserve me from thinking that it is a matter of indifference whether subjects become Protestants or remain Catholics, still less whether they believe or at least observe the religion derived from their fathers. I would give all I possess if all the Protestants of your states could become Catholics!'[7] We know from his private Memorandum of 1765 that Joseph believed in freedom of conscience and deplored any compulsion to change one's religion. Missionary endeavours like those of St Francis Xavier in China would, he noted, do no good in Europe. 'In matters of faith and customs, no punishment or violence does any good; one's own conviction is essential.'[8] He hoped that Protestants allowed to settle in a Catholic country would be attracted towards Catholicism, but he defined his conception of tolerance thus: 'For me tolerance means only that in purely temporal matters, without regard to religion, I would employ, allow to own lands, practise trades and become citizens those who are competent and would bring advantage and industry to the State.'[9]

Many Enlightenment thinkers felt, as Joseph did, that pragmatic arguments for toleration coincided with moral ones. Toleration was particularly needful in Prussia, where, since the public conversion of the Elector John Sigismund in 1613, the Hohenzollern of Prussia had professed the Reformed religion amid a largely Lutheran population.[10] Pressure from the Lutheran Church and the Brandenburg Estates obliged John Sigismund to abandon any hope of mass conversions to Calvinism and to grant official toleration to Lutheranism. Frederick William, the Great Elector (reigned 1640–88), did his best to strengthen the Reformed church, partly by inviting Calvinist immigrants such as the Huguenots, some 15,000 of whom escaped to Prussia from Louis XIV's persecutions. His successor, Frederick III (reigned 1688–1713), sought reconciliation between Lutheran and Reformed churches, and accordingly invited into Prussia the Pietist leaders who dissented from mainstream Lutheranism. Besides Huguenots, Jews and sectarians were allowed to settle. Frederick the Great showed his tolerance by accepting a Roman Catholic as citizen in the second week of his reign (June 1740), with the note: 'All religions are equal and good, as long as the persons who profess them are decent; and even if Turks and Heathen were to come and populate the country, we will be ready to build mosques and churches for them.'[11]

---

6 *Maria Theresia und Joseph II: Ihre Correspondenz*, ed. by Alfred Ritter von Arneth, 3 vols (Vienna: Gerold, 1867), II, 146–47.

7 Ibid., II, 151–52.

8 Ibid., III, 352; discussed by Beales, *Joseph II*, p. 168.

9 Ibid., II, 152.

10 See Richard L. Gawthrop, *Pietism and the Making of Eighteenth-Century Prussia* (Cambridge: Cambridge University Press, 1993).

11 Quoted in Wilhelm Grossmann, 'Religious Toleration in Germany, 1684–1750', *Studies on Voltaire and the Eighteenth Century*, 201 (1982), 115–41 (p. 127).

Toleration was supported by natural law. Thus Pufendorf insisted that natural law gave the secular authority no power over individual consciences, and it could only urge clergymen to see that God's laws were observed; but the state's tolerance should not extend to atheists or advocates of immorality.[12] Spinoza declares that 'no man's mind can possibly lie wholly at the disposition of another, for no one can willingly transfer his natural right of free reason and judgment, or be compelled to do so'.[13] Hence a government that denies freedom of thought must be a tyranny. Similarly, Locke assumes that the Church must be quite separate from civil society. Religion becomes a purely private, individual matter: 'the care of each man's salvation belongs only to himself'.[14] The ruler must not interfere with his subjects' religious beliefs and practices, unless they endanger the peace of society.

The claims of the individual conscience were also advanced by the mystical writer and Church historian Gottfried Arnold (1666–1714). In his *Impartial History of the Church and Heretics from the Beginning of the New Testament down to the Year of our Lord 1688* (1699–1700), Arnold depicted the history of the Church as a process of decline from the original purity and simplicity of early Christianity. The decline began with the appointment of bishops and the development of doctrinal differences. The true spirit of Christianity has been maintained by an invisible Church of obscure mystics whose importance Arnold seeks to restore: 'For the Kingdom of God has always been inward and thus invisible to the bodily eye, and has consisted in a few despised outcasts who recognized one another only by the inward connection and affinity of their spirit, not by outward forms, ceremonies, doctrines, festivals, and other circumstances.'[15] Even Muhammad receives sympathetic attention. His popularity is taken as testimony to the corruption of the Christian Church: 'The causes of his popularity were no doubt that he left everyone his freedom of conscience in religion and elsewhere, and prohibited all disputation on pain of death; whereas among the Christians there was nothing but strife, heresy-hunting, abuse and persecution.'[16] Stressing the illumination of the individual, Arnold demanded freedom of conscience and denounced any attempt to compel belief, whether by violence or excommunication (itself a relic of Judaism). His book was widely read throughout the eighteenth century and profoundly influenced, among others, the young Goethe, who was inspired by it to construct a private religion of his own based on Neoplatonism and Gnosticism.[17]

Alongside this emphasis on subjectivity, there was a search for common ground,

---

12   See Klaus Schreiner, 'Toleranz', in *Geschichtliche Grundbegriffe: Historisches Lexikon zur politisch-sozialen Sprache in Deutschland*, ed. by Otto Brunner, Werner Conze, and Reinhart Koselleck, 7 vols (Stuttgart: Klett-Cotta, 1972–92), VI, 445–605 (p. 503).

13   Benedict de Spinoza, *A Theologico-Political Treatise; A Political Treatise*, trans. by R. H. M. Elwes (New York: Dover, 1951), p. 257.

14   Locke, *A Letter on Toleration*, p. 125.

15   *Gottfrid Arnolds Unparteyische Kirchen- und Ketzer-Historie / von Anfang des Neuen Testaments biß auff das Jahr Christi 1688*, 2 vols (Frankfurt a.M.: Thomas Fritsch, 1699 and 1700), II, 846.

16   Ibid., I, 275.

17   Johann Wolfgang Goethe, *Dichtung und Wahrheit*, in *Sämtliche Werke: Briefe, Tagebücher und Gespräche*, ed. by Friedmar Apel and others, Deutsche Klassiker-Ausgabe, 40 vols (Frankfurt a.M.: Deutscher Klassiker Verlag, 1986–2000), XIV, 382.

for basic truths on which all Christians could agree. Even in Catholic regions, where people were sharply aware of the dangers of indifference, toleration was promoted by Reform Catholicism, which opposed the excesses of baroque piety — Mariolatry, saints' cults, processions — and wished Christian teaching to be based on rational conviction, study of Scriptures, and simple morality. These are the ideals proposed in the most popular text of Reform Catholicism, *Della regolata divozione dei Cristiani* (On well-ordered Christian devotion, 1747) by the historian Lodovico Antonio Muratori. In 1777 the German version of this book was adopted as a textbook in pastoral theology at the University of Vienna.[18]

Elsewhere, however, the common ground might take the form of 'natural religion' which was Deist rather than Christian, and stressed morality at the expense of speculation. 'By *Natural Religion*,' wrote Matthew Tindal, 'I understand the Belief of the Existence of a God, and the Sense and Practice of those Duties, which result from the Knowledge, we, by our Reason, have of him, and his Perfections; and of ourselves, and or own Imperfections; and of the Relation we stand in to him, and to our Fellow-Creatures; so that the *Religion of Nature* takes in every Thing that is founded on the Reason and Nature of Things.'[19] On this basis it was possible to extend toleration to atheists: Pierre Bayle argued that speculative opinions had no influence on conduct, and that contemplative atheists like Spinoza were harmless, while boastful atheists were atheists because they were depraved, not vice versa.[20] In Frederick the Great's Prussia, religious opinions were a private matter, provided one obeyed the rules of citizenship: 'All these sects', wrote Frederick, 'live here in peace and contribute equally to the happiness of the state; no religion deviates much from the others on the subject of morals; hence they may all be equal in the sight of the government, which consequently leaves each man at liberty to go to heaven by whatever path he pleases; all that is asked of him is to be a good citizen.'[21]

The dismissive indifferentism of Frederick the Great resembled the firmly Catholic tolerance shown by Joseph II in that both rested in varying degrees on economic grounds. The economic advantages of toleration took some time to be recognized. In the late seventeenth century, Catholic and some Lutheran states refused to admit immigrants of a different religion, even though the immigrants' entrepreneurial skills were needed to develop new industries, e.g. making luxury goods for the prince's court. Theories of mercantilism, however, maintained that a state should as far as possible be economically self-sufficient. Arguing that a state's wealth depends on the happiness and prosperity of its subjects, mercantilism concluded that their lives should be regulated in considerable detail by a benevolent 'police state' (*Polizeistaat*), recently defined as 'a state in which the good of the ruler is indistinguishable from the good of the populace; the administrative apparatus is devoted to the increase of

18   James Van Horn Melton, *Absolutism and the Eighteenth-Century Origins of Compulsory Schooling in Prussia and Austria* (Cambridge: Cambridge University Press, 1988), p. 78.

19   Matthew Tindal, *Christianity as Old as the Creation* (London, 1731), p. 11.

20   Elisabeth Labrousse, *Bayle*, trans. by D. Potts (Oxford: Oxford University Press, 1983), pp. 80–81.

21   [Frederick the Great], *Mémoires pour servir à l'histoire de la Maison de Brandenbourg* (Berlin, 1751), p. 396.

the ruler's wealth through the optimization of the happiness of his subjects.'[22] For mercantilism, it was convenient to regard religion as a private matter. Hence the economically ill-advised expulsions of Jews from Vienna, Huguenots from France, and (in 1686 and 1689) Waldensians from Piedmont worked to the advantage of Prussia. The Great Elector responded to the revocation of the Edict of Nantes by issuing the Edict of Potsdam (29 October 1685) which invited religious refugees to settle in Prussia and even offered them help with travel. Earlier, he granted extensive legal protection to Jews by an edict of 1671 inviting forty to fifty families to settle in Brandenburg. In doing so, as Wanda Kampmann points out, he was impelled not by religious tolerance but by mercantilism.[23] Similar considerations lay behind Joseph II's path-breaking Edicts of Toleration from October 1781 on. He allowed Lutherans, Calvinists and Greek Orthodox to worship: in any community where their numbers exceeded 100 families or 500 individuals they could build a church and appoint a clergyman. They were also permitted to buy property, join guilds, take part in local government, graduate at universities, and enter the civil service. Another series of decrees allowed Jews to attend Christian schools and universities, practise trades, open factories, rent houses, employ Christian servants, and attend the theatre. Particularly in the case of Jews, Joseph assured his ministers that his object was not to increase their numbers but to maximize their usefulness.[24]

The tolerance dictated by pragmatic and economic reasoning did not necessarily imply respect for different beliefs. Thus Frederick describes the Quakers and the Moravian Brethren as 'sects each more ridiculous than the other'.[25] In reaction to such reductiveness, Goethe demanded not only toleration but 'Anerkennung', positive respect. 'Tolerance should really be only a passing outlook; it must lead to respect. To put up with another faith is to insult it [Dulden heißt beleidigen].'[26] Some Enlighteners, knowing how limited rationality was, inquired into the emotional grounds for accepting others' beliefs. And they increasingly proposed a common ground of humanity which was not fixed and static, but open to development as humankind progressed in unforeseeable ways.

Enlightenment means not just accepting precepts but imitating models. In a searching essay, Christian Thomasius (1655–1728) argued that prejudices resulted partly from intellectual impatience, partly from misdirected love which caused people to imitate models before they were intellectually mature enough to choose models worthy of imitation.[27] A century later, enlightenment through love and imitation is the theme of Goethe's drama *Iphigenie auf Tauris* (1787). Here prejudice is represented by the barbarian king Thoas, civilized humanity by the Greek priestess Iphigenie who has found refuge in his kingdom. Learning that other Greeks have

22   Keith Tribe, *Governing Economy: The Reformation of German Economic Discourse, 1750–1840* (Cambridge: Cambridge University Press, 1988), p. 34.

23   Wanda Kampmann, *Deutsche und Juden: Die Geschichte der Juden in Deutschland vom Mittelalter bis zum Beginn des Ersten Weltkrieges* ([1963]; Frankfurt a.M.: Fischer, 1979), p. 57.

24   See T. C. W. Blanning, *Joseph II*, Profiles in Power (London: Longmans 1994), pp. 72–75.

25   [Frederick the Great], *Mémoires*, p. 396.

26   Goethe, *Sämtliche Werke*, I xiii 249.

27   Christian Thomasius, 'De Praejudiciis oder Von den Vorurteilen', in *Aus der Frühzeit der Aufklärung*, ed. by F. Brüggemann (Weimar, Leipzig, Vienna: Böhlau, 1928), pp. 29–59.

arrived to take her home, the jealous Thoas threatens to restore the blood-sacrifices which he abolished under her humane influence, and ignores his promise to let her leave for Greece as soon as an opportunity should arise. To persuade him to keep his word, Iphigenie appeals to a moral authority, 'the voice of truth and humanity', which is not the prerogative of any one nation but available to anyone 'through whose breast the spring of life flows pure and unimpeded'.[28] By dissuading Thoas from bloodshed, she overcomes the inherited curse of the Atrides and thus represents a humanity which is not shackled to the past but able to grow towards new ideals. In eventually keeping his promise to let her go, Thoas acknowledges the natural law which contributes to the play's framing assumptions; and in being won over by his affection and her sincerity, he implicitly confirms Thomasius' insight that people benefit less from rational arguments than from finding worthy and lovable models for imitation.

By subsuming the antithesis between Greeks and barbarians under a common humanity, Goethe shows that toleration is now a cultural as well as a religious issue. A major problem of cultural toleration facing the German Enlightenment was the social integration of the Jews. The old view that Jews had been rejected by God, and survived as a 'witness people', still had its spokesman within Lutheran orthodoxy, but such views were difficult to sustain within the rational theology which the German Enlightenment owed above all to Christian Wolff. Intellectual obstacles bulked larger. To the Enlighteners, Judaism seemed rigid, intolerant, and superstitious, an impression reinforced in the 1750s by the much-publicized dispute between Jonathan Eybeschütz and Jacob Emden, two eminent rabbis living in Altona. Emden accused Eybeschütz of supplying pregnant women with protective amulets containing covert references to the magic powers supposedly exercised by the seventeenth-century pseudo-Messiah Sabbatai Zvi. This controversy, which drew in the Senate of Hamburg and the King of Denmark, encouraged both Jews and Gentiles to regard mainstream Judaism as hopelessly out of touch with real moral and intellectual issues. There remained a social barrier. Forbidden to own or farm land, to practise most professions, and to attend Gentile schools or universities, the Jews of eighteenth-century Germany still formed a separate community, distinguished not only by their enforced concentration on trade and finance but by their distinctive dress and German-Jewish language. To become socially integrated, they had to adopt Western clothes and manners and use standard German — a tendency already evident by the mid-century — and demonstrate their intellectual fitness to participate in the culture of the Enlightenment. The great exemplar of Jewish capacity for enlightenment was the Berlin philosopher Moses Mendelssohn, who persuaded his friend, the Prussian civil servant Christian Wilhelm von Dohm, to publish a treatise advocating the extension of civil rights to the Jews. A better-known spokesman for the acceptance of Jews, and for toleration in general, was the freelance writer, dramatist, critic and scholar Gotthold Ephraim Lessing, whose contribution to religious toleration in eighteenth-century Germany is now to be briefly examined.

---

28 Goethe, *Sämtliche Werke*, I v 612.

Lessing's religious thought is difficult to describe because he never expounded it systematically but expressed it in controversies, where prudent evasions and polemical point-scoring obscure what may have been his real opinions. Nevertheless, at least one constant can be identified: an appeal to reason and morality rather than faith or revelation as the criteria of religious truth. For Lessing, it was an insoluble problem that Christianity made historical claims — namely, that God's revelation occurred at a particular time and place in history — instead of being based on the universal claims of reason. The resurrection of Christ was a contingent historical fact, based on historical testimony but not underwritten by reason. Reason and revelation were disjoined: 'That is the ugly, broad ditch that I cannot cross, no matter how often and how seriously I have tried to leap it', he wrote in 1755.[29] Unable to accept revelation, and hostile equally to ecclesiastical dogmatism and to the shallow irreligion current in Enlightenment Berlin, Lessing restlessly pursued religious inquiries with a number of assumptions that were not widely shared.

Like Gottfried Arnold, Lessing sympathizes with the unorthodox and seeks truth especially in the writings of those who have incurred official condemnation. He wrote a series of 'vindications' ('Rettungen') of such figures as the Renaissance philosopher Jerome Cardan of Milan, whose book *De Subtilitate* (1552) compared Christianity with Judaism, Islam, and paganism, and brought its author the reputation of atheism; Simon Lemnius, an opponent of Luther; and the eleventh-century theologian Berengar of Tours, who was charged with heresy for his views on the Real Presence in the Eucharist. Among his own contemporaries he published and defended the sceptical researches into the authenticity of Biblical texts by Hermann Samuel Reimarus. Unlike Arnold, however, Lessing saw how easily the unorthodox can set up their own repressive counter-orthodoxy. He wrote to his brother Karl on 22 April 1774:

> I hate all those who want to establish sects from the bottom of my heart. For it is not error, but sectarian error, indeed sectarian truth, that makes people unhappy; or would do, if the truth could establish a sect.[30]

Like the Goethe of *Iphigenie*, Lessing thinks that truth emerges in the course of history. In *The Education of the Human Race* (1780) Lessing supposes that the revelations of Moses and Christ are valid, and that they are God's (or Providence's) way of gradually educating humankind; their content could have been discovered by unaided human reason, but the providential process of education speeds things up. Thus the revelation of Moses was made to 'the most rude and the most ferocious' people in the appropriately crude language of rewards and punishments; but when these moral lessons were in danger of being obscured by rabbinical over-ingenuity, 'a better instructor must come and tear the exhausted primer from the child's hands — Christ came!'[31] Christ taught the new lesson of the immortality of the soul; but

29 G. E. Lessing, *Werke*, ed. by H. G. Göpfert et al., 8 vols (Munich: Hanser, 1970–79),VIII, 13. For an introduction to Lessing's theology with selected texts, see *Lessing's Theological Writings*, ed. by Henry Chadwick (London: A. & C. Black, 1956).

30 Quoted in Harald Schultze, *Lessings Toleranzbegriff: Eine theologische Studie* (Göttingen: Vandenhoeck & Ruprecht, 1969), p. 41.

31 Lessing, *Werke*, VIII, 491, 501.

the New Testament also promises a new gospel (Revelation 14. 6), and Lessing ends his account with speculations about the millennium and even the transmigration of souls. This has often been taken as Lessing's final statement about religion and as matching the message of toleration proclaimed in *Nathan der Weise*. The doctrine of progressive revelation was gratefully taken up by liberal theologians such as F. W. Robertson and Frederick Temple in nineteenth-century England. Instead of treating different religions as equal, however, it presents Judaism as primitive and Christianity as a slightly less childish precursor of a future religion of reason. Thus Lessing's treatise debunks all actual religions, relativizing them by a standard about which, as it is located in the future, nothing can as yet be known.

In Lessing's search for religious truth, what matters is not the result of the search but the serious and sincere process of inquiry. 'The value of a person lies not in the truth that he possesses, or thinks he possesses, but in the honest efforts he has made to get at the truth', writes Lessing in his controversy with the ultra-orthodox Pastor Goeze.[32] But while the search for truth is an antidote to dogmatic certitude, it may become an end in itself, an excuse for ultimately frivolous speculations.[33]

Forestalling this objection, Lessing stresses that the test of religious truth is moral action. In 1750 the twenty-one-year-old Lessing wrote: 'Man was made to act and not to speculate'.[34] Thus, like many other Enlighteners, including Bayle and Frederick the Great, Lessing disjoins truth from action. Moral action is not founded on correct opinions but on some more obscure basis.

These principles underlie Lessing's treatment of religious toleration, especially towards the Jews, in *Nathan der Weise*.[35] The play brings Jews, Christians and Muslims together in the Jerusalem of the Crusades. Its centre is generally taken to be the parable of the three rings. Thanks to his reputation for wisdom, the Jewish merchant Nathan is summoned before Saladin and asked which of the three religions is the true one. Nathan sidesteps this embarrassing conundrum by telling how a ring that made its possessor pleasing to God and man was handed down through the generations till it came to a father with three sons. He had two externally similar rings made, so that each son received one. Wondering which was the true ring, they took their problem to a judge, who told them that the authenticity of the ring could only be demonstrated by the upright conduct of its owner, and advised each to assist the ring's power by his benevolence, peacefulness and devotion. Thus moral action becomes the test of a religion's truth.

The parable implies, not that the other two rings are as good as the true one, but that all three rings are false. For all three sons behaved equally badly in their dispute: 'each wants to be the prince of the house', though the owner of the true ring ought to have behaved more magnanimously than the other two.[36] Indeed the judge speculates that the true ring may have been lost and that each facsimile

---

32 Lessing, *Werke*, VIII, 32–33.

33 See H. B. Nisbet, 'Lessing and the Search for Truth', *Publications of the English Goethe Society*, 43 (1972–73), 72–95.

34 'Gedanken über die Herrnhuter', *Werke*, III, 683.

35 For a more detailed study, see my '"Dies hohe Lied der Duldung"'? The Ambiguities of Toleration in Lessing's *Die Juden* and *Nathan der Weise*', *Modern Language Review*, 93 (1998), 105–20.

36 Lessing, *Werke*, II, 277.

will serve provided its possessor lives up to it. The inner truth of each religion is its incitement to moral action. Tradition (the historical content of religion) cannot establish any absolute religious truth, because everyone believes the traditions in which he was brought up; rather, the historical element of religion is a fiction, and the only proof of any religious pudding is in the eating.

This parable might seem to assist religious toleration by discouraging unproductive disputes about the truth-claims of different religions. The character of the tolerance exemplified in the play is thrown into doubt by Nicholas Boyle's aside in his biography of Goethe: 'The representatives of the three major religions, Judaism, Christianity, and Islam, are not here shown to tolerate one another's differences, for it is only temporary misunderstanding that prevents them from recognizing that they all think alike: they are shown rather to be agreed in a fourth, secret, religion of agnostic humanism.'[37] The parable implies that the cognitive element in religion is also fictive. Revelation does not survive sceptical examination, just as the ring fails of its effect when put to the test. The historical and traditional basis of religion is revealed as simply a fairy-story, no different in principle from the 'Märchen' with which Nathan fobs off Saladin. We have a toleration based on indifference. One can tolerate opinions because one assumes that none of them are true anyway, as in Gibbon's well-known account of the religious toleration practised under the Roman Empire: 'The various modes of worship, which prevailed in the Roman world, were all considered by the people, as equally true; by the philosopher, as equally false; and by the magistrate, as equally useful.'[38] However, Lessing's position is more complex than Gibbon's urbane scepticism. In a posthumously published fragment, variously dated to the 1750s or the 1760s, he maintains: 'All positive and revealed religions are [...] equally true and equally false.'[39] Their falsity consists in the local and historical modifications which mediate but also falsify their 'inner truth'. Lessing prudently avoids offering any blunt definition of this 'inner truth'; but *Nathan der Weise* would imply that the inner truth of religion is the degree to which it promotes rational morality.

Nathan der Weise not only combines seriousness with scepticism, but succeeds by embodying its rational morality in the person of Nathan, whose goodness is apparent even to the initially surly and bigoted Templar. Only late in the play do we learn how Nathan's character has been purified by bereavement: after his wife and seven sons were burnt in a pogrom by Christians, Nathan finally accepted this loss as God's will and adopted the infant Recha as compensation for his loss. It is psychologically convincing that Nathan's goodness should rest on inner strength acquired by the acceptance of suffering; and that, as Thomasius and Goethe realized, moral lessons here are inculcated not by precept but by the quietly commanding presence of true personal goodness. Thus the Enlightenment as represented by Lessing and Goethe has passed beyond rationalism into a fuller conception of humanity as founded on mystery which would eventually burst the Enlightenment's own boundaries.

---

37 Nicholas Boyle, *Goethe: The Poet and the Age*, vol. I: *The Poetry of Desire* (Oxford: Clarendon Press, 1991), p. 33; cf. p. 273.

38 Edward Gibbon, *The Decline and Fall of the Roman Empire*, 6 vols (London: Dent, 1910), I, 29.

39 Lessing, *Werke*, VII, 283.

CHAPTER 2

Virtue versus 'Schwärmerei' in Lessing's *Emilia Galotti*

Emilia Galotti is a major example of the favoured eighteenth-century theme of 'virtue in distress', in which a virtuous woman is in danger from a male seducer.[1] Samuel Richardson's *Clarissa*, the archetypal and monumental instance, also establishes a powerful precedent by making the antagonism one of class as well as gender. The middle-class Clarissa Harlowe falls victim, after resisting for many hundreds of pages, to the determination, the ruthlessness, and the obsessiveness of the aristocratic libertine Lovelace. The compelling dramatic power of Richardson's writing made his novel the template for innumerable other narratives of seduction, from Lessing's *Miß Sara Sampson* (1755) down to Heinrich von Kleist's *Die Marquise von O...* (1808). These narratives are particularly fascinating when, as often, the danger to the heroine is not only external but internal: when her own attraction to the seducer undermines her virtue and helps him to overcome her. *Emilia Galotti* is notoriously such a case: in the impassioned monologue by which she seeks to persuade her father to kill her, Emilia declares that she is afraid, not of external violence, but of her own susceptibility to seduction: 'Verführung ist die wahre Gewalt' [the seducer is the true tyrant] (v. 7).[2] And this makes one wonder about the virtue of which we hear so much throughout the play. If it is so ineffectual in a crisis, perhaps it is already a flawed ideal? Perhaps in fact it is simply the expression of the over-excitable disposition known as 'enthusiasm' in eighteenth-century England and as 'Schwärmerei' at the same period in Germany?

An unavoidable fact about the word 'Tugend' [virtue] is that it now sounds dated, and has done for a very long time. One can hardly use it without ironic detachment or a sense of quoting an obsolete term. In Thomas Mann's *Der Zauberberg* (1922) Hans Castorp is astonished to hear this outdated word used seriously.[3] Its datedness

---

1 See R. F. Brissenden, *Virtue in Distress: Studies in the Novel of Sentiment from Richardson to Sade* (London: Macmillan, 1974).

2 Quotations from *Emilia Galotti* are identified by act and scene number. All quotations from Lessing are from Gotthold Ephraim Lessing, *Werke und Briefe*, ed. by Wilfried Barner and others, 12 vols (Frankfurt a.M.: Deutscher Klassiker Verlag, 1989–94). References to other works by Lessing, and to reception documents quoted by the editors, are identified as L with volume and page number. Translations from *Emilia Galotti* are taken from *Five German Tragedies*, trans. by F. J. Lamport (Harmondsworth: Penguin, 1969).

3 Thomas Mann, *Der Zauberberg*, ed. by Michael Neumann (Frankfurt a.M.: Fischer, 2002), p. 156.

is already apparent in some famous nineteenth-century occurrences of the word. When Georg Büchner's Robespierre blandly insists: 'Die Tugend muß durch den Schrecken herrschen' [virtue must rule through terror], and Danton denounces his bloodless and priggish 'Tugend', we see the word being distorted by Danton into a narrower sense of primarily sexual virtue, and used by Robespierre in a manner that calls out for criticism.[4] When Fontane's Effi Briest soliloquizes: 'Mich ekelt, was ich getan. Aber was mich noch mehr ekelt, ist eure Tugend' [I loathe what I did, but what I loathe even more is your virtue], the 'virtue' attributed to her ex-husband, her parents, and the whole of respectable society is clearly presented as an outworn and inadequate conception of morality.[5] The problematic character of 'Tugend' as a moral term is, I want to argue, already apparent in Lessing's text.

The word 'Tugend' may be used in the singular or the plural. In the singular, 'Tugend' denotes a disposition — virtue — which is prior to specific 'Tugenden' or virtues. Nowadays, this use of 'Tugend' sounds particularly dated. We might still praise someone for having specific virtues, but we would be unlikely to say that somebody possessed virtue or 'Tugend' *tout court*. The process by which 'Tugend' becomes unusable as a moral term accompanies the dissolution of the unitary concept of virtue.

'Tugend' is a rich and complex concept, derived from Christian and classical sources. The theological virtues defined by St Paul as faith, hope and love (1 Cor. 13. 13) were placed by Augustine and other Church Fathers just above the cardinal virtues (prudence, temperance, fortitude and justice) taken from Plato and Aristotle. In the early eighteenth century the ideal of 'Tugend', as Wolfgang Martens has shown in detail, was propagated by the moral weeklies and the popular philosophers.[6] 'Tugend' will be shown above all in action: in looking after one's family, in doing one's work honestly and efficiently, and in helping the unfortunate. It will take the form of moderation and self-restraint, especially in sexual matters. This ideal, while compatible with Christianity, is somewhat detached from Christian teaching. The virtuous person is not required to be a saint, or to have a deep conviction of original sin, or to rely on divine grace. St Paul's strenuous conception of the moral life as conflict, in which one is constantly fighting against the old Adam, is considerably toned down. In the philosophy of Christian Wolff, which underlay that of the moral weeklies, the Christian soul struggling against temptation is replaced by the rational person who is able to weigh up the consequences of his actions and overcome the temptations arising from the passions and the senses. This is still a cognitive concept of virtue: to do what is right I have to know what is right. But we no longer have the intellect disciplining and coercing the recalcitrant, sensual

---

4   Georg Büchner, *Sämtliche Werke*, ed. by Henri and Rosemarie Poschmann, 2 vols (Frankfurt a.M.: Deutsche Klassiker Verlag, 1992–99), I, 32. The translation is taken from Georg Büchner, *Complete Plays, 'Lenz' and Other Writings*, trans. by John Reddick (London: Penguin, 1993), p. 23.

5   Theodor Fontane, *Romane, Erzählungen, Gedichte*, ed. by Walter Keitel, 6 vols (Munich: Hanser, 1962), IV, 75. The translation comes from *Effi Briest*, trans. by Mike Mitchell, World's Classics (Oxford: Oxford University Press, 2015), p. 222.

6   Wolfgang Martens, *Die Botschaft der Tugend: Die Aufklärung im Spiegel der deutschen moralischen Wochenschriften* (Stuttgart: Metzler, 1968), esp. the section 'Der der Tugend fähige Mensch', pp. 231–46.

will. Instead, the intellect and the will are in agreement. Both are naturally drawn towards the good. The will keeps being distracted by mistaken desires for things that are really not good for it, and the business of the intellect is to dispel those desires by showing them to be intellectually misguided.

Alongside this conception of 'Tugend' there are harsher and milder possibilities. A harsher version of virtue which enjoyed great popularity till the early eighteenth century was associated with Stoicism.[7] The Stoic firmly subjected his passions to the iron rule of reason. His virtue took the form especially of steadfastness, self-control, rigorous performance of duty. If he closely followed classical Stoicism, he might cultivate *apatheia*, or insensibility towards emotion and pain. Stoic morality, with the emphasis on steadfastness, was popularized by Justus Lipsius in his widely read treatise *De constantia* (1584). Many of Shakespeare's plays both display Stoicism and criticize it. Horatio is 'not passion's slave'; by his own assertion, he is 'more an antique Roman than a Dane'. Julius Caesar is 'constant as the northern star'. But Coriolanus takes Stoicism to churlish extremes, refusing to solicit votes for the consulship, and eventually has his inflexible persona dissolved by his dependence on his mother. Moving forward to the eighteenth century, the Stoic hero reappears in Johann Christoph Gottsched's *Der sterbende Cato* [*The Death of Cato*] (1732) as a patriot to whom the fate of the Roman republic is far more important than that of his family. By now, Stoicism looked old-fashioned and incredible. People did not behave like that. Fielding introduces into *Tom Jones* (1749) a Stoic philosopher called Square who is always talking about the eternal fitness of things and the insignificance of pain: 'In pronouncing these [sentiments] he was one Day so eager, that he unfortunately bit his Tongue; and in such a Manner, that it not only put an End to his Discourse, but created much Emotion in him, and caused him to mutter an Oath or two.'[8]

However, while the particular moral practice recommended by Stoicism might be dismissed, Stoicism made an essential contribution to the eighteenth-century conception of virtue. For while Christianity advocated various virtues, Stoicism argued that all virtues were interlinked by mutual entailment. You could not have one virtue without having all the rest. Hence the good person possessed not just virtues, but virtue. The unitary concept of 'Tugend' comes from Stoicism, and is set out clearly in Zedler. The author of the article on Stoic philosophy, having explained that the principal virtues are 'Klugheit, Mäßigkeit, Tapfferkeit und Gerechtigkeit' [prudence, moderation, courage, and justice], adds: 'Diese Tugenden haben alle einerley Endzweck, und einerley Regeln und Lehr-Sätze (*praecepta*) derowegen sie auch nicht von einander geschieden werden, sondern wer eine hat, hat alle' [These virtues all have the same final goal, and the same rules and precepts, wherefore they cannot be separated, but whoever has one, has them all].[9] It follows that if

---

7 See Gerhard Oestreich, *Neostoicism and the Early Modern State* (Cambridge: Cambridge University Press, 1982); Geoffrey Miles, *Shakespeare and the Constant Romans* (Oxford: Clarendon Press, 1996).

8 Henry Fielding, *The History of Tom Jones, a Foundling*, ed. by Martin C. Battestin and Fredson Bowers, 2 vols (Oxford: Clarendon Press, 1974), I, 217.

9 Johann Heinrich Zedler, *Großes vollständiges Universal-Lexikon*, 64 vols (Leipzig and Halle: Verlegts Johann Heinrich Zedler, 1732–50), vol. XL (1744), col. 342.

you prefer some virtues to others — for example, if you exalt the virtues shown in domestic life and disparage those shown in public life — you risk fragmenting and demolishing the unitary conception of virtue.

A milder conception of virtue was also, and increasingly, available. If for the popular philosophy of 'Tugend' reason and will are really on the same side, and reason has only to clear away irrational obstacles that block the will's natural inclination towards the good, the next step must be to make reason subordinate to feeling. Our knowledge of the good depended on our feeling for the good. This was the step taken by Shaftesbury with his concept of the 'moral sense'.[10] For him, the knowledge of right and wrong is innate. Virtue is a feeling, an affection: 'a certain just disposition or proportionable affection of a rational creature towards the moral objects of right and wrong'.[11] The relation between the words 'affection' and 'rational' in this sentence is a little unclear, for the tendency of Shaftesbury's arguments is to reduce the role of reason and increase that of feeling. And if you make feeling, rather than reason, the guarantor of virtue, you move away from a standard — reason — that is in principle available to everyone, and move towards a standard — the moral sense — that rather few people have. Virtue risks becoming available only to an elite.

In order to detect some of the strains lurking in the concept of virtue, I want briefly to consider a phrase that is common in eighteenth- and nineteenth-century German literature, the phrase 'rauhe Tugend' [rough virtue]. Its first occurrence that I know of is in Christoph Martin Wieland. In 1752 the eighteen-year-old Wieland completed four cantos of an epic poem entitled *Hermann* and sent them to the famous Swiss critic Johann Jakob Bodmer, who so admired the poem that he invited Wieland to stay with him in Zürich. Early in the poem, Wieland tells us that Hermann was brought up virtuously in lonely forests:

> Hier gewohnte sein unverfälscht Herz, den höfischen Lastern
> Unzugänglich, die rauhe Tugend und Arbeit zu lieben.[12]

[Here his uncorrupted heart, inaccessible to the courtly vices, became accustomed to love rough virtue and work.]

Clearly Hermann's virtue is the better for being rough. It forms an extreme contrast to the vices practised at courts, where of course people are polished. Courtiers, constantly currying favour with their prince and jockeying for position with one another, are also devious and insincere, in contrast to Hermann's 'unverfälscht Herz'. In Wieland's poem Rome centres on a deeply corrupt imperial court whose denizens are prey to sexual vices and lust after Germanic women. Hermann's wife, the desirable Thusnelda, is abducted on the orders of the Emperor Tiberius, who is described as 'Wütend vor alter Brunst, (zur Zärtlichkeit war er zu viehisch!)' [raging

---

10   Anthony Ashley Cooper, third Earl of Shaftesbury, *Characteristics of Men, Manners, Opinions, Times*, ed. by Lawrence E. Klein (Cambridge: Cambridge University Press, 1999), p. 180.

11   Ibid., p. 177.

12   *Wielands Gesammelte Schriften*, ed. by the Deutsche Kommission der Königlich Preußischen Akademie der Wissenschaften, 23 vols (Berlin: Weidmannsche Verlagsbuchhandlung, later Akademie-Verlag, 1909–69), I: *Poetische Jugendwerke. Erster Teil*, ed. by Fritz Homeyer (1909), p. 139.

with carnal desire (he was too bestial to feel tenderness!)].[13] Hermann rescues her, but later she and the other Germanic women find themselves in danger from the Roman commander Varus, who is presented as a serial rapist and murderer. Here we have the opposition, familiar from the literature of pastoral and idyll, between the court and the country, between sophisticated vice and the honest unpolished virtue of rough diamonds. Albrecht von Haller in *Die Alpen* (1729) expresses it neatly in praising the industrious virtue of the rural Swiss:

> Hier herrscht kein Unterschied, den schlauer Stolz erfunden,
> Der Tugend untertan und Laster edel macht;
> Kein müßiger Verdruß verlängert hier die Stunden,
> Die Arbeit füllt den Tag und Ruh besetzt die Nacht.[14]

[Here no distinction prevails, invented by crafty pride, which subordinates virtue and ennobles vice; here no idle vexation lengthens the hours, works fills the day and rest occupies the night.]

Another rough diamond appears in Lessing with the Templar in *Nathan der Weise*. He is virtuous in saving Recha from the fire, but decidedly rough in rudely rejecting Nathan's attempts to thank him. Hence Nathan says: 'Fast macht | Mich seine rauhe Tugend stutzen' [His rough virtue almost disconcerts me] (II. 5). Here the roughness seriously detracts from the virtue. To be truly effective, virtue needs some degree of polish: not to make its possessor into a courtier, but to enable him or her to converse civilly with others and to develop the affections which, as Shaftesbury argued, hold society together.

When, in *Emilia Galotti*, Claudia says about her husband: 'O, der rauhen Tugend!' [O what rough virtue!] (II. 5),[15] this is the second of three references to Odoardo's virtue. Two scenes later his virtue is praised extravagantly by his prospective son-in-law Appiani: 'Welch ein Mann, meine Emilia, Ihr Vater! Das Muster aller männlichen Tugend!' [Emilia, what a man your father is! The image of all manly virtue!] II. 7) And earlier Claudia has deplored his 'strengen Tugend' [strict virtue] (II. 4). Clearly Odoardo is a test case of virtue. His virtue is, as Stoicism requires, a compound of all the virtues, at least all those proper to a man. If there is anything wrong with his virtue, the whole concept is in danger.

What kind of virtue does Odoardo embody? By the standards of Stoicism he falls short. He is passionate and impulsive. He is capable of self-restraint, as when he refrains from saying anything unpleasant to Claudia on learning that Emilia has met and talked to the Prince (II. 4). His virtue is 'rauh' or uncouth, like Hermann's, in being uncourtly. The Prince describes him as 'Ein alter Degen; stolz und rauh; sonst bieder und gut!' [An old soldier, and a rough diamond; an honest man, though!] (I. 4). He has taken the lead in opposing the Prince's claims to land at Sabionetta. He disapproves of court life, because it is vicious and it requires one to defer to worthless people like Marinelli in the hope of obtaining an office which somebody as upright as Appiani would not want anyway. He is attached to his prospective son-

---

13 Ibid., p. 170.
14 Albrecht von Haller, *Die Alpen und andere Gedichte* (Stuttgart: Reclam, 1965), p. 6.
15 Lamport has 'unyielding virtue', which misses the connotation of uncourtly roughness.

in-law — with an enthusiasm that Hermann Weigand described as 'schwärmerisch', over-enthusiastic — because of their shared ideals.[16] Odoardo chooses to live in the country at Sabionetta, a few miles from the city. He likes living in the country because it offers 'Unschuld und Ruhe' [innocence and peace], and he likes Appiani especially for his decision to live in the even remoter region of the Alpine foothills of Piedmont — 'in seinen väterlichen Tälern sich selbst zu leben' [to live his own life in the valleys where his fathers lived] (II. 4). This preference for rural life places him in a long tradition going back to Horace's second Epode, praising rural retirement, and beginning 'Beatus ille' ['Happy the man...'].[17] But in Odoardo's case it is strangely negative.

Odoardo's virtue seems somewhat empty, especially when refracted through Appiani. Earlier I quoted part of Appiani's eulogy of Odoardo. Here is some more:

> Zu was für Gesinnungen erhebt sich meine Seele in seiner Gegenwart! Nie ist mein Entschluß immer gut, immer edel zu sein, lebendiger, als wenn ich ihn sehe — wenn ich ihn mir denke. Und womit sonst, als mit der Erfüllung dieses Entschlusses kann ich mich der Ehre würdig machen, sein Sohn zu heißen, — der Ihrige zu sein, meine Emilia? (II. 7)

> [What aspirations fill my soul in his presence! My resolve always to be noble and good is never stronger than when I see him, than when I think of him. And how other than with the fulfilment of that resolve can I make myself worthy of the honour of being called his son; of being yours, my Emilia!]

Appiani seems in fact much more enthusiastic about Odoardo than about Emilia. He tells us that he and Odoardo have just torn themselves from each other's arms, yet he makes no move to embrace Emilia, and she comments on his low spirits. When he first appears (II. 7) he is pensive, with downcast eyes. He seems to have a melancholy, phlegmatic temperament. It takes the quarrel with Marinelli to stir him up; after it he says: 'Mein Blut ist in Wallung gekommen. Ich fühle mich anders und besser' [It set my blood racing. I feel a different and a better man] (II. 11) A contemporary commentator, Matthias Claudius, speaks of 'die melancholische Schwärmerei des Grafen Appiani' [Count Appiani's melancholy enthusiasm] (L VII, 891). One should hesitate, therefore, before taking Appiani, as Helmuth Kiesel does, as a straightforward embodiment of the type of virtue that prefers rural innocence to courtly corruption.[18] Nor is he just 'empfindsam' [sensitive], as Marinelli describes him (I. 6), a description which Wolfgang Martens agrees with.[19] Rather, he seems to want to retreat to the country in order to indulge his melancholy.

---

16   Hermann J. Weigand, 'Warum stirbt Emilia Galotti?' in his *Fährten und Funde: Aufsätze zur deutschen Literatur*, ed. by A. Leslie Willson (Bern and Munich: Francke, 1967), pp. 39–50 (p. 42).

17   See Anke-Marie Lohmeier, *Beatus ille: Studien zum 'Lob des Landlebens' in der Literatur des absolutistischen Zeitalters* (Tübingen: Niemeyer, 1981), esp. her 'Ausblick' into the eighteenth century, pp. 405–32.

18   Helmuth Kiesel, *'Bei Hof, bei Höll': Untersuchungen zur literarischen Hofkritik von Sebastian Brant bis Friedrich Schiller* (Tübingen: Niemeyer, 1979), p. 231.

19   Wolfgang Martens, *Der patriotische Minister: Fürstendiener in der Literatur der Aufklärungszeit* (Weimar, Cologne, Vienna: Böhlau, 1996), p. 272. Contrast the account of Appiani's melancholy in Matthew Bell, *The German Tradition of Psychology in Literature and Thought, 1700–1840* (Cambridge: Cambridge University Press, 2005), pp. 45–46.

The virtue which Appiani praises in Odoardo, and vice versa, seems less an expression of moral principle than of the respective temperaments of its exponents. Odoardo is choleric, Appiani melancholy. Both Appiani and Odoardo must come under suspicion of 'Schwärmerei', a disposition defined by Wieland as 'eine Erhitzung der Seele von Gegenständen, die entweder gar nicht in der Natur sind, oder wenigstens das nicht sind, wofür die berauschte Seele sie ansieht' [the soul being heated by objects that either are not in nature or at least are not what the intoxicated soul considers them].[20]

What about Emilia? Originally Lessing conceived her story as a tragedy of virtue: 'das Schicksal einer Tochter, die von ihrem Vater umgebracht wird, dem ihre Tugend werter ist, als ihr Leben' [the fate of a daughter killed by her father, to whom her virtue is dearer than her life] (letter to Nicolai, 21 January 1758, L 11/1, p. 267). In the play of 1772, her virtue has been narrowed down to 'Unschuld' [innocence], as she calls it — yet commentators from Lessing's time till now have had great difficulty in making sense of the climactic scene. Goethe, according to his friend Riemer, complained in blunt language that the play never made clear whether Emilia did or did not love the Prince, and thus left her conduct open to multiple interpretations:

> Die Liebe ist zwar angedeutet, erstlich in der Art wie sie den Prinzen anhört, wie sie nachher ins Zimmer stürzt: denn wenn sie ihn nicht liebte, so hätte sie ihn ablaufen lassen; zuletzt sogar ausgesprochen, aber ungeschickt, in ihrer Furcht vor des Kanzlers Hause: denn entweder sey sie eine *Gans*, sich davor zu fürchten, oder ein *Lüderchen*. So aber, wenn sie ihn liebe, müsse sie sogar zuletzt lieber fordern zu sterben, um jenes Haus zu vermeiden.[21]

> [Love is certainly suggested, first in how she listens to the Prince and how she afterwards rushes into the room; for if she did not love him, she would have sent him packing; finally, explicitly but clumsily, in her fear of the Chancellor's house: for either she is a silly girl to be afraid of it, or else a little slut. But if she does love him, she should finally demand to die, in order to avoid that house.]

When one reads the final scene in cold blood, not carried away by the characters' frenzied emotions, it seems strange and contrived, inviting such speculations as those voiced by Goethe. Lessing earlier criticized Wieland's drama *Lady Johanna Gray* for not humanizing virtue: 'er hat die Tugend gemalt, *aber nicht in Handlungen, nicht nach dem Leben*' [he has painted virtue, *but not in action, not from life*].[22] *Miß Sara Sampson* was by contrast intended as a lifelike depiction of 'Tugend', and seemed so to its audiences, if we may judge from its spell-binding and emotional effect.[23] Emilia's behaviour is more extreme, yet less convincing.

20 Wieland, *Der Teutsche Merkur* (1775), quoted in Manfred Engel, 'Die Rehabilitation des Schwärmers. Theorie und Darstellung des Schwärmens in Spätaufklärung und früher Goethezeit', in *Der ganze Mensch: Anthropologie und Literatur im 18. Jahrhundert*, ed. by Hans-Jürgen Schings (Stuttgart and Weimar: Metzler, 1994), pp. 469–98 (p. 472).

21 Friedrich Wilhelm Riemer, *Mittheilungen über Goethe, aus mündlichen und schriftlichen, gedruckten und ungedruckten Quellen*, 2 vols (Berlin: Duncker & Humblot, 1841), II, 663–64, dated 4 March 1812.

22 '63. Literaturbrief', L 4, p. 646; emphasis in original.

23 Thus Ramler told Gleim how an audience at Frankfurt had sat stock still, weeping, through a three-and-a-half-hour performance: L 3, p. 1221.

One objection that is difficult to answer is that Emilia has not previously seemed a determined character, yet now she forces her father into the morally outrageous action of killing his own daughter. Claudia describes her as 'die Furchtsamste und Entschlossenste unsers Geschlechts' [the most timid and yet the most determined of our sex] (IV. 8). But telling us that she is resolute is a poor substitute for displaying her resolution, whereas her fearfulness was apparent when she came rushing back from church after her encounter with the Prince. Commentators have also been puzzled by Emilia's assertion that she has a sensual nature — 'Ich habe Blut, mein Vater; so warmes, so jugendliches Blut, als eine. Auch meine Sinne, sind Sinne' [I have blood in my veins too, father, warm young blood like any other girl] (v. 7). We have not seen her sensuality before. Instead, we have seen an excessively pious young woman who, to her father's astonishment, goes to mass on her wedding morning, who declares herself to be dependent on divine grace, who prays to her guardian angel to make her deaf, if necessary for all the rest of her life, so that she cannot hear the Prince's advances, and who thinks that in the sight of heaven, the wish to sin is equivalent to the deed: 'Und sündigen wollen, auch sündigen' [And the will to sin [will be taken] for sin] (II. 6). Appiani professed to be glad that in her he would have 'eine fromme Frau' [a pious woman] (II. 7). But the play's first readers were less pleased. The playwright's brother Karl Lessing found something contemptible in her passive piety — but then, he added, 'Sie ist eine Katholikin' [She is a Catholic] (L VII, 873). He made sense of her by maintaining that she was an extreme example of Catholic piety which kept her in the naïve belief that chastity was the highest form of virtue.

The play not only reminds us that of course Emilia is a Catholic — she attends mass in the Church of the Dominicans — but also suggests the specifically Catholic character of her piety in her appeal to her guardian angel and in 'die strengsten Übungen der Religion' [the severest religious exercises] (v. 7) with which she tries to erase the impression made on her by the goings-on in the Grimaldi household. Yet her piety also seems confused. It is puzzling that although she relied on divine grace when the Prince accosted her in church she makes no reference to grace in the final act. Instead she talks wildly of thousands of women who flung themselves into the water and were canonized. This may refer to the legend of St Ursula and the eleven thousand virgins who were put to death beside the Rhine; but as Colin Walker says, there is no suggestion that they jumped into it.[24] Her recourse to suicide is explicitly forbidden by Augustine and Aquinas, as Walker demonstrates.[25] Lessing too expressed disapproval of suicide. Reviewing Moses Mendelssohn's *Über die Empfindungen* [*On the Emotions*] (1755), he says that Mendelssohn has proved that no category of believer or unbeliever can rationally commit suicide:

> Er beweiset nicht nur, daß dem Gläubigen die Religion, und dem Ungläubigen sein eigenes System der Zernichtung nach dem Tode von dem Selbstmorde abhalten müsse; sondern beweiset auch, daß ihn so gar der Weltweise sich untersagen müsse, welcher den Tod nicht als eine Zernichtung, sondern als

24 Colin Walker, '"So tief ließ mich die Gnade nicht sinken": On the Absence of Divine Grace in *Emilia Galotti*', *Publications of the English Goethe Society*, 57 (1986–87), 75–94 (p. 85).

25 Ibid., pp. 79–80.

einen Übergang in eine andere und vielleicht glücklichere Art von Fortdauer betrachtet. (L III, 419)

[He proves not only that the believer must be restrained from suicide by religion, and the unbeliever by his own conception of annihilation after death; but also that suicide must be rejected even by the philosopher who regards death not as annihilation but as a transition into another and perhaps a happier kind of continued existence.]

And writing to Heinrich Wilhelm von Gerstenberg on 25 February 1768, he says that Ugolino, the hero of Gerstenberg's drama, was right not to commit suicide, because reason requires one to submit to providence: 'Die Vernunft befiehlt mir, mich der Vorsicht in allen Vorfällen geduldig zu unterwerfen' [Reason commands me to submit patiently to Providence in all eventualities] (L XI/i, 505–06).

Emilia, more generally, seems, like Appiani, to illustrate 'Schwärmerei'. But while his is the melancholy type, hers is the religious variant. If so, then her sudden profession of sensuality need not be a surprise, because it illustrates the widespread assumption that 'Schwärmerei' and sensuality are opposite sides of the same coin. Wilhelm Dilthey implies such a connection when he says of Emilia: 'Sie ist das Geschöpf eines heißen südlichen Naturells, frühreifer Erfahrungen des Beichtstuhls und der Träume, die Guastala [sic] und sein Hof in einer so gearteten Natur hervorbrachten' [She is a creature of a warm southern temperament, precocious experience of the confessional and of the dreams that Guastalla and his court produced in such a character].[26] The revelation of her sensuality is not even as unexpected as it seems. If we look back, there are numerous hints at Emilia's sensual nature. She even applies to her devotion the word 'brünstig' [fervid] which more commonly has a sexual connotation. Thus Wieland's Thusnelda feels for her husband Hermann 'die edle, brünstige Liebe' [noble, fervid love].[27] Emilia says: 'Nie hätte meine Andacht inniger, brünstiger sein sollen, als heute' [Never should my devotions have been more heartfelt, more fervid than they were to have been today] (II. 6). The word 'Sinne' [senses] links the Emilia we first meet with the Emilia of the death scene. She tells her mother how, when accosted by the Prince, she became insensible: 'Meine Sinne hatten mich verlassen' [My senses had taken leave of me] (II. 6). Another link between earlier and later scenes is the highly sensual image of the rose which she intends to wear in her hair. Yet another is her repeated physical tussling with the Prince: first when he seizes her arm to delay her leaving the church, then at Dosalo when he leads her, 'nicht ohne Sträuben' [despite her evident unwillingness] (III. 5) to a room from which her 'Gequieke' and 'Gekreische' are heard [shrieking and crying] (IV. 3). Subliminally at least, Lessing has after all suggested a sensual excitability which can be seen as related to her excessive piety.[28]

---

26   Wilhelm Dilthey, *Das Erlebnis und die Dichtung* (Leipzig and Berlin: Teubner, 1921), p. 80.

27   *Wielands Gesammelte Schriften*, I: *Poetische Jugendwerke. Erster Teil*, ed. by Fritz Homeyer (1909), p. 154.

28   On Emilia's sensuality, see Gloria Flaherty, 'Emilia Galotti's Italian heritage', *Modern Language Notes*, 97 (1982), 497–514.

There was by Lessing's time an extensive literature criticizing religious enthusiasm, in which a frequent target was the conduct of devout Catholic women, particularly nuns who had visions, stigmata, and the like. The Counter-Reformation produced many examples. Thus Meric Casaubon, in *A Treatise concerning Enthusiasme* (1655), describes a French Carmelite nun, Sister Catherine of Jesus, who was very devout from her childhood, and 'strangely addicted to bodily pennances and voluntary chastisements'.[29] Casaubon ascribes her visions of heaven and hell to her own melancholy temperament:

> Truly I do not see any cause to believe that in any of these many Visions or Ecstasies, there was any thing at all supernaturall, either divine or diabolicall, more then is in every common disease: wherein we acknowledge as the hand of God alwayes; so the ministry of the Devil, if not alwayes, very often, as was before declared. I conceive them all, both Visions and Ecstasies, to have been the effect of pure melancholy; very agreeable to what hath happened unto other melancholick persons, in other places.[30]

Pierre Bayle likewise insists on the power of the imagination in producing, especially among nuns, the illusion of demonic possession:

> Une semblable persuasion peut facilement tomber dans l'esprit de ces Religieuses devôtes, qui lisent beaucoup de traittez remplis d'histoires de tentations & d'apparitions. Elles attribuent à la malice de Satan les mauvaises pensées qui leur viennent, & si elles remarquent une forte opiniatreté dans leurs tentations, elles s'imaginent qu'il les persecute de plus près, qu'il les obsede, & enfin qu'il s'empare de leurs corps.[31]

> [A similar conviction can easily enter the minds of those devout nuns who read many treatises filled with stories about temptations and apparitions. They ascribe the bad thoughts that occur to them to the malice of Satan, and if they find their temptations very persistent, they imagine that he is persecuting them at close quarters, that he is besetting them, and finally that he is taking possession of their bodies.]

Bayle instances the mystic St Angela of Foligno. By her own account, the devils who entered her body inflamed her with intolerable sexual desire: 'Ils excitoient dans son corps une telle flamme d'impureté, qu'elle ne s'en pouvoit reprimer la force, que par le feu materiel, mais son confesseur lui defendit ce remede' [They excited in her body such a flame of impurity, that she could not resist its force except by material fire, but her confessor forbade her this remedy].[32] The Latin original, which Bayle prints in the margin, speaks unmistakably of 'ignem concupiscentiae', fire of lust.

It is then hard to see Emilia's suicide (if that is what it is) as the expression of virtue. Rather, a combination of intense piety, intense sensuality, and a powerful imagination persuades her that she must die to escape the Prince. Lessing held to

29 Meric Casaubon, *A Treatise concerning Enthusiasme* (1655), facsimile edition by Paul J. Korshin (Gainsville, FL: Scholars' Facsimile Reprints, 1970), p. 158.

30 Ibid., p. 164.

31 Pierre Bayle, *Réponse aux questions d'un provincial*, 5 vols (Rotterdam: Reinier Leers, 1704), I, 287–88.

32 Ibid., p. 288.

a cognitive conception of ethics, as H. B. Nisbet has shown, derived from Leibniz and Wolff, in which 'virtue consists primarily in rational knowledge of the good', though this is sometimes in tension with his theory of tragic pity as the beneficial effect of drama on the spectator.[33] Yet Emilia's suicide and her father's killing of her are in no way rationally considered. They occur in a tumult of emotion.

Emilia forms a sharp contrast to Sara Sampson. For both, virtue is bound up with piety. 'Ist Liebe vielleicht die Eigenschaft, die am meisten in die Augen springt, ist Saras Frömmigkeit für das Bild ihrer Tugendhaftigkeit von kaum geringerer Bedeutung. Sara sieht alle Dinge unter religiösem Aspekt' [If love is perhaps her most conspicuous quality, Sara's piety is of scarcely less importance for the picture of her virtuous character. Sara sees all things under the aspect of religion], writes Ferdinand von Ingen.[34] But Sara's is a Protestant piety; Emilia's is Catholic. Sara's virtue is innate to her. Sir William says: 'Solche Vergehungen sind besser, als erzwungene Tugenden' [Such misdemeanours are better than enforced virtue] (I. 1). By contrast, Emilia's virtue is forced. She has to tame her physical desires by the severest exercises of religion — presumably, as Colin Walker suggests, the Spiritual Exercises of St Ignatius Loyola.[35] Since she is represented as living in Counter-Reformation Italy, she will have been told by her confessor how seriously the Church regards any deviation, in thought as well as deed, from the sexual purity to which, as Jean Delumeau has shown, it attached such overwhelming importance, and her sense of guilt will thus have been heightened.[36] Sara submits to Providence; Emilia takes Providence into her own hands by persuading her father to kill her. Lessing disapproved of suicide and admired the Stoic virtue of steadfastness: he praised Gerstenberg's Ugolino for facing death with 'Standhaftigkeit und Unterwerfung' [steadfastness and submission] (L XI/i, 506).

The more we examine the Galotti family, the more extraordinary they seem. They are not just 'von gleichem Schrot und Korne' [of the same stuff as ourselves], as Lessing said dramatic characters ought to be in order to engage the audience's empathy (L VI, 559). They verge on the pathological, with Odoardo's impulsiveness and lack of self-control, Appiani's melancholy, and Emilia's religious 'Schwärmerei'. And the relation between Odoardo and Emilia looks peculiar too. He is suspicious when he learns that Emilia has gone to mass; that seems to him inappropriate on her wedding day; and a single step is 'genug zu einem Fehltritt' [enough to put a foot wrong] (II. 2) — does that imply suspicion of her? She fears loss of her virginity: so does Odoardo. He says that is the place where he (why *he*, rather than she?) is most easily wounded (II. 4). His killing of her, expressed as breaking a rose, has, as Peter Horst Neumann says, a 'Hauch von Inzest' [breath of incest].[37] Breaking the rose suggests a symbolic defloration.

33   H. B. Nisbet, 'Lessing's Ethics', *Lessing Yearbook*, 25 (1993), 1–40 (p. 3).

34   Ferdinand van Ingen, 'Tugend bei Lessing. Bemerkungen zu *Miß Sara Sampson*', *Amsterdamer Beiträge zur Neueren Germanistik*, 1 (1972), 43–73 (p. 46).

35   Walker, p. 78.

36   See Jean Delumeau, *Le Péché et la Peur: la culpabilisation en Occident, XIIIe-XVIIIe siècles* (Paris: Fayard, 1983), esp. pp. 486–97.

37   Peter Horst Neumann, *Der Preis der Mündigkeit: Über Lessings Dramen* (Stuttgart: Klett-Cotta, 1977), p. 49.

Helmut J. Schneider has recently shown how Kleist undermines the apparent Enlightenment certainties of Lessing's work by treating such themes as the family in a radical manner that exposes raw nature underlying culture.[38] Thus while in *Nathan der Weise* the adoption of a stranger strengthens the family, the adoption of Nicolo in *Der Findling* [*The Foundling*] serves to unleash the passions of lust and hatred which the institution of the family was meant to control. Following Schneider, I want to suggest a similar argument concerning *Emilia Galotti* and *Die Marquise von O...*. The family is held together by emotional bonds in which raw desire is constrained by the incest taboo. Family love may be called a compromise formation. The threat to Emilia's chastity from the libidinous Prince — a very different person from the dismal, pious, unerotic Appiani — arouses Odoardo's sexual passion for his daughter. As we know from René Girard and many others, desire is the desire of the other: that is, something looks much more desirable when another person desires it. But Odoardo's way of coping with this upsurge of passion is to get rid of it by killing Emilia, and it is important that he contemplates killing her even before she urges him to do so. In *Die Marquise von O...*, the Colonel — an officer with the very same rank as Odoardo — reacts to the news of his daughter's pregnancy by violently throwing her out of the house; then, when his wife has by a very extraordinary stratagem reassured herself of their daughter's innocence, the Colonel takes his daughter on his knee, sheds tears, and kisses her, 'gerade wie ein Verliebter!' [exactly like a lover!].[39] We have moved far beyond the Enlightenment. The family ought to be the abode of virtue, controlled by the incest taboo. But, early in Kleist's story, such a virtuous family proved to be dysfunctional. By insisting on conventional morality, the Colonel split the family apart. Later, by taking back his daughter and admitting and enacting his incestuous love for her, he ought to be rendering his family dysfunctional, requiring the immediate attention of social workers, but in fact the family is now far happier. The Galotti family, ostensibly dedicated to middle-class ideals of 'Tugend', are in fact dysfunctional, and it only takes the Prince's intervention to throw their ideals into utter disarray.

Emilia stands in contrast to the Prince's previous mistress, Gräfin Orsina, presented as a highly intelligent woman who reads books (I. 6), defends a woman's right to think, and has, as Marinelli mockingly says, the reputation of a 'Philosophin' [female philosopher] (IV. 3). Ironically, it is with Orsina that, as Wilfried Barner has shown, Lessing's debt to Seneca is clearest — not, however, to Seneca the Stoic philosopher, but to Seneca the dramatist, author of *Medea*, which also provides the model for Marwood in *Miß Sara Sampson*.[40] In Lessing's day the philosopher and the dramatist were widely thought to be different persons. When Orsina sarcastically asks: 'Ist es wohl noch Wunder, daß mich der Prinz verachtet? Wie kann ein Mann

---

38   Helmut J. Schneider, 'The Facts of Life: Kleist's Challenge to Enlightenment Humanism (Lessing)', *A Companion to the Works of Heinrich von Kleist*, ed. by Bernd Fischer (Rochester, NY: Camden House, 2003), pp. 141–63.

39   Heinrich von Kleist, *Sämtliche Werke und Briefe*, ed. by Ilse-Maria Barth and others, 4 vols (Frankfurt a.M.: Deutscher Klassiker Verlag, 1989), III, 181.

40   Wilfried Barner, *Produktive Rezeption: Lessing und die Tragödien Senecas* (Munich: Beck, 1973), esp. pp. 76–82.

ein Ding lieben, das, ihm zum Trotze, auch denken will?' [Is it any wonder that the Prince scorns me? How can a man love a creature that insists, as if to spite him, on having her own thoughts?] (IV. 3), she presents herself as an intellectually as well as morally emancipated woman. She thus puts into perspective the submissiveness of Emilia to religious and patriarchal authority. And she behaves in a way to which the conventional concepts of 'Tugend' and 'Laster' seem wholly inadequate. Deeply hurt on being discarded by the Prince and treated with casual indifference, she proposes to take her revenge by getting Odoardo to murder the Prince with the dagger she gives him. While Marwood, in threatening to murder her child, comes across as inhuman and criminal, Orsina belongs to a larger sphere. Yet Odoardo persists in clinging to his simple scheme of 'Tugend' versus 'Laster', virtue versus vice, assigning Emilia to the first and Orsina to the latter: 'Was hat die gekränke Tugend mit der Rache des Lasters zu schaffen?' [What has offended virtue to do with the revenge of vice?] (V. 2).

What do we make now of Odoardo's 'rauhe Tugend'? Claudia deplores his virtue as not only 'rauh' — rough, uncouth — but also 'streng' — harsh, severe. Once again, 'rauhe Tugend' is opposed to courtly polish. Claudia is half wrong and half right. Odoardo has been proved right in worrying about the Prince's striking up an acquaintance with his daughter. Claudia thinks Odoardo is excessively suspicious; that such uncouth virtue hardly deserves the name of virtue; that, if Odoardo shows knowledge of people, such knowledge is not worth having — a hint that he is misanthropic; and that he is charging the Prince with making up to Emilia merely in order to disgrace him (Odoardo). All these responses evade Odoardo's central concern — that Emilia is in danger from the Prince because 'Ein Wollüstling, der bewundert, begehrt' [A rake who admires also desires] (II. 4). This is unjust inasmuch as the Prince is not a mere debauchee. Rather than an old-style cynical libertine, he is a new-style 'empfindsam' seducer, given to emotional self-indulgence almost in the manner of Goethe's Werther. Even so, Emilia is certainly in danger from him. However, rough virtue is not the way to rescue her. His uncourtly bluntness leaves Odoardo at a loss when faced by the smooth talk of the Prince and Marinelli. He cannot speak their language. Hence, when they tell him that Emilia's abduction needs to be investigated and she must be kept separate from her family, he fails even to protest. His failure has often been seen as a sign of his inability to cope with the atmosphere of the court. Thus Herder, defending Lessing's characterization against hostile critics, said of the climactic scene: 'Der Alte hat eben so wohl, als das erschrockene Mädchen in der betäubenden Hofluft den Kopf verloren; und eben diese Verwirrung, die Gefahr solcher Charaktere in solcher Nähe wollte der Dichter schildern' [The old man, just like the frightened girl, lost his head in the dizzying atmosphere of the court; and it was this confusion, the danger posed to such characters in such a setting, that the poet wanted to depict].[41]

---

41 Johann Gottfried Herder, *Briefe zur Beförderung der Humanität*, 37, in Herder, *Werke*, ed. by Günter Arnold and others, 10 vols (Frankfurt a.M.: Deutscher Klassiker Verlag, 1985–2000), vol. VII, ed. by Hans Dietrich Irmscher (1991), p. 200.

Rather than pitting middle-class virtue against aristocratic vice — as in so many Sturm und Drang tragedies modelled on it — the play, more interestingly, examines the weaknesses latent in that very virtue on which the middle-class characters so pride themselves. The Galottis' virtue proves fragile, because when it is tested the characters are guided by emotion rather than principle. Odoardo is a victim of his own hasty and choleric temperament, Appiani of his melancholy, while Emilia shows an incongruous but plausible combination of sensuality and religious enthusiasm. However unconvincing as representatives of middle-class virtue, they are fascinating studies in the various types of emotional excess that were grouped together as 'Schwärmerei'.

CHAPTER 3

Literary Techniques and Complex Words in Goethe's *Faust*

1. Dramatic Poetry

Faust is a dramatic poem, and to appreciate it one needs to understand its poetic language. The reader without German need not despair, for the many translations include some masterpieces — here I would single out those by David Luke — which provide real access to the poem. This essay, however, is written for the reader who knows German, or at least enough German to tackle Goethe's text with a translation to hand.

Such a reader will soon notice the variety of Goethe's dramatic poetry. In some poetic dramas, especially those committed to a high or dignified style, all the characters speak a broadly homogeneous language, which only incidentally, and through nuance, serves the expression of individuality. That is the case in Racine, in Schiller, and in Goethe's own neoclassical dramas *Iphigenie auf Tauris* and *Torquato Tasso*. *Faust*, however, is quite differently conceived. Each of the main characters is a distinct person inhabiting a distinct world which in turn expresses his or her individuality. 'Die Natur bildet den Menschen,' wrote Goethe in 1775, 'er bildet sich um, und diese Umbildung ist doch wieder natürlich; er, der sich in die große weite Welt gesetzt sieht, umzäunt, ummauert sich eine kleine drein, und staffiert sie aus nach seinem Bilde.'[1] Hence Part One repeatedly emphasizes the 'world' that a character inhabits. Looking round his Gothic study, Faust laments: 'Das ist deine Welt! das heißt eine Welt!' (409). He imagines Gretchen, whose domestic peace he had disrupted, 'Umfangen in der kleinen Welt' (3355). And since the characters inhabit different worlds, they often fail to understand one another. Barker Fairley pointed out how often in *Faust* apparent dialogues are really competing monologues: 'It is a case of people not quite talking to one another.'[2] Thus Faust's discourses are lost on his pedantic assistant, Wagner; the profession of faith that Gretchen extorts from him clearly goes over her head; and in his many conversations with Mephisto, Faust

---

1   Goethe, 'Anteile an Lavaters *Physiognomischen Fragmenten*', in *Sämtliche Werke*, ed. by Friedmar Apel et al., 40 vols (Frankfurt a.M.: Deutscher Klassiker Verlag, 1986–2000), XVIII: *Ästhetische Schriften, 1771–1805*, ed. by Friedmar Apel (1998), p. 142. *Faust* is quoted from vol. VII, ed. by Albrecht Schöne (1994).

2   Barker Fairley, *Goethe's 'Faust': Six Essays* (Oxford: Clarendon Press, 1953), p. 24.

is slow to register that he has thrown in his lot with a devil, showing considerable obtuseness even in the recognition scene 'Trüber Tag. Feld'. With these different worlds of consciousness side by side in the play, Goethe's dramatic verse assumes an extraordinary variety and flexibility, which is sustained in Part Two. Here we move further from familiar drama of human interaction into pageantry, mystery, allegory, and a vast display of what the aged Goethe called 'ernst gemeinte Scherze' (letter to Sulpiz Boisserée, 24 Nov. 1831). But in both Parts, as Eckermann noted, the separate scenes are 'little world-circles, each existing alone' ('für sich bestehende kleine Weltenkreise', 13 Feb. 1831), each with its own atmosphere conveyed through poetic language.

Lack of space requires me to concentrate mainly on the dramatic poetry of Part One. I shall briefly survey the main metrical forms Goethe uses, keeping to a minimum the counting of syllables, and aiming to bring out how metre expresses character and mood. I shall then show, with some reference to Part Two, how Goethe's language was enriched by the Bible, by his study of world literature, and by the language of the liturgy. Finally, returning to Part One, I shall look closely at the poetic deployment of some key words, aiming to show how Goethe exploits the tension and instability in the range of meanings they can have, and thus poetically suggests yet further implications which hover, as it were, on the edge of the text.

The staple metre of both parts of *Faust* is madrigal verse ('Madrigalvers'), which, according to the invaluable study of *Faust*'s metres by Markus Ciupke, accounts for 2642 lines out of 4612 in Part One and for 2127 out of 7498 in Part Two.[3] As its name suggests, madrigal verse originated as a song metre; it was also used in the eighteenth century for chatty verse narratives such as fables. It is basically iambic, with a varying number of stressed syllables, usually four to six, but sometimes fewer; additional unstressed syllables can be inserted, and many variations on the iambic pattern are possible. Thus a line can acquire an energetic start from an initial trochee:

> Wenn ihr's nicht fühlt, ihr werdet's nicht erjagen (534);

haste can be suggested by dactyls:

> Stürzen wir uns in das Rauschen der Zeit (1754);

and solemn emphasis can be supplied by a spondee:

> Zwei Seelen wohnen, ach! in meiner Brust (1112).

Madrigal verse is the *lingua franca* of *Faust*. It is used especially for conversation, even when the characters talk past each other. It is flexible in line length, permitting even such short lines as 'So tausendfach' (2025) and 'Mein Bruder ist Soldat' (3120). It is flexible also in its rhymes, permitting couplets ('Paarreim'), alternating rhymes ('Kreuzreim', abab), and 'embracing rhymes' ('umarmender Reim' or 'Blockreim': abba). It is the medium in which the Lord converses with Mephisto, and Faust with Wagner, Mephisto and Gretchen. To see its dramatic potential, consider the

---

3   Markus Ciupke, *Des Geklimpers vielverworrner Töne Rausch: Die metrische Gestaltung in Goethes 'Faust'* (Göttingen: Wallstein, 1994), pp. 234–35. I am very much indebted to this excellent book.

following exchange:

DER HERR.	Hast du mir weiter nichts zu sagen?
	Kommst du nur immer anzuklagen?
	Ist auf der Erde ewig dir nichts recht?
MEPHISTO.	Nein, Herr! ich find' es dort, wie immer, herzlich schlecht.
	Die Menschen dauern mich in ihren Jammertagen,
	Ich mag sogar die armen selbst nicht plagen.
DER HERR.	Kennst du den Faust?
MEPHISTO.	Den Doktor?
DER HERR.	Meinen Knecht! (293–99)

The Lord's first words are dignified, reserved, impatient and gruff. In each of his three lines, the first few words are lightly stressed, preparing for an irritated emphasis on 'weiter', 'immer' and 'ewig' — three words which themselves form a crescendo by stating Mephisto's constant dissatisfaction ever more strongly. The first two lines have four beats, the third has five, and Mephisto outdoes his master by replying with a six-beat line which, moreover, starts with an emphatic, defiant spondee ('Nein, Herr!') and ends by answering the Lord's rhyme with a word that is antithetical in meaning ('schlecht' to 'recht'). His following couplet, however, proves to be embraced by a 'Blockreim'. Its last line is an antilabe, that is, a line divided among more than one speaker, which quickens the dramatic tempo (there are several antilabes later in the fight scene with Valentin: 3708–20). The line ends with the description of Faust as 'Meinen Knecht!' uttered firmly by the Lord, whose laconic, almost military manner suggests the habit of command, in extreme contrast to Mephisto's almost unstoppable loquacity.

When our attention moves from heaven to earth, we find ourselves listening to the first of Faust's great monologues. Several of these deserve separate discussion. The first, delivered in his study, includes some of the most famous lines in a play which, like *Hamlet*, is full of quotations, and moreover introduces the atmosphere of sixteenth-century Germany in which the Faust legend originated:

FAUST.	Habe nun, ach! Philosophie,
	Juristerei und Medizin,
	Und leider auch Theologie
	Durchaus studiert, mit heißem Bemühn.
	Da steh' ich nun, ich armer Tor,
	Und bin so klug als wie zuvor! (354–59)

Goethe found verse like this in the work of the Nuremberg shoemaker-poet Hans Sachs (1494–1576). As early as the seventeenth century, conscientious metrists dismissed such rough verse as 'Knittelvers' (literally 'cudgel verse'), but Goethe adopted it for his early comic plays (e.g. *Hanswursts Hochzeit*, 1773–75) and used it in a tribute to its master, 'Hans Sachsens poetische Sendung' (1776). 'Knittelvers' has four (occasionally five) beats and a varying number of unstressed syllables; it can begin with a trochee ('Habe', 'Durchaus') or an iamb ('Und leider auch'); and it is most often a sequence of rhyming couplets. It sounds rough, blunt, even naive; it is often used to address the audience directly. Goethe uses it for the Student who has his leg pulled by Mephisto, for Gretchen on her first appearances, and for her brother Valentin. But it was a bold stroke to adapt 'Knittelvers' to express Faust's frustration at having traversed the whole circle of scholarship without having learnt anything worth knowing. Great poets, said Heine, express despair through a comic mask, as Shakespeare does with the Fool in *King Lear*; and 'den großen Denkerschmerz, der seine eigne Nichtigkeit begreift, wagt Goethe nur in den Knittelversen eines Puppenspiels auszusprechen.'[4]

If the study of poetry really were a matter of counting syllables, one might discern no great difference between the 'Knittelvers' of Faust's opening monologue and the language of his Easter monologue in 'Vor dem Tor' (903–40):

> FAUST.   Vom Eise befreit sind Strom und Bäche
> Durch des Frühlings holden, belebenden Blick;
> Im Tale grünet Hoffnungsglück;
> Der alte Winter, in seiner Schwäche,
> Zog sich in rauhe Berge zurück.
> Von dorther sendet er, fliehend, nur
> Ohnmächtige Schauer körnigen Eises
> In Streifen über die grünende Flur;
> Aber die Sonne duldet kein Weißes [...]

Here again the fluency comes from the varying number of unstressed syllables, the liberty of beginning a line with a trochee or an iamb, and the movable rhymes. These lines, however, differ from 'Knittelvers' in their lyrical profusion of adjectives, their colours (green, white), their discreet vowel-pattering ('Vom Eise befreit') and alliteration ('belebenden Blick'), and in the personification of natural phenomena: winter, now old and feeble, retreats to the mountains before the gaze of the spring and the refusal of the sun to tolerate any snow or hail. A purist would query some of the rhymes: the impure rhyme of 'Blick' with 'Glück' is common enough to pass, but 'Eises' does not properly rhyme with 'Weißes'. Elsewhere Goethe notoriously rhymed words which were pronounced similarly in Frankfurt and Leipzig, and may not have seemed provincial in the eighteenth century, but sound incongruous now: 'Buch' with 'genug' (419, 421), 'nach' with 'Tag' (698, 701), and 'neige' with 'Schmerzensreiche' (3587–88).

Faust again evokes nature lyrically in his monologue in 'Wald und Höhle' (3217–50). Here the metre is blank verse, the iambic pentameter familiar from Shakespeare and from Lessing's *Nathan der Weise* (1779), and developed into a subtle instrument of lyrical and psychological exploration by Goethe himself in the neoclassical plays, *Iphigenie* and *Tasso*, which he composed in the same years as this passage. Why the passage should thank the Earth Spirit for giving Faust what he asked for, when we have already seen the Earth Spirit dismissing Faust scornfully, and why it should blame the Earth Spirit for saddling him with Mephisto who, as the 'Prolog' tells us, is the emissary of the Lord — these much-discussed enigmas need not concern us here.[5] The lines reveal a contemplative Faust whom we have not seen before, except

---

4   *Ideen. Das Buch Le Grand*, in Heinrich Heine, *Sämtliche Schriften*, ed. by Klaus Briegleb, 6 vols (Munich: Hanser, 1968–76), II, 282.

5   See Eudo C. Mason, *Goethe's 'Faust': Its Genesis and Purport* (Berkeley and Los Angeles:

very briefly when he summoned up the Macrocosm:

> Du führst die Reihe der Lebendigen
> Vor mir vorbei, und lernst mir meine Brüder
> Im stillen Busch, in Luft und Wasser kennen.
> Und wenn der Sturm im Walde braust und knarrt,
> Die Riesenfichte stürzend Nachbaräste
> Und Nachbarstämme quetschend niederstreift,
> Und ihrem Fall dumpf hohl der Hügel donnert,
> Dann führst du mich zur sichern Höhle, zeigst
> Mich dann mir selbst, und meiner eignen Brust
> Geheime tiefe Wunder öffnen sich. (3225–34)

In this quotation, natural violence is framed within peaceful contemplation, enhanced by the regularity of the metre. In the first and last few lines, the adjectives are all static ('still', 'sicher', 'geheim', 'tief'). Faust is a passive onlooker; none of the verbs has him as its subject. Only in the central passage do violent, onomatopoeic verbs convey how the huge fir-tree is blown down by the gale; the three successive stresses in 'Fall dumpf hohl' themselves enact, as Ciupke finely observes, the crashing of the tree-trunk.[6]

A more familiar Faust appears in 'Marthens Garten', explaining his religious creed to Gretchen, who, not being entirely naive, is suspicious of his orthodoxy. Here Faust turns to 'free rhythms' ('freie Rhythmen'), a verse-form pioneered in the 1750s by Klopstock to express an ecstatic devotion to God, and adopted by Goethe in such famous early hymnic poems as 'Prometheus' and 'Ganymed'. Free rhythms are normally unrhymed; Faust here uses rhymes (3432–33, 3435–36) only to underline the futility of theistic or atheistic affirmation, and goes on to express, in a series of short lines varying in length and stress, his sense that divinity is present and active around and within us. The loose metre and lack of rhyme are compensated by intricate verbal repetition ('Der Allumfasser, | Der Allerhalter, | Faßt und erhält er nicht | Dich, mich, sich selbst?'; 3438–41) and sound-patterning ('Und steigen freundlich blickend | Ewige Sterne nicht herauf?'; 3444–45). The excited mood is heightened by exclamations and rhetorical questions.

One last illustration of Faust's metrical versatility, and also of Goethe's response to poetic tradition, comes from Part Two. In the opening scene, 'Anmutige Gegend', Faust, having been cast into a therapeutic sleep by kindly spirits, wakes and delivers a monologue in iambic pentameter and *terza rima* modelled on Dante's *Divine Comedy*. Before writing this scene in 1826, Goethe had been studying Dante in the new German translation by Karl Streckfuss. Its setting recalls the Earthly Paradise which Dante's Pilgrim enters in *Purgatorio* xxviii, before drinking from the river Lethe and being led through it by Matilda to meet Beatrice.[7] The rhyme-scheme of *terza rima* (ababcbcdcdede, etc.) creates a continuity which can only be

---

University of California Press, 1967), ch. 5; Rolf Christian Zimmermann, *Das Weltbild des jungen Goethe*, 2 vols (Munich: Fink, 1969, 1979), II, 261–64.

6   Ciupke, *Des Geklimpers vielverworrner Töne Rausch*, p. 73.

7   See Willi Hirdt, 'Goethe und Dante', *Deutsches Dante-Jahrbuch*, 68/69 (1993/94), 31–80 (esp. pp. 76–77).

ended by a final and all the more emphatic 'Kreuzreim'. While Dante's cantos often end in a rather understated way, Goethe uses all the available emphasis to end this scene. Having contemplated the natural energies embodied in the waterfall, Faust considers how it nevertheless refracts the sunlight:

> Allein wie herrlich, diesem Sturm entsprießend,
> Wölbt sich des bunten Bogens Wechseldauer,
> Bald rein gezeichnet, bald in Luft zerfließend,
> Umher verbreitend duftig kühle Schauer.
> <u>Der</u> spiegelt ab das menschliche Bestreben.
> Ihm sinne nach, und du begreifst genauer:
> Am farbigen Abglanz haben wir das Leben. (4721–27)

Here we see Goethe moving from the evocation of nature via his studies of light and colour to the didacticism which so pleased his Victorian admirers. The continuous tercets are well suited for meditation. The regularity of the pentameters is broken only by the initial trochee 'Wölbt sich', underlining the activity of the refracted light and alliterating significantly with 'Wechsel'. The tercets then reach a powerful closure by rhyming two of the poem's key words, '(Be)streben' and 'Leben'. The last word picks up the opening line of this soliloquy: 'Des Lebens Pulse schlagen frisch lebendig' (4679), a line which is, strictly speaking, tautological; but if Shakespeare can get away with pleonasm in writing about 'a strange invisible perfume' (*Antony and Cleopatra*, II. 2. 219), Goethe's example further confirms that great poetry can override the ordinary rules of expression.

Of the other major characters, Mephisto is remarkable for his ability to adapt to whoever he is talking to. He picks up the 'Knittelvers' used by the student; he adopts the madrigal verse and the coarse humour of the drinkers in 'Auerbachs Keller'; and he uses the full flexibility of madrigal verse in his tense, spiky, competitive, only superficially companionable exchanges with Faust. When luring Faust back to Gretchen in the 'Wald und Höhle' scene, he modifies madrigal verse to represent Gretchen's yearning in a brilliant imitation of love poetry:

> Die Zeit wird ihr erbärmlich lang;
> Sie steht am Fenster, sieht die Wolken ziehn
> Über die alte Stadtmauer hin.
> Wenn ich ein Vöglein wär'! so geht ihr Gesang
> Tage lang, halbe Nächte lang. (3315–19)

With its two dactyls ('Über die', 'Stadtmauer') and the emphasis on 'hin' required by the rhyme with 'ziehn', the third line has a slow, dragging motion which expresses Gretchen's absorption in Faust and her weariness in waiting for him. The following line becomes irregular by incorporating the song-line 'Wenn ich ein Vöglein wär', and the last is again slowed by the leisurely opening trochee ('Tage') and the internal rhyme on 'lang'.

Here Mephisto acts, in keeping with the dialectical scheme of *Faust*, as the unwitting agent of life, tempting Faust away from sterile melancholy and back into involvement with others. Often his language is bracing and vigorous, as when he urges Faust to leave his study:

> Drum frisch! Laß alles Sinnen sein,
> Und grad' mit in die Welt hinein!
> Ich sag' es dir: ein Kerl, der spekuliert,
> Ist wie ein Tier, auf dürrer Heide
> Von einem bösen Geist im Kreis herumgeführt,
> Und rings umher liegt schöne grüne Weide. (1828–33)

In comparing Faust's studious seclusion to bewitchment by an evil spirit, Mephisto is bold to the point of insolence. For he is himself an evil spirit who proposes to lead Faust on a futile and circular journey. Moreover, his simile illustrates his constant tendency — appropriate to the Spirit of Negation — to reduce and degrade. In his study, Faust was at least using his reason, the highest human faculty, yet Mephisto compares him to an animal, and offers as an alternative only sensual satisfaction.

Faust himself calls Mephisto an animal, or worse — 'Untier' — in the scene 'Trüber Tag. Feld', where the two come most directly into conflict. This scene is written in prose, as other scenes ('Auerbachs Keller', 'Kerker') originally were, and may have been written as early as 1772. Faust's furious rhetoric, typical of the Sturm und Drang of the 1770s, rebounds against Mephisto's indifference, shown first by his 'Sie ist die erste nicht' and then by his cool 'Endigst du?' ('Have you finished yet?'), and is revealed as the bombast of a guilt-stricken and powerless man. He has no reply to Mephisto's irritated reproach: 'Wer war's, der sie ins Verderben stürzte? Ich oder du?' But the vigorous prose brings out, not only Faust's moral desperation, but also the wider implications of the confrontation. Faust equates Mephisto with the serpent of Eden, and seems to see in him a fiendish monster with bared teeth: 'Fletsche deine gefräßigen Zähne mir nicht so entgegen!' — while Mephisto acutely observes in Faust the tendency of all tyrants (that is, irresponsible and self-willed rulers) to discharge their own frustrations onto others. Faust has not quite attained insight, either into his own faults or into the fatal consequences of allying himself with the devil. Only the 'Kerker' scene will bring him as close as possible to understanding that he has done something wrong that can never be put right in this world.

Gretchen, his victim, has already widened her powers of expression. Although she first speaks in the homely simplicity of 'Knittelvers' (and returns to it in the scene 'Am Brunnen'), with Faust she uses madrigal verse, implying a greater sophistication which will help to betray her. Her depth of feeling is conveyed first by her folk-song 'Es war ein König in Thule', whose theme of loyalty ironically fails to predict her own fate, and later by her monologue at the spinning-wheel. Although its loosely iambic four-beat lines, arranged in quatrains, resemble a folk-song metre, and although it has been set to music by Schubert and many others, this monologue is not sung by Gretchen but recited, following the rhythm of the spinning-wheel. With its mounting passion, it prepares us for the free metres into which she breaks when her situation becomes desperate and her feelings unbearable. While in her address to the Virgin Mary ('Zwinger') her utterances are still shaped partly by liturgical rhythms, partly by those of folk-song, her agony in the Cathedral scene, where she comes close to fainting, is conveyed by free rhythms, speeded by enjambements:

Mir wird so eng!
Die Mauernpfeiler
Befangen mich!
Das Gewölbe
Drängt mich! — Luft! (3816–20)

The 'Kerker' scene shows Gretchen at her lowest and her highest points. Having
borne and drowned her child, and been driven mad by guilt, betrayal, social
ostracism, and (no doubt) official brutality, she nevertheless resists the invitation
to flee with Mephisto, whose evil nature she has already recognized, and throws
herself on the divine mercy. The scene is hard to match anywhere in world
literature. Shakespeare's mad Ophelia arouses pity, but Gretchen passes through
utter distress to tragic heroism by rejecting Faust for the God who, according to the
harsh version of Christianity purveyed by the Evil Spirit in the 'Dom' scene, must
already have condemned her. No wonder that Goethe, having originally written
the scene in prose, felt obliged to versify it in order to reduce 'die unmittelbare
Wirkung des ungeheuern Stoffes' (letter to Schiller, 5 May 1798). After her song,
which reveals her identification with her dead child, Gretchen speaks in rhyming
lines of irregular length, varying from five beats to one ('O weh! deine Lippen sind
kalt, | Sind stumm', 4493–94). The basically iambic pattern lets the ebb and flow
of emotion be expressed through variation with dactyls ('Niemand wird sonst bei
mir liegen!', 4528), amphibrachs ('Sie winkt nicht, sie nickt nicht, der Kopf ist ihr
schwer', 4570), and trochees ('Lagert euch umher, mich zu bewahren!', 4609). As
Gretchen obsessively re-lives their love-affair, her flight, infanticide and arrest, and
anticipates her imminent execution, Faust is reduced to uttering single lines which
gradually cease to rhyme with anything Gretchen says ('Der Tag graut! Liebchen!
Liebchen!' finds no rhyme, 4579).

Throughout Part One, Gretchen, for all her simplicity, shows a greater range of
expression than Faust. She speaks, recites, sings and prays. Faust never sings. Even
Mephisto, in 'Auerbachs Keller', sings the Song of the Flea, thus satisfying the coarse
tastes of the drinkers who have previously been singing about a poisoned rat. The
supernatural beings either sing, or speak in song-like metres. The opening praise of
the universe uttered by the archangels is modelled on versified psalms. The choruses
who celebrate Easter utter basically dactylic verses, modelled on medieval Latin
hymns, with prominent 'gleitende Reime', that is, rhymes extending over more
than one syllable:

Tätig ihn Preisenden,
Liebe Beweisenden,
Brüderlich Speisenden [...] (801–03)

A very similar metre, the Adonic, is used by the spirits who sing Faust to sleep by
evoking a beautiful Mediterranean landscape:

[...] Decken die Laube,
Wo sich fürs Leben,
Tief in Gedanken,
Liebende geben. (1466–69)

2. Biblical and Literary Allusion

Goethe's intimacy with the Bible is obvious, especially in his earlier works.[8] It pervades the texture of *Faust*. Thus when Faust calls himself 'Ebenbild der Gottheit' (516, 614), he is recalling how God made man in His own image and likeness (Gen. 1. 26); when he tells Wagner not to be a 'schellenlauter Tor' (549), he echoes the 'tinkling cymbal' ('klingende Schelle' in Luther's translation) of 1 Cor. 13. 1; and his visionary 'Feuerwagen' (702) suggests the fiery chariot which carries Elijah up to heaven (II Kings 2. 11). From many possibilities, I will single out three striking allusions.

As a young man Goethe studied the Old Testament intently with the aid of such Hebrew as he knew and of the new historical approach to its composition and context (FA XIV, 300–03). In particular, he attempted a new translation of the Song of Songs, which he considered 'die herrlichste Sammlung liebes Lieder die Gott erschaffen hat' (to Merck, 7 Oct. 1775), and this lyricism helped to inspire Gretchen's poetry of yearning.[9] The phrase which the Authorized Version renders 'my bowels were moved for him' (Song of Solomon 5. 4) was translated by Goethe as 'mich überliefs', which appears in *Faust* as Gretchen's exclamation 'Mich überläuft's!' (3187). The cynical Mephisto adapts the Song (4. 5: 'Thy two breasts are like two young roes that are twins, which feed among the lilies') in telling Faust:

> Ich hab' Euch oft beneidet
> Ums Zwillingspaar, das unter Rosen weidet. (3336–37)

When Goethe was completing *Faust: Der Tragödie erster Teil*, he decided to frame the drama in a heavenly prologue which he modelled on the Book of Job. The scene is contained *in nuce* in Job 2. 1:

> Again there was a day when the sons of God came to present themselves before the Lord, and Satan came also among them to present himself before the Lord.

The subsequent dialogue, in which the Lord calls Job 'my servant' and Satan undertakes to destroy his piety, forms a template for the conversation between the Lord and Mephisto, in which Mephisto engages in a one-sided wager that he will divert Faust from his divinely appointed path. Ironically, the analogy with Job rebounds on Mephisto; for much later, when angels descend to carry off Faust's immortal part and frustrate his hopes, the roses they throw bring him out in sores which he himself compares to Job's:

> Wie wird mir! — Hiobsartig, Beul' an Beule
> Der ganze Kerl. (11809–10)

---

8 See Osman Durrani, *Faust and the Bible: A Study of Goethe's Use of Scriptural Allusions and Christian Religious Motifs in 'Faust I' and 'II'* (Bern: Peter Lang, 1977); Gerhard Kaiser, 'Goethes Faust und die Bibel', *Deutsche Vierteljahrsschrift*, 58 (1984), 391–413.

9 See Otto Pniower, 'Goethes Faust und das Hohe Lied', *Goethe-Jahrbuch*, 13 (1892), 181–98; James Simpson, *Goethe and Patriarchy: Faust and the Fates of Desire* (Oxford: Legenda, 1998), esp. pp. 16–24.

The parts of the Bible that Goethe especially draws on, the Song of Solomon and the Book of Job, are those which have traditionally seemed most incongruous within the Old Testament canon. Thus Goethe foregrounds those parts of the Bible which orthodox commentators have preferred to marginalize. In dealing with the New Testament he does something similar, for in 'Bergschluchten' two female penitents from the Gospels, the sinful woman of Luke 7 and the Samaritan woman of John 4, are placed alongside Mary of Egypt, who figures in the saints' legends collected by the Jesuits. Here Goethe is implicitly questioning the special status of the sacred text.

Goethe draws not only on the Bible but on his wide reading in world literature. *Faust* has been called 'a "restitution of all things" (Acts 3. 21) in the continuity of the world's literature'.[10] Sometimes mythical figures appear conscious of their literary status: thus Helena, on first appearing, mentions her posthumous reputation, and the witch Erichtho introduces the 'Klassische Walpurgisnacht' by assuring us that despite the libels of later poets (Lucan and Dante) she is

> Nicht so abscheulich, wie die leidigen Dichter mich
> Im Übermaß verlästern [...] (7007–08)[11]

Goethe's interest, however, extended far beyond Europe. The conversation in the 'Vorspiel auf dem Theater' among Director, Poet, and Clown is modelled on the dialogue between dramatist and actress that opens the Indian play *Sakuntala* by Kalidasa (*c.* 400 CE), which Goethe knew in the translation that Georg Forster had made from an English version. Although Goethe's fascination with the Muslim world found expression mainly in his *West-östlicher Divan* (1819), at least one scholar has detected many echoes of the *Arabian Nights* in *Faust II*, though her case often seems overstated.[12]

The most varied literary allusions come in the third act of Part Two, a version of which was published separately in 1827 as *Helena: Zwischenspiel zu Faust*. The literary references are part of Goethe's project, which he described as follows to an admirer, the scholar Carl Jacob Ludwig Iken: 'Es ist Zeit, daß der leidenschaftliche Zwiespalt zwischen Klassikern und Romantikern sich endlich versöhne' (27 Sept. 1827). The Act accordingly moves from classical verse forms to those of modern Europe: Goethe, like his contemporaries, regarded Romantic literature as a continuation of medieval poetry, and had already displayed this conception in the masque entitled 'Die romantische Poesie' which he composed for the Duchess Luise of Weimar in 1810.[13] At the outset, Helena speaks in iambic trimeters, a verse-form drawn from Greek tragedy:

> Bewundert viel und viel gescholten, Helena,
> Vom Strande komm' ich, wo wir erst gelandet sind (8488–89)

---

10   E. R. Curtius, *European Literature and the Latin Middle Ages*, trans. by Willard Trask (New York: Pantheon, 1953), p. 189.

11   See Dante, *Inferno*, ix. 23. Erichtho first appears in Book 7 of the epic *Pharsalia* by Lucan (39–65 CE) as a Thessalian witch consulted by Pompey before the battle of Pharsalia.

12   Katharina Mommsen, *Natur- und Fabelreich in 'Faust II'* (Berlin: de Gruyter, 1968).

13   See Friedrich Sengle, *Das Genie und sein Fürst: Die Geschichte der Lebensgemeinschaft Goethes mit dem Herzog Carl August* (Stuttgart and Weimar: Metzler, 1993), pp. 279–80.

The Chorus replies in irregular metres which range from two stresses to five. Mephisto, appearing in the guise of Phorkyas, moves from iambic trimeters to trochaic tetrameters, lines with eight feet of which the last is catalectic (i.e. consisting only of one syllable):

> Tritt hervor aus flüchtigen Wolken, hohe Sonne dieses Tags,
> Die verschleiert schon entzückte, blendend nun im Glanze herrscht.
>
> (8909–10)

It should be noted that Goethe's classical metres are far from mechanical: both Helena's and Phorkyas' diction allows for extra syllables (as in 'flüchtigen' above) which make for a quicker, lighter delivery. According to Kurt May's reckoning, 118 out of 484 lines contain a foot with an extra syllable.[14] These additions often draw attention to emotionally charged words, as in the line

> Denn Ruf und Schicksal bestimmten fürwahr die Unsterblichen
> Zweideutig mir (8531–32),

From 'bestimmten' onwards, we practically have three amphibrachs.

After the transformation scene, Faust appears in medieval armour and speaks in blank verse, the staple metre of Northern European languages from Shakespeare onwards. A new and distinctively 'Romantic' note is introduced by Lynkeus, the lynx-eyed watchman who apologizes for neglecting his duty in short trochaic quatrains:

> Laß mich knieen, laß mich schauen,
> Laß mich sterben, laß mich leben,
> Denn schon bin ich hingegeben
> Dieser gottgegebnen Frauen.
>
> Harrend auf des Morgens Wonne,
> Östlich spähend ihren Lauf,
> Ging auf einmal mir die Sonne
> Wunderbar im Süden auf. (9218–25)

Here we have a familiar lyric form, anticipated especially in the trochaic four-line stanzas (*redondillas*) found in Calderón and other classical Spanish writers, and used especially for the subject of love.[15] We also recognize the hyperbolic homage characteristic of Petrarchan poetry. Helena's beauty eclipses the sun; later she darts arrows of love at all who see her (9260–63) and the glow of her cheeks turns rubies pale (9311–12).[16]

As ancient metres yield to modern verse forms, the reconciliation of Classicism and Romanticism is achieved in the justly famous and touching scene where Helena, having noticed an unfamiliar symmetry in Faust's language, learns to speak in rhyme:

---

14   May, *'Faust II' in der Sprachform gedeutet* (Munich: Hanser, 1962), pp. 161–62.

15   Stuart Atkins, 'Goethe, Calderon, and *Faust: Der Tragödie Zweiter Teil*', *Germanic Review*, 28 (1953), 83–98 (p. 91).

16   See Leonard Forster, *The Icy Fire: Five Studies in European Petrarchism* (Cambridge: Cambridge University Press, 1969), pp. 148–68.

FAUST.	Nun schaut der Geist nicht vorwärts, nicht zurück,
	Die Gegenwart allein —
HELENA.	ist unser Glück.
FAUST.	Schatz ist sie, Hochgewinn, Besitz und Pfand;
	Bestätigung, wer gibt sie?
HELENA.	Meine Hand. (9381–84)

Many strands of meaning come together in this passage. First, since we are inquiring into Goethe's use of world literature, we may notice that it unites not only Helena and Faust, Classicism and Romanticism, but also East and West. For the story of rhyme being invented to express the harmony of two lovers is an Eastern one, which Goethe found in the works of the Orientalist Hammer-Purgstall and adapted for one of the poems in his *West-östlicher Divan*:

> *Behramgur*, sagt man, hat den Reim erfunden,
> Er sprach entzückt aus reiner Seele Drang;
> *Dilaram* schnell, die Freundin seiner Stunden,
> Erwiderte mit gleichem Wort und Klang.[17]

Next, this exchange signifies Helena's full development into an individual. When she first appeared, she spoke of herself in her social roles: 'Komm' ich als Gattin? komm' ich eine Königin?' (8527).[18] By now, however, the encounter with Faust has brought her into full presence as an individual. Her presence is registered in language, as a recent subtle reading of the rhyming episode has brought out.[19] But it is not only a linguistic creation, for the interchange between Faust and Helena ends by embodying their union in a hand-clasp ('Meine Hand'). And this gesture evokes reminiscences. It reminds us how often in Goethe — the dramatist of the embodied self — emotional contact is rendered in touch rather than words. Lotte takes Werther's hand in the moment of emotional communion indicated by the name 'Klopstock!';[20] at the end of *Iphigenie* the friendship between Greeks and 'barbarians' is sealed by a handshake ('reiche mir [...] deine Rechte').[21] *Tasso* ends with a wordless gesture. But within the architectonics of *Faust*, the true alliance of Faust and Helena recalls by contrast the deceitful wager between Faust and Mephisto, which was sealed by the two parties placing their hands on top of each other with the words 'Schlag auf Schlag!' (1698).

One further example of Goethe's homage to world literature deserves attention: the evocation of Arcadia that ends the scene 'Innerer Burghof'. Ancient pastoral poetry, in which happy shepherds sing of love, was reshaped by Virgil in his Eclogues and situated in Arcadia, a valley of the Peloponnese — the 'Nichtinsel' (9512) where Faust establishes his realm jointly with Helena. Mythical and natural motifs from

---

17   Goethe, *Sämtliche Werke*, III: *West-östlicher Divan*, ed. by Hendrik Birus (1994), p. 92.

18   More examples in May, '*Faust II*', pp. 166–67.

19   Anthony Phelan, 'Deconstructing Classicism: Goethe's *Helena* and the Need to Rhyme', in *New Ways in Germanistik*, ed. by Richard Sheppard (New York, Oxford, Munich: Berg, 1990), pp. 192–210 (esp. p. 206).

20   Goethe, *Sämtliche Werke*, VIII: '*Die Leiden des jungen Werthers*', '*Die Wahlverwandtschaften*', *Kleine Prosa, Epen*, ed. by Waltraud Wiethölter (1994), p. 52.

21   Goethe, *Sämtliche Werke*, V: *Dramen, 1776–1790*, ed. by Dieter Borchmeyer (1988), p. 619.

Virgil — Apollo, Pan, nymphs and shepherds, goats cropping the bushes — all reappear in the leisurely quatrains (9506–73) which return to the flexible madrigal verse of Part One.[22] Faust's monologue culminates in the reconciliation of culture and nature, thrones and bowers:

> Gelockt, auf sel'gem Grund zu wohnen,
> Du flüchtetest ins heiterste Geschick!
> Zur Laube wandeln sich die Thronen,
> Arkadisch frei sei unser Glück! (9570–73)

We might be tempted to read these lines as expressing the supreme moment of happiness which Faust told Mephisto he could never experience (1688–1700). But we should notice that Faust uses the subjunctive voice ('sei'), not stating a fact but voicing a desire. Later, when he does speak of 'den höchsten Augenblick' (11,586), it is with reference to the free society of the future which he hopes to found on land reclaimed from the sea. In Arcadia, likewise, Faust's happiness depends on the future, for there is another Virgilian allusion in his phrase 'das holde Kind' (9555), anticipating the birth of his son Euphorion, but also recalling Virgil's 'child, under whom the iron brood shall first cease, and a golden race spring up throughout the world'.[23] This passage, probably intended as a hyperbolic compliment to one of Virgil's patrons, has often been construed as an unwitting prophecy of the birth of Christ. In *Faust*, the child Euphorion overreaches himself and dies, disrupting the idyll and confirming that earthly happiness can only be short-lived.

3. Liturgy

As we move through *Faust*, we find that scenes focused on Faust himself, or on Faust and one interlocutor (Wagner, Mephisto, Gretchen), alternate with crowd and ceremonial scenes. First we have the crowd enjoying Easter Sunday in 'Vor dem Tor'. Later we have a church service ('Dom') and its antithesis, the witches' celebration of Walpurgisnacht. In Part Two ceremonial scenes predominate: the masque of Plutus in Act I, the Classical Walpurgisnacht culminating in the triumphal pageant of Galatea, Faust's wooing and wedding of Helena in Act III, and finally Faust's heavenly apotheosis. The appreciation of the *Helena* episode offered in 1828 by Thomas Carlyle — still an outstanding essay in the sympathetic interpretation of an enigmatic text — applies to much of Part Two:

> In fact, the style of *Helena* is altogether new; quiet, simple, joyful; passing by a short gradation from Classic dignity into Romantic pomp; it has everywhere a full and sunny tone of colouring; resembles not a tragedy, but a gay gorgeous mask.[24]

---

22 See Curtius, *European Literature*, ch. 10; Horst Rüdiger, 'Weltliteratur in Goethes *Helena*', *Jahrbuch der Deutschen Schiller-Gesellschaft*, 8 (1964), 172–97 (esp. pp. 188–94); and for the immediate context, M. Kay Flavell, '"Arkadisch frei sei unser Glück": The Myth of the Golden Age in Eighteenth-Century Germany', *Publications of the English Goethe Society*, n.s., 43 (1972–73), 1–27.

23 Fourth Eclogue, in Virgil, *Eclogues, Georgics, Aeneid I–VI*, trans. by H. Rushton Fairclough, Loeb Classical Library (Cambridge, MA, and London: Harvard University Press, 1935), p. 29.

24 Carlyle, *Critical and Miscellaneous Essays*, 4 vols (London: Chapman & Hall, 1888), I, 124.

For his dramatic spectacles, Goethe drew especially on Calderón, a dramatist whom he ranked alongside Shakespeare (see Eckermann, 28 March 1827). Calderón's Baroque theatre specialized in visual displays, such as sudden transformations of scenery, the appearance of armies on the stage (as in 'Innerer Burghof'), and the use of stage machinery like the cloud effect at the beginning of Act IV and the opening of Hell-mouth on the stage in Act V.

I want, however, to concentrate on how Goethe increases his range of poetic forms by exploiting the Roman Catholic liturgy. In the 'Dom' scene we hear the 'Dies irae', used in requiem masses, and composed by the Franciscan Thomas of Celano (*c.* 1200–*c.* 1255). It warns of the Day of Judgement (the 'day of wrath') when the divine judge shall discern and punish all secret sins. The stanzas Goethe chooses to quote present Christianity as harshly retributive; he omits the long sequence of verses invoking the divine mercy. No wonder Gretchen faints.

Gretchen's prayer to the Virgin in 'Zwinger' seems to have been suggested by a thirteenth-century hymn which also forms part of the Catholic liturgy and is uncertainly ascribed to the Franciscan poet Jacopone da Todi (1230–1306). It begins:

> Stabat mater dolorosa
> Juxta crucem lacrimosa
> Dum pendebat filius.
>
> Cujus animam gementem,
> Contristantem et dolentem,
> Pertransivit gladius.

> [The sorrowful mother was standing weeping beside the Cross while her Son was hanging on it. Through her lamenting, anguished and sorrowing soul the sword had passed.][25]

Gretchen is about to be a mother; her child will die, at her own hand; she too will feel intense sorrow. To complicate yet further the pattern of resemblances and divergences, we have the figure of Frau Marthe, her accommodating neighbour, whose Christian name is that of another Mary's sister (Luke 10. 38–42) and whose surname, 'Schwerdtlein' (2899), recalls the image of the sword piercing the Virgin's soul (Luke 2. 35). Comic pastiche is suggested when we encounter Marthe lamenting the death of her husband, mainly because she has no death certificate. One should neither ignore nor over-interpret these similarities; but they give Frau Marthe a semi-comic place in the sequence of real and mythical female figures leading from the witches in Part One via Helena and the sea-nymph Galatea up to the appearance of the Virgin Mary at the end of Part Two.[26]

The final scene, 'Bergschluchten', purporting to depict Faust's ascent to heaven, has particularly puzzled commentators. The Christian imagery, with saints, hermits, angels, and the Virgin Mary, comes strangely from someone who desc-

25 Text and translation from *The Penguin Book of Latin Verse*, ed. by Frederick Brittain (Harmondsworth: Penguin, 1962), p. 246.

26 On the parallels between Galatea and the Virgin Mary, see Cyrus Hamlin, 'Tracking the Eternal-Feminine in Goethe's *Faust II*', in *Interpreting Goethe's Faust Today*, ed. by Jane K. Brown (Columbia, SC: Camden House, 1994), pp. 142–55.

ribed himself as 'kein Widerkrist, kein Unkrist aber doch ein dezidierter Nichtkrist' (to Lavater, 29 July 1782).[27] Goethe's belief in immortality, in the survival of a personal essence or entelechy, draws on Aristotle and Leibniz rather than Christian sources. The thought behind 'Bergschluchten' is deeply eclectic, and its imagery is no less original.[28] Just as Goethe, in the 'Klassische Walpurgisnacht', made free use of Greek mythology to express the variety of natural forces, so here he makes analogous use of Christian mythology to express man's aspirations to the transcendent. His imagery derives from Renaissance painting, from Dante, and from the account of the angelic hierarchies provided by Dionysius the Areopagite, a fifth-century Neoplatonic writer to whom Dante pays tribute in *Paradiso* 10. 115–17 and 28. 130–32.[29]

The scene shows Goethe's empathy with the spirit of Counter-Reformation Catholicism, not only in the visual similarity between Faust's ascent and the illusionistic perspectives of a Baroque church ceiling, but in the verse, the keynote being set by the bold dactylic metres of the Chorus and the Pater Ecstaticus:

> Ewiger Wonnebrand,
> Glühendes Liebesband,
> Siedender Schmerz der Brust,
> Schäumende Gotteslust [...] (11854–57)

These lines gain added vitality from a residual uncertainty about how to read them. Dactyls usually tail off into two unstressed syllables, but these end with a syllable ('brand', 'band' etc.) which demands more emphasis both by its semantic content and its accumulation of consonants. Precedents for this metre have been found in medieval and Renaissance Latin hymns.[30] A different kind of dactylic verse, interspersed with iambs, is used later by the chorus of Younger Angels:

> Nebelnd um Felsenhöh'
> Spür' ich soeben,
> Regend sich in der Näh',
> Ein Geisterleben. (11966–69)

Here the initially dactylic pattern is disturbed by the need to stress 'in' and 'Geist-'.

The metrical variety continues. A simpler, trochaic metre is used by the Doctor Marianus in his invocation to the Virgin, underlining the direct intensity of his emotion. The three female penitents speak in trochaic tetrameters:

27 [On Goethe's meaning, see now T. J. Reed, 'Goethe as Secular Icon', in *The Present Word: Culture, Society and the Site of Literature. Essays in Honour of Nicholas Boyle*, ed. by John Walker (London: Legenda, 2013), pp. 44–51 (p. 46).]

28 See most recently Jochen Schmidt, 'Die "katholische Mythologie" und ihre mystische Entmythologisierung in der Schluß-Szene des Faust II', *Jahrbuch der Deutschen Schiller-Gesellschaft*, 34 (1990), 230–56, and Dieter Bremer, ' "Wenn starke Geisteskraft [...]": Traditionsvermittlungen in der Schlußszene von Goethes *Faust*', *Goethe-Jahrbuch*, 112 (1995), 287–307. Schmidt's arguments reappear in condensed form in his *Goethes Faust, Erster und Zweiter Teil. Epoche — Werk — Wirkung* (Munich: Beck, 1999).

29 On Dionysius and his influence, see C. A. Patrides, *Premises and Motifs in Renaissance Thought and Literature* (Princeton, NJ: Princeton University Press, 1982), ch. 1.

30 See Ciupke, *Des Geklimpers vielverworrener Töne Rausch*, p. 195.

> Bei der Liebe, die den Füßen
> Deines gottverklärten Sohnes [...] (12037–38)

The initial stress starts each line with a quiet energy that builds up to their final chorus (12061–68). And after that the penitent formerly named Gretchen repeats not only the metre but also the very words of her earlier prayer to the Virgin, except that now 'Not' has been transformed into 'Glück' (12072). Finally the Chorus Mysticus, a choir without visible singers, which one imagines filling the heavens, again exploits the resources of the dactyl: 'Alles Vergängliche' (12104) can be read as a slow and solemn dactyl, but 'Das Ewig-Weibliche' needs a stress on the second syllable which decelerates it further, giving us an emphatic amphibrach ('Das Ewig-') which rises to freedom in the increasingly light syllables of the closing dactyl ('Weibliche').

4. Complex Words

Any reader of *Faust* notices that a rather small number of key words keeps recurring: 'Herz', 'Sinn', 'Kraft', 'Geist', 'Tat', 'Wort', 'Liebe', 'schaffen', 'wirken'. Such recurring words enrich poetic drama by thickening its texture. Their connotations change subtly in different contexts; and when one remembers the same word from different passages, one discerns new relationships, new implications. Long ago the American New Critics and their British counterparts showed us how to read Shakespeare with attention to what William Empson called 'complex words'. Empson's reflections on the word 'honest' in *Othello*, and Cleanth Brooks' study of the word 'man' in *Macbeth*, disclose an exploration that Shakespeare was semi-consciously conducting as part of his creative activity.[31] In Goethe's case, although his recorded statements are valuable evidence for the meaning of *Faust*, they are not themselves its meaning; the text is not simply a poetic restatement of convictions formulated in prose, but restlessly explores the implications and limitations of these convictions. External evidence for Goethe's intentions must not be used (as it often has been) to petrify the live process of debate going on within the text.

I want now to examine certain complex words in Part One of *Faust*. These are words with a range of meaning and with tensions among their various meanings, tensions which are enacted both in the dramatic structure of the play and on the micro-level of its poetic texture. From numerous possibilities I have selected 'Gott', 'Geist', 'Brust', 'Busen' and 'Leib'.

The Prologue in Heaven presents us with a divine being who, however, is never called God, but 'the Lord', as in the Old Testament. Mephisto calls him 'Lord' to his face and refers to him behind his back as 'the Old Man' ('der Alte'). The ordinary Christian term 'Gott' is used by Faust when he prepares to translate St John's Gospel; ('Die Liebe Gottes', 1185), and otherwise, only by Gretchen ('Glaubst du an Gott?' 3426), by Faust replying to her in the scene 'Marthens Garten', and again

---

31 See William Empson, *The Structure of Complex Words* (London: Chatto & Windus, 1951); Cleanth Brooks, 'The Naked Babe and the Cloak of Manliness', in his *The Well Wrought Urn* (New York: Reynal & Hitchcock, 1947), pp. 21–46.

at the end where Gretchen appeals to the 'Gericht Gottes'. Elsewhere, Mephisto speaks circumspectly of 'ein Gott' (1781, 2441) or (mocking Faust) 'einer Gottheit' (3285). Faust himself, contemplating the sign of the Macrocosm, asks: 'Bin ich ein Gott? Mir wird so licht!' (439). He often uses the word in the plural to denote a state of being to which he vainly aspires (652, 3242): 'Götterleben' (620), 'Götterwonne' (706), 'Götterhöhe' (713). Clearly Faust has no actual belief in a single Supreme Being, even though he unwittingly serves that Being; his self-description as 'der Gottverhaßte' may be taken as a bitter metaphor (3256). Faust considers himself to be the 'Ebenbild der Gottheit' (516, 614), the image of God, not simply as a human being created by God, but as an exceptional being whose powers exceed those of the angels ('Ich, mehr als Cherub', 618). He wishes to transcend human limits, to become a god, to cast off what is earthly ('abgestreift den Erdensohn', 617), an ambition duly mocked by Mephisto (3266, 3290). The Earth Spirit derides his pretensions to be an 'Übermensch' (490).

The vainglorious character of such ambitions is intimated by Mephisto when he writes in the Student's album the words in which the Biblical serpent tempted Eve to eat the forbidden fruit: 'Eritis sicut Deus, scientes bonum et malum' (2048) — 'ye shall be as God, knowing good and evil'. The intellectual ambitions shown by the Student must lead eventually to Faust's overweening desire for 'Gottähnlichkeit' (2050). When Faust utters his despairing curse upon the three cardinal virtues, the spirits proclaim him a demi-god:

> Weh! weh!
> Du hast sie zerstört,
> Die schöne Welt,
> Mit mächtiger Faust;
> Sie stürzt, sie zerfällt!
> Ein Halbgott hat sie zerschlagen! (1607–12)

Here we are reminded that Faust is a symbolic figure, signifying by his intellectual drive the Enlightenment's rejection of the Christian cosmos still inhabited by Gretchen. The spirits, later described by Mephisto as his lesser servants, flatter Faust's vanity by punning on his name and calling him a demi-god. Their hint is developed by Mephisto when he compares Faust specifically to the demi-god Prometheus, punished for his excesses by having a vulture devour his liver daily:

> Hör auf, mit deinem Gram zu spielen,
> Der, wie ein Geier, dir am Leben frißt. (1635–36)

What does Faust understand by becoming a god? His exclamation 'Mir wird so licht!' (439) suggests radiance; it implies substituting spiritual existence for physical life. He also senses a frustrated divinity within himself:

> Der Gott, der mir im Busen wohnt,
> Kann tief mein Innerstes erregen;
> Der über allen meinen Kräften thront,
> Er kann nach außen nichts bewegen. (1566–69)

Both these suggestions — spiritual existence and inner powers — are developed by Goethe's uses of 'Geist', a word whose semantic range makes it notoriously hard to translate. At one extreme it means 'mind', though with suggestions of energy and emotion that distinguish it from 'Verstand' (intellect) or 'Vernunft' (reason). Faust often uses the word in this sense, e.g. 'des Geistes Flügeln' (1090), 'Des Geistes Flutstrom' (698). At the other extreme, 'Geist' means a supernatural being that does not need physical embodiment: the Spirit of the Earth ('Erdgeist'), the crowds of spirits that attend Mephisto, and the spirits of the air whose existence is to Wagner unquestionable (1130) and to Faust a matter of hypothesis ('O gibt es Geister in der Luft ...', 1118). In the early modern period, when Faust is supposed to live, the widespread belief in an invisible world of spirits found learned support in Neoplatonic writings; and Goethe knew not only these but probably also the more recent account of the spiritual realm by the seer Emanuel Swedenborg.[32]

Beside these two meanings of 'Geist', the subjective and the supernatural, there are other meanings which mediate between them. The Earth Spirit is a distinct being, but also a force of nature. He represents the creative and destructive energies that animate the physical universe. As such, the Spirit is not simply external: Faust, himself a natural being, feels his heart, senses and emotions powerfully stirred by the approach of the Earth Spirit. Later, when Faust begins translating St John's Gospel, he needs to be 'inspired by the Spirit', 'vom Geiste recht erleuchtet' (1228), and this implies the Holy Spirit. The Holy Spirit is personified — 'Mir hilft der Geist!' (1236) — but it works through Faust's own mental and emotional powers and is thus not sharply distinct from the subjective sense of 'Geist'.

Despite these mediations, the complexity of the word 'Geist' lies in its range from the subjective to the supernatural. Its use implies the question whether the restless human spirit ('eines Menschen Geist, in seinem hohen Streben', 1676) can aspire to enter the 'Geisterwelt' (443). Can man's inner, mental, emotional powers carry him beyond human limits?

The mark of human limitation is the body. Spirits are disembodied; Mephisto merely assumes such human forms as suit his needs — a wandering scholar, a nobleman — though like the traditional devil he always seems to be lame (cf. 2184, 2499). To be human is to be embodied. The human spirit needs material embodiment, just as light, according to Mephisto, needs material objects ('Körper', 1354–58) in order to exist at all.

Goethe frequently uses two words which have literal, corporeal and also mental meanings: 'Busen' and 'Brust'. These have to cover a semantic range for which in English there are three words: 'bosom', 'breast' and 'chest'. The 'Busen' is especially the seat of the emotions, be they fearful (411), ecstatic (3287), melancholy (3654), or passionate: 'Mein Busen fängt mir an zu brennen!' says Faust, enraptured by the Witch's picture of a beautiful woman (2461). 'Busen' can imply both physical and emotional intimacy, as when Gretchen wishes to lie on Faust's 'Busen' (4465), or when she exclaims 'Mein Busen drängt | Sich nach ihm hin' (3406–07); this is a milder version of the *Urfaust*'s rawly physical and passionate 'Mein Schoos! Gott! drängt | Sich nach ihm hin'.

---

32   On early modern doctrines of spirits, see Harold Jantz, *Goethe's Faust as a Renaissance Man: Parallels and Prototypes* (Princeton, NJ: Princeton University Press, 1951), pp. 27–35, 63.

The word 'Brust', which in the plural also means a woman's breasts, juxtaposes the emotional and the physical yet more sharply. It can again be the seat of emotions, Faust's 'tiefbewegte Brust' (307; cf. 3233, 3247). It is narrowly physical when Gretchen asks for her child (or her baby sister?) to be buried 'mir an die rechte Brust' (4528). It can connote the physical intimacy between the lovers (1682, 3346); Faust, in an outburst of fetishism, tells Mephisto to bring 'ein Halstuch von ihrer Brust' (2661); and we have a glimpse of the lovers' amorous play when Faust, seeing a vision of Gretchen, exclaims: 'Das ist die Brust, die Gretchen mir geboten' (4197). But since the breast is what the mother offers the child, Faust is also revealing the male fantasy of being a child again, and he repeats this fantasy in relation to Mother Nature, into whose 'tiefe Brust' he acquires insight (3223). His longing for contact with Nature is most ardently expressed in some lines of almost Shakespearean richness early in the play:

> Wo fass' ich dich, unendliche Natur?
> Euch Brüste, wo? Ihr Quellen alles Lebens,
> An denen Himmel und Erde hängt,
> Dahin die welke Brust sich drängt —
> Ihr quellt, ihr tränkt, und schmacht' ich so vergebens? (455–59)

Mother Nature's breasts are an overflowing source of life (as the polyptoton of 'Quellen' and 'quellt' conveys), sustaining heaven and earth; these briefly seem like twins, being suckled side by side, till the singular verb 'hängt' unifies them into a single cosmos. The withered breast ('welke Brust') suggests Faust's own emotional desiccation and hints at a constant process of renewal in which the male breast, full of lofty aspirations but without its own source of life, has to be repeatedly nourished by the milk-filled breasts of feminine Nature.

Together, 'Busen' and 'Brust' convey a complex understanding of bodily existence. Mental life — the thoughts and feelings within one's bosom — is continuous with physical life; lovers embracing communicate at once emotionally and physically; and the polyvalence of 'breast(s)' says much about the interdependence of men and women and the shared humanity of both. The man with lofty thoughts in his breast was nourished at his mother's breasts and seeks sustenance at the breast of his lover.

For the body itself, Goethe uses the word 'Leib'. 'Körper' is used only by Mephisto, referring to material objects in general (1354–58). 'Leib' is used casually in numerous set phrases (2603, 3277, 3419, 3754) which nevertheless recall and confirm that human life has to be embodied. The word acquires more prominence when Goethe exploits its rhyme with 'Weib' (2436/38, 2603–04, 3327/29). Faust's sensual desire, his physical appetite, are thrust on the reader's attention. But there are significant shifts of tone. His carnal appetite is brutally evident when he reproaches Mephisto:

> Bring die Begier zu ihrem süßen Leib
> Nicht wieder vor die halb verrückten Sinnen! (3328–29)

But the same phrase acquires passionate lyricism when Faust, rapt by his Walpurgis-nacht vision, says:

> Das ist die Brust, die Gretchen mir geboten,
> Das ist der süße Leib, den ich genoß. (4197–98)

And carnality is connected with incarnation, as Faust has earlier acknowledged:

> Ich bin ihr nah', und wär' ich noch so fern,
> Ich kann sie nie vergessen, nie verlieren;
> Ja, ich beneide schon den Leib des Herrn,
> Wenn ihre Lippen ihn indes berühren. (3332–35)

Superficially, this is a libertine jest. Looked at more closely, it expresses two understandings of the Eucharist. Gretchen presumably accepts the Church's teaching on the sacrament and believes that in swallowing the Host she is making contact with Christ's body beneath the accidental guise of bread. Thus for her the miracle of incarnation is repeated whenever she receives communion. Goethe himself was more sceptical. Even when he took communion as a young man, he described its purpose as remembrance: 'mich an des Herren Leiden und Tod zu erinnern' (letter to Susanna von Klettenberg, 26 Aug. 1770). Faust's relation to Gretchen is similarly one of intense remembrance, and though he can and does forget her, he remembers her vividly at the Walpurgisnacht in a visionary premonition of her death.

In its texture, then, *Faust* shows us a profound and subtle meditation on what it is to be human, to be incarnate. Faust may fantasize about becoming a disembodied spirit, but the play in fact leads him from the merely intellectual existence of a scholar to a richer experience of human life as lived in and through his body. By its complex words, the play discourages us from a dualistic view of spirit and body. Mephisto may be a spirit assuming a temporary embodiment, but to be human means not just being in a body but being a body. At the end of Part Two, when Faust, 'das edle Glied | Der Geisterwelt' (11934–35), does enter the spiritual world, the angels proclaim the indissoluble unity of spirit and matter:

> Wenn starke Geisteskraft
> Die Elemente
> An sich herangerafft,
> Kein Engel trennte
> Geeinte Zwienatur
> Der innigen beiden.
> Die ewige Liebe nur
> Vermag's zu scheiden. (11958–65)

Not only are these themes woven into the texture of the play; they are visible also in its structure. Faust's opening monologue is delivered on Easter Eve. He is prevented from suicide by the choruses on Easter Sunday. Just as he imagined that in summoning up spirits he was becoming a god, so he conceives death as being swept up in a fiery chariot to higher spheres of 'Götterwonne' and 'Götterhöhe' (706, 713). By contrast, the choruses tell of another person who really did die but overcame human limitations and rose from the grave to immortal life. These Easter choruses are not simply decorative. They round off a long scene of some 450 lines in which Faust has repeatedly tried to transcend ordinary human life: by becoming a god, by summoning up spirits and treating them as equals, and then by planning suicide in the hope of thus attaining a higher existence. All these aspirations are implicitly rebuked by contrast with the death and resurrection of Christ. Beyond that, how we are to interpret the juxtaposition is left open. Faust cannot share the choruses' faith, but their songs reanimate memories of his childhood, stir his emotions, and make him want to go on living. Different readers will see different kinds and degrees of irony in the paradoxical couplet:

> O tönet fort, ihr süßen Himmelslieder!
> Die Träne quillt, die Erde hat mich wieder! (783–84)

We may find in it an anticipation of Zarathustra's injunction: 'Ich beschwöre euch, meine Brüder, *bleibt der Erde treu* und glaubt denen nicht, welche euch von überirdischen Hoffnungen reden!'[33] But we should also note how Faust's unrealistic ambitions correspond to those that later kill his son Euphorion. Though warned that his strength, like that of the giant Antaeus, depends on staying in touch with the solid ground (9611), Euphorion insists on attempting ever loftier flights, and eventually crashes to the ground like Icarus. Thus he repeats, with fatal consequences, the attempt to transcend earthly life from which Faust was dissuaded by the Easter choruses.[34] Even in his apotheosis, Faust does not discard his body, but acquires a purified body. The whole poem recalls a letter of Goethe's about a friend's efforts to interest him in the secrets of the Book of Revelation: 'ich bin ein sehr irdischer Mensch [...] Ich dencke auch aus der Wahrheit zu seyn, aber aus der Wahrheit der fünf Sinne und Gott habe Geduld mit mir wie bisher' (to Lavater, 28 Oct. 1779).

---

33   *Also sprach Zarathustra*, Vorrede 3, in Friedrich Nietzsche, *Werke*, ed. Karl Schlechta, 3 vols (Munich: Hanser, 1956), II, 280.

34   The parallel is pointed out by Harold Jantz, *The Form of Faust: The Work of Art and its Intrinsic Structures* (Baltimore, MD, and London: Johns Hopkins University Press, 1978), p. 35.

CHAPTER 4

Wallenstein: Man of Destiny?

Wallenstein is a reflective, almost a philosophical tragedy. Every so often the main characters stand back, reflect on what is happening to them, and try to interpret it with a range of concepts among which 'fate' and 'revenge' predominate. In Greek tragedy, this interpretation would have been done by the chorus. In this modern tragedy, it is voiced by the characters in moments of insight, and expressed in soliloquies. These soliloquies are crucial to the understanding of the play. For when the characters speak to one another, they are generally expressing their hopes and wishes, trying to persuade or deceive one another, and often trying to deceive themselves. When they are alone on stage, or when they seem to think aloud, ignoring anyone else present, they utter the unwelcome forebodings that are borne out by the tragic action. Thus Wallenstein, after listening to his sister's argument that he owes the Emperor no loyalty and should have no scruples about rebellion, asserts that both he and the Emperor are being manipulated by an evil spirit which carries out revenge:

> It is his evil genius, and mine,
> Punishing him through me, the tool of his ambition,
> And I expect that vengeance is already
> Whetting its blade to pierce my heart as well. (p. 345; W 645–48)[1]

His daughter Thekla, joined by love to the young officer Max Piccolomini, speaks confidently about their prospects in Max's presence, but when she is alone she expresses her premonitions of a grim fate ('Schicksal') that threatens her entire family:

> A spirit dark upon our house does brood,
> And destiny would strike us from its roll. (p. 287; P 1899–1900)

And the agent of Wallenstein's murder, Buttler, soliloquizes, once Wallenstein is trapped inside the fortified town of Eger: 'He's here. His destiny has brought him in' (p. 416; W 2428).

---

1 This and future translations of passages longer than a few words are taken from Friedrich Schiller, *The Robbers; Wallenstein*, trans. by F. J. Lamport (Harmondsworth: Penguin, 1979), and referred to by page number only. Other translations are my own. The German text used for this and other works by Schiller is *Sämtliche Werke*, ed. by Gerhard Fricke and Herbert G. Göpfert, 5 vols (Munich: Hanser, 1958), cited by volume and page number for works other than *Wallenstein*. *Wallenstein* is cited as follows: L = *Wallensteins Lager*; P = *Die Piccolomini*; W = *Wallensteins Tod*.

A remarkable feature of these commentaries is that although the characters are supposed to be living in the seventeenth century, are all Christians and mostly Roman Catholics, they make no use of specifically Christian concepts. The concept of providence occasionally crops up in the play, but it is voiced only by marginal characters whose words carry little weight. We hear nothing about sin, forgiveness, atonement, or redemption. The apparatus of Christianity — churches, priests, even the Virgin Mary — is present as a necessary part of the historical setting, but the concepts and images used by the characters are thoroughly pagan. The insistent language of fate, guilt and revenge recalls Greek tragedy. The atmosphere of gathering doom towards the end of the trilogy is reminiscent of Aeschylus' *Oresteia*.[2]

The characters' reflections on fate, however, are not to be taken as authoritative, final explanations of the drama. They are not expressions of some philosophical doctrine which the play serves merely to illustrate. Even when spoken with great conviction, they are in some measure tentative. They are attempts to make sense of the pattern of events in which the characters feel themselves to be trapped. And the reader or spectator is invited to take part in the active process of sense-making. In this essay I shall look as closely as space permits at a number of key words, arranged in semantic groups. There is first the group of words for 'fate' or 'destiny' ('Schicksal', 'Verhängnis', 'Geschick'), and then an associated group in which the ideas of 'chance' ('Zufall'), 'fortune' ('Glück') and 'game', 'play' or 'gamble' ('Spiel') are prominent. Set against these are a number of words for human impulses, above all 'heart' ('Herz') and 'impulse' ('Trieb'). Their implications of human agency are in conflict with recurrent suggestions that people are no more than the instrument ('Werkzeug', 'Spielzeug') of higher powers. These powers in turn are evoked with a wide range of eclectic imagery, including such words as 'Mächte' (powers), 'Geist' (spirit), 'Dämon' (demon), 'Engel' (angel), 'Gott' (god) and 'Göttin' (goddess), and with the enormously rich and suggestive references to astrology which Schiller built into the play at a late stage of composition. In order not to reduce the play to a mere pattern of words, however, I want also to focus on the enigmatic and many-sided character at its centre.

Wallenstein describes himself as a man of destiny. Addressing the delegation of soldiers who are seeking reassurance that he is loyal to the Emperor, he declares that he is the man of destiny: 'I feel I am the man that fate has chosen' (p. 397; W 1989). Though Wallenstein is an actor and a rhetorician, this statement is not simply for the soldiers' benefit. It matches the conviction, which he has had ever since he was a rather eccentric young man at military academy, that he is special, unusually gifted, singled out by fate for an exceptional purpose. Seeing Wallenstein from the inside, as Schiller allows us to do via his soliloquies, we can tell that this sense of mission is not wholly secure. In particular, it suffered a severe blow, some three and a half years before the action of the play, when Wallenstein, then the leading

---

2   This comparison was made by the earliest commentators, notably by Wilhelm von Humboldt in his letter to Schiller of September 1800 (FA 747). Comments on the play by Schiller and his contemporaries are readily available in Schiller, *Werke und Briefe*, Bibliothek deutscher Klassiker, ed. by Otto Dann and others (Frankfurt a.M.: Deutscher Klassiker Verlag), vol. IV: *Wallenstein*, ed. by Frithjof Stock (2000), and are quoted from it with the abbreviation FA (Frankfurter Ausgabe).

military commander of the Imperial forces, was dismissed for insubordination at the Electoral Convention at Regensburg in 1630. Since then, Wallenstein has taken up astrology and gained from it the assurance that, since his guardian planet is Jupiter, he must be a privileged mortal, gifted with insight into the workings of the cosmos, and a natural ruler, one of 'Jupiter's fair children, born in light' (p. 254; P 985).

This view of himself as a cheerful, regal character is in conflict with the depression that frequently assails Wallenstein during the play, and, still more, with the picture of Wallenstein that Schiller draws in his *History of the Thirty Years War*.[3] The historical Wallenstein, we learn there, was a stern, gloomy, reserved, taciturn character who never smiled and spoke only in an unpleasant tone. His generosity was only a device to retain the loyalty of his terrified adherents: 'A dreadful, fear-inspiring gravity sat on his brow, and only his excessive rewards could retain his trembling servants' (IV, 492). The Wallenstein of the play is not like that. He governs people, not through terror, but through his charisma. The many recipients of his generosity do not tremble before him. His general Isolani, whose gambling debts he has paid three times, says that his disposition is kingly (P 65). The soldiers of fortune Devereux and Macdonald, who are hired to murder him, contrast the meanness of the Imperial court with his magnificent gifts (W 3253). His old acquaintance Gordon, now commandant of the fortress at Eger, says he has made thousands of people happy (W 2517). Above all, Max Piccolomini, an enthusiastic young man, shows a devotion to Wallenstein which the dismal tyrant of the *History* could never have earned; he declares that Wallenstein constantly seeks to bestow happiness on people (P 782), delighting them and astonishing them like a god (P 1706–08). Thus, in return for accompanying his wife and daughter from Carinthia to Bohemian, Wallenstein presents Max with a team of hunting horses. Granted, Max is naive: he overlooks the scheming side of Wallenstein's character; and his enthusiasm is heightened by his being in love with Wallenstein's daughter; but his and other testimonies do suggest that Wallenstein's munificence is more than calculating, that it is the expression of a large, generous disposition which is one side of Wallenstein's complex personality.

Max is an invented character with no historical counterpart. One of his functions to bring out the expansive side of Wallenstein's character, both by praising it for the audience's benefit, and by eliciting Wallenstein's affection. Wallenstein typically expresses his feelings about Max in astrological imagery:

> You always were to me
> The bringer of some most especial joy;
> And now, like that fair star that heralds day,
> You bring my life's own sun to shine on me. (p. 246; P 755–58)

---

3   This discrepancy was already noted by Humboldt (letter to Schiller, Sept. 1800, FA 752). Dieter Borchmeyer develops Humboldt's insight in *Macht und Melancholie: Schillers 'Wallenstein'* (Frankfurt a.M.: Athenäum, 1988), arguing that Wallenstein is wrong to identify with Jupiter and is really a melancholy character under the sign of Saturn. Though Borchmeyer's is far the most important study of the astrological motif in *Wallenstein*, I would rather see the jovial and saturnine as different aspects of Wallenstein's personality. The latter has evidently been dominant since Regensburg.

By comparing Max to Venus, the morning star which heralds the sun, Wallenstein hints at the quasi-homosexual feelings which often appear when Schiller depicts close bonds among men.[4] When Max finally turns against him, Wallenstein responds alternately with fury and with pathetic appeals, recalling how he tended the boy Max as a nurse ('Wärterin', W 2149) with feminine solicitude ('Mit weiblich sorgender Geschäftigkeit', W 2151). After Max's death, Wallenstein feels that life has lost its bloom and now stretches ahead, cold and colourless (W 3644). Max clearly means far more to him than his timorous wife or the daughter whom he has not seen for several years.

Wallenstein's charisma is that of a great military leader. In the *History* Wallenstein is contrasted, to his disadvantage, with his antagonist King Gustav Adolf of Sweden, whom Schiller calls the greatest general of his century (IV, 496). Not only does Gustav Adolf, unlike Wallenstein, make creative innovations in the art of war, but his devoutly Protestant, well-disciplined troops refrain from plundering the territories they traverse, whereas the Imperial forces led by Wallenstein and Tilly devastate the lands of allies and enemies alike. Since Gustav Adolf fell at the battle of Lützen in 1632, he cannot appear in Schiller's play, which is set in February 1634, and so Wallenstein appears as an unrivalled military genius. Gustav Adolf is represented by proxy, however, through the Swedish colonel Wrangel who negotiates with Wallenstein, and who pays him the dubious compliment of comparing him as a military leader to Attila and Pyrrhus. Both of these, especially Attila the Hun, are notorious for their devastations, and the reference to Attila, known as God's Scourge, is picked up later when Wallenstein's sister describes him passing through Germany with fire and sword and wielding the scourge over all its territories (W 605).

While ruthless towards the civilian population, however, Wallenstein earned the loyalty of his own troops by providing for them with 'paternal care' (P 193), and has thus assembled a multinational, multi-denominational army whose loyalty is to him, not to the Emperor. He remembers the name of every soldier he has ever spoken to (W 1841–42). At the same time, he has a low opinion of human nature in general. In his view, people follow the herd and are loyal only to fortune (W 1434–35, 1802–03). He is not surprised or disappointed when Isolani, whom he has saved from disgrace, is pressured by Octavio Piccolomini, the Emperor's double agent, to desert his cause. When Buttler accuses him of manipulating people like chessmen (W 2853–56), we need to discount something for Buttler's own resentment, but that resentment is founded on the evidence, supplied by Octavio, that Wallenstein actually frustrated Buttler's hopes of ennoblement while pretending to support them. If the letter from Wallenstein that Octavio produces is genuine — and since Wallenstein elsewhere says he puts nothing in writing (P 854), it may be a forgery[5] — such a deception is at least compatible with Wallenstein's political dealings. Having been restored to his position of command because the Empire cannot

---

4   For an overview of how Schiller's commentators have handled this theme, see Robert Tobin, *Warm Brothers: Queer Theory and the Age of Goethe* (Philadelphia: University of Pennsylvania Press, 2000), chapter 8.

5   See W. F. Mainland, *Schiller and the Changing Past* (London: Heinemann, 1957), pp. 38–39.

manage without him, he has been languid in his military campaign and active in his secret negotiations with the Empire's enemies, the Swedes and Saxons. His plan to transfer his army to the Swedish side involves treachery on such a massive scale that the upright Protestant Wrangel is dumbfounded.

Yet it would not be adequate to call Wallenstein a cynical politician. For one thing, he is too unsuccessful. His negotiations with the Swedes are so prolonged that his closest associates, Terzky and Illo, become frantic with impatience and urge him desperately to commit himself. To them, his hesitation is mere inexplicable indecision. In addition, the charge of cynicism would place Wallenstein on a level with Octavio. As the Emperor's secret emissary in Wallenstein's camp, enjoying Wallenstein's confidence and reporting all he hears back to the court in Vienna, Octavio is the successful manipulator that Wallenstein fails to be. For him, politics is a matter of calculation ('Kalkul', W 970), and he relies on his correct calculations as he prepares to pressure first Isolani, then Buttler, into abandoning Wallenstein.

In contrast to his small-minded associates Terzky and Illo, and to his skilful but blinkered enemy Octavio, Wallenstein is a visionary. Besides the charismatic general, we have, as Lesley Sharpe says, 'the possibility that Wallenstein is a far-sighted statesman who can look beyond the pursuit of minor territorial advantages for his Emperor'.[6] If the treachery he contemplates is on a vast scale, so is the outcome for which he hopes. By joining forces with the Swedes, he intends to compel the Imperial court to end the war which has by now tormented Central Europe for sixteen years. He reveals this plan to the delegation of soldiers (W 1950), and it is attested also by both Max and Octavio Piccolomini. What he does not tell the Swedes, of course, is that having achieved this purpose he intends to break with them and drive them back across the Baltic. Nor does he tell Max that he hopes to gain for himself the throne of Bohemia, thus rising from his present position of duke to that of king. Max's hope that Wallenstein will allow him to marry Thekla is a delusion, encouraged, in order to bind him to Wallenstein, by the scheming Countess Terzky. Indifferent to Thekla's wishes, Wallenstein intends to find a husband for her on one of Europe's thrones (W 1513).

But all this, as Wallenstein himself admits, is a dream. In a famous soliloquy, early in *Wallensteins Tod*, he expresses his discomfort at actually having to go through with it. He twists and turns like a man in a trap, staring at the threshold across which the Swedish negotiator is about to step, bringing with him an irrevocable decision. A key word in this soliloquy is 'Herz'. Wallenstein's dream sprang from his heart, from his emotions. He fed his heart with it (W 141–42), was led by his overflowing heart (W 174) into talking imprudently about it, and has thus released it from the safe corner of his heart (W 187–88) which was its proper place. Nothing could be less like a calculating politician. Wallenstein has too little calculation and too much imagination for his own good. Moreover, his dream of kingship within a peaceful Europe springs from the 'maternal soil' of his heart (W 188), from the 'feminine', emotional, creative side of his personality.

---

6 Lesley Sharpe, *Friedrich Schiller: Drama, Thought and Politics* (Cambridge: Cambridge University Press, 1991), p. 228.

The visionary side of Wallenstein may seem hard to reconcile with the tough, down-to-earth pragmatism he displays when requiring Max to choose between allegiance to the Emperor and to himself. The Wallenstein who proclaims his crudely material ambitions and mocks Max's idealism has often been interpreted as a realist, bearing in mind the distinction Schiller draws in *On Naive and Sentimental Poetry* between the realist and the idealist as two opposed types of person.[7] But the pragmatist and the visionary are two complementary sides of Wallenstein's character. In the previous Act, his visionary tendency was painfully brought up against the hard choice presented to him by Wrangel. He now copes with his discomfort by transferring it to someone else. He assumes towards Max the tough, cynical attitude which Wrangel inflicted on him. The sadism he shows here is that of a disappointed visionary.

Ironically, the visionary aspect of Wallenstein, with his emphasis on the heart, aligns him with the two people whose lives his ambition will ruin, Max and Thekla. Having fallen in love on the journey to Bohemia, and confirmed their mutual commitment by a passionate embrace, they are the play's main representatives of the heart. For Max, the experience of love also illuminates other aspects of life. He tells Countess Terzky how, driven about restlessly by his emotions, he entered the church of the 'Himmelspforte' ('Heaven's Gate') monastery:

> There I went in, and found myself alone.
> Above the altar hung the Virgin Mother;
> A simple image, but it was the friend
> That I was seeking in this very moment.
> How often have I seen Her in her glory
> And splendour, seen her worshippers adore Her —
> It had not touched me; now at once I knew
> The meaning of devotion and of love. (p. 272; P 1463–70)

Here we have a glimpse of Schiller's anthropology, his understanding of human nature. Religious devotion springs from the same source as love between people. It may be seen as a displacement or extension of such love. Love also strengthens the imagination: his love for Thekla enables Max to understand what the faithful feel about the Virgin Mary. Corresponding to the 'maternal soil' from which Wallenstein's dream of kingship grew, we have here a maternal figure who is the focus for art and devotion, two kinds of imaginative construction growing from love.

The love between Max and Thekla, however, is doomed, as Thekla suspects from the outset. Having learnt with horror of Wallenstein's intended treachery, and having been rejected scornfully as a suitor, Max turns against his former idol and denounces him with the exaggerated bitterness that comes from disillusionment. Thekla then sums up their situation: 'Fate parts us, but our hearts remain united'

---

7 Schiller himself said that as the historical Wallenstein was in no way great, he could not be idealized, and therefore it was necessary to make him into a great dramatic character by realistic means (letter to Humboldt, 21 March 1796, FA 590); but this view, expressed early in the composition of the play, should not be taken as a complete guide to Wallenstein's character as it developed, as in E. L. Stahl, *Friedrich Schiller's Drama: Theory and Practice* (Oxford: Clarendon Press, 1954).

(p. 411; W 2379). Max is killed in a heroic cavalry charge; Thekla secretly runs away in order to commit suicide on his grave. It seems as if the warmth of the heart cannot survive in the cold world of 'Schicksal'. Two decades later, Hegel was to say of the novel that it typically showed 'the conflict between the poetry of the heart and the opposing prose of circumstances' and to illustrate this claim from Goethe's *Wilhelm Meisters Lehrjahre* (1795–96), where the poetic figure of Mignon dies as the hero prepares to assume practical responsibilities.[8] The same seems to apply to the drama *Wallenstein*. Wallenstein's dream, and the young couple's love, both perish in what is variously called 'life's strangeness' (W 189) and 'the common clarity of things' (p. 455; W 3447).

Certainly fate seems an irresistible force. It appears in several guises. There is 'Glück', fortune, sometimes called 'Fortuna' (e.g. L 421, W 3239), a series of unpredictable alternations traditionally represented by the image of Fortune's wheel (W 2789). Another sense is 'luck': an individual, such as a skilled commander who seizes opportunities invisible to his followers and enemies, may have a run of luck, as does Wallenstein, who his soldiers think has 'das Glück' at his command (L 349); but unpredictable events are sure to intervene and change one's fortune. The concept of 'Glück' overlaps with that of 'Spiel', meaning gambling. To the irresponsible Terzky, Wallenstein's pact with the Swedes is a gamble ('Spiel', P 830), and if it succeeds, he does not care who pays, while Wallenstein is aware that his followers are betting on him, as on a lottery number which will gain a big prize (W 914).[9] Since consequences are unpredictable, any action is a lottery, dipping one's hand into 'fate's mysterious urn' (W 185). And events are subject to blind chance. Thus the capture of Wallenstein's messenger Sesina, which reveals his plans to the Imperial court and forces his hand, is 'an evil chance' (W 92).

All these terms imply that the future is open. But another set of words implies, even more disturbingly, that the future is already determined, in ways that we cannot know. Here the word 'Schicksal' is used. Sometimes it means simply 'the course of events', as when Gordon says that he and Wallenstein, having attended military academy together, were separated by 'Schicksal' (W 2571). Sometimes, however, it means a predetermined outcome to which the individual is subject, as in Thekla's words about her family's fate quoted at the beginning of this essay, or as when she tells the Swedish captain who reports Max's death: '[Y]ours was but the voice of my own fate' (p. 437; W 3012). Fate imposes on people brutal choices which bear the mark of necessity ('Notwendigkeit', W 183) and compels them to act in self-defence ('Notwehr', W 269).

However, the concept of fate is related to human agency in complex ways that were analysed by the Weimar philosopher Johann Gottfried Herder. In 1795, when planning *Wallenstein*, Schiller had published in his journal *Die Horen* an essay by Herder, 'Das eigene Schicksal' ('One's own fate'), which distinguishes several

---

8   G. W. F. Hegel, *Aesthetics: Lectures on Fine Art*, trans. by T. M. Knox (Oxford: Clarendon Press, 1975), p. 1092.

9   On 'Spiel', see the *Wallenstein* chapter in Karl S. Guthke, *Schillers Dramen: Idealismus und Skepsis* (Tübingen: Francke, 1994).

meanings commonly attached to the word fate.[10] There is the sequence of cause and effect, which operates in the moral world as it does in nature. Our good and evil actions lead, not always immediately, but ultimately, to predictable results. When our misdeeds result in disasters, we often ascribe these outcomes to an external force, which we call 'Nemesis'. And we sometimes use this concept, or that of fate, in order to deny responsibility for the disastrous outcomes of our own actions.

Buttler, who arranges Wallenstein's assassination from resentment at having his prospects frustrated, likes to transfer responsibility from himself to fate. According to him, it is Wallenstein's 'Verhängnis' [doom] that has led him to Eger, and it is the 'goddess of fate' (W 2434) who has decided he shall go no further. Talking to Gordon, who is shocked by the prospect of Wallenstein's murder, Buttler unfolds a philosophy of determinism:

> It is not hate makes me his murderer.
> It is his evil fate. Ill fortune drives me,
> The hostile confluence of circumstance.
> Man thinks that he is free to do his deeds,
> But no! He is the plaything of a blind
> Unheeding force, that fashions what was choice
> Swiftly into a grim necessity. (p. 432; W 2873–79)

In an obvious way, this is untrue. As soon as Octavio told him about Wallenstein's deceit, Buttler, in a fury, resolved to kill him. Nobody asked him to do so. But it would be too simple to see this as a self-exonerating lie. Rather, in order to carry out the deed, Buttler has to persuade himself that he is not doing it of his own free will, but is the helpless instrument of blind necessity. This is an extreme example of what an existentialist would call bad faith, especially as, having done the deed for which he thus disclaims responsibility, Buttler hastens to Vienna to claim his reward. But it reveals the psychological pressures that sometimes lie behind the concept of fate.

Other passages suggest more clearly that fate is not something externally imposed on people, but a compulsion springing from their own desires. Thekla expresses this neatly when she tells her aunt that by opting for Max, her own heart has determined her fate: 'Our own heart's prompting is the voice of fate' (p. 285; P 1840). In contrast to Buttler, Thekla is a good existentialist who takes responsibility for her own life and death. Wallenstein, just before his fateful meeting with Wrangel, also juxtaposes 'heart' and 'fate', but more cryptically:

> Fate always wins, for our own heart within us
> Imperiously furthers its designs. (p. 346; W 655–56)

Unlike Thekla, for whom the heart is the intimate place of personal decisions, Wallenstein here talks as if the heart were something alien, the part of us occupied by the external force of fate. Towards fate, the heart is subservient, the executor of its commands, but to the hapless individual the heart issues orders on behalf of

10   The essay 'Das eigene Schicksal' is in Johann Gottfried Herder, *Werke*, ed. by Günter Arnold and others, 10 vols (Frankfurt a.M.: Deutscher Klassiker Verlag, 1985–2000), vol. VIII (1998), pp. 241–56.

fate. But even if the heart has thus been colonized by an alien force, it is still the seat of our emotions, the most intimate part of us, and we cannot help obeying it and feeling that what it commands, even if unwelcome, is also right. So fate always wins, because it operates not just on us but through us.

In the same speech, Wallenstein reflects on the moral causality operating through fate. His act of treachery will not go unavenged. Like the Greek hero who sowed dragon's teeth and harvested a crop of armed men, it will inevitably have bad consequences which will rebound upon him. Similarly, Octavio admits to Max that his deception of Wallenstein is wrong, but partially exonerates himself by describing it as one of the consequences of Wallenstein's misdeed:

> This namely is the curse of evil deeds,
> That they will never cease to breed and bring forth evil. (p. 310; P 2452)

Wallenstein also contemplates a moral symmetry in which he and the Emperor are each being used to punish the other. Wallenstein, previously the instrument of the Emperor's ambition, is, through his treachery, like a tool that turns against its user. But even if his treachery is predetermined, Wallenstein does not share Buttler's notion that predetermined acts are morally neutral. He is a person of enough stature to confront, in a tone of dogged endurance, the tragic paradox whereby 'it must needs be that the [evil] occasions come; but woe to that man through whom the occasion cometh!' (Matt. 18. 7).

These bleak reflections are reinforced by many references to pagan beings which help Schiller to import the atmosphere of classical tragedy into the modern world. Max talks about the Furies ('Erinnyen', W 2322), the spirits of revenge. In this atmosphere, even the 'god of joy' (P 1911) becomes a blind, fire-raising fury. The goddesses of war, revenge, and fate are variously invoked (L 452, W 2425, W 2434). Wallenstein strikes a positive note by acknowledging the goddess of hope (W 3561), but elsewhere laments that an evil demon is beating black wings around his head (W 1473), a standard image for melancholy, and calls Buttler his 'evil demon' for spoiling his efforts to win round the delegation of soldiers (W 2003). He ascribes the workings of fate to the agency of an evil spirit (W 645). He unfolds to Max an almost Gnostic theology, in which the 'divine beings' on high (W 800) provide only radiant but insubstantial ideals; the earth is the province of the evil spirit; and to gain substantial goods on earth, one must descend below it and make a pact with deceitful subterranean powers that require one to sacrifice the purity of one's soul. These sound like the 'malicious powers' (W 190) to which Wallenstein earlier felt he was surrendering by turning his fantasies into action. But whereas, in the earlier passage, the 'powers' could be interpreted as another reference to the incalculable workings of fate, in the address to Max there is a strong suggestion of a demonic pact. Indeed there is a hint that Wallenstein's agreement with the Swedish envoy was a kind of pact with the devil, for afterwards Wrangel disappears as suddenly as though he were the Evil One himself (W 850).

Christian imagery of the supernatural only appears, as here, with reference to evil beings. Wallenstein denounces the double-dealing Octavio as an evil spirit sent from hell (W 2105–09). Buttler is determined to be Wallenstein's evil angel, not his guardian but his destroyer (W 1181–82). In a moment of sober reflection, Wallenstein asserts that every misdeed generates its own avenging angel (W 650–51). Other than in conventional exclamations ('Great God in Heaven!', p. 328; W 146), God is not invoked except by two characters: the Capuchin, who is professionally obliged to do so, and the pious, feeble and ineffectual Gordon. Gordon retains the Christian conception of providence, suggesting that 'divine providence' (W 3627) may have appointed him the means of saving Wallenstein, but disproving his own suggestion by his pusillanimous failure to act on it. Questenberg, the emissary from the Imperial court, shows the appropriate mind-set by declaring that Wallenstein's failure to perceive Octavio's duplicity is the visible work of Heaven (P 354), but he again discredits such a superstitious belief by making God complicit in Octavio's dishonesty. The Christian belief that one can see the hand of God, or at least divine providence, in worldly affairs is treated with extreme scepticism.

Rather than simply submit to an inscrutable universe, however, it may be possible to come to understand its workings by other means than those offered by Christianity. For Wallenstein, the belief in providence has been replaced by belief in a fate into whose operations some gifted mortals can occasionally gain insight. He thinks that he himself is such a person and has experienced privileged moments when he was close to the 'Weltgeist', the spirit animating the world (W 898), and able to put a question to fate. One such moment occurred before the battle of Lützen: wanting to know who was his most faithful follower, Wallenstein asked fate to bring that person before him when he next opened his eyes; and when he awoke, there stood Octavio, who moreover reported a dream warning that Wallenstein would be killed if he rode his usual horse. Accordingly, Wallenstein changed to another horse, and his life was saved. What clearer sign could fate have given? Having taken up astrology, Wallenstein has also cast Octavio's horoscope, and found that the two of them were born under the same stars. Confident in his superior insight, he dismisses the warnings of Terzky and Illo that Octavio is not to be trusted.

This creates a problem in interpreting Wallenstein. For, since Octavio is plotting against him, his reliance on astrology heightens the impression of his political naivety, and risks making him look downright foolish.[11] Despite their small, mean souls, Terzky and Illo seem to have a better understanding of people and affairs than Wallenstein has. Besides, Wallenstein is so attached to astrology that he refuses to accept that it has misinformed him about Octavio. Octavio's treachery, he claims, is the kind of perverse action which the stars could not be expected to predict. And when, shortly before his death, his astrologer Seni urges him to flee from the impending disaster foretold by the stars, Wallenstein pooh-poohs this warning, though it is soon to be borne out by his assassination. Is his belief in astrology just a weak-minded superstition? Or is it something in which he does not really believe deep down, but which serves to prop up the self-confidence that was so shaken by his dismissal at Regensburg?

11 The anonymous reviewer in the *Allgemeine Literatur-Zeitung* (Jena and Leipzig, 30 and 31 January 1801) found Wallenstein obviously inexperienced (a 'Neuling') in his dealings with Wrangel, and 'almost childish' in his ambition to be a king (FA 927, 929).

Astrology in the play counts for more than that. Schiller introduced it when the play was nearly complete, encouraged by Goethe, who pointed out that 'the astrological superstition rests on the indistinct feeling that the world is a vast whole' (letter to Schiller, 8 Dec. 1798, FA 674–75). As Wallenstein describes it, astrology reveals the rhythms of the universe. The stars, most obviously, determine the rhythms of the natural world — day and night, spring and summer, seed-time and harvest — but they also disclose similar rhythms underlying human character and actions (P 985–89). They show that a person's actions are not random but arise from character as predictably as fruit from a tree (W 957).

> Deeds of men as well
> Are sown by fate, in future's darkness broadcast,
> In trust and hope to destiny surrendered.
> He who would reap must seek to learn the times,
> To read and choose the star-appointed hour. (p. 255; P 989–94)

Just as seeds must be sown in spring, so important actions must be undertaken at a propitious time, at an hour dictated by the stars, so that they will succeed and bear fruit in the future.

Although Wallenstein's astrology proves wrong, we are not to think that it is merely a mistake. It corresponds to another conception of fate as analysed by Herder. Since life is dependent on times and seasons, mastery of fate means doing things at the proper time: 'Throughout history it was the heroes of fate who could form a sound judgement of the course of events, the critical days of an illness, and the ripeness of things in general' (Herder, p. 252). Wallenstein's astrology is an unsuccessful attempt to judge when the time is ripe for action. In practical terms, it is certainly less useful than the shrewdness of Octavio, or even of Terzky and Illo. But it is not just an alternative way of seeking practical guidance. Rather, it is a grandiose attempt to grasp the hidden forces governing the universe, and to understand both the great world of the cosmos, and the little world or microcosm (W 955) of humankind, as subject to the same gigantic rhythms. In his confident moods, Wallenstein believes that his success is ensured by his being aligned with those rhythms. He may seem defeated, but he will rise again, as surely as the high tide follows the ebb:

> Today indeed it seems I am sunk low,
> But I shall rise again; a flowing tide
> Will follow swiftly on this present ebb. (p. 459; W 3573–75)

Similarly, Wallenstein believes that occult science puts him in contact with the hidden forces both under and above the earth. The former are often referred to by the imagery of springs. Thus Wallenstein rebukes Illo's talk of chance by saying that to the adept, there is no such thing as chance:

> What seems to us but blind coincidence,
> *That* from the deepest springs of all is sprung. (p. 355; W 944–45)

The microcosm is the deep shaft from which man's actions spring ('quellen', W 956); elsewhere Wallenstein speaks of 'the pure deed from a pious source' (W 162). The period of his indecision, apparently, was the ascendancy of Saturn, the planet that presides over the mysterious birth of things in the depths both of the earth and of the heart ('Gemüt', W 27). Astrology also discloses a spiritual ladder ascending from our earthly dust (P 978) to the world of the stars. On this ladder heavenly forces pass between earth and the higher world. As an adept, Wallenstein can perceive the powers fermenting under the earth, and he can discern the moment when their work is ready to be drawn up into the realm of light which is dominated by Jupiter, the planet with which he identifies (W 30).

All this makes Wallenstein sound remarkably like a creative artist.[12] Such a person may be subject to spells of lethargy, depression, creative withdrawal, when something is taking shape in his unconscious. Then the moment comes when his conceptions have been formed and are ready to be given plastic form. Wallenstein's dream of peace and kingship is a creative fantasy which could conceivably be realized by decisive action. But because it arises from the well-springs of his unconscious, the 'maternal soil' of his heart (W 188), it follows the rhythms of his imagination, and is not easily adjusted to the constantly shifting circumstances of political and military action. As soon as Wallenstein feels ready to take the decisive step, he learns that his plans have been discovered and that he therefore must commit himself to the Swedes, like it or not. Instead of enjoying the freedom of the creative artist, he has to suffer the constraints of the politician practising the art of the possible.

If, in seeking contact with the natural forces of the cosmos, Wallenstein tries to step beyond the limits of humanity, he does so also in another, more negative sense. There are repeated suggestions that Wallenstein is an elemental being, a force of nature, which is most likely to be destructive. When Wallenstein tried to capture the port of Stralsund, where Wrangel was the Swedish commander, he was struggling not just against another army but against the element of the sea (W 228). It was then, as the Capuchin recalls, that he uttered his famous boast that he would take Stralsund even if it were attached by a chain to heaven (L 605–06); Schiller tells the story in the *History*, saying that Wallenstein sought to conquer nature itself (IV, 479). Max imagines that having made peace in the Empire, Wallenstein will retire to his estates and battle with the elements by diverting rivers, blowing up rocks and building roads (P 1672). This is a misjudgement which Wallenstein himself does not make. He knows that he cannot retire into inactivity: 'If I can no more act, then I am nothing' (p. 342; W 528). The word 'wirken' in this line is often used of natural and spiritual forces, as when Wallenstein talks about heavenly powers at work ('wirkend', P 981). When Max turns against his fallen idol, he denounces him as a destructive natural force, a volcano whose eruption overwhelms the innocent people all around, blind and unfeeling — 'Like the blind element that mindless rolls' (p. 402; W 2091). The image may remind us that Wallenstein has caused the deaths of innumerable people by ravaging large tracts of Germany with fire and sword. Later Buttler compares Wallenstein to another natural phenomenon, a

---

12 Borchmeyer calls him the model of an aesthetic dilettante ('das Musterbeispiel eines ästhetischen Dilettanten' (p. 139)); I would rather see him as a potentially powerful creative artist who is frustrated by his own weaknesses and others' machinations.

meteor (W 2435), which, having flashed across the skies to the general wonderment, is about to fall to earth.

In his denunciation of Wallenstein, Max twice uses the word 'wild'. Wallenstein is said to follow only the wild impulse of his heart (W 2093), represented by the image of the volcano disgorging its 'wild torrent' of lava (W 2101). The word 'wild' aligns Wallenstein with nature as opposed to civilization. A natural force is not just a destructive one, like the volcano; it is something with which no alliance can be formed (W 2092). Civilization depends on alliances, on treaties, on bonds. The bonds of affection and loyalty between parents and children, husbands and wives, subjects and rulers, are the mortar with which civilization is built. And here the word 'nature' can be used in another sense, for such bonds are natural, and to deny them is to place oneself outside natural human society in an asocial state of wild nature. In the *History* Schiller describes how the overthrow of governments recreates the pre-civilized state of nature in which each individual must survive by 'Selbsthilfe', self-preservation at the expense of others (IV, 510).

Self-preservation at others' expense is also the message impressed on Wallenstein by the amoral and cynical Terzkys. In his only memorable utterance, the colourless Count Terzky affirms that the world is governed by self-interest: 'It is advantage rules the world's affairs' (p. 339; W 443). His wife is convinced that Wallenstein, having been badly treated by the Emperor, no longer owes him any loyalty; further, she encourages Wallenstein to consider himself a force of nature, superior to the restrictions of civilization. Nature, she says, is a 'giant spirit' (589) which obeys only itself and cannot be bound by treaties. Wallenstein should align himself with nature and follow the imperatives of his own character. The only fault he can commit is to be inconsistent. This seductive doctrine of anarchism, if accepted, would soon destroy all civilization.

In *Wallenstein*, Max contrasts the ties of civilization with the destructive activity of its antithesis, barbarism:

> Oh, but the free and gracious impulses
> Of hospitality, and loyalty to friend,
> Give to the heart a sacred, pious duty,
> And nature will exact a grim revenge
> On the barbarian who would defile them. (p. 411; W 2331–35)

Here Max is asking Thekla whether, in order to regain her father's favour, he should turn against the Emperor and his father and support Wallenstein's treachery. He evokes the layers of mutual obligation which constitute civilization. Hospitality, friendship, and religion are all based on the heart and exist, not as abstract principles, but as feelings ('Regungen'); indeed such feelings are religion (in the etymological sense of 'binding'), and can be called 'heilig' (sacred) and 'fromm', a word that is often inadequately translated as 'pious' but here implies a heartfelt loyalty to tradition. By joining Wallenstein, Max would break the bonds of a subject and a son: he would betray the Emperor and have to try to kill his father. Only a barbarian violates such ties; nature shudders at the violation, and the feelings that bind people together ensure that it will be punished.

This passage resonates throughout the play, which offers so many examples of loyalty and betrayal. The loyalty that the soldiers and officers feel for Wallenstein is exploited by Terzky and Illo, and indeed by Wallenstein himself. Octavio takes advantage of Wallenstein's friendship with very little scruple, justifying himself to Max with the feeble argument that he did not seek Wallenstein's friendship but had it forced on him. Wallenstein is contemplating an act of massive disloyalty to the Emperor, one that its beneficiaries, the Swedes, are prepared to accept but not to condone. At the same time, the Empire hardly inspires devotion. Schiller was well aware that the Imperial government under Ferdinand II promoted a bigoted Catholicism, persecuted religious dissenters, and waged war with total disregard for the well-being of its subjects. The play makes clear the Emperor's ambition ('Herrschsucht'), his bigotry, and his unscrupulous methods. Besides, the Imperial court has treated Wallenstein shabbily. But then Wallenstein, even before Regensburg, was an insubordinate subject, and since his recall he has been playing a double game which makes him morally similar to Octavio.

Two key passages reflect on political order. To Max's claim that Wallenstein's personal rule is aligned with nature and must override regulations written down in books, Octavio replies that the complex, indirect methods prescribed by an ancient civilization are safer than the direct, drastic route taken by lightning or the cannon-ball (P 463–70). Here again Wallenstein is being compared to the destructive forces of nature. Of course Octavio, who is using indirect methods to betray Wallenstein, has an axe to grind, but his argument may be valid irrespective of his motives for advancing it. The response to this passage comes in Wallenstein's soliloquy when he reflects that a civilization may be founded on no deeper value than habit, and yet be almost unassailable because so many people accept it with child-like faith (W 197). The tension between the conservative Octavio and the revolutionary Wallenstein is not resolved in the play. On the one hand, the Empire, as a legally constituted government, dignified by age and tradition, however shoddy, is infinitely better than anarchy. On the other, by relying on Octavio's deceit and eroding the bonds of trust that hold civilization together, the Empire itself risks plunging into anarchy.

Looking at *Wallenstein* in the context of Schiller's work as a whole, we may say that it dramatizes two opposed conceptions of nature. One is nature as a blind, amoral, destructive force. 'The world, as a historical object,' Schiller writes in the late essay *On the Sublime* (1801), 'is basically nothing but the conflict of natural forces with one another and with human freedom' (v, 803). We see these natural forces at work as early as *The Robbers*, embodied respectively in the passions of Karl Moor and the amoral, malevolent intellect of his brother Franz, who, angry with nature for denying him physical attractions, resolves to use another natural gift, his reason, to compensate for his disadvantages. Both brothers are judged not only by moral standards but also by the positive natural bonds embodied in the family. This sense of nature as constructively joining people together through physical needs (the infant's need for its mother, affection between parents and children, between husband and wife) is most fully developed in *Wilhelm Tell*. Tell's assassination of Gessler is a crime, but justified by Gessler's assault on family ties, whereas Johannes

Parricida, who killed his uncle the Emperor, has committed the most unnatural of crimes, recalling Franz Moor's cruelty towards his father. Hence Tell can rightly say: 'I have avenged the sacred nature which you have violated' (II, 1025). Wallenstein's activity, and his inactivity, are likewise to be seen against the background of nature as embodied in family ties, in the love between Max and Thekla, in the loyalty due even to an unattractive Emperor, and finally in the rhythms of the cosmos.

CHAPTER 5

Schiller and the Jesuits

'Wohl ausgesonnen, Pater Lamormain!' is Wallenstein's immediate reaction (line 1233) when Questenberg, in Act II of *Die Piccolomini*, gives him the Emperor's order to supply eight cavalry regiments to accompany the Spanish 'Kardinal-Infant' with his army from Milan to the Netherlands.[1] We have already learnt this news from the soldiers in *Wallensteins Lager*, who realize that it is intended to weaken Wallenstein's forces and nip in the bud any independent action he may wish to undertake. The key role played by Father Lamormain at the Imperial court has been intimated earlier in the same Act, when the Duchess of Friedland reports to her husband, Wallenstein, on the cool reception that she has found in Vienna. The gracious and friendly treatment she received in the past has been replaced by chilly formality and oppressive silence. Nobody spoke of Wallenstein, even to criticize him. The only explanation for this reserve came from Father Lamormain. As soon as this person's name is mentioned, Wallenstein cuts in quickly: 'Lamormain! Was sagt der?' (line 690). Apparently Lamormain revealed that Wallenstein was charged with disobeying orders and was in danger of again being dismissed from his post, as happened in 1630 at Regensburg, only this time with still more disgrace. Even if we know nothing else about Father Lamormain, we can tell that he is a key figure at the Viennese court, privy to the most secret information, and authorized to impart it, albeit indirectly by hints ('Winke', line 690). More than that, Wallenstein's response to Questenberg implies that Lamormain not only communicates policy but devises it, that he not only advises the Emperor but guides him, with a cunning that arouses Wallenstein's reluctant admiration:

> Wär der Gedank nicht so verwünscht gescheit,
> Man wär versucht, ihn herzlich dumm zu nennen. (lines 1234–35)

Father Lamormain, familiar to historians as the Jesuit confessor to the Emperor Ferdinand II, is one of many Catholic characters who are negatively portrayed in Schiller's works. In *Die Räuber*, Franz Moor appears to be a Catholic: he threatens to

---

1   Schiller's texts are quoted whenever possible from *Friedrich Schiller: Sämtliche Werke*. ed. by Gerhard Fricke and Herbert G. Göpfert, 5 vols (Munich: Hanser, 1958). Quotations from verse plays are identified by line number, others by *Werke* with volume and page numbers, others by HA with volume and page numbers. Letters from and to Schiller are quoted from the *Schillers Werke: Nationalausgabe*, ed. by Julius Petersen et al. (Weimar: Hermann Böhlaus Nachfolger, 1943–2010). They are identified by NA with volume and page numbers.

put Amalia in a convent; while Karl is anti-Catholic, burning down a town which is twice described as 'bigott'. This town sends out the bullying 'Pater', a Catholic priest who tells Karl that if he gives himself up to the civil authorities, they will, in their great mercy, do nothing more than break him on the wheel. In *Don Carlos* Schiller exploits to the full the 'Black Legend' of Spain as a country not only in economic decline but in servitude to rigid ceremonial and religious bigotry.[2] The Inquisition is in full swing, and about to extend its operations to the Spanish Netherlands. The King is shown to be under the thumb not only of his confessor Domingo but of the entirely inhuman Grand Inquisitor. The fanaticism shown in *Don Carlos* by Alba, 'Des Fanatismus rauher Henkersknecht' (line 162), is transferred in *Maria Stuart* to Mortimer and his unseen backers, the Guise family in France, who were partly responsible for the Massacre of St Bartholomew's Night. Mortimer and his bravos will stop at nothing to rescue Maria and have been absolved in advance for whatever crimes they may commit. There is a strong element of fanaticism too in Schiller's Joan of Arc, who, inspired by her voices and visions, slaughters every Englishman (and Welshman) in her path (unlike her historical prototype, who encouraged the troops but did not fight, let alone kill) until stopped in her tracks by her love for Lionel and her realization that she has overstepped the divine command. And in Schiller's fiction, we have in *Der Geisterseher* a conspiracy, masterminded by an Armenian, to secure a prince's fortune by inducing him to become a Catholic.[3]

To make his allegiances even clearer, Schiller regularly contrasts his Catholic fanatics with morally upright Protestants. The greatest Protestant hero in his work is Gustav Adolf, King of Sweden, who is presented in the *Geschichte des Dreißigjährigen Krieges* as the greatest military commander of his century, as a responsible leader who goes to war only after unbearable provocation, as sharing the privations of his soldiers, and, above all, as leading a disciplined and devout army which, unlike the Imperial forces, refrains from plundering, and which forms a circle round its preacher every morning and evening. Gustav Adolf's spontaneous piety, his 'ungekünstelte lebendige Gottesfurcht', is placed in sharp relief against the superstitious devotion of the Emperor Ferdinand — 'der kriechenden Andächtelei eines Ferdinands, die sich vor der Gottheit zum Wurm erniedrigt und auf dem Nacken der Menschheit trotzig einherwandelt' (HA IV, 497). Gustav Adolf does not appear in *Wallenstein*, for he was killed in battle some fifteen months before the action of the play begins, but his representative is the Swedish Colonel Wrangel, who in Act I, scene 5 of *Wallensteins Tod* engages in tough negotiations with Wallenstein and has too much

2 See Barbara Becker-Cantarino, 'Die schwarze Legende: Ideal und Ideologie in Schillers *Don Carlos*', *Jahrbuch des Freien Deutschen Hochstifts* (1975), 153–73.

3 Considering its prominence in his works, remarkably little has been written about Schiller and the Catholic Church. Jeffrey L. Sammons, 'Mortimer's Conversion and Schiller's Allegiances', *Journal of English and Germanic Philology*, 72 (1973), 155–66, is perceptive and still invaluable, as is Jill Berman's study of the psychology of Mortimer's conversion, 'Mortimer and the Gods of Italy', *Oxford German Studies*, 8 (1973–74), 47–59. Yet both are absent from the bibliography of Manfred Misch's chapter 'Schiller und die Religion' in *Schiller-Handbuch*, ed. by Helmut Koopmann (Stuttgart: Kröner, 1998), pp. 198–215, which does not discuss Schiller's attitude to Catholicism. This chapter is largely though not wholly identical with Misch, 'Schiller und die Religion', in *Schiller heute*, ed. by Hans-Jörg Knobloch and Helmut Koopmann (Tübingen: Francke, 1996), pp. 27–43.

integrity to hide his disapproval of the latter's proposal to lead an entire army away from their legitimate ruler. Earlier, in *Die Räuber*, the ranting 'Pater' is contrasted with the dignified Pastor Moser, who tries in vain to induce Franz Moor to repent; and in *Maria Stuart* Mortimer cuts a poor figure beside his uncle, Sir Amias Paulet, a staunch old Puritan who indignantly rebuffs Burleigh's suggestion that he should make away with Maria in prison.

Although Schiller's characters are much too lifelike to be called stereotypes, many of them do have their origins in religious stereotypes that were current in the Enlightenment. Thus the 'Pater', and still more the Capuchin in *Wallensteins Lager*, represent a variety of popular preaching that was considered by the Aufklärer to be hectoring, intellectually trivial, and full of tasteless puns. The model that Schiller drew on was Abraham a Sancta Clara, the Viennese preacher (actually from Bavaria) who for many years chastised his flock entertainingly for their faults; another figure often pilloried by the enlightened was Pater Cochem, a seventeenth-century devotional writer from the Rhineland, whose colloquial life of Christ and collections of legends were hugely popular throughout Catholic Germany even at the end of the eighteenth century. Priests who meddled in politics, like Domingo in *Don Carlos*, had many prototypes. One example, featured briefly but vividly in the *Geschichte des Dreißigjährigen Krieges*, was Père Joseph, the Capuchin who was Cardinal Richelieu's diplomatic emissary, and who encouraged Ferdinand II to dismiss Wallenstein, thus weakening the Imperial cause, while actually promoting an alliance between France and the Empire's arch-enemy Sweden (HA, IV, 488–89). But the most popular stereotype, the one surrounded by the most sensational stories and the most productive one for literature, was that of the scheming Jesuit, who could also be a political conspirator and a terrorist. Enlighteners in both Protestant and Catholic countries regarded the Jesuits with a horrified fascination which went back to the sixteenth century and was to become even more intense in the nineteenth.

The Jesuits were originally a group of students at the University of Paris centring on Ignatius de Loyola.[4] His name was really Iñigo Lopez de Loyola, but when he matriculated it was wrongly transcribed as Ignatius. As the Society of Jesus, dedicated to propagating the Catholic faith through education and missionary work, they were officially founded by a Papal bull in 1540. In the 1560s they assumed

---

4 For the history, political philosophy, and mythology of the Jesuits, I have drawn heavily on the following: J. C. H. Aveling, *The Jesuits* (London: Blond & Briggs, 1981); John W. O'Malley, *The First Jesuits* (Cambridge, MA: Harvard University Press, 1993); Harro Höpfl, *Jesuit Political Thought: The Society of Jesus and the State, c. 1540–1630* (Cambridge: Cambridge University Press, 2004); Robert Bireley, *The Jesuits and the Thirty Years War: Kings, Courts, and Confessors* (Cambridge: Cambridge University Press, 2003); Richard van Dülmen, 'Antijesuitismus und katholische Aufklärung in Deutschland', in his *Religion und Gesellschaft: Beiträge zu einer Religionsgeschichte der Neuzeit* (Frankfurt a.M.: Fischer, 1989), pp. 141–71; Derek Beales, 'The Suppression of the Jesuits', in his *Prosperity and Plunder: European Catholic Monasteries in the Age of Revolution, 1650–1815* (Cambridge: Cambridge University Press, 2003), pp. 143–68; Peter Burke, 'The Black Legend of the Jesuits: An Essay in the History of Social Stereotypes', in *Christianity and Community in the West: Essays for John Bossy*, ed. by Simon Ditchfield (Aldershot: Ashgate, 2001), pp. 165–82; Geoffrey Cubitt, *The Jesuit Myth: Conspiracy Theory and Politics in Nineteenth-Century France* (Oxford: Clarendon Press, 1993).

the additional task of combating Protestantism. Sinister stories about them soon sprang up. They were said to be organized on the lines of an absolute monarchy or military regiment, and to use their educational system to brainwash their members into a condition of blind obedience. One of the main charges against them was moral laxity. In the seventeenth century many Jesuits maintained the doctrine of probabilism. That said that when you had to choose between two courses of action, either of which was probably but not certainly right, you could choose the one that suited you best, even if it was less probably right than the other.[5] This doctrine was opposed and satirized by Pascal in the *Lettres provinciales*. Jesuits were thought to defend themselves under interrogation by equivocation, and under oath by mental reservations. They were also credited with encouraging tyrannicide. The Jesuit Juan de Mariana in *De Rege et regis institutione* (1599) argued that a legitimate ruler who persistently abused his power could be killed by an individual. This was a highly unpopular doctrine in the age of absolutism, when divinity was thought to hedge a king, and the Parlement de Paris had Mariana's book burned by the public hangman on 8 June 1610. Jesuits were also credited with the doctrine that the end justifies the means, another view combated by Pascal. By putting forward these lax doctrines, it was argued, the Jesuits made themselves popular as confessors and gained positions of influence, for it was thought that a confessor could even direct the public policy of his charge. Voltaire wrote of the typical Jesuit confessor (noting that Jesuits were also popular because princes did not need to worry about rewarding them with bishoprics): 'C'est un ministère secret qui devient puissant à proportion de la faiblesse du prince.'[6]

In 1614 a book appeared called the *Monita secreta Societatis Iesu*, purporting to be a set of secret rules governing the Jesuits' pursuit of power, influence, and wealth. It was in fact written by a renegade Polish Jesuit called Zaharowski as a satire, and its satirical intention is, or should be, obvious, though it was widely taken as serious. For example, it advises Jesuits to cultivate rich widows, who must be prevented from remarrying and induced to leave their property to the Order. If they have daughters, these must be encouraged to become nuns; it is recommended to make the mother embitter her daughter's life by scolding her and by telling her of the hardships of marriage. Sons, if at all suitable, should be encouraged to enter the Order, with the aid of a sympathetic tutor. Young men should not be admitted to the Order till they have received their inheritances, which they can then give to the Order.[7]

It was widely believed that the Jesuits put their lax morals and their theory of tyrannicide into practice. They were thought to be behind the murders of William the Silent in 1584 and Henri III of France in 1588, the assassination attempts on Henri IV in 1593 and 1594, the successful murder of Henri IV in 1610, and the attempt by

---

5   The best explanation of probabilism that I have found is in Henry Charles Lea, *A History of Auricular Confession and Indulgences in the Latin Church*, 3 vols (London: Swan Sonnenschein, 1896), vol. II, ch. 21: 'Probabilism and Casuistry', pp. 285–411.

6   Voltaire, *Essai sur les mœurs*, ed. by René Pomeau, 2 vols (Paris: Garnier, 1963), II, 287.

7   There have been many editions; I used *Geheime Vorschriften des Jesuiter-Ordens. Aus dem Lateinischen* ([Vienna], 1782).

Damiens to assassinate Louis XV in 1757. They were thought to have murdered two Popes (Clement VIII and Clement XIV) and to have poisoned Cardinal Tournon with chocolate at Macao in 1709. In 1758 an attempt to assassinate King Dom José of Portugal, probably by the jealous husband of his mistress, gave the enlightened minister Pombal a pretext to crush the Jesuits by implausibly charging them with complicity.[8] In Britain, they allegedly instigated the Gunpowder Plot in 1605 and the Popish Plot in 1678. On the Continent, they were blamed for helping to cause the outbreak of the Thirty Years' War. For a handy summary of these allegations, one need look no further than the article 'Jésuite' in that central Enlightenment text, the *Encyclopédie*.[9]

When such charges were widely believed, it is not surprising that satire against the Jesuits should be vitriolic. A notable English example is Donne's essay 'Ignatius his Conclave', in which the soul of Ignatius is represented in hell, competing with other dead villains for Lucifer's favour, and which already denounces 'the *Jesuites Assassinates*, and *King-killings*'.[10] Another is John Oldham's *Satyrs upon the Jesuits*, first published in full in 1679, in one of which the ghost of Henry Garnett, who was hanged for alleged involvement in the Gunpowder Plot, appears to later conspirators and encourages them in all wickedness:

> The blackest, ugliest, horrid'st, damned'st deed,
> For which Hell flames, the Schools a Title need,
> If done for *Holy Church* is sanctified.
> This consecrates the blessed Work and Tool,
> Nor must we ever after think 'em foul.[11]

These myths were still powerful in the nineteenth century. They appear in the *Schiller-Lexikon* published at Berlin in 1869, on the eve of unification and the Kulturkampf. The entry on 'Jesuiten' tells us that the society has a monarchical constitution ('eine vollkommen monarchische Verfassung'), and exercises influence by installing its members as confessors and tutors to princes; moreover: 'In dem Grundsatz: "der Zweck heiligt die Mittel" fanden sie eine vollkommene Beschönigung für die abscheulichsten Handlungen'.[12]

Where did these notions come from? One cannot but notice their similarity to fantasies that later circulated about Jews. Both Jesuits and Jews have been supposed to form a huge monolithic international organization, plotting to dominate the world by unscrupulous means. Even the *Monita secreta* have their more recent counterpart in the *Protocols of the Elders of Zion*. We have in fact a fully developed

---

8   See Kenneth Maxwell, *Pombal: Paradox of the Enlightenment* (Cambridge: Cambridge University Press, 1995), pp. 79–86.

9   See the *Encyclopédie ou Dictionnaire raisonné des sciences, des arts et des métiers* (Neuchâtel: Faulche, 1765), vol. VIII, pp. 512–16. The author of the article was Jean d'Alembert. These and other charges were systematically examined and rejected in Bernhard Duhr, SJ, *Jesuiten-Fabeln: Ein Beitrag zur Culturgeschichte* (Freiburg i.Br.: Herder, 1891).

10   John Donne: *Ignatius His Conclave*, ed. by T. S. Healy, SJ (Oxford: Clarendon Press, 1969), p. 61.

11   *The Poems of John Oldham*, ed. by Harold F. Brooks and Raman Selden (Oxford: Clarendon Press, 1987), p. 21.

12   Ludwig Rudolph, *Schiller-Lexikon: Erläuterndes Wörterbuch zu Schiller's Dichterwerken*, 2 vols (Berlin: Nicolaische Verlagsbuchhandlung, 1869), I, 458.

conspiracy theory, whose only relation to empirical reality is that tiny grains of truth are magnified into a huge paranoid structure which is ultimately self-confirming. The various murders, for example, have only the remotest link to the Jesuits. Before Baltazar Gerard murdered William the Silent, he had told a Jesuit in Trier of his intention, so the Jesuits were held responsible. The first of Henri IV's would-be assassins, Pierre Barrière, said under interrogation that he had been encouraged by the Jesuits; the second, Jean Chastel, had studied at the Jesuit college of Clermont. François Ravaillac, who did kill Henri IV in 1610, had tried to enter the order, but been turned down; from the records of his interrogation, he sounds like the type of emotionally disturbed lone killer who often undertakes assassinations at the present day.[13] Henry Garnett seems to have known some months in advance about the Gunpowder Plot and to have done nothing to prevent it, but he was certainly not its instigator.[14]

As for meddling in politics, some Jesuits did, some didn't. The official view of the Society in the seventeenth century was that they should stay out of politics. In 1602 its General, Acquaviva, published an Instruction for Confessors of Princes ('De Confessariis Principum') intended to preserve the advantages of gaining princes' support for the Society but to avoid harming the Society's reputation by interfering in politics: the confessor was not to become involved in political matters or court factions, not to exercise any political power, and to require the prince to hear him out if he criticized abuses in the prince's government. However, it was difficult to draw a clear line between private and political issues, and difficult also to resist the temptation to steer political discussions in a direction favourable to the Church in general and the Society in particular.

Father Lamormain seems seldom to have resisted. He was an international figure, born in Luxembourg and educated in Prague, whose name is variously given as Wilhelm Lamormain or Guillaume Lamormaini. C. V. Wedgwood describes him as 'a lean, tall man with an ugly limp, the deformity which had driven him as a boy into the shelter of the seminary. His manners were austere, his habits simple, his convictions fanatical.'[15] As early as 1615, when he was rector of the University of Graz, the papal nuncio in Graz, Paravicini, wrote angrily of him: 'Er ist ganz und gar politisch eingestellt', and fifteen years later Eggenberg, the Imperial first minister, complained to Vitelleschi, the General of the Jesuits, that Lamormaini interfered too much in politics.[16] He was confessor to the Emperor from 1624 until the latter's death in 1637. He managed to ensure that no Jesuit other than himself had access to the Emperor. Such was his influence that even the Emperor's

---

13   See Roland Mousnier, *L'Assassinat d'Henri IV: Le Problème du tyrannicide et l'affermissement de la monarchie absolue* (Paris: Gallimard, 1964). These associations are listed in Burke, 'The Black Legend', p. 173.

14   Mark Nicholls, *Investigating Gunpowder Plot* (Manchester: Manchester University Press, 1991), p. 72.

15   C. V. Wedgwood. *The Thirty Years War* (London: Cape, 1938), p. 166.

16   Quoted from Andreas Posch, 'Zur Tätigkeit und Beurteilung Lamormains', *Mitteilungen des Instituts für österreichische Geschichtsforschung*, 63 (1955), 375–90 (p. 378); Robert Bireley, *Religion and Politics in the Age of the Counterreformation: Emperor Ferdinand II, William Lamormaini, S.J., and the Formation of Imperial Policy* (Chapel Hill: University of North Carolina Press, 1981), p. 94.

brother, when seeking a favour, wrote to Lamormain asking him to put his request to the Emperor. His influence over Ferdinand was assisted by the latter's extreme piety. Schiller quotes Lamormain, without naming him, in the *Geschichte des Dreißigjährigen Krieges*: ' "Nichts auf Erden", schreibt sein eigener Beichtvater, "war ihm heiliger als ein priesterliches Haupt. Geschähe es, pflegte er zu sagen, daß ein Engel und ein Ordensmann zu *einer* Zeit und an *einem* Orte ihm begegneten, so würde der Ordensmann die erste und der Engel die zweite Verbeugung von ihm erhalten." ' (HA, IV, 489) This is taken from the eulogy of the Emperor that Lamormain published after his death (*Ferdinandi II Virtutes*, 1638).[17]

Initially Lamormain got on well with Wallenstein, who was a generous benefactor to the Jesuits and in 1628 was named, at Lamormain's urging, a Founder of the Society, which entitled him to a special share in the Society's prayers. However, at the Electoral Convention at Regensburg in 1630 Lamormain supported Wallenstein's dismissal, because he feared that the Catholic Electors would otherwise break with the Emperor. He was an extreme supporter of the Edict of Restitution which so antagonized the Protestant princes. After Wallenstein was recalled, Lamormain tried to repair his relations with Wallenstein, but Wallenstein continued to resent the Jesuits' share in his dismissal. Schiller makes his Wallenstein tell the Mayor of Eger, 'Ich hasse | Die Jesuiten' (WT 2595–96). Lamormain was party to the decision, reached early in 1634, that Wallenstein should be removed from office for insubordination, and, if he refused to come under guard to Vienna for a hearing, then killed along with his fellow-conspirators. He reassured Ferdinand that his conscience could permit Wallenstein's execution. He shared the widespread view that Wallenstein had become too powerful and was a threat to the Emperor's authority, and indeed was part of a conspiracy to seize power in the Habsburg lands and depose the Emperor. His letter to Vitelleschi, setting this out, is an important source of information about Wallenstein's downfall.[18]

We must imagine Father Lamormain, therefore, as an important person behind Schiller's scenes. Just as Wrangel stands for the Protestant spirit best represented by Gustav Adolf, so Lamormain stands in for a large body of Jesuit intrigue, to which Schiller refers in the *Geschichte des Dreißigjährigen Krieges*. There we are told that after the Treaty of Augsburg, divisions between Lutherans and Calvinists were exploited by the 'Machinationen der Jesuiten' (HA, IV, 381). Rudolf II's melancholy temperament and Spanish upbringing exposed him to 'den schlimmen Ratschlägen der Jesuiten' (HA, IV, 384). Protestant suspicions of Catholic good faith were increased by '[d]as unbesonnene Eifer der Jesuiten' (HA, IV, 395). The Jesuits were expelled from Bohemia and believed to be the originators ('Urheber') of its misfortunes (HA, IV, 423). Ferdinand, educated by the Jesuits at Ingolstadt (HA, IV, 427), is described as 'der Sklave Spaniens und der Jesuiten' (HA, IV, 432). Maximilian

---

17   See the anonymous German translation, P. Wilhelm Lamormaini, *Ferdinand II: Ein Tugend-Spiegel für alle Stände* (Vienna: Ueberreuter, 1857), p. 41. The quotation comes from Chapter 9, 'Seine Ehrerbietung gegen den Priesterstand'.

18   The letter (in Latin) is reproduced in Heinrich Ritter von Srbik, *Wallensteins Ende: Ursachen, Verlauf und Folgen der Katastrophe*, 2nd edn (Salzburg: Otto Müller, 1952), pp. 310–13. A partial translation appears on pp. 108–09.

of Bavaria was persuaded partly by 'die Eingebungen der Jesuiten' (HA, IV, 437) to support Ferdinand in 1619, and Ferdinand is swayed by 'die giftvolle Beredsamkeit der Jesuiten' (HA, IV, 565); indeed Schiller speaks in one breath of the 'Gunst des Kaisers und der Jesuiten'. And since Lamormain and the Jesuits have turned against Wallenstein, we may assume that when, shortly before his death, he says: 'Von falschen Freunden stammt mein ganzes Unglück' (line 3511), he is referring to them as well as to Octavio.

There is a final association between Wallenstein and the Jesuits. I mentioned that they were widely blamed for the assassination of Henri IV in 1610. On the evening of his death, Wallenstein is thinking about this very event, which has long been on his mind:

> Es machte mir stets eigene Gedanken,
> Was man vom Tod des vierten Heinrichs liest.
> Der König fühlte das Gespenst des Messers
> Lang vorher in der Brust, eh sich der Mörder
> Ravaillac damit waffnete. Ihn floh
> Die Ruh, es jagt' ihn auf in seinem Louvre,
> Ins Freie trieb es ihn, wie Leichenfeier
> Klang ihm der Gattin Krönungsfest, er hörte
> Im ahnungsvollen Ohr der Füße Tritt,
> Die durch die Gassen von Paris ihn suchten. (lines 3490–99)

Although Wallenstein denies feeling any similar premonition, he is clearly uneasy. This is not the first time he has compared himself to other historical figures. He justified his plans to revolt against the Emperor by recalling how Caesar led the legions against Rome (lines 835–39). And he accepted Wrangel's double-edged comparison of him to the military leaders Attila and Pyrrhus (line 287). The comparison with Henri IV is in one way inappropriate: Wallenstein is not a king, and his assassination is not regicide; he is, rather, an over-mighty subject whose murder is being plotted by his monarch.[19] In evoking Henri IV, he is inadvertently confirming his own ambitions. Moreover, he is referring to someone who resembles himself in several respects. Henri IV, like Wallenstein, converted to Catholicism. He brought peace to France after prolonged religious wars, as Wallenstein imagines doing for the Empire. And he was thought to have fallen victim to reactionary Catholic forces including the Jesuits. The same is being suggested about Wallenstein: the Empire, a force for unenlightened conservatism, with Jesuits among its politicians, ensures his downfall.

Lamormain is not the only scheming priest mentioned in the play. There is also Father Quiroga, who pops up briefly when one of the attendants at the banquet of Wallenstein's supporters in *Die Piccolomini*, Act IV, says to another: 'Pass ja wohl auf, Johann, dass wir dem Pater | Quiroga recht viel zu erzählen haben. | Er will dafür uns recht viel Ablass geben' (lines 2127–29). In being paid for their information in

---

19   This point is made by Ilja Mieck, 'L'Assassinat de Wallenstein', in *Complots et conjurations dans l'Europe moderne*, ed. by Yves-Marie Bercé and Elena Fasano Guarini (Rome: École française de Rome, 1996), pp. 507–34 (p. 507). A closer analogy would be with Henri III's decision in 1588 to have the Guise brothers assassinated as rebellious subjects.

indulgences, these servants contribute to Schiller's portrayal of pitiable and ignorant Catholic superstition, as do Devereux and Macdonald later when, in order to overcome the charm that supposedly makes Wallenstein invulnerable, they decide to ask an Irish Dominican to dip their swords and pikes in holy water. The Imperial side relies heavily on priests: when Isolani goes to Vienna to ask for new horses for his regiment, he is amazed to find himself required to deal with the incongruous figure of a Capuchin (P line 173); and the courier who brings Octavio news that Wallenstein's messenger Sesina has been captured has been admitted privately by Capuchin monks through a little door in their monastery (P lines 2589–90).

The motif of Jesuit intrigue points both backwards and forwards through Schiller's work. The clerics in *Don Carlos* are Dominicans, as the name of the King's confessor, Domingo, indicates, though in the Mannheim production of the play, Dalberg, to Schiller's annoyance, made him into a Jesuit, thus causing the audience to suspect an allusion to the powerful and arch-conservative Jesuit Father Ignaz Frank, confessor to the Elector of Bavaria and the Palatinate.[20] But the most Jesuit-like character is the Marquis Posa, even though, at first glance, nobody could seem less like a Jesuit schemer. He is avowedly an anachronistic figure, a man of the Enlightenment who (as Hans-Jürgen Schings has shown) has read deeply in the political theories of Montesquieu.[21] The sixteenth century is not yet ready for his ideal. He considers himself a citizen of future centuries (lines 3076–78). The intrigue he initiates, with Carlos as its instrument, is intended to liberate the Dutch, the Spaniards, and ultimately the whole of humanity from the despotism of the Catholic Church. Yet, as Schiller himself points out in the *Briefe über Don Carlos*, Posa's noble intentions lead him astray into 'Wahn' and 'Verblendung' (HA II, 245, 246). Moreover, the goal that Posa seeks to accomplish single-handed, that of placing an enlightened monarch on the throne, is that which the Masons and Illuminati of Schiller's day tried to achieve through their international network ('durch eine geheime Verbindung mehrerer durch die Welt zerstreuter tätiger Glieder', HA, II, 257). And the methods of the Illuminati, many of whom Schiller knew personally, were modelled on those of the Jesuits. Thus the founder of the Illuminati, Adam Weishaupt, required all the members to spy on one another, a practice imitating the Jesuits' use of the confessional for mutual surveillance (Schings, p. 27). Schiller expressly associates Posa's methods with those ascribed to the Jesuits when the Queen, having learnt about his plans, exclaims: 'Kann | Die gute Sache schlimme Mittel adeln?' The doctrine that the end justifies the means has been attributed to the Jesuits at least since Pascal.[22] Schiller's friend Körner alluded to it when warning Schiller against attempts to recruit him for the Masons

20   See Schiller's letter to Körner, 25 April 1788, in NA, xxv, 49 (and note). I thank Lesley Sharpe for drawing this to my attention.

21   Hans-Jürgen Schings, *Die Brüder des Marquis Posa: Schiller und der Geheimbund der Illuminaten* (Tübingen: Niemeyer, 1996), pp. 101–29. Schiller associates Posa with Montesquieu in the *Briefe über Don Carlos* (HA, II, 258).

22   See Pascal in *Les Provinciales*, letter 7, where a Jesuit is made to say: 'nous corrigeons le vice du moyen par la pureté de la fin'; Pascal, *Œuvres complètes*, ed. by Jacques Chevalier (Paris: Gallimard, 1954), p. 729. Schings notes that this is a 'Devise, stereotyp den Jesuiten zugeschrieben' (p. 121).

or the Illuminati: 'Der edelste Zweck in den Händen einer Gesellschaft, die durch *Subordination* verknüpft ist, kann nie vor einem Misbrauch gesichert werden, der den Vortheil weit überwiegt.'[23]

The Jesuits also appear in *Maria Stuart*. Telling Maria about his conversion, Mortimer not only describes how her uncle, the Cardinal de Guise, persuaded him that reason could only lead people astray, that the Church needed a visible head in the Pope, and that the early Church councils had been inspired by the spirit of truth; he also recounts how he was sent from Rome to the English College at Rheims,

> Wo die Gesellschaft Jesu, fromm geschäftig,
> Für Englands Kirche Priester auferzieht. (lines 494–95)

There he was shown the picture of Maria, told about her unjust captivity, and eventually encouraged to go to England in the hope of liberating her. He and his twelve companions have received the sacrament; all the crimes they may commit are forgiven in advance, including Mortimer's projected murder of his uncle. This last is tantamount to parricide, since Amias Paulet is his 'zweiter Vater' (line 2520). Parricide is 'the most heinous of sins in Schiller's moral universe' (Sammons, p.162), because it tears apart the natural bond between father and son; it is committed by his greatest villains, from Franz Moor to Johannes Parricida, and its counterpart, the killing of a son by his father, is commanded at the end of *Don Carlos* by the Grand Inquisitor. It seems that the Jesuits have trained Mortimer not only in dissimulation ('der Verstellung schwere Kunst', line 545), but also in political assassination. The attempt on Elisabeth's life is carried out by a Barnabite monk, a member of another of the religious orders founded in the Counter-Reformation (at Milan in 1530; the order's official name is the Clerks Regular of St Paul). Having heard that Elisabeth was excommunicated by the Pope, this monk, who apparently became dangerously introspective ('tiefsinnig', line 2625), concluded that he should free the Church from its enemy and gain the crown of martyrdom by killing her.[24] We have here an allusion to the doctrine of tyrannicide and a figure who recalls the series of political assassins such as Clement and Ravaillac who were supposed to have been prompted by the Jesuits.[25]

There are further, fleeting allusions to Jesuit intrigue in an earlier play, *Die Verschwörung des Fiesco zu Genua* (published in 1783). Fiesco's factotum, the semi-comic villain and arch-intriguer Muley Hassan, is repeatedly associated with the Jesuits. In Act II, scene 4 he mentions that a Jesuit has been cunning enough to

---

23   Letter to Schiller, 18 September 1787, NA, xxxi, 145–46.

24   The word 'tiefsinnig', associated with 'Anwandlungen des Wahnsinns', is also applied to Wallenstein just before his conversion to Catholicism (*Wallensteins Tod*, lines 2564–65). Grimm's dictionary uses the quotation from Maria Stuart to illustrate the word's use 'besonders von trübsinnigen, schwermütigen gedanken und von personen, die sich solchen hingeben, darin versunken sind, melancholicus'.

25   Allowing for Schiller's bias, he may still have captured something of the atmosphere of Elizabethan conspiracy. In 1584 a spy reports a would-be assassin declaring that if he kills Queen Elizabeth for the sake of the Catholic religion, his soul will go straight to heaven. Even if slanderous, this report had to be plausible. See John Bossy, *Giordano Bruno and the Embassy Affair* (New Haven, CT, and London: Yale University Press, 1991), p. 112.

see through Fiesco's pretended indifference to Genoan politics ('Ein Jesuit wollte gerochen haben, daß ein Fuchs im Schlafrocke stecke'), to which Fiesco replies: 'Ein Fuchs riecht den andern' (HA, I, 354); the Jesuits thus appear exceptionally sly. Later he is found trying to set fire to a Jesuit church (HA, I, 741) and we are reminded later that he was hanged next to it (HA, I, 749). Schiller had no need to mention the Jesuits: at the date of Fiesco's conspiracy, January 1547, the church which Schiller twice calls the 'Jesuiterdom', to the right of the ducal palace, was dedicated to St Ambrose; only after being rebuilt by the Jesuits, at the expense of the wealthy Genoese nobleman and Jesuit priest Marcello Pallavicino, between 1589 and 1637, did it become known as the Chiesa del Gesù, and a church belonging to a religious order would not, strictly speaking, be a cathedral ('Jesuiterdom' is the word Schiller twice uses); but the crucial point is the firm association in Schiller's mind between Jesuits and intrigue.

Schiller wrote more fully about Catholic intrigue in his unfinished novel *Der Geisterseher*, which he began in July 1786 and published in instalments in his journal *Thalia* between 1786 and 1789. The central figure of this tantalizing fragment is a Protestant German Prince who is induced by an elaborate intrigue to enter the Catholic Church, evidently with the prospect of placing a Catholic on the throne of a German principality. The Prince's conversion is assisted by his lack of religious and moral principle. Brought up in a gloomy version of Protestantism to view God as a 'Schreckbild' (HA, V, 105), he encounters in Venice a society of libertines and materialists whose doctrines bring him to a state of despair. The society includes a wealthy Cardinal and the latter's debauched 'nephew' who encourages the Prince to lose his money by gambling and thus makes him financially dependent. But the presiding figure of the intrigue is a mysterious 'Armenian' who first arranges for the Prince to attend an apparent necromantic conjuration, then induces him to fall in love with a beautiful woman, the illegitimate daughter of a German noble, after whose death the despairing Prince enters the Church. The Jesuits are referred to only once, when an Englishman suggests that the necromancer should summon up 'Papst Ganganelli' who can explain how he met his death (HA, V, 61); Ganganelli is the family name of Pope Clement XIV (reigned 1769–74) who in 1773 dissolved the Jesuit order and was rumoured to have been murdered by the Jesuits. The story was written at the height of anxieties about the Illuminati in Germany, and soon after the Diamond Necklace affair in Paris had been revealed. Fear of Jesuits mingled with other anxieties: 'Das Wort Krypto-Katholik wurde das neueste Schlagwort, und mit einer geradezu fieberhaften Angst witterte man überall verkleidete Jesuiten.'[26] The story's genesis is surrounded by fears of Jesuit plots. Schiller's native Württemberg was ruled by the Catholic Duke Karl Eugen, who, being childless, would be succeeded by his Protestant younger brother; of this brother's children, however, two girls converted to Catholicism, and one son (the third, Friedrich Eugen) was thought in danger of being persuaded by the Jesuits to convert likewise. One reason for these suspicions was that in July 1786 Friedrich Eugen published in the *Berlinische Monatsschrift* an essay defending the conjuration of spirits on religious

---

26 See Adalbert von Hanstein, *Wie entstand Schillers Geisterseher?* (Berlin: Duncker, 1903), p. 45.

grounds. Two months earlier, in May 1786, the *Berlinische Monatsschrift* contained an essay on Cagliostro by Elisa von der Recke, accusing him not only of charlatanry but of being secretly in league with the Jesuits, and another essay on secret societies which warned against the Jesuits' influence.[27] Schiller's Venice is not only full of monks and friars (Benedictines, Minorites, Carmelites and Dominicans all feature) but is the setting for precisely the kind of politically motivated intrigue ascribed to the Jesuits.

The course of the Prince's conversion also bears a remarkable resemblance to Mortimer's. Mortimer tells Maria how he was brought up 'in strengen Pflichten', and was glad to escape 'Der Puritaner dumpfe Predigtstuben'. Soon after his conversion, he was shown Maria's picture and told her story, which made him resolve to free her from her martyrdom. His enthusiasm clearly results from sensual excitement in religious guise. The Prince, on seeing the beautiful woman, is reminded of a painting of the Madonna by a Florentine artist who also painted an Héloïse and an almost naked Venus (HA, v, 132). This reminds us of the well-known aesthetic problem that Catholic religious art appeals to the senses in a way that has sometimes been called distractingly irreligious.[28] The beautiful woman is praying; the Prince's feelings for her are sensuality disguised as religious devotion: 'Sie betete zu ihrer Gottheit, und ich betete zu ihr — Ja, ich betete sie an' (HA, v, 133). In both cases, the convert moves from an unattractive version of Protestantism via sensuality to a Catholicism that seems deficient in morality and philosophy.

Soon after beginning *Der Geisterseher*, Schiller wrote explicitly about the Jesuits in a short article for the *Teutscher Merkur*, published in October 1786 under the heading 'Jesuitenregierung in Paraguay'. It recounts an episode from the history of the Jesuit reductions in Paraguay.[29] Over a vast area, covering not only modern Paraguay but much of southern Brazil and northern Argentina, the Jesuits, from 1610 onwards, established settlements for the Indians in order to save them from the forced labour and slavery imposed by the Spanish and Portuguese colonists. In 1750 Spain ceded a large territory to Portugal, including seven Jesuit towns with over 30,000 Indians. All were ordered to move to Spanish territory. Although the Jesuits reluctantly tried to persuade the Indians to obey royal orders, the Indians tried to defend their homes by fighting the combined Spanish and Portuguese forces. They were defeated, and by the end of May 1756 all the seven towns were conquered and occupied. Many strange stories about these events reached Europe. It was widely believed that the Jesuits held a vast and wealthy empire with an Indian as its nominal ruler, and that the Jesuits had commanded the Indian army. These slanders were enthusiastically propagated by Pombal, the enlightened autocrat of Portugal, and

27   See Marion Beaujean, 'Zweimal Prinzenerziehung: *Don Carlos* und *Geisterseher*. Schillers Reaktion auf Illuminaten und Rosenkreuzer', *Poetica*, 10 (1978), 217–35 (esp. p. 218). Extracts from some of these publications are now available in Friedrich Schiller, *Werke und Briefe*, ed. by Otto Dann et al. (Frankfurt a.M.: Deutscher Klassiker Verlag, 2002), vol. VII, pp. 1021–23.

28   See David Freedberg, *The Power of Images: Studies in the History and Theory of Response* (Chicago, IL: University of Chicago Press, 1989), pp. 345–46.

29   See Philip Caraman, *The Lost Paradise: An Account of the Jesuits in Paraguay, 1607–1768* (London: Sidgwick & Jackson, 1975); and (for a more critical view) Gilberto Freyre, *The Masters and the Slaves: A Study in the Development of Brazilian Civilization*, trans. by Samuel Putnam (New York: Knopf, 1956).

his ally Count Aranda in Spain. Voltaire drew on them in Chapter XIV of *Candide*, where the hero arrives in Paraguay among wealthy Jesuits holding military rank, and has to kiss the Jesuit colonel's spurs when he returns from the parade. Schiller also exploited them. In the story he tells, two Europeans fighting on the Indian side are captured by Spanish forces and turn out, under interrogation, to be Jesuits. One of them has a notebook with coded but decipherable principles for governing the Indians. The Indians are to believe that the Jesuits are superhuman beings and that obedience to them will be rewarded with eternal life in which the Indians can have all the women they want. This story, much too good to be true, is taken from the Brunswick professor Johann Christoph Harenberg's encyclopaedic *Pragmatische Geschichte des Ordens der Jesuiten*, a relatively sober account of the Jesuits which nevertheless finds room for many historical slanders.[30] In fact, the war was carried on by the Guaraní Indians without Jesuit assistance. The Austrian Jesuit chronicler of these events, Martin Dobrizhoffer, says that the lack of Jesuit leadership is proved by the failure of the Indians' campaign: 'If the Guarany insurgents were indeed encouraged by the Jesuits, could they not have effected more against the royal forces? Destitute of the counsels and presence of the Fathers, they did their business stupidly and unprosperously.'[31] Schiller, like Voltaire, has uncritically accepted the stories circulating in Europe about the Jesuits' Paraguayan empire, and is using them for a journalistic item.

The comparison between Schiller and Voltaire is worth pursuing, because it allows us to locate Schiller more precisely within the Enlightenment and in relation to other Enlighteners. Voltaire knew a great deal about the Jesuits at first hand. Having been educated by Jesuits at the college of Louis-le-Grand, Voltaire respected their excellent education, and long remained loyal to them. On 14 December 1749 he wrote to Father Vionnet: 'Il y a longtemps que je suis sous l'étendard de votre Société. Vous n'avez guère de plus mince soldat, mais vous n'en avez pas de plus fidèle.'[32] However, Voltaire came out openly against the Jesuits in 1759, when official permission to publish the *Encyclopédie* was withdrawn as a result of Jesuit lobbying (though it continued surreptitiously), and he himself was attacked as an enemy of religion and the state in the Jesuits' *Journal de Trévoux*. In 1759 he published the 'Relation de la maladie, de la confession, de la mort et de l'apparition du jésuite Berthier' in which Father Berthier, editor of the *Journal*, is supposed to die of poison emanating from its pages, and to be denied the sacraments by a Jansenist, on the grounds that his journal has stirred up hatred and he himself has read so many bad Jesuit books.[33]

30 Johann Christoph Harenberg, *Pragmatische Geschichte des Ordens der Jesuiten, seit ihrem Ursprunge bis auf gegenwärtige Zeit* (Halle and Helmstädt: Carl Hermann Hemmerde, 1760), pp. 2243–49. Schiller has simply abridged the section headed 'Neueste Relation von der Schlacht in Paraguay 1759. 1. Oct. zwischen der jesuitischen und den vereinigten spanischen und portugiesischen Armeen. Aus dem Spanischen übersetzt.'

31 Martin Dobrizhoffer, *An Account of the Abipones, an Equestrian People of Paraguay*, trans. by Sara Coleridge, 3 vols (London: John Murray, 1822), I, 27.

32 Voltaire, *Complete Works and Correspondence*, ed. by Haydn Mason et al., 135 vols (Oxford: Voltaire Foundation, 1968–), vol. 95, p. 210. Henceforth cited as *OCV*.

33 See Voltaire, *Mélanges*, ed. by Jacques van den Heuvel (Paris: Gallimard, 1961), pp. 337–46.

Even so, Voltaire did not support the expulsion of the Jesuits from France in 1762. His essay on the occasion, entitled 'Balance égal', cites, half-jokingly, twelve reasons for removing the Jesuits for education, the first being that some have sexually abused boys, a standard accusation against Jesuits.[34] Others are charges of instigating assassinations and provoking revolt in Paraguay. Then follow seven reasons for keeping them: they themselves expel pederasts if major scandal threatens; they no longer plot assassinations; they can be kept under control, and punished if necessary by the law; and they are good teachers. Finally, a balance must be kept between two extreme religious groups, the Jesuits (or more generally Molinists, adherents of the doctrine of free will) on the one hand, and Jansenists on the other. The Jansenists, after all, had made great claims for the sanctity of the convulsionaries who, in 1731–32, had gone into fits in the cemetery of Saint-Médard and in some cases performed or undergone miraculous cures.[35] Are Jesuits any worse than convulsionaries? 'Les jésuites flattent les passions des hommes, pour les gouverner par ces passions mêmes: les St. Médardiens s'élèvent contre les goûts les plus innocents, pour imposer le joug affreux du fanatisme.'[36] And although Voltaire shared the Enlightenment's disapproval of Jesuit rule in Paraguay, he was prepared to admit that although it amounted to slavery, it was also humane: 'à quelques égards le triomphe de l'humanité'.[37]

Some of Voltaire's best friends were Jesuits. Not only did he stay in touch with his old schoolteachers, but at Ferney he made friends with four local Jesuits who were good at chess. One of them, Father Antoine Adam, became his personal priest and stayed in his house for some fourteen years until his abrupt and unexplained dismissal, though even then Voltaire gave him a pension of 700 livres. Admittedly, Father Adam seems to have been a somewhat delinquent Jesuit and on bad terms with his order: when he visited his superiors at Dijon they refused to receive him, and he was rumoured to have a mistress in the village. Voltaire made fun of him, and used to introduce him with the words: 'Voici Adam, le premier et le dernier des hommes'.[38] He presented him to James Boswell in English as 'a broken soldier of the Company of Jesus'.[39]

The touchstone for one's attitude to the Jesuits was one's belief about the assassination of Henri IV. If one believed that Ravaillac had been set up by the Jesuits, then one was opening the door to the kind of conspiracy theory represented

---

34   See [Johann Pezzl]: *Briefe aus dem Novizziat*, 2 vols (n.p. [Zürich],1780, 1781), II, 88; [Johann Friedel], *Heinrich von Walheim oder Weiberliebe und Schwärmerey*, 2 vols (Frankfurt a.M. and Leipzig, 1785), I, 52–53; [René Pomeau, *D'Arouet à Voltaire, 1694–1734* (Oxford: Voltaire Foundation, 1985), p. 213; David Wootton, 'Unhappy Voltaire, or "I shall never get over it as long as I live"', *History Workshop Journal*, 50 (2000), 137–55].

35   For a short account, see Ronald Knox, *Enthusiasm* (Oxford: Clarendon Press, 1950), ch. 16.

36   'Balance égal' (1762), *OCV* 56A, pp. 241–46 (esp. pp. 245–46).

37   *Essai sur les mœurs*, II, 387.

38   See Jean Orieux, *Voltaire ou La Royauté de l'esprit* (Paris: Flammarion, 1966), p. 594. For the rumoured mistress, see Ian Davidson, *Voltaire in Exile: The Last Years, 1753–78* (London: Atlantic Books, 2004), p. 222.

39   See *Boswell on the Grand Tour: Germany and Switzerland, 1764*, ed. by Frederick A. Pottle (London: Heinemann, 1953), p. 274.

by Nicolai and earlier by d'Alembert's article in the *Encyclopédie*. Although Henri IV was among his heroes, Voltaire's stance on this question was much more judicious. His 'Dissertation sur la mort de Henri IV' dismisses as unproven all suggestions that Ravaillac was part of a conspiracy. Monkish ideas about tyrannicide, combined with fanaticism, were sufficient: 'il suffisait alors d'avoir été moine, pour croire que c'était une œuvre méritoire de tuer un prince ennemi de la religion catholique' (*OCV* II, 344). Similarly in the *Essai sur les mœurs*, Voltaire examines the assassination of Henri IV at some length, but is certain that Ravaillac was a lone, insane killer, 'un furieux imbécile' (II, 555), inflamed by monks and preachers, but without accomplices: 'On voit par les actes de son procès, imprimés en 1611, que cet homme n'avait en effet d'autres complices que les sermons des prédicateurs, et les discours des moines' (II, 556). 'Ravaillac ne fut que l'instrument aveugle de l'esprit du temps, qui n'était pas moins aveugle' (II, 557).[40] And in 'Dialogue entre un brachmane et un jésuite' Voltaire uses Ravaillac's deed to illustrate determinism, or the idea that all events form part of a chain of cause and effect, in contrast to the Jesuit doctrine of free will: the Brahmin maintains that he himself caused Ravaillac's deed by beginning a stroll on the Malabar coast with his left foot instead of his right.[41]

Voltaire's balanced and differentiated attitude to the Jesuits contrasts with that of some other *lumières*, notably Jean d'Alembert, author not only of the article about them in the *Encyclopédie* but of a treatise, *Sur la Destruction des Jésuites en France*, published in 1765, at a time when the order had been suppressed in France but its members were allowed to stay there as secular priests (a concession withdrawn in 1767). In his preface, D'Alembert claims to be detached and impartial. He avoids speculation about the Jesuits' association with Ravaillac, though he charges them with involvement in several attempts to assassinate Henri IV. He gives the Jesuits full credit for their excellent educational methods and their achievements in literature and science. Yet he also hesitates uneasily between ridicule and fear. The founder of the Society, Ignatius of Loyola, is mocked for having his head turned by chivalric romances and books of devotion and for resolving to become 'le Don Quichotte de la Vierge'.[42] Yet the organization he founded is said to be a perfectly constructed monolith, 'le chef d'œuvre de l'industrie humaine en fait de politique' (p. 12). However much they may hate one another, Jesuits can be relied on to unite against an enemy, and to sacrifice their own members ruthlessly to the common good. As an elite corps, he compares them to the Janissaries who guard the Ottoman Sultan, and he attributes to them the goal of world domination: '*Gouverner l'univers*, non par la force, mais *par la religion*, telle parait avoir été la devise de cette société dès son origine' (p. 14). D'Alembert did far more than Voltaire to assemble a repertoire of images and concepts that sustained fear of Jesuits.

One might have expected, however, that the Jesuits would vanish from people's minds after the dissolution of their order in 1773. Surely they were no longer of any interest except as characters in a historical drama? Far from it. To many

---

40   *Essai sur les mœurs*, II, 556, 557.
41   *Mélanges*, pp. 311–15 (p. 312).
42   Jean d'Alembert, *Sur la Destruction des Jésuites en France* ([Paris], 1765), p. 11.

writers of the Enlightenment, the Jesuits had become more dangerous, not less, since the dissolution of their order. They still existed as 'Exjesuiten', still formed an international network, and were still gathering influence in the hope of returning to power under some future Pope (as indeed did happen in 1814). The Austrian poet Joseph Ratschky, in his mock-heroic poem *Melchior Striegel* (1793–95), developed the widespread comparison of the Jesuits to the Jews in exile:

> So harrt des Messias ein Israelit,
> Und ein gebeugter Exjesuit
> Der Wiedergeburt der Jünger Loyolens,
> Die Ganganelli *nolens volens*
> Gleich irrenden Schäfchen weit und breit
> Zerstreute, doch nur auf kurze Zeit.
> Bald werden sie Königen wieder *ad latus*
> Sich setzen; bald wird durch ihren *Status*
> *In Statu* von neuem (wie sich's gebührt,
> Wenn's gut gehn soll) die Welt regiert.[43]

In North Germany, the most dedicated, indeed obsessive opponent of the Jesuits was the militant spokesman of the Berlin Enlightenment, Friedrich Nicolai. His enormous account of his travels through the Catholic regions of Germany includes many warnings against them. His fears were strengthened during his three-week stay in Vienna in 1781, when his main local contacts, Tobias von Gebler and Heinrich von Bretschneider, both immigrants from Prussia, fed his paranoia to an extent that some other Viennese writers thought absurd.[44] By training their pupils in blind obedience, the Jesuits seek to found a state within the state and enrich their order at the expense of the countries they inhabit. 'Ihr *blinder Gehorsam* gegen ihre Obern, der Esprit de Corps, der ihnen von Jugend auf zur andern Natur geworden ist, ihr *Zusammenhang* von einem Ende der Erde zum andern, ihre vielen öffentlichen und geheimen *Verbindungen,* die feine *Politik* und das tiefe *Geheimniß* mit dem sie ihr Hauptgeschäft die *Fortpflanzung ihres Ordens* betreiben, machen ihr Institut zum merkwürdigsten, aber zum schädlichsten für die menschliche Gesellschaft.'[45] In the preface to volumes V and VI, Nicolai quotes a letter from an unnamed friend in Vienna, warning him that the Jesuits, who murder kings and popes, may also murder him for what he has said about them (p. xiii). His obsession came to be called 'Jesuitenriecherei' and got him ridiculed in *Faust I* as 'der steife Mann' whose constant snuffling is explained thus: 'Er spürt nach Jesuiten' (lines 4319–22).

Nicolai, however, was only repeating what many representatives of the Enlightenment, especially in Austria, maintained. He derived much information from a book by Johann Rautenstrauch which gives a systematic account of the Jesuits' immoral theory and practices, under the title *Jesuitengift, wie es unter Clemens XIII.*

---

43 Joseph Franz Ratschky, *Melchior Striegel*, ed. by Wynfrid Kriegleder (Graz: Akademische Druck- und Verlagsanstalt, 1991), p. 91.

44 See the introduction to *Aus dem josephinischen Wien: Geblers und Nicolais Briefwechsel während der Jahre 1771–1786*, ed. by Richard Maria Werner (Berlin: Hertz, 1888), pp. 11–18.

45 See Friedrich Nicolai, *Beschreibung einer Reise durch Deutschland und die Schweiz im Jahre 1781: Nebst Bemerkungen über Gelehrsamkeit, Industrie, Religion und Sitten*, 8 vols (Berlin and Stettin: no pub., 1783–87), V, 163.

entdeckt, unter Clemens XIV. unterdrükt, und unter Pius VI. noch fortschleicht, oder der Jesuit in fünferlei Gestalten, allen Christen zur Warnung, vorgestellt, als Probabilist, Beichtvater, Ketzermacher, Fürstenhasser und päbstlicher Soldat.[46] From the innumerable denunciations of Jesuits written in the 1780s, I will quote a sample of the more hysterical style:

> Der ganze Erdboden ist voll von ihnen, ihr Gift fliegt wie eine pestilenzialische Seuche von einem Pol zum andern, überall wirkt es, nur geheimer hier, und dort öffentlicher. Ganganelli konnte diesem zahllosen Heer von Heuschrecken wohl die äußerliche Hülle abstreifen, aber die immer aus ihrem eignen Blut fortwachsende Hydra konnte er nicht bis auf den letzten Kopf erschlagen. Diese Hydra ist noch so vielköpfig als sie sonst war, sie hat Fürstenköpfe, Ministerköpfe, Papstköpfe, Bischofsköpfe, Weibesköpfe, Pfaffenköpfe, Juden-köpfe, Banditenköpfe, Hurenköpfe — mit einem Worte, Köpfe von allen Orden, Ständen, Geschlechtern, Zünften, Innungen aller Provinzen und Nationen.[47]

Meanwhile in Germany this view of the Jesuits found expression in the huge history of the Society by Philipp Wolf, who retails all the familiar slanders.[48] This book provided the basis for the long article 'Jesuiten' in the encyclopaedia by Ersch and Gruber which was a standard account for the nineteenth century.[49] And to see how long-lived fears of Jesuits were, one need only read Eugène Sue's enormously long but engrossing novel *Le Juif errant* [*The Wandering Jew*], serialized in the Liberal paper *Le Constitutionnel* from June 1844 to June 1845.

Against this background, we can certainly ascribe to Schiller a lasting suspicion of organized Catholicism and a recurrent interest in supposed Jesuit conspiracies. But this interest appears to have been primarily literary. In real life he was far less worried about Jesuits and ex-Jesuits than Nicolai was. In September 1787 the prominent Illuminatus Joachim Christoph Bode arrived in Weimar and told Schiller how the Jesuits, in alliance with the Moravian Brethren, were hard at work wrecking the Enlightenment in Berlin. Schiller seems to have been astonished but not very concerned:

> Er [Bode] ist sehr mit den Berlinern über die drohende Gefahr des Catholizismus einig. Ich habe aber schon vergeßen, was er mir alles darüber gesagt hat. [...] Die Jezige Anarchie der Aufklärung meynt er wäre hauptsächlich der Jesuiten Werk. Die Jesuiten und Herrnhuter behauptet er wären von Anfang an verbündet gewesen.[50]

---

46 Published anonymously at 'Philadelphia' (i.e. Vienna, 1784).

47 Anon. [Leopold Aloys Hoffmann], *Zehn Briefe aus Oesterreich an den Verfasser der Briefe aus Berlin* (Gedruckt an der schlesischen Gränze, 1784), pp. 135–36.

48 Peter Philipp Wolf, *Allgemeine Geschichte der Jesuiten von dem Ursprunge ihres Ordens bis auf gegenwärtige Zeiten*, 4 vols (Lisbon: bei Pombal und Compagnie, 1792). The place of publication and the publisher are clearly fictitious: Pombal was the enlightened Portuguese minister who expelled the Jesuits from his country.

49 J. S. Ersch, J. G. Gruber, *Allgemeine Encyklopädie der Wissenschaften und Künste*, 148 vols (1819–92; reprint Graz: Akademische Druck- und Verlagsanstalt, 1981), vol. XV (1838), pp. 427–61.

50 Letter to Körner, 10 September 1787, NA, XXIV, 153.

As for Nicolai, Schiller and his friends were willing to joke about the Berlin critic's obsession with Jesuits. Ludwig Ferdinand Huber warned Schiller in 1786 that if a recent letter, written in a mystical vein, were to fall into Nicolai's hands, he would undoubtedly think Schiller a secret Jesuit.[51] Schiller's interest in Jesuits was primarily literary. Their sinister reputation added spice to plays that expressed Schiller's fascination with conspiracies. Thus in March 1783 he wrote from Bauerbach to the Meiningen librarian Wilhelm Reinwald, requesting books about Jesuits and similar topics to provide material for a tragedy:

> Die Bücher, wovon wir sprachen über *Jesuiten*, und *Religionsveränderungen* — überhaupt, über den Bigotismus und seltne Verderbnisse des Karakters, suchen Sie mir doch mit dem bäldsten zu verschaffen, weil ich nunmehr mit starken Schritten auf meinen *Friderich Imhof* los gehen will. Schriften über Inquisition, Geschichte der Bastille, dann vorzüglich auch (was ich vorgestern vergeßen habe) Bücher worinn von den unglüklichen Opfern des *Spiels* Meldung geschieht, sind ganz vortreflich in meinen Plan.[52]

Though nothing more is known of this abortive *Imhof*, it sounds, with its themes of moral corruption, debauchery, and conversion, like a prelude to *Der Geisterseher*. Seeking sensational material for plays and fiction, Schiller readily thought of Jesuits among other topics. Similarly, Voltaire exploits slanders against the Jesuits in fiction, as when he introduces the allegedly warlike and oppressive Paraguayan Jesuits into *Candide*, but is decidedly balanced and judicious when writing about the Jesuits' real activities in a discursive context.

With the help of the triangle of Schiller, Nicolai and Voltaire, we can draw some tentative conclusions, not only about Enlightenment attitudes to the Jesuits, but, more generally, about the genesis and development of conspiracy theories.[53] First, the paranoia which finds expression in conspiracy theories easily accompanies the practice of Enlightenment in unfavourable conditions. In the eighteenth century, Enlighteners disseminated doctrines that were unpopular with the state and the Church, and formed societies to discuss and pursue their aims. While some of these societies belonged to the growing 'public sphere', others, notably the Freemasons and the Illuminati, were partially or entirely secret. Their founders may have believed that secrecy would allow them to spread Enlightenment ideals without interference by the authorities, but in fact secrecy enormously increased both danger and the consciousness of danger, for a secret organization was liable both to be infiltrated by spies and to be betrayed by disaffected ex-members. If one creates a conspiracy, one

---

51   Letter from Huber to Schiller, 11 May 1786, NA, XXXI, 99.

52   Letter to Reinwald, March 1784, NA, XXIII, 69–70.

53   On this surprisingly neglected subject, see *Changing Conceptions of Conspiracy*, ed. by Carl F. Graumann and Serge Moscovici (New York and Berlin: Springer 1987); also G. T. Cubitt, 'Conspiracy Myths and Conspiracy Theories', *JASO: Journal of the Anthropological Society of Oxford*, 20 (1989), 12–26. There is much valuable information in Johannes Rogalla von Bieberstein, *Die These von der Verschwörung, 1776–1945: Philosophen, Freimaurer, Juden, Liberale und Sozialisten als Verschwörer gegen die Sozialordnung* (Bern: Peter Lang, 1976); *Conspiracies and Conspiracy Theories in Early Modern Europe*, ed. by Barry Coward and Julian Swann (Aldershot: Ashgate, 2004); [Ralf Klausnitzer, *Poesie und Konspiration: Beziehungssinn und Zeichenökonomie von Verschwörungsszenarien in Publizistik, Literatur und Wissenschaft, 1750–1850* (Berlin: de Gruyter, 2007)].

must live in dread of counter-conspiracies. It appears that in the early 1780s Nicolai was actively involved with the Illuminati (Schings, p. 42), while Schiller, though he received overtures from their emissaries, remained at a critical distance and was able not only to portray the moral double-dealing of a high-minded conspirator in *Don Carlos* but to comment on their practices in the *Briefe über Don Carlos*. Both Nicolai and Bode illustrate how someone involved in a conspiracy can become credulous and even paranoid about other conspiracies.

Secondly, conspiracy theories are excellent material for fiction. The connection between 'plot' meaning conspiracy and 'plot' meaning a fictional narrative is accidental, but significant. A plot is an admirable basis for a plot. Schiller's work in particular deals in plots and conspiracies with exceptional frequency. Two of his plays have such words in their titles (*Die Verschwörung des Fiesco zu Genua* and *Kabale und Liebe*). Others too turn on plots and counterplots: Franz Moor's plot to disinherit his brother, Posa's plot to save the Netherlands, Wallenstein's intrigues with the Swedes, the Imperial Court's schemes to disempower him, Mortimer's plot to rescue Maria Stuart, and the (fragmentary) plot involving the manipulation of Demetrius. *Der Geisterseher* can be assigned to the then popular genre of the 'Geheimbundroman', traces of which can be found in *Wilhelm Meisters Lehrjahre*. Subsequent popular novels, especially thrillers, turn on conspiracies. The most familiar model is that in which the villain is plotting world domination and the hero is either counter-plotting against him or by-passing intrigue through decisive action. Fictional conspiracies can provide material for supposedly real ones: the most striking example is the novel *Biarritz* (1868) by 'Sir John Retcliffe' (Hermann Goedsche), containing an account of a secret conspiratorial meeting in the Jewish cemetery at Prague, which was reprinted in St Petersburg as a pamphlet allegedly based on fact, and was later adapted by the Tsarist secret police as *The Protocols of the Elders of Zion*, the infamous 'exposure' of a Jewish world conspiracy.[54]

While most readers can of course distinguish fiction from extra-textual reality, fictional plots and narrative structures provide us with models which can help to shape our experience of reality. There is an interplay, though a difficult one to track, between fictional structures and the structures by which we interpret the world around us. The conspiracy is such a structure. In complex modern society, it is easy to believe that the world is controlled by authorities who keep their activities secret. Such beliefs offer the reassurance that at least someone is in charge, a sense of the connectedness of things, and sometimes (as in the Cold War) clear binary patterns which simplify the confusion around us. In Schiller's work we can see real-life beliefs about conspiracies providing material not only for openly fictional works such as *Der Geisterseher* but also for historical works such as *Wallenstein* which suggest that plot and counter-plot are major motive forces in history.

---

54 See Norman Cohn, *Warrant for Genocide: The Myth of the Jewish World-Conspiracy and the Protocols of the Elders of Zion* (London: Eyre & Spottiswoode, 1967).

CHAPTER 6

Women Warriors
and the Origin of the State:
Werner's *Wanda* and Kleist's *Penthesilea*

In the film *The Terminator*, Sarah Connor asks her lover: 'What kind of women do you have in the future?' and gets the reply: 'They're good fighters.' Whatever the future may hold, women in the past were often imagined as good fighters, indeed as Amazons. Patrick Geary has recently argued that medieval narratives about the founding of states almost always include Amazons. He dwells especially on the sixth-century *History of the Goths* by Jordanes and the twelfth-century *Bohemian Chronicle* by Cosmas of Prague. The defeat of Amazons, Geary argues, marks the 'beginning or reconstitution of the proper order of the world'.[1]

Geary's thesis corresponds in some measure to the representation of Amazons in modern German literature.[2] In particular, it receives partial support from a body of Romantic and post-Romantic drama that presents Amazons and warrior women as primitive societies that must be overcome so that male-dominated states may be firmly established. A group of plays from this period focuses on the legendary Czech princess Libussa (Libuše) who was said to have ruled an ancient state with a company of warlike maidens before submitting to domesticity on marrying Primislaus, the founder of Prague.[3] This myth provided material for Zacharias Werner's *Wanda, Königin der Sarmaten* [Wanda, Queen of the Sarmatians] (1810), where the warrior queen Wanda is supposed to have been one of Libussa's martial maidens, and also for Clemens Brentano's *Die Gründung Prags* [The Founding of Prague] (1815) and Franz

---

1 Patrick J. Geary, *Women at the Beginning: Origin Myths from the Amazons to the Virgin Mary* (Princeton, NJ: Princeton University Press, 2006), p. 34.

2 Thus in Carl Spitteler's epic *Olympischer Frühling* (1910), loosely based on Greek mythology, which gained him the Nobel Prize for Literature in 1919, the wedding of Hera, Queen of the Amazons, to Zeus, symbolizing the establishment of civilization, is immediately followed by the slaughter of the Amazons at the insistence of the three goddesses of civilization, Pallas, Artemis, and Aphrodite: Spitteler, *Gesammelte Werke*, 10 vols, ed. by Gottfried Bohnenblust, Wilhelm Altwegg, and Robert Faesi (Zürich: Artemis-Verlag, 1945–58), II: *Olympischer Frühling* (1945), pp. 250, 252.

3 For the Libussa myth and its literary treatments, see František Graus, *Lebendige Vergangenheit: Überlieferung im Mittelalter und in den Vorstellungen vom Mittelalter* (Cologne: Böhlau, 1975), pp. 89–109.

Grillparzer's *Libussa* (1848).[4] These plays create myths about the transition from nature to culture, the founding of the state, and the accompanying (re)allocation of gender roles. Both Werner's *Wanda* and his drama *Das Kreuz an der Ostsee* [The Cross on the Baltic] (1806), in which the Polish noblewoman Agaphia, in her husband's absence, takes charge of defending the fortress of Plozk against an attack by the pagan Prussians, stand somewhat apart, as they do not present an Amazon society, only individual Amazon women.

Heinrich von Kleist's *Penthesilea* (written 1807, published 1808) is different again. It draws on classical myths about the Amazon state which Kleist found in the popular mythographic compilation by Benjamin Hederich.[5] It informs us about the origin and the working of the Amazon state in such detail that one commentator, Hans M. Wolff, was able to provide a political and constitutional analysis of this society.[6] It does not present the Amazons as a primitive society which must be superseded by male rule before civilization proper can begin. Rather, it shows their state as a coherent and well-functioning polity. Wolff maintains that it is an Enlightenment utopia: 'Der Amazonenstaat ist der Idealstaat der Aufklärung und eine kühne dichterische Verwirklichung jener Utopie, um deren Durchführung die französische Revolution vergebens gerungen hatte' [The Amazon state is the Enlightenment's ideal state and a bold poetic realization of the utopia which the French Revolution had striven in vain to create].[7] I will argue below that it is depicted positively enough to make this a plausible claim. But if so, Kleist (as Wolff also argues) problematizes the Enlightenment's social ideals by showing, in the person of Penthesilea, that the passions of the exceptional individual cannot be confined within the framework of the state. Only in his last play, *Prinz Friedrich von Homburg* (completed 1810, published 1821), would Kleist imagine a reconciliation between the rational representative of the state (the Elector) and the passionate individual (the Prince), and even there the enigmatic words uttered by Kottwitz in the last scene, 'Ein Traum, was sonst?' [A dream, what else?] may indicate that this solution too is only utopian.[8]

Wanda and *Penthesilea* were written almost simultaneously. Having written the first three acts of *Wanda* in the summer of 1807, Werner read them aloud to Goethe and others in Jena on 3 December 1807. Goethe was sufficiently impressed both by Werner and by the play to decide to stage it on the gala night celebrating the Duchess Luise's birthday. As this was on 30 January 1808, Werner wrote the last two acts at high speed in early January, and the performance was a great success. Having been a *Theaterintendant* [theatre director] in Königsberg and worked with the

4 See Ritchie Robertson, 'On the Threshold of Patriarchy: Brentano, Grillparzer and the Bohemian Amazons', *German Life and Letters*, 46 (1993), 203–19.

5 Benjamin Hederich, *GründlichesLexikon mythologicum* (Leipzig: Gleditsch, 1724).

6 See Hans M. Wolff, *Heinrich von Kleist als politischer Dichter* (Berkeley and Los Angeles: University of California Press, 1947), pp. 438–43; an earlier version is his 'Kleists Amazonenstaat im Lichte Rousseaus', *PMLA*, 53 (1938), 189–206.

7 Wolff, *Kleist als politischer Dichter*, p. 450.

8 Heinrich von Kleist, *Sämtliche Werke und Briefe*, ed. by Ilse-Maria Barth and others, 4 vols (Frankfurt a.M.: Deutscher Klassiker Verlag, 1989), ii, 644. All quotations from *Penthesilea* are taken from this edition and are cited by line number only.

famous actor and director Iffland, Werner understood the demands of the theatre. Verse in varying meters, music, and stage effects, culminating in the radiant lily that appears in the morning sky after Wanda's death, gave his play the appeal of opera.[9] Kleist meanwhile had begun *Penthesilea* probably in August 1806; arrested as a spy at the gates of Berlin on 30 January 1807, he was sent first to a prison and then to a prisoner-of-war camp in France, where he worked further on the play, completing it after his return to Germany some time in autumn 1807.[10] On 24 January 1808 he sent Goethe the version of *Penthesilea* which had just appeared in his journal *Phöbus*, begging him humbly 'auf den "Knien meines Herzens"' [on the bended knees of my heart] for some encouragement.[11] On 1 February, however, two days after the premiere of *Wanda*, Goethe sent a dusty answer, bluntly dismissing Kleist's play as unsuitable for the stage in Weimar or indeed any conceivable theatre.[12]

The two plays coincide not only in their composition but also in their adherence to the genre of mythic drama favoured by the German Romantics. Although Kleist's material is classical, his treatment of it is overwhelmingly passionate, physical and violent, and his presentation of the Amazon state goes far beyond the suggestions in his sources. Many Romantics drew on Christian legend, as in Tieck's *Leben und Tod der heiligen Genoveva* [The Life and Death of St Genevieve] (1800) and Werner's *Das Kreuz an der Ostsee* which features St Adalbert, or on Germanic myth, as in the trilogy *Der Held des Nordens* [The Hero of the North] (1810) by Friedrich de la Motte Fouqué. Werner in *Wanda*, like Brentano and Grillparzer later, turned instead to Slav myth.

In Slav myth the Romantic dramatists found a body of material that was intriguingly novel but could be related to familiar patterns, in line with the emerging discipline of comparative mythology. Such endeavours were important also as a counterweight to the German 'Drang nach Osten' [eastward drive] which since the early Middle Ages had established colonial domination throughout much of Eastern Europe. In line with this historical tendency, 'Slavs' were often identified with slaves: 'The German tribes in their eastward expeditions sought to capture slaves for sale. Indeed, the earlier documents do not speak of the inhabitants of the eastern regions as *Slavi*, but as *Sclavi*.'[13] In 1803, in lectures delivered in Berlin, August Wilhelm Schlegel asserted 'daß die Slaven überall und unter allen Umständen zur Sklaverei bestimmt sind' [that the Slavs everywhere and in all circumstances are destined for slavery].[14] Yet elsewhere, an increased interest in Slav culture, its past

---

9 See Elisabeth Stopp, '"Ein Sohn der Zeit": Goethe and the Romantic Plays of Zacharias Werner', in her *German Romantics in Context: Selected Essays 1971–1986*, collected by Peter Hutchinson, Roger Paulin and Judith Purver (London: Bristol Classical Press, 1992), pp. 1–25 (originally published in *Publications of the English Goethe Society*, 40 (1970): 123–50).

10 'Ich habe die Penthesilea geendigt': letter to Marie von Klein, 'Spätherbst 1807', in Kleist, *Sämtliche Werke und Briefe*, IV, 395.

11 Letter to Goethe (24 January 1808), in Kleist, *Sämtliche Werke und Briefe*, IV, 407.

12 Letter to Kleist (1 February 1808), in Johann Wolfgang Goethe, *Sämtliche Werke: Briefe, Tagebücher und Gespräche*, Deutscher Klassike-Ausgabe, 40 vols (Frankfurt a.M.: Deutscher Klassiker Verlag, 1986–2000), XXXIII, 273–74 (also in Kleist, *Sämtliche Werke und Briefe*, IV, 409–10).

13 F. L. Carsten, *The Origins of Prussia* (Oxford: Clarendon Press, 1954), pp. 1–2.

14 Quoted in Josef Körner, 'Die Slaven im Urteil der deutschen Frühromantik', in *Historische*

and its potential for the future, was developing. In a famous passage of his *Ideen zur Philosophie der Geschichte der Menschheit* [Ideas for a Philosophy of Human History] (1784–91), Herder examined the history of the Slavs and foretold that they would succeed the Germans as the leaders of civilization.[15] With this prophecy, Herder raised the prestige of a group of peoples who, since the partitions of Poland, had been without political independence (except for Russia); in addition, although the speakers of Slavonic languages were geographically scattered and culturally diverse, Herder's pages helped to construct the image of the Slavs as a unitary people, and to lay the foundations for later Slavophile movements.[16]

Amazon myth provided ways of thinking afresh about gender relations. The Greeks believed in the existence of a society of female warriors, who equipped themselves for warfare by having their right breast seared away. They were most commonly located in Scythia, on the northern shore of the Black Sea. Sometimes they were thought to live entirely without men, except for an annual occasion when they mated promiscuously with the men of a neighbouring tribe, after which they would return the resulting male children and keep the females; sometimes they were thought to keep men in subjection and confine them to household work. They had conducted an unsuccessful attack on Athens soon after Theseus had made it the capital of Attica; the ninth labour of Hercules was to obtain the girdle of the Amazon Queen Hippolyta, which he accomplished by killing her; and another Amazon queen, Penthesilea, intervened against the Greeks during the siege of Troy, but was killed by Achilles and subjected to a necrophiliac assault.[17] There is unlikely to be any historical basis for these legends, though the discovery in the southern Ukraine of numerous graves, dating from the fourth to the sixth centuries BC, containing female skeletons with weapons, may support Herodotus's assertion that among the Scythians female warriors fought alongside men.[18] The Slav counterparts to the Amazon legend are the myths of Libussa and Wanda, imagined as queens respectively of the early Czechs and the Poles, and (especially Wanda) as female warriors.

These plays are not related in any straightforward way to the reality of gender

---

Vierteljahrschrift, N.F. 31 (1938), 565–76 (p. 569). For more early nineteenth-century examples, see Michael Burleigh and Wolfgang Wippermann, *The Racial State: Germany, 1933–1945* (Cambridge: Cambridge University Press, 1991), p. 26.

15 Johann Gottfried Herder, *Ideen zur Philosophie der Geschichte der Menschheit*, in his *Werke*, ed. by Günter Arnold and others, 10 vols (Frankfurt a.M.: Deutscher Klassiker Verlag, 1985–2000), VI, 698–99.

16 On German images of Slavs, see Ritchie Robertson, 'Zum deutschen Slawenbild von Herder bis Musil', in *Das Eigene und das Fremde: Festschrift Urs Bitterli*, ed. by Urs Faes and Béatrice Ziegler (Zurich: NZZ-Verlag, 2000), pp. 116–44.

17 On the Amazon myth and its interpretations, see W. B. Tyrrell, *Amazons: A Study in Athenian Mythmaking* (Baltimore, MD: Johns Hopkins University Press, 1984); Josine H. Blok, *The Early Amazons: Modern and Ancient Perspectives on a Persistent Myth* (Leiden: Brill, 1995); and, for a richly documented study of Amazon lore in relation to Pope's Thalestris, Howard D. Weinbrot, *Britannia's Issue: The Rise of British Literature from Dryden to Ossian* (Cambridge: Cambridge University Press, 1993), pp. 311–17.

18 See Renate Rolle, *The World of the Scythians*, trans. by Gayna Walls (London: Batsford, 1980), pp. 86–91.

relations in Germany circa 1800. The association of women with domesticity, and the disapproval of energetic activity by women in the public sphere, are memorably stated in Schiller's 'Das Lied von der Glocke' [The Song of the Bell] (1800), which idealizes the 'zücht'ge Hausfrau' [the virtuous housewife] in contrast with women who regressed to raw nature by participating in revolutionary upheavals like those of the French Revolution: 'Da werden Weiber zu Hyänen [...]' [Here women become hyenas]. [19] But Schiller's polemical extremes may tell us less about actual gender relations than the ambivalences of a text such as Johann Heinrich Campe's *Väterlicher Rat für meine Tochter* [Fatherly Advice for my Daughter] (1791). The schoolteacher and radical Enlightenment thinker Campe warns his daughter that she will live in a state of dependency and oppression which will be painful, even if disguised by external signs of respect, and that even a good man is likely to be irascible and domineering, requiring constant patience and self-denial from his wife. This inequality may be founded on the greater physical strength with which nature has endowed the male sex; but Campe's obeisance to 'den weisen und mütterlichen Absichten der Natur' [Nature's wise and motherly intentions] sounds ironic when placed alongside his acknowledgement that society, in its current form, *makes* women subordinate:

> Dazu ward bei allen kultivierten Nationen die ganze Erziehungs- und Lebensart der beiden Geschlechter dergestalt eingerichtet, daß das Weib schwach, klein, zart, empfindlich, furchtsam, kleingeistig — der Mann hingegen stark, fest, kühn, ausdauernd, groß, hehr und kraftvoll an Leib und Seele würde. Die stille sitzende Lebensart, wozu ihr nun einmal verdammt seid von früher Jugend an, eure, jede freie und rasche Bewegung hindernde, unnatürliche Kleidung, welche die despotische Staatsklugheit der Männer nicht umsonst so zweckmäßig für euch ausgesonnen hat, eure Sitten, eure Beschäftigungen, eure ganze Art zu leben und zu sein, zwecken alle auf jenes, unsere eigene freiere Lebensart hingegen, unsere Spiele, Übungen und Geschäfte zwecken auf dieses ab. [20]

> [All cultivated nations have arranged the education and life of the two sexes in such a way that the female should be weak, small, delicate, sensitive, timid, small-minded, whereas the male should be strong, firm, bold, hardy, large, lofty and vigorous in body and soul. The sedentary way of life to which you are condemned from your earliest youth, the unnatural clothing which obstructs any free and spontaneous movement, and which man's despotic political reason has deliberately devised for you, your customs, your occupations, your whole way of living and being, are all intended to promote the former [character], whereas our freer way of life, our games, exercises and responsibilities, are intended to promote the latter.]

By indicating how far gender difference is reinforced by deliberate social arrangements, Campe hints that things might be otherwise. And this instability, in

19   Friedrich Schiller, *Sämtliche Werke*, ed. by Gerhard Fricke and Herbert G. Göpfert, 5 vols (Munich: Hanser, 1958), I, 440.

20   Extract from Johann Heinrich Campe, 'Väterlicher Rat an meine Tochter', in *Ob die Weiber Menschen sind: Geschlechterdebatten um 1800*, ed. by Sigrid Lange (Leipzig: Reclam, 1992), pp. 24–37 (quotations from pp. 29, 26, 27).

which gender relations come to seem at once unalterable and provisional, underlies
the many literary works of the time which feature spirited and dominant women
exercising a degree of freedom that can rarely have been available in life. Surveying
German literature 1790–1830, Nicholas Saul applies the term 'Amazon' to a great
variety of female figures who show strength of character or even simply ride a
horse.[21] By using 'Amazon' in this diluted sense, Saul is following German usage
around 1800. Thus Therese Huber lets a character sum up the gender ideology of
the time as follows (distancing herself from it by an ironic narratorial comment):
'Der feste, treue, eiserne Mann kann nur der sanftesten Weiblichkeit huldigen;
Schwächlinge lieben Amazonen' [The firm, true man of iron can only revere the
softest femininity; weaklings love Amazons]. But the frequency with which the
term can be applied conveys how easily the literary imagination of both male and
female authors could conceive women playing more varied and more active roles
than were allowed them by the ideology of domesticity.

Wanda, Königin der Sarmaten

Werner's imagination carries him back, even before political structures, to the
emergence of culture from nature. In thinking about this borderline, Werner,
like his contemporaries, draws on the 'four stages' theory of history developed in
the Scottish Enlightenment, especially by Adam Ferguson, and transmitted to a
number of German thinkers, among them Herder and Schiller.[22] In this historical
scheme, the stages of social development were each defined by the dominant
mode of subsistence. The most primitive stage, that of hunting, was followed by
herding, then by agriculture, and finally by commerce. The idea of the dominant
mode of subsistence looks forward to Marx's idea of defining historical stages by
the dominant mode of production (though Marx sees each stage as emerging from
the other through conflict). Accordingly, the plays we are dealing with turn on
the transition from nature to culture, which is imagined as the transition from a
nomadic way of life to a settled way of life based on agriculture. Here the regulation
of relations between the sexes serves as a synecdoche for the regulation of social
relations in general.

The passage from one state of society to another is particularly clear in Werner's
Das Kreuz an der Ostsee. The Prussian warrior Silko deplores the peaceful present
and praises the warlike past of hunting, before agriculture, marriage and religion,
when women were companions to men:

---

21   Nicholas Saul, 'Aesthetic Humanism (1790–1830)', in *The Cambridge History of German Literature*,
ed. by Helen Watanabe-O'Kelly (Cambridge: Cambridge University Press, 1997), pp. 202–71 (esp.
pp. 218–19, 222, 223, 225, 239). To this list one should add the heroine of Therese Huber's *Die Familie
Seldorf* (1795–96) who disguises herself as a man and fights furiously in the French revolutionary army.

22   For an introductory account, see Karen O'Brien, *Narratives of Enlightenment: Cosmopolitan
History from Voltaire to Gibbon* (Cambridge: Cambridge University Press, 1997), pp. 132–36; on its
transmission to Germany, Fania Oz-Salzberger, *Translating the Enlightenment: Scottish Civic Discourse
in Eighteenth-Century Germany* (Oxford: Clarendon Press, 1995).

> Die Männin dem Krieger
> Nicht sklavisch gekettet,
> Sie war ihm im Jagen ein munt'rer Gesell;
> Nicht Gräber noch Pflüger,
> In Höhlen gebettet,
> Erkämpften sie Nahrung und tranken am Quell;
> Kein heiliger Hain! — selbst waren sie Götter! —
> Sie tobten, wie Wetter,
> Des Vaterlands Retter,
> Und Leben durchzuckte sie sprudelnd und hell![23] (W, 14)

[The she-man, not slavishly bound to the warrior, was his cheerful companion on the hunt; they did not dig or plough, they slept in caves, fought for their food and drank from the spring. No sacred grove! — they themselves were gods! — they raged like thunderstorms, saviours of the fatherland, and life filled them, gushing and clear!]

These cave-dwelling humans were at one with nature; they made no distinction between the human and the divine, and hardly any between male and female, as the word 'Männin' [virago] suggests. Silko then tells how, some eighty years before, Waidewuthis, by pointing to the admirable organization of the bees, persuaded the free Prussians to make him their king and to believe in the gods Percun, Potrympos and Picollos, whose priest he was; he also established agriculture, divided the land into fields, and enforced monogamy.

In the later *Wanda*, the progress of society is suggested by the references to different civilizations superseding one another by conquest. The Poles under Wanda have defeated and enslaved the Wends, a Slavonic peasant people who formerly inhabited north-eastern Europe. The name 'Sarmatians' is that of an ancient steppe people mentioned by Greek and Roman ethnographers; sixteenth-century Polish historians fancifully alleged that the Polish nobility, the *szlachta,* was descended from them, in order to claim that the aristocracy was not just socially but also racially distinct from its social inferiors.[24] The Poles, though more advanced than the primitive Prussians, are in a relatively early social state. In *Das Kreuz an der Ostsee* Sarmatians are explicitly equated with the nobility ('Adel', W, 93), while below them they have only peasants; not having yet attained mercantile society, they have to ask what 'Bürger' [citizens] are (W, 93). In neither play are the Poles presented in a flattering light. The Polish republic of nobles, in which a single dissenting voice could annul a decision (as Sapieha's veto does in the first act of Schiller's *Demetrius*), was a byword for disorder. In *Das Kreuz an der Ostsee* Werner makes the Duchess Agaphia deplore the Poles' ungovernability (W 130–31). In *Wanda*, three Polish nobleman vie for Wanda's hand in marriage, and a riot breaks

---

23 *Zacharias Werner's ausgewählte Schriften: Aus seinem handschriftlichen Nachlasse herausgegeben von seinen Freunden,* 5 vols (Grimma: Verlags-Comptoir, 1840; repr. Bern: Herbert Lang, 1970), VII, 14. All future quotations from Werner are taken from this volume, and will be identified as W and page number.

24 Norman Davies, *Heart of Europe: A Short History of Poland* (Oxford: Oxford University Press, 1986), p. 324.

out among their followers which is described as 'tumultuarisch' [tumultuous] (W, 207), a standard term for Polish unruliness.[25] When the Germans under Prince Rüdiger set out to conquer the Poles, such an outcome would be understood by Werner's contemporaries as a step forward in civilization.

Within this framework, does the play show us female rule as something that must be superseded by male domination? It certainly implies that the conquest of the Poles would establish male along with German dominance. There is a suggestion that people as ungovernable as the Poles require a female ruler, not being ready yet for the quasi-paternal discipline of a king. Wanda calms their turbulence by her moral authority and presents herself as a mother-figure, telling them: 'Ehrt Eurer treuen Fürstin reinen Muttersinn!' [Honour the pure motherliness of your faithful princess] (W, 207) Wanda also says that she has overstepped the destined limits of her sex in becoming queen of the Sarmatians:

> Als ich, ein Weib, zur Zartheit nur geboren,
> Es wagte, mehr als mein Geschick zu sein [...]. (W, 224)

[When I, a woman, born to tenderness, dared to go beyond my destiny ...]

To that extent Nicholas Saul may be right in calling the play 'the explicit confirmation of the epoch's misogynist anthropology' because it shows that 'sexuality threatens a woman's exercise of power, which is sustained only by the transfer onto her nation of the unfulfilled erotic passion for a lost lover.'[26] One might add, however, that the play is realistic in showing that for a female ruler her sexuality has to be managed as part of her image. In real life, Catherine the Great manipulated her favourites in order to consolidate her power, while Maria Theresia cultivated a domestic identity as mother of her nation.

However, the play veers away from political into spiritual themes. Its central message is linked with Werner's unorthodox Christianity. When he wrote it, Werner was not yet among German Romanticism's numerous converts: he joined the Catholic Church only in 1811, and was ordained a priest three years later. He declared in 1806 that his main theme was 'Vergöttlichung der Menschen durch die Liebe [...]. Wahrhaft Liebende sind sich gegenseitig Heyland' [The deification of human beings through love [...]. True lovers are saviours to each other].[27] The play's message is that people can redeem each other and attain salvation through love. Wanda's love was originally for Rüdiger, whom she met seven years earlier at Libussa's court but now believes to be dead. She swears to remain unmarried and to devote herself to her people, while Rüdiger has sworn to his men, at the beginning of the play, that he will win Wanda or die. Thus their vows are tragically conflicting: he *must* marry her, she *cannot* marry him. When he makes himself known to her, she protects him from the wrath of the Poles but leads her troops in battle against his. The Germans flee, leaving only Rüdiger and his confidante, the minstrel Balderon. Rüdiger and Wanda fight, each hoping to be killed by the

25 Compare Schiller, *Demetrius*: 'Es entsteht ein tumultuarisches Getöse' (*Sämtliche Werke*, III, 23).
26 Saul, 'Aesthetic Humanism', p. 250.
27 Werner, letter to Tina, Gräfin von Brühl (May 1806), quoted in Stopp, ' "Ein Sohn der Zeit" ', p. 5.

other. Libussa's ghost declares obscurely that they must triumph through suffering. Eventually Wanda kills Rüdiger; his last word is 'Dank!' [thanks] (W, 256). In the final scene, Wanda has overcomes despair and, in a great ceremonial, plunges to her death in the Vistula.

At first sight, Wanda's suicide may seem, like Penthesilea's, to be an expression of defeat. Werner, however, invites us to understand it as a spiritual triumph. Ostensibly torn between her love for Rüdiger and her duty to her people, Wanda in reality has to renounce sexual union with Rüdiger for the sake of a higher destiny, announced by the spirit of Libussa: 'Leben ist der Liebe Spiel, | Tod der Liebe Weg zum Ziel' [life is a game of love, death is love's path to its goal] (W, 245). The same message is conveyed by the High Priest's story of an eagle which dies in flames; when a dove brings a myrtle (symbol of erotic love) to the ashes, both birds reappear in transfigured form. This allegory, suggesting the story of the Phoenix, indicates that death is the consummation of love and the precondition for spiritual rebirth (W 266). Accordingly, Wanda's sacrificial death carries a powerful erotic charge:

> Das Opfer muß
> Durch seines Priesters Hände fallen! —
> Ich Unglückseligste von Allen! —
> Und doch allmächtig, schwelgend im Genuß! —
> Du, Bräutigam, Du warst mein erstes Lallen;
> Als ich mit Dir entquoll den Rosenhallen! —
> Und jetzt! — Noch einen ew'gen Kuß! (W, 256)

[The victim must die at the hands of its priest! I am the unhappiest person of all! And yet all-powerful, revelling in pleasure! You, bridegroom, my lips first lisped your name, when with you I left the halls of roses! And now! One more everlasting kiss!]

Staging her death with elaborate ceremonial, she presents it, in her final words, as a triumphant spiritual and erotic union with the divine:

> Des Morgens Strahlen ballen sich zusammen;
> Auf ihnen fahr' ich zu dem Urlicht auf! —
> Seyd *Eins*, Ihr Völker, die Ihr auf mich schaut,
> Wie sich dem Bräut'gam eint die Götterbraut! — (W, 270)[28]

[The rays of dawn converge; on them I shall rise to the primal light! — Be one, you nations who behold me, as the divine bride is one with the bridegroom!]

Even Wanda's suicide may be seen as an act of female empowerment. In throwing herself into the Vistula, she resembles the heroine of Franz Grillparzer's *Sappho*, who throws herself into the sea after the end of her love-affair with Phaon. Both Wanda and Sappho are pagans. They are therefore not affected by the Christian ban on suicide as offending against the commandment 'Thou shalt not kill'. Although the ancients were ambivalent about suicide, they all agreed that it was permissible in order to escape shame or tyranny. A widespread view was that man was like a sentry, assigned by the divinity to his post and forbidden to desert it. Yet Socrates,

---

28 On Werner's 'Todeserotik' and its indebtedness to Schleiermacher, see Gerard Koziełek, *Friedrich Ludwig Zacharias Werner: Sein Weg zur Romantik* (Wrocław: no pub., 1963), p. 129.

in the *Phaedo*, says that divinity may impose a necessity upon him which justifies suicide, such as the death sentence passed on Socrates by the Athenians; while Cicero says that we may depart from this life when divinity has given us a valid reason for doing so, and that we are entitled to leave life's theatre when the play has ceased to please us.[29] There were famous examples of female suicide in the ancient world. Porcia, the wife of Brutus, killed herself by putting burning charcoal in her mouth and stifling herself.[30] Arria persuaded her husband Caecina Paetus to commit suicide when both were in prison, by 'piercing her breast, extracting the dagger, passing it to her husband, and crowning all with the immortal, almost godlike words "Paetus, it does not hurt."'[31]

Werner's version of Christianity is quite eclectic enough for him to import a classical justification of suicide, especially as Wanda is not a Christian. She does however grasp what he at that time considered the essence of religion — the ascent to a higher life accompanied by an eroticism of death that partly recalls Novalis, partly shows an affinity to the close of *Die Wahlverwandtschaften* [Elective Affinities] (1809), which Goethe wrote when he was in close contact with Werner. Wanda, like Ottilie in Goethe's novel, shows her autonomy by suicide: Ottilie starves herself, Wanda leaps into the river, and both are glorified: Wanda unequivocally, Ottilie with teasing narratorial ambiguity.

Penthesilea

If Werner illustrates how much Romantic thought was based on ideas developed in the Enlightenment, Kleist is a post-Enlightenment writer in more complex ways. Until his identification with German and Prussian nationalism (*Die Hermannsschlacht* [Arminius's Battle] (written 1808–09, published 1821), 'Katechismus der Deutschen' [A German Catechism] (1809), *Prinz Friedrich von Homburg*), he does not reject the Enlightenment, but in various respects he questions it, problematizes it, and goes beyond it.[32] Within the dense, often contradictory web of his thought and imagination, we can find many strands of sympathy with the Enlightenment, and

29   See Miriam Griffin, 'Philosophy, Cato and Roman Suicide', *Greece and Rome*, 22 (1986), 64–77, 192–202 (esp. p. 70 for Socrates); Lester G. Crocker, 'The Discussion of Suicide in the Eighteenth Century', *Journal of the History of Ideas*, 13 (1952), 47–72 (esp. p. 52 for Cicero); more generally: Ian Donaldson, *The Rapes of Lucretia: A Myth and its Transformations* (Oxford: Clarendon Press, 1982); Michael MacDonald and Terence R. Murphy, *Sleepless Souls: Suicide in Early Modern England* (Oxford: Clarendon Press, 1990); Roger Paulin, *Der Fall Wilhelm Jerusalem: Zum Selbstmordproblem zwischen Aufklärung und Empfindsamkeit* (Göttingen: Wallstein, 1999); Nicholas Saul, 'Fragmentästhetik, Freitod und Individualität in der deutschen Romantik: Zu den Morbiditätsvorwürfen', in *Zwischen Aufklärung und Romantik: Neue Perspektiven der Forschung. Festschrift für Roger Paulin*, ed. by Konrad Feilchenfeldt et al. (Würzburg: Königshausen & Neumann, 2006), pp. 232–51.

30   'Marcus Brutus', in *Plutarch's Lives*, trans. by John Dryden, Everyman's Library, 3 vols (London: Dent, 1910), III, 412.

31   Pliny the Younger, *Complete Letters*, trans. by P. G. Walsh, World's Classics (Oxford: Oxford University Press, 2006), p. 75 (= Book 3, letter 16).

32   See Helmut J. Schneider, 'The Facts of Life: Kleist's Challenge to Enlightenment Humanism (Lessing)', in *A Companion to the Works of Heinrich von Kleist*, ed. by Bernd Fischer (Rochester, NY: Camden House, 2003), pp. 141–63.

particularly with those writers, critical of religion and supportive of egalitarian democracy and women's emancipation, whom Jonathan Israel has termed the 'radical Enlightenment'.[33] This has two important consequences for our understanding of *Penthesilea*.

First, although we hear much about the gods, they do not appear in person, any more than they do in Goethe's *Iphigenie*, with which *Penthesilea* has often been compared and contrasted.[34] The language of theophany, as Bernhard Böschenstein has shown, is applied by human characters to each other, as when Achilles addresses Penthesilea as a radiant apparition ('Glanzerscheinung', l. 1809) who seems to have descended from the ethereal realm (l. 1810), while to her he seems like a hero from the stars (ll. 2180–82), or even like Mars himself, a dazzling apparition from Elysium (ll. 2208–16).[35] The motor of the play, as in *Iphigenie*, is not divine agency, but human agency. Even the passions which gain control of the two central characters can be explained in psychological terms, not as divine intervention. There is no need to suppose that Penthesilea, by seeking Achilles and invoking Aphrodite (l. 1231), has broken the law of Mars, the Amazons' god, and is therefore punished with the madness that makes her devour Achilles.[36] We are in a world shaped by human agency.

Second: human agency is shown in the creation of the Amazon state. Unlike the stages of society shown by Werner, the Amazon state is the product, not of some immanent logic of historical development, but of deliberate human action. In this respect it resembles Rousseau's conception of the social contract and very likely shows the influence of Rousseau. Kleist was familiar with Rousseau's works: in 1801 he promised to give his fiancée Wilhelmine von Zenge Rousseau's complete works and tell her the order in which she should read them.[37] The social contract is a 'just so story', explaining how people move from the primitive state of nature to the body politic. It enables them to find 'a form of association which will defend and protect with the whole common force the person and goods of each associate, and in which each, while uniting himself with all, may still obey himself alone, and remain as free as before.'[38] Rousseau also thought, however, that an early stage of social development was most conducive to virtue and happiness. The progress of

---

33   See Jonathan Israel, *Radical Enlightenment: Philosophy and the Making of Modernity, 1650–1750* (Oxford: Oxford University Press, 2001); *Enlightenment Contested: Philosophy, Modernity, and the Emancipation of Man, 1670–1752* (Oxford: Oxford University Press, 2006).

34   e.g. in Gerhard Kaiser, 'Mythos und Person in Kleists *Penthesilea*', in his *Wandrer und Idylle* (Göttingen: Vandenhoeck & Ruprecht, 1977), pp. 209–39 (p. 219); Roger Paulin, 'Kleist's Metamorphoses: Some Remarks on the Use of Mythology in *Penthesilea*', *Oxford German Studies*, 14 (1983), 35–53 (p. 40).

35   Bernhard Böschenstein, 'Der "Gott der Erde". Kleist im Kontext klassischer Dramen: Goethe, Schiller, Hölderlin', *Kleist-Jahrbuch* (1991), 169–81.

36   Paulin, 'Kleist's Metamorphoses', p. 45; Kaiser, 'Mythos und Person in Kleists *Penthesilea*', p. 229, likewise invokes the myth of Dionysus.

37   Letter of 22 March 1801, in Kleist, *Sämtliche Werke und Briefe*, IV, 203.

38   Jean-Jacques Rousseau, *The Social Contract and the Discourses*, trans. by G. D. H. Cole, revised by J. H. Brumfitt and John C. Hall, Everyman's Library (London: Dent, 1973), 190–91. On Rousseau's importance for Kleist, see Wolff, *Kleist als politischer Dichter*, pp. 360–62, 437–51, and Bernhard Böschenstein, 'Kleist und Rousseau', in *Kleist-Jahrbuch* (1981–82), 145–56.

the arts and sciences, and the increasing complexity and subordination of society, generated hypocrisy, dissimulation, artificial wants, and moral corruption. Hence in his *Discourses* he holds up as examples of virtue and happiness such simple societies as the ancient Persians, the ancient Germans, the modern Swiss, and 'the Scythians, of whom such wonderful eulogies have come down to us'.[39] Kleist's Amazons, who are Scythian women, represent a Rousseauesque polity.

In far the longest scene of Kleist's play, Scene 15, Penthesilea explains to Achilles, who listens with astonishment mixed with irony, how the Amazon state originated. She tells how a Scythian tribe was defeated by the Ethiopians under Vexoris, who killed all the men and seized their women; but the women secretly prepared daggers, and, when Vexoris was due to marry their queen Tanaïs, they suddenly killed all the men and set up a 'Frauenstaat':

> Ein Staat, ein mündiger, sei aufgestellt,
> Ein Frauenstaat, den fürder keine andre
> Herrschsücht'ge Männerstimme mehr durchtrotzt,
> Der das Gesetz sich würdig selber gebe,
> Sich selbst gehorche, selber auch beschütze:
> Und Tanaïs sei seine Königin. (Lines 1957–62)

[A state, a mature one, shall be established, a women's state which henceforth not be bullied by any other domineering male voice, and shall make its own laws with dignity, obey itself, protect itself as well, and Tanais shall be its queen.]

The word 'mündig' is crucial. It means that one has come of age and is able to act for oneself without the tutelage of a guardian ('Vormund'). It is a key word of the Enlightenment, made famous by Kant's definition of 'Aufklärung' [Enlightenment] as the abandonment of one's 'selbst verschuldete Unmündigkeit' [immaturity which is one's own fault] and acquiring the courage to think for oneself.[40] Heine writes in *Zur Geschichte der Religion und Philosophie in Deutschland* [*On the History of Religion and Philosophy in Germany*] (1835), in an ostensibly religious context but with obvious political implications: 'Wir sind frei und wollen keines [*sic*] donnernden Tyrannen. Wir sind mündig und bedürfen keiner väterlichen Vorsorge' [We are free and don't want a thundering tyrant. We are mature and don't need paternal care].[41]

Maintaining an all-female state is shown to be difficult. Kleist's independent women were warned by a supernatural voice that, if they formed their own state, they would have to guard it against conquest by a foreign power, yet their weapon of choice, the bow, was difficult to use for women encumbered by heavy breasts. Queen Tanaïs responded decisively by tearing off her right breast and renaming her people, just before she collapsed, the Amazons, which by an uncertain etymology

---

39   Rousseau, 'A Discourse on the Moral Effects of the Arts and Sciences', in *The Social Contract and the Discourses*, pp. 1–29 (p. 9). Kleist talks about this text in detail in his letter to Wilhelmine von Zenge of 15 August 1801: in Kleist, *Sämtliche Werke und Briefe*, IV, 260–62.

40   Immanuel Kant, 'Beantwortung der Frage: Was ist Aufklärung?' in Kant, *Werke*, ed. by Wilhelm Weischedel, 6 vols (Darmstadt: Wissenschaftliche Buchgesellschaft, 1964), VI, 53–61 (p. 53).

41   Heinrich Heine, *Sämtliche Schriften*, ed. by Klaus Briegleb, 6 vols (Munich: Hanser, 1968–76), III, 571.

was supposed to mean 'the breastless ones' ('Die Amazonen oder Busenlosen', l. 1989). Warfare was required not only to defend the state but also to propagate its population by bringing back male captives to impregnate the women; this is done at an annual ceremony, the 'Rosenfest', or festival of roses, and when the women are pregnant, the 'Fest der reifen Mütter' [festival of mature mothers] is held and the men are sent home with gifts. The constant warfare on which the Amazons depend for their continued existence may sound incompatible with an ideal state, but Rousseau insists that his simple and virtuous societies were also tough, hardy, and warlike, whereas highly cultured states have always become feeble and easy to conquer. Thus Sparta was able to defeat Athens, the Swiss were able to gain their independence from the Austrians, and 'the Scythians, the poorest of all nations, were able to resist the most powerful monarchs of the universe'.[42]

The Amazon state, however, has found little sympathy among most Kleist critics. Some agree with Achilles, who considers it unfeminine and unnatural (l. 1903). Thus Walter Müller-Seidel condemns its 'Unnatur und Unnatürlichkeit' [transgression against nature and its unnaturalness], arguing that when Penthesilea, just before her death, dissociates herself from it, that implies a criticism of the state (surely rather of Penthesilea?), and that for Kleist, 'Humanität' [humaneness] meant breaking with the 'Unnatur, Konvention und Anonymität' [unnatural, conventional and anonymous practice] expressed in the Amazon law that women may not choose their male partners.[43] Gerhard Kaiser likewise criticizes it as 'unmenschlich' and 'unnatürlich' [inhuman and unnatural] on the grounds that the law forbidding partner choice turns both men and women into instruments.[44] H. M. Brown deplores the Amazon state as 'repressive' and thinks it wrong to suppose that all men are as bad as the Ethiopians, ignoring the 'nobility and magnanimity' of other races such as the Greeks (though Achilles and his companions hardly show such qualities).[45] Catherine Rigby goes further, calling the Amazon state 'a perverted version of patriarchal oppression' on the grounds that the Amazons, by forbidding partner choice and enjoining self-mutilation, exercise as harsh a tyranny as the men they killed.[46] Yet repressiveness, let alone tyranny, does not seem to be an issue in the play. Admittedly, Penthesilea says the Amazons are sad when the men leave after impregnating them (ll. 2083–87), but otherwise they do not seem to chafe under their law. As Ruth Angress points out, theirs is a stable and well-functioning society: 'Peculiar as it is, the Amazon state has proved its viability since its inception, and apart from Penthesilea in the grip of her passion, none of the Amazons ever question the strength of their institutions.'[47]

---

42   Rousseau, 'A Discourse on the Moral Effects of the Arts and Sciences', p. 18.

43   Walter Müller-Seidel, 'Penthesilea im Kontext der deutschen Klassik', in Kleists Dramen: Neue Interpretationen, ed. by Walter Hinderer (Stuttgart: Reclam, 1981), pp. 144–71 (pp. 147, 149).

44   Kaiser, 'Mythos und Person in Kleists Penthesilea', p. 211.

45   H. M. Brown, Kleist and the Tragic Ideal (Bern: Peter Lang, 1977), p. 65.

46   Catherine E. Rigby, Transgressions of the Feminine: Tragedy, Enlightenment and the Figure of Woman in Classical German Drama (Heidelberg: Winter, 1996), p. 152.

47   Ruth Angress, 'Kleist's Nation of Amazons', in Beyond the Eternal Feminine, ed. by Susan L. Cocalis and Kay Goodman (Stuttgart: Heinz, 1982), 99–134 (p. 114).

The Amazon state is founded not only on a voluntary agreement among its citizens but also on a successful rebellion against intolerable oppression. In that respect it illustrates a general law of human society which Penthesilea enunciates as follows:

> Doch Alles schüttelt, was ihm unerträglich,
> Der Mensch von seinen Schultern sträubend ab. (ll. 1934–35)

> [For human beings resist whatever they find intolerable, and shake it from their shoulders.]

It also has a number of contemporary resonances. Kleist, who wrote part of *Penthesilea* in a French prison at Châlons-sur-Marne, and whose native country was under French occupation, shows here the sympathy for resistance to oppression which is also apparent in his play *Die Hermannsschlacht* [Arminius's Battle] and in his novella *Die Verlobung in St. Domingo* [The Betrothal on St Domingo].[48] Resistance to male oppression was also a theme of the French Revolution: many women, notably Olympe de Gouges, author of *Déclaration des droits de la femme et de la citoyenne* [Declaration of the Rights of the Woman and the Female Citizen] (1791), who was guillotined in 1793, demanded that the Revolution should take the principles of the Enlightenment to their logical conclusion by extending equality to both sexes.[49] These are the revolutionary women whom Schiller called 'Hyänen' [hyenas], and the same term is applied to Penthesilea by one of the Greeks who hear with stupefaction about her incomprehensible pursuit of Achilles: 'seht die Hyäne, die blind-wütende!' [behold the hyena in her blind fury!] (l. 331). Kleist is not here inviting us to compare Penthesilea to a hyena, or equate her pursuit of Achilles to the savagery of a beast of prey; he is showing that the Greeks, who have already been established as conventional and obtuse in their outlook, can only denigrate what they cannot understand, just as conservative onlookers denigrated revolutionaries. And the Amazons, as Elystan Griffiths has recently pointed out, recall, in their united commitment to warfare on behalf of their state, the French revolutionary armies, a new phenomenon resulting from the *levée en masse* in contrast to the mercenary armies that fought previous wars; while the amazement of the Greeks on beholding this new fighting force recalls the perplexity of Europe's conservative rulers faced with aggressive popular armies.[50]

---

48   See Ruth Angress, 'Kleist's Treatment of Imperialism: *Die Hermannsschlacht* and *Die Verlobung in St Domingo*', in *Monatshefte*, 69 (1977), 17–33; also Michael Perraudin, 'Babekan's 'Brille' and the Rejuvenation of Congo Hoango: A Reinterpretation of Kleist's Story of the Haitian Revolution', *Oxford German Studies*, 20–21 (1991–92), 85–103. Brown (*Kleist and the Tragic Ideal*, p. 30) links *Penthesilea* with German patriotic writings.

49   See Inge Stephan, '"Da werden Weiber zu Hyänen...": Amazonen und Amazonenmythen bei Schiller und Kleist', in *Feministische Literaturwissenschaft*, ed. by Inge Stephan and Sigrid Weigel (Berlin: Argument-Verlag, 1984), 23–42. For a guide to the extensive feminist commentary on *Penthesilea*, see Jost Hermand, 'Kleist's *Penthesilea*: Battleground of Gendered Discourses', in *A Companion to the Works of Heinrich von Kleist*, ed. by Fischer, pp. 43–60.

50   Elystan Griffiths, *Political Change and Human Emancipation in the Works of Heinrich von Kleist* (Rochester, NY: Camden House, 2005), p. 57, also p. 101.

It is notable also that the Amazons (except for the High Priestess) communicate in a polite, dignified, and egalitarian manner, and that although few of them are named in the *dramatis personae*, they frequently address each other by name, suggesting a network of warm personal ties: besides the major characters Penthesilea, Prothoe, Meroe, and Asteria, we briefly meet Glaukothoe, Charmion (l. 945), Ornythia (946), Parthenion (948), Arsinoe (1047), Oterpe (1439), Megaris (1598), 'Ananke, Führerin der Hunde' [Ananke, leader of the dogs] (2408, also 2445), Thyrroe, who is in charge of the elephants (2410), Hermia (2677), Phania, and Terpi (2839).[51] Nor does the absence of men preclude close emotional relationships: commentators have paid strangely little attention to the tender and touching relations between Penthesilea and Prothoe, who call each other 'Meiner Seelen Schwester' [sister of my soul] (l. 873), 'Schwesterherz' [sister-heart] (l. 2843), and 'Geliebte' [beloved] (ll. 1687, 2905). Penthesilea even says to Prothoe: 'Nun, meines Blutes bess're Hälft' ist dein' [Well, my blood's better half is yours] (l. 1685). Their relationship, in particular, ought to correct the impression given by some critics that the Amazons have a kind of impersonal beehive state. Thus Wolff asserts: 'Der Amazonenstaat ist der Idealstaat reiner Vernünftigkeit, der alle irrationalen Elemente unterdrückt' [The Amazon state is the ideal state of pure rationality, suppressing all irrational elements].[52] Does the absence of Penthesilea's and Prothoe's relationship from critical discussion imply that for most readers, affectionate or homoerotic relationships between women in literature have been invisible?[53]

The play offers ample evidence that men, including the Greeks, are indeed domineering ('herrschsüchtig') and that women need to protect themselves against them. A single, chilling example is Scene 11, in which an unarmed Achilles encounters a party of Amazons aiming their arrows at him.[54] Rather like a colonialist facing down a party of rebellious natives, he gains control of the situation by issuing a bantering challenge and addressing them as 'ihr Jungfrau'n' [you maidens] (l. 1406), which sounds superior and patronizing (in effect: 'You wouldn't shoot an unarmed man, would you, girls?'). As the Amazons are under orders from Penthesilea to spare him, they shoot their arrows over his head. Achilles, feeling that he has won, and unaware that he really owes his life to Penthesilea, resorts to the conventional language of gallantry, declaring that they can strike him more surely with their eyes and that he is already disarmed:

> Ich fühle mich im Innersten getroffen,
> Und ein Entwaffneter, in jedem Sinne,
> Leg ich zu euren kleinen Füßen mich. (ll. 1414–16)

51 The names are listed by the editor in Kleist, *Sämtliche Werke und Briefe*, II, 784, mistakenly including 'Alcest' among the Amazons: from line 947 it should be clear that Alcest is a Greek warrior defeated by the Amazon Ornythia.

52 Wolff, *Kleist als politischer Dichter*, p. 457. One of the few commentators to appreciate Prothoe is Seán Allan, *The Plays of Heinrich von Kleist* (Cambridge: Cambridge University Press, 1996), pp. 159–61.

53 See the pioneering book by Angela Steidele, *'Als wenn Du mein Geliebter wärest': Liebe und Begehren zwischen Frauen in der deutschsprachigen Literatur, 1750–1850* (Stuttgart and Weimar: Metzler, 2003), where an 'intimes Verhältnis' is mentioned briefly (p. 296).

54 There is an excellent account of this scene in Angress, 'Kleist's Nation of Amazons', p. 128.

[I feel struck in my inmost soul, and, disarmed in every sense, I prostrate myself at your little feet.]

However, Achilles does not rely solely on rhetoric to save himself. While he tells the Amazons that they are too lovely and delicate to attack him, his soldiers aim spears at them from behind the scenes, immediately killing three women. The survivors prepare to set their mastiffs on him; Achilles asserts that if the dogs appeared, the women would rush to save him because they know he is in love with them. The Amazons do not fall for this flattery, but just as a princess is aiming at him, Achilles tells a Greek to shoot her, and she falls. This scene indicates that Achilles is utterly unscrupulous, and, more generally, that the shopworn Petrarchan rhetoric he deploys was always a way of crediting women with symbolic power in order to consolidate the real power exercised by men which, in turn, reveals its true foundations in the brutal violence orchestrated by Achilles.[55] Kleist's Achilles is as repulsive as other versions of this figure, from the Homeric original who endangers the Greek war effort by sulking in his tent (and was criticized by Plato for his avarice, cruelty, and impiety), via the Shakespearean Achilles who gloats over his unarmed victim Hector in Shakespeare's *Troilus and Cressida*, to the sadistic war criminal 'Achill das Vieh' [Achilles the Beast] in Christa Wolf's *Kassandra* [Cassandra].[56]

The 'Frauenstaat' or women's polity therefore looks a good idea in principle. It is no criticism of the state to say that it cannot contain the individual with powerful desires. Penthesilea's passion for Achilles not only destroys herself and him, but harms the state, first by letting a number of her fellow Amazons be killed, and then by allowing all the Greek captives to escape. Kleist is both exploring the possibility of a radically different social order, and suggesting that any social order will be vulnerable to the force of individual passion.

In practice, however, the Amazon state inevitably has its own internal tensions.[57] It seems to reproduce the strains of heterosexual society by imposing a twofold identity on women. If one ideal role is that of the warrior, the other is that of the docile young woman, represented by the young girls who wind wreaths of roses for the 'Rosenfest' under the governess-like tutelage of the High Priestess. This character is bossy, authoritarian, insensitive, and inept. Being absurdly literal-minded, she misinterprets a casual utterance by Penthesilea as an instruction to prepare the 'Rosenfest'. Later, when Penthesilea has been rescued by the Amazons from the Greeks, the High Priestess ignores her distress and gives her a severe telling-off for losing all the Greek captives. After the death of Achilles, the High Priestess forces Penthesilea to realize that she herself killed him. Her example shows

---

55   For a searchingly critical account of Achilles, as well as a positive account of the Amazon state which develops Angress's arguments, see Allan, esp. pp. 246–54.

56   See *The Republic*, 390e–391c, in *The Dialogues of Plato*, trans. by B. Jowett, 4th edn, 4 vols (Oxford: Clarendon Press, 1953), II, 236–37; Shakespeare, *Troilus and Cressida*, v. 8; Christa Wolf, *Kassandra: Vier Vorlesungen, eine Erzählung* (Berlin: Aufbau-Verlag, 1983), p. 233.

57   H. M. Brown finds a series of contradictions within the Amazon state: see *Kleist and the Tragic Ideal*, pp. 64–74, and more briefly her *Heinrich von Kleist: The Ambiguity of Art and the Necessity of Form* (Oxford: Clarendon Press, 1998), pp. 312–13. But equal or greater contradictions could be found in *any* polity.

that 'Herrschsucht' [domineering] is not only a masculine trait. Fortunately, she has an antagonist in Penthesilea's devoted friend Prothoe, who puts up with Penthesilea's wild mood swings and shows increasing irritation with the High Priestess (ll. 1281, 2813). In the High Priestess we can see an expression of the anticlericalism which is part of Kleist's debt to the Enlightenment.

The model of the docile girl is represented also by Penthesilea herself. After she has killed Achilles, the priestesses remark on what a well-behaved and charming girl she was:

> Solche eine Jungfrau, Hermia! So sittsam!
> In jeder Kunst der Hände so geschickt!
> So reizend, wenn sie tanzte, wenn sie sang!
> So voll Verstand und Würd' und Grazie! (ll. 2677–80)

> [Such a maiden, Hermia! So well-behaved! So skilful in all manual occupations! So charming when she danced or when she sang! So full of sense and dignity and grace!]

This makes Penthesilea sound like the perfect product of a finishing school for young ladies. We learn also, not only that she sang like a nightingale, but that she was too tender-hearted to tread on a worm (ll. 2683, 2689). The priestesses do not reflect that such qualities are unlikely to survive combat training. Moreover, Penthesilea has been put through a painful set of conflicting emotions. Heartbroken by the death of her dearly loved mother Otrere, she spent a month weeping at the grave until her people, eager to go to war, compelled her to mount the throne and lead the army. Penthesilea, by her own admission, was torn by emotional conflict ('Wehmütig strebender Gefühle voll' [full of sorrowful conflicting feelings] (l. 2158). She is obliged to lead her people before she has properly mourned her mother. To reconcile her two responsibilities — to her mother's memory and to her nation's future — she interprets her task as first and foremost the fulfilment of her mother's orders. And since her mother ordered her to seek out Achilles, she does so with an extraordinary vehemence: not because Achilles is so very attractive in his own right, but because, in gaining him, she will have gained a symbolic substitute for her lost mother.

In mourning, one idealizes the lost object.[58] Penthesilea not only speaks with uncritical devotion about Otrere, but also idealizes the substitute for her, Achilles. Yet this idealization is precarious. She seems fascinated by Achilles's reputation for cruelty, particularly by his treatment of Hector, whom Achilles killed and dragged round the walls of Troy. According to Hederich's compilation of myths, there was a link between Hector and Penthesilea, in that Hector set out to welcome her to Troy and thus fell into Achilles's hands and was killed, causing Penthesilea such distress that she nearly went straight back home.[59] In Kleist, this distress is transmuted into fascinated curiosity. She asks him about his treatment of Hector, rewards him with

---

58 See Sigmund Freud, 'Trauer und Melancholie', in Freud, *Studienausgabe*, ed. by Alexander Mitscherlich et al., 10 vols (Frankfurt a.M.: Fischer, 1970), III, 197–212.

59 Kleist, *Sämtliche Werke und Briefe*, II, 688; on Kleist's use of Hederich, see Paulin, 'Kleist's Metamorphoses'.

a kiss, and calls him 'Du junger Kriegsgott' [You young god of war] (l. 1807). Later she hails him as 'Den Lieben, Wilden, Süßen, Schrecklichen, | Den Überwinder Hektors!' [The dear, fierce, sweet, terrible one, the conqueror of Hector] (ll. 2185–86). Achilles' treatment of Hector is for Penthesilea the key action that expresses his character and makes him both frightening and attractive. She is right to focus on it, for dragging a dead or dying enemy behind him is something that Achilles very much enjoys. Earlier, he has elaborated in sadistic detail the prospect of doing this to Penthesilea:

> den Wagen dort
> Nicht ehr zu meinen Freunden will ich lenken,
> Ich schwör's, und Pergamon nicht wiedersehn,
> Als bis ich sie zu meiner Braut gemacht,
> Und sie, die Stirn bekränzt mit Todeswunden,
> Kann durch die Straße häuptlings mit mir schleifen. (ll. 610–15)

[I shall not drive that carriage back to my friends, I swear it, nor see Pergamon again, till I have made her my bride, and can drag her head first through the streets, her forehead wreathed with deadly wounds.]

And he has even told Prothoe in so many words that he means to treat Penthesilea as he did Hector (ll. 1513–14). Faced with Prothoe's understandable horror, he replies inconsistently with an equivocal profession of love: 'sag' ihr, daß ich sie liebe' [tell her that I love her] (l. 1520). This suggests that in Achilles emotional attraction is closely linked to sadism. And Achilles' sadism meets in Penthesilea with a corresponding masochism, shown in the fantasy she unfolds of Achilles treading on her neck, dragging her home behind his horses, and feeding her body to his dogs and to carrion birds (ll. 1244–52).[60] Since masochism and sadism are dynamically linked, it is appropriate that when she kills Achilles she does so in just the cannibalistic manner that Achilles himself threatens in the *Iliad*. Hence her killing of Achilles is a form of identification with Achilles.[61]

To the limited extent that Penthesilea's idealization of Achilles is related to Achilles himself, and not just to an image of him as heroic warrior and her mother's choice, it is based on the very qualities that most people would find repulsive: the actual and potential brutality that seems so much to fascinate her. We can expect that when Achilles' brutal and domineering character forces itself on her attention, her idealization of him will swing round into its opposite. And it does. Even in the idyllic Scene 15, in which Penthesilea is under the happy illusion that she has captured Achilles, not vice versa, he shows a detached sarcasm that does not wholly

---

60   Inge Stephan misreads this as Penthesilea's wish to drag Achilles home (Stephan, ' "Da werden Weiber zu Hyänen ..." ', p. 38). Syntactically, this reading is possible though strained, but the context rules it out. As a result, Stephan wrongly attributes to Penthesilea a character as barbarous as that of Achilles.

61   *Iliad*, Book 22, lines 344–47, in Voss's translation: 'Finster schaut' und begann der mutige Renner Achilles: | Nicht beschwöre mich, Hund, bei meinen Knien und den Eltern! | Daß doch Zorn und Wut mich erbitterte, roh zu verschlingen | Dein zerschnittenes Fleisch für das Unheil, das du mir brachtest!'; Homer, *Ilias / Odyssee in der Übersetzung von Johann Heinrich Voss* (Munich: Winkler, 1957), p. 386. The connection is pointed out by Angress, 'Kleist's Nation of Amazons', p. 104.

escape her notice, infatuated though she is. When she tells him how the Amazons killed the male invaders, he comments: 'solch' eine Tat der Weiber läßt sich denken' [One can imagine women doing something like that] (l. 1952). This glib ascription of murderous deceit to the people he disparagingly calls 'Weiber' [wenches] (Penthesilea uses the word 'Frauen' [women]) is a thoughtless piece of conventional misogyny, the obverse of the conventional gallantry which Achilles himself used, deceitfully and murderously, in Scene 11.[62] When she begins recounting, perhaps in a naively solemn tone, how the Amazons increase their population, she notices him smiling (more likely grinning) and asks why, but gets an evasive answer. However, these signs are not enough to alarm her. In a rapid sequence, Penthesilea is forced to realize that she is actually Achilles's captive and that he wants, not to accompany her to the Amazon capital of Themiscyra, but to make her his queen in Greece. Rescued by the Amazons, she is angry with them, since they have after all separated her from the man she (however ill-advisedly) loves. In a state of emotional turmoil, heightened by the High Priestess's tongue-lashing, she receives a challenge from Achilles to single combat. She has no way of knowing that Achilles, who has begun to feel something like love for her, means to let her overcome him and take him to Themiscyra. She feels that he has ignored everything she said, rejected her love, and mockingly invited her to a fight she is bound to lose, so that their union can take place on *his* terms:

> Der mich zu schwach weiß, sich mit ihm zu messen,
> Der ruft zum Kampf mich, Prothoe, ins Feld?
> Hier diese treue Brust, sie rührt ihn erst,
> Wenn sie sein scharfer Speer zerschmetterte?
> Was ich ihm zugeflüstert, hat sein Ohr
> Mit der Musik der Rede bloß getroffen? (ll. 2384–89)

[Knowing that I'm too weak to contend with him, Prothoe, does he really summon me into the field? Will this faithful breast not stir his feelings until his sharp spear smashes it? Did what I whispered to him touch his ear only with the music of speech?]

Achilles, for his part, is so deep in narcissism that he has not even begun to realize that she wants to define the terms of their relationship. Although he is prepared to accompany her to Themiscyra, he means to stay there only for a month or two, and is sure that she will then follow him to Greece (ll. 2474–82). He believes that she will not hurt him in the duel (l. 2471), and even when warned that she is approaching with dogs and elephants, he asserts: 'O! Die sind zahm, wie sie' [Oh, they're as tame as she is] (l. 2548).

In the event there is no combat: Penthesilea sets her dogs on Achilles and joins them in tearing and devouring his flesh. This reverses the myth, in which Achilles killed Penthesilea (and, in some versions, abused her corpse). It horrifies all the Amazons. What are we to make of it? Is it so far off the scale of human emotions as

---

62   Kaiser aptly comments: 'Penthesileas Offenbarung über Ursprung und Sinn des Amazonenstaates quittiert Achill auf dem Niveau eines Gardeleutnants, der seine Erfahrungen mit den Weibern quasi als Sorte hat'. Kaiser, 'Mythos und Person in Kleists *Penthesilea*', p. 217.

to be unintelligible? Must we resort to calling Penthesilea insane? She does, after all, set out for the duel 'mit allen Zeichen des Wahnsinns' [with every sign of madness] (stage direction after line 2427), and she is subject not only to mood swings — as when, in scene 5, she first curses and then embraces the long-suffering Prothoe — but to alternating states of consciousness, in which her previous actions are either temporarily forgotten or seem dream-like. Probably, however, we are not to think of her as a pathological case, but as a person with unusually labile emotions, subject to intense emotional pressures, and endowed with the depth and intensity of feeling that distinguishes other tragic figures such as Racine's Phèdre. Her infatuation with Achilles can be understood better if we interpret it as fulfilling her mother's order, and Achilles as partly a symbolic substitute for her mother. Her love for her mother is projected on to Achilles, but as such love is intrinsically ambivalent, it turns into its opposite. This supports the Kleinian reading recently proposed by Simon Richter. Richter relies heavily on Melanie Klein's attempt to explain ego development from the child's ambivalent attitude to the breast: the pleasurable, full, 'good' breast and the frustrating, dry, 'bad' breast shape one's emotional life. In this perspective, Achilles represents for Penthesilea not only her mother but more specifically her mother's breast. The good breast which she wants to kiss turns into the bad breast which she wants to bite. Hence her famous explanation of her conduct as a mistaken substitution of 'Bisse' [bites] for the rhyming 'Küsse' [kisses].[63]

Penthesilea's tragedy is first and foremost personal. To what extent is it also national? She brings about the deaths of several Amazons, and, by losing the captives, defeats the purpose of their expedition to Troy. Commentators seem to assume further that the play ends with the dissolution of the Amazon state. Gerhard Kaiser takes for granted that the end of the play shows the 'Ende des Amazonenstaates' [the end of the Amazon state], H. M. Brown perceives 'the total disbandment of the institution and its traditions', while Anthony Stephens affirms, a little hesitantly: 'It seems clear that the state ends with Penthesilea's suicide'.[64] This conclusion appears to be based on the fact that after killing Achilles Penthesilea lets the great golden bow, the emblem of the former Scythian kings, which Tanaïs received on the state's foundation, slip from her hand to the ground, where it is said to die: 'Und stirbt, | Wie er der Tanaïs geboren ward' [And dies, as it was born to Tanaïs] (ll. 2771–72). Yet this need mean only that Penthesilea renounces her queenship of the Amazons, a decision confirmed by her later declaration: 'Ich sage vom Gesetz der Fraun mich los' [I disown the law of women] (l. 3012) and by her secret instruction to Prothoe to scatter Tanaïs's ashes in the air. The Amazons draw no wider conclusion, and the fragility of any such inference is admitted in the older study by E. L. Stahl: 'With the destruction of the bow, *we may surmise*, the power of the Amazons has gone.'[65] I have to agree with Angress: 'The Amazon state remains intact at the end. The

63 Simon Richter, *Missing the Breast: Gender, Fantasy, and the Body in the German Enlightenment* (Seattle: University of Washington Press, 2006), pp. 219–47.

64 Kaiser, 'Mythos und Person in Kleists *Penthesilea*', p. 235; Brown, *Kleist and the Tragic Ideal*, p. 108; Anthony Stephens, *Heinrich von Kleist: The Dramas and Stories* (Oxford: Berg, 1994), p. 122.

65 E. L. Stahl, *Heinrich von Kleist's Dramas* (Oxford: Blackwell, 1961), p. 89. My emphasis.

women have lost their Greek prisoners but they are free to return home.'[66] Why have so many critics (not all male) thought otherwise on flimsy evidence? Could it be a conservative prejudice that makes them disbelieve that an all-female state, even in fiction, could possibly be viable?

The age of aesthetic humanism was one in which people were uneasily conscious that female subordination was not natural but created. Texts that explore female autonomy, even when they dwell on its limitations, show how things could be otherwise. Werner's *Wanda* may help to reinforce received opinions, but it also exposes them as the expressions of society rather than nature, and of power rather than justice; while Kleist's portrayal in *Penthesilea* of a viable all-female society, retaining the virtuous simplicity and the martial toughness that Rousseau ascribed to certain small nations, is so radical that commentators have tended to avoid its challenge.

---

66 Angress, 'Kleist's Nation of Amazons', p. 132.

CHAPTER 7

Theophanies in German Classicism

A theophany is the visible appearance of a god. In ancient literature theophanies are common. A famous example is the appearance to Aeneas of his mother, Venus, in Book 1 of Virgil's *Aeneid*. Aeneas and his men have been driven by a storm to the North African coast, and Aeneas has gone out to reconnoitre, when Venus, disguised as a huntress, meets him and gives him advice. The gods do not appear in their full glory, for mortals would be unable to stand the sight, like the foolish Semele who was burnt up when Zeus, at her request, showed her his real form. Despite Venus' disguise, however, Aeneas discerns in her some quality more than human:

> o — quam te memorem, virgo? namque haud tibi voltus
> mortalis, nec vox hominem sonat; o dea certe!

[B]ut by what name should I call thee, O maiden? for thy face is not mortal nor has thy voice a human ring: O goddess surely![1]

Venus reveals her identity only when their conversation is over and she can give Aeneas a glimpse of her real radiance.

In German classical drama, even in plays set in the ancient world, gods appear only rarely. In Goethe's *Iphigenie auf Tauris* we hear much about the gods, but in contrast to the original play by Euripides, where Artemis appears in person, Goethe allows us to think that the gods are only the projections of human desires. The Amazons in Kleist's *Penthesilea* are called the daughters of Mars, but Mars himself is not seen on stage. The great exception is *Amphitryon*, set in ancient Greece, where Kleist, adapting a legend already dramatized by Plautus, and partially following the version by Molière, shows Jupiter and Mercury creating havoc in Amphitryon's household. In several other works by Kleist, however, one character seems to another to have a semi-divine radiance. In *Die Marquise von O...*, the heroine's rescuer, Graf F..., at first seems to be an angel from heaven. Penthesilea and Achilles appear to one another as radiant beings; in *Das Käthchen von Heilbronn*, which Kleist described as a companion piece to *Penthesilea*, Käthchen is similarly entranced by the Graf von Strahl; and in Kleist's last play, *Prinz Friedrich von Homburg*, the Prince, while sleepwalking, perceives a godlike radiance in the Elector. If *Amphitryon* is a bitterly comical travesty of a theophany, where the gods behave in a distinctly

---

1 Virgil, *Eclogues, Georgics, Aeneid I–VI*, trans. by H. Rushton Fairclough, Loeb Classical Library(Cambridge, MA: Harvard University Press, 1935), pp. 264, 265.

ungodlike manner, the other plays present us with illusory theophanies. The radiance that characters ascribe to one another indicates the intensity of their love. It also expresses the wish that something beyond the ordinary might really exist on earth. Thus it may be seen as a compensation for the fact that a supernaturalist religious belief was felt to be no longer tenable.

Theophanies in the Ancient World and Since

In the ancient world, the earthly appearance of a god was not just a literary motif. It was often felt to be something that could actually happen. Pausanias, writing in the second century CE, reports that the inhabitants of Elis were convinced that their festival was attended by the god Dionysus in person.[2] In the following century, an inscription on a stone at Miletus expresses wonder at the recent sharp increase in the number of divine visitations.[3] The third-century pagan author Celsus thinks that gods really do descend to earth, instancing the many appearances by the divine healer Asclepius, but he regards some such claims as fraudulent, dismissing the claims made by Christians for the divinity of Jesus along with the similar claims made by the followers of Simon Magus.[4] In the Bible, we find a curious episode in the Acts of the Apostles where Paul and Barnabas, having healed a cripple at Lystra in Asia Minor, are acclaimed by the inhabitants as gods who have descended to earth:

> And when the multitude saw what Paul had done, they lifted up their voice, saying in the speech of Lycaonia, The gods are come down to us in the likeness of men.
> And they called Barnabas, Jupiter; and Paul, Mercury, because he was the chief speaker.[5]

Paul of course insists that he and Barnabas are fellow mortals, and with great difficulty, restrains the crowd from sacrificing oxen to them. But the incident reveals how deeply belief in the gods was rooted in popular consciousness. It suggests that the many epiphanies in ancient literature — especially in Homer, but also in some tragedies — may have been appreciated as something more than literary fictions, and may have stimulated a sense of religious awe.

It may be asked whether Jesus himself should be understood as a theophanic presence. He has, after all, traditionally been understood as God incarnate. But the New Testament suggests otherwise. In the Gospel narratives, Jesus is not seen by his disciples as a divine being, but as an extraordinary human. Even in the Resurrection narratives he is not seen as a god. When New Testament authors try

---

2   Robin Lane Fox, *Pagans and Christians* (London: Penguin, 1988), p. 115. See also the article 'Epiphany' in *The Oxford Classical Dictionary*, 3rd edn, ed. by Simon Hornblower and Antony Spawforth (Oxford: Oxford University Press, 1990), p. 546.

3   Lane Fox, p. 102. More examples from late antiquity are in Jacob Burckhardt, *The Greeks and Greek Civilization*, trans. by Sheila Stern (London: HarperCollins, 1998), p. 34.

4   Frances Young, 'Two Roots or a Tangled Mass?', in *The Myth of God Incarnate*, ed. by John Hick (London: SCM Press, 1977), pp. 87–119 (pp. 88–89).

5   Acts 14. 11–12.

to formulate his relation to God, they use a variety of terms — 'the Son of God' (Mark 1. 1), 'the Word became flesh' (John 1. 14), 'taking the form of a servant' (Philippians 2. 7), 'the image of the invisible God' (Colossians 1. 15) — which imply, not a fixed conception, but a series of attempts to define the indefinable.[6] None of them amounts to a theology of incarnation, such as was put forward by Athanasius early in the fourth century and defined at the Council of Chalcedon in 451. And it has been argued that this theology owes something to the pagan belief that exceptional mortals, such as Hercules, were born under miraculous circumstances and were carried off to heaven instead of dying. Frances Young reports the theory 'that it was the Greek-speaking Gentile converts who transformed Jesus, the Jewish Messiah of Palestine, into an incarnate divine being'. She surveys the analogous beliefs in Jewish tradition — for example, about Elijah being transported to heaven in a fiery chariot — which might have assisted such a syncretistic development of belief. So the conception of Jesus as an incarnation of God may after all have some connection with pagan theophanies.[7]

In the Gospels themselves, the only episode that does resemble a pagan theophany is the Transfiguration, recounted in all three of the Synoptic Gospels. Having ascended a mountain with some of his disciples, Jesus 'was transfigured before them; and his face did shine as the sun, and his garments became white as the light' (Matthew 17. 2; cf. Mark 9. 2–3, Luke 9. 29). Kleist's characters sometimes perceive one another as transfigured in a similar way.

In more recent times, a sense of religious awe is still present in literary texts where a beautiful stranger is at first thought to be divine. A well-known example occurs in *The Tempest* when Ferdinand and Miranda first set eyes on each other. Miranda thinks he is 'a spirit', 'A thing divine', while Ferdinand declares her to be 'Most sure the goddess | On whom these airs attend!' (1. 2. 412–23). In *Wilhelm Meisters Lehrjahre*, Wilhelm, after being attacked by robbers, is helped by the 'fair Amazon' Natalie, her uncle, and their doctor. About to faint, he imagines the beautiful unknown woman enveloped in radiant light:

> In diesem Augenblicke, da er den Mund öffnen und einige Worte des Dankes stammeln wollte, wirkte der lebhafte Eindruck ihrer Gegenwart so sonderbar auf seine schon angegriffenen Sinne, daß es ihm auf einmal vorkam, als sei ihr Haupt mit Strahlen umgeben, und über ihr ganzes Bild verbreite sich nach und nach ein glänzendes Licht.[8]

> [At that moment, as he tried to open his mouth and stammer a few words of thanks, the vivid impression of her presence had such a strange effect on his already disordered senses that he suddenly thought her head was surrounded by rays, and a radiant light gradually spread over her whole image.]

6 See Adrian Hastings, 'Incarnation', in *The Oxford Companion to Christian Thought*, ed. by Adrian Hastings, Alistair Mason and Hugh Pyper, pp. 321–24; Frances Young, 'A Cloud of Witnesses', in *The Myth of God Incarnate*, ed. by Hick, pp. 13–47.

7 Young, 'Two Roots', p. 98.

8 Johann Wolfgang Goethe, *Sämtliche Werke: Briefe, Tagebücher und Gespräche*, ed. by Friedmar Apel et al., Deutsche Klassiker-Ausgabe, 40 vols (Frankfurt a.M.: Deutscher Klassiker Verlag, 1986–2000), IX: *Wilhelm Meisters theatralische Sendung, Wilhelm Meisters Lehrjahre, Unterhaltungen deutscher Ausgewanderten*, ed. by Wilhelm Vosskamp and Herbert Jaumann (1992), p. 590.

Here the associations are not classical but Christian. The rays that seem to surround Natalie's head are those of a halo. As the light spreads to envelop her whole body, she appears like an angel. The word 'Bild' (image) makes her seem like a visionary apparition. Wilhelm's vision is explained in medical terms, since he is still confused after being beaten up by robbers, but his delusion is only superficial, for Natalie, as is confirmed later when Wilhelm gets to know her, is indeed a figure of angelic goodness.

In some other apparent theophanies, however, the religious aura that at first seems to surround a character is more seriously misleading. A complex case occurs in *Iphigenie auf Tauris*. On meeting Iphigenie for the first time, Pylades addresses her as 'du Göttliche' [divine one] (l. 823) and asks about her 'göttergleiche Herkunft' [godlike ancestry] (l. 814).[9] Like Wilhelm's vision of Natalie as a saint, this testifies to Iphigenie's transparent nobility, but it also suggests that Pylades, who has a good deal of crude cunning, wishes to flatter her, for his conversation with Orest in the previous scene shows his awareness that she is not a goddess but simply 'ein fremdes göttergleiches Weib' [an alien godlike woman] (l. 712).

That Iphigenie is human is not just a self-evident truth. For the play strongly suggests that Iphigenie — with her humanity, her instinctive truthfulness, and her moral courage, shown when she stands up to King Thoas in Act v — is *better* than the gods. Her belief that the gods love humanity — 'Denn die Unsterblichen lieben der Menschen | Weitverbreitete gute Geschlechter' [For the Immortals love mankind | Spread far and wide in goodly kindreds] (ll. 554–55)[10] — testifies to her good nature, but is not borne out by what we hear of them. She herself admits that the gods behaved badly towards her ancestor Tantalus in treating him as an equal when, being a mere mortal, he was too weak to endure their company, and in punishing him and his descendants for an (unspecified) offence which was really a human failing. The gods have in fact placed Tantalus' descendants under a curse which means that a member of each generation must subject a relative to a horrible death. When Iphigenie fears that her turn is about to come, since Thoas commands her to make her brother a human sacrifice, she recalls an old song about the gods' callous indifference towards humanity, and begs the gods to prove it untrue. Pylades' confident statement, 'Die Götter rächen | Der Väter Missetat nicht an dem Sohn' [The Gods do not avenge | The misdeeds of the fathers on the sons] (ll. 713–14)[11] is plainly false. The Greek gods in the play resemble the God of the Old Testament, whose professed compassion does not prevent him from 'visiting the iniquity of the fathers upon the children, and upon the children's children, upon the third and upon the fourth generation' (Exodus 34. 7). Even worse, it is suggested that the gods themselves lead humanity into evil.[12] Iphigenie stands up

---

9   Goethe, *Sämtliche Werke*, v: *Dramen, 1776–1790*, ed. by Dieter Borchmeyer, p. 578.

10   Goethe, *Sämtliche Werke*, v, 570. Translations from *Iphigenie* are taken whenever possible from Johann Wolfgang von Goethe, *Iphigenia in Tauris*, trans. by Roy Pascal (London: Angel Books, 2014); here, p. 50.

11   Goethe, *Sämtliche Werke*, v, 575; *Iphigenia*, p. 55.

12   See Wolfdietrich Rasch, *Goethes 'Iphigenie auf Tauris' als Drama der Autonomie* (Munich: Beck, 1979).

for humanity — both for human beings against divine ones, and for humane values against inhuman religious conceptions — and thus incarnates central values of the Enlightenment. Without openly defying the gods, she is just as much in revolt against them as Goethe's Prometheus, who, in a well-known poem, mocks the impotence of the tyrant Zeus and asserts his autonomy down on earth.[13] And it is Iphigenie's brother Orest, not the goddess, who brings about the resolution of the action by concluding that the oracle which told him to bring 'the sister' back from Tauris to Greece was referring not to the statue of Artemis, Apollo's sister, preserved at Tauris, but to Orest's own flesh-and-blood sister Iphigenie. The play thus traces humankind's route from servile submission to maturity, autonomy, and self-reliance. No theophany is wanted or needed.

Another illusory theophany occurs in a later writer who was deeply indebted to German classical drama — Franz Grillparzer. In *Die Argonauten*, the second part of his trilogy *Das goldene Vließ* (published 1822), Medea, daughter of the King of Colchis, has an unexpected encounter with the Greek adventurer Jason. She supposes him to be the Colchian god of death:

> *Heimdar* war es, der Todesgott.
> Bezeichnet hat er sein dunkles Opfer,
> Bezeichnet mich mit dem ladenden Kuß,
> Und Medea wird sterben, hinuntergehn
> Zu den Schatten der schweigenden Tiefe.[14]

[It was Heimdar, the god of death. He marked down his dark victim, marked me down with the inviting kiss, and Medea will die and descend to the shadows of the silent depths.]

Like Wilhelm with Natalie, Medea's perception is literally mistaken but morally accurate. Jason is no god, but a mortal, and her acquaintance with him will prove fatal for her. He will exploit Medea's help to obtain the golden fleece, marry her reluctantly, and then desert her for Kreusa, daughter of the King of Corinth, regarding Medea as inferior because a 'barbarian'; Medea will then take a barbarous revenge. Grillparzer's play is in many respects a pessimistic rewriting of *Iphigenie*. Both turn on the relations between Greeks and barbarians. In *Iphigenie* the distinction is annulled, for all are shown to be capable of humanity; in *Das goldene Vließ* both sides are shown to be capable of treachery, but it is maltreatment by the Greeks that drives Medea to take revenge. In both cases, the illusory theophany points to the true nature of the human mistaken for a god. But in Grillparzer's play, in contrast to Goethe's, the nature or existence of the gods is not at issue; he develops the story of Jason and Medea into a searing portrayal of a relationship gone sour, including problems like the custody of the children which are familiar from modern divorce cases.

---

13 'Prometheus' in *Sämtliche Werke*, I: *Gedichte, 1756–1799*, ed. by Karl Eibl, pp. 203–04; see also Jonas Jølle, ' "prince poli & savant": Goethe's Prometheus and the Enlightenment', *Modern Language Review*, 99 (2004), 394–415.

14 Franz Grillparzer, *Sämtliche Werke*, ed. by Peter Frank and Karl Pörnbacher, 4 vols (Munich: Hanser, 1960–65), I, 839.

A different criticism of the gods from that expressed in *Iphigenie* is hinted at in a late story by Christoph Martin Wieland, 'Daphnidion'. The story, written in 1803, forms part of *Das Hexameron von Rosenhain*, a group of six stories within a narrative frame that Wieland wrote early in the nineteenth century and published as a whole in 1805. For this story Wieland has adopted the ancient genre of the 'Milesian tale', an erotically tinged narrative including both human and supernatural beings. However, there are no actual gods in 'Daphnidion'. Their place is taken by a young man called Phöbidas, who is said to be descended from Phoebus Apollo, and the shepherdess Daphnidion who is the object of his lust. Although Phöbidas is not himself divine, he is so handsome that he is mistaken for a god: a nymph, taken by surprise, sees him as 'einen Jüngling, den sie seiner Schönheit wegen für einen der ewig jugendlichen Götter, Merkur, Apollo oder Bacchus, ansehen mochte'.[15] The story clearly alludes to that of Apollo and his lust for Daphne, who, to escape his clutches, was turned into a laurel tree. And in the person of the incorrigibly conceited Phöbidas it criticizes the cruelty of the gods who exploit humans in order to satisfy their desires.

Both Phöbidas and Daphnidion resort to magical aid. Daphnidion is under the protection of a woman with magical powers called Dämonassa. When Phöbidas pursues the girl into a cave, Dämonassa intervenes and tells him he may approach Daphnidion with only one of his senses. He can either see her, hear her voice, or touch her. The sensual Phöbidas chooses the last option, but goes too far by embracing Daphnidion, whereupon he is magically transported out of the cave and left unconscious. Undeterred, he enlists the aid of a magician, Hippalektor, who promises to give him the semblance of a girl so that he can dance with Daphnidion and steal from her a ring that protects her from magic. Dämonassa, however, foresees this move and replaces Daphnidion with another girl; Phöbidas' attempt fails, he is exposed in his true form, whereupon all the young women fall upon him, beat them, and threaten him with castration. Thanks to Dämonassa's humane intervention, Phöbidas escapes this penalty, but the women give him a symbolic punishment by making a stuffed dummy in his likeness and beating it in an annual ritual. So the original story of Apollo and Daphne is reversed: the Apollo figure is ridiculed and abused instead of being worshipped.[16]

Not only does the story condemn Phöbidas' lustfulness — and, by implication, that of his divine ancestor — but it also treats magic in an ironic and perfunctory way, showing that it is first and foremost Dämonassa's intelligence, rather than her magical powers, that enables her to outsmart her antagonist. Hippalektor meanwhile is something of a charlatan: although he professes to obtain his knowledge about Daphnidion's circumstances from a magical book, he seems in fact to depend on skilfully gathering information. In this way, too, Wieland, like Goethe in *Iphigenie*, transfers the emphasis from magical to human powers. The gods, or their descendants, are not needed or wanted.

15   Wieland, *Ausgewählte Werke*, ed. by Friedrich Beissner, 3 vols (Munich: Winkler, 1965), III, 277.
16   See Peter Haischer, '*Das Hexameron von Rosenhain*', in *Wieland-Handbuch*, ed. by Jutta Heinz (Stuttgart: Metzler, 2008), pp. 333–44 (p. 336).

Goethe's 'Der Gott und die Bajadere'

The late eighteenth century had access to other ancient worlds besides that of Greece and Rome. Sir William Jones, who was sent to India in 1783 to learn Sanskrit, understand Indian laws, and reduce the power of Indian lawyers, soon went beyond his original remit to explore (as did some other British scholars) the rich world of early Sanskrit literature. Charles Wilkins published his translation of the *Bhagavad Gita* in 1785; a German version by Friedrich Majer, based on Wilkins's translation, appeared in 1802. In 1789 Jones provided an English version of the drama *Sakuntala*, which was then turned into German by Georg Forster. The great epics, the *Ramayana* and the *Mahabharata*, were still known only in excerpts, but enough was available by the 1790s to indicate a literature and mythology which could rival those of the Greeks.[17] In the visual arts, too, a taste which had learnt to appreciate Gothic architecture and the archaic Greek temples at Paestum was able to respond to Indian building and sculpture, so that, as Partha Mitter says: 'To an antiquarian of the late eighteenth century Indian antiquities were as worthy of investigation as those of Britain or of Greece.'[18]

Goethe was an Indophile only with reservations. He shared the enthusiasm for *Sakuntala*. From an early age, thanks to reading travel books, he knew the story of the *Ramayana*. He was grateful to 'the incomparable Jones' for making so much interesting material known in the West.[19] But in his later years he repeatedly criticized Indian philosophy as being abstruse and Indian art as being grotesque;[20] Indian literature succeeded when it overcame the conflict between these two forces, 'weil sie sich aus dem Conflict mit der abstrusesten Philosophie auf einer und mit der monstrosesten Religion auf der andern Seite im glücklichsten Naturell durchhelfen und von beiden nicht mehr annehmen, als ihnen zur inneren Tiefe und äußern Würde frommen mag' [because thanks to a happy natural endowment they escape from the conflict between the most abstruse philosophy on the one hand, and the most monstrous religion on the other, taking no more from either than provides them with inner profundity and external dignity].[21]

'Der Gott und die Bajadere' has the subtitle 'Indische Legende'; the word 'Legende' suggests especially an edifying narrative taken from the life of a saint, and feels at least faintly incongruous. The poem arouses attention first by its unusual

---

17 See A. Leslie Willson, *A Mythical Image: The Ideal of India in German Romanticism* (Durham, NC: Duke University Press, 1964); Suzanne L. Marchand, *German Orientalism in the Age of Empire: Religion, Race, and Scholarship* (Cambridge: Cambridge University Press, 2009), esp. p. 18; Michael J. Franklin, *Orientalist Jones: Sir William Jones, Poet, Lawyer, and Linguist, 1746–1794* (Oxford: Oxford University Press, 2011), esp. ch. 7: 'Europe Falls in Love with Śakuntalā'.

18 Partha Mitter, *Much Maligned Monsters: History of European Reactions to Indian Art* (Oxford: Clarendon Press, 1977), p. 141.

19 Goethe, 'Indische Dichtungen', in *Werke*, ed. by Bernhard Suphan et al., IV sections, 143 vols (Weimar: Böhlau, 1887–1919), I, vol. 42/II, pp. 50–53 (p. 51). For his positive view of Indian philosophy, see *Sämtliche Werke*, XXXIX: Johann Peter Eckermann, *Gespräche mit Goethe in den letzten Jahren seines Lebens*, ed. by Christoph Michel (1999), p. 310.

20 See e.g. *Zahme Xenien* II, *Sämtliche Werke*, II: *Gedichte, 1800–1832*, ed. by Karl Eibl (1988), p. 635.

21 'Indische Dichtungen', p. 50.

metre. Each stanza consists of two quatrains, rhyming abab, followed by three lines in amphibrachs ('Und <u>hat</u> er / die <u>Stadt</u> sich | als <u>Wand</u>rer | be<u>trach</u>tet'). This metre is that of a well-known Lutheran chorale, 'Eins ist not' [One thing is needful], composed in 1695 by Johann Heinrich Schröder (1666–97), set to music by Johann Sebastian Bach, and popular in Goethe's day.[22] So the poem is not only given Christian associations by having the word 'Legende' in its subtitle, but is written in a distinctively Christian metrical form.

The poem is based on an anecdote which Goethe found in Pierre Sonnerat's account of his travels in India and China, originally published in 1782 and in German translation the following year. Sonnerat's story concerns 'Dewendren' [Devendra], who is said to be king of the Hindu demi-gods. It needs to be quoted in full to show how Goethe altered it:

> Dewendren gieng nämlich einst unter der Gestalt eines schönen Jünglings aus, und suchte eine solche Tochter der Freude auf, um zu erfahren ob sie ihm getreu seyn würde. Er versprach ihr ein hübsches Geschenk, und sie machte ihm die ganze Nacht herrliche Freude. Am Morgen stellte sich Dewendren als ob er todt wäre; und das Mädchen glaubte es so ernstlich, daß sie sich ohne weiteres mit ihm wollte verbrennen lassen, obschon man ihr vorstellte, der Verstorbene sey ja nicht ihr Mann. Eben wie sie sich in die Flamme stürzen wollte, erwachte Dewendren wieder aus seinem Schlaf und gestand ihr seinen Betrug; aber zum Lohn ihrer Treue nahm er sie nun zum Weibe, und führte sie mit sich in das Paradies.[23]

> [For Devendra once went out in the form of a handsome young man and sought out a daughter of pleasure in order to find out whether she would be faithful to him. He promised her a fine present, and she gave him a wonderful time the whole night. In the morning Devendra pretended to be dead; and the girl believed this so seriously that she wanted at once to be burnt alongside him, although it was pointed out to her that the dead man was not her husband. Just as she was about to leap into the flames, Devendra awoke from his sleep and confessed his deception to her; but to reward her faithfulness he made her his wife and took her with him to Paradise.]

The first change Goethe made is that the god of the poem is no mere demi-god but 'Mahadöh' (correctly Mahadeva or 'great god'), in whom Goethe seems to conflate two members of the supreme Hindu pantheon, Vishnu and Shiva. The title belongs to Shiva, but it is Vishnu who descends to earth in nine incarnations or *avatars*, with a tenth yet to come.[24] The 'bayadere' (from the Portuguese *baiadeira*, 'dancer'), is a *devadāsī*, i.e. ritual dancer and temple prostitute. Of these people, Butler says: 'From childhood dedicated to the service of the gods, and therefore of the priests, their function sanctifies them in Hindu eyes; and even when their term of office expires and they become public dancers and courtesans, they remain the servants or slaves

22   This is pointed out by Norbert Mecklenburg, 'Balladen der Klassik', in *Balladenforschung*, ed. by Walter Müller-Seidel (Königstein/Ts.: Athenäum, etc., 1980), pp. 187–203 (p. 200).

23   Quoted from Sonnerat, *Reise nach Ostindien und China*, 2 vols (Zurich, 1783), in Goethe, *Sämtliche Werke*, I, 1238.

24   E. M. Butler, 'Pandits and Pariahs', in *German Studies presented to Leonard Ashley Willoughby* (Oxford: Blackwell, 1952), pp. 26–51 (pp. 31–32).

of the gods and are admitted to dance at their festivals' (p. 29). But in the poem, just as Goethe elevates the god, so he degrades the dancing-girl. She seems a mere common prostitute with painted cheeks, who has been thoroughly though not hopelessly corrupted by her profession. It takes the god's insight to perceive 'Durch tiefes Verderben, ein menschliches Herz' [through deep corruption, a human heart]. The god arouses her capacity to love, but to test it he demands of her unspecified acts which have a disturbing suggestion of sadism: 'Lust und Entsetzen und grimmige Pein' [pleasure and horror and terrible pain]. At all events, his behaviour softens the heart of the prostitute, so that she sheds tears for the first time. She kneels before him with a feeling of love which is neither mercenary nor merely physical:

> Sinkt zu seinen Füßen nieder,
> Nicht um Wollust noch Gewinst,
> Ach! und die gelenken Glieder,
> Sie versagen allen Dienst.[25]

[[S]he sinks down at his feet, not for pleasure nor profit, and alas! her supple limbs refuse their service.]

Here some commentators have found a clear allusion to Mary Magdalene. According to long-standing Christian tradition, though not according to the Gospels, Mary Magdalene was a prostitute who was brought by Jesus to repentance. St Luke's Gospel includes 'Mary called Magdalene' (i.e. from the town of Magdala) among 'certain women, which had been healed of evil spirits and infirmities', specifying that 'seven devils' went out of her (Luke 8. 2; cf. Mark 16. 9). Mary Magdalene was present at the crucifixion, and testified to Jesus's resurrection (Matt. 28. 1 and elsewhere). She was conflated with the unnamed woman, 'a sinner', who anointed Jesus' feet (Luke 7. 37–39), and of whom Jesus said: 'Her sins, which are many, are forgiven, for she loved much' (Luke 7. 47) — a statement which has prompted many blasphemous jokes identifying carnal with spiritual love.[26]

   Goethe's allusion to Mary Magdalene seemed obvious to Hegel, who said in his lectures on aesthetics:

> We find here the Christian story of the repentant Magdalene cloaked in Indian modes of thinking: the Bayadere shows the same humility, the like strength of love and faith; God puts her to the proof, which she completely sustains, and now her exaltation and reconciliation follow.[27]

According to the twentieth-century scholar, E. M. Butler, 'It has always been recognized that the spirit of this lovely ballad is essentially Christian; and no one can read it without realizing that the exotic garment covers a modern Mary Magdalene.'[28] Butler suggests that by drawing attention to Christ's forgiveness of Mary Magdalene, the poem rebukes Weimar society for its condemnation of Christiane, the lower-class woman with whom Goethe lived for many years before

---

25   Goethe, *Sämtliche Werke*, I, 694.
26   e.g. the ending of Heine's poem about a Parisian prostitute, 'Pomare': Heine, *Sämtliche Schriften*, ed. by Klaus Briegleb, 6 vols (Munich: Hanser, 1968–76), VI, 31.
27   *Hegel's Aesthetics*, trans. by T. M. Knox, 2 vols (Oxford: Clarendon Press, 1975), I. 393.
28   E. M. Butler, 'Pandits and Pariahs', p. 31.

marrying her.[29] Other commentators, however, have flatly denied that Goethe's poem has anything to do with Christianity.[30]

By this denial, such commentators at least avoid a problem that Butler seems innocently not to have noticed. For if the Bayadere corresponds to Mary Magdalene, then Mahadöh must correspond to Jesus. And if so, Goethe is independently hinting at a speculation that has recurred down the ages, and been voiced in the twentieth century by Robert Graves and in the twenty-first by Dan Brown: that Jesus, far from being the celibate person portrayed in the Gospels, really had sexual relations (whether marital or non-marital) with Mary Magdalene.[31] Mahadöh, as a god incarnate in human form, comes much closer than Jesus did to experiencing the full range of human life. So the poem asks to be read as a cheeky, only just implicit criticism of Christianity for its imperfectly physical version of incarnation. Neither Hegel, who assimilates the poem to Christianity and treats the Indian setting as merely superficial, nor Butler, acknowledges the poem's critical thrust, and many other commentators over the centuries have managed to ignore it.[32]

The associations with Jesus are strengthened in the next part of the poem. While in the source anecdote Devendra only pretended to be dead, Goethe makes it clear that Mahadöh, as a human being, really has died. The Bayadere cannot rouse him to life. The priests carry his body to be burnt. The Bayadere wants to practise suttee by being burnt with him, claiming that he is her husband, but the priests point out that he was not her husband and that she is merely a bayadere; her love for him counts for nothing in their eyes. In Sonnerat's anecdote, the bayadere's claims were rejected by unspecified persons, referred to impersonally only as 'one' ('man'). Goethe has given the story a powerful anticlerical twist by introducing the priests, giving them a prominent role, and presenting them as inhuman persons who refuse to recognize the possibility of love outside marriage. Their chorus, 'ohn' Erbarmen' [without pity], makes her even more distressed than she was before ('mehret ihres Herzen Not').

The suicide of the loving Bayadere prompts the resurrection of Mahadöh, who carries her to heaven in his arms. It is at least suggested, not that her suicide makes his resurrection possible, since he is after all a god and presumably omnipotent, but that she occasions it by thus demonstrating her faithfulness. Thus the Bayadere has some agency, some power of action. She recalls Gretchen, who in the last scene of *Faust I* effectively commits suicide by rejecting the escape route that Faust offers her, and thereby demonstrates her independence and resolve. It was only many years later that Goethe wrote the closing scene of *Faust II*, in which Gretchen's intercession turns out to have played a part in the redemption of Faust. So in 'Der Gott und die Bayadere' we have a hint of what will become a perennial theme in

29   Butler, p. 35; similarly Mecklenburg, p. 199.

30   e.g. Hartmut Laufhütte, 'Formulierungshilfe für Haustyrannen? Goethe Der Gott und die Bajadere', in *Gedichte und Interpretationen 3: Klassik und Romantik*, ed. by Wulf Segebrecht (Stuttgart: Reclam, 1984), pp. 117–43 (pp. 129, 141).

31   See Robert Graves, *King Jesus* (London: Cassell, 1946); Dan Brown, *The Da Vinci Code* (London: Bantam Press, 2002).

32   See the survey of critical comment by Mecklenburg, pp. 199–200.

German tragedy, the redemption of man by woman. Senta in Wagner's *The Flying Dutchman* redeems the Dutchman through her suicide; the death of Mieze in Alfred Döblin's *Berlin Alexanderplatz* is essential in inducing Franz Biberkopf to give up his criminal career. But in Goethe's poem there is a powerful Christian echo at the very end:

> Es freut sich die Gottheit der reuigen Sünder;
> Unsterbliche heben verlorene Kinder
> Mit feurigen Armen zum Himmel empor.[33]

These lines emphatically recall Jesus' parable of the lost sheep, which similarly ends with a general assertion: 'I say unto you, that likewise joy shall be in heaven over one sinner that repenteth, more than over ninety and nine just persons, which need no repentance' (Luke 15. 7).

The poem ends with a motif that occurs in Goethe's poetry several significant contexts: death and transcendence through fire. We find it at the close of a poem written a few days before 'Der Gott und die Bajadere', the ballad 'Die Braut von Corinth'. This ballad is much more explicitly anti-Christian. It is set early in the Christian era. A young pagan, coming from Athens to Corinth to meet his destined bride, finds that her parents have converted to Christianity, replacing the colourful diversity of paganism with gloomy subjection to a single God. The new religion too demands sacrifices, but not merely of oxen: her parents have compelled the young woman to accept perpetual celibacy as a sacrifice to the new God. Here Goethe draws on a familiar Enlightenment polemic against the institution of convents, of which the most famous example is Diderot's novel *La Religieuse*. Goethe and Schiller both knew this novel; in 1795 Schiller contemplated getting it translated and published in his journal *Die Horen*; and a German translation finally appeared in 1797, about the time when Goethe was writing this poem.[34] The young woman visits her bridegroom at night. He offers her bread and wine, the gifts of Ceres and Bacchus (a pagan counterpart to the Eucharist); she accepts the wine, and they make love, but after her mother has interrupted the proceedings the young woman reveals that she is dead and has returned in the form of a vampire. Having given her a lock of his hair, her bridegroom will sicken and die. Christianity appears as a cult of death. The only way to save the couple is described by the young woman in her last appeal to her mother:

> Höre, Mutter, nun die letzte Bitte:
> Einen Scheiterhaufen schichte du;
> Öffne meine bange kleine Hütte,
> Bring' in Flammen Liebende zur Ruh.
> Wenn der Funke sprüht,
> Wenn die Asche glüht,
> Eilen wir den alten Göttern zu.[35]

---

33 Goethe, *Sämtliche Werke*, I, 695.
34 Schiller, letter to Goethe, 29 November 1795, in *Der Briefwechsel zwischen Schiller und Goethe*, ed. by Emil Staiger (Frankfurt a.M.: Insel, 1966), p. 164; Mecklenburg, p. 198.
35 Goethe, *Sämtliche Werke*, I, 692.

A purifying death on a funeral pyre will purge the couple from the deadly pollution which, it is implied, Christianity has brought upon the world, and reunite them with the ancient gods.

Transcendence through fire features also in the later *West-östlicher Divan* (1819). The poem 'Vermächtniß altpersischen Glaubens' [Legacy of ancient Persian belief] celebrates the reverence paid by the ancient Persians and their descendants, the modern Parsees, to the sun and to fire, which, as Goethe knew from travelogues, they regarded as the sun's earthly counterpart. Here fire is a life-giving force which lights up the night and, in cooking, brings out the juices of animals and plants and makes them edible. But the most famous expression of this theme is the poem entitled 'Selige Sehnsucht', where the fatal attraction of a moth to a flame stands for humanity's desire to rise to a higher existence through a fiery death.

Commentators have been somewhat reluctant to recognize how sharply Goethe criticizes Christianity in 'Der Gott und die Bajadere' and its companion poem.[36] Goethe's attitude to religion was inevitably complex.[37] He favoured an undogmatic natural religion and rejected the intolerance he found in his friend Lavater, to whom he wrote that he was 'zwar kein Widerkrist, kein Unkrist aber doch ein dezidierter Nichtkrist'.[38] By this he means that he is not a Voltairean mocker of religion ('Widerkrist'), nor an immoral person ('Unkrist'), but indifferent to Christianity.[39] He objected to clerical authority, elaborate religious ceremonies, and the Christian devaluation of the body except as Jesus' suffering 'Jammerbild am Holze' [miserable image on the cross].[40] So the incarnation of Mahadöh asks to be read as a better alternative to the half-hearted incarnation taught by the Churches.

Amphitryon

Kleist's play about theophany, *Amphitryon*, adapted from the comedy of the same title by Molière, has a possible link with Wieland's 'Daphnidion'. About the time when Wieland was writing the story, early in 1803, Kleist, a friend of his son Ludwig, was staying in his house at Ossmannstedt outside Weimar. It is likely that he read 'Daphnidion' and that the motif of a quasi-divine figure appearing as an unscrupulous seducer lodged in his imagination. Another consequential piece of reading from this period can be documented. Kleist, together with Ludwig

36   See Mecklenburg, p. 199.

37   For useful overviews, see Wolfgang Binder, 'Grundformen der Säkularisation in den Werken Goethes, Schillers und Hölderlins', *Zeitschrift für deutsche Philologie*, 83 (1964), Sonderheft, 42–69; H. B. Nisbet, 'Religion and Philosophy', in *The Cambridge Companion to Goethe*, ed. by Lesley Sharpe (Cambridge: Cambridge University Press, 2002), pp. 219–31.

38   Letter to Lavater, 29 July 1782, in Goethe, *Sämtliche Werke*, XXIX: *Das erste Weimarer Jahrzehnt: Briefe, Tagebücher und Gespräche vom 7. November 1775 bis 2. September 1786*, ed. by Hartmut Reinhardt (1997), p. 436.

39   T. J. Reed, 'Goethe as Secular Icon', in *The Present Word: Culture, Society and the Site of Literature. Essays in Honour of Nicholas Boyle*, ed. by John Walker (London: Legenda, 2013), pp. 44–51 (p. 46).

40   Goethe, *Sämtliche Werke*, III: *West-östlicher Divan*, ed. by Hendrik Birus (1994), p. 509; cf. 'Das Tagebuch', in *Sämtliche Werke*, II, 847.

Wieland, also read Richardson's *Clarissa*. Ludwig recalled that they were absorbed by Clarissa's story for a whole week.[41] Although Clarissa never supposes her eventual seducer, Lovelace, to be divine, she does see in him a rescuer from the oppression of her family, and he provides a model of the untrustworthy rescuer whom we later find in Graf F. So in 'Daphnidion' and *Clarissa* we have two different narratives of seduction or attempted seduction, which entered Kleist's imagination and helped to shape his own works. The theme of the divine seducer reappears in *Amphitryon*, with Jupiter, instead of Apollo, playing the key role.

Kleist's drama, like Molière's original, presents a literal theophany. Jupiter, attended by Merkur [Mercury], descends to earth in order to make love to Alkmene while her husband Amphitryon is away at war. Since Alkmene is an impeccably faithful wife, Jupiter assumes the form of her husband, and persuades the sun-god to delay so that the night will last much longer than usual. Amphitryon's return then initiates a comedy of mistaken identity: Alkmene, thinking he has just left her after their rapturous night of love, is surprised to see him back so soon, whereupon Amphitryon, who has been away for five months, takes great offence at this casual and seemingly indifferent greeting. The confusion is heightened by the fact that Merkur assumes the guise of Amphitryon's servant Sosias. Confronted by Sosias, Merkur maintains that *he* is the real Sosias, confirms his claim by revealing (supernatural) knowledge of everything Sosias has done privately, and finally enforces it by beating Sosias up.

These and the succeeding events might seem, as they are in Molière, little more than a comedy inspired by Jupiter's notorious amorous adventures among mortals, and accompanied by a broadly humorous knockabout subplot centring on Sosias and Merkur. With Kleist, however, matters soon become much more intricate and more serious. Their interpretation has given rise to a controversy probably more extreme and more bitter than any other in the contested history of Kleist studies. On the one hand, we have Lawrence Ryan, who maintains that Jupiter's true purpose is educative.[42] Alkmene has an unnatural, unspontaneous view of love as simply part of her marital duty; by granting her a night of sexual ecstasy with a person she believes to be her husband, Jupiter educates her into an individual, erotic relationship with him. He is not only a sexual but a religious instructor: the long fifth scene of Act II, which is entirely Kleist's addition to Molière's original, is to be read as a lesson in theology.

Against Ryan's reading, Wolfgang Wittkowski maintains that the play enacts a Promethean revolt against the authority of the gods.[43] Jupiter is essentially exploitative and abusive. His arguments in II. 5 are a series of sophistries. He suppresses Alkmene's incipient revolt by finally promising Amphitryon a semi-

41 'Kleist und ich lasen hier die *Clarissa*, und lebten in und mit ihr ganze acht Tage', *Heinrich von Kleists Lebensspuren: Dokumente und Berichte der Zeitgenossen*, ed. by Helmut Sembdner (Munich: Hanser, 1996), p. 83.

42 Lawrence Ryan, 'Amphitryon: Doch ein Lustspielstoff!', in Claude David et al., *Kleist und Frankreich* (Berlin: Schmidt, 1969), pp. 83–121.

43 Wolfgang Wittkowski, 'Der neue Prometheus: Kleists *Amphitryon* zwischen Molière und Giraudoux', in David et al., *Kleist und Frankreich*, pp. 27–82.

divine son, named Hercules. Only Alkmene fails to accept this conclusion, but her distress is expressed only by her ambiguous 'Ach!' which is the play's final word. Subsequent interpretations of the play have tended to fall into two camps, labelled by Jeffrey Sammons 'Jupiterists' and 'Alkmenists'.[44] The camps are so far apart that one wonders how it is possible for people to read the same text in such different ways. 'Both read the Bible day and night, | But thou read'st black where I read white.'[45]

Although 'Promethean' may be going too far, the reading I mean to offer is close in spirit to Wittkowski's. I want to trace the emotional nuances of Jupiter's interaction with Alkmene. Suppose that a god who descends to earth turns out to be wicked, and wicked in an all-too-human way? Suppose he is emotionally needy and manipulative, exploiting mortals not just for his sexual but also for his emotional satisfaction, and ultimately not caring about the state in which he leaves his victims?

The material that Jupiter has to play with is Alkmene's love for her husband. She recalls that when the supposed Amphitryon first entered her room, he seemed even more handsome than usual. This is how she describes what was in fact a theophany:

> Du müßtest denn de Regung mir mißdeuten,
> Daß ich ihn schöner niemals fand als heut.
> Ich hätte für sein Bild ihn halten können,
> Für sein Gemälde, sieh, von Künstlershand,
> Dem Leben treu, ins Göttliche verzeichnet.[46]
> Er stand, ich weiß nicht, vor mir, wie im Traum,
> Und ein unsägliches Gefühl ergriff
> Mich meines Glücks, wie ich es nie empfunden,
> Als er mir strahlend, wie in Glorie, gestern
> Der hohe Sieger von Pharissa nahte.
> Er wars, Amphitryon, der Göttersohn!
> Nur schien er selber einer schon mir der
> Verherrlichten, ich hätt ihn fragen mögen,
> Ob er mir aus den Sternen niederstiege. (ll. 1189–1200)[47]

> [Do not misunderstand me when I say
> I never found him handsomer than now.

---

44   Jeffrey L. Sammons, 'Jupiterists and Alkmenists: *Amphitryon* as an example of how Kleist's texts read interpreters', in *A Companion to the Works of Heinrich von Kleist*, ed. by Bernd Fischer (Rochester, NY: Camden House, 2003), pp. 21–41.

45   'The Everlasting Gospel' (*c.* 1818), in William Blake, *Complete Writings*, ed. by Geoffrey Keynes (London: Oxford University Press, 1972), p. 748.

46   As Gerhard Kurz points out, 'verzeichnet' sounds negative: it can mean 'falsch, verzerrt, ungetreu zeichnen'. Kurz, ' "alter Vater Jupiter": Zu Kleists Drama *Amphitryon*', in *Gewagte Experimente und kühne Konstellationen: Kleists Werk zwischen Klassizismus und Romantik*, ed. by Christine Lubkoll und Günter Oesterle (Würzburg: Königshausen & Neumann, 2001), pp. 169–85 (p. 178). Hence my translation as 'distorted'.

47   Quotations are from Heinrich von Kleist, *Sämtliche Werke und Briefe*, ed. by Ilse-Maria Barth et al., 4 vols (Frankfurt a.M.: Deutscher Klassiker Verlag, 1989), identified wherever possible by line number.

> I could have taken him for his own image,
> His picture, by an artist, true to life
> And yet distorted to divinity.
> He stood before me, somehow, like a dream,
> And I had an unspeakable sensation
> Of happiness I never felt before,
> When yesterday Pharissa's lofty victor
> Approached me, radiant, as though in glory.
> It was Amphitryon, son of the gods,
> And yet he seemed already to have joined
> Those splendid beings, I'd have liked to ask
> If he descended to me from the stars.]

What Alkmene saw was a transfigured version of Amphitryon, and yet, such is her love for her husband, she is certain that it was him, differing only in degree from the Amphitryon she knows.

Jupiter's agenda has already been made clear. He does not just want Alkmene's body; he also wants her love. The trouble is that all her declarations of love refer, as far as she is concerned, to her husband. Their love-making, which she thinks took up only two hours, in fact lasted for seventeen hours, but Alkmene is so devoted to Amphitryon that she feels nothing remarkable in this superhuman prowess. So, when leaving her, Jupiter tries to drive a wedge between her erotic love and her wifely duty by asking:

> Ob den Gemahl du heut, dem du verlobt bist,
> Ob den Geliebten du empfangen hast? (ll. 456–57)

> [Was it the spouse to whom your troth is plighted,
> Was it the lover you received last night?]

When Alkmene refuses to admit any such distinction, Jupiter (in the guise, we must remember, of Amphitryon) disparages the husband and public figure Amphitryon as 'the fool who thinks he has a right to you', 'the Thebans' vain commander', 'that public idiot'. Alkmene takes these remarks for strange jokes that Amphitryon is making at his own expense (whereas in fact Jupiter is going as far as he dares in running down his emotional rival). She promises Jupiter that she will regard the 'Göttertag' [divine day] (l. 496) they have spent together as something special, set apart from the ordinary routine of their marriage.

However, Jupiter wants to go further. He has to break it to Alkmene that she has spent the night with someone other than Amphitryon, and to divert her love from Amphitryon to him, without making her feel guilty at committing adultery. She is already worried by some apparent jokes the visitor let slip in which he called himself her lover and even a thief. Worse still: he gave her a diadem, pillaged from the enemy, with an A (for Amphitryon) inscribed on it; but now, as both she and her servant Charis can see, the diadem instead bears a J. So, despite her love for Amphitryon, she admits it is possible that the visitor was an impostor and that she has unwittingly committed adultery.

The crucial scene is the following one (Act II, scene 5) between Alkmene and Jupiter, which is entirely Kleist's invention. Alkmene asks Jupiter for reassurance, confessing that she now has the horrible suspicion that someone other than Amphitryon has visited her. Being a dutiful wife, Alkmene is horrified by the idea that she might unwittingly have committed adultery, but in reply, Jupiter gives her a lesson in pantheism. For divinity is everywhere, pantheism is true, and since Jupiter is everything that exists, he must also be Amphitryon — so in sleeping with him, she has really slept with her husband: 'wer wäre außer mir, Geliebte?' [Who could exist apart from me, beloved?] (l. 1268). At the end of the play, Jupiter will assert this pantheism more boldly, proclaiming that he is Amphitryon and also everyone and everything else (ll. 2297–2300). For the present, Alkmene does not understand his lesson and is not reassured. She is now convinced that she has been deceived by an impostor. Jupiter now tries another argument, assuring her that she is *subjectively* innocent, and that the impostor was deceived, because he could obtain only her body, not her love. (This of course is an expression of Jupiter's own bitterness at finding Alkmene so loyal to her husband.) Her obstinacy at length induces him to reveal that her visitor was Jupiter himself. But, once again, Alkmene fails to react in the way he wants. Being not only a virtuous wife but a devout worshipper of the gods, she rebukes the supposed Amphitryon for imputing such a crime ('Frevel') to Jupiter. This word enrages Jupiter; he commands her to be silent, and upbraids her for failing to appreciate the glorious destiny of being chosen by Jupiter. To this bullying, Alkmene responds with sheer bafflement, but eventually she convinces herself that Amphitryon is generously inventing excuses for her and resolves nonetheless to leave him and hide her shame in some lonely place. Jupiter replies by pointing to the diadem that she has in her hand. This persuades Alkmene that she did a divine visitor, and that precisely because she was so faithful to her husband, he was obliged to assume Amphitryon's form in order to deceive her. So Alkmene is now much happier, and prepared to forget the 'pain' that Jupiter inflicted on her, if her marriage to Amphitryon can be restored to what it was.

Jupiuter is now back where he started. By telling the truth, he has only reinforced Alkmene's loyalty to her husband, while Jupiter himself is even further from being the recipient of her love — instead, he has caused her pain. So he attempts another method, suggesting to Alkmene that she may have offended Jupiter by her imperfect devotion. Perhaps, when she thought she was worshipping the god, she was really adoring the image of her husband? To the devout Alkmene, this suggestion is very upsetting, and eventually she promises to think only of Jupiter, not of Amphitryon, when praying:

> Gut, gut, du sollst mit mir zufrieden sein.
> Es soll in jeder ersten Morgenstunde
> Auch kein Gedanke fürder an dich denken:
> Jedoch nachher vergess ich Jupiter. (ll. 1486–89)

> [All right, all right, I'll do what makes you happy.
> Henceforth, when praying first thing every morning,
> I will not think a single thought of you:
> But after, Jupiter will be forgotten.]

This again is not what Jupiter wants to hear, so he tries another way of making her desire him for himself. Suppose Jupiter were to appear to her in his full glory ('in seinem vollen Glanze'), or even if he just touched her soul, would she not weep with disappointment at being unable to follow him to heaven? No, she wouldn't. If she could turn time back, and keep herself free from any contact with gods and heroes, she would be only too pleased. All she wants is ordinary life with her husband, and she wishes that the encounter with Jupiter had never happened. This response reduces Jupiter to despair, and he utters his only aside: 'Verflucht der Wahn, der mich hieher gelockt!' [Cursed be the madness that drew me hither!] (l. 1522). Since neither bullying nor temptation has worked, he becomes pathetic, asking Alkmene to sweeten Jupiter's lonely life with a little bit of love:

> Ach Alkmene!
> Auch der Olymp ist öde ohne Liebe.
> Was gibt der Erdenvölker Anbetung,
> Gestürzt in Staub, der Brust, der lechzenden?
> *Er* will geliebt sein, nicht ihr Wahn von ihm.
> In ew'ge Schleier eingehüllt,
> Möcht' er sich selbst in einer Seele spiegeln,
> Sich aus der Träne des Entzückens wiederstrahlen. (ll. 1518–25)

> [Oh, Alkmene!
> It's dreary on Olympus without love.
> The worship of the nations of the earth
> Can't satisfy the yearning in his breast.
> *He* wants their love, not their conception of him.
> Swathed in eternal veils,
> He'd like to be reflected in a soul,
> To see himself in an enraptured tear.]

It is impossible to tell how much this is mere pathetic oratory, how much Jupiter really does feel lonely on Olympus, but he undermines his own case by admitting his narcissism: he wants to be loved so that he can see his own image reflected back to him. There is again a suggestion that the god envies the ordinary life led by mortals, but also that he doesn't understand this ordinary life because he can't step outside his huge childish ego.

Jupiter's pathos has some effect on Alkmene. If she were singled out for the sacred duty of comforting the god, she would rise to the occasion. Jupiter presses further. If the god were actually embracing her, and Amphitryon suddenly appeared, what would she feel then? Alkmene still prefers her husband:

> Wenn du, der Gott, mich hier umschlungen hieltest,
> Und jetzo sich Amphitryon mir zeigte,
> Ja — dann so traurig würd ich sein, und wünschen,
> Daß er der Gott mir wäre, und daß du
> Amphitryon mir bliebst, wie du es bist.

> [If you, the god, here held me in your arms,
> And now Amphitryon appeared to me,
> Well, I'd be sad, and I would wish for him
> To be the god to me, while you remained
> Amphitryon for me, the way you are.]

Jupiter professes to be pleased with this answer, though he cannot really be. Commentators have differed about how to interpret his apparently positive response.[48] Most likely, seeing that the inflexibly faithful Alkmene cannot be persuaded to prefer him to her husband, he is putting a good face on a bad job.

Finally, Jupiter as Amphitryon appears alongside the real Amphitryon before Alkmene and all the Theban officers. Obliged to decide which is the real Amphitryon, they incline towards Jupiter but refer the final decision to Alkmene, who plumps for Jupiter and rejects the real Amphitryon as a clumsy impostor who has practised a 'schnöde List' [vile deception] on her. Jupiter crowns the confusion by declaring that Amphitryon is Amphitryon but that he too is Amphitryon, with the pantheistic argument that, as the god, he is not only Amphitryon but everyone and everything else. There is nothing classical about this claim; it reads more like a parody of the modern pantheism associated with Spinoza, for whom God was equivalent to nature. Spinoza's pantheism had already been ridiculed by Pierre Bayle. If everything real is only a modification of God, Bayle argued, then one should not say 'the Germans have killed ten thousand Turks' but 'God modified into Germans has killed God modified into ten thousand Turks'.[49]

Before anyone can raise such objections, however, Jupiter manifests himself in his true form, in a real theophany, and everyone falls flat on their faces, apart from Amphitryon, who is supporting the swooning Alkmene. Jupiter then pronounces his decree: he has had a good time in Amphitryon's house, and Amphitryon will in future enjoy fame and have his dearest wish fulfilled. Amphitryon wishes for a heroic son, and gets his wish: he will have a son called Hercules, who will accomplish superhuman tasks and finally ascend to heaven. Jupiter specifically says 'a son will be born to you' ('Dir wird ein Sohn geboren werden'), whereas his counterpart in Molière only says that a son will be born 'in your house' ('chez toi').[50] The effect is to make Amphitryon look like a gullible cuckold, since obviously the son will not be his but Jupiter's. All this while Alkmene's state is apparently of no concern to Jupiter, but only to Amphitryon, who asks anxiously 'Alkmene!' and receives only her famously ambiguous 'Ach!' which closes the play.

One conclusion to be drawn from Kleist's version of these events is that divine intervention is unwelcome. Mortals would rather be left alone to get on with their ordinary lives. Amphitryon and Alkmene are perfectly happy together; she idolizes her husband, and he, though a bit pompous, is in the last scene the only person to show concern for her. Wittkowski even calls him 'a great lover' ('ein großer Liebender'), which may be over-generous but at least points in the right direction.[51] Jupiter intervenes in their lives, not simply for physical pleasure, but for the more

48   See Wittkowski, p. 50: 'Er macht gute Miene zum bösen Spiel'; Anthony Stephens thinks that either Jupiter is impressed by Alkmene's persistence, or 'he has consistently pretended that all his defeats are really wins, and now does so again'; *Heinrich von Kleist: The Dramas and Stories* (Oxford: Berg, 1994), p. 94.

49   Bayle, 'Spinoza', Note N, *Dictionnaire historique et critique*, 4 vols (Amsterdam: Brunel, etc., 1730), IV, 261.

50   Molière, *Amphitryon*, in *Œuvres complètes*, ed. by Georges Couton, 2 vols (Paris: Gallimard, 1971), II, 441.

51   Wittkowski, p. 53, cf. Kurz p. 171.

interesting reason (assuming we can believe his protestations) that he feels lonely and wants to receive the love of a mortal directed towards himself, not to the more or less inadequate conception of him that mortals inevitably have. To extort a declaration of love, he resorts to all manner of emotional manipulation and does not scruple to break apart a happy marriage, making up for his disruption afterwards by means of a bribe in the form of Hercules.

The entry of the divine into human life readily calls to mind the Christian story. Jupiter's announcement to Amphitryon calls to mind the annunciation made by the archangel Gabriel to Mary (Luke 1. 26–38). Goethe spoke of Kleist's 'Deutung der Fabel in Christliche, in die Überschattung der Maria vom Heiligen Geist' [Christian interpretation of the fable, into the overshadowing of Mary by the Holy Ghost], alluding to the Bible verse: 'The Holy Ghost shall come upon thee, and the power of the Highest shall overshadow thee' (Luke 1. 35).[52] Kleist's friend Adam Müller, a Catholic convert, who arranged for the play's publication, wrote to Friedrich Gentz: 'Der Amphitryon handelt ja wohl ebensogut von der unbefleckten Empfängnis der heiligen Jungfrau, als von dem Geheimnis der Liebe überhaupt'] *Amphitryon* is just as much about the immaculate conception of the Holy Virgin as about the mystery of love in general].[53] He associated it not with the virgin birth of Jesus but with the immaculate conception of the Virgin, a concept that was much debated in the Middle Ages; it was affirmed by the Council of Basel in 1439, became widespread from the sixteenth century on, and would later be proclaimed as a dogma by Pope Pius X's bull 'Ineffabilis Deus' in 1854. More generally, Gerhard Kurz has noticed how much Kleist Christianized the classical material:

> Tatsächlich hat Kleist den antiken Mythos synkretistisch ins Christliche gedeutet: Die mythische Zeugung eines göttlichen Kindes durch den Gott und eine irdische Frau wird mit vielen Anspielungen und Zitaten auf das christliche Muster der Menschwerdung Gottes bezogen. Angespielt wird z.B. auf die unbefleckte Empfängnis von Maria (V. 1285f.); auf die Verkündigung von Jesus in Jupiters Worten, "Dir wird ein Sohn geboren werden, | Deß Namen Herkules". (V, 2335f.) Aus der christlichen Religion kommen Wörter wie Offenbarung, Teufel, Sünderin, Heilige, Klause, Götze, Abgott, Geschöpf, Gott, Vater. Jupiter sagt einmal: "Ist hier nicht Wunder alles, was sich zeigt?" (V. 1387)[54]

> [Kleist has in fact put a syncretistic Christian interpretation on the classical myth. The mythical generation of a divine child by the god and an earthly woman is related through many allusions to the Christian model of God's incarnation. Reference is made, for example, to Mary's immaculate conception and to the Annunciation in Jupiter's words 'A son will be born to you whose name is Hercules'. The Christian religion supplies words such as revelation, devil, sinner, saint, cell, graven image, idol, creature, god, father. Jupiter says at one point: 'Is not everything we see a miracle?']

52 Goethe, conversation recorded by Riemer, in *Sämtliche Werke*, XXXII: *Napoleonische Zeit: Briefe, Tagebücher und Gespräche vom 10. Mai 1805 bis 6. Juni 1816*, Teil I: *Von Schillers Tod bis 1811*, ed. by Rose Unterberger (1993), p. 205. Also quoted in Kleist, *Sämtliche Werke und Briefe*, I, 878.

53 Quoted in Kleist, *Sämtliche Werke und Briefe*, I, 873.

54 Kurz, p. 170.

But it would be a mistake to put a pious or proto-Catholic interpretation on the events and thereby miss the element of satire. For while Gabriel made the annunciation to Mary, the future mother of Jesus, Jupiter makes his to Amphitryon, the prospective father. (In St Matthew's Gospel, too, the annunciation is made not to Mary but to Joseph, in a dream: Matt. 1. 20.) So Amphitryon looks like a cuckold who has been bought off and has forgotten that the mother might have a view on the matter. Kleist thereby links up with the medieval tradition of portraying St Joseph as a semi-comic character, a willing cuckold.[55]

The main thrust of the satire, however, is against Jupiter. As in Goethe's *Iphigenie*, the gods' intervention in human life is cruel and mischievous. Goethe himself observed that Alkmene was left in a painful situation and Amphitryon in a cruel one.[56] Thomas Mann in 1928 noted the contrast between Jupiter's duplicity ('Doppelzüngigkeit') and Alkmene's sincerity.[57] Wittkowski maintains that Jupiter's final operatic triumph is placed 'ins Licht einer scharf gezielten, satirischen Polemik gegen die religiöse Autorität' [a sharply focused satirical polemic against religious authority].[58] Hans Robert Jauss calls Jupiter a 'genius malignus' or evil spirit who puts Alkmene through a series of emotional tortures.[59] Peter Michelsen similarly remarks that Jupiter shows a 'Grausamkeit, wie sie nur eines Gottes würdig ist' [a cruelty worthy only of a god].[60] Rather than an ultimately benign educator, we have here an emotionally needy and selfish god who exploits mortals for his sensual pleasure but is uneasily conscious of his estrangement from the shared emotional life of humanity and uses his power to disrupt the relationships in which he can have no part.

Divine Radiance in Kleist

Perhaps the best-known case of the supposed superhuman visitant occurs in *Die Marquise von O...* As the fortress which her father commands falls to its assailants, and the Marquise is about to be gang-raped by a group of soldiers, a rescuer, Count F..., appears who repels them and carries the Marquise to safety. To her he seems

55   J. Huizinga, *The Waning of the Middle Ages*, trans. by F. Hopman (Harmondsworth: Penguin, 1955), p. 164. Hopman's 'a comic type' slightly mistranslates Huizinga's 'een half-komische figuur'; *Herfsttij der Middeleeuwen* [1919] (n.p. [Amsterdam]: Olympus, 2011), p. 223. See Martin W. Walsh, 'Divine Cuckold / Holy Fool: The Comic Image of Joseph in the English "Troubles" Play', in *England in the Fourteenth Century: Proceedings of the 1985 Harlaxton Symposium*, ed. by W. M. Ormrod (Woodbridge: The Boydell Press, 1986), pp. 278–97. The cuckold Joseph reappears in Joyce's *Ulysses* (1922) as 'God's little joke': James Joyce, *Ulysses*, ed. by Jeri Johnson, World's Classics (Oxford: Oxford University Press, 1993), p. 79.

56   Goethe, *Sämtliche Werke*, XXXII, 205.

57   Thomas Mann, 'Kleists *Amphitryon*: Eine Wiedereroberung', in his *Gesammelte Werke*, 13 vols (Frankfurt a.M.: Fischer, 1974), IX, 187–228 (p. 208).

58   Wittkowski, p. 35.

59   Hans Robert Jauss, 'Von Plautus bis Kleist: *Amphitryon* im dialogischen Prozeß der Arbeit am Mythos', in *Kleists Dramen: Neue Interpretationen*, ed. by Walter Hinderer (Stuttgart: Reclam, 1981), pp. 114–43 (pp. 136–37).

60   Peter Michelsen, 'Umnachtung durch das Licht. Zu Kleists *Amphitryon*', *Kleist-Jahrbuch* (1996), 123–39 (p. 126).

an angel sent from heaven. But before he restores her to her family, and while she is unconscious, something else happens at which the text drops only a hint, admittedly a broad one. A few months later, the Marquise finds herself inexplicably pregnant. She places an advertisement in the newspaper asking the perpetrator to make himself known on a certain date. When the day comes, who should appear but Count F... The Marquise rejects him with horror, declaring that she did not expect a devil. Ultimately, by roundabout means, the two are reconciled; the Count is allowed to marry her, on condition that he does not live with her; eventually, thanks to his impeccable behaviour, this condition is relaxed, they have a large family, and the Marquise confesses to her husband that she would not have thought him a devil if she had not initially taken him for an angel.

In part, Kleist is adapting and rewriting an episode from Lessing's *Nathan der Weise*, the pre-eminent drama of the German Enlightenment.[61] At the start of the play, Nathan returns from a journey to find that in his absence his (adoptive) daughter Recha has been rescued from a fire by a young man, a Knight Templar, who has rejected all attempts to thank him. Recha's gratitude to her deliverer has grown into erotic passion, which, lacking an outlet, issues in the emotional, semi-hysterical state of delusion that the Enlightenment called 'Schwärmerei'. Nathan tries, with some success, to reason Recha out of her belief. He points out that while it is unlikely that a Christian Knight Templar should be at large in the Jerusalem ruled by Saladin, the intervention of an angel is even more unlikely. Although Kleist's Marquise, already a widow with two children, must be a good deal older than Recha, the story portrays her as almost equally naïve. On hearing an inaccurate rumour that Graf F... has been killed on the battlefield, crying as he falls 'Julietta! This bullet avenges you!', she remarks how odd it is that the woman thus apostrophized should have the same name as she does. The rape itself is signalled to the alert reader by Kleist's punctuation. After Count F... has carried the Marquise to safety, we are told:

> Hier — traf er, da bald darauf ihre erschrockenen Frauen erschienen, Anstalten, einen Arzt zu holen; versicherte, indem er sich den Hut aufsetzte, daß sie sich bald erholen würde; und kehrte in den Kampf zurück.

> [Then — the officer instructed the Marquise's frightened servants, who presently arrived, to send for a doctor; he assured them that she would son recover, replaced his hat and returned to the fighting.][62]

How had his hat fallen off? Evidently during the sexual act indicated by the dash. When the story was first published, in February 1808 in the magazine *Phöbus*, the dash was no mere line but a great thick bar that in itself was bound to attract the reader's attention.[63] The story therefore is not a mystery story except for the

61   On Kleist's rewriting of Lessing, see Helmut J. Schneider, 'The Facts of Life: Kleist's Challenge to Enlightenment Humanism (Lessing)', in *A Companion to the Works of Heinrich von Kleist*, pp. 141–63.

62   Heinrich von Kleist, *The Marquise of O— and Other Stories*, trans. by David Luke, ed. by Nigel Reeves (Harmondsworth: Penguin, 1978), p. 70.

63   Jürgen Stenzel, *Zeichensetzung: Stiluntersuchungen an deutscher Prosadichtung* (Göttingen: Vandenhoeck & Ruprecht, 1966), p. 64.

unsuspecting Marquise; the attentive reader is immediately placed in a position of superior knowledge. Thus the collusion between author and reader reproduces the structure of the 'Zote' or dirty joke in which a male teller and a male hearer share a joke at the expense of an absent woman.

As this example indicates, there are (at least) two incongruous discourses at work in Kleist's story. One discourse concerns extremes of good and evil. The same person, Graf F..., is angelic as a rescuer and devilish as a rapist. Another discourse deals with sexual matters in a down-to-earth, indeed earthy way. Both discourses are juxtaposed when, the Marquise having been banished from her family home to a country estate, her mother resolves to test whether she has really been guilty, as her father thinks, of an illicit sexual liaison. She visits the Marquise and spins her a yarn to the effect that her rapist was really the servant Leopardo. The Marquise promptly recalls how she once woke from a midday nap and saw Leopardo walking away from her divan, so she concludes that he must indeed be the perpetrator. Knowing that her story is false, her mother, convinced of the Marquise's innocence, asserts it in the most high-flown terms: 'you are purer than an angel'.[64] They return home, and on the way they make many jokes about Leopardo, who drives their carriage: 'the Marquise's mother said she noticed how her daughter blushed every time she looked at his broad shoulders'.[65] Clearly the Marquise's angelic purity doesn't prevent her from wondering about the sexual potency of the burly Leopardo, whose name moreover significantly conflates 'Leopoldo', a plausible name for somebody who, as he does, comes from the partly Italian-speaking Tyrol, with the animal associations of 'leopard'.[66]

In several of Kleist's later plays, characters perceive one another as godlike. In these apparent theophanies, the adored object is perceived as bathed in radiant light, for which the word 'Glanz' is used. As in *Die Marquise von O...*, there is a contrast between perception and reality, but the contrast takes a different form in each play. The simplest case is *Das Käthchen von Heilbronn*, which is categorized by its subtitle as 'ein großes historisches Ritterschauspiel' [a great historical drama of chivalry], but is really a dramatic fairy-tale set in medieval Germany. Käthchen, daughter of an armourer in Heilbronn, becomes enamoured of Count Wetter von Strahl the instant she sees him, and follows him around with dog-like devotion. The Count's names are significant: 'Wetter' can mean 'thunderstorm', and 'Strahl' means 'ray' or 'beam'; contemporary theories concerning magnetism and electricity are thereby invoked to gesture towards an up-to-date explanation for her attraction. The Count meanwhile is also in love with Käthchen. Each has dreamt about the other. The Count, however, cannot confess his love because he is betrothed to the noble Kunigunde von Thurneck. In the course of the action, Kunigunde's castle is set on fire by attackers; Kunigunde is chiefly concerned about a picture, given her by the Count, which is locked in her desk; the devoted Käthchen enters the burning building and rescues the picture thanks to the protection of a cherub who

64   Kleist, *The Marquise of O—*, p. 104.
65   Kleist, *The Marquise of O—*, pp. 104–05.
66   See Heinz Politzer, 'Der Fall der Frau Marquise: Beobachtungen zu Kleists *Die Marquise von O...*', *Deutsche Vierteljahrsschrift*, 51 (1977), 98–128 (pp. 100–01).

makes a brief appearance on stage. Kunigunde, disappointed that Käthchen has not been burnt alive, tries but fails to poison her. Finally Käthchen is revealed to be the illegitimate daughter of the Emperor, and hence a suitable match for the Count; the play ends with their marriage, while Kunigunde departs vowing revenge. Here, because it is a fairy-tale, the visionary transfiguration of the beloved person is allowed to be a version of the truth.

Things are very different in *Penthesilea*, which Kleist famously described as a contrasting companion-piece to *Käthchen*. 'Denn wer das Käthchen liebt,' he wrote to the Austrian dramatist Heinrich von Collin, 'dem kann die Penthesilea nicht ganz unbegreiflich sein, sie gehören ja wie das + und das — der Algebra zusammen und sind ein und dasselbe Wesen, nur unter den entgegengesetzten Beziehungen gedacht.'[67] ['For anyone who loves Käthchen cannot wholly fail to understand Penthesilea; they belong together like plus and minus in algebra, only in opposed relations.'] If Käthchen pursues Count von Strahl, so Penthesilea pursues the Greek warrior Achilles. But where Käthchen is submissive, Penthesilea, Queen of the Amazons, is aggressive. The rule of the Amazon state is that every year the women make war on a different nation in order to capture men and take them back to the Amazon capital Themiscyra. There, at the annual Feast of Roses, the prisoners copulate with their captors and impregnate them, after which they are sent away with presents. Amazons are supposed to choose their partners at random, but Penthesilea's mother, on her death-bed, told her to single out Achilles. So when the Amazons intervene in the Trojan War, not to support either side but for purposes which the Greeks find wholly incomprehensible, Penthesilea does her best to capture Achilles. Finally, in the fifteenth of the play's twenty-four scenes, they get the chance to talk. Penthesilea is under the illusion that she has captured Achilles, but in fact he has followed her into the Amazon camp out of curiosity about this magnificent female warrior whose actions seem to have no rational motive. As he admits, she seems to him like a radiant apparition from another world:

> O du, die eine Glanzerscheinung mir,
> Als hätte sich das Aetherreich eröffnet,
> Herabsteigst, Unbegreifliche, wer bist du?
> Wie nenn ich dich, wenn meine eigne Seele
> Sich, die entzückte, fragt, wem sie gehört? (Scene 15, ll. 1805–13)

> [O you, who like the vision of a dream,
> As if the realms of aether opened wide,
> Stranger than strange, descend to me, who are you?
> How shall I name your name when my own soul
> Enraptured asks to whom it now belongs?][68]

By way of answer, Penthesilea explains to him the origin and constitution of the Amazon state, and how she has transgressed its laws by choosing him as her partner. Although she had heard much about Achilles' heroic deeds, the actual sight of him

---

67 Kleist, letter to Heinrich von Collin, 8 December 1808, *Sämtliche Werke und Briefe*, IV, 424.
68 *Penthesilea*, in *Five German Tragedies*, trans. by F. J. Lamport (Harmondsworth: Penguin, 1969), p. 380.

surpassed her expectations. She is no less dazzled by him than he by her:

> PENTHESILEA.   Wie aber ward mir,
> O Freund, als ich dich selbst erblickte — !
> Als du mir im Skamandros-Thal erschienst,
> Von den Heroen deines Volks umringt,
> Ein Tagsstern unter bleichen Nachtgestirnen!
> So müßt' es mir gewesen sein, wenn er
> Unmittelbar, mit seinen weißen Rossen,
> Von dem Olymp herabgedonnert wäre,
> Mars selbst, der Kriegsgott, seine Braut zu grüßen!
> Geblendet stand ich, als du jetzt entwichen,
> Von der Erscheinung da — wie wenn zur Nachtzeit
> Der Blitz vor einen Wandrer fällt, die Pforten
> Elisiums, des glanzerfüllten, rasselnd,
> Vor einem Geist sich öffnen und verschließen. (Scene 15, ll. 2203–16)

> [But what then must I feel,
> O friend, when you yourself at last I saw!
> When in Scamander's valley you appeared,
> Surrounded by the heroes of your nation,
> Day-star amid the paler stars of night!
> It could not have been otherwise if he
> Himself had come with his white chariot-team,
> Driving in thunder from Olympus' heights,
> Ares, the god of war, to greet his bride!
> Dazzled I stood, when you escaped from me,
> By such an apparition — as at night
> When lightning strikes before a wanderer,
> The gates of bright Elysium with din
> Fly open for a spirit, and are closed.][69]

The word 'dazzled' sums up Penthesilea's tragedy. Endowed with exceptionally powerful emotions and imagination, she is not content with ordinary life — and it must be stressed in passing that the Amazon state, however extraordinary, is presented by Kleist as a well-functioning and civilized society based on a successful revolt against oppression.[70] Emotionally volatile, she is so much governed by her imagination that she often misperceives the world around her. No wonder her anxious and loyal friend Prothoe says to her:

> Penthesilea! O du Träumerin!
> In welchen fernen Glanzgefilden schweift
> Dein Geist umher [...]?
>
> [Penthesilea! What is it you dream?
> In what far distant shining realm now dwells
> Your spirit [...]?][71]

69 *Five German Tragedies*, p. 392.

70 For this view, a minority one among Kleist's commentators, see Ruth Angress, 'Kleist's Nation of Amazons', in *Beyond the Eternal Feminine*, ed. by Susan L. Cocalis and Kay Goodman (Stuttgart: Heinz, 1982), pp. 99–134.

71 *Five German Tragedies*, p. 371.

The dazzling light of her imagination, used to 'Glanzgefilden' [shining or radiant realms], blinds her to reality. She cannot see that although Achilles shows signs of a better self in conversation with her, he is really a coarse-grained person, unscrupulous and murderous. His plan is to let her capture him and go off with her to Themiscyra for a few months, after which he fancies, with no justification, that she will be willing to give up her warrior identity and accompany him to Greece as his queen. When he issues a challenge to Penthesilea, she, unaware of its ulterior motive, feels insulted and arrives on the scene with dogs and elephants which Achilles naively imagines to be tame beasts that will eat out of his hand. The dénouement is very different: Penthesilea, temporarily demented, flings herself on him and joins with her dogs in tearing him to pieces and devouring his flesh.

In this unlikely place we may have another reminiscence of Lessing. The scene — only reported, not presented on stage — is like the realization of the fantasy expressed by Countess Orsina in *Emilia Galotti* when she imagines all the Prince's discarded mistresses banding together like Maenads and tearing him to pieces:

> Ha! (*wie in der Entzückung*) welch eine himmlische Phantasie! Wann wir einmal alle — wir, das ganze Heer der Verlassenen — wir alle in Bacchantinnen, in Furien verwandelt, wenn wir alle ihn unter uns hätten, ihn unter uns zerrissen, zerfleischten, sein Eingeweide durchwühlten — um das Herz zu finden, das der Verräter einer jeden versprach und keiner gab! Ha! das sollte ein Tanz werden! das sollte![72]

> [Ah! [*as if in ecstasy*] what a heavenly fantasy! If we one day — all of us, his victims — a whole army of deserted women — transformed into Bacchantes, into furies — if we could have him in our midst, tear him to pieces, dismember him, hunt through his entrails to find the heart that he promised to every one of us, the traitor, and gave to none! Ah! what a dance that would be!][73]

The violence that was latent in Lessing, expressed only in horrific fantasies by a woman on the verge of insanity, has in Kleist become real and is acted out by another woman who alternates between reason and madness.

In *Penthesilea*, then, the visionary power to see reality transfigured in quasi-divine radiance is the gift of an exceptional person, but a gift that tragically debars her from perceiving the imperfect world around her. In Kleist's last play, *Prinz Friedrich von Homburg*, the visionary power is again the gift of an unusual individual, and seems likely to prove a fatal delusion, till Kleist at the end stages a utopian, consciously artificial reconciliation between vision and reality. The play is Kleist's considered response to the present situation of Prussia, which, after humiliating defeats by Napoleon's troops at the battles of Jena and Auerstedt in 1806, was under French occupation. Kleist's first reactions took the form of bloodthirsty patriotic poems, pamphlets, and the drama *Die Hermannsschlacht*, which is close to the more extreme wing of the Prussian reform movement in its advocacy of resistance to the occupying forces by all possible means irrespective of humanity or morality. By

---

72 *Emilia Galotti*, in Gotthold Ephraim Lessing, *Werke*, ed. by Herbert G. Göpfert et al., 8 vols (Munich: Hanser, 1970–79), II, 189–90.

73 *Emilia Galotti*, in *Five German Tragedies*, p. 89.

1810 Kleist's patriotic frenzy had abated somewhat. He shared the views of his friend Adam Müller who argued in *Elemente der Staatskunst* [*Elements of Statecraft*] (1809) that a reformed Prussian state should strike a balance between impersonal law and patriotic emotion.[74] *Prinz Friedrich von Homburg* offers an idealized model of a united Prussia, in which the visionary patriotism of the Prince is finally reconciled with the astute statecraft of the Elector.

In the huge secondary literature on *Prinz Friedrich von Homburg*, there is a division similar to that which divides commentators on *Amphitryon* into Jupiterists and Alkmenists. Many would see the Elector as a wise and fatherly leader who educates the headstrong young Prince and shows him how to channel his patriotic enthusiasm into effective action. A minority of critics — of whom I am one — find the Elector to be a flawed figure who himself learns in the course of the play that statecraft is not enough to rally a patriotic community.[75]

Although *Prinz Friedrich von Homburg* centres on the battle of Fehrbellin in 1675, when Prussian forces defeated the Swedes, its opening scene is strikingly incongruous with the military background. The Prince — who in historical reality was forty-two, married for the second time, and had a wooden leg (still on display in the palace at Bad Homburg) — is here presented as a young man who shares with Penthesilea a dangerously powerful imagination. As the curtain rises we see him in a sleepwalking state, plaiting a wreath, in a French-style formal garden behind the mansion of Fehrbellin. Behind him, on a staircase leading down from the mansion, the Elector and many members of the Prussian court are watching him in astonishment. They include Princess Natalie, whom the Prince has met only briefly. Intrigued, despite himself, by the Prince's strange state, the Elector takes the wreath from him, puts his own chain round it, and hands it to Natalie, whereupon the Prince rises and follows Natalie with outstretched arms, whispering that she is his 'bride', and seizes her glove. The Elector and his court retreat in consternation, leaving the Prince alone with his friend Count Hohenzollern. On regaining his senses, the Prince describes a dream:

> Welch einen sonderbaren Traum träumt ich?! —
> Mir war, als ob, von Gold und Silber strahlend
> Ein Königsschloß sich plötzlich öffnete,
> Und hoch von seiner Marmorramp' herab,
> Der ganze Reigen zu mir niederstiege,
> Der Menschen, die mein Busen liebt:
> Der Kurfürst und die Fürstin und die — dritte,
> — Wie heißt sie schon?

---

74   See Klaus Peter, 'Für ein anderes Preußen: Romantik und Politik in Kleists *Prinz Friedrich von Homburg*', *Kleist-Jahrbuch* 1992, pp. 95–125.

75   For surveys of research, see Fritz Hackert, 'Kleists *Prinz Friedrich von Homburg* in der Nachkriegs-Interpretation', *LiLi*, 3 (1973), 53–80; Bernd Hamacher, ' "Darf ichs mir deuten, wie es mir gefällt?" 25 Jahre *Homburg*-Forschung zwischen Rehistorisierung und Dekonstruktion (1973–1998)', *Heilbronner Kleist-Blätter*, 6 (1999), 9–67. I must acknowledge a particular debt to John M. Ellis, *Kleist's 'Prinz Friedrich von Homburg': A Critical Study* (Berkeley: University of California Press, 1970), which first helped me to understand this play.

[What a strange dream I dreamt!
I thought a royal palace, gleaming bright
With gold and silver, opened suddenly,
And down its lofty marble stairway came
Down to me the entire assembled throng,
The people whom my bosom loves:
Both the Elector and his princess, and
The third — what is her name?]

Waking, he cannot remember Natalie's name, but in his unconscious he is already in love with her. He continues to recount events as a transfigured version of reality, mentioning especially the 'Kurfürst, mit der Stirn des Zeus' [the Elector with the brow of Zeus]. The stairway leading down from the mansion seemed to stretch up to 'the gate of heaven'. Evidently the Prince's imagination is filled with dreams of patriotic devotion, heroism, affection, and romantic love.

The reality which occupies most of the rest of the play is considerably different. The Prince's imagination, again like Penthesilea's, makes him less effective than he should be on the battlefield. He fails to listen properly to the battle orders, which require him to remain with his cavalry in reserve and to attack only when the Swedish enemy is already in flight, in order to turn their retreat into a rout. Carried away by patriotic enthusiasm, he charges prematurely, so that the victory is less than complete. The Elector in *Prinz Friedrich von Homburg* — based on Friedrich Wilhelm (1620–88), the Great Elector — is both an inspiring leader and a Machiavellian politician. Not yet knowing who led the charge prematurely, the Elector declares that the culprit, whoever he may be, must be executed for disobeying orders. On learning that it is the Prince, his relative, he stands by his principles. This inflexibility provokes a mutiny among his officers, one of whom, Colonel Kottwitz, rebukes him for his 'kurzsicht'ge Staatskunst', his short-sighted and over-abstract conduct of affairs.[76] The play invites us to see the Elector as cold and mechanistic in his execution of justice — rather as he insists on sticking to his preconceived battle plan irrespective of changing circumstances on the battlefield.

The Elector is not only rigid, but also a Machiavellian in the sense of being amoral and unscrupulous. Another relative, the strange, Mephistophelean character Hohenzollern, suggests to the Prince that the Elector may have political reasons for wanting him out of the way. An ambassador has arrived from the Swedes with an offer of peace, to be sealed by a dynastic marriage of a Swedish prince to the Princess Natalie. Natalie is said to object to the match because she has set her heart on somebody else, and the Elector has reason to believe that that person is the Prince. Is Hohenzollern right in his suspicions? The play does not allow us to be absolutely sure. But when Natalie goes to the Elector to plead for the Prince's life, she begs him not to insist on a marriage which will require the death of the Prince as a sacrifice, and the Elector does not disclaim such intentions. Finally the Elector resolves the difficulty with apparent statesmanlike wisdom. He hands responsibility over to the Prince. If the Prince really thinks the sentence passed on him is unjust, he will be set free. The Prince concludes that the sentence is just and announces

76 Kleist, *Sämtliche Werke und Briefe*, II, 632.

his intention to die as a sacrifice to the laws of war. Thus, if the Elector is really a Machiavellian who wants rid of the Prince, he is close to achieving his purpose without incurring blame, because the Prince himself proclaims publicly that he deserves and wants to die.

However, if the Elector is a Machiavellian, he also has another, emotional side which is not under his control and interferes with his responsibilities. In the opening scene, where we see the Prince sleepwalking, the Elector is so intrigued that he draws Natalie into the action to see what the Prince will do. At the battle the Elector unwisely rides on a conspicuous white horse, and his life is only saved because an officer asks to ride the white horse instead and is himself killed, mistaken for the Elector. In Act v, the mischievous Hohenzollern presents evidence that the Prince's culpable action was in fact the fault of the Elector, since if the Elector had not encouraged the dreams of love and victory that the Prince revealed when sleepwalking, the Prince would not have been distracted when the battle plan was being announced and would not have disobeyed orders. The Elector ridicules this argument, but nevertheless seems affected by it, as well he might. For Hohenzollern reveals the Elector as a type of figure that occurs elsewhere in Kleist, the guilty judge. He is another, more dignified version of Judge Adam in *Der zerbrochene Krug*, who judges the case of the broken jug and tries to conceal the fact that he himself broke the jug when scrambling out of a young woman's bedroom window. In the background we can see the pattern of a Shakespeare play that is considered a stimulus for Kleist's drama, namely *Measure for Measure*, which shows us both the corrupt judge Angelo and the 'old fantastical duke of dark corners' who governs Vienna in an eccentric fashion. I have not yet seen it pointed out that the impish Hohenzollern resembles the mischievous character Lucio who talks about the Duke's weaknesses and may not always be wrong.[77]

Going, as he thinks, to his execution, the Prince shows that he fully retains his power of imaginative transfiguration, signalled by the word 'Glanz' [radiance]. His dreams of glory have been transferred to the next world:

> Nun, o Unsterblichkeit, bist du ganz mein!
> Du strahlst mir, durch die Binde meiner Augen,
> Mit Glanz der tausendfachen Sonne zu!

> [Now, immortality, you're fully mine!
> And through the blindfold on my eyes you shine
> A thousand times more radiant than the sun!]

Meanwhile, the Elector, having resolved to spare his life, has not only torn up the death-sentence but re-staged the setting with which the play opened. The Prince finds himself back in the French-style garden, with the Elector and all his court on the stairway, and torchlight providing the nearest possible approximation to the radiance he imagines. This time the Elector gives the wreath and chain to Natalie, who descends the stair, gives them to the Prince, and places his hand on her heart.

---

77   *Measure for Measure*, IV. 3. 152, in *William Shakespeare, The Complete Works*, ed. by Peter Alexander (London and Glasgow: Collins, 1951), p. 107. See Meta Corssen, *Kleist und Shakespeare* (Weimar: Duncker, 1930).

Not surprisingly, the Prince faints, but he is awakened by the thunder of cannon and the shouts of all present hailing him as the hero of Fehrbellin. Still puzzled, he asks Colonel Kottwitz whether it is all a dream, to which Kottwitz replies: 'Ein Traum, was sonst?' [A dream, what else?]. And of course it *is* a dream, that is, a reconciliation of ardent patriotism with rational statecraft, possible only in fiction. Nevertheless, the fiction is intended as an ideal to strive towards. In *Prinz Friedrich von Homburg*, therefore, the imaginative transfiguration of reality, which is the form that theophany usually takes in Kleist, is not an illusion, as in *Die Marquise von O...*, nor a fatal error, as in *Penthesilea*, but is affirmed by the play's ending, albeit only as a magnificent dream.

CHAPTER 8

Cosmopolitanism, Patriotism, and Nationalism in the German-speaking Enlightenment

One of the services that Jonathan Israel has rendered to the study of the Enlightenment has been to reaffirm the essential unity of the movement. Against a recent tendency to dissolve the Enlightenment into a congeries of national 'Enlightenments', Israel boldly asserts that the Enlightenment brought a degree of cohesion into European intellectual culture that had not been seen since the Roman Empire:

> For it was then [in the late seventeenth and early eighteenth centuries] that western and central Europe first became, in the sphere of ideas, broadly a single arena integrated by mostly newly invented channels of communication, ranging from newspapers, magazines and the salon to the coffee-shop and a whole array of fresh cultural devices of which the erudite journals (invented in the 1660s) and the 'universal' library were particularly crucial.[1]

Within this international framework, it was possible to regard oneself as a cosmopolitan, a citizen of the world. The purpose of this paper is to explore the meanings of cosmopolitanism, particularly in eighteenth-century Germany, and to show how it was able to coexist with a certain conception of patriotism until it was displaced at the end of the century by a much more militant national sentiment which formed one of the components in nineteenth-century nationalism. Two aspects of this development, which have received little notice, will be foregrounded here. One is that far from being a product of the Napoleonic Wars, as commonly thought, this patriotic fervour can be traced back to the writings generated by the Seven Years' War. The other is that in the Napoleonic period this fervour flourished not only — as is notorious — in Germany but also, with significant differences, in Austria.

The cosmopolitan infrastructure of the Enlightenment to which Israel refers in the quotation above was often called the republic of letters. Pierre Bayle adopted this term for his journal *Nouvelles de la République des Lettres*, which first appeared in March 1684. Networks of correspondence among scholars, journals which carried

---

1 Jonathan Israel, *Radical Enlightenment: Philosophy and the Making of Modernity, 1650–1750* (Oxford: Oxford University Press, 2001), p. vi. On disputes over the unity of the Enlightenment, see John Robertson, *The Case for the Enlightenment: Scotland and Naples, 1680–1760* (Cambridge: Cambridge University Press, 2005), pp. 2–9.

reviews of new publications, forms of sociability such as clubs and Masonic lodges, and libraries which arranged books according to their discipline instead of their confessional affiliation, all made possible an exchange of information and ideas across national boundaries. Not all the scholars who exchanged information were proponents of Enlightenment, and of those who were, not all saw their 'republic' as an alternative political structure; for many, as Noel Malcolm has reminded us, it was a synonym for *orbis litterarum* or the 'world of learning'.[2] But these networks made possible the active propagation of Enlightenment by means of collective projects such as the *Encyclopédie*, and gave its proponents a sense of cohesion and solidarity which helped them to resist their more or less unenlightened national governments. Thomas J. Schlereth has catalogued the ways in which they looked across national boundaries and acquired an international, even global perspective: the study of science, supported by correspondence; interest in explorations which encouraged the geographical study of the world as a whole; an eclectic and relativistic attitude in philosophy; natural religion and universal tolerance; opposition to narrow patriotism, a view of the state as merely utilitarian, a positive attitude to international trade as opposed to mercantilism, and even an aspiration towards the regulation of conflicts by international law.[3] Hence Voltaire could write — appropriately in English — in 1727: 'Since all Europe hath set up the Greek, and Roman Authors for Models of Writing, Homer and Demosthenes, Virgil and Tully, have in some Measure united under their Laws our European Nations, and made of so many and different Countries, a single Commonwealth of Letters.'[4] And in a letter of 1745 he declared: 'La pacifique république des gens qui pensent est répandue par toutte [*sic*] la terre.'[5] Between these two statements one can see a significant shift. A republic of learning, of erudition, has become a republic of free intellectual activity more generally.

Cosmopolitanism did not of course originate with the Enlightenment. The Stoic philosopher Seneca advocates involvement in public life, not simply to serve one's own relatives or one's own polity, but to benefit all mankind 'in claiming the world as our country'.[6] In Sir Philip Sidney's *Old Arcadia* (probably completed in 1580) a judge cites the authority of 'the universal civility, the law of nations (all mankind being as it were coinhabiters or world citizens together)'.[7] The theory of natural law,

2   Noel Malcolm, 'Private and Public Knowledge: Kircher, Esotericism, and the Republic of Letters', in *Athanasius Kircher: The Last Man Who Knew Everything*, ed. by Paula Findlen (New York and London: Routledge, 2004), pp. 297–308 (p. 300). On the relation between the Republic of Letters and the Enlightenment, see L. W. B. Brockliss, *Calvet's Web: Enlightenment and the Republic of Letters in Eighteenth-Century France* (Oxford: Oxford University Press, 2002), pp. 5–13.

3   Thomas J. Schlereth, *The Cosmopolitan Ideal in Enlightenment Thought* (Notre Dame, IN, and London: University of Notre Dame Press, 1977).

4   *Les Œuvres complètes de Voltaire / The Complete Works of Voltaire*, 135 vols (Geneva: Institut et Musée Voltaire; Oxford: Voltaire Foundation, 1968–), 3B: *The English essays of 1727*, ed. by David Williams (Oxford: Voltaire Foundation, 1996), p. 308.

5   Letter to Cardinal Domenico Passionei, 12 October 1745, D3234, *OCV: Correspondence and related documents*, ed. by Theodore Besterman, ix. 344.

6   Seneca, 'On Tranquillity of Mind', in *Moral Essays*, trans. by John W. Basore, Loeb Classical Library, 3 vols (London: Heinemann; Cambridge, MA: Harvard University Press, 1970), II, 229; cf. 207.

7   Sir Philip Sidney, *The Old Arcadia*, ed. by Katherine Duncan-Jones (Oxford: Oxford University Press, 1985), p. 349.

elaborated by Hugo Grotius (1583–1645) on the basis of the ethical theories of Plato, Aristotle, and Aquinas, applied to all people irrespective of nationality, and included an attempt to regulate relations between states. Thus, from several directions, the thinkers of the Enlightenment found encouragement to look beyond parochial and national boundaries and to regard themselves as citizens owing responsibility to a larger, indeed the largest possible, public. Hence when Schiller in 1784 announced a new periodical, the *Rheinische Thalia*, he made a virtue of the enforced exile from his native principality of Württemberg (whose duke had forbidden him to write any more plays after *Die Räuber*) to describe himself as, perforce, a citizen of the world: 'Ich schreibe als Weltbürger, der keinem Fürsten dient. Frühe verlor ich mein Vaterland, um es gegen die große Welt auszutauschen' [I write as a citizen of the world who does not serve any prince. At an early age I lost my fatherland, to exchange it for the great world].[8] And in the drama *Don Carlos*, when the enlightened Marquis Posa appeals to his old friend Don Carlos to help restore the religious freedom of the Netherlanders from Spanish oppression, Posa is allowed to describe himself anachronistically as 'Ein Abgeordneter der ganzen Menschheit' [a delegate of all humanity].[9] Similarly, in his history of the revolt of the Netherlands, Schiller draws a contrast between Count Egmont, who was never more than a Fleming, that is, concerned with the interests of his own region, and the successful leader of the revolt, William the Silent, who looked beyond local issues to wider questions and was thus a 'Bürger der Welt' [citizen of the world].[10]

To be a 'citizen of the world' — in German, a 'Kosmopolit' or 'Weltbürger' — meant acquiring foreign languages and, if possible, encountering foreign cultures and in particular foreign intellectuals. Thus Voltaire, in his enforced three years' residence in Britain, learnt the English language so well that he not only published books in impeccable English but many years later astonished his visitor James Boswell by his command of the language.[11] Boswell himself sought out well-known intellectuals and writers — Voltaire, Rousseau, Gottsched and Gellert — and while on the Continent not only learnt to speak French fluently and write it respectably, but also spoke and wrote Dutch and Italian, and managed a little German. He affirmed his cosmopolitanism by writing, in the preface to his account of the tour to the Hebrides he undertook with Samuel Johnson:

> I am, I flatter myself, completely a citizen of the world. — In my travels through Holland, Germany, Switzerland, Italy, Corsica, France, I never felt myself from home; and I sincerely love 'every kindred and tongue and people and nation'.[12]

8   Friedrich Schiller, 'Ankündigung der *Rheinischen Thalia*', in his *Sämtliche Werke*, ed. by Gerhard Fricke and Herbert G. Göpfert, 5 vols (Munich: Hanser, 1958), v, 855. Translations are my own unless otherwise stated.

9   Schiller, *Don Carlos*, l. 157, in *Sämtliche Werke*, II, 14.

10   Schiller, *Geschichte des Abfalls der Vereinigten Niederlande von der spanischen Regierung*, in *Sämtliche Werke*, IV, 97.

11   *Boswell on the Grand Tour: Germany and Switzerland, 1764*, ed. by Frederick A. Pottle (London: Heinemann, 1953), p. 292.

12   *Johnson's Journey to the Western Islands of Scotland, and Boswell's Journal of a Tour to the Hebrides with Samuel Johnson, LL.D.*, ed. by R. W. Chapman (London: Oxford University Press, 1924), p. 172.

Boswell's compatriot David Hume, as ambassador in Paris, was fêted by his French acquaintances, even though, according to the unkind testimony of Horace Walpole, 'his French is almost as unintelligible as his English'.[13] Diderot, having deplored how unreal distinctions between nations tend to curb a benevolence that ought to be universal, wrote to Hume: 'Mon cher David, vous êtes de toutes les nations, et vous ne demanderez jamais au malheureux son extrait baptistaire. Je me flatte d'être, comme vous, citoyen de la grande ville du monde' [My dear David, you belong to all nations, and you will never ask an unfortunate person for an extract from his baptismal register. I pride myself on being, like you, a citizen of that great city, the world].[14]

In Germany, the word 'Kosmopolit' makes an early appearance in a mildly satirical context. Lessing's early comedy *Der junge Gelehrte*, written in 1747, satirizes the conceit of the young scholar Damis, who despises everyone who is not a scholar. He assures his servant Anton that it is not too late to join the republic of learning. But when Anton naively asks where this republic is situated, Damis gets cross:

> Ich rede von der Republik der Gelehrten. Was geht uns Gelehrten Sachsen an, was Deutschland, was Europa an? Ein Gelehrter, wie ich es bin, ist für die ganze Welt; er ist ein Cosmopolit; er ist eine Sonne, die den ganzen Erdball erleuchten muß —.[15]

> [I am talking about the republic of scholars. What do we scholars care about Saxony, about Germany, about Europe? A scholar like myself is for the whole world; he is a cosmopolitan; he is a sun who must illuminate the entire globe.]

This satire on academic vanity, however, is not directed against the cosmopolitan ideal of the republic of learning, of which Lessing was a distinguished example, as H. B. Nisbet emphasizes in his recent biography.[16] Besides having a thorough classical education, Lessing knew all the major Western European languages and published translations from French, English and Spanish. But it does point to an instability in the concept of the 'Weltbürger' or 'Kosmopolit'. Such a person can easily forget, like Damis, that he does lead a physical and social existence in a certain place. He can confine himself in an ivory tower, maintaining relations with other people only on paper. Ideally, however, a 'Weltbürger' is conscious both of his duties towards humanity at large and of his duties towards his fellow-citizens.

Such an ideal 'Weltbürger' is Democritus, the hero of Christoph Martin Wieland's novel *Geschichte der Abderiten* (1781). Democritus, famous as the 'laughing philosopher', is in this novel a loyal citizen of Abdera, a town notorious in ancient times for the folly of its population:

13 Quoted in E. C. Mossner, *The Life of David Hume* (Oxford: Clarendon Press, 1954), p. 445.

14 Denis Diderot, *Correspondance*, ed. by Georges Roth, 16 vols (Paris: Les Éditions de Minuit, 1955–70), VIII, 16.

15 Gotthold Ephraim Lessing, *Der junge Gelehrte*, II iv, in *Werke und Briefe*, ed. by Wilfried Barner et al., 12 vols (Frankfurt a.M.: Deutscher Klassiker Verlag, 1987–98), I, 178.

16 H. B. Nisbet, *Lessing: Eine Biographie*, trans. by Karl S. Guthke (Munich: Fink, 2008), p. 12.

> Und wiewohl er glaubte, daß der Charakter eines *Weltbürgers* Verhältnisse in sich schließe, denen im Kollisionsfall alle andere weichen müßten: so hielt er sich doch darum nicht weniger verbunden, als *ein Bürger von Abdera*, an dem Zustande seines Vaterlandes Anteil zu nehmen, und, so viel er konnte, zu dessen Verbesserung beizutragen.[17]

> [And although he believed that the character of a *citizen of the world* implies relationships which, in case of conflict, must take precedence over all others, yet he considered himself none the less obliged, as a *citizen of Abdera*, to take an interest in the condition of his fatherland, and to contribute to its improvement as much as he could.]

He has a hard time of it, however, among the foolish Abderites, who especially love trivial legal and religious disputes, and who distrust Democritus because he has travelled so widely:

> 'So geht es', sagten sie, 'wenn man naseweisen Jünglingen erlaubt, in der weiten Welt herum zu reisen, um sich ihres Vaterlandes schämen zu lernen, und nach zehn oder zwanzig Jahren mit einem Kopfe voll ausländischer Begriffe als *Kosmopoliten* zurück zu kommen, die alles besser wissen, als ihre Großväter, und alles anderswo besser gesehen haben, als zu Hause.'[18]

> ['That's what happens,' they said, 'when you allow cheeky boys to travel all over the wide world, in order to learn to be ashamed of their fatherland, and to come back after ten or twenty years as *cosmopolitans* with their heads full of foreign notions, knowing better than their grandfathers about everything, and having seen that everything elsewhere is better than at home.']

To them, a cosmopolitan is simply (as in *The Mikado*) an 'idiot who praises in enthusiastic tone | All centuries but this and every country but his own'. Wieland himself, by contrast, in his essay 'Das Geheimnis des Kosmopolitenordens' [The Secret of the Cosmopolitan Order] (1788), in his journal *Der Teutsche Merkur*, defines a cosmopolitan as follows:

> Die Kosmopoliten führen ihren Namen (Weltbürger) in der eigentlichsten und eminentesten Bedeutung. Sie betrachten alle Völker des Erdbodens als eben so viele Zweige einer einzigen Familie, und das Universum als einen Staat, worin sie mit unzähligen andern vernünftigen Wesen Bürger sind, um unter allgemeinen Naturgesetzen die Vollkommenheit des Ganzen zu befördern, indem jedes nach seiner besondern Art und Weise für seinen eigenen Wohlstand geschäftig ist.[19]

> [Cosmopolitans bear their name (citizens of the world) in the most genuine and significant sense. They regard all the nations of the earth as so many branches of a single family, and the universe as a state in which they are citizens along with innumerable other rational beings, in order to promote the welfare of the whole

---

17   Christoph Martin Wieland, *Werke*, ed. by Fritz Martini and Hans Werner Seiffert, 5 vols (Munich: Hanser, 1964–68), II, 188.

18   Ibid., II, 170. For a summary of Wieland's cosmopolitan ideal, based on the novel *Sokrates Mainomenos oder die Dialogen des Diogenes von Sinope* (1770) and the earliest published version of the *Geschichte der Abderiten*, see Andrea Heinz, 'Der Kosmopolitismusgedanke bei Wieland um 1770', *Wieland-Studien*, 4 (2005), 49–61.

19   Wieland, III, 556.

under the universal laws of nature by each of them working in his particular manner for his own well-being.]

There was no necessary contradiction between cosmopolitanism, as Wieland understood it, and patriotism. One could be a patriot, and nurture a special affection for one's own country or region, without any lack of interest or concern for other countries. Thus Goethe introduces into his unfinished novel *Wilhelm Meisters theatralische Sendung* [*Wilhelm Meister's Theatrical Mission*], written in the early 1780s, a German officer who represents 'einen wahren Patrioten' [a true patriot] because he follows the development of German literature without overrating it, and hopes for its improvement, while being familiar with several foreign literatures. His attachment to his own country is an emotional one which does not diminish his sympathy for the superior products of other nations.[20] In Schiller's *Kabale und Liebe* (1784), the scheming President, who manages a petty court on behalf of its ducal ruler, is induced to fear that his son will abandon filial obedience and assume 'die Pflichten eines Patrioten' [the duties of a patriot][21] — that is, somebody who seeks the welfare of his own country, without reference to selfish interests.

Wieland similarly sought to promote German national self-awareness by founding the journal *Der Teutsche Merkur*, a partial counterpart to the *Mercure de France*, but the patriotism shown by founding what he called a 'National-Journal' in no way contradicted his cosmopolitanism.[22] In his essay 'Über teutschen Patriotismus' [On German Patriotism] (1793), inspired by the German responses to the excesses of the French Revolution, Wieland doubted whether the new 'Modetugend' [fashionable virtue] known as patriotism at all corresponded to the sense of belonging to the German nation which his journal was intended to promote. He contrasts German patriotic feeling with the ancient virtue of patriotism. He recalls how the Greeks were united against Persian aggression by a common 'Vaterlandsliebe' [love of the fatherland], and how the normally distinct character of each Greek state was counterbalanced by national festivals such as the Olympic Games. He thinks that although in Germany there are people who feel patriotic devotion towards their particular German state, be it Saxony, Bavaria, or Württemberg, there is nobody who feels such devotion towards Germany as a whole. The present strength of feeling, he thinks, does not arise from devotion to Germany, but rather from justified opposition to the mad egalitarianism of the French revolutionaries who have invaded the western regions of Germany.[23]

By now it had become still more important to defend the concept of a 'Weltbürger' against its detractors. For in Germany there were a large number of secret societies, notably Freemasons and Illuminati, dedicated to Enlightenment ideals of progress,

20   Johann Wolfgang Goethe, *Sämtliche Werke: Briefe, Tagebücher und Gespräche*, ed. by Friedmar Apel and others, 40 vols (Frankfurt a.M.: Deutscher Klassiker Verlag, 1986–2000), IX, 166.

21   Schiller, I, 799.

22   This is made clear by Hans-Peter Nowitzki, 'Der "menschenfreundliche Cosmopolit" und sein "National-Journal": Wielands *Merkur*-Konzeption', in *'Der Teutsche Merkur': Die erste deutsche Kulturzeitschrift?*, ed. by Andrea Heinz (Heidelberg: Winter, 2003), pp. 68–107 (esp. pp. 101–02). On Wieland's use of the term 'National-Journal', see ib., pp. 93–94.

23   Wieland, III, 744–54 (Greek 'Vaterlandsliebe', p. 746).

but suspected of plotting to undermine society. Adolph Freiherr von Knigge, who was a leading member of the Illuminati from 1779 to 1784, writes:

> Man wird heutzutage in allen Ständen wenig Menschen treffen, die nicht [...] wenigstens eine Zeitlang Mitglieder einer solchen geheimen Verbrüderung gewesen wären.[24]

> [Nowadays few people will be found in any social rank who have not, at least for a while, been members of such a secret brotherhood.]

When it became known that the Illuminati professed radical republicanism and religious scepticism, the authorities took fright: in 1785 an edict by the Elector of Bavaria banned Freemasons and Illuminati there. Fantasies developed concerning a worldwide Masonic conspiracy. On 17 August 1790, alarmed by the early stages of the French Revolution, Marie Antoinette wrote to her brother, the Habsburg Emperor Leopold II:

> prenez bien garde là-bas à toute association de franc-maçons. On doit déjà vous avoir averti; c'est par cette voie que tous les monstres d'ici comptent d'arriver dans tous les pays au même but.[25]

> [Be on your guard against any association of Freemasons there. You must already have been warned; it is by that route that all these monsters here count on reaching the same goal in all countries.]

In keeping with their Enlightenment principles, Masons and Illuminati often called themselves 'Weltbürger'. Thus the Jena Masons described themselves as 'tugendhafte edle Welt-Bürger' [virtuous noble citizens of the world].[26] When unease developed about their supposedly subversive activities, the term 'Weltbürger' fell into discredit. Knigge says that 'Weltbürgergeist' [the spirit of cosmopolitanism] is among the 'große Wörter' [big words] which are mere baits used by Illuminatism to attract the naïve.[27] As conspiracy theorists drew up terrifying accounts of the international network of subversion of which the Illuminati allegedly formed part, 'Weltbürger' become a term of downright abuse, as in the anonymously published revelations by Ernst August Anton von Göchhausen, *Enthüllung des Systems der Weltbürger-Republik* [*Exposure of the System of the Cosmopolitan Republic*] (1786).[28]

It was against this background of panic that Wieland put forward his defence of cosmopolitanism in the essay ironically entitled 'Das Geheimnis des Kosmopolitenordens' (1788). A true cosmopolitan, he says, cannot be a member of a secret society, because he aims to benefit all humanity and has no reason to shun the

---

24   Adolph Freiherr von Knigge, *Über den Umgang mit Menschen*, ed. by Gert Ueding (Frankfurt a.M.: Insel Verlag, 1977), p. 391.

25   Quoted in J. M. Roberts, *The Mythology of the Secret Societies* (London: Secker & Warburg, 1972), p. 168.

26   Quoted in W. Daniel Wilson, *Unterirdische Gänge: Goethe, Freimaurerei und Politik* (Göttingen: Wallstein, 1999), p. 54.

27   Knigge, p. 126.

28   On Göchhausen, see Ralf Klausnitzer, *Poesie und Konspiration: Beziehungssinn und Zeichenökonomie von Verschwörungsszenarien in Publizistik, Literatur und Wissenschaft, 1750–1850* (Berlin: de Gruyter, 2007), pp. 294–321.

light. Nor do cosmopolitans seek to form a state within a state (an accusation made against the recently dissolved Society of Jesus). A cosmopolitan, moreover, is always a quiet and peaceful citizen of whatever state he inhabits; he may criticize political conditions and seek to improve them, but he will be aware that violence always does more harm than good. He believes that the ideal state is perfectly rational, but he thinks that this rational state is to be reached, not through sudden innovation, but as the asymptotic, hence never completely attainable end-point of a long and gradual progress in which all actual forms of government are temporary but necessary stages. The cosmopolitan therefore avoids taking sides in actual political conflicts, with two exceptions. A cosmopolitan could not have failed to take the side of the Netherlands against the tyranny exercised by Philip II of Spain through his regent the Duke of Alba (the subject of Schiller's drama *Don Carlos*, published in 1787, the previous year); and if the future representatives of the French nation should subject the arbitrary power of their king and his ministers to suitable restraints, that too would be a measure which cosmopolitans could only applaud.[29]

But this was already a rearguard defence of cosmopolitanism. The French Revolution would soon go far beyond Wieland's hopes for liberal reform, calling forth violent displays of patriotism and ending what Franco Venturi calls 'the cosmopolitan century', replacing it with an age of nationalism.[30] At the turn of the century Friedrich von Hardenberg, known as Novalis, wrote a series of aphorisms headed *Glauben und Liebe oder Der König und die Königin* [*Faith and Love or The King and the Queen*], outlining a mystical theory of monarchism. Those people at the present day, he said, who advocate a republic founded on representative democracy, are lacking in imagination and emotion. The cosmopolitanism they profess is merely a disguise for their shallowness. They are:

> armselige Philister, leer an Geist und arm an Herzen, Buchstäbler, die ihre Seichtigkeit und innerliche Blöße hinter den bunten Fahnen der triumphie-renden Mode, unter der imposanten Maske des Kosmopolitismus zu verstecken suchen.[31]

> [wretched Philistines, spiritually empty and emotionally impoverished, who read only the letter, and who try to conceal their shallowness and inner barrenness behind the colourful banners of triumphant fashion, beneath the outwardly imposing mask of cosmopolitanism.]

The emotional patriotism represented by Hardenberg did not emerge only at the end of the eighteenth century. An outburst of fervent patriotism, appealing especially to ancient ideals of Roman patriotism, appeared at the time of the Seven Years' War (1756–63). This patriotism drew also on the republican tradition. This tradition of thought goes back to the 'civic humanism' of the Renaissance, when it was articulated especially by Machiavelli in deploring the destruction of the Italian

---

29 Wieland, III, 566.

30 See Franco Venturi, *Italy and the Enlightenment: Studies in a Cosmopolitan Century*, trans. by Susan Corsi (London: Longman, 1972).

31 Novalis, *Schriften*, ed. by Paul Kluckhohn and Richard Samuel, 5 vols (Stuttgart: Klett-Cotta, 1960–88), II, 490–91.

city-states and their replacement by tyrannies. It passed to eighteenth-century Germany via the sympathetic presentations of republican thought by Montesquieu in *L'Esprit des lois* (1748) and Adam Ferguson in *An Essay on the History of Civil Society* (1767), both of whom found many German readers. Its key principle was that a republic depends on active political participation by a large body of citizens who must qualify themselves for political activity by republican virtue, placing the common good above their private interests.[32] Republican virtues were often considered compatible with the presence of a monarch, provided his powers stopped well short of tyranny. Thus it was possible for Thomas Abbt, a professor of philosophy in Frankfurt an der Oder, to import republican ideals into the Prussia of Frederick the Great. Abbt's essay, *Vom Tode fürs Vaterland* [*On Death for the Fatherland*] (1761), was inspired by the cosmopolitan essay *Vom Nationalstolz* [*On National Pride*] (1758) by Wieland's friend Johann Georg Zimmermann, but Abbt replaced Zimmermann's cosmopolitanism with ardent patriotism.[33] He argues that patriotism should be based not on rational reflection but on passionate enthusiasm, and that one's country has the right to claim one's life. Patriotism frees one from the narrow circle of one's egotistic interests and makes one aware that one is part of a greater national whole. Abbt sets out to dispel the idea that patriotism can flourish only in republics, not in monarchies, and to contest Montesquieu's argument that in monarchies the driving motive is honour. He maintains that patriotism, attached to the figure of a popular monarch who shares his people's dangers, can be inculcated from childhood onwards and provide a conception of honour open to the entire population.

> Man weiß es, daß nicht alle Menschen ihre Glückseligkeit in der Ehre suchen: aber diese Ehre kann man mit der Liebe fürs Vaterland vereinigen, und dadurch alle Seelen gleichsam adeln. Dieses war eben der Kunstgriff in den Republiken. Die Ehre, die sie ertheilten, war so beschaffen, daß jeder darauf Anspruch machen konnte: und das Mittel, darauf Anspruch zu machen, war nichts anders, als der Zweck, den sie suchten — der Tod fürs Vaterland.[34]

> [We know that not everyone seeks his happiness in honour: but honour can be combined with love for one's fatherland and thus all souls can, so to speak, be ennobled. This was the technique practised in republics. The honour they bestowed was of such a nature that anyone could lay claim to it; and the means of claiming it was nothing other than the goal they sought to attain — death for one's fatherland.]

This patriotic spirit, according to Abbt, existed in the Roman Republic, among the followers of Alexander the Great, and above all in ancient Sparta, and was still alive in Switzerland, where the names of national heroes were recited at

---

32 See *Machiavelli and Republicanism*, ed. by Gisela Bock, Quentin Skinner and Maurizio Viroli (Cambridge: Cambridge University Press, 1990); Frederick Beiser, *Schiller as Philosopher: A Re-examination* (Oxford: Clarendon Press, 2005), p. 125.

33 See Annie Bender, *Thomas Abbt: Ein Beitrag zur Darstellung des erwachenden Lebensgefühls im 18. Jahrhundert* (Bonn: Friedrich Cohen, 1922), pp. 56–57.

34 Thomas Abbt, *Vom Tode fürs Vaterland* (1761), in his *Vermischte Werke*, 6 vols (Berlin and Stettin: Nicolai, 1768–80), II, 81.

annual celebrations. Against the charge that such patriotism is 'enthusiastic' (in the negative sense the word had in the eighteenth century), Abbt compares it to the unimpeachable sacrificial spirit of Christian martyrs, and ranks it far above the readiness of Muslims to die for the sake of sensual enjoyments in paradise, and above the absurdities of such saints as Francis of Assisi and Ignatius Loyola. He advocates a new, potentially democratic outlook which, focused on the person of a monarch, can provide a modern form of social cohesion and moral nobility without distinction of classes.

Abbt's essay, published late in the Seven Years' War, was read and admired throughout Germany. He clinched his argument by a stirring quotation from the poet Ewald von Kleist, who had not only published patriotic poetry but given his own work a special authority by taking part heroically in combat and dying of wounds received at the battle of Kunersdorf. Abbt quoted some lines from Kleist's heroic poem in three cantos, *Ciβides und Paches* (1759), focusing on two Macedonian warriors, former followers of Alexander the Great, who after his death steadfastly though vainly defend a fortress against the expansionism of Athens. Paches voices the poem's guiding sentiments in the words:

> Tod ist unser Wunsch und Glück,
> Wenn wir dadurch des Vaterlandes Wohl
> Erkaufen können.[35]

[Death is our desire and happiness, if by it we can purchase the good of our fatherland.]

And this message is underlined by the passage that Abbt quotes (in fact slightly misquotes) from near the end of the poem:

> Der Tod fürs Vaterland ist ewiger
> Verehrung werth. — Wie gern sterb ich ihn auch
> Den edlen Tod, wenn mein Verhängniß ruft![36]

[Death for the fatherland deserves everlasting honour. — How gladly I too shall die the noble death, when my destiny calls!]

Admittedly, not everyone shared the mood of Kleist and Abbt. Lessing responded to this wave of patriotism with the claim: 'ich habe überhaupt von der Liebe des Vaterlandes [...] keinen Begriff, und sie scheinet mir aufs höchste eine heroische Schwachheit, die ich recht gern entbehre' [I have not the least conception of love for one's fatherland, and it seems to me, at most, a heroic weakness, which I am very glad to be without].[37] But forty years later, when Prussia was attacked and defeated by French forces under Napoleon, it was not Lessing's scepticism but the passion of Thomas Abbt that resurfaced. By now, however, Abbt's militant patriotism was transmuted into nationalism. Abbt's *Vaterlandsliebe* is not yet nationalism, for patriots of this stamp demand devotion to the fatherland just because it is the fatherland,

---

35 Ewald Chr. von Kleist, *Sämtliche Werke*, ed. by Jürgen Stenzel (Stuttgart: Reclam, 1971), p. 149.
36 Ibid., p. 152.
37 Letter to Gleim, 14 February 1759, in Lessing, xi/1. 311–12.

not because of any specific qualities ascribed to the nation. By the early nineteenth century, however, Hardenberg was among numerous writers who urged that an enlightened devotion to humanity as a whole and to abstract ideals including that of patriotism could never appeal to the emotional depths that were stirred by the national community in which one actually lived, moved and had one's being. Nationalists called for devotion to the specific qualities they ascribed to the nation or 'Volk' in whose name they professed to speak.

The spirit of nationalism, in ascribing peculiar and outstanding virtues to the spirit of one's own nation, is clear in the Berlin lectures by Johann Gottlieb Fichte. Lecturing in the winter of 1807–08, against the background of France's defeat of Prussia, Fichte assured his Berlin audience that only the Germans were a 'Volk' [nation], indeed an 'Urvolk' or primal nation. A 'Volk' is eternal; it is a continuity extending before the birth and after the death of the individual; this sense of belonging to a larger whole is the foundation of patriotism, of devotion to 'Volk und Vaterland', which can inspire one to die for one's country.[38] The Germans' profundity and authenticity distinguishes them from the superficial French, and the distinction is embodied in the two nations' respective languages: while the Germans still speak their original language, the French speak a version of Latin, the language of their conquerors, and this superficial language, imposed on them externally by the Romans, can never spring from the heart as German does. The Prussian dramatist and journalist Heinrich von Kleist meanwhile wrote patriotic poems urging his fellow-Germans to slaughter vast numbers of Frenchmen and dam the Rhine with their corpses.[39] While, two generations earlier, the patriotism of Ewald von Kleist and Thomas Abbt was focused on defending the nation, with Heinrich von Kleist the defence of the nation is readily transmuted into bloodthirsty aggression. The century of nationalism was dawning in stark colours.

What was happening meanwhile in Austria? The Habsburg Monarchy might seem an unpromising setting for either cosmopolitanism or patriotism. Participation in the Republic of Letters was prevented by the censorship, which admittedly was inefficient and leaky. It was intended to keep books prejudicial to faith and morals out of the Habsburg Monarchy. Travellers had their books confiscated at the frontier. As Derek Beales says, 'The Monarchy's list of prohibited books was longer than the pope's.'[40] Until 1753, censorship was in the hands of the Jesuits. After that Maria Theresia appointed a 'Zensurkommission' chaired by Gerhard van Swieten. By placing him in charge, Maria Theresia was supporting a policy of permitting writers now regarded as safe (Montesquieu, Leibniz, Wolff, Thomasius, Newton, Locke), but preserving Austria from radical influences (such as Voltaire, Hume, Diderot and Spinoza). The censorship was still full of anomalies, resulting in part from van Swieten's wish to admit enlightened works of political science

38   Johann Gottlieb Fichte, *Reden an die deutsche Nation* (Hamburg: Meiner, 1978), p. 106.
39   Heinrich von Kleist, 'Germanias Aufruf an ihre Kinder' (1809) in his *Sämtliche Werke und Briefe*, ed. by Ilse-Maria Barth and others, 4 vols (Frankfurt a.M.: Deutscher Klassiker Verlag, 1989), III, 431.
40   Derek Beales, *Enlightenment and Reform in Eighteenth-Century Europe* (London: Tauris, 2005), p. 69.

without alarming Maria Theresia, who could override the 'Zensurkommission'. Hence trade-offs were required: the price of admitting Montesquieu's *L'Esprit des lois* was the banning of his *Lettres persanes*.[41] However, the existence of censorship itself aroused curiosity about censored works — so much so that in 1777 the index of prohibited books had itself to be prohibited.[42] Moreover, the censorship was notoriously permeable. Almost any prohibited book could be obtained for a high enough price. The library in the Benedictine abbey at Melk had a second-hand copy of the *Encyclopédie*, though it was officially banned.[43] In 1778, the young Ignaz Fessler, training for the priesthood in Wiener Neustadt, managed to read works by Hobbes, Machiavelli, Tindal, Bacon, and Reimarus, which he borrowed from friends in Vienna.[44]

As for patriotism, the Monarchy consisted of a patchwork of territories, most acquired by a haphazard process of dynastic inheritance and marriage, including what is now Belgium and 'Vorderösterreich' (the Breisgau), others, like Transylvania, conquered or reconquered from the Turks. After defeat by Prussia, the Monarchy tried to catch up with Frederick the Great by creating a modern, centralized, economically self-sufficient state. This included trying to inculcate a spirit of patriotism among the population, a task which fell to the Enlightener Joseph von Sonnenfels. Unlike Fichte a generation later, Sonnenfels could not appeal to the discourse of the 'Volk'. Although speakers of German exercised political and cultural hegemony in the Austrian domains, account had to be taken of the sensibilities of the other, and increasingly articulate, nations that inhabited the Habsburg territories. Thus Joseph II not only knew the standard Western European languages (German, French, Italian, and Latin) but had a passable knowledge of Czech, and, on his travels in remote parts of his domains, was able to communicate with some of his subjects in Romanian.[45] Linguistic or racial nationalism was not an option here.

In order to praise the Austrian 'Vaterland', Sonnenfels had first to warn against cosmopolitanism — an ironic and unsuitable position for a professed Enlightener. In his periodical *Der Mann ohne Vorurtheil* [*The Man without Prejudice*] (1765–67), an Austrian counterpart to the German moral weeklies, a perhaps fictitious correspondent writes in 1766 that the concept of 'Vaterland' is virtually extinct, and that the now fashionable word is 'Kosmopolit' or 'Weltbürger':

> Alle Welt ist heut zu Tage kosmopolitisch gesinnt, und sie werden nicht leicht jemanden finden, der seinem Vaterlande so sehr zugethan wäre, daß er demselben die geringsten Vortheile aufopferte. Im Gegentheil werden sie aber

41   See Joseph von Sonnenfels, 'Die erste Vorlesung in dem akademischen Jahrgange 1782', in *Sonnenfels gesammelte Schriften*, 10 vols (Vienna: no pub., 1786), VIII, 103–46 (pp. 112–13).

42   See Grete Klingenstein, *Staatsverwaltung und kirchliche Autorität im 18. Jahrhundert: Das Problem der Zensur in der theresianischen Reform* (Vienna: Verlag für Geschichte und Politik, 1970), p. 201.

43   Johannes Frimmel, *Literarisches Leben in Melk: Ein Kloster im 18. Jahrhundert im kulturellen Umbruch* (Vienna, Cologne, Weimar: Böhlau, 2004), p. 147.

44   [Ignaz-Aurelius Fessler], *Dr. Fessler's Rückblicke auf seine siebzigjährige Pilgerschaft: Ein Nachlass* [sic] *an seine Freunde und an seine Feinde* (Breslau: Korn, 1824), p. 58.

45   See Derek Beales, *Joseph II*, 2 vols (Cambridge: Cambridge University Press, 1987–2009), I: *In the Shadow of Maria Theresa, 1741–1790* (1987), pp. 63–64, 361–62.

auch nicht läugnen können, daß dieses Vaterland für seine Bürger heute nichts, als ein Schall, ohne Bedeutung und Innhalt, ist. Warum sollen die Menschen ihr Vaterland lieben, fragt der Bürger von Genf, wenn das Vaterland für sie nichts mehr, als für jeden Fremden ist, und wenn dasselbe ihm weiter nichts zugesteht, als was es niemandem versagen kann?[46]

[Everyone nowadays has a cosmopolitan outlook, and it would be hard to find anyone who is so attached to his fatherland that he would sacrifice the slightest advantage for it. Indeed, it cannot be denied that this fatherland now means nothing to its citizens but a sound without meaning or content. Why should people love their fatherland, asks the citizen of Geneva [Rousseau], if the fatherland is no more for them than it is for any foreigner, and if it gives him only what it can deny to nobody?]

Sonnenfels developed this theme in his book *Ueber die Liebe des Vaterlandes* [*On the Love of one's Fatherland*] (1771). Its main inspiration is Rousseau. Sonnenfels quotes from the *Discours sur les origines de l'inégalité parmi les hommes* [*Discourse on the Origins of Human Inequality*] on how Hottentots would rather persist in their own poverty than adopt an easier life in Dutch settlements at the Cape of Good Hope.[47] In ancient times, similarly, the Spartans preferred domestic poverty to foreign luxury. The Spartans provide Sonnenfels, as they did Rousseau, with an example of patriotism diffused among the population. But their state was flawed by the existence of helots, a slave caste who could not be patriotic. The foundation of patriotism must be a class of farmers who own their own land (here Sonnenfels is indirectly attacking the institution of serfdom): 'Der Ackersmann allein ist der versicherte Bürger seines Staats, alle übrigen Stände sind Kosmopoliten' [Only the farmer is the assured citizen of his state, all other ranks are cosmopolitans]. [48] Ownership of land, a stake in the country, is essential for the making of a patriot: 'Eigenthum des Bodens, und persönliche Freyheit machen ein feldbauendes Volk zu Patrioten. Die Iloten sahen Sparta nicht als ihr Vaterland an' [Ownership of land and personal freedom make an agricultural nation into patriots. The Helots did not regard Sparta as their fatherland].[49]

A contented citizen, however, is not yet a patriot: he must be proud of his country, as the Romans were of the title of a Roman citizen. Even the culinary conceit of the French, who consider their ragouts superior to anything offered on German dinner-tables, is endurable as a sign of attachment to their own country. When people are brought to identify happiness with the qualities of their own country, a firm foundation is laid for patriotism. Sonnenfels introduces a note of cynicism when he declares that it does not matter whether such attachment is based on truth.

Wer wagt nicht alles, um *seiner* Glückseligkeit willen? Es verschlägt nichts, ob diese Glückseligkeit *an sich* wahr ist, oder nicht; genug daß sie es in der Meynung des Bürgers ist.[50]

46   *Der Mann ohne Vorurtheil*, II. Jahrgang (1766), XVI. Stück, pp. 127–28.
47   Sonnenfels, *Ueber die Liebe des Vaterlandes* (Vienna: Kurzböck, 1771), p. 27.
48   Ibid., pp. 45–46.
49   Ibid., p. 46.
50   Ibid., p. 26.

[Who would not risk everything for his *own* happiness? It does not matter whether this happiness is true in itself, or not, provided it is so in the opinion of the citizen.]

Similarly, it does not matter what form of government prevails, whether republican or monarchical — here Sonnenfels quotes famous lines from Pope:

> *Laßt* sprech ich mit Popen *die Thoren sich über den Vorzug der Regierungsformen zanken! die, welche am besten verwaltet wird, ist die beste.* [...] Die Republikaner also, und der Unterthan des Monarchen können sich dadurch, daß jener in einer Republik lebt, dieser in einer Monarchie, vorzüglich beglückt halten, und ganz wohl überzeugt seyn, daß ihr Glück genau von der Verfassung des Staates abhängt, dessen Bürger sie sind.[51]

> ['For forms of government,' I say with Pope, 'let fools contest! Whate'er is best administered, is best.' [...] Thus the republican and the subject of a monarch can each think himself specially fortunate because the one lives in a republic, the other in a monarchy, and be perfectly convinced that their happiness depends on the constitution of the state whose citizens they are.]

For this and other reasons, Sonnenfels's *Ueber die Liebe des Vaterlandes* is a problematic text. Its patriotism is inevitably devotion to an abstract entity. Goethe criticized it for its abstractness in a review in the *Frankfurter Gelehrte Anzeigen*: he complained that Sonnenfels' concept of patriotism was abstracted from different cultures, without attending to the particular historical circumstances under which such patriotism could develop. He wanted us all to be Romans, an idea Goethe abhorred: '*Römerpatriotismus*! Davor bewahr uns Gott, wie vor einer Riesengestalt!' [Roman patriotism! May God protect us from it, as from a giant!].[52] More recent commentators have praised Sonnenfels for radicalism in advocating peasant proprietorship.[53] They have not noticed how much Sonnenfels' concept of patriotism depends on illusions of national uniqueness which are to be instilled in the population by manipulative rulers.

  Sonnenfels played little part in the truly radical measures carried out by Joseph II, including the abolition of religious discrimination, serfdom, and censorship. To promote his reforms, Joseph urged his civil servants to work patriotically for the common good. But he did not compare them to Romans or Spartans, or advocate death for the fatherland. Such extravagances appear, however, in the extraordinary novel *Dya-Na-Sore*, published in three volumes between 1787 and 1791, and professing to be a translation from Sanskrit. Schiller, reviewing the first volume of this unreadable novel, deservedly tore it to shreds, calling it a 'Zwitter von Abhandlung und Erzählung' [a hybrid of treatise and narrative].[54] Its teaching

---

51 Ibid., p. 75.

52 Goethe, xviii, 26–29 (p. 27).

53 See especially Ernst Wangermann, 'Joseph von Sonnenfels und die Vaterlandsliebe der Aufklärung', in *Joseph von Sonnenfels*, ed. by Helmut Reinalter (Vienna: Verlag der Österreichischen Akademie der Wissenschaften, 1988), pp. 157–69. Sonnenfels's *Der Mann ohne Vorurtheil* contains moving revelations of the wretchedness of peasants compelled to do forced labour as well as work their own fields: see II. Jahrgang, 1. Stück, dated from '...stein den 31 May 1766'.

54 Schiller, v, 924–25 (p. 925).

consists in heroic patriotism:

> Der Mensch ist nur groß durch den Begrif eines Vaterlandes. [...] Gelehrter, Dichter, Krieger oder Künstler — das Vaterland ist seine Geliebte, sie allein ists, wofür er Volkommenheit sucht.[55]

> [Man is great only through the concept of a fatherland. [...] Be he scholar, poet, warrior or artist — the fatherland is his beloved, it is for her alone that he seeks perfection.]

The fatherland is best served on the battlefield, and to fight for its cause is morally improving: 'Das Schlachtfeld ist ein Land, das tausendfältige Früchte trägt. Kein guter Mann ging noch ins Treffen, der nicht besser heraus kam' [The battlefield is land that bears thousandfold fruits. No good man ever went into combat without emerging as a better one].[56] One of the numerous hermits who counsel the main characters praises war, scorning their feeble inclination towards pacifism:

> Eben der Krieg, antwortete er, der bei euch so sehr in Verruf steht, ist die Quelle der edelsten Handlungen. Der Ort, wo die menschliche Seele in ihrer erhabensten Stärke sich zeigt.[57]

> [War, he replied, of which you hold such a low opinion, is the source of the noblest actions. The place where the human soul manifests itself in its sublimest strength.]

Meyern at least put his money where his mouth was. He had been a professional soldier from 1783 till 1786. The publication of *Dya-Na-Sore* may have been intended to support Austria's war against Turkey which began in August 1787.[58] Meyern's writing can thus be seen as a continuation of his military activities by other means. He returned to them when he organized a volunteer corps to resist Napoleon's threat to Austria in 1796–98. After Napoleon's troops defeated an Austrian army at Ulm in 1805, Vienna was occupied. The Austrian campaign against France in the spring of 1809 ended in a futile victory at Aspern and a decisive defeat at Wagram. Meyern helped to organize the patriotic resistance. He shared this intense patriotism with numerous writers, notably Caroline Pichler, Therese von Artner, Heinrich von Collin and Josef von Hormayr. Hormayr, a historian, compiled a series of seventy-six biographies of Austrian rulers, statesmen, generals and scholars entitled *Österreichischer Plutarch* (1807–14) which was intended to awaken Austrian national consciousness and provide material for artists and poets.[59]

If we want to find something distinctive in Austrian, as opposed to German, patriotism at this era, we might look at the national hero held up for emulation. In

---

55   W. Fr. Meyern, *Dya-Na-Sore, oder die Wanderer. Eine Geschichte aus dem Sam-skritt übersezt* (Frankfurt a.M.: Zweitausendeins, 1979), p. 881. Original spelling.

56   Ibid., p. 660.

57   Ibid., p. 111.

58   See Beales, *Joseph II*, vol. II: *Against the World, 1780–1790* (2009), p. 580.

59   On this patriotic movement, see André Robert, *L'Idée nationale autrichienne et les guerres de Napoléon: L'Apostolat du baron de Hormayr et le salon de Caroline Pichler* (Paris: Alcan, 1933), and on Artner, Wynfrid Kriegleder, 'Therese von Artner und ihr vaterländisches Heldengedicht *Die Schlacht von Aspern*', in *Deutsche Sprache und Kultur, Literatur und Presse in Westungarn/Burgenland*, ed. by Wynfrid Kriegleder and Andrea Seidler (Bremen: edition lumière, 2004), pp. 249–66.

Germany, the discourse of the 'Urvolk' provided a national hero in Arminius or Hermann, the ancient Germanic leader who defeated three Roman legions under Varus in AD 9. 'Hermann' had been a symbol of German national consciousness since the Renaissance.[60] His many appearances in German literature include an early epic poem by Wieland, *Hermann* (1752); the Hermann dramas by Friedrich Gottlob Klopstock, which present him (like the protagonist of Goethe's *Götz von Berlichingen*) both as a defender of the nation and as an upholder of family values; and, most notoriously, Kleist's bloodthirsty nationalist drama *Die Hermannsschlacht* [*Hermann's Battle*] (1808–09). Hermann connotes the supposedly ingrained domestic and military virtues of the Germans displayed in self-defence against the over-civilized decadence, barbarity and imperialism of the Romans.

By contrast, the hero repeatedly invoked by Austrian patriotic writers is actually a Roman. We hear constantly about Regulus, who was taken prisoner by the Carthaginians in 255 BC and sent by them on parole to Rome to negotiate peace terms. He advised the Romans to refuse the terms but kept his parole, knowing that on his return he would be tortured to death. (Modern scholarship, alas, considers this a legend: more likely Regulus died of natural causes in captivity and his widow in revenge tortured two Carthaginian prisoners, whereupon the legend was invented to palliate her conduct.) Alongside the Spartan hero Leonidas, Regulus is among the star examples of patriotism cited by Sonnenfels in *Ueber die Liebe des Vaterlandes*. Hormayr invokes Regulus in his account of Joseph II in *Österreichischer Plutarch*, saying:

> Er war ganz durchdrungen von jenem Geist, welcher *Regulus* aus der langent-behrten Umarmung der Gattin, Kinder und Freunde forttrieb, nach Karthago, obwohl er wohl wußte: quae sibi barbarus tortor pararet![61]

> [He was permeated by the spirit that drove Regulus forth from the long-denied embrace of his spouse, children and friends, to Carthage, although he well knew that the barbarian was preparing tortures for him!]

Regulus is not primarily a military hero but rather an instance of passive endurance. In sacrificing himself for his country, he provided an apt analogy to the dedication to the good of his subjects shown in the tireless activity of the reforming Emperor Joseph II.

The discourse of Roman patriotism appears most emphatically in the play by Heinrich von Collin, *Regulus* (1802). The prologue summarizes the plot in patriotic language: 'Es will ein Dichter nun die erste Gabe | Auf den Altar des Vaterlandes legen' (ll. 4–5).[62] In the play, the Carthaginians want to exchange Roman captives,

---

60   See *Arminius und die Varusschlacht: Geschichte — Mythos — Literatur*, ed. by Rainer Wiegels and Winfried Woesler (Paderborn: Schöningh, 1995).

61   Joseph Freyherr von Hormayr, *Politisch-historische Schriften, Briefe und Akten*, ed. by Helmut Reinalter and Dušan Uhlić (Frankfurt a.M.: Peter Lang, 2003), pp. 75–76. Regulus also makes a brief appearance in Abbt, p. 47.

62   The text used is Heinrich von Collin, *Regulus*, in *Das Drama der klassichen Periode*, Zweiter Teil, Zweite Abteilung: Kotzebue und Collin (Deutsche National-Litteratur, 139), ed. by Adolf Hauffen (Stuttgart: Union Deutsche Verlagsgesellschaft, n.d.). On this play, see Roger Bauer, 'Das stoisch-josephinische Tugendideal in der österreichischen dramatischen Literatur der Grillparzerzeit', in his

including Regulus, for Carthaginian captives. But while the Romans have adopted Carthaginian ways and lost their national spirit, the Carthaginian captives in Rome have acquired warlike Roman ways, and their return would give the enemy an advantage. Hence Regulus insists that he must not be ransomed, even though Bodostor, the Carthaginian envoy, threatens him with death by unheard-of tortures. Before the Senate, Regulus offers himself as a sacrifice to his country: 'Das Opfer ist bereit' (l. 935). He opposes the pleading of his family, insisting: 'Der Tod wird Pflicht, wenn er dem Staate frommt' [Death becomes a duty when it serves the state] (l. 1104). His self-sacrificing patriotism places him also in opposition to Bodostor, who turns out to be a spokesman of the Enlightenment. Bodostor advocates cosmopolitanism, speaking of 'der Menschheit Recht' [the rights of humanity] (l. 1219) and condemning Regulus's patriotism as narrow. Regulus declares that his sacrifice for Rome is entirely voluntary: 'Ich will für Rom ein freies Opfer bluten!' [I want to bleed for Rome as a free sacrifice!] (l. 2378). Finally he is led away and sets off for Carthage and death. He lays down his life for his fatherland Rome in an exalted discourse of sacrifice that anticipates the Prussian nationalism of Kleist's *Prinz Friedrich von Homburg*.

There is, nevertheless, a difference worth stressing between Collin and Kleist, and it can be described with the help of the distinction made by contemporaries between patriotism and nationalism. This distinction is sharply drawn by Samuel Bredetzky, a Protestant clergyman, educationalist, and geologist who worked some reflections on the subject into a travel book he published in 1809. Bredetzky, an Austrian subject, had been born and brought up in Hungary, and the targets of his criticism would appear to be early Hungarian nationalists. He feels that patriotism, in the sense of selfless devotion to one's country, is being displaced by nationalism, which noisily proclaims the unique virtues of one's country and people. Although Bredetzky had attended university at Jena, and conceived a great admiration for Fichte, his experience there predated Fichte's nationalist turn. He complains:

> Nichts wird in unsern Zeiten leichter mit einander verwechselt als diese zwei ungleichartigen Zwillingsschwestern, *Nationalismus* und *Patriotismus*. Patriotismus ist das heilige Feuer, welches den *edlen*, guten Staatsbürger zu edlen Handlungen antreibt, ein Feuer, das, auf dem Altar des Vaterlandes dargebracht, die höchste Ehre und das größte Lob erwirkt. *Nationalismus* ist jene verderblich schleichende Glut, welche ungesehen die Stütze der Gebäude verkohlt und zum Einsturz vorbereitet. Der Patriot kennt Eigenliebe und Eigendünkel nicht, er liebt und befördert, was dem Vaterlande frommt, was seine Mitbrüder glücklich macht, ohne Geräusch, mit Nachdruck und Würde.[63]

> [No two things are more readily confused in our times than these two unhappy twin sisters, *nationalism* and *patriotism*. Patriotism is the sacred fire that impels the *noble* and good citizen to noble actions, a fire that, offered on the altar of the fatherland, produces the highest honour and the greatest praise. *Nationalism*

Laßt sie koaxen, Die kritischen Frösch' in Preußen und Sachsen! Zwei Jahrhunderte Literatur in Österreich (Vienna: Europaverlag, 1977), pp. 47–60; Peter Skrine, 'Collin's *Regulus* reconsidered', in *Bristol Austrian Studies*, ed. by Brian Keith-Smith (Bristol: Bristol University Press, 1990), pp. 49–72.

63 Samuel Bredetzky, *Reisebemerkungen über Ungern und Galizien*, 2 vols (Vienna: Anton Doll, 1809), I, 185–86.

is that pernicious creeping heat that, unseen, chars the pillars of the building and brings about its collapse. The patriot knows nothing of self-love and vanity, he loves and promotes whatever serves the fatherland and makes his brethren happy, without noise, with force and dignity.]

Part of Bredetzky's case against nationalists is that they elevate national devotion from a dignified religion into an enthusiastic cult. The altar of the fatherland is not enough for them. They wield a censer ('Rauchpfanne') from which clouds of incense arise as a sacrifice to their nation.[64]

This national religion animates Kleist's play. The Prince of Homburg has offended against the law of war by ignoring his orders and leading a charge prematurely. Since the charge was successful, he feels it to be monstrously unjust that he should be imprisoned and condemned to death for disobedience in the field. His sovereign, the Elector of Brandenburg, offers to release him if he can affirm that his sentence is undeserved. Having reflected, the Prince concludes that he does indeed deserve death, and resolves to perish in order to glorify the sacred law of war:

> Ich will das heilige Gesetz des Kriegs,
> Das ich verletzt', im Angesicht des Heers,
> Durch einen freien Tod verherrlichen![65]

[I wish to glorify the sacred law of war, which I have broken, before the face of the army, by a voluntary death!]

Although the word 'Opfer' [sacrifice] is not used here, the concept of sacrifice is clearly present. The Prince intends to lay down his life, not in order to produce any benefit for his country, but in order to glorify the military code on which his country's fame is founded. He wants to bear witness to the patriotism which has become his religion. As such, he is a martyr. The word 'martyr' is derived from the Greek for 'witness', and many of the early Christian martyrs resembled the Prince in voluntarily seeking out a death by which they could publicly bear witness to the glory of their religion.[66]

By contrast, Collin's Regulus is a voluntary sacrificial victim but not, or not mainly, a martyr or witness. His self-sacrifice serves a purpose, that of securing favourable peace terms for the Romans in their negotiations with Carthage. Rather than a military hero, an embodiment of an 'Urvolk', or a martyr to a religious cause, he represents the exemplary conduct of the conscientious, self-sacrificing bureaucrat, such as Joseph II tried to bring into being. Hence Waltraud Heindl, in her study of the Austrian bureaucracy, describes Collin's Regulus as the 'Leitfigur' [exemplar] of the Josephinian bureaucrat.[67] The ideal bureaucrat is prepared to sacrifice his personal happiness for the good of his country. Thus the administrative reforms of Joseph II, combined with the patriotic upsurge of the early nineteenth century, helped to establish the bureaucrat as a central, sometimes tragic figure in

---

64 Ibid., I, 187.
65 *Prinz Friedrich von Homburg*, lines 1750–52, in Kleist, II, 638.
66 See G. W. Bowersock, *Martyrdom and Rome* (Cambridge: Cambridge University Press, 1995).
67 Waltraud Heindl, *Gehorsame Rebellen: Bürokratie und Beamte in Österreich 1780 bis 1848* (Vienna, Cologne, Graz: Böhlau, 1990), p. 43.

Austrian literature. Famous examples include the loyal bureaucrat Bancban in Franz Grillparzer's tragedy, *Ein treuer Diener seines Herrn* [*A Faithful Servant of his Master*] (1826) and the stoical Bezirkshauptmann in Joseph Roth's *Radetzkymarsch* [*The Radetzky March*] (1932).[68] Between patriotic militarism and patriotic bureaucracy, the latter would seem to be the lesser evil.

---

68   I have discussed the figure of Bancban in 'Der patriotische Minister in Grillparzers *Ein treuer Diener seines Herrn und Hebbels Agnes Bernauer*', *Hebbel-Jahrbuch 2010*, pp. 95–119.

PART II

The Austrian Enlightenment

CHAPTER 9

Joseph II in Cultural Memory

This paper offers an initial account of the Austrian Emperor Joseph II and the ways in which his personality, achievements, and failures survived in cultural memory. It is a literary rather than a historical study, with no ambition to rival the historians at their own work. However, the historiography of Joseph II's reign is curiously incomplete. The Cambridge historian Tim Blanning has recently produced an incisive study of Joseph's reign within the rather narrow limits of the 'Profiles in Power' series. His colleague Derek Beales earlier published a very detailed biographical account of Joseph's early life and of the period (1765–80) in which he reigned jointly with his mother Maria Theresia. The promised second volume, dealing with the decade from 1780 to 1790 in which Joseph ruled alone, has yet to appear. For a really thorough account of this decade one must still rely on the study by Paul von Mitrofanov, written a century ago in Russian and translated into German in 1910.[1]

In literary history, two major studies of the cultural impact of Joseph and Josephinism appeared in the 1970s. One was Werner M. Bauer's study of the eighteenth-century Austrian novel, which includes numerous works that used fiction to present Joseph's enlightened principles. The other was Leslie Bodi's *Tauwetter in Wien*, a deeply researched and engagingly written study of prose in the Josephinist decade, covering not only fiction but also the deluge of pamphlet literature (the *Broschürenflut*) released by Joseph's relaxation of the censorship.[2] In 1990 Edward Timms and I sought to take this research further by commissioning a volume of essays on the Austrian Enlightenment and its aftermath. Beginning with an essay by Derek Beales on the question whether Joseph was an enlightened despot, the volume examined the presence of Josephinism in a number of writers from the 1780s down to Stifter and Ebner-Eschenbach, rounding the survey off

1 See T. C. W. Blanning, *Joseph II*, Profiles in Power (London: Longman, 1994); Derek Beales, *Joseph II*, I: *In the Shadow of Maria Theresa, 1741–1780* (Cambridge: Cambridge University Press, 1987); Paul von Mitrofanov, *Joseph II. Seine politische und kulturelle Tätigkeit*, trans. by V. von Demelić (Vienna and Leipzig: C. W. Stern, 1910). [Since this paper was written, Derek Beales's second volume has appeared: *Joseph II*, II: *Against the World, 1780–1790* (Cambridge: Cambridge University Press, 2009); I reviewed it in *European History Quarterly*, 41 (2011), 109–10.]

2 Werner M. Bauer, *Fiktion und Polemik: Studien zum Roman der österreichischen Aufklärung* (Vienna: Verlag der Österreichischen Akademie der Wissenschaften, 1978); Leslie Bodi, *Tauwetter in Wien: Zur Prosa der österreichischen Aufklärung*, 2nd edn (Vienna, Cologne, Weimar: Böhlau, 1995); originally published in 1977.

with an article by the Oxford historian R. J. W. Evans on the survival of Josephinist ideals in the Austrian Vormärz and the 1848 revolution, and with a bibliographical survey by Leslie Bodi of research on the Austrian Enlightenment since his own book.[3] Our volume was an exploration, and I now want to move further into the territory it opened up.

Part of my purpose is to explore the legacy of the Austrian Enlightenment which has in various ways been minimized in the constructions of Austrian cultural history by Claudio Magris, Roger Bauer and Carl Schorske. Magris depicts an Austria dominated by myths of imperial glory disguising actual stagnation.[4] Bauer stresses the continuing dominance of the Baroque heritage.[5] Schorske explores the lasting appeal of a culture of grace, of aristocratic manners, which he contrasts with the rational, bureaucratic culture inherited from Josephinism.[6] All three play down the heritage of the Enlightenment, the ideal of rational government and liberal Catholicism, which were preserved, even if they could only imperfectly be realized, throughout the nineteenth century against much resistance. The image of a cheerfully decadent Austria is only part of the truth, but it has been propagated in the twentieth century as the whole truth, especially by Hugo von Hofmannsthal, with his ideal Baroque Austria suggested by Josef Nadler's literary histories, and perhaps even more by Hermann Bahr, who in the 1920s denounced Josephinism as an attempt to impose rationalism on the essentially conservative and Baroque Austrian character.[7]

Joseph had ruled jointly with his mother, Maria Theresia, since 1765. On her death in 1780 he became sole ruler of the Habsburg Empire. He was determined to introduce reforms, and did so rapidly. A series of decrees concerning the relations between lords and peasants did not quite abolish serfdom but did give former serfs freedom to move about and choose a trade or profession, though they still owed dues and services to their masters. The powers of lords to punish peasants were regulated. Even fox-hunting was considered: Joseph tried to set an example by closing down his own hunt and retraining the huntsmen as foresters or footmen.

Joseph's most famous reforming measures are his Patents of Toleration, which, beginning in October 1781, granted freedom of worship to communities of Lutherans, Calvinists and Greek Orthodox and removed the restrictions on their buying property, joining guilds and attending university. Similar measures removed the much more extensive restrictions on Jews. In dealing with the Church, Joseph ordained that all ecclesiastical appointments required the approval of the state;

---

3   *The Austrian Enlightenment and its Aftermath*, ed. by Ritchie Robertson and Edward Timms, Austrian Studies, 2 (Edinburgh: Edinburgh University Press, 1991).

4   Claudio Magris, *Der habsburgische Mythos in der österreichischen Literatur*, trans. by Madeleine von Pasztory (Salzburg: Otto Müller, 1966).

5   Roger Bauer, *La Réalité, royaume de Dieu* (Munich: Max Hueber, 1965).

6   Carl E. Schorske, *Fin-de-siècle Vienna: Politics and Culture* (Cambridge: Cambridge University Press, 1981); 'Grace and the Word: Austria's Two Cultures and their Modern Fate', in his *Thinking with History: Explorations in the Passage to Modernism* (Princeton, NJ: Princeton University Press, 1998), pp. 125–40.

7   See Hermann Bahr, *Adalbert Stifter. Eine Entdeckung* (Zürich, Leipzig, Vienna: Amalthea, 1919), p. 12; *Selbstbildnis* (Berlin: Fischer, 1923), p. 244.

he dissolved the contemplative monastic orders and transferred their property to charitable use; and he reorganized the training of the clergy into twelve seminaries following a rigorous and uniform curriculum.

All these measures caused such alarm in Rome that in the spring of 1782 Pope Pius VI visited Vienna in person in order to remonstrate with the Emperor. To many contemporaries this seemed the greatest event of the century and a reversal of Canossa, where the Emperor did penance in 1077 before Pope Gregory VII.[8] Relations with the Church, and most other subjects, could be freely discussed thanks to Joseph's relaxation of the censorship. The resulting flood of pamphlets ranged from trivia (Johann Rautenstrauch's *Über die Stubenmädchen in Wien*) to serious historical discussions, notably *Was ist der Pabst?* (1782) by the church historian Johann Valentin Eybel.

Joseph seemed to fulfil the ideal of an enlightened despot, even a philosopher-king. He never uttered the statement attributed to him, 'I have made philosophy the legislator of my empire', but the mistake was significant. Whatever people might have imagined, Joseph had little interest in the *philosophes*.[9] Although he met many of them, including Buffon, d'Alembert, Grimm, and Turgot, in Paris in 1777, it was well known that on his return journey through Switzerland he visited Albrecht von Haller but passed the gates of Ferney without calling on Voltaire, even though the latter was expecting him, had arranged a dinner-party in his honour, and placed peasants in the trees to provide an ovation.[10] His conception of enlightenment, as often in the late eighteenth century, was not intellectual but practical. Goethe says of the progressive landowner in *Wilhelm Meisters Lehrjahre* (V, xvi) that by encouraging agriculture he had promoted 'die wahrste Aufklärung'.[11] Joseph talks constantly about utility ('Nutzen') and the general good. In his decrees, he never began 'So ist unser Wille', but always, 'Das allgemeine Beste [...]'. His reforming measures were justified not on abstract principle but on utilitarian grounds. Thus his decree for abolishing serfdom in Bohemia and Moravia begins:

> Daß die allgemeine Aufhebung der Leibeigenschaft in den Böhmischen Ländern und die Einführung einer gemäßigten nach dem Beispiel der Österreichischen Lande eingerichteten Untertänigkeit auf die Verbesserung der dortendigen Cultur und Industrie den nützlichsten Einfluß nehmen würde, daß auch die Vernunfts- und Menschenliebe selbst für diese Abänderung das Wort spreche, kann nach reiferer Überlegung nicht wohl einem gegründeten Widerspruch mehr unterliegen.[12]

8   See Elisabeth Kovács, *Der Pabst in Teutschland: Die Reise Pius VI. im Jahre 1782* (Vienna: Verlag für Geschichte und Politik, 1983).

9   See Derek Beales, 'Christians and *philosophes*: The Case of the Austrian Enlightenment', in *History, Society and the Churches: Essays in Honour of Owen Chadwick*, ed. by Derek Beales and Geoffrey Best (Cambridge: Cambridge University Press, 1985), pp. 169–94.

10   Letter by Joseph, 16–17 July 1777, quoted in Beales, *Joseph II*, p. 382.

11   Johann Wolfgang Goethe, *Werke*, Hamburger Ausgabe, ed. by Erich Trunz, 14 vols, Hamburg 1949–60, VII, 348. On this version of the Enlightenment, see Franco Venturi, *Utopia and Reform in the Enlightenment* (Cambridge: Cambridge University Press, 1971).

12   Resolution Josephs II. 'Gründe zur Aufhebung der Leibeigenschaft in Böhmen und Mähren', 23 April 1781, in *Der Josephinismus: Ausgewählte Quellen zur Geschichte der theresianisch-josephinischen Reformen*, ed. by Harm Klueting (Darmstadt: Wissenschaftliche Buchgesellschaft, 1995), p. 240.

His edicts of toleration were similarly intended to release the productive capacity of his Protestant and Jewish subjects by admitting them to a full range of occupations. These measures accompanied a drive towards homogenization and Germanization.

With Jews, Joseph was not respectful towards their institutions: he suppressed the rabbinical courts and had Hebrew replaced by the official languages (German in most provinces, Latin in Hungary) in contracts, wills, court proceedings, and education. Other regulations concerning dress, beards, and names, and the requirement to attend the public schools, sought to make Jews outwardly indistinguishable from other people. Joseph aimed to weld his diverse subjects into a single nation which should ultimately resemble more homogeneous nations such as France. The abbé Georgel, secretary to the French embassy, reports the following utterance: 'C'est un rude métier, me disoit un jour l'Empereur Joseph II, que d'avoir à manier des peuples si éloignés du centre et de caractère si opposés; on ne peut les contenir ou les mouvoir qu'avec une chaîne de fer.'[13]

Joseph's enlightened reforms were based on his own selfless devotion to what he considered his subjects' good. He shared the ideal formulated by Frederick the Great, who in many respects was his role model, of being 'only the first servant of the state, obliged to act with honesty, wisdom, and with a complete lack of self-interest'.[14] In practice, however, his reforms were hampered by his methods, which included excessive haste and severity, along with a tendency to micro-management and workaholism. His ideals and his management style can be illustrated from the famous 'Hirtenbrief' he issued to his civil servants on 13 December 1783, exhorting them in schoolmasterly tones to devote themselves whole-heartedly to the common good:

> Aus diesem folgt, dass bey allen stellen ohne ausnahm jederman [sic] einen solchen trieb zu seinem geschäft haben muss, dass er nicht nach stunden, nicht nach tägen, nicht nach seiten seine arbeit berechnen, sondern alle seine kräften anspannen muss, wenn er geschäfte hat, um selbe vollkommen nach der erwartung und nach seiner pflicht auszuführen und, wenn er keine hat, auch derjenigen erholung, die man so billig doppelt empfindet, wenn man seine pflicht erfüllt zu haben sich bewusst ist, geniesse.
> Der nicht liebe zum dienst des vaterlandes und seiner mitbürger hat, der für erhaltung des guten nicht von einem besonderen eifer sich entflammt findet, der ist für geschäfte nicht gemacht und nicht werth, ehrentiteln zu besitzen und besoldungen zu ziehen.[15]

Since he depended on support from the civil service, it was not a shrewd move to deprive civil servants of 'Hofquartiere', free accommodation in the city. The parents of Caroline Pichler, the famous salonnière and memoirist, got off lightly:

---

13 *Mémoires pour servir à l'histoire des événements de la fin du dix-huitième siècle depuis 1760 jusqu'en 1806–1810, par un contemporain impartial, Feu M. l'abbé Georgel* (Paris: Alexis Eymery, 1820), vol. 1, p. 368.

14 Quoted in T. C. W. Blanning, *The Culture of Power and the Power of Culture: Old Regime Europe, 1660–1789* (Oxford: Oxford University Press, 2002), p. 195.

15 Klueting, p. 335.

Hofrat Greiner and his family managed to rent a pleasant flat on the Neuer Markt.[16] Others, however, had to move to the suburbs, and those on pensions had to move to the provinces. Joseph showed similar insensitivity when he ordained that, because of the timber shortage in Vienna, corpses should be sewn into linen sacks instead of being buried in coffins — an edict which aroused such fury that it had to be withdrawn. Leslie Bodi argues that the public rejection of this measure marked a turning-point in Joseph's reform campaign and rendered him permanently disillusioned and embittered. Certainly Joseph's resentment is clear from his written instructions to his chancellor:

> Da ich sehe und täglich erfahre, daß die Begriffe der Lebendigen leider! noch
> so materiel sind, daß sie einen unendlichen Preis darauf setzen, daß ihre Körper
> nach dem Tode langsamer faulen, und länger ein stinkendes Aas bleiben: so
> ist mir wenig daran gelegen, wie sich die Leute wollen begraben lassen; und
> werden Sie also durchaus erklären, daß nachdem ich die vernünftigen Ursachen,
> die Nutzbarkeit und Möglichkeit dieser Art Begräbnisse gezeigt habe, ich
> keinen Menschen, der nicht davon überzeugt ist, zwingen will, vernünftig zu
> seyn, und daß also ein jeder, was die Truhen belangt, frey thun kann, was er
> für seinen todten Körper zum voraus für das Angenehmste hält.[17]

Joseph's toleration required all Christians to register with one of the three tolerated Churches. The peasant Deists of Bohemia professed belief in one God, and the immortality of the soul, but denied the Trinity and had no visible church but worshipped in their own homes. They refused to register as Lutherans, as the Hussites had done. So on 8 March 1783 Joseph ordered the young men to be conscripted into the army, the other adults transported to Hungary and Transylvania, and the children under fifteen placed with Catholic guardians. They were persecuted essentially because they did not fit into neat categories. (Since persecution only increased their numbers, Joseph had later to abate his severity.) Joseph's criminal code commuted the death penalty to hard labour on the grounds that convicts could thus be made useful to the state. Joseph usually found conditions in prison too mild. He insisted that prisoners should sleep in chains on straw pallets in unheated rooms and live on bread and water. Those who reported sick had the periods they spent in hospital added to the length of their sentence. In 1783 Joseph proposed that prisoners should make themselves useful by hauling barges up the Danube, sleeping at night in unlit underground bunkers with only air-holes along the bank. Over six years, 721 out of 1100 men died while hauling barges.[18]

His obsessive devotion to the service of his state led Joseph to concern himself with such trifling matters that Blanning has called him 'a terrible busy-body who could not mind his own business'.[19] He issued a resolution against making a noise in public (1 Aug. 1781): 'Das muthwillige Schreien und Händeklatschen auf der Gasse

---

16   Caroline Pichler, *Denkwürdigkeiten aus meinem Leben*, ed. by Emil Karl Blümml, 2 vols (Munich: Georg Müller, 1914), I, 63–64.

17   Quoted in Bodi, *Tauwetter in Wien*, p. 245.

18   See Paul P. Bernard, *The Limits of Enlightenment: Joseph II and the Law* (Urbana, Chicago and London: University of Illinois Press, 1979).

19   Blanning, *Joseph II*, p. 62.

ist bey angemessener Strafe jedermann ohne Rücksicht verboten.'[20] He ordered that street lights should use brass lamps, not copper ones. He told his chief of police, Count Pergen, that a Jewish woman named Neuhauser had acquired a bar of silver of dubious origin; Joseph had himself organized a search for the bar, and he told Pergen to round up the woman's accomplices. Pergen himself, not to be outdone, held four hearings to establish that one Elisabeth Eberlein had offered for sale some overripe beans, and Joseph commended his zeal.[21] He worked at least ten hours, sometimes eighteen hours a day. In summer he rose at 5, in winter at 6. He went to bed at 11, but if there was urgent business he would work at it till late at night. He always had three or four secretaries to hand, and when he went on travels, usually had a carriage with a desk installed in it.

In conscious opposition to the Baroque tradition of magnificent representation, Joseph's manners were simple. The British ambassador, Lord Stormont, reports enthusiastically: 'He often runs about with a single Servant behind Him; likes to converse with men of all Ranks, puts those he talks to, quite at their Ease; loves easy, familiar Conversations, as much as He hates to talk in a circle.'[22] He generally wore a simple uniform without decorations. He called most people 'Sie', which was then unusual; on journeys he would stay at inns, instead of lodging in noble mansions or in town halls where they were received with elaborate ceremonies; he ate simply, and sometimes had his coat mended while travelling. He slept on straw-filled sacks, covered with a deerskin; even when staying with noblemen, he would have the bed removed from his room and would lie on the straw. Even when his health was declining in 1789 it was very difficult to persuade him to sleep on a mattress.[23] But some observers found this simplicity affected, and of course it was itself a form of public display. A famous occasion when Joseph staged his simplicity was the incident on his journey through Moravia in 1769 when he took a peasant's plough and drove it himself for a whole furrow. Pictures of Joseph driving the plough were widely distributed, and over a century later they served the purposes of Pan-German propaganda in the Vienna inhabited by the young Hitler.[24]

Regarding himself as responsible to the entire population, Joseph made himself unusually accessible. He received his subjects in the Controlorgang, a long corridor on the first floor of the Leopoldinischer Trakt; they would wait with petitions, and he would come out of his office several times a day (not at fixed times) and hear them; some petitioners were taken into a small room for private discussions. Being willing to hear all his subjects, he naturally wasted some time with cranks, such as

20   Decree of 1 August 1781, quoted in Mitrofanov, p. 271.

21   Paul P. Bernard, *From the Enlightenment to the Police State: The Public Life of Johann Anton Pergen* (Urbana and Chicago: University of Illinois Press, 1991), p. 132.

22   Quoted in Beales, *Joseph II*, I, 308.

23   These and many other personal details come from Johann Pezzl, *Charakteristik Josephs des Zweiten*, 3rd edn (Vienna: Degen, 1803). Pezzl's account, and much else, is reprinted in Franz Gräffer (ed.), *Josephinische Curiosa; oder ganz besondere, theils nicht mehr, theils noch nicht bekannte Persönlichkeiten, Geheimnisse, Details, Actenstücke und Denkwürdigkeiten der Lebens- und Zeitgeschichte Kaiser Josephs II.* (Vienna: Klang, 1848).

24   On the incident, Beales, *Joseph II*, I, 338; on its later exploitation, Brigitte Hamann, *Hitlers Wien: Lehrjahre eines Diktators* (Munich: Piper, 1996), pp. 163–64.

one Baron Calistus, who told him that the Hungarian town of Komorn suffered from an earthquake every five years; but as there are no earthquakes in Egypt, and Egypt differs from other countries only in having pyramids, the best defence against earthquakes was to build pyramids.[25] He showed his benevolence by often walking alone in Vienna, speaking affably to ordinary people. He had the Prater and the Augarten opened to the public. He was always first on the scene at disasters such as fires and floods, and for this purpose kept a horse ready saddled night and day. The Prussian ambassador Riedesel, who was hostile to Joseph, reports how in 1785 he appeared among the people rendered homeless by the flooding of the Danube. The people declared that he was responsible, because his attacks on the Church had called down God's punishment. The Emperor merely shrugged his shoulders.[26]

This little incident epitomizes Joseph's tragedy. Sincerely devoted to his people's welfare, he forced on them unwanted (though often salutary) reforms, and received little thanks. No wonder that he became morose and suspicious. Moreover, his devotion to public government was in part a displacement of private emotional frustrations. His first wife, Isabella of Parma, died after three years. According to Caroline Pichler, who had good sources of information at court, after her death, Joseph's sister Christina, in whom Isabella had confided, tried to cure his grief by showing him private letters in which Isabella revealed that she did not love him. The effect of this clumsy therapy was what one might imagine (Pichler, I, 123–24). Joseph's second marriage to Princess Maria Josefa of Bavaria was political, loveless, and childless, and likewise short. Thereafter Joseph satisfied his sensual desires with what chroniclers discreetly call 'Nymphen'. He was not a cultivated man, though he appreciated music and played the cello, and his notorious remark that Mozart had too many notes was not, in its context, so silly as it sounds. The court composer and official Ditters von Dittersdorf reports him as saying: 'Nur in Theaterstücken dünkt mich, daß er öfters zu viele Noten anbringt, worüber die Sänger sich sehr beklagen' (Gräffer, II, 172).

Joseph died on 20 February 1790 of tuberculosis which he had contracted during the unpopular and largely unsuccessful campaign against Turkey. To preserve support, he had already had to repeal some of his reforms, especially those affecting Hungary. He felt on his death-bed that his career had been a failure. He received official eulogies, but according to the diplomat Hammer-Purgstall, his funeral not only failed to provoke grief among the people but was even an indecently cheerful occasion.[27] A contemporary satire, inspired by sympathy with the insurgents in the Austrian Netherlands, runs:

> Que me restera-t-il pour ma gloire et mes peines?
> — Peines.
> Mais qu'auront mes sujets et les Belges surtout?
> — Tout.

25 This anecdote comes from 'Josephinische Memorabilien von dem 1810 verstorbenen Hofrath von Bretschneider' in Gräffer, I, 106–27 (pp. 124–25).

26 Mitrofanov, p. 107, following Riedesel's dispatch of 3 August 1783.

27 Joseph Freiherr von Hammer-Purgstall, *Erinnerungen aus meinem Leben, 1774–1852* (Vienna and Leipzig: Holder-Pichler-Tempsky, 1940), p. 25.

Et que deviendront donc mes peuples malheureux?
— Heureux.
Et qui suis-je donc moi, qui me croyait immortel?
— Mortel.
L'Univers n'est-il plus tout rempli de mon nom?
— Non.
Tous mes peuples soumis ne me craigneront donc plus?
— Plus.
Autrefois mon seul nom inspirait terreur.
— Erreur.
Laisse-moi, je te prie, je souffre et je me meurs.
— Meurs.[28]

After a time, however, Joseph came to be idealized. Goethe represents him in the anti-revolutionary drama *Die Aufgeregten* as a ruler who, like Frederick the Great, could have averted revolution by imposing reforms from above (Goethe, v, 202). Other writers, inside and outside Austria, celebrated the 'Volkskaiser', the modest emperor who went about incognito quietly doing good, and thus assimilated him to the image of the ruler as man of the people best illustrated by Shakespeare in *Henry V*. In 1810 Johann Peter Hebel wrote the story 'Ein gutes Rezept' of how Joseph discreetly gave charity to a sick man. The Austrian Jewish writer Leopold Kompert introduces Joseph into his first published story, 'Judith die Zweite' (1846) as a philanthropist, and likewise into the later story 'Die beiden Schwerter' (1861), though here Kompert is more critical, implying that Joseph's emancipation of the Jews was too half-hearted.[29] Liberals regarded him as an ideal. Anastasius Grün included in his *Spaziergänge eines Wiener Poeten* (1831) a poem addressed to the Emperor's statue, defending his enlightened despotism:

Ein Despot bist du gewesen! Doch ein solcher, wie der Tag,
Dessen Sonne Nacht und Nebel neben sich nicht dulden mag.[30]

And in 1848 Joseph was a hero of the Revolution, particularly as a 'German Emperor' who anticipated the ideal of 'Großdeutschland'. On the morning of 2 April 1848 the academic legion marched to the statue of Joseph II to demonstrate their German nationalism, and thence to the Hofburg in order to deliver a German flag to the Emperor.[31] Many poems were addressed to his memory. 'Kaiser Joseph', by Freiherr von Lazarini, described the Revolution as the culmination of Josephinism: 'Du großer Kaiser, des Lichtes Heiland, | Der Wahrheit Apostel und König! | Wir haben erreicht der Freiheit Eiland, | Ihr Lied gehört wundertönig.'[32]

---

28   Quoted in Friedrich Engel-Jánosi, 'Josephs II. Tod im Urteil der Zeitgenossen', *Mitteilungen des Instituts für österreichische Geschichte*, 44 (1930), 324–46 (p. 332).

29   See M. Theresia Wittemann, *Draußen vor dem Ghetto. Leopold Kompert und die 'Schilderung jüdischen Volkslebens' in Böhmen und Mähren* (Tübingen: Niemeyer, 1998), p. 176.

30   *Anastasius Grün's gesammelte Werke*, ed. by Ludwig August Frankl (Berlin, 1877), II, 370.

31   R. J. Rath, *The Viennese Revolution of 1848* (Austin: University of Texas Press, 1957), pp. 133–34.

32   Joseph Alexander Freiherr von Helfert, *Der Wiener Parnaß im Jahre 1848* (Vienna, 1882; repr. Hildesheim: Olms, 1977), p. 127.

Grillparzer, who has been plausibly described as 'Josephiner im innersten Grunde seines Herzens',[33] noted in his diary that Joseph had set about his reforms too hastily, but the reaction against him had also been over-hasty, and that his despotism, like those of Louis XIV and Frederick the Great, formed 'ein notwendiges Mittelglied in dem seit Luther begonnenen Fortschreiten der Emanzipation der Menschheit' (Grillparzer, III, 987). In public, he had his say about Joseph in two poems, 'Des Kaisers Bildsäule' (1837) and 'Kaiser Joseph' (1855), in both of which the statue of Joseph by Zauner outside the National Library is supposed to contrast current events with his own rule. In the former poem, Joseph contrasts his own devotion to equality and justice with the state of affairs in which a nobleman can escape trial for injuring a policeman by riding him down. Joseph in fact so valued justice that even noblemen might as convicted criminals be seen among the chain-gangs that in his day kept Vienna's streets clean. Grillparzer also holds up Joseph as an exemplar of religious toleration and cultural Germanization, rebuking the nationalism of the Vormärz.

> Und über meine Völker, vieler Zungen,
> Flog hin des deutschen Adlers Sonnenflug,
> Er hielt, was fremd, mit leisem Band umschlungen,
> Vereinend, was sich töricht selbst genug. (Grillparzer, I, 252–53)

If, however, we want to trace the afterlife of Josephinism, we need to look much further than literary texts where Joseph is explicitly named, and I want to suggest three areas for investigation. First: although Joseph encountered obstruction from his civil service, they also gave his reforms much support. The bureaucrat Joseph Rohrer, who around 1800 wrote the first three volumes of a projected ethnographic account of all the nations of the Empire, declares himself still an ardent Josephinist. He describes the inscription which has been placed, with (as he emphasizes) official permission, on the house of a wealthy Greek in the Fleischmarkt. Beneath a likeness of Joseph II the following verse is inscribed in golden letters:

> Vergänglich ist dies Haus
> Doch Josephs Nachruhm nie
> Er gab uns Toleranz
> Unsterblichkeit gibt sie.[34]

Robert Evans has written about the networks of bureaucrats who continued to adhere to Josephinism. Many writers were themselves bureaucrats, including Grillparzer, Bauernfeld and Castelli. In such writings, including reminiscences by non-literary people, I suspect that much evidence of Joseph's continuing popularity can be found. Waltraud Heindl's work on the Austrian bureaucracy suggests further sources to look at.[35]

---

33   Peter Kuranda, 'Grillparzer und die Politik des Vormärzes', *Jahrbuch der Grillparzer-Gesellschaft*, 28 (1926), 1–21 (p. 3).

34   Joseph Rohrer, *Neuestes Gemählde von Wien* (Vienna: Doll, 1797), p. 12.

35   R. J. W. Evans, 'Josephinism, "Austrianness", and the Revolution of 1848', *Austrian Studies*, 2 (1991), 145–60; Waltraud Heindl, *Gehorsame Rebellen: Bürokratie und Beamte in Österreich 1780 bis 1848* (Vienna, Cologne, Graz: Böhlau, 1990).

Secondly, we need to look at the afterlife of the Catholic Enlightenment in Austria. Joseph shared the aspirations of the Catholic reform movement which had developed in the Habsburg territories by the mid-eighteenth century.[36] The reformers were influenced by Jansenism, which, originating in seventeenth-century France as a theological movement stressing man's need for God's free grace and the inefficacy of human works, developed into a broad movement opposed to the Baroque cults of saints and the Virgin Mary promoted by the Jesuits; they preferred a simple liturgy in a bare hall, focusing on an unadorned altar, and presided over by the parish priest, whose role they considered much more valuable than that of monastic orders. In urging austerity and inwardness, they agreed with the well-known historian Ludovico Antonio Muratori (1672–1760), who in *Della regolata divozione de' Christiani* (1747) condemned processions, pilgrimages and festivals as leading to disorder and impiety; church services should be orderly, with beggars and animals excluded from services; devotion should be inward, focusing on the word of Scripture rather than images, under the guidance of well-educated parish priests. The Catholic Enlightenment had a lasting influence in Austria, typified by Bernard Bolzano, but in tension both with a popular inclination to Baroque piety and with the Romantic revival of Catholicism centred on the figure of Clemens Maria Hofbauer. Another strand of Josephinism is the anticlericalism that animated many of its supporters. The history of literary anticlericalism in Austria has been sketched by Peter Horwath,[37] but much remains to be explored, including the anticlericalism found in Grillparzer with the figure of the Priest in *Des Meeres und der Liebe Wellen* and, much more blatantly, thanks to the temporary relaxation of censorship around 1848, by Nestroy in depicting the expulsion of the Redemptorists in *Freiheit in Krähwinkel* and in satirizing superstition and pilgrimages in *Höllenangst*.[38]

Thirdly, I want to look at the figure of the ideal ruler in literary works to see if such a person shows Josephinist traits even if not explicitly compared to Joseph. We find such ideal rulers in comedy, with Astragalus in Raimund's *Der Alpenkönig und der Menschenfeind*, whom Wendelin Schmidt-Dengler has recently described as 'den idealen josephinischen Herrscher'.[39] I would argue that such a figure is present also in fiction in the person of Risach, whose estate in *Der Nachsommer* is a model of the Josephinist state, run autocratically but humanely in a spirit of practical enlightenment and utility that finds expression above all in the promotion of agriculture: 'Ich besuche auch um meiner Nachbarn willen gern diesen Platz; denn [...] außerdem daß ich hier unter meinen Arbeitern bin, sehe ich von hier aus alle, die mich umgeben, es fällt mir manches von ihnen ein, und ich ermesse, wie ich ihnen nützen kann, oder wie überhaupt das Allgemeine gefördert werden möge'.[40]

36   For an introduction, see Owen Chadwick, *The Popes and European Revolution* (Oxford: Clarendon Press, 1981), ch. 6. [*A Companion to the Catholic Enlightenment in Europe*, ed. by Jeffrey D. Burson and Ulrich L. Lehner (Leiden: Brill, 2010).]

37   Peter Horwath, *Der Kampf gegen die religiöse Tradition: Die Kulturkampfliteratur Österreichs, 1780–1918* (Bern: Peter Lang, 1978).

38   See Colin Walker, 'Nestroy and the Redemptorists', in *Bristol Austrian Studies*, ed. by Brian Keith-Smith (Bristol: Bristol University Press, 1990), pp. 73–116.

39   Wendelin Schmidt-Dengler, *Nestroy: Die Launen des Glückes* (Vienna: Zsolnay, 2001), p. 48.

40   Adalbert Stifter, *Gesammelte Werke*, ed. by Konrad Steffen, 14 vols (Basel and Stuttgart:

An indirect response to Joseph which I now want to examine more closely is Grillparzer's *König Ottokar*. The play is no longer seen as a glorification of the Habsburgs. Rather, the positive presentation of Rudolf embodies an indirect reproof to Franz I by standards that were still current among middle-class audiences who remained sympathetic to Josephinism.[41] The negative portrayal of Ottokar is seen as a portrait of Napoleon, since Grillparzer acknowledged an 'entfernte Ähnlichkeit' between Ottokar and Napoleon, at least as regards his territorial ambitions and his private life. The play is still often seen as turning on a static opposition between the proud, self-centred tyrant Ottokar and the wise, restrained, selfless ideal monarch Rudolf.[42] Like many commonplaces, however, these need revision. Not only have both kings undergone a process of development: Rudolf from a headstrong young man to a wise monarch; Ottokar, now a tyrant, used to be, in the eyes of Seyfried von Merenberg, 'ein Muster, Vorbild [nicht] | Von jedem hohen Tun' (ll. 20–21). The opposition is qualified, as Edward McInnes noted in 1978, by many hints in the play that political events have their own dynamism, and that Ottokar's failure to build alliances, Rudolf's seeming not to pose a threat to the electors, and Rudolf's activity in uniting princes 'Durch kluge Heirat und durch kräftges Wort' (line 1487), affect the outcome as much as Ottokar's vices and Rudolf's virtue.[43] Above all, Ottokar's ambitions are not solely personal. He wants to make Prague a capital comparable to Cologne, Vienna, London and Paris. He inquires minutely into the building of walls and bridges in Prague. And, despite being king of the Bohemians, he has imported German artisans and caused a suburb of Prague to be reserved for them, the original inhabitants being transferred to another territory at the state's expense. This is often taken as an example of Ottokar's tyranny, but it is never censured elsewhere in the play. It gives some justification for the Marxist critic who accordingly interpreted Ottokar as a progressive figure.[44] This activity also assists the Germanization of Central Europe; and it is extremely high-handed. In all these ways it resembles the hasty reforming policies of Joseph II.

If the reforming aspect of Joseph II is projected into Ottokar, Joseph's public persona is adopted by Rudolf. Like Joseph, Rudolf rejects elaborate representation. Ottokar arrives at their meeting magnificently arrayed; Rudolf is discovered in his tent, hammering at a helmet to remove the dents (rather as Joseph used to have his coat mended while travelling), and this duly impresses the public, who whisper to

Birkhäuser, 1965), VI, 73–74.

41   See Harald Steinhagen, 'Grillparzers *König Ottokar*: Drama, Geschichte und Zeitgeschichte', *Jahrbuch der Deutschen Schiller-Gesellschaft*, 14 (1970), 456–87 (p. 482).

42   See e.g. Jutta Greis, 'Fürstenutopie im literarischen Gestern: *König Ottokars Glück und Ende*', in *Gerettete Ordnung: Grillparzers Dramen*, ed. by Bernhard Budde and Ulrich Schmidt (Frankfurt a.M., Bern, New York: Peter Lang, 1987), pp. 106–25 (p. 112); Jürgen Schröder, ' "Der Tod macht gleich": Grillparzers Geschichtsdramen', in *Franz Grillparzer: Historie und Gegenwärtigkeit*, ed. by Gerhard Neumann and Günter Schnitzler (Freiburg i.Br.: Rombach, 1994), pp. 37–57 (p. 45).

43   See Edward McInnes, '*König Ottokar* and Grillparzer's Conception of Historical Drama', in Bruce Thompson and Mark Ward (eds), *Essays on Grillparzer*, New German Studies, 5 (Hull: Hull University German Department, 1978), pp. 25–36.

44   Claus Träger, 'Geschichte, "Geist" und Grillparzer: Ein klassischer Nationalautor und seine Deutungen', *Weimarer Beiträge*, 7 (1961), 449–519.

each other: 'Gevatter Grobschmied, saht ihr wohl? Der Kaiser, | Den Hammer in der Hand! Vivat Rudolphus!' (ll. 1614–15). He talks familiarly and affably to the people, as Joseph did. Rudolf combines the ancient notion of the king who, as such, never dies with the more recent image of the 'Volkskaiser'. And the play *König Ottokar* thus explores both the weaknesses and the strengths associated with Joseph II.

   Here is a final example of how the memory of Joseph II could live on in disguised form. Joseph Roth includes in *Radetzkymarsch* the story of how the Emperor Franz Joseph receives homage from his Jewish subjects in Galicia:

> 'Gesegnet bist du!' sagte der Jude zum Kaiser. 'Den Untergang der Welt wirst du nicht erleben!' Ich weiß es! dachte Franz Joseph. Er gab dem Alten die Hand. Er wandte sich um. Er bestieg seinen Schimmel.
> Er trabte nach links über die harten Schollen der herbstlichen Felder, gefolgt von seiner Suite. Der Wind trug ihm die Worte zu, die Rittmeister Kaunitz zu seinem Freund an der Seite sprach: 'Ich hab' keinen Ton von dem Juden verstanden!' Der Kaiser wandte sich im Sattel um und sagte: 'Er hat auch nur zu mir gesprochen, lieber Kaunitz!' und ritt weiter.[45]

The name of the officer, Kaunitz, is a giveaway. For it is the name of the statesman, Prince Wenzel Anton von Kaunitz, who advised both Maria Theresia and Joseph II. It reveals that Roth has superimposed his image of Franz Joseph on that of the earlier Volkskaiser, Joseph II, a complex case of cultural memory.

---

45 Joseph Roth, *Werke*, ed. by Klaus Westermann and Fritz Hackert, 6 vols (Cologne: Kiepenheuer & Witsch, 1989–91), V, 350.

CHAPTER 10

Curiosity in the
Austrian Enlightenment

Madame de Staël, who visited Vienna in 1808, thought that a combination of natural sluggishness, Catholicism, and censorship had kept the Austrians immune to the Northern spirit of Enlightenment, apart from a brief and unproductive flash during the reign of Joseph II: 'L'esprit du catholicisme qui dominait à Vienne, quoique toujours avec sagesse, avait pourtant écarté sous le règne de Marie-Thérèse ce qu'on appelait les lumières du dix-huitième siècle.'[1] This was less than fair: the Austrian Enlightenment extends back to the reign of Maria Theresia, many of its proponents were loyal though reform-minded Catholics, and they were driven, as much as their German counterparts, by a spirit of curiosity.

The medieval Church approved of wonder but disapproved of curiosity, which St Augustine condemned as 'the concupiscence of the eyes'.[2] But just how far did these strictures against curiosity last into the eighteenth century? Here an important dual role was played by the Jesuits. As the spearhead of the Counter-Reformation, they had a particular responsibility for education. They relied heavily on visual media — images of saints, church architecture, spectacular plays — and discouraged intellectual inquiry by the laity. Yet they were also keenly interested in science and languages, especially as missionaries. By the mid-eighteenth century, however, their educational methods, which relied heavily on rote-learning, looked outdated. The sweeping university reforms undertaken by Gerard van Swieten at the request of Maria Theresia in 1749–52 were intended partly to reduce the Jesuits' dominance and to introduce a wider range of well-qualified teachers.[3] So while the Jesuits in some ways promoted curiosity, in others they tended to stifle it.

Another potential deterrent to curiosity was censorship. It was intended to keep books prejudicial to faith and morals out of the Habsburg Monarchy. Travellers had

1   Germaine de Staël, *De l'Allemagne*, 2 vols (Paris: Garnier-Flammarion, 1968), I, 79.

2   Quoted in Lorraine Daston and Katharine Park, *Wonders and the Order of Nature, 1150–1750* (New York: Zone Books, 1998), p. 123.

3   See Rudolf Kink, *Geschichte der kaiserlichen Universität in Wien*, 2 vols (Vienna: Gerold, 1854), esp. I, 424–25 for the detailed criticism of Jesuit education; further Winfried Müller, 'Der Jesuitenorden und die Aufklärung im süddeutsch-österreichischen Raum', in *Katholische Aufklärung: Aufklärung im katholischen Deutschland*, ed. by Harm Klueting (Hamburg: Meiner, 1993), pp. 225–45 (esp. pp. 229–33).

their books confiscated at the frontier: 'The Monarchy's list of prohibited books was longer than the pope's.'[4] Until 1753 censorship was in the hands of the Jesuits. After that Maria Theresia appointed a 'Zensurkommission' chaired by Gerard van Swieten. By placing him in charge, she supported a policy of permitting writers now regarded as safe (Montesquieu, Leibniz, Wolff, Thomasius, Newton, Locke), but preserving Austria from radical influences (such as Voltaire, Hume, Diderot and Spinoza). The censorship was still full of anomalies, resulting in part from van Swieten's wish to admit enlightened works of political science without alarming Maria Theresia, who could override the 'Zensurkommission'. Hence trade-offs were required: the price of admitting Montesquieu's *L'Esprit des lois* was the banning of his *Lettres persanes*.[5] However, the existence of censorship itself aroused curiosity about censored works — so much so that in 1777 the index of prohibited books had itself to be prohibited.[6]

Moreover, the censorship was notoriously permeable. Almost any prohibited book could be obtained for a high enough price. Johann Baptist de Terme, a leading Jansenist in Vienna, obtained them via a merchant who allowed books to be concealed among the goods he imported from Holland.[7] Father Rudolf von Graser, of the Benedictine monastery at Kremsmünster, obtained German works of rationalist theology through a scythe-dealer from Wels who got them at the Leipzig book fair and smuggled them into the monastery.[8] The library in the Benedictine abbey at Melk had a second-hand copy of the *Encyclopédie*, though it was officially banned.[9] In 1778, the young Ignaz Fessler, training for the priesthood in Wiener Neustadt, managed to read works by Hobbes, Machiavelli, Tindal, Bacon, and Reimarus, which he borrowed from friends in Vienna.[10]

In any case, the Habsburg Monarchy could not have been cordoned off from European influences, because so many of its leading figures were themselves immigrants from Western Europe. The best-known was Gerard van Swieten himself. A Dutchman, summoned to Vienna as a professor of medicine, he was a fellow countryman and family friend of the chemist and botanist Nikolaus Joseph Jacquin, and encouraged Jacquin to move to Vienna to complete his studies. These and many other Catholic 'Wahlösterreicher' were among the dynamic figures of the Austrian Enlightenment.[11]

---

4   Derek Beales, *Enlightenment and Reform in Eighteenth-Century Europe* (London: Tauris, 2005), p. 69.

5   See Joseph von Sonnenfels, 'Die erste Vorlesung in dem akademischen Jahrgange 1782', *Sonnenfels gesammelte Schriften*, 10 vols (Vienna: no pub., 1786), VIII, 103–46 (pp. 112–13).

6   See Grete Klingenstein, *Staatsverwaltung und kirchliche Autorität im 18. Jahrhundert: Das Problem der Zensur in der theresianischen Reform* (Vienna: Verlag für Geschichte und Politik, 1970), p. 201.

7   Peter Hersche, *Der Spätjansenismus in Österreich* (Vienna: Verlag der Österreichischen Akademie der Wissenschaften, 1977), p. 233.

8   Johann Willibald Nagl, Jakob Zeidler and Eduard Castle, *Deutsch-Österreichische Literaturgeschichte*, 4 vols (Vienna: Fromme, 1914–37), II, 22.

9   Johannes Frimmel, *Literarisches Leben in Melk: Ein Kloster im 18. Jahrhundert im kulturellen Umbruch* (Vienna, Cologne, Weimar: Böhlau, 2004), p. 147.

10   [Ignaz-Aurelius Fessler], *Dr. Fessler's Rückblicke auf seine siebzigjährige Pilgerschaft: Ein Nachlass* [*sic*] *an seine Freunde und an seine Feinde* (Breslau: Korn, 1824), p. 58.

11   For many examples, see R. J. W. Evans, 'The Origins of Enlightenment in the Habsburg Lands', in his *Austria, Hungary, and the Habsburgs: Central Europe c. 1683–1867* (Oxford: Oxford

One should also remember that the Habsburg Monarchy included substantial Italian territories, among them, from 1737 onwards, the Grand Duchy of Tuscany. Lombardy, a Habsburg possession, was one of the focal points of Enlightenment in Italy. The great historian and Church reformer Lodovico Antonio Muratori, based in Modena, was very close to Habsburg territory. Thus part of the Enlightenment took place virtually in the Habsburg domains.

Three areas of curiosity will be briefly surveyed here.[12] The first is religion: the textual study of the Bible, and the early history of the Church. The second is natural science, and the third is ethnography.[13]

Religion

Curiosity led some Enlighteners to inquire into the textual, historical and intellectual bases of Christianity. The textual bases are a set of documents which postdate, sometimes by many centuries, the events they purport to recount, and which, having been translated and transcribed many times, show a large number of internal inconsistencies and probable errors. To investigate these is the task of textual criticism. The study of the Bible text, often thought particularly a Protestant activity, was in fact pioneered by the Catholic Richard Simon. His *Histoire critique du Vieux Testament* (1678) argued against the orthodox view that the first five books of the Old Testament, the Pentateuch, had been written by Moses, pointing out that these books include an account of Moses' death. Closer to Austria, Giovanni Lami, professor of Church history at Florence and theological adviser to the Grand Duke of Tuscany, discussed biblical exegesis in *De eruditione apostolorum liber singularis* (1738); though convinced of John's authorship of the Fourth Gospel and the first Epistle, he thought that 5. 7–8 of the latter (important and controversial as the only Biblical evidence for the doctrine of the Trinity) were interpolated, and doubted whether John was the author of the other two Epistles and the Revelation.[14] Even enlightened clerics in Austria itself, however, did not admit such doubts. The liberal Abbot Franz Stephan Rautenstrauch, Joseph II's adviser on theological matters,

University Press, 2006), pp. 36–55 (pp. 41–43).

12   On the history of curiosity and collecting, see Neil Kenny, *The Uses of Curiosity in Early Modern France and Germany* (Oxford: Oxford University Press, 2004); Arthur MacGregor, *Curiosity and Enlightenment: Collectors and Collections from the Sixteenth to the Nineteenth Century* (New Haven, CT, and London: Yale University Press, 2007).

13   It may fairly be asked how far curiosity in the Austrian Enlightenment was gendered, i.e. permissible for men but reprehensible in women. A complex picture emerges from the memoirs of Caroline Pichler (1769–1843), which feature several women interested in serious studies. Pichler's mother studied natural science and comparative religion; Pichler's friend Baroness von Matt studied astronomy and had an observatory built in her house — Caroline Pichler, *Denkwürdigkeiten aus meinem Leben*, ed. by Emil Karl Blümml, 2 vols (Munich: Georg Müller, 1914), I, 47–48, 408–09. Yet Pichler herself expresses disapproval of learned ladies, implying that women themselves tended to internalize and perpetuate conventional prejudices. I have explored these contradictions in 'The Complexities of Caroline Pichler: Conflicting Role Models, Patriotic Commitment, and *The Swedes in Prague* (1827)', *Women in German Yearbook*, 23 (2007), 34–48.

14   See Lionel Gossman, *Medievalism and the Ideologies of the Enlightenment: The World and Work of La Curne de Sainte-Palaye* (Baltimore, MD: Johns Hopkins University Press, 1968), pp. 78–79.

rejected the Protestant idea that the story of the Fall in Genesis was allegorical, and preferred to think that not only Genesis but the entire Bible must be literally true.[15]

The most comprehensive criticism of the Church and its texts and doctrines produced on Austrian soil was the *Triregno*, written in Viennese exile by the Neapolitan lawyer Pietro Giannone. Giannone had already incurred the anger of the Church by his anticlerical *Istoria civile del regno di Napoli* (1723); the Austrian viceroy, Cardinal Althann, enabled him to flee via Trieste to Vienna, where he lived until 1734 with the help of a pension provided by the Emperor Karl VI. He was friendly with Prince Eugen, who also corresponded with the English deist John Toland and enjoyed Voltaire's anticlerical play *Œdipe*; it is unlikely, however, that Eugen's heterodox circle had any wider impact.[16] On returning to Italy, Giannone had several narrow escapes from the Inquisition, but was finally captured in 1736 and imprisoned for the remaining twelve years of his life, an exemplary warning to any others who might feel like criticizing the Church publicly. The *Triregno*, which he wrote in Vienna between 1731 and 1734 but which was not published till 1895, aims to correct the ill-founded doctrines and political claims of the Church. It gives a critical examination of the Pentateuch, arguing that a narrative with so many inconsistencies cannot be divinely inspired. It addresses a sore point of theology, the fact that a central doctrine of Christianity, the immortality of the soul, is entirely unmentioned in the Old Testament, and argues that the early Hebrews knew no such doctrine until it was imported from Egypt. It questions the official doctrines of heaven, hell, and purgatory, and argues that the last is a mere invention by clerics with no Biblical warrant.[17]

Later in the century, adherents of Joseph II had urgent reason to inquire into Church history for the bases of Papal claims to authority. Joseph challenged the authority of the Church on numerous fronts: he abolished monastic schools and arranged for the clergy to be trained rigorously in twelve seminaries (*Generalseminare*). This measure placed the education of the clergy in the hands of the state, which prescribed the curriculum. Monasteries that were devoted only to the contemplative life were abolished; those occupied with pastoral or educational work were spared. He also asserted his control over the Church hierarchy, requiring all bishops to give an oath of allegiance to the Crown, and improving the education and pay of parish priests. Most famously, he instituted a large measure of toleration, allowing Lutheran, Calvinist and Greek Orthodox communities to have their own churches and enjoy civil rights, and also removing civil restrictions on Jews. The immediate cause of his conflict with the Papacy was his insistence on appointing

---

15   See Beda Franz Menzel, OSB, *Abt Franz Stephan Rautenstrauch von Břevnov-Braunau: Herkunft, Umwelt und Wirkungskreis* (Königstein/Ts.: Königsteiner Institut für Kirchen- und Geistesgeschichte der Sudetenländer e.V., 1969), pp. 191–92.

16   See Derek McKay, *Prince Eugene of Savoy* (London: Thames & Hudson, 1977), pp. 201–02; Evans, p. 41.

17   See Jonathan Israel, *Radical Enlightenment: Philosophy and the Making of Modernity, 1650–1750* (Oxford: Oxford University Press, 2001), p. 675; a fuller account in Dino Carpanetto and Giuseppe Ricuperati, *Italy in the Age of Reason, 1685–1789*, trans. by Caroline Higgitt (London: Longman, 1987), pp. 106–13.

abbots in Austrian Lombardy, and, in principle, all bishops and abbots throughout the Monarchy. Pope Pius VI visited Vienna in person in the spring of 1782 in order to remonstrate — the first time a Pope had visited any German territory since 1415.[18] In support of Joseph's stand, scholars undertook inquiries into early Church history to see what foundation there was for the Pope's pretensions to authority.[19] The text usually cited was John 18. 36: 'My kingdom is not of this world', as evidence that Christ had not intended Peter and his successors as heads of the Church to wield temporal power.[20]

Perhaps the most serious of these inquiries was the polemical treatise *Was ist der Pabst?* by Johann Valentin Eybel, professor of Church law at Vienna, who in the 1780s was placed in charge of the dissolution of monasteries in Upper Austria. Presenting himself as neither a simple-minded 'Schwärmer', nor an impious 'Freygeist', but as 'der vernünftige und wohl unterwiesene Christ',[21] Eybel scrutinizes the text of the New Testament to argue that Jesus conferred no special powers on Peter to forgive sins and govern the Church, but addressed him only as the representative of all the disciples. Thus Jesus did not found a Church with a single head, but authorized a number of bishops. The status of the Pope is not founded on divine authority but on practical convenience, which requires one bishop to act as a kind of chairman. The Pope is only the Bishop of Rome — a view in which Eybel concurs with 'Febronius', the pseudonym of Nikolaus Hontheim, suffragan bishop of Trier, who in *De statu ecclesiae et legitima potestate Romani pontificis* (1763) had argued for the restriction of papal jurisdiction. Hontheim had been compelled to recant in 1778, but Eybel (without naming him) takes up his arguments and supports them by surveying the illegitimate extension of papal power in the course of the Middle Ages.

Did any of these inquiries introduce radical Enlightenment, in Jonathan Israel's sense — Spinozist, Deist, or materialist — into Austria? A case in point is Ignaz Fessler. Fessler's early reading, which included Reimarus' *Fragmente eines Ungenannten* and the work of the radical Pietist Johann Christian Edelmann, brought him close to Deism. Ordained a priest in 1779, he celebrated his first Mass in a state of complete unbelief. He hoped however that he could retain the core of Catholic faith while rejecting all its superstitious accretions without falling prey to Deism.[22] In the 1780s, however, he read Helvétius and found himself again on the verge of Deism, a tendency strengthened subsequently by reading Spinoza and Kant and making an

---

18   See Elisabeth Kovács, *Der Pabst in Teutschland: Die Reise Pius VI. im Jahre 1782* (Vienna: Verlag für Geschichte und Politik, 1983).

19   These were probably written in consultation with Joseph and/or his associates: see Ernst Wangermann, *Die Waffen der Publizität: Zum Funktionswandel der politischen Literatur unter Joseph II.* (Vienna: Verlag für Geschichte und Politik, 2004).

20   *Ueber die Ankunft Pabst Pius des Sechsten in Wien*. Von J. v. Sonnenfels und [Johann] Rautenstrauch (Vienna: no pub., 1782), p. 15; earlier in Abbot Franz Stephan Rautenstrauch's *Institutiones iuris eccl. Germaniae accomodatae* (1772), quoted in Menzel, p. 186.

21   [Johann Valentin Eybel], *Was ist der Pabst?* (Vienna: no pub., 1782), p. 6. On the reception of this pamphlet, see Kovács, p. 60.

22   Fessler, pp. 59, 79.

intensive study of Stoic ethics.[23] In 1791 he became a Lutheran, without making a formal confession of faith, and after a profound inward illumination in 1816, he became Bishop of Saratov, responsible for the German Protestant community on the Volga.

Radical approaches to the Bible had some currency in Masonic circles. The ex-Barnabite Karl Ludwig Reinhold, later son-in-law of Wieland, friend of Schiller and Herder, and expositor of Kant, who remained in close touch with Viennese Masons after his departure for Leipzig in 1783, argued in *Hebräische Mysterien* (1786) that Moses had fused the Hebrew Jehovah with the Egyptian recognition of the divinity of Nature and had thus anticipated Spinoza.[24] These speculations played some part in the genesis of Schikaneder's text for Mozart's *Zauberflöte*, though their role and significance is still controversial.[25]

The most radical critique of the Bible and of Christianity to emerge from the Austrian Enlightenment is Johannes Pezzl's *Marokkanische Briefe*, purporting to be a series of letters from Sidi, an Oriental visitor to Vienna, to his friend Hamid, on the model of Montesquieu's *Lettres persanes*. Even under the relaxed censorship introduced by Joseph II, this book was banned.[26] Its comments on the Bible include a highly sceptical account of the early chapters of Genesis, a list of the massacres and murders which are not only recounted but approved in the Old Testament, and a reference to the awkward fact that the Old Testament shows no knowledge of the immortality of the soul. Discussing the New Testament, Pezzl's spokesman implies a general diffusion of Deism by claiming that Protestants now think that Jesus was only human:

> Die Katholiken glauben mit dogmatischem Eifer, daß Kristus der wahre Sohn Gottes sey. Die Protestanten fangen allmählich an, laut zu sagen, daß Kristus ein Mensch war wie jeder andre, der aber mit guten Gaben ausgerüstet Moral predigte, und in diesem Verstande ein Sohn Gottes, das heißt, ein guter Mensch war.[27]

Pezzl shows familiarity with the most radical Deist writings of the Enlightenment, including the notorious *Treatise of the Three Impostors* which charged Moses, Jesus and Muhammad with fraud.[28] Pezzl had easier access to these books than other people, since he spent some of his life outside Austria. A Bavarian, originally destined for the priesthood, he got into trouble in Vienna for his scathing account of a novitiate, *Briefe aus dem Novizziat*, published at Zürich in 1780–81, and prudently spent the years from 1782 to 1785 in Switzerland before returning to Vienna.

---

23   For Helvétius, see ibid., pp. 169, 199. On Fessler's Spinozism, see Peter F. Barton, *Ignatius Aurelius Feßler: Vom Barockkatholizismus zur Erweckungsbewegung* (Vienna, Cologne, Graz: Böhlau, 1969), pp. 169–70.

24   See Jan Assmann, *Moses the Egyptian: The Memory of Egypt in Western Monotheism* (Cambridge, MA: Harvard University Press, 1997), pp. 115–25.

25   See now Jan Assmann, *Die Zauberflöte: Oper und Mysterium* (Munich: Hanser, 2005).

26   See Wangermann, pp. 113–14.

27   [Johann Pezzl], *Marokkanische Briefe. Aus dem Arabischen* (Frankfurt a.M., Leipzig: no pub., 1784), p. 91.

28   Now available in *Le 'Traité des trois imposteurs' et 'L'Esprit de Spinosa': Philosophie clandestine entre 1678 et 1768*, ed. by Françoise Charles-Daubert (Oxford: Voltaire Foundation, 1999).

Natural Science

As we know, in early modern Europe scientific curiosity often took the form of collecting. Collections might include geological specimens, fossils, plants, and animals of many kinds. In Central Europe, such collections were often made by intelligent and inquisitive monks. Members of the contemplative orders especially had plenty of time on their hands, and while some devoted themselves to prayer, others to quarrelling, yet others pursued hobbies, often on a large scale. When the Carthusian monastery at Gaming in Lower Austria was dissolved in 1782, one inmate, according to the inventory taken by the commissioners, had three sheds full of equipment, including carpentry tools, an electricity generator, a magic lantern, eleven bird-cages, and two thousand five hundred flower-pots, many containing foreign plants.[29] Clearly there was a fund of intellectual curiosity here which, if encouraged and channelled, could produce significant results. The study of the natural world was no longer seen as impious curiosity. It could be a way of praising God and helping one's neighbour. In 1777 the funeral sermon for Abbot Gussmann of Seitenstetten justified such inquiry with the imagery of enlightenment: 'Die Ordensmänner sind ein Licht, das mitten in den Finsternissen leuchten soll; sie müssen nicht nur voll der Tugend und Frömmigkeit, sondern auch von der Wissenschaft ganz erleuchtet seyn.'[30]

By the early eighteenth century the Benedictines had overtaken the Jesuits in scholarship. While the Jesuits clung to an increasingly arid Aristotelian and Thomist philosophy, the Benedictines were open to the new philosophy of Christian Wolff and also to experimental science. They had their own university at Salzburg. Although higher education in early eighteenth-century Austria was still controlled by the Jesuits, Salzburg was not part of the Habsburg Monarchy but an independent principality ruled by its prince-bishop. The Benedictine university was forward-looking in its educational methods. In the 1740s its Dean, Anselm Desing, renewed the curriculum and the methods of study, discouraging the old-fashioned method by which lecturers dictated notes to their students, and promoting the use of textbooks on which lecturers gave explanatory commentaries. A chair of experimental physics was founded. The university's most distinguished scientist was Father Dominikus Beck (1732–91), who erected the first lightning-conductors in Salzburg, and whose works include treatises explaining the lightning-conductor to ordinary readers — an example of scientific popularization.[31]

Another Benedictine centre was Kremsmünster, the wealthiest abbey in Upper Austria, which had a famous *Gymnasium*. Some of its monks did historical research in the spirit of the French Benedictine Jean Mabillon, author of the treatise on

29 Brunhilde Hoffmann, *Die Aufhebung der Kartause Gaming* (Salzburg: Institut für Anglistik und Amerikanistik, Universität Salzburg, 1981), pp. 67–68.

30 Quoted in Friedrich Polleross, 'Auftraggeber und Funktionen barocker Kunst in Österreich', in *Geschichte der bildenden Kunst in Österreich*, 6 vols (Munich, London, New York: Prestel, 1997–2003), IV: *Barock*, ed. by Hellmut Lorenz (1999), pp. 17–50 (p. 29).

31 See Virgil Redlich, 'Die Salzburger Benediktiner-Universität als Kulturerscheinung', in *Benediktinisches Mönchtum in Österreich*, ed. by Hildebert Tausch, OSB (Vienna: Herder, 1949), pp. 79–97 (p. 94).

historical method *De re diplomatica* (1681). Their work was animated by curiosity, inasmuch as mere historical writing gave way to the discovery of previously unknown facts.[32] But Kremsmünster was particularly known for research in natural science, thanks to the polymath Father Placidus Fixlmillner (1721–91). Fixlmillner was a doctor of philosophy and a doctor of theology; besides mathematics, physics, and theology, he studied law, and taught canon law and history at Kremsmünster; he wrote equally fluently in Latin, German and French. In 1762 he was appointed as the abbey's astronomer. He was thus placed in charge of the eight-storey 'mathematical tower', forty-seven metres high, designed by Anselm Desing, and completed in 1759. The lower storeys housed scientific collections, while the observatory was above them.[33] Fixlmillner had a share in one of the great astronomical events of the time, the discovery of the planet Uranus. The actual discovery was made by the Anglo-German astronomer Sir William Herschel on 13 March 1781. Fixlmillner's contribution was to calculate the orbit of the newly discovered planet. His achievement was acknowledged internationally. It is important to note also that Fixlmillner corresponded with other astronomers throughout Europe. In the eighteenth-century republic of letters, learned correspondence not only served the transmission of knowledge but involved a social and academic etiquette and marked one's place in the hierarchy of learning.[34] It therefore says much for Fixlmillner's reputation that he corresponded with distinguished astronomers including the Jesuit Maximilian Hell, and Jérôme Lalande, professor at the Collège de France.

Maximilian Hell (1720–92) was even more eminent than Fixlmillner. At the age of thirty-five he was put in charge of the new observatory at the University of Vienna, where he calculated ephemerides, i.e. exact predictions of the movements of the sun, the moon, and the planets. His reputation was confirmed when in 1767 he was invited by King Christian VII of Denmark to observe the solar transit of Venus. It was for this purpose that James Cook sailed to Tahiti. Hell, by contrast, was required to make his observations on the Arctic island of Vardö, where, after a long and arduous journey through Germany, Denmark and Norway, he arrived on 11 October 1768 and began building an observatory. The observation was duly made on 3 June 1769, but Hell's results differed from those of other observers, and he got involved in a scholarly dispute with Lalande. Back in Vienna, he was invited by Maria Theresia in 1774 to draw up a plan for an academy of sciences. His plan included only natural sciences, viz. astronomy, geometry, mechanics, physics, botany, anatomy and chemistry, since he considered the humanities 'nicht

---

32   See Anna Coreth, *Österreichische Geschichtsschreibung in der Barockzeit (1620–1740)* (Vienna: Holzhausen, 1950), pp. 97–101; Georg Heilingsetzer, 'Die Benediktiner im 18. Jahrhundert: Wissenschaft und Gelehrsamkeit im süddeutsch-österreichischen Raum', in *Katholische Aufklärung*, pp. 208–24.

33   See Johann-Christian Klamt, *Sternwarte und Museum im Zeitalter der Aufklärung: Der Mathematische Turm zu Kremsmünster (1749–1758)* (Mainz: Verlag Philipp von Zabern, 1999).

34   See Anne Goldgar, *Impolite Learning: Conduct and Community in the Republic of Letters, 1680–1750* (New Haven, CT, and London: Yale University Press, 1995); Laurence W. B. Brockliss, *Calvet's Web: Enlightenment and the Republic of Letters in Eighteenth-Century France* (Oxford: Oxford University Press, 2002), pp. 96–102.

Wissenschaft im eigentlichen Verstande'.[35] Although his plan was approved in principle, nothing came of it: Maria Theresia thought there were not enough eminent scientists to fill it, and was perhaps also deterred by the likely cost. Hell was a member of the scientific societies of Copenhagen, Göttingen, Stockholm, Trondheim and Bologna, and a corresponding member of that of Paris. After the Society of Jesus was dissolved in 1773, Hell was offered a post in London, but refused because he did not wish to live among heretics.

Research was promoted also by the Imperial Court.[36] Prince Eugen kept exotic birds and plants at his palace, the Belvedere, and assembled a large library, which, when he died intestate, was bought by the Emperor Karl VI and formed the nucleus of the National Library.[37] Franz Stephan of Lorraine, consort of Maria Theresia and (as Franz I) Emperor from 1745, was himself an enthusiastic amateur scientist who conducted many chemical and physical experiments. In these he was helped by the Jesuit Father Joseph Franz (1704–76), who lectured on mathematics, astronomy and experimental physics at Vienna University, and whose observations of the comet of February 1743 were reported in the journal of the Royal Society of London.[38] In 1749 Franz Stephan bought and had transported to Vienna the world's largest natural history collection, that of Johann de Baillou in Florence. Baillou, who agreed to the sale on condition that he and his descendants should be made hereditary keepers of the collection, displayed it, systematically arranged, in glass cases in what is now the Augustiner-Lesesaal of the National Library. It formed the core of the Imperial collections and eventually of the Naturhistorisches Museum. In addition, Franz Stephan established a menagerie at Schönbrunn in 1752 and in the following year a botanical garden, directed by the aforementioned Nikolaus Joseph Jacquin with the assistance of two of his Dutch fellow-countrymen, Adrian van Stekhoven and Richard van der Schot.

The Court was also able to finance scientific expeditions. There was of course plenty to discover in the Habsburg domains, especially in remote regions like the Carpathians. Early in the century Luigi Ferdinando Marsigli (1658–1730), a Bolognese who entered the service of Emperor Leopold I, was commissioned to explore these regions and determine the boundaries between Hungary and the Turkish and Venetian territories. His extensive scientific interests, ranging from geology to botany, brought him membership of the Royal Society of London and

---

35   Quoted in Hermann Haberzettl, *Die Stellung der Exjesuiten in Politik und Kulturleben Österreichs zu Ende des 18. Jahrhunderts* (Vienna: Verband der wissenschaftlichen Gesellschaften Österreichs, 1973), p. 184.

36   Much of the information in this and the following paragraphs comes from Günther Hamann, 'Zur Wissenschaftspflege des aufgeklärten Absolutismus: Naturforschung, Sammlungswesen und Landesaufnahme', in *Österreich im Zeitalter des aufgeklärten Absolutismus*, ed. by Erich Zöllner (Vienna: Österreichischer Bundesverlag, 1983), pp. 151–77; see also Renate Zedinger, 'Auf ah. Befehl Ihro Majestät des Kaisers Franz I. Beispiele naturwissenschaftlicher Herausforderungen und deren Bewältigung im Lothringischen Kreis', *Das achtzehnte Jahrhundert und Österreich*, 14–15 (2000), 135–54.

37   McKay, pp. 196, 243.

38   'Observationes Cometæ, a R. P. Frantz Soc. Jes. factæ, mense Februario anni MDCCXLIII, Viennæ Austriæ', *Philosophical Transactions*, 42 (1742–43), 457–58.

culminated in the publication of a six-volume geographical work on the Danube, *Opus Danubiale* (1726).[39] In 1748–50 the court mathematician Johann Anton Nagel travelled through much of the Monarchy, as well as France, the Netherlands, and England, in order to collect mineral samples for the Imperial collection; he also explored caves and made mathematical calculations concerning earthquakes. Even more ambitious and more exotic was the four-year journey to the Caribbean made in 1755–59 by Jacquin to collect plant and animal specimens. Accompanied by van der Schot and two Italian hunters and taxidermists, Jacquin visited most of the West Indian islands, besides 'New Granada' (now Venezuela) and Colombia, and sent back sixty-seven chests of specimens, including the first piece of platinum sent from America to Europe, besides large numbers of plants and animals, among them a 'Löwentiger' (a puma). The expedition was hazardous: Jacquin almost died of yellow fever, was twice captured and robbed by pirates, and once nearly perished at the hands of mutineers.[40]

In the 1780s, Joseph II financed an expedition to North America (Pennsylvania, New Jersey, North Carolina), the Caribbean and Caracas, led by Franz Joseph Märter (professor of natural history at the *Theresianum*) and the Schönbrunn gardener Franz Boos. Despite faulty organization and inadequate equipment (they had not even suitable shoes for exploring the American countryside), the gardeners brought a total of eighty-eight chests of plants back to Schönbrunn.[41] In 1785 Boos was sent on another expedition, this time to the Cape of Good Hope, Mauritius and Réunion. Besides many plants, shells and butterflies, he brought back the body of a giraffe, the first ever seen in Vienna. The zoological museum on the Josephsplatz had to be partially rebuilt so that such an enormous creature could be displayed.

Although successive emperors were willing to finance expeditions, they were reluctant to put scientific research on a solid footing by founding an academy of sciences. Maximilian Hell's unsuccessful plan for an academy was simply one of Austria's many failures to institute an academy which would promote research by bringing different scientists together, like the Royal Society in London, founded in 1662, and the Académie des Sciences in Paris, founded in 1654. Leibniz, shortly before his death in 1716, advocated the establishment of a similar body in Vienna, but without success. In 1746 the ex-officer Freiherr Josef von Petrasch in Olmütz in Moravia founded the *Societas eruditorum incognitorum in terris austriacis*, a private academy whose members included not only distinguished scholars throughout Austria, such as the Benedictine historian Hieronymus Pez of Kremsmünster and Johann von Baillou, the keeper of the Imperial natural history collection, but foreigners and Protestants such as Johann Christoph Gottsched. However, with its members so scattered, the Society existed largely on paper. It issued a monthly

39   See John Stoye, *Marsigli's Europe, 1680–1730: The Life and Times of Luigi Ferdinando Marsigli, Soldier and Virtuoso* (New Haven, CT, and London: Yale University Press, 1994).

40   See Otto Nowotny, 'Die Forschungs- und Sammelreise des Nikolaus J. Jacquin in die Karibik und zu den Küsten Venezuelas und Kolumbiens 1755–1759', in *Österreich und die Neue Welt*, ed. by Elisabeth Zeilinger (Vienna: Österreichische Nationalbibliothek, 1993), pp. 89–94.

41   See Helga Hühnel, 'Kaiserliche "Gärtnergesellen" bereisen Amerika', in *Österreich und die Neue Welt*, pp. 95–102.

journal and planned a series of editions to be called the *Bibliotheca scriptorum Bohemiae*, but it fell victim to the intrigues of the Jesuits, who wanted their school in Olmütz to be upgraded and feared competition, and to Maria Theresia's disapproval of its tolerance towards Protestants.[42]

In view of official indifference, any further attempt to found an academy of sciences would clearly depend on the enthusiasm and organizational ability of an exceptional private individual. Such an individual appeared in the person of Ignaz von Born (1742–91). Having begun a Jesuit novitiate, Born abandoned it after sixteen months and took up the study, first of law, then of mineralogy and mining. In 1769 he was appointed to a post at the important mining academy at Schemnitz in Hungary. He also had a private estate at Alt-Zedlitz in Bohemia, where he set up his own natural history collection, library, coin cabinet, and botanic garden. Being highly sociable, he gathered around him a circle of scholars who in 1770 founded the *Böhmische gelehrte Privatgesellschaft*. Besides establishing a botanic garden and a natural history cabinet, they had a weekly journal, the *Prager gelehrte Nachrichten*, largely consisting of reviews of scholarly works. Although the journal ceased publication after a year, the society stayed in existence and in 1784, as the *Böhmische Gesellschaft der Wissenschaften in Prag*, gained the patronage of Joseph II, though never the official standing of a state academy. Born meanwhile had in 1777 been made keeper of the Imperial natural history collection. His extensive publications, especially on mineralogy, brought him international recognition and membership of many learned societies, including the Royal Society in London.[43]

Born's chief claim to fame, however, is connected with his Freemasonry. Freemasonry, as the main form of associational life in late eighteenth-century Austria, constituted a kind of public sphere. For Born, it offered some compensation for the many frustrations he suffered in his personal and public life. He suffered from polyneuritis, the result of severe lead poisoning in a Transylvanian mine. His work as keeper of the natural history collection was demanding and unrewarding, since Joseph II was very stingy about financing academic publications, and the catalogue of the collection had to be abandoned after the appearance of the first volume in 1778. However, Born was in his element as master of the Masonic lodge *Zur wahren Eintracht*, whose membership is a roll call of the leading figures of the Austrian Enlightenment, including Haydn, Sonnenfels, Alxinger, and Blumauer. It also includes more exotic figures: Franz Zauner, the sculptor whose equestrian statue of Joseph II still stands on the Josephsplatz, Graf Saurau, later ambassador to St Petersburg and governor of Milan, and Angelo Soliman, an African from the Galla people who had been sold into slavery as a child, given to an Austrian general in Italy, and employed by Prince Liechtenstein as secretary, interpreter,

---

42 For a detailed account of this society, see Menzel, pp. 83–85.

43 Most of the information in this and the following paragraphs comes from Edwin Zellweker, *Das Urbild des Sarastro: Ignaz v. Born* (Vienna: Dr. G. Borotha-Schoeler Verlag, 1953), and Helmut Reinalter, 'Ignaz von Born: Aufklärer, Freimaurer und Illuminat', in *Aufklärung und Geheimgesellschaften: Zur politischen Funktion und Sozialstruktur der Freimaurerlogen im 18. Jahrhundert*, ed. by Helmut Reinalter (Munich: Oldenbourg, 1989), pp. 151–71.

and eventually tutor to the Prince's nephew.[44] The lodge also contained female Masons, among them Born's daughter Maria Gräfin Bassegli. Its interest in the wider world is illustrated by the dinner it held in honour of Georg Forster when he visited Vienna in 1784, and its reception of Lafayette, the French officer famous for fighting in the American War of Independence, when he visited Vienna on a diplomatic mission in 1785. The lodge issued a scientific journal, the *Physikalische Arbeiten der einträchtigen Freunde in Wien* (1783–88), and a periodical of wider appeal, the *Journal für Freymaurer* (1784–87). Georg Forster wrote to Sömmering with his impression: 'Man [...] hat die ganze Sache zu einer Gesellschaft wissenschaftliche Aufklärung liebender, von allem Vorurteil freier Männer umgeschaffen.'[45]

The spirit of scientific Enlightenment could also take the form of satire. Knowing that Maximilian Hell was hostile to the Freemasons, Born and his associates composed an absurd spoof professing to advertise a forthcoming book by Hell, the *Telescopium Christiano-Hellianum*, and got it published in a serious journal, Schlözer's *Staats-Anzeiger*. Born's best-known satire, however, was his *Specimen monachologiae methodo Linnaeano,* published under the name Joannes Physiophilus in 1783. A German translation, attributed to 'Ignaz Loyola Kuttenpeitscher', soon followed, and sold two thousand copies in three weeks in Vienna alone; it was also translated into English and French. In it monks are assigned to the class of 'Vieher (Bruta, vernunftloser Thiere)' and subdivided into 'Fleisch, Fisch, und Früchte fräßige Mönche'.[46] The author explains that now that princes have begun to exterminate not only creatures that harm their hunting and their crops, such as wolves, hawks, and sparrows, but also creatures harmful to humanity, namely the various species of monks, it is desirable that an illustrated account of these creatures should be preserved for posterity. The text begins with a definition: 'Der Mönch ist ein menschenartiges, bekuttetes, zu Nachts heulendes, durstiges Thier' (p. 21). The 'Mönchinn' differs from her male counterpart only by covering her head, being cleaner, and never going out. Generally, monks differ from human beings by lacking judgement and will, obeying only the will of their superiors; by bowing their heads instead of standing upright; by idleness and solitude. The monk is 'ein Mittelding zwischen Menschen und Affen' (p. 24). After this introduction, the diverse orders are described as various species. While the Benedictine is treated mildly (St Benedict's rule was constantly held up as a standard of poverty and labour which contemporary monks disgracefully ignored), the Dominican, associated with the Inquisition, is portrayed as a dangerous predator, able to smell wine and heresy from a long distance. Others are represented as physically disgusting. The Franciscan is greedy and stinks like a he-goat; the Discalced Augustinian Monk is drunken, his

---

44   The members are listed in Ludwig Abafi, *Geschichte der Freimaurerei in Österreich-Ungarn*, 5 vols (Budapest: Ludwig Aigner, 1890–99), III, 308–18. They did not include Mozart, who belonged to the lodge 'Zur Wohlthätigkeit': ibid. III, 333.

45   Quoted in Zellweker, p. 73.

46   *Johann Physiophilus's Versuch einer Mönchologie nach Linnäischer Methode mit dreien Kupfern geziert* [etc.] (AUGSBURG, auf Kosten P. Aloys Merzens Dompredigers, 1786), p. 12. The false ascription is part of the joke: Aloys Merz was a notoriously conservative and militant preacher in Augsburg. All quotations in the following paragraphs are taken from this volume.

face 'trunkenboldisch' (p. 44); the Capuchin searches for lice, sniffs and snorts, and wipes his backside with the cord of his cassock; and the Pauline or 'Paulanermönch' is particularly smelly because of his diet of fish and vegetables cooked in oil, which gives special pungency to his farts: '[er] dampft einen schmerkelnden Geruch aus, der zum Erbrechen reizt, und Eckel macht, wie verschüttetes Oel. Nichts ist gräuserlicher, als der Wind, den er läßt' (p. 62).

Ethnography

When expeditions were undertaken for scientific purposes, their records include observations not only of physical phenomena but of the exotic peoples encountered by the travellers. From his journey to the Caribbean, Jacquin brought back not only plants and animals, but artefacts made by indigenous peoples who were soon to die out.[47]When Maximilian Hell made his arduous journey to Lapland, he and his companion, Father Johann Sajnovics, took an interest in the Lapps. Sajnovics's extremely circumstantial diary describes their appearance, their dress (which reminds him of Hungarian peasants), their houses, their practice of measuring their wealth in reindeer, and their habit of wrapping their babies in fur and tree-bark.[48] Hell and Sajnovics made a study of the Lapps' language and concluded that it resembled Hungarian, thus anticipating the concept of the Finno-Ugric language family. Born's account of his Carpathian travels contains something of social rather than strictly ethnographic interest — an arresting description of male and female convicts at Temesvar setting off in a chain-gang to do forced labour, something which the enlightened Austrian state had substituted for the death penalty.[49]

Till the end of the century, we do not find Austrian writers concentrating wholly on ethnography, with the exception of Jesuits. While Father Florian Paucke fits considerable ethnographic detail into a historical narrative of his experiences in Paraguay, his fellow Jesuit Martin Dobrizhoffer takes the step forward into systematic ethnography with his detailed account of the Abipon, an equestrian people of the Chaco.[50] To include these Jesuit authors, despite their merits, in an account of the Enlightenment, might however be stretching the concept too far.

47   Hamann, p. 155.

48   Carl Ludwig Littrow, *P. Hell's Reise nach Wardoe bei Lappland und seine Beobachtung des Venus-Durchgangs im Jahre 1769: Aus den aufgefundenen Tagebüchern geschöpft und mit Erläuterungen begleitet von Carl Ludwig Littrow* (Vienna: Gerold, 1835), pp. 122, 124.

49   Ignaz Born, *Briefe über Mineralogische Gegenstände, auf seiner Reise durch das Temeswarer Bannat, Siebenbürgen, Ober- und Nieder-Hungarn, an den Herausgeber derselben, Johann Jacob Ferber, Mitglied der Königl. Großherzogl. Akademie der Wissenschaften zu Siena, und der Ackerbau-Gesellschaft zu Vicenza und zu Florenz, geschrieben* (Frankfurt a.M., Leipzig: no pub., 1774), p. 9.

50   Florian Paucke, SJ, *Zwettler-Codex 420: Hin und Her. Hin süsse, und vergnügt, Her bitter und betrübt. Das ist: Treu gegebene Nachricht durch einen im Jahre 1748 aus Europa in West=America, nahmentlich in die Provinz Paraguay abreisenden und im Jahre 1769 nach Europa zurükkehrenden Missionarium*, ed. by Etta Becker-Donner, 2 vols (Vienna: Braumüller, 1959); the work of Martin Dobrizhoffer, originally published in Latin, was translated into German, and is also available in English as *An Account of the Abipones, an Equestrian People of Paraguay*, trans. by Sara Coleridge, 3 vols (London: John Murray, 1822). On these texts, see Wolfgang Neuber, 'Florian Paucke S.J. und sein Reisebericht über Paraguay', in *Österreich und die Neue Welt*, pp. 67–79.

For different reasons, one might question the Enlightenment credentials of a writer who gives considerable space to ethnography. Belsazar Hacquet, another 'Wahlösterreicher', was born in Brittany, travelled extensively in the Carpathian region and published many books about it, foregrounding its geography and geology but also saying a good deal about its inhabitants. Yet although Hacquet was a friend of Gerard van Swieten and Ignaz von Born, as well as an admirer of Joseph II, his books show him as singularly unenlightened in his hostile and scornful attitude to most of the people he describes. German colonists in Transylvania are idle and incompetent, Poles are slovenly, Hungarians are lazy and stupid, Romanians are deceitful and murderous, and as for Jews, Hacquet recommends that they should be made to disappear as a distinctive race by being forbidden to marry, or by encouraging Jewish girls to marry Christians.[51] For an Aufklärer and a scientist, he has some remarkably primitive notions: he thinks that children who are suckled by gypsies acquire black skins, and that venereal disease originates from animals and is spread by women who have sex with dogs.[52] He gives much valuable information about costumes and customs, but the unsympathetic coldness of his ethnographic gaze is always apparent, especially when he looks on coolly at a Ruthenian woman giving birth unassisted. The passage is worth quoting both for its substance and to illustrate the dehumanizing effect of Hacquet's observations:

> Ich hatte hier, wie schon anderwärts, die Gelegenheit in einer Hütte zu sein, wo ein Weib entbunden wurde. Da ich merkte, daß sie zur Geburt gieng, so blieb ich so lang, bis sie ihrer Bürde los wurde. Ich fragte sie, ob sie dann keine Weiber zur Hilfe hätte. O nein, war die Antwort, zu so was ist es nicht notwendig, und in der That in Zeit von einer halben Stunde war alles vorüber. Das Weib kam in einem Winkel der Hütte bey ihrem Bette stehend, nieder. Das Kind fiel ihr zur Erde, auf ein wenig Heu, wo dann beym Fall die Nabelschnur zerriß, und nicht unterbunden wurde; sie gieng nun zu Bette, und ein junges Mensch, welches sie bey sich hatte, gab ihr das Kind und ein Glaß Brandwein, das war alles.[53]

In his old age, however, Hacquet seems to have mellowed, for his later ethnographic account of the Slavs treats their shortcomings, such as drunkenness, or the Montenegrin blood-feud, with relative mildness, and is indeed partisan enough to assert that the Slavs, whose population extends from Austria to Kamchatka, cover a territory larger than China and far greater than the much-lauded Roman Empire.[54] This handsomely produced volume has coloured illustrations of many Slav peoples in their customs, which help to make it an important ethnographic source.

51 Belsazar Hacquet, *Hacquet's neueste physikalisch-politische Reisen in den Jahren 1788 und 1789 durch die Dacischen und Sarmatischen oder Nördlichen Karpathen*, 4 vols (Nuremberg: Raspe, 1790–96), I, 202; III, 223, 232.

52 Ibid., I, 124; III, 112.

53 Ibid., III, 59–60.

54 Belsazar Hacquet, *Abbildung und Beschreibung der südwest- und östlichen Wenden, Illyrer und Slaven[,] deren geographische Ausbreitung von dem adriatischen Meere bis an den Ponto, deren Sitten, Gebräuche, Handthierung, Gewerbe, Religion u. s. w. nach einer zehnjährigen Reise und vierzigjährigem Aufenthalte in jenen Gegenden* (Leipzig: im Industrie-Comptoir, n.d. [1805]), p. 2; the blood-feud, p. 9.

A far more engaging writer, and the first Austrian to undertake a systematic ethnography of the Monarchy's peoples, was the civil servant Joseph Rohrer.[55] He published in 1804 accounts of the German, the Slav, and the Jewish inhabitants of the Monarchy. Each is divided into eight sections. The first four describe in turn the physical character, the diet, the dress, and the occupations of the people in question; the next four deal with cultural and moral matters, namely their aesthetic sense ('Kunstsinn'), their mentality ('Denkart'), their religion, and their moral character. They are based largely on direct observations made during Rohrer's extensive travels in the Habsburg domains. Their motivation is partly curiosity about the diverse inhabitants of the Monarchy, partly a desire to describe the Monarchy's human resources as a basis for the pursuit of enlightenment and improvement. Rohrer is an enthusiastic Aufklärer, a believer in humanity's progress towards perfection, and an upholder of the reforming ideals of the lamented Joseph II. A cultivated and widely read author, he often shows a divided attitude towards his subject. Dealing with the Morlaks of Dalmatia, he deplores, like a true Aufklärer, their superstitious belief in vampires, but when he describes the 'Klagefrauen' whom he has heard keening for the dead at their funerals, he shows a sympathy for primitive culture reminiscent of Herder.[56] In this respect Rohrer may be considered to stand at the cusp of Enlightenment and Romanticism, and to herald a new sensibility that would displace that of the Aufklärung.

Finally, and more generally, how far do the inquiries examined here signal a change in mentality? Very obviously, they form part of an epochal process of secularization, in which a search for final causes — the meaning of an event within a divine providential order — yields to a search for efficient causes and an agnosticism about their ultimate meaning. Earthquakes provide a spectacular example. In 1590, after a severe earthquake in Neulengbach in Lower Austria, the Bishop of Vienna accused the populace of incurring God's anger through their wicked and un-Christian language. But when the court mathematician Johann Anton Nagel investigated the earthquake of 27 February 1768, which severely damaged the town of Wiener Neustadt, he did not ask about its providential purpose but about the diffusion of forces from its epicentre.[57] However, the change in mentality was uneven. That can be illustrated by referring to the symbol of enlightenment, the lightning conductor, which could be seen as using scientific knowledge to frustrate divine punishment. 'Daß in Kirchen gepredigt wird', said Lichtenberg, 'macht deswegen die Blitzableiter auf ihnen nicht unnötig.'[58] When Father Dominikus Beck put up lightning conductors in Salzburg, he had clearly

55   For a detailed account of him, see Ritchie Robertson, 'Joseph Rohrer and the Bureaucratic Enlightenment', *Austrian Studies*, 2 (1991), 22–42.

56   Joseph Rohrer, *Versuch über die slawischen Bewohner der österreichischen Monarchie*, 2 vols (Vienna: Kunst- und Industrie-Comptoir, 1804), II, 30, 74. On Enlightenment interest in the Morlaks, see Larry Wolff, *Venice and the Slavs: The Discovery of Dalmatia in the Age of Enlightenment* (Stanford, CA: Stanford University Press, 2001).

57   See Christa Hammerl, 'Zur Rekonstruktion der Erdbeben von Wiener Neustadt (1768) und Leoben (1794)', *Das achtzehnte Jahrhundert und Österreich*, 14–15 (2000), 163–79.

58   Georg Christoph Lichtenberg, *Schriften und Briefe*, ed. by Wolfgang Promies, 4 vols (Munich: Hanser, 1967–72), I, 860.

accepted a broadly scientific view of the universe as working for the most part without divine intervention. But when an observatory with a lightning conductor was erected on the Hohenpeissenberg in Bavaria, the site of a famous pilgrimage church, the ordinary inhabitants continued with their pilgrimages and retained the practice of ringing the church bells ('Wetterläuten') in order to ward off lightning.[59] Different and incongruous mentalities existed side by side, and the victory of curiosity was slow.

59 Rebekka Habermas, *Wallfahrt und Aufruhr: Zum Wunderglauben im Bayern der frühen Neuzeit* (Frankfurt a.M., New York: Campus, 1991), pp. 109–14.

CHAPTER 11

Johann Pezzl:
Enlightenment in the Satirical Mode

Johann Pezzl was born in Mallersdorf, near Straubing in southern Bavaria, on 30 November 1756. The son of a baker, he was educated at the Lyzeum in Freising and in September 1775 began a novitiate in the Benedictine monastery of Oberalteich.[1] He left it in August 1776 and then studied law at the Benedictine university of Salzburg, which was run in a relatively enlightened spirit: an obsolete scholasticism had been replaced by the philosophy of Christian Wolff, and the study of experimental science was encouraged.[2] At Salzburg Pezzl got to know Johann Kaspar Riesbeck (1754–1786), a congenial spirit, who was writing his own *Briefe über das Mönchswesen* [*Letters on Monasticism*], published in 1779. Riesbeck encouraged him to read Enlightenment texts and introduced him to Freemasons and Illuminati. By publishing the first volume of his *Briefe aus dem Novizziat* [*Letters from the Novitiate*] in 1780, Pezzl obtained a dangerous notoriety. The book was banned in Bavaria, and even in relatively enlightened Salzburg it became the subject of a judicial investigation, which ended by compelling Pezzl to recant his errors. In August 1780 Pezzl moved to Zurich, where in 1781 and 1782 he issued the second and third parts of the *Briefe* and in spring 1783 his humorous novel *Faustin oder das philosophische Jahrhundert* [*Faustin or the Philosophical Century*].

From 1784 onwards, however, Pezzl found a secure home in the enlightened Vienna of Joseph II. Joseph had ruled jointly with his mother, Maria Theresia, since 1765. Freed by her death in 1780 from her maternal authority, he became sole ruler of the Habsburg Empire. He was determined to introduce reforms, and did so rapidly. His most famous reforming measures are his Patents of Toleration, which, beginning in October 1781, granted freedom of worship to communities of Lutherans, Calvinists and Greek Orthodox and removed the restrictions on their buying property, joining guilds and attending university. Similar measures removed

---

1   See Clarissa Höschel, 'Wie Johann Pezzl vom Benediktinernovizen zum Freimaurer, Satiriker und Staatsbeamten wurde: Ein biographischer Abriss zu Pezzls 250. Geburtstag (2006)'. *Literatur in Bayern*, 85 (Sept. 2006), 38–46; '"Candidatus Johann Pezzl": Auf den Spuren eines konspirativen Salzburger Studentenlebens', *Salzburg Archiv*, 32 (2007), 187–208. I thank Ulrich L. Lehner for providing me with copies of these articles.

2   See Ulrich L. Lehner, *Enlightened Monks: The German Benedictines, 1740–1803* (Oxford: Oxford University Press, 2011).

the much more extensive restrictions on Jews. In dealing with the Catholic Church, Joseph tried to bring it under state control by ordaining that the appointment of bishops should require his approval; and he dissolved the contemplative monastic orders, transferring their property to charitable use. These measures caused such alarm in Rome that in the spring of 1782 Pope Pius VI took the unprecedented step of visiting Vienna in person in order to remonstrate with the Emperor, who remained steadfast.[3]

In Vienna, Pezzl lived by his pen, and also worked as a librarian to Wenzel Anton, Prince Kaunitz, who was Austria's state chancellor from 1753 to 1792. Pezzl socialized with Freemasons, becoming a member of the lodge 'Zur Wohltätigkeit', to which Mozart also belonged.[4] More noteworthy publications followed, notably his *Reise durch den Baierschen Kreis* [*Journey through Bavaria*] (1784), his *Marokkanische Briefe* [*Moroccan Letters*] (1784), and the topographical *Skizze von Wien* [*Sketch of Vienna*] (six parts, 1786–90). On Joseph II's death in 1790 Pezzl published a biographical sketch, *Charakteristik Josephs II.* [*The Character of Joseph II*], which has considerable interest as a historical source. Even combined with journalism and translation, these works seem not to have provided him with an adequate living, and — perhaps also to make up for his earlier espousal of Josephinism — at the time of the political reaction after Joseph's death he took up a post in the 'Chiffre-Kanzlei', a government office concerned with intercepting and deciphering mail. He married the well-to-do Anna Maria Kurz (1764–1844) in 1793; they had no children. Pezzl published some further satirical novels and historical works, but otherwise concentrated on his career, which culminated in his becoming deputy director of the 'Chiffre-Kanzlei' in 1820, three years before his death from dropsy on 9 June 1823.

Concerning Pezzl's personal appearance and character we have the testimony of Caroline Pichler (1769–1843), the Viennese salon hostess, novelist and memoirist, who as a girl met most of the leading figures of the Austrian Enlightenment in the house of her father, the distinguished civil servant Franz Sales von Greiner: 'In the early days of his residence in Vienna, Pezzl was a frequent visitor to my parents' house — a small, stocky man, rather ordinary-looking if one considered only his outward appearance, but full of wit, liveliness and knowledge.'[5] Other witnesses confirm that though Pezzl looked like a Bavarian farmer, he was also highly intelligent, with notably bright eyes, and simple in his attire and lifestyle.[6]

The best way to present Pezzl's contribution to the Catholic Enlightenment and to the reforming ambitions of Joseph II is by surveying his main works.

---

3   See T. C. W. Blanning, *Joseph II* (London: Longman, 1994); Derek Beales, *Joseph II*, vol. II: *Against the World, 1780–1790* (Cambridge: Cambridge University Press, 2009).

4   Ludwig Abafi, *Geschichte der Freimaurerei in Österreich-Ungarn*, 5 vols (Budapest: Ludwig Aigner, 1890–99), III, 333.

5   Quoted by Wolfgang Greip in the introduction to his edition of Pezzl, *Faustin oder das philosophische Jahrhundert* (Hildesheim: Gerstenberg, 1982), p. 118*. (Pages in the introduction have asterisks to distinguish them from the main text.)

6   Leslie Bodi, *Tauwetter in Wien: Zur Prosa der österreichischen Aufklärung, 1781–1795*, 2nd edn (Vienna, Cologne, Weimar: Böhlau, 1995), p. 191.

Briefe aus dem Novizziat

These letters are presented as an authentic document, sent to Pezzl by a slightly older friend during his year as a novice in a Benedictine monastery in Bavaria. This profession of authenticity is usual in eighteenth-century fiction, particularly epistolary fiction. Thus the fictitious letters in Goethe's *Die Leiden des jungen Werthers* [*The Sorrows of Young Werther*] (1774) are presented by an editor who claims to have assembled them and also to have collected information about Werther from the latter's friends, and who increasingly intervenes in the text when Werther's mental disturbance requires another viewpoint to counterbalance his own. In Pezzl's *Briefe*, the narrator's introduction also explains how the letters came into his hands. The novice was able to get them smuggled out, first by a good-natured monastic servant, and later by a cousin of his who was in the same monastery. Nevertheless, since we are repeatedly told that the inmates are under constant surveillance, it is somewhat implausible that the novice could write his letters in the first place, let alone send them without having them intercepted by the authorities.

However, Pezzl's profession of authenticity should not be wholly disregarded. He also tells us that the book will not be yet another scurrilous attack on monasticism. Instead, it is to be a serious and informative work based directly on experience. And although the *Briefe* amount to a very severe attack on monasticism, they are also extremely factual, presenting in circumstantial detail the training to which a novice is subjected, and drawing conclusions about the moral and physical harm that must normally result. There is no reason to doubt that they are a broadly faithful record of Pezzl's own experience.

The novice finds himself subjected to subordination, solitude, strict routine, and inquisitorial discipline. On requesting admission to the Benedictine order, he is obliged to kneel before the prelate. Later, the novices are often made to sit on the floor as an exercise in humility. Apart from services, meals, and an hour set aside each day for conversation, they are confined to their sparsely furnished cells. They are required normally to remain silent, to keep their eyes on the floor, to avoid looking anyone, especially superiors, in the eye, and to walk with their hands folded on their chests. These practices prevent the monks from developing the social virtues by which the Enlightenment set particular store. It was a standard element of anti-monastic critiques that solitude led to dire consequences, including madness. Pezzl emphasizes how the monks nourish resentment against each other, play malicious tricks, engage in petty quarrels, and gather supporters, until what should be Christ's flock turns into a pack of ravening wolves. The artificial solitude imposed by monastic life is the worst possible setting to acquire the social virtues, which are also Christian virtues: 'Everyone must admit that people who live in solitude cannot possibly have the chance to learn social virtues, benevolence, brotherly love, and compassion.'[7]

The monks' daily routine starts at 3.30 a.m., when they are roused by the servant hammering on their cell doors, and continues, parcelled up into small units, until bedtime at 8 p.m. or soon after. The time is spent in idleness which is

---

7 Pezzl, *Briefe aus dem Novizziat* ([Zürich], 1780–82), I, 45.

much less healthy than work in the fields would be. The novices are allowed no privacy: anyone can look into their cells through apertures in the door, and the area reserved for them contains a screen with holes through which they can be watched. Their inner lives are kept under equally close surveillance. They make frequent confession, though they are too tired and harassed to have any time for sinning, and each day ends with a general examination of their consciences, in which they are asked questions to which it would be very imprudent to give an honest answer — for example, which of the monastic rules they find most difficult, whether they dislike any of their fellow novices or superiors — so that they rapidly become accomplished hypocrites. They are supplied with a *cilicium* or wire belt, full of points turned inwards, which after a few hours becomes agonizing to wear, and with whips consisting of numerous cords, with which they are required to practise ritual flagellation. They are under the direction of a novice-master, who in Pezzl's hands becomes a memorable comic tyrant. We are given a dramatic scene in which a series of novices confess their faults in Latin and the novice-master replies 'auf gut hausknechtisch' [like a porter] (I, 120) with abusive tirades. They are required to practise mortification by undergoing unnecessary discomfort, denying themselves food that they like, refraining from drinking when they are thirsty, and so forth. In these practices they have the examples of the saints to follow, and the feats of asceticism recorded in saints' lives are recounted with due ridicule: how St Francis talked with donkeys, rolled in the snow, and slept in a chimney, all to mortify the body; how Passidea of Siena knelt on thorns, thistles, red-hot nails, or a large grater when she prayed, and had herself hung upside down in a chimney, like a ham, to be smoked; how St Macarius lay buried in earth up to his throat for three years, eating nothing but the grass that was within reach. The narrator concludes: 'Am I wrong, dear brother, in maintaining that the actions formerly praised as deeds of spiritual heroism, as superhuman virtues worthy of heaven, would now get one put in a madhouse?' (II, 117).

The *Briefe* are not just a factual report but a literary work, and literature provides a touchstone by which monastic life is condemned as unnatural and absurd. The narrator is an enthusiast for literature. Before he enters the monastery, he describes escaping from uncongenial society into the enjoyment of nature, in a manner strongly reminiscent of *Werther*:

> I bow, go to a hill near the wood, read my Wieland, and in the light of the setting sun I contemplate the industrious people who must spend their days sweating in unpaid obligatory labour, in order to provide nourishment for twenty praying layabouts, while their own children at home are wailing with hunger. (I, 14)

The original rule of St Benedict required the monks themselves to do manual labour, but now it is left to the labourers who are required to cultivate the monks' fields in addition to their own. This reflection on social injustice is coupled with a display of sensibility recalling Goethe, with the difference that where Goethe's hero reads Homer at sunset, Pezzl's narrator reads Wieland. Christoph Martin Wieland, the great humorous writer of the German Enlightenment, was a favourite of Pezzl's, and is frequently cited in the *Briefe* and elsewhere. When the narrator and his cousin acknowledge to each other the sexual content of their dreams, they do so by adapting some well-known lines from 'Diana und Endymion', one of Wieland's *Comische Erzählungen* (I, 161):

> Sie sind auch hier von jener Art,
> Die oft, trotz Skapulier und Bart,
> Sankt Franzens fette Seraphinen
> In schwüler Sommernacht bedienen.[8]

> [Here too they [the dreams] are of the kind often employed by St Francis' plump seraphs, despite their scapulars [over-garments worn by monks] and beards, on sultry summer nights.]

The theme of suppressed sexuality surfaces repeatedly in the *Briefe*. The narrator notices that a hymn usually sung in the evenings contains a line which is clearly a warning against nocturnal emissions (I, 70). When the novices sleep in a dormitory, the narrator notes that it is visited at night by a monk, and wonders ironically whether he is in search of homosexuals: 'surely one cannot suppose that some novices have had a fit that makes them go together at night into the stalls and do what Jupiter did to Ganymede, Socrates to Alcibiades, and what even nowadays the Jesuits have so often done to their young students' (II, 88). Pederasty was a standard charge against Jesuits in Enlightenment polemic.[9]

The narrator's literary tastes contrast sharply with those permitted in the monastery. He reads Wieland, Goethe, Voltaire, Sterne's *Sentimental Journey*, Friedrich Nicolai's novel *Sebaldus Nothanker*, the poems of Albrecht von Haller, and the antimonastic satire *Le Balai* [*The Broom*] (1762) by Henri-Joseph du Laurens (1719–93). This poem provides the whole book with an epigraph, taken from an allegorical episode set in the Temple of Monasticism:

> Tyran des cœurs, la Moinerie affreuse
> Est de ces lieux la Souveraine heureuse.
> Son diadème est la crédulité,
> Son triste sceptre est l'inhumanité.[10]

> [Tyrant of hearts, frightful Monasticism is the happy ruler of this place. Her diadem is credulity, her sad sceptre is inhumanity.]

In the monastery library, however, Pezzl's narrator finds the Church Fathers, theologians from Aquinas to Busenbaum, and sermons, though instead of French and German sermons which have some literary merit, there are the popular sermons by Abraham a Sancta Clara and Martin Cochem, which Enlighteners despised. Hidden

---

8 Christoph Martin Wieland, *Werke*, ed. by Fritz Martini and Hans Werner Seiffert, 5 vols (Munich: Hanser, 1964–68), IV, 113.

9 [Johann Friedel], *Heinrich von Walheim oder Weiberliebe und Schwärmerey*, 2 vols (Frankfurt a.M. and Leipzig, 1785), I, 52–53; [René Pomeau, *D'Arouet à Voltaire, 1694–1734* (Oxford: Voltaire Foundation, 1985), p. 213; David Wootton, 'Unhappy Voltaire, or "I shall never get over it as long as I live"', *History Workshop Journal*, 50 (2000), 137–55].

10 Henri-Joseph du Laurens, *Le Balai: Poème héroï-comique en XVIII chants* (Constantinople [i.e. Amsterdam]: De l'Imprimerie du Mouphti, 1762), p. 118.

away at floor level are expurgated editions of the classics. (Pezzl gives broadly the same impression when describing the library at Oberalteich, where he spent his own novitiate.)[11] Though excluded from the room with prohibited books, he learns that it contains Ovid, Luther's Bible, 'Febronius', 'Lochstein', 'Neuberger', and a history of the papal bull *In coena domini* (I, 27). The joke here is that several of these works were anti-monastic treatises which would probably not have been in a monastery at all. The pseudonymous work by 'Febronius' argued that papal power should be restricted; those by 'Lochstein' and 'Neuberg' argue that church property ought to be subject to taxation, while the bull *In coena domini*, issued in 1627 and read every Holy Thursday, declared that church property was inviolate.[12]

Towards the end, the *Briefe* abandon the pretence of fiction and turn into a treatise on monasticism. The narrator recounts the history of monasticism from its origins in Egypt, and tries to calculate its demographic ill effects. In a period when the economic doctrine of mercantilism urged that each state should maximize its population and make the entire population productive, one of the charges against monasticism was that it took large numbers of healthy adults out of economic life and forbade them to reproduce. Pezzl says that in 1549 there were 225,044 monasteries in the world. If each had 36 inmates, the total was over eight million. Spread over three generations, that makes 24,304,752 'Klosterleute' (II, 63). If each of these had married and had five children, the population would have increased in a single generation by forty million. These figures may be treated with scepticism. Contemporary estimates of the numbers of monks and nuns were very unreliable. Pezzl tells us elsewhere that in 1780 there were about 63,000 monks and nuns in the Austrian territories, but according to Derek Beales, the leading historian of the Austrian Enlightenment, these territories contained fewer than 2000 monastic houses with about 40,000 regular clergy of both sexes, a disproportionate number being located in the Monarchy's Belgian and Italian territories.[13]

Pezzl's critique of monasticism was very much in the spirit of the times. Even earlier, under Maria Theresia, her chancellor Kaunitz had argued on economic grounds for reducing the number of regular clergy. One of Joseph II's first acts was to issue a decree dissolving the monasteries of contemplative orders and imposing restrictions on the rest. Satires on monastic life were popular and were sometimes written by liberal-minded monks, such as Ulrich Petrak of Melk and Anselm Edling of St Paul in Carinthia.[14] Pezzl was astute in making use of his own experiences to launch himself into literature with a distinctive contribution to a familiar genre.

11   Pezzl, *Reise durch den Baierschen Kreis* (Salzburg and Leipzig, 1784), p. 36.

12   For detailed accounts, see Michael Printy, *Enlightenment and the Creation of German Catholicism* (Cambridge: Cambridge University Press, 2009).

13   Pezzl, *Charakteristik Josephs des Zweiten*, 3rd edn (Vienna: Degen, 1803), p. 72; Derek Beales, *Prosperity and Plunder: European Catholic Monasteries in the Age of Revolution, 1650–1815* (Cambridge: Cambridge University Press, 2003), p. 180.

14   See Johannes Frimmel, *Literarisches Leben in Melk: Ein Kloster im 18. Jahrhundert im kulturellen Umbruch* (Vienna, Cologne, Weimar: Böhlau, 2004); Erich Nussbaumer, *Geistiges Kärnten: Literatur- und Geistesgeschichte des Landes* (Klagenfurt: Kleinmayr, 1956); Hans-Wolf Jäger, 'Mönchskritik und Klostersatire in der deutschen Spätaufklärung', in *Katholische Aufklärung: Aufklärung im katholischen Deutschland*, ed. by Harm Klueting (Hamburg: Meiner, 1993), pp. 192–207.

Faustin oder das philosophische Jahrhundert

Pezzl's novel *Faustin oder das philosophische Jahrhundert* is an updated version of Voltaire's *Candide*. The naive hero, Faustin, comes at an early age under the influence of Father Bonifaz, an enlightened cleric. Just as Voltaire's Pangloss persists in believing, despite all evidence to the contrary, that this is the best of all possible worlds, so Bonifaz is convinced that the age he lives in is the philosophical century in which enlightenment has triumphed. Faustin goes on a whirlwind and largely involuntary tour of Europe and America which proves overwhelmingly that ignorance, superstition and barbarity are still rampant. In South Germany he finds people flocking to the alleged exorcist and miraculous healer Gassner.[15] In Venice, he is expelled for mocking the ceremony in which the Doge marries the sea. In Naples, where Freemasons are persecuted, he is denounced as one, and flees to Genoa. There he gets caught up in a scheme for sending German colonists to Spain and becomes secretary to the enlightened minister Olavide, but when the latter is arrested by the Inquisition, Faustin flees to supposedly enlightened France. There he learns that the *Encyclopédie* is in the Bastille (this is literally true, as offending books, as well as people, were confined there), and that on Voltaire's death the clergy refuse to permit his burial in a cemetery. Enlightened England is no better: an imposing monument there, which Faustin thinks must be the tomb of some Enlightener such as Locke or Shaftesbury, turns out to commemorate a racehorse, and on a later visit Faustin finds London convulsed by the anti-Catholic Gordon Riots, which he considers a Protestant counterpart to the massacre of St Bartholomew's Night. The world still drives a trade in human beings. Forcibly recruited as a soldier, Faustin arrives in America and witnesses the horrors of the slave trade, as well as seeing how European immigrants are obliged to sell themselves as indentured labourers. His disgust at European colonialism is strengthened by reading the Abbé Raynal's famous anti-colonial text, *Histoire des deux Indes* (1770).

Fortunately, this benighted world has two spots of light. One is Berlin, where under Frederick the Great tolerance prevails to such an extent that a mass is said in a Catholic church for the soul of Voltaire. The other is Vienna, where Joseph II has just assumed sole rule and instituted his edicts of toleration. Faustin declares that with Joseph's accession in 1780 a new era has begun — 'the era of enlightened southern Germany, the Josephian era':[16] this is apparently the first use of an adjective derived from the Emperor's name, anticipating the later 'josephinisch'.[17] The end of the novel sees Faustin and a like-minded friend living quietly in Vienna and greeting each of Joseph's reforms with the exclamation: 'Under Joseph's government, we have the universal victory of reason and humanity, and an enlightened, tolerant, truly philosophical century!'[18]

15 On Gassner, see H. C. Erik Midelfort, *Exorcism and Enlightenment: Johann Joseph Gassner and the Demons of Eighteenth-Century Germany* (New Haven, CT, and London: Yale University Press, 2005).

16 Pezzl, *Faustin*, p. 378.

17 Derek Beales, *Enlightenment and Reform in Eighteenth-Century Europe* (London: Tauris, 2005), pp. 289–90.

18 Pezzl, *Faustin*, p. 281.

Faustin shares the episodic structure of *Candide*. Just as Voltaire transports Candide all over the globe, from Westphalia to the Black Sea and to South America, taking in such newsworthy destinations as earthquake-ruined Lisbon and the much-discussed Jesuit reductions in Paraguay, so Pezzl sends Faustin on the slightest of pretexts to every place where superstition and oppression can be observed. Though it lacks the polish of *Candide*, Pezzl's novel is a lively narrative which especially shows how closely he followed contemporary events: all his references, even the monument to the racehorse, can be traced to newspaper reports and travel books.

Pezzl's eye for detail is still more evident in *Reise durch den Baierschen Kreis*, which he published anonymously soon after arriving in Vienna, and which attracted considerable interest. It is a lively travel book in a series of letters in which the author, modelling himself explicitly on Sterne's Yorick, undertakes to report on 'morality, enlightenment, the people's character and the national mentality' in Bavaria from Passau to near Salzburg.[19] Towns and important buildings are characterized, the state of universities such as Ingolstadt is examined in detail, and we learn such items, valuable for the historian, as the fact that Regensburg, like all Imperial cities, is full of Austrian, Prussian and Danish recruiting officers, of which the Austrians generally get the best recruits and the Danes the worst. Monastic and religious life is the main topic. Many anecdotes are told about life in various monasteries, their financial management, their reputation for learning, the state of their libraries, and the extent to which they still promote vulgar superstition. Thus we learn that the chapel at Oberalteich, where Pezzl did his novitiate, contains 'the most disgusting picture that a plebeian monk's head could ever devise' in which monks spray holy water as Doctor Luther flees through the air on a pig, carrying a Bible, a full glass, and a sausage.[20] Equally tasteless is the statue of a pregnant Madonna, in whose belly a window has been opened allowing the spectator to see the infant Jesus as a half-formed embryo. These are among many examples of superstition heightened by vulgarity.

Oriental Fictions: *Marokkanische Briefe* and *Abdul Erzerums neue persische Briefe*

Pezzl's *Marokkanische Briefe* are the most radical critique of Christianity to emerge from the Austrian Enlightenment. They were suggested by a Moroccan embassy that visited Vienna in 1783, but, like several of his other works, their literary inspiration is French. While *Faustin* is modelled on *Candide*, the *Marokkanische Briefe* are inspired by Montesquieu's *Lettres persanes* (1721), in which two Persians visiting France comment satirically, from an outsider's perspective, on French manners and customs. In Pezzl's version, 'Sidi' reports to his friend 'Hamid', back home, on his impressions of Vienna. He favours monarchy, and approves of the freedom of the press introduced by Joseph II; but his main interest is in Christianity. He pillories not only the superstitious excesses of Baroque Catholicism, a standard target of enlightened critique, but the very foundations of Christianity in the Bible. The Old Testament is both fanciful and immoral. He illustrates the former by a

19   Pezzl, *Reise*, p. 3.
20   Pezzl, *Reise*, p. 37.

sceptical résumé of the early chapters of Genesis, and the latter by listing the many massacres from sacred history which, he says, have inspired assassins down the ages. The murder of Eglon, king of Moab, by Ehud with his two-edged sword (Judges 3. 15–23), and Samuel hewing Agag in pieces 'before the Lord' (1 Samuel 15. 33), were among the Enlightenment's favourite examples of Old Testament barbarity (e.g. Voltaire's article 'Fanatisme' in his *Dictionnaire philosophique*). He knows such radical writers on the Bible as Lessing, who in *Die Erziehung des Menschengeschlechts* [*The Education of the Human Race*] (1780) argues that revelation is a gradual and still incomplete process; he mentions the Italian Deist Alberto Radicati, who compared Islam with Christianity, arguing that the original purity of both religions had been corrupted by priests;[21] and even the notorious *Treatise of the Three Impostors*, which represented Moses, Muhammad and Jesus as equal charlatans. As this suggests, the New Testament comes in for sharp criticism as well. Sidi knows the arguments presented by the Hamburg Orientalist Reimarus, and published after his death by Lessing, that Jesus was a political revolutionary whose intentions were reinterpreted after his death by his followers. He questions the divinity of Christ:

> The Catholics believe with dogmatic zeal that Christ was the true son of God. The Protestants are gradually beginning to say that Christ was a human being like any other, but a gifted preacher of morality, and in that sense a son of God, i.e. a good person.[22]

Here Pezzl steps over the boundaries of the Catholic Enlightenment, illustrating Ernst Wangermann's contention that 'Reform Catholicism could be the gateway to natural religion, deism and atheism'.[23] As for the institutions of the Catholic Church, Sidi is as severe as Pezzl could wish against monastic orders, Jesuits, and the practices of auricular confession and celibacy. The boredom suffered by the novice in *Briefe aus dem Novizziat* is echoed in his critique of the Church Fathers:

> One is alarmed at the sight of the monstrous folio volumes of Augustine, Ambrose, Jerome, Thomas, etc., etc. Apart from occasional scraps of a kind of eloquence or chattiness, everything else is unreadable. Nonsense and contra-dictions are in their rightful place on every page. For a thinker of our time I could imagine no more painful punishment than condemning him to read the complete works of a Church Father: a *bel esprit* would burst, as though he had taken rat-poison.
>   Most patristic scribblings consist of sophistical hair-splitting, word-plays, allegories taken to the point of absurdity, exaggerated morality, eccentric Bible commentaries, nonsensical monastic notions, empty platitudes, foolish

---

21   See Jonathan Israel, *Enlightenment Contested: Philosophy, Modernity, and the Emancipation of Man 1670–1752* (Oxford: Oxford University Press, 2006), p. 97.

22   [Pezzl], *Marokkanische Briefe: Aus dem Arabischen*. Neue vermehrte und verbesserte Auflage (Frankfurt a.M.and Leipzig, 1784), p. 91.

23   Ernst Wangermann, 'Reform Catholicism and Political Radicalism in the Austrian Enlightenment', in *The Enlightenment in National Context*, ed. by Roy Porter and Mikuláš Teich (Cambridge: Cambridge University Press, 1981), pp. 127–40 (p. 133); cf. Harm Klueting, 'The Catholic Enlightenment in Austria or the Habsburg Lands', in *A Companion to the Catholic Enlightenment in Europe*, ed. by Ulrich L. Lehner and Michael Printy (Leiden: Brill, 2010), pp. 127–64 (p. 143).

declamations, and occasional deliberate absurdities and distortions. Now and
again some sensible sentences are visible, but they are far from outweighing the
mass of useless stuff.[24] (Pezzl 1784b, 99–100)

No wonder that such a harsh and sweeping critique was too much even for the
freedom of publication instituted by Joseph II. Deistical works were in any case
treated with caution; the anti-Christian thrust of the *Marokkanische Briefe* caused
their publication in Vienna to be prohibited, and care was taken to confiscate any
copies that were smuggled in from abroad.[25]

It has been claimed by Gustav Gugitz that Pezzl also wrote the anonymous *Abdul
Erzerums neue persische Briefe* (1787), which are based on the fiction that the grandson
of Usbek, the letter-writer in Montesquieu's *Lettres persanes*, likewise visits Europe
and writes reports to his friends and relatives at home.[26] However, the ascription
is dubious.[27] Unlike Pezzl's other works, the *Neue persische Briefe* are very short on
specific contemporary detail. They are a tirade in which Abdul Erzerum expresses
the disillusionment which, as the prefatory letter informs us, led him after his travels
to drown himself. Although an acquaintance met while travelling gives Abdul
high hopes of the Viennese Enlightenment, Abdul notes, even before reaching
Vienna, the misery of the rural population, a topic to which he frequently recurs.
In Vienna itself he concludes that the humane treatment of the citizens results not
from genuine philanthropy but the mercantilist ambition to maximize the number
and productivity of the population. The very project of enlightenment strikes
him as dubious, because it means treating everyone by the same standard and thus
spreading uniformity and mediocrity, and because it deprives people of traditional
beliefs while offering nothing in return. The spirit in which Abdul forms these
judgements echoes that of the Sturm und Drang, and particularly *Werther*:

> It is simply impossible for me to limit myself to quiet civil life, waiting for the
> wealth of domestic happiness to provide me with the small quantity of joy that
> I long impatiently to seize for myself. Why should I hide it? A heart like mine
> cannot easily be appeased.[28]

Passages like this suggest that Abdul's disillusionment is not the result of his
Austrian experiences, however disheartening they may be, but is programmed from
the outset.

Skizze von Wien

The *Skizze von Wien* appeared in six instalments between 1786 and 1790. In its
method of describing a city, it acknowledges a debt to the *Tableau de Paris* (1781–88)
by Louis-Sébastien Mercier (1740–1814). Beginning with statistical information
about Vienna's situation, climate, population, commerce, and consumption of

24   [Pezzl], *Marokkanische Briefe*, pp. 99–100.
25   See Ernst Wangermann, *Die Waffen der Publizität: Zum Funktionswandel der politischen Literatur
unter Joseph II* (Vienna: Verlag für Geschichte und Politik, 2004), pp. 113–14.
26   Gustav Gugitz, 'Johann Pezzl', *Jahrbuch der Grillparzer-Gesellschaft*, 16 (1906), 164–217 (p. 195).
27   Bodi, *Tauwetter*, p. 315.
28   *Abdul Erzerums neue persische Briefe* (Vienna and Leipzig: Stahel, 1787), p. 28.

commodities, the *Skizze* continues with a miscellaneous collection of mini-essays on Viennese localities and on such aspects of urban life as theatres, newspapers, coffee-houses, prostitutes, venereal diseases, and many more. By this superficial disorder, the genre of the *tableau* differs from the older genre of the urban topography, and conveys the juxtaposition of heterogeneous realities that is characteristic of the great city.[29] It was so popular that Pezzl later wrote a sequel, *Neue Skizze von Wien*, in three parts (1805–12), which differs from the first series in its more negative emphases, notably on the cost of living and the growth of luxury.[30]

Part of Pezzl's purpose is to defend great cities as such against the strictures of moralists, who denounce them as haunts of vice, and the primitivism of Rousseau, who is here dismissed as a fantasist. Cities, Pezzl insists, are centres of arts, learning, refinement, culture and humanity. Vienna in particular needs to be defended against the complaints of the Berlin Enlightener, Friedrich Nicolai (1733–1811), who in his account of his travels in southern Germany and Austria attacked the Viennese for their self-indulgent hedonism and their attachment to Catholic superstitions.[31] Pezzl defends the ordinary Viennese against the charge of excessive eating and drinking, undue enjoyment of theatre, excursions to the country, and other pleasures. After all, Vienna lies in a fertile region, the average Viennese is comfortably off; why should the Viennese not enjoy the abundant products of nature?

The charge of superstition is harder to rebut, for Pezzl himself, an ardent Josephinist, shares the disapproval of Catholic 'Andächtelei' or superstitious piety.[32] He welcomes the reduction in the number of regular clergy, whose establishments, he claims, used to take up one-sixth of Vienna's surface area. Surveying the state of religion in Vienna, he finds that the majority of the population are warmly attached to a religion which is a medley of truths, half-truths, and untruths, and that they reject any criticisms of it, while many, especially the clergy, practise religion mainly from self-interest. Among so-called freethinkers, he distinguishes those who remain Catholics but wish to purify their religion from superstitious practices; those who, loyal to Christianity, wish to modify some of its doctrines; deists, who are rare in Vienna; and French-style atheists, who have yet to appear there.

Pezzl naturally praises also the secular achievements of Josephinism. Besides freedom of speech and abolition of censorship, he includes accounts of the Allgemeines Krankenhaus [General Hospital], the school for the deaf and dumb, and other institutions founded by Joseph. His overall commitment to the cause of enlightenment appears in a section headed 'Aufklärung', where he says that many people identify enlightenment with the removal of religious abuses, but it means much more:

> For me, an enlightened man is one whose moral feeling is properly formed;
> who finds contentment in the profession in which chance or the laws have

29 See Kai Kauffmann, *'Es ist nur ein Wien!' Stadtbeschreibungen von Wien 1700 bis 1783* (Vienna, Cologne, Weimar: Böhlau, 1994), pp. 210–12, 225.

30 Kauffmann, p. 241.

31 Friedrich Nicolai, *Beschreibung einer Reise durch Deutschland und die Schweiz im Jahre 1781: Nebst Bemerkungen über Gelehrsamkeit, Industrie, Religion und Sitten*, 8 vols (Berlin and Stettin, 1783–87).

32 Pezzl, *Skizze von Wien*, 6 vols (Vienna and Leipzig: Kraus, 1786–90), p. 92.

placed him; who acts honestly and on reflection; who has become accustomed to loving his work, reverencing the laws, readily accepting instruction, loving order in his domestic and professional affairs, and observing moderation in his diet and taking care of his health; who never longs to spend more than he can afford; who seeks constantly to perfect the talents necessary for his destined role within society; who knows and practises the virtues of the citizen, friend, husband and father; who knows that in civil society one must inevitably bear one's individual burden and sacrifice one's private advantage for the sake of the greater whole; who never makes an immodest attack on the religion publicly sponsored by the state, and, if he has acquired different beliefs, holds them in private; who, finally, enjoys his existence with pleasure, and knows how to enjoy it comfortably, quietly, and for a long time.[33]

This is a decidedly conservative conception of enlightenment. The enlightened person, imagined only as male, is first and foremost a good citizen. He should be contented with his lot, accept his place in society, perform his domestic and public duties, and, whatever his private beliefs may be, conform to the official religion of his country. These are the ideals recommended to the middle-class readers of the moral weeklies which flourished in eighteenth-century Germany, and of which Sonnenfels's *Der Mann ohne Vorurtheil* was an Austrian counterpart.[34] The advice about religious conformity, in particular, suggests that the author of the *Marokkanische Briefe* had by now returned within the fold of the Catholic Enlightenment. Although the *Skizze* makes clear that Pezzl still opposes monasticism, pilgrimages, and other customs defined as superstitious, he no longer wishes to question the foundations of Christianity.

Conclusion

Where, finally, are we to place Pezzl on a map of the Catholic Enlightenment? He undoubtedly belongs on the outside left. He agrees with the Catholic reformers of late eighteenth-century Austria in attacking credulity, superstition, and intolerance. In his polemic against monasticism, he goes beyond Joseph II, who closed down the monasteries of contemplative orders, and attacks the entire institution of monasticism as useless to society and damaging to its inmates. His perspective is close to that of Protestant polemics against monasticism. Similarly, in his most radical text, the *Marokkanische Briefe*, he moves beyond the limits of Catholicism by questioning the divinity of Christ, and seems closer in spirit to the liberal developments within German Lutheranism. The liberal wing of Protestant theology known as Neology did its best to dismantle the supernatural aspects of Christianity while maintaining a façade of orthodoxy; Lessing in his theological polemics sought unsuccessfully to induce the Neologists to admit that their official orthodoxy was intellectually dishonest. Pezzl refers to Lessing with sympathy. He also accepts the historical criticisms of the Old and New Testaments made by Reimarus and published after

33 Pezzl, *Skizze von Wien*, pp. 350–51.
34 See Wolfgang Martens, *Die Botschaft der Tugend: Die Aufklärung im Spiegel der deutschen moral-ischen Wochenschriften* (Stuttgart: Metzler, 1968).

Reimarus' death by Lessing as 'Fragments of an Anonymous Writer'. His adoption of a non-Christian perspective in the *Briefe*, and his sympathy for such extreme views as those of Radicati, imply a deism close to that of Voltaire.

However, Pezzl remained within the Catholic Church. This contrasts him with his contemporary, Ignaz-Aurelius Fessler (1756–1839), whose autobiography recounts his entry into the Capuchin order, his consecration as a priest just when he had lost his faith, his reading in radical writers such as Helvétius and Spinoza, and his conversion to Protestantism.[35] Pezzl took a less intense interest in strictly religious questions, and was more interested in moral and political reform. Hence, writing under his own name in *Skizze von Wien*, he prudently recommends that anyone whose private beliefs differ from the religion supported by the state should keep his beliefs to himself and refrain from attacking the state religion — a sign that Josephinism had by then reached its high-water mark, and also that many of its reforming aims, such as the reduction of superstitious practices and the dissolution of monasteries belonging to contemplative orders, had in fact been achieved. Although he approaches the boundaries of the Catholic Enlightenment, he does not — publicly at least — go beyond them.

---

35   *Dr. Fessler's Rückblicke auf seine siebzigjährige Pilgerschaft. Ein Nachlass [sic] an seine Freunde und an seine Feinde* (Breslau: Korn, 1824).

CHAPTER 12

Joseph Rohrer and the Bureaucratic Enlightenment

Our understanding of the Enlightenment has recently changed in emphasis. In 1932, Ernst Cassirer's influential *The Philosophy of the Enlightenment* described a purely intellectual movement.[1] He did not inquire how the ideas of the *philosophes* affected the practice of eighteenth-century absolute monarchs. In fact, eighteenth-century rulers were largely hostile to theorizing. Maria Theresia frequently denounced the *philosophes*. Her son Joseph II maintained the ban on the writings of Voltaire and Hume, ostentatiously refrained from visiting Voltaire when passing through Ferney, and brusquely rebuffed offers of advice from Joseph von Sonnenfels, the most prominent intellectual of the Austrian Enlightenment.[2] Scarcely any of the reforms introduced under enlightened absolutism can be shown to have been directly inspired by specific doctrines of the *philosophes*. They are due rather to the spread of enlightened thinking among the vast numbers of bureaucrats who ran the eighteenth-century 'police states'.[3] The importance of these universitytrained and reform-minded administrators as bearers of the Enlightenment has been demonstrated above all by the historian Franco Venturi.[4] If Cassirer presented the

1 Ernst Cassirer, *The Philosophy of the Enlightenment,* trans. by F. C. A. Koelln and J. P. Pettegrove (Princeton, NJ: Princeton University Press, 1951); originally *Die Philosophie der Aufklärung* (Tübingen: Mohr Siebeck, 1932).

2 See Paul von Mitrofanov, *Joseph II: Seine politische und kulturelle Tätigkeit,* trans. by V. von Demelić (Vienna and Leipzig: C. W. Stern, 1910), pp. 90–93, and Derek Beales, 'Christians and Philosophes: The Case of the Austrian Enlightenment', in *History, Society and the Churches: Essays in Honour of Owen Chadwick,* ed. by Derek Beales and Geoffrey Best (Cambridge: Cambridge University Press, 1985), pp. 169–94, who argues that the *philosophes* exercised very little influence on the Enlightenment in Austria. [On Joseph's sole reign from 1780 to 1790, see now Derek Beales, *Joseph II,* vol. II: *Against the World, 1780–1790* (Cambridge: Cambridge University Press, 2009).]

3 On the eighteenth-century meaning of 'Polizei' and 'Polizeistaat', see Keith Tribe, *Governing Economy: The Reformation of German Economic Discourse, 1750–1840* (Cambridge, 1988), pp. 32–34. 'The Polizeistaat is a state in which the good of the ruler is indistinguishable from the good of the populace; the administrative apparatus is devoted to the increase of the ruler's wealth through the optimization of the happiness of his subjects' (p. 34).

4 See Franco Venturi, *Utopia and Reform in the Enlightenment* (Cambridge: Cambridge University Press, 1971); H. M. Scott, 'The Problem of Enlightened Absolutism', in *Enlightened Absolutism: Reform and Reformers in Later Eighteenth-Century Europe,* ed. by H. M. Scott (Basingstoke: Macmillan, 1990), pp. 1–35.

philosophical Enlightenment, Venturi has transferred attention to the bureaucratic Enlightenment.

This is the context in which to see the work of Joseph Rohrer (1769–1828), a member of the new class of enlightened bureaucrats, who was also a cultivated man and an entertaining and idiosyncratic writer. His major literary project was an ethnographic study of all the peoples of the Habsburg domains, three volumes of which were completed. And he upheld the ideals of Josephinism long after the anti-Josephinian reaction of the 1790s. The virtually complete neglect of his work by modern historians is difficult to understand.[5] He deserves to be rescued from oblivion.

Although born in Vienna, Joseph Rohrer was brought up in the Tyrol, where he attended the Haupt-Gymnasium at Innsbruck.[6] After attending the University of Vienna, where his studies included mathematics, he entered the civil service in 1791, initially as a bookkeeper at Bregenz. Soon, however, he was transferred to Vienna, where he evidently mixed in literary circles: he knew Johann Baptist Alxinger personally, and some of his early essays were published in the *Österreichische Monatsschrift* (1793–94), a shortlived periodical edited first by Alxinger and then by Gottlieb Leon and Joseph Schreyvogel.[7] He also published two books: *Uiber die Tiroler* (1796), a first effort at ethnographic writing, and *Neuestes Gemählde von Wien* (1797), intended as an updated successor to Johann Pezzl's *Skizze von Wien* (1789). By 1797 he must already have moved into the police service, for his second book goes into detail about the functioning of the police and includes much sociological information about the behaviour of thieves and prostitutes. In 1800 he went as a commissioner of police to Lemberg (now Lvov), capital of Galicia, the province which had been added to the Habsburg domains in 1772 by the first partition of Poland.[8] Commissioners of police had extensive powers. They were supposed

5   The only extended account of Rohrer I have found in any modern work is in Wolfgang Häusler, *Das galizische Judentum in der Habsburgermonarchie im Lichte der zeitgenössischen Publizistik und Reiseliteratur von 1772–1848* (Vienna, 1979), where Rohrer's attitude to the Jews is discussed on pp. 53–60. He is mentioned in *Deutsch-österreichische Literaturgeschichte*, ed. by J. W. Nagl, Jakob Zeidler and Eduard Castle, 4 vols (Vienna: Fromme, 1914–37).

6   Besides incidental references scattered throughout Rohrer's works, this biographical information comes from Constant von Wurzbach, *Biographisches Lexikon des Kaiserthums Österreich*, 60 vols (Vienna: Druck und Verlag der k. k. Hof- und Staatsdruckerei, 1857–90), XXVI, 284, and Ludwik Finkel and Stanisław Starzynski, *Historya uniwersytetu lwowskiego* (Lwów, 1894); I am grateful to Dr Andrzej Olechnowicz for translating the passage about Rohrer for me. Wurzbach, by a strange oversight, attributes to Rohrer a catalogue of the Imperial collection of paintings, which he elsewhere correctly ascribes to Johann Rosa.

7   Rohrer's contributions to the *Österreichische Monatsschrift* were: 'Über die Wanderungen der Tiroler', *Österreichische Monatsschrift*, 1 (March 1793), 221–50; 'Über die Industrie in Vorarlberg', *Österreichische Monatsschrift*, 2 (June 1794), 251–56; 'Von der Denkart in den Wälschen Confinen', ib., 257–62.

8   On Galicia at this period, see Wasyl Gawlitsch, 'Ostgalizien im Spiegel der deutschen Reiseliteratur am Ende des 18. Jahrhunderts' (diss., Vienna, 1943); Horst Glassl, *Das österreichische Einrichtungswerk in Galizien (1772–1790)* (Wiesbaden, 1975); Maria Klańska, 'Erkundungen der neuen österreichischen Provinz Galizien im deutschsprachigen Schrifttum der letzten Dezennien des 18. Jahrhunderts', in *Galizien als gemeinsame Literaturlandschaft*, ed. by Fridrun Rinner and Klaus Zerinschek (Innsbruck: Institut für Sprachwissenschaft der Universität Innsbruck, 1988), pp. 35–48.

not only to forestall and punish crime, but to prevent people from being idle or making a noise in public. From 1801 they were also in charge of censorship.[9] Even with wide powers, however, Rohrer's job cannot have been easy. A travel account of the 1780s describes Lemberg as full of brothels which the police at that time made no attempt to control; another, from the early 1790s, denounces the town's administration as exceptionally slow and inefficient.[10]

Rohrer's ethnographic project probably antedates his move to Lemberg. He mentions (B 146) that one of his books, the *Versuch über die slawischen Bewohner der österreichischen Monarchie*, was completed in 1801 and delivered to the Court Censorship, which evidently took three years to deal with it. The oddities of Habsburg bureaucracy presumably account for his publishing five books in a single year (1804). These included a statistical account of the Tyrol and neighbouring regions, concentrating on physical rather than human geography, and an account in letter form of a journey from Moldavia, just across the southeastern frontier of the Habsburg territories, via the Bukovina to Galicia, and from there through Silesia and Moravia to Vienna. The journey was begun on 20 November 1802 and ended in Vienna in April 1803. More important, however, are the three ethnographic works dealing respectively with the Germans, the Slavs, and the Jews. These three books, amounting together to more than a thousand pages, give evidence not only of extensive travel, but also of wide reading and remarkable industry.

In 1806, no doubt thanks to his publications, Rohrer was appointed professor of statistics at the University of Lemberg. After repeated requests for a transfer, he received a similar post in Olmütz (Olomouc in Moravia) in 1816, but returned to his position in Lemberg two years later. He knew the playwright Franz Kratter, who was living in rural retirement outside Lemberg, and was the leading figure in its German-language literature. Rohrer's own writing seems to have been hindered by his teaching duties, for he published nothing more until 1827, when the first volume of a planned statistical account of the entire Habsburg dominions appeared. Ill-health, particularly an illness of the chest, obliged him to retire prematurely in 1822, and his statistical project was cut short by his death on 21 September 1828.[11]

---

9   Mitrofanov, *Joseph II*, p. 270; Ernst Wangermann, *From Joseph II to the Jacobin Trials*, 2nd edn (Oxford: Oxford University Press, 1969), p. 175.

10   Franz Kratter, *Briefe über den itzigen Zustand von Galizien*, 2 vols (Leipzig: Wucherer, 1786), II, 191; Belsazar Hacquet, *Hacquet's neueste physikalisch-politische Reisen durch die Dacischen und Sarmatischen oder Nördlichen Karpathen*, 4 vols (Nuremberg: Raspe, 1790–96), III, 178–80.

11   Rohrer published the following books:
— *Uiber die Tiroler. Ein Beytrag zur österreichischen Völkerkunde* (Vienna: Doll, 1796). Cited as T.
— *Neuestes Gemählde von Wien* (Vienna: Doll, 1797). Cited as G.
— *Abriß der westlichen Provinzen der österreichischen Monarchie* (Vienna: Camesina, 1804).
— *Bemerkungen auf einer Reise von der Türkischen Gränze über die Bukowina durch Ost und Westgalizien,*
— *Schlesien und Mähren nach Wien* (Vienna: Pichler, 1804). Cited as B.
— *Versuch über die deutschen Bewohner der österreichischen Monarchie*, 2 vols (Vienna: Kunst- und Industrie-Comptoir, 1804). Cited as D.
— *Versuch über die jüdischen Bewohner der österreichischen Monarchie* (Vienna: no pub., 1804). Cited as J.
— *Versuch über die slawischen Bewohner der österreichischen Monarchie*, 2 vols (Vienna: Kunst- und Industrie-Comptoir, 1804). Cited as S.
— *Statistik des österreichischen Kaiserthums*, vol. 1 (Vienna, 1827); no more published.

Throughout his life Rohrer travelled extensively within the Habsburg domains. By 1804, when he published his major ethnographic works, he had travelled widely in the German-speaking lands, Bohemia, Moravia, Carniola, Silesia, and of course Galicia. From his last book it appears that by 1827 he had also become familiar with Hungary, which is seldom mentioned in the earlier books. However, he seems scarcely ever to have been outside Habsburg territory. He tells us that he had visited Regensburg (D 1, 114), but despite his enthusiasm for English life and literature, only one reference suggests that he had actually visited Britain. In *Uiber die Tiroler* he tells how Tyrolean canary-sellers travel as far as London, where 'in the City, in the handsome square Moorfields, [they] have a special booth to sell their birds; since this booth stands between two madhouses, St Luke's Hospital and Goldbedlam [*sic*], it makes a strange impression on the feelings of the onlooker' (T 44). This could, however, be a second-hand account.

To read systematically through Rohrer's works is to become aware of a tension between his bureaucratic calling and his imagination. With part of his mind he enthusiastically appreciates the human diversity of the Habsburg domains. Another part of his mind, however, wants to judge that diversity by the single standard of progress towards enlightenment, and to substitute uniformity and discipline. In propagating enlightenment, he comes close to regarding people not as Kantian ends in themselves but as objects of administration who must if necessary be disciplined into happiness.

Similar tensions are obvious in the career of Rohrer's hero, the other Joseph. In his enthusiasm for enlightened reform, Joseph II failed to realize that rational arguments were not sufficient to win people for his reforms. Though sincerely devoted to his conception of his people's good, he was also a friendless workaholic, tactless and often wounding in dealing with relatives, associates, and subjects.[12] He showed his insensitivity when in 1784 he ordained that the Hungarian Crown of St Stephen should be transferred from Pressburg (Bratislava) to Vienna, thus arousing a storm of protest from the Hungarians whom Maria Theresia had worked so hard to conciliate; and when he ordained that, because of the timber shortage in Vienna, corpses should be sewn into linen sacks instead of being buried in coffins — an edict which aroused such fury that it had to be withdrawn.[13] Hence his subjects felt no affection for him, as a contemporary pamphleteer pointed out.[14] Rohrer's writings, like Joseph's career, illustrate the tensions generated by the Enlightenment with its promise of happiness under the rule of reason.

Unlike the Emperor, Rohrer was a highly cultivated man. He had a remarkable knowledge of languages, being familiar not only with Latin and Greek but with

12   See the character sketches in Mitrofanov, *Joseph II*, pp. 97–112; Derek Beales, *Joseph II*, Vol. 1: *In the Shadow of Maria Theresa, 1741–1780* (Cambridge: Cambridge University Press, 1987), pp. 306–37.

13   See Leslie Bodi, *Tauwetter in Wien: Zur Prosa der österreichischen Aufklärung*, 2nd edn (Vienna, Cologne, Weimar: Böhlau, 1995), p. 245.

14   Joseph Richter, 'Warum wird Kaiser Joseph von seinem Volke nicht geliebt?' reprinted in *Literatur der Aufklärung, 1765–1800*, ed. by Edith Rosenstrauch-Königsberg (Vienna, Graz, Cologne: Böhlau, 1988), pp. 69–81.

English, French, Italian, Polish, and at least one South Slavonic language. In Galicia he was able to communicate with servants and peasants in Ukrainian. In later life he appears also to have mastered Hungarian. His reading in classical and modern languages was extensive, though his taste was conservative. He speaks familiarly of the literature of the Austrian Enlightenment, praising Alxinger, Blumauer, Denis and Mastalier, and though he considers Austrian literature to be in decline, he commends the writings of Gabriele von Baumberg and Caroline Pichler (D II, 9–10). Although he praises the good taste of Schiller's periodical *Die Horen* and knows the Schlegels' *Athenäum*, he never mentions Goethe. His heroes among German writers are Lessing and Kant; he also refers appreciatively to the idylls of Salomon Gessner. In the theatre he praises Lessing's *Minna von Barnhelm* and the domestic comedies of Iffland and Kratter. He dislikes the vulgarity of Viennese popular comedy, complaining:

> [...] daß unsere Damen und Fräulein in den vorstädtischen Theatern die zottenhaften Reden, Gebärdenspiele und Gassenlieder in dem Fagottisten, den Nymphen der Silberquelle, den Waldmännern u. m. s. mit vollen Händen beklatschen, und immer noch lieber als eine Minna von Barnhelm im Nazional-Theater besuchen. (G 179)[15]

> [Our married and unmarried ladies clap their hands vigorously at the obscene speeches, gestures and popular songs in *The Fagottist*, *The Nymph of the Silver Spring*, *The Woodmen*, etc., and would still far rather see them than go to *Minna von Barnhelm* in the National Theatre.]

Shakespeare is never mentioned: the mutilated versions of *Hamlet* and *Macbeth* performed on the eighteenth-century Viennese stage would hardly arouse enthusiasm. Rohrer's preferences in English literature are those usual in Vienna in the 1780s: he likes Pope, who provides epigraphs to two of his books, and Macpherson's 'Ossian', which had been translated into German by the Austrian poet Denis.[16] He also quotes Gibbon, Hume, and Sterne's *Tristram Shandy*, while the drunkenness in Galicia reminds him of Hogarth's punch-drinkers.

A large proportion of Rohrer's extensive reading, especially in English, consists of political and statistical works. Like many contemporaries, from Voltaire and Diderot to the Italian nobleman Alberto Radicati and the Bavarian-born novelist Johann Pezzl, he saw Britain as the birthplace of enlightenment.[17] His reading ranges from Adam Smith and the zoologist Thomas Pennant to William Marshall's

---

15   Two of these plays, Perinet's *Kaspar der Fagottist* and Schikaneder's *Die Waldmänner*, are discussed in Otto Rommel, *Die Alt-Wiener Volkskomödie* (Vienna: Schroll, 1952), but he does not mention *Die Nymphe der Silberquelle*.

16   See William Steedman, 'Die Aufnahme der englischen Literatur im 18. Jahrhundert in Österreich' (diss.. Vienna, 1938).

17   See Roy Porter, 'The Enlightenment in England', in *The Enlightenment in National Context*, ed. by Roy Porter and Mikuláš Teich (Cambridge: Cambridge University Press, 1981), pp. 1–18; for Germany, Michael Maurer, *Aufklärung und Anglophilie in Deutschland* (Göttingen: Vandenhoeck & Ruprecht, 1987); Johann Pezzl, *Faustin oder das philosophische Jahrhundert* (Zürich, 1783), p. 292: 'Es sind dort [in England] die ehrwürdigen Grabstätten des Kerns der neuern Philosophie, sagte er; die Grabstätte eines Bacon, Newton, Steele, Addison, Loke [*sic*], Swift, Bolingbroke, und unsers unvergleichlichen Pope.'

Rural Economy (1788) and James Robertson's *View of the Agriculture in the County of Perth*. His favourite periodical was evidently the *Staatsanzeigen* (1783–93) edited by the Göttingen historian A. L. Schlözer; this enjoyed such favour among the enlightened that Blumauer, in his anticlerical travesty of the *Aeneid*, has it read by the sanctified philosophers inhabiting his enlightened heaven.[18] Schlözer's studies of Russia are themselves important early contributions to ethnography or 'Völkerkunde', a word which Schlözer apparently coined.[19] Rohrer also kept up with travel writing, including not only well-known accounts of Pacific voyages by Cook and Forster but even such an obscure work as Martin Martin's *A Late Voyage to St Kilda* (1698; often reprinted), which Rohrer quotes in order to compare the St Kildans to the isolated, eaglehunting inhabitants of Plangross in the Tyrol.

Rohrer also enjoyed the other arts. He proclaims his love of music, especially that of Haydn and Mozart, and tells us: 'It is my own playing of several stringed instruments that has enabled me to forget many unmerited slights' (D II, 12). He took a guitar on his journey to Moldavia and back, and at an inn near Vienna was glad to be able to dispel his low spirits by playing a piano. His love of music is evident also from the account he gives of the musical gifts of the Czechs (S II, 24). In *Statistik des österreichischen Kaiserthums* he enthusiastically praises the architecture of Palladio and others, and lists the buildings to be seen in and near Vicenza, including the Villa Rotonda and the tomb of Canova. *Uiber die Tiroler* includes a long list of painters born in the Tyrol, notably the famous Angelika Kauffmann, who is mentioned with great pride (T 69). His taste in landscape runs to romantic mountain scenery and the picturesque disorder of English gardens. 'Romantisch' and 'mahlerisch' [picturesque] are terms of praise. Rohrer has even read theorists of the picturesque, for he recommends Addison and Home (D II, 45).[20]

In discussing Rohrer's writings, I shall say little about the *Abriß der westlichen Provinzen des österreichischen Staates* and the *Statistik des österreichischen Kaiserthums*, since these are drily factual books which can interest only the economic historian. His travel narrative also consists largely of information about geography and agriculture, interspersed with brief references to the hospitality he receives and the

18   ...Hier schmauchen Solon, Wilhelm Penn,
       Confuz und Zoroaster,
       Und Montesquieu beim himmlischen
       Bierkrug ihr Pfeifchen Knaster,
       Und lesen dann, wenn ihnen sehr
       Die Zeit lang wird, den Erlanger,
       Und Schlözers Staatsanzeigen.

Virgil's Aeneis, travestirt, in *Aloys Blumauer's gesammelte Werke* (Stuttgart: J. Scheible's Buchhandlung, 1839), part I, p. 161.

19 See Justin Stagl, 'Der wohl unterwiesene Passagier: Reisekunst und Gesellschaftsbeschreibung vom 16. bis zum 18. Jahrhundert', in *Reisen und Reisebeschreibungen im 18. und 19. Jahrhundert als Quellen der Kulturbeziehungsforschung*, ed. by B. I. Krasnobaev, Gert Robel and Herbert Zeman (Berlin: U. Camen, 1980), pp. 353–84 (p. 375).

20 'Home' is Henry Home, Lord Kames (1696–1782), author of *Elements of Criticism* (1762). Rohrer also mentions 'Whentley', presumably a mistake for Thomas Whateley, author of *Observations on Modern Gardening* (1770).

discomforts of his journey. I shall concentrate on the ethnographic works, which most deserve attention for their informational and literary value.

Since Rohrer's was the first attempt in Austria to compose ethnography, in his preface to his study of the German-speaking subjects of the Habsburgs he is at pains to define his undertaking. It was not a history, he insists, but a descriptive account (not 'Völkergeschichte' but 'Völkerbeschreibung'; D 1, 13). He usually describes his work as 'Völkerkunde'. Its purpose, he explains, is to inform patriots about the resources and present state of their country and indicate how people's material and moral condition may be improved. Elsewhere, he defends his discursive and personal style by explaining that he is not writing simply for scholars, but has in mind a wide readership, in whom he wants to inculcate an appreciation of beauty and sublimity and an interest in the size and resources of their fatherland.[21] Each of his three ethnographic books is divided into eight sections. The first four describe in turn the physical character, the diet, the dress, and the occupations of the people in question; the next four deal with cultural and moral matters, namely their aesthetic sense ('Kunstsinn'), their mentality ('Denkart'), their religion, and their moral character. He tells us that, having found very few written sources of any value, his knowledge is drawn mainly from observation.

Despite his reliance on first-hand experience, Rohrer still needed literary models to organize his material. Very few books were of direct use. His closest model appears to be the survey of non-Slavic peoples of the Russian Empire by Johann Gottlieb Georgi.[22] Georgi's book systematically and informatively examines the material and cultural life of numerous peoples, but is much more concise and impersonal than Rohrer's. Rohrer explains that his task is harder, since the peoples surveyed by Georgi were all at a primitive level, whereas those in Austria are at many different points along the scale running from 'savagery' via 'civilization' to 'sophistication' (D 1, 7).

Rohrer's ethnographic works are a bold and sometimes uneasy hybrid of two forms of writing: the travel narrative and the statistical account. Travel narrative is a familiar genre. It foregrounds personal experience, mediated to us by the voice of the narrator. It narrates direct encounters between the traveller and other people. The statistical account originated from the desire to impose method on travel writing. In the early modern period, travellers were encouraged to make their observations systematic. Manuals called apodemics told them what to look for and what questions to ask.[23] The apodemic developed into the statistical account, which is severely impersonal and factual; although it does not consist solely of figures (as the modern sense of 'statistics' might suggest), it does present information as far as possible in quantitative and tabular form. Where a persona can be discerned, it is that of the dispassionate scientific enquirer or the public-spirited civil servant.

---

21   Rohrer, *Abriß*, pp. iv–v.

22   Johann Gottlieb Georgi, *Beschreibung aller Nationen des Rußischen Reichs, ihrer Lebensart, Religion, Gebräuche, Wohnungen, Kleidungen und übrigen Merkwürdigkeiten* (St Petersburg: no pub., 1776).

23   See Justin Stagl, 'Die Apodemik oder "Reisekunst" als Methodik der Sozialforschung vom Humanismus bis zur Aufklärung', in *Statistik und Staatsbeschreibung in der Neuzeit*, ed. by Mohammed Rassem and Justin Stagl (Paderborn: Schöningh, 1980), pp. 131–87.

Statistical accounts of the Habsburg domains, in which short accounts of various peoples are squeezed between lists of geographical and agricultural data, were already available in Rohrer's day, the best-known being by J. A. Demian.[24] Rohrer's ethnographic project was original in trying to combine factual and personal modes of writing.

On the one hand, Rohrer is writing as a traveller. His experiences in the Tyrol and Galicia, like Forster's in the Pacific, have appealed to his imagination, and he uses his literary talent to record them vividly. Hence his ethnographic works contain numerous anecdotes and personal reflections, especially in the footnotes. These interfere with his other intention, which is to provide a methodical survey of the human resources of the Habsburg domains. While Georgi's book is his main ethnographical model, his principal model of statistical writing, if a single one can be isolated, is the *Statistical Account of Scotland* edited by Sir John Sinclair.[25] This massive project surveys the material and cultural state of every parish, the entries being written in each case by the parish minister. Rohrer refers admiringly to this work, but adds mournfully: 'Where, save in Scotland and Bohemia, is the clergy so far advanced in the love of sciences as to include not only theological but also profane knowledge (as it is called) among its intellectual interests?' (D ii, 107). Another model which is frequently apparent is the moral essays of the popular philosophers which were widely read in eighteenth-century Germany and helped considerably to diffuse enlightened ideas. Rohrer had evidently read many of these, and refers admiringly to the best known of the popular philosophers, Christian Garve, whose knowledge of human nature he praises (D i, 224; G 191). That he is writing in part as a moralist is signalled by the epigraph to his *Versuch über die deutschen Bewohner der österreichischen Monarchie*, which comes from Book i of Pope's *Essay on Man*:

> Eye Nature's walks, shoot Folly as it flies,
> And catch the Manners living as they rise;
> Laugh where we must, be candid where we can —

Rohrer's literary talents are best displayed in some lyrical descriptive passages, especially the descriptions of female beauty which figure prominently in his sections on the physical character of the various peoples, and his account of the festivities held on the first Sunday in August on the Brigittenau near Vienna. These passages bring us to the centre of his imaginative world. His ideal landscape, his *locus amoenus*, is a meadow surrounded by water. The Brigittenau is a 'romantic island', a 'meadow embraced by the double arm of the Danube' (D ii, 159), while the Linz area, whose girls Rohrer particularly admires, is 'this romantic landscape embraced by two rivers' (D i, 51). In this setting, culture and nature are reconciled. The Viennese enjoy themselves in a manner which is 'relaxed, natural and cordial' (D ii, 159), while deer graze unafraid in their presence. The repeated word 'embraced'

24 Johann Andreas Demian, *Darstellung der österreichischen Monarchie nach den neuesten statistischen Beziehungen*, 4 vols (Vienna: no pub., 1804–07).

25 *The Statistical Account of Scotland, drawn up from the communications of the ministers of the different Parishes*, ed. by Sir John Sinclair, 21 vols (Edinburgh: Creech, 1791–99).

('umschlungen'), with its sexual connotation, gently eroticizes the landscape. The union of nature and culture is embodied in female beauty: the Bregenzerwald girl is 'this untroubled daughter of Nature' (D I, 64). Natural beauty surpasses art: Linz girls have 'cheeks whose rosy colour shifts with their changing emotions through all possible shades, now into darker, now into lighter tones, so charmingly that no painter can imitate it' (D I, 52), while the Bregenzerwald girl has 'features which only Angelika Kauffmann, who was born here, contrived to express in her painting of Elisa as a nun' (D I, 64). Literature, however, can convey these suggestions: the description of Linz girls ends by alluding to Rousseau's *La nouvelle Héloïse* (D I, 52), and the charms of Viennese girls invite the reflection: 'but O Montaigne! it is the cats who play with us, not we with them' (G 173).[26] Here the literary reference reintroduces animal imagery as the expression of nature at one with culture. In such passages we see Rohrer's share in the late eighteenth-century sensibility which gave a heartfelt response to natural beauty: the sensibility of Rousseau and the young Goethe.

The literary persona Rohrer usually adopts is that of an unprejudiced friend of humanity ('unbefangener Menschenfreund'; D I, 100), who combines reason and feeling in the service of his country. Although a Catholic, he considers the essence of Christianity to lie in toleration and right action ('Rechthandeln'; D II, 119). He shares, in other words, the Enlightenment ideal of undogmatic, practical religion most famously expressed in Lessing's *Nathan der Weise* (1779).

Rohrer makes no secret of his Josephinism. His writings are filled with references to 'the unforgettable Joseph' (e.g. D I, 38), 'this creative monarch, at whose urn, sunk in profound reverence, I silently mourn' (S I, 52). Maria Theresia is also mentioned with respect, as is Joseph's successor Leopold II and even the enlightened Portuguese minister Pombal, but references to Franz I, who ruled Austria from 1792 to 1835 (seven years after Rohrer's death), are few and lukewarm.

It was perhaps foolhardy, however, to stress one's Josephinism in the aftermath of the Jacobin trials, as Rohrer does in *Neuestes Gemählde von Wien*. In 1794 Jacobin conspiracies were uncovered in Vienna, Graz, and Budapest. Eight of the principal accused were executed the following year, while numerous others received long prison sentences. Accordingly, Rohrer declares his Josephinism in a manner which, while unmistakable, is also inoffensive. Early in the book he describes the inscription which has been placed, with (as he emphasizes) official permission, on the house of a wealthy Greek in the Fleischmarkt. Beneath a likeness of Joseph II the following verse is inscribed in golden letters:

> Vergänglich ist dies Haus
> Doch Josephs Nachruhm nie
> Er gab uns Toleranz
> Unsterblichkeit gibt sie. (G 12)

[This house will pass away, but Joseph's fame never will: he gave us toleration, and that gives immortality.]

---

26 'Quand je me joue à ma chatte, qui sait si elle passe son temps de moi plus que je ne fais d'elle?' Michel de Montaigne, *Apologie de Raymond Sébond*, in *Œuvres complètes*, ed. by Robert Barral (Paris: Gallimard, 1967), p. 188.

Later in *Neuestes Gemählde von Wien* Rohrer forthrightly blames the censorship for the poor state of contemporary literature. He shows some discomfort over the reintroduction of capital punishment, half-heartedly justifying it by reference to the troubled times and 'the turbulent will of the people' which has clamoured for it (G 137). He notes a general change in the Viennese character in the 1790s: they have become unsociable and suspicious of foreigners. This he attributes to 'the events in France and the intensified vigilance of the government which these have rendered necessary' (G 171): again, his defence is so lame as to imply a criticism. At the end of the book Rohrer firmly asserts his own patriotism and comments cautiously on the political disposition of the Viennese. All want peace and order, but want to achieve these by different means: 'some pay traditional reverence to the legal and monarchical constitution, others want to establish and strengthen it by better understanding' (G 203–04). This is a plea for an intelligent patriotism.

In all his works, Rohrer's patriotism is that of a state official concerned for the public weal. He holds the economic assumptions of cameralism: that it is important for a state to be wealthy, that wealth depends on the happiness and prosperity of its subjects, and that the state should therefore regulate its subjects' lives in considerable detail.[27] He also takes for granted the mercantilist principle that a state should as far as possible be economically self-sufficient. His writing follows the tradition founded by the Habsburg bureaucrat Philipp Wilhelm von Hörnigk, author of *Österreich über alles, wenn es nur will* [Austria above all others, if only it wants to be] (1684). A more immediate model, praised as an 'ardent patriot' (G 112), is the reformer Sonnenfels, who in 1763 was appointed by Maria Theresia to the newly founded chair of government ('Polizeiwissenschaft') at Vienna. Besides a standard textbook on the principles of administration, which Rohrer would undoubtedly have read, Sonnenfels wrote an influential moral weekly, *Der Mann ohne Vorurteil* [The Man Without Prejudice] (1765–67). The two enterprises were linked by the conviction, which Rohrer also held, that private morality is essential to public welfare.[28]

In both public and private life, Rohrer is concerned to describe and promote the progress of enlightenment. For him, as usually in eighteenth-century German usage, enlightenment is not the name of a period but denotes a process of intellectual, moral and cultural advance. Like his mentor Kant, Rohrer emphasizes the spread of intellectual autonomy, the development of the ability to think for oneself.[29] 'Selbstdenken' [intellectual autonomy] is one of Rohrer's favourite words. His enlightenment is also, by implication, politically radical. This appears from the definition of 'true enlightenment' that Rohrer quotes from an anonymous work, the *Geschichte der Vervollkommnung des menschlichen Geschlechts* [History of the Perfecting

27   See Scott, 'The Problem of Enlightened Absolutism', p. 18; Tribe, *Governing Economy*.

28   See James J. Sheehan, *German History, 1770–1866* (Oxford: Clarendon Press, 1989), p. 196, where Sonnenfels's periodical is wrongly called *Der Mann ohne Vorteil*; Tribe, *Governing Economy*, pp. 78–90.

29   See Immanuel Kant, 'Beantwortung der Frage: Was ist Aufklärung?' (1783) in *Werke*, ed. by Wilhelm Weischedel, 6 vols (Darmstadt: Wissenschaftliche Buchgesellschaft, 1958), VI, 53–61; H. B. Nisbet, '"Was ist Aufklärung?": The Concept of Enlightenment in Eighteenth Century Germany', *Journal of European Studies*, 12 (1982), 77–95.

of the Human Race] (1788): 'Where true enlightenment rules, no one demands more than his due; there is a true estimation of property and merit. A person's inner worth decides everything; appearance gives nothing' (S ii, 49–50n).

Rohrer is convinced that the world is governed by Providence, and perceives its workings in the discovery of the potato, which nourishes the poor, and in the propensity even of animals to put sociability above self-preservation. Although writing during the Napoleonic wars, he maintains a Panglossian conviction that we live in 'the best of worlds' (D ii, 97). The cultivated shores of Lake Constance support his belief in history as progress:

> Einst erschienen den gebildeten Römischen Kriegern, als sie zum ersten Mahle in diese Gegenden vordrangen, die streifenden Allemannischen Horden, welche hier ihnen aufstießen, wahrscheinlich in eben jenem Bilde, in welchem wir Deutsche vor nicht langer Zeit die nordamerikanischen Wilden ansahen. (D i, 197)

> [When the civilized Roman warriors first penetrated into these regions, the wandering Alemannic hordes which encountered them probably presented the same image as we Germans, not long ago, beheld in the North American savages.][30]

Disasters still happen, but people's increased readiness to help one another demonstrates the spread of humanity and confutes the 'disparagement of enlightenment' practised by those 'watchers of Zion ('Zions-Wächter') who threaten us with the Last Judgement' (D ii, 169–70). This is a shallow conception of progress: it compares poorly with Herder's remark that the progress of civilization resembles a mountain torrent rather than a gently flowing river, or Kant's conception of the progress of society through the mutual antagonism of its members.[31]

Though unimpressive as an amateur philosopher, Rohrer deserves respect when he deals with the diffusion of enlightenment among ordinary people ('Volks-aufklärung'; D ii, 78). This interest distinguishes him from many proponents of enlightenment who thought that ordinary people could not benefit from it.[32] He gives credit to individuals who work for the enlightenment of the people, like the South Tyrolean Abbate Tartarotti with his campaign against belief in witchcraft,[33] and the Lutheran clergyman Magliarik who introduced cotton-spinning among the Slovaks (S i, 108).

---

30   Cf. the comparison between ancient Germans and present-day primitives in Schiller's 'Was heißt und zu welchem Ende studiert man Universalgeschichte?'.

31   Johann Gottfried Herder, *Werke*, ed. by Günter Arnold and others, 10 vols (Frankfurt a.M.: Deutscher Klassiker Verlag, 1985–2000), vol. vi: *Ideen zur Philosophie der Geschichte der Menschheit*, ed. by Martin Bollacher (1989), p. 655; Kant, 'Idee zu einer allgemeinen Geschichte in weltbürgerlichen Absicht' (1784), in *Werke*, vi, 31–50.

32   Examples from Germany in Sheehan, *German History*, pp. 203–04; from elsewhere in Harvey Chisick, *The Limits of Reform in the Enlightenment: Attitudes towards the Education of the Lower Classes in Eighteenth-Century France* (Princeton, NJ: Princeton University Press, 1981); 'David Hume and the Common People', in *The 'Science of Man' in the Scottish Enlightenment*, ed. by Peter Jones (Edinburgh: Edinburgh University Press, 1989), pp. 5–32.

33   On Girolamo Tartarotti and his book *Del congresso notturno delle lammie* (1749), see Franco Venturi, *Settecento riformatore: Da Muratori a Beccaria* (Turin: Einaudi, 1969), pp. 359–63.

In Rohrer's ethnographic treatises, the chapters on 'Kunstsinn' deal principally with popular culture. A people's aesthetic sense, he says, cannot be judged by their knowledge of great artists, of whom they have seldom heard, but by the construction of their houses, furniture, and domestic utensils. Music and dancing are also discussed: Carniolan dances, for example, are praised as 'no less lively than skilful' (S II, 12). For Rohrer, aesthetic culture also includes activities like the mechanical ingenuity of the Tyroleans. As an example of their ingenuity, Rohrer describes a cradle being rocked by remote control:

> So traff ich zufällig einmahl in einer Alpenhütte des Zillerthales eine sanft und gleichförmig geschaukelte Wiege, ohne in der ganzen Wohnung außer dem schlummernden Kinde und einer heimischen Dohle eine andere Seele zu entdecken. Dies brachte mich auf den Einfall, die Schnur, welche hinaus ins Freye ging, zu verfolgen. In einer Entfernung von etwa 50 Schritten fand ich dann dieselbe mit einer kleinen Verrichtung, welche das Gepräge der simplen Natur trug, an einem Rade festgemacht, welches von einer Felsenquelle herumgetrieben wurde. (T 60–61)

> [Thus I once, in an Alpine cottage in the Zillerthal, came upon a cradle rocking gently and regularly, although there was not another soul to be found in the entire house besides the sleeping baby and a pet jackdaw. This made me think of following the string which led out of doors. At a distance of some fifty paces I then found the string attached by a small device, which bore the mark of simple nature, to a wheel which was turned by a rocky brook.]

(Rohrer's literary skill is shown by the delightful though strictly unnecessary detail of the pet jackdaw, which brings the little episode to life.)

An important aspect of popular enlightenment is the attack on superstition. Rohrer rejects the idea that popular superstitions should be tolerated. He deplores the Tyroleans' fondness for going on pilgrimages to Venice, Einsiedeln in Switzerland, the Wieskirche in Bavaria, and Weingarten in Swabia (T 82). He reports with horror that even within the last half-century an alleged witch was burnt at Würzburg (T 84).[34] Such superstitions have been adequately explained, Rohrer considers, by the popular philosopher Zimmermann in his account of the hallucinations arising from solitude.[35] As for more primitive peoples, the belief in vampires still held by the Morlaks of Dalmatia proves to Rohrer that they are at a rudimentary stage of development (S II, 30).

For Rohrer, enlightenment extends beyond religious belief into personal morality: 'The treatment of the female sex, of servants in general, and of strangers are practically the correct standard by which to judge a nation's degree of moral culture' (S II, 96). This idea underlies Rohrer's sharp criticism of the Polish nobility, who display a veneer of French culture but no genuine enlightenment. Although they are servile when paying formal calls on officials, they treat the same officials

---

34   This occurred in 1749. It is mentioned in Pezzl, *Faustin*, p. 45; for details, see the reprint edited by Wolfgang Griep (Hildesheim: Olms, 1982), p. 28.

35   Johann Georg Zimmermann, *Über die Einsamkeit*, 4 vols (Leipzig: no pub., 1784–85). This immensely popular work was also translated into French and English. Rohrer cites it at D II, 96. Much of it is a scurrilous attack on monasticism, which would appeal to an adherent of Joseph II.

rudely when they pass them in the street (S II, 130): Rohrer no doubt speaks from personal experience. He castigates their habits of idleness and luxury, and their brutality towards their servants.

More generally, enlightenment means, as it did for the French Encyclopaedists and for the classical Goethe, the diffusion of useful knowledge.[36] Rohrer takes a keen interest in industrial and agricultural methods, deploring the backward state of Styrian mining (D II, 70) and the primitive agricultural implements used in Dalmatia (S I, 91). He offers many suggestions about how the Galicians could exploit their land by planting grass on the sandy banks of the Vistula, extracting oil from sunflowers, and growing hops and cherries (S I, 131–38). He proposes a vast system of canals, connecting the Elbe with the Vltava and the March (east of Vienna) with the Oder, and extending into Lower Austria and Hungary (D I, 239). He complains that human excrement pollutes streams and rivers, when it might be used to manure fields, as is done by the peasants around Linz (D I, 147). A sign that Galicians are 'unenlightened' ('unaufgeklärt') is that they do not know what precautions to take against cattle disease (S II, 43–44). Humans, too, require medical precautions: Rohrer repeatedly advocates inoculation for smallpox and cowpox. Rohrer's advocacy of popular enlightenment of course has political implications. It is incompatible with serfdom: people can hardly think for themselves if they cannot work for themselves. In describing the Galician peasants Rohrer points out how the compulsion to labour for their feudal lord makes the peasants careless, lazy, and prone to do wanton damage (S I, 125–27). He praises Joseph II for granting peasants civil rights and reducing their compulsory labour. And he makes much of the happiness of the Tyroleans, clearly his favourites, who had managed to retain their ancient freedom when the rest of central Europe was reduced to a second serfdom:

> Patriarch auf seinem sonnigen Hügel oder im Thalschrunde führt der tirolische Bauer eine abgesonderte Wirtschaft, und weiß von Hörigkeit nichts. [...] Bey solch einem Grad politischer und bürgerlicher Freyheit, welchen diese Bergbewohner unstreitig größtentheils der Humanität ihrer Oesterreichischen Beherrscher zu verdanken haben, ergiebt sich von selbst der Schluß, daß die Tiroler — wenn anders Glückseligkeit hienieden unter dem Monde gesucht werden kann, ein glückliches Volk in ihrem Felsenrund sind. (T 136, 139)

> [Patriarch on his sunny hill or in the deep valley, the Tyrolean peasant manages an independent household and knows nothing of feudal servitude. [...] With such a degree of political and civil freedom, which these mountaineers unquestionably owe in large part to the humanity of their Austrian rulers, it is natural to conclude that, if indeed happiness can be sought in this sublunary world, the Tyroleans are a happy nation within their rocky circle.]

This makes manifest one of the tensions in Rohrer's commitment to enlightenment. Although he is strongly attached to the Tyroleans, he has to admit that they have

36   See John Lough, The 'Encyclopédie' (London: Longman, 1971); Johann Wolfgang Goethe, Wilhelm Meisters Lehrjahre, v, xvi: 'so hatte er in Zeit von zwanzig Jahren sehr viel im stillen zur Kultur mancher Zweige der Landwirtschaft beigetragen und alles, was dem Felde, Tieren und Menschen ersprießlich ist, in Bewegung gebracht und so die wahrste Aufklärung befördert'.

not been receptive to enlightened influences. Their widespread illiteracy and their inability to speak High German have debarred them from high culture. Many of them display what Rohrer tactfully calls 'ein gewisser mit vieler Behaglichkeit verbundener Ideenstillstand' [a certain comfortable fixity of ideas] (T 77). They do not even know their own history. One curious instance he gives of their backwardness in civilization is that in certain districts children address their parents by the familiar pronoun 'du' (T 104).

Moreover, the Tyroleans were not sympathetic to Joseph II's reforms. As devout Catholics, they objected to the dissolution of contemplative monasteries (twenty-three were dissolved in the German Tyrol alone). They resented the sharp diminution in the powers of their provincial Estates. Having been exempt from compulsory military service, they resented Joseph II's introduction of a uniform conscription throughout his domains. On Joseph II's death, the Tyroleans successfully appealed to Leopold II to restore their former constitution and their exemption from conscription.[37]

Rohrer gives an instance in which Joseph II's reforms threatened to cause serious harm. Since all Tyroleans expect to marry, the priests can ensure that a young man who gets a girl pregnant will marry her once he is able to support her. Here a diminution in priestly authority would have caused great unhappiness, had not the older custom been firmly enough rooted to prevail (T 117). As a proponent of enlightenment, however, Rohrer ought consistently to oppose the irrational force of tradition. It is strange to find him admitting that tradition can be a valuable safeguard against imprudent enlightenment.

When Rohrhe writes about the Tyrol, he is close to another author he admires, Justus Möser (T 58–59), whose *Patriotische Phantasien* (1774–78), dealing with the laws and customs of Osnabrück, defended traditional communities as repositories of national feeling and political wisdom, superior to the abstract uniformity which academic theorists wished to impose. Rohrer's attachment to the Tyrol has much in common with Möser's to Osnabrück. He is, for example, fascinated by Tyrolean customs. In *Uiber die Tiroler* he gives detailed descriptions of the sports practised in the Tyrol, such as wrestling, racing each other up mountains, ball-games, and shooting. Elsewhere he describes tobogganing and yodelling. A long and vivid footnote in *Uiber die Tiroler* deals with transhumance and describes how the inhabitants of Vorarlberg move in processions to the mountain pastures where they spend the summer (T 24–26). In his love of ancient customs, Rohrer aligns himself with the Counter-Enlightenment represented by such writers as Moser and Herder; and he provides support for the argument, recently advanced by Jonathan Knudsen, that the Counter-Enlightenment should not be seen as a distinct movement but as a reaction proceeding dialectically from within the Enlightenment itself.[38]

---

37   See Mitrofanov, *Joseph II*, pp. 363–65 and 588; Helmut Reinalter, *Aufklärung–Absolutismus–Reaktion: Die Geschichte Tirols in der 2. Hälfte des 18. Jahrhunderts* (Vienna: Schendl, 1974), pp. 75 137.

38   See Isaiah Berlin, 'The Counter-Enlightenment', in his *Against the Current: Essays in the History of Ideas* (Oxford: Clarendon Press, 1989), pp. 1–24; Jonathan B. Knudsen, *Justus Möser and the German Enlightenment* (Cambridge: Cambridge University Press, 1986), esp. p. 148.

Elsewhere, too, Rohrer has to acknowledge that the methods of enlightenment may do harm, and that its aims may conflict with one another. The decline of superstition does not necessarily promote the advance of morality. 'The level of intellectual autonomy ('Selbstdenken') on which the Italian Tyroleans are at present is not the most favourable for morality' (T 90): the decline of traditional belief has encouraged frivolous impiety and weakened the sanctions against perjury, theft, and gambling. Similar objections were raised by opponents of Joseph II's Edict of Toleration, who accepted that freedom of thought was suitable for the nobility and urban middle classes, but thought it could only harm 'rude and uncivilized peasants in the country' by filling their minds with doctrines they could not understand.[39] Dealing with more primitive people, Rohrer admits to having been much moved by a Serbian funeral ceremony, and describes the keeners ('Klagefrauen') still found among the Morlaks and in Istria and Friuli. This is one superstition which Rohrer respects, even at the price of inconsistency. 'Let the wit deride the superstition of simple nations. The psychological inquirer ('Seelenforscher') thinks and feels more than he laughs and sneers; and therefore sees nothing more in the conduct of the Slavs than still unspoiled human nature, seeking to give relief to its oppressed heart' (S II, 74).

A similar tension is apparent when Rohrer writes as a moralist. He reveals a conservatism which makes him defend the old and criticize anything newfangled. Dignified old men among the Saxon colonists in Transylvania put him in mind of the semi-mythical past, populated by 'honourable German knights' (D I, 73) — the era evoked by Goethe in *Götz von Berlichingen* (1773). Rohrer also praises the traditional character of the 'Austrian of the old stamp' (D II, 159), and compares traditional hospitality in Upper Austria to that of the ancient Germans recorded by Tacitus, deeming it much superior to the ascetic primitivism of Rousseau.

Rohrer the moralist tends to locate virtue in the country and vice in Vienna. Vienna is the home of luxury, affectation, and worse. Rohrer gives a detailed account of how young women drift into prostitution (G 186–91) which throws valuable light on the social type celebrated in literature as the 'Mädel aus der Vorstadt' or the 'süßes Mädel'. More typically, however, he denounces Viennese gormandizing ('Schwelgerey'; G 163), especially their habit of eating a three-course breakfast. The greatest bestseller in the city's history is a cookery book which went through twenty-two impressions in twenty-five years. Yet Viennese girls, he says, starve themselves in order to be fashionably slender:

> Sie tanzen so federleicht selbst in Orten, deren Inneres Ehrfurcht gebietet, von einem Stuhle zum andern, als kaum eine Wassersumpfspinne von einer Pflanze zur andern flatter. (D I, 49–50)

> [They dance from one chair to another with even more feathery lightness, even in places whose interior commands reverence, than a waterspider fluttering from one plant to another.]

The Viennese spend too much time indoors, and suffer from pallor, short-sightedness, rheumatism, and haemorrhoids. Young women spend their time reading horror stories and romances set in the Middle Ages (a familiar complaint at the

39   Mitrofanov, *Joseph II*, p. 770.

end of the eighteenth century). They injure their health by dancing, especially by waltzing, which Rohrer claims causes coughs, stitches, haemorrhages and consumption. Rohrer dismisses ballet as 'erotic hopping about' and recounts at second hand an anecdote about Lessing praising Joseph II for abolishing ballet in Vienna (D II, 18n). And yet elsewhere he warmly defends dance-halls as a recreation for artisans (D II, 43n).

To counter luxury, Rohrer offers the Viennese a drastic austerity programme. They are to take swimming lessons and mountain walks. Girls should learn to spin flax instead of playing the piano. Education should also change: instead of Latin rhetoric, schoolboys should study agriculture and domestic economy; instead of mythology, schoolboys should study the science of fruit-growing ('anstatt der Mythologie die Pomologie'; D II, 54).

Rohrer's criticisms and recommendations result in part from his mercantilism. He disapproves of the Viennese because they consume without producing, and because their luxurious tastes have to be satisfied by costly imports. Hence he recommends that, to save importing sugar, a native species of grass should be found which can serve to flavour food (D I, 85). His attacks on luxury, along with his emphasis on useful skills, are close to the doctrines professed a few years earlier by the Austrian Jacobins. The alleged ringleader of the 'Jacobin Conspiracy', Andreas Riedel, who in 1795 was sentenced to sixty years' imprisonment, went further in desiring the abolition of the nobility; and he sounds like Rohrer when he declares that the true noble is someone 'who goes forth into the wild plains of the Banat [...] and of Podolia to teach its primitive inhabitants the blessings of civilisation [...] and how to till the soil'.[40]

Another theme in Rohrer's criticism of luxury is his stress on disciplining the body. His attacks on excessive eating and unconstrained dancing are linked: in both, the body is being released from control. Instead, Rohrer recommends English dances, because they have 'more method' (D II, 16). He contrasts the constant changes of fashion in Vienna with the uniformity of country clothing. Uniformity symbolizes control and discipline, the repression of individuality. Rohrer's ideal is represented by a Tyrolean mining colony where there is no over-indulgence in food and drink, no quarrelling or fighting: 'One day passes like the next in the sweat of one's brow. Here or nowhere is found a confirmation of the doctrine that only work and moderation can preserve mankind's original goodness' (D I, 96). It sounds as though Rohrer is, inconsistently, advocating a Rousseauian asceticism. But the truth is rather that this inconsistency results from the high value he sets on hard work and therefore on discipline, which he sees as an instrument of civilization. Discipline can be exercised as part of communal living: he notes that Slavonians used to live in isolated houses, but were ordered to live in villages, 'where one neighbour, as it were, naturally observes the other, and the Slavonian is gradually elevated from his rude state by greater vigilance' (S II, 4). All this strongly recalls Foucault's account of the exercise of discipline through surveillance and the production of 'docile bodies'.[41]

40 Quoted in Wangermann, *From Joseph II to the Jacobin Trials*, p. 13.
41 Michel Foucault, *Discipline and Punish*, trans. by Alan Sheridan (London: Penguin, 1977).

Rohrer often points to Britain as a country whose prosperity is founded on hard work and on the full exploitation of natural resources. He admires the agricultural improvements in Britain, and wishes that Austrian noblemen would import some shepherds from Lincolnshire or Leicestershire, along with their flocks, instead of 'Jokeys' (D 1, 111), or that some English farmers would settle in Austria, as some Scottish farmers have settled near Copenhagen. He praises the enterprise of the colonists from southern and western Germany who settled in Transylvania, and commends the mechanical skills practised in the Tyrol, the Black Forest, and by German emigrants to Galicia. Such skills, he notes, deserve every encouragement, for machinery has proved the basis of Britain's wealth. Once again, the Tyrolese are his model: he describes how their cottage industries (spinning and lacemaking) were encouraged by Joseph II; and he devotes much attention to the Tyroleans' skill as mechanics, and to the enterprising spirit which takes them all over Europe to sell their wares. The Slovaks are similarly praised for being industrious, spinning cotton and travelling around the Empire as pedlars.

Rohrer not only commends hard work but wants it to be maximized. He advises that after working in the fields, farmers and their families should occupy the evening by spinning or knitting, giving the example of the Hessian peasant who 'would feel intolerable tedium on coming home from his ploughing, if he could not occupy himself in knitting' (D 1, 169). Instead of idly minding cattle, children should be set to work — thus Rohrer carries out a pre-emptive strike against the later Romantic pastorals of Eichendorff and Heine. One reason he gives for deploring Tyroleans' habit of going on pilgrimages is the loss of working time; he calculates how much they might have earned by spinning cotton during the eighteen days devoted annually to 'pious idleness' (T 82n.). He describes with pleasure how the Schottenfeld, formerly an empty space used for cavalry exercises, is now a 'dainty little factory town':

> Es zählt nicht weniger als 394 Häuser, wovon jedes mit einem Garten versehen ist. Diese Häuser sind fast alle lediglich von Seidenzeug Band Düntuch und Flormachern bewohnt, und haben grosse geräumige Säle, in welchen viele hundert Kehlen der an ihren Stühlen arbeitenden Mädchen deutsche Opernlieder singen, und sich hierdurch zur Arbeit wechselweise ermuntern. Wenn man bey heiteren Sommertagen des Morgens um 6 Uhr auf diesen Strassen wandelt, so wird man umgeben von dem Schalle dieser singenden Chöre, und seines Lebens doppelt froh. (G 8)

> [It numbers no less than 394 houses, each of which is provided with a garden. These houses are almost all occupied solely by makers of silk, ribbons, gauze and crape, and have large, spacious rooms in which a hundred throats of the girls working at their chairs sing songs from German operas, and thus stimulate one another to work. When one passes along these streets at six o'clock on bright summer mornings, one is surrounded by the sound of these choirs, and feels twice as glad to be alive.]

This piece of urban georgic[42] makes one wonder how the girls felt about being hard

42 On the late eighteenth-century shift from pastoral (portrayal of rural leisure) to georgic (portrayal of rural industry), see John Barrell, *The Dark Side of the Landscape* (Cambridge: Cambridge

at work at six o'clock on a summer morning. Rohrer is so convinced of the virtue of industry, however, that he does not raise such questions.

His high valuation of hard work colours Rohrer's attitude to the Jews, who are the subject of one of his ethnographic treatises. Throughout his writings there are casual and gratuitous anti-Jewish remarks. The commerce of Jewish innkeepers in Galicia is dismissed as 'the busy idleness of the dirty Jews' (S 1, 141). In *Statistik des österreichischen Kaiserthums* Rohrer recommends to his readers a Viennese coffee-house which is not frequented by Jewish 'Stockjobler' [i.e. stockjobbers].[43] The Armenians, a number of whom lived in Galicia, also annoy him by their alleged 'selfish profit-seeking' (D II, 149). He seems not to have liked the large Jewish presence in Lemberg, which contained some 15,000 Jews in a total population of 40,000.[44] After describing the Jews' costume, he says:

> Denkt man sich nun noch zu dieser düstern und schwerfälligen Kleidungsart ein verstörtes Gesicht hinzu, in welcher Furcht, Neid und Schadenfreude ihre Züge eingruben; so kann man sich beyläufig einen Begriff machen, wie dem empfindsamen Deutschen durch die ersten Jahre seines Aufenthaltes in einem Lande zu Muthe seyn muß, in welchem ein solches, sich selbst verunstaltendes Volk mitten zwischen lachenden, grünen Fluren die Meisterrolle spielt! (J 52)

> [If, in addition to this gloomy and heavy garb, one imagines a distraught face in which fear, envy and malice have etched their signs, then one can form some notion of how the sensitive German must feel during the first years of his residence in a country where such a self disfiguring people plays the leading role amid smiling green meadows!]

Although Rohrer's study of the Jews later provided material for at least one anti-Semitic pamphleteer,[45] it is not itself an anti-Semitic tirade. For the most part, it is an unusually cool and descriptive work with much detail about the Galician Jews' physical appearance, their dress, their characteristic ailments, and their occupations. He corrects the stereotyped notion that Jews are all innkeepers or procurers (the impression given by Kratter's *Briefe über den itzigen Zustand von Galizien*, for instance) by noting that many are tailors, moneylenders, or dealers in small goods, while in the Bukovina (though nowhere else) a number practise agriculture (J 59). Some animus is apparent in his condemnation of the Talmud as 'enthusiastic nonsense' (J 123) and of 'Kassidim', i.e. Hasidim, as 'proud fanatics' (J 150). He knew little about either, and relies for his information largely on the autobiography of the Polish Jew Salomon Maimon.[46] He thinks highly of the Karaites, who reject the Talmud, and in his travel book he records a long conversation with a Karaite Rabbi. Although disappointed to find that this man retained some superstitions, like avoiding contact with a dying person, Rohrer expresses great esteem for him.

University Press, 1980).

43   Rohrer, *Statistik*, p. 279n.

44   *Hacquets neueste physikalisch politische Reisen*, III, 176.

45   Friedrich Rühs, *Über die Ansprüche der Juden an das deutsche Bürgerrecht*, 2nd edn (Berlin: In der Realschulbuchhandlung, 1816).

46   *Salomon Maimons Lebensgeschichte von ihm selbst geschrieben* (Berlin, 1792–93); Salomon Maimon, *An Autobiography*, trans. by J. Clark Murray (Paisley and London: no pub., 1888).

Rohrer's distance from anti–Semitism becomes clear if one compares his account of the Jews with that given by the naturalist Belsazar Hacquet. Hacquet, generally bilious when he turns from botany and geology to human affairs, descends to senseless rantings against the Jews as 'filthy', 'stinking', 'parasites', 'scum of the human race', oppressors of Christians and adherents of 'Talmud-mishmash'.[47] Rohrer's criticism of the Jews is based not on insensate hatred but on the rational and cameralistic argument that they are not useful to the state. They are for the most part employed unproductively; their health is too poor for them to provide useful soldiers; and their religion separates them from the rest of society and disqualifies them from their civic duties. Since the Talmud is said to contain a 'casuistry which flies in the face of all the requirements of sound reason' (J 123), Rohrer evidently regards it as a form of clerical obscurantism.

Rohrer declares his admiration for Moses Mendelssohn and associates himself with the Berlin philosemite Christian Wilhelm von Dohm, author of *Über die bürgerliche Verbesserung der Juden* [On the Civil Improvement of the Jews] (1781).[48] Dohm argued that the Jews' character had been degraded by isolation, and that it would be improved by their admission to civil society. Rohrer differs from Dohm in thinking it more difficult to reform the Jews' character. He points out that in Galicia not all are innkeepers or businessmen: many are manual workers, and yet their character shows no signs of improvement. His own proposals for the reform of the Jews are at least better than Hacquet's, who thinks they should be extirpated by being forbidden to marry till after the age of childbearing; but perhaps not much better. Jews prepared to take up productive work should be placed in forced labour institutions ('Zwangs-Arbeitsanstalten'; J 100) modelled on English workhouses or the Philadelphia penitentiary. 'Immoral' Jews should be sent abroad to settlements resembling those at Sydney Cove and Norfolk Island, which Rohrer greatly admires; he proposes that Austria should enter into an agreement with a colonial power like Britain or Holland to establish penal settlements overseas. Alternatively, they should be confined in prisons using the Philadelphia system of solitary confinement; if they have to work with other prisoners, these should be forbidden to speak to them.

These proposals reveal the inhumanity of which enlightened reformers were capable. The Australian penal settlements were in fact a fair anticipation of the Soviet gulag.[49] The Philadelphia penitentiary was denounced by Dickens and used by Schopenhauer to illustrate the tortures induced by boredom; and an extract from its regulations forms part of the arresting introduction to Foucault's *Discipline and Punish*.[50] In Rohrer we see a friend of humanity proposing, in all good faith, to

47 *Hacquets neueste physikalisch-politische Reisen*, III, 204–34.
48 Christian Wilhelm von Dohm, *Über die bürgerliche Verbesserung der Juden* (Berlin and Stettin: Nicolai, 1781). See Jacob Katz, *Out of the Ghetto: The Social Background of Jewish Emancipation, 1770–1870* (Cambridge, MA: Harvard University Press, 1973).
49 See Robert Hughes, *The Fatal Shore* (London: Collins Harvill, 1987).
50 Charles Dickens, *American Notes* (London: Oxford University Press, 1957), esp. p. 99: 'I hold this slow and daily tampering with the mysteries of the brain, to be immeasurably worse than any torture of the body'; Arthur Schopenhauer, *Die Welt als Wille und Vorstellung*, ed. by Julius Frauenstädt, 2 vols (Leipzig: Brockmann, 1923), I, 369–70; Foucault, *Discipline and Punish*, pp. 6–7; Michael Ignatieff, *A Just Measure of Pain: The Penitentiary in the Industrial Revolution, 1750–1850* (New

transform people into happy and useful citizens by placing them in concentration camps and forcedlabour battalions.

We have now reached the far end of Rohrer's imaginative world. If his world has at its centre the paradisal union of culture and nature, at its outer rim there is an archipelago of penal settlements where recalcitrant nature is being civilized through discipline. His emphasis on discipline derives largely from the cameralist assumption of responsibility for regulating people's lives in order to increase their happiness. The dangers attending that assumption are apparent in Rohrer's limited tolerance for other people, his assumption that they do not necessarily know what is good for them, and that if necessary they must be forced to be happy. This assumption was consistent with the principles of cameralism and was common in enlightened absolutism. As an anonymous writer puts it in the *Journal Général de L'Europe* in 1785: 'It is not surprising that reforms meet with contradiction and give rise to complaints. But an enlightened and firm government places itself above complaints and continues to do good to people despite themselves.'[51]

York: Pantheon Books, 1978). For further examples of well-meant alternatives to capital punishment, including life imprisonment, forced labour, and vivisection, see Venturi, *Utopia and Reform*, p. 113; John McManners, *Death and the Enlightenment* (Oxford: Clarendon Press, 1981), pp. 399–401.

51 'Il n'est pas étonnant que les reformes éprouvent des contradictions et causent des murmures. Mais un gouvernement éclairé et ferme se met au dessus des murmures et continue de faire le bien au peuple malgré lui.' Quoted in Mitrofanov, *Joseph II*, p. 292, n. 2.

CHAPTER 13

Poetry and Scepticism in the Wake of the Austrian Enlightenment: Blumauer, Grillparzer, Lenau

I

The Austrian Enlightenment did not intend to promote religious scepticism. Its ill-fated leader, Joseph II, convincingly professed himself as loyal to the Church as was his mother Maria Theresia.[1] The measures which brought him into conflict with the Church, and induced Pope Pius VI to take the unprecedented step of visiting Vienna in person to remonstrate with him, were economic and political rather than doctrinal. They included the dissolution of the contemplative monastic orders, the attempt to subject ecclesiastical appointments to state control, and, most famously, the series of Edicts of Toleration which removed the restrictions on religious worship, occupations and education that had previously affected Lutherans, Calvinists, Greek Orthodox and Jews. But toleration did not mean pluralism. Joseph had no intention of weakening the dominance of the Catholic Church in his Empire. He did, however, seek to weaken the Baroque piety that found expression in elaborate ceremonies, Mariolatry, Corpus Christi processions, pilgrimages and barnstorming sermons, and to promote instead the simple, orderly and rational devotion advocated especially by the Jansenists.

Most of the intellectuals who supported Josephinism were broadly sympathetic to this Reform Catholicism. The Professor of Jurisprudence at Vienna, Johann Valentin Eybel, whose pamphlet *Was ist der Pabst?* [*What is the Pope?*] aroused great attention in the year of the Pope's visit, describes himself as 'der vernünftige und wohl unterwiesene Christ' [the rational and well-instructed Christian], equally distant from the enthusiast or 'Schwärmer', superstitiously awestruck by the Pope, and from the freethinker or 'Freygeist' who subjects the Pope's mitre and saints' legends to shallow mockery.[2] The Josephinist poets associated with the

---

1 See *Maria Theresia und Joseph II: Ihre Correspondenz*, ed. by A. von Arneth (Vienna: Gerold, 1867), pp. 151–52, and the discussion in Derek Beales, *Joseph II*, vol. 1: *In the Shadow of Maria Theresa, 1741–1780* (Cambridge: Cambridge University Press, 1987), p. 469. For Beales's more recent thoughts on this subject, see his *Prosperity and Plunder: European Catholic Monasteries in the Age of Revolution, 1650–1815* (Cambridge: Cambridge University Press, 2003), chapter 8.

2 Anon. [Johann Valentin Eybel], *Was ist der Pabst?* (Vienna: Kurzbeck, 1782), p. 6.

Wienerischer Musenalmanach similarly espoused a middle-of-the-road Christianity. The freethinking denounced by Eybel ('dieses Unkraut schießt auch bey uns auf' [These weeds flourish with us too])[3] is also rebuked by Johann Baptist Alxinger in 'Der Freygeist', a poem recommending virtue and religion as antidotes to scepticism. The poetry of Alxinger and his fellows alternates between quiet cheerfulness ('Heiterkeit') and quiet melancholy, accepting the world in either mood as providentially ordered for the best.[4] It becomes forceful, however, in the polemical anti-clericalism that was an essential part of Josephinism. Alxinger's religion is Josephinist in its praise of toleration and its hostility towards the papacy's pretensions to political and intellectual authority, as well as to monasticism; the latter institution is said to withdraw able-bodied men and women from work and motherhood, encouraging pederasty and reserving unfortunate young women 'fürs Serail von Gottes Sohn' [for the seraglio of God's son].[5] In 'Der Priester Gottes', Alxinger warns that, though priests no longer burn heretics or instigate wars, they still exercise covert influence and denounce the truth from the pulpit — but that is because they know their days are numbered:

> Recht so! denn hat bey einer Nation
> Aufklärung ihre Fakel aufgesteckt,
> Da stürzt sein Götzentempel krachend ein.[6]

[Quite right! for once Enlightenment has lit her torch in any nation, its idolatrous temple will come crashing down.]

There is much more violent polemic, and little serenity, in the work of Aloys Blumauer, a leading Josephinist poet. Educated by Jesuits, and briefly a member of the Society of Jesus before its suspension in 1773, in the early 1780s he became a Mason and was employed as official censor. He was also a journalist, who edited the *Wienerischer Musenalmanach* together with Johann Franz Ratschky from 1781 to 1792, and single-handed in 1793–94; from 1782 to 1784 he also edited the *Wiener Realzeitung*, a major organ of liberalism; and from 1784 to 1787 he edited the *Journal für Freymaurer* issued by the lodge 'Zur wahren Eintracht' [True Harmony], to which he was secretary. Blumauer was long famous for his mock epic, *Virgils Aeneis travestirt*, which appeared in instalments from 1782 to 1788. This ferocious, sometimes scatological satire seeks to support Joseph's stand against the Church by ridiculing Aeneas, the founder of Rome who, in Blumauer's version, is supposed thereby to have founded the papacy. Aeneas not only descends to Hell, finding it full of Jesuits, but also visits Heaven and finds it populated by heroes of Enlightenment from Solon to Montesquieu and William Penn. Such satirical aggression had its counterpart in the depression with which Blumauer was often

---

3 Ibid. p. 5.

4 See Herbert Zeman, 'Die österreichische Lyrik des ausgehenden 18. und des frühen 19. Jahrhunderts: Eine stil- und gattungsgeschichtliche Charakteristik', in *Die österreichische Literatur: Ihr Profil im 19. Jahrhundert (1830–1880)*, ed. by Herbert Zeman (Graz: Akademische Druck- und Verlagsanstalt, 1982), pp. 513–47.

5 'Der Cölibat', in *J. B. Alxingers sämmtliche poetische Schriften* (Leipzig: no pub., 1784), 'Anhang', p. 15.

6 *Alxingers sämmtliche poetische Schriften*, p. 28.

afflicted. In one of his verse epistles to Johann Pezzl he calls himself a 'Grämler' and 'Grübler', a melancholy brooder (B II, 165, 169).[7] Blumauer's life was summed up in an alphabetical obituary:

> Aloys Blumauer
> Censor, Dichter
> Epikuräer, Freigeist, Genie, Hagestolz, Jesuit
> Kenner Latiums
> Maurer
> Naso Österreichs
> Pfaffenfeind
> Quälte Rom
> Spöttelte
> Travestirte
> Unsterblich Virgils Werk
> Xenophthalmisch, Ybischartig
> Zollte der Natur den Tribut.[8]

[Aloys Blumauer: censor, poet; Epicurean, freethinker, genius, confirmed bachelor, Jesuit; expert on Latium; Mason; Austria's Ovid; priest-hater; tormented Rome; mocked, travestied immortally Vergil's work; xenophthalmic, poplar-like; paid his dues to Nature.]

Blumauer's large body of lyric verse gives ample evidence of his pessimism. The poem 'O-Tahiti', dedicated to the explorer Georg Forster, questions whether the Tahitians are as happy as Enlightenment primitivists claimed, suggesting that they too suffer from irrational restrictions such as political oppression, subjection to fashion, superstition and government by priests. He addresses his doubts to the Tahitian people:

> Hat deine Seele keine Abentheuer
> Des tollen Aberglaubens ausgeheckt?
> Hast du nicht Pfaffen, deren Hand den Schleier
> Der heil'gen Lüge dir um's Auge legt? (B II, 133)

[Has your soul contrived no adventures of mad superstition? Have you no priests whose hand covers your eyes with the veil of pious mendacity?]

More personal reasons for his gloomy temperament are suggested by the poems 'An den Magen' [To the Stomach] and 'Ode an den Leibstuhl' [Ode to the Chaise Percée]. But his main philosophical poem is the long 'Glaubensbekenntniß eines nach Wahrheit Ringenden' [Confession of Faith by a Seeker after Truth]. It has attracted remarkably little attention from modern readers. One of the few who

7   The edition quoted is *Aloys Blumauer's gesammelte Werke*, 3 parts (Stuttgart: J. Sceible's Buchhandlung, 1839), cited as B with part and page number. See also Ritchie Robertson, 'Heroes in their Underclothes: Aloys Blumauer's Travesty of Virgil's *Aeneid*', *Austrian Studies*, 9 (1998), 24–40 [now in Robertson, *Mock-Epic Poetry from Pope to Heine* (Oxford: Oxford University Press, 2009), pp. 260–81].

8   Constant von Wurzbach, *Biographisches Lexikon des Kaiserthums Österreich*, 60 vols (Vienna: Druck und Verlag der k. k. Hof- und Staatsdruckerei, 1856–90), II, 439. He explains that 'xenophthalmisch' refers to Blumauer's eye trouble, while 'ybischartig', meaning 'like a tall yellowish poplar', alludes to his yellow complexion and tall thin build.

even mention it complains that it is too 'poorly conceived and executed' to count as poetry, and merely 'perpetuate[s] the abstract and barren "Gedankenlyrik" of his rationalistic century'.[9] We shall soon find that there is at least a little more to the poem than that.

Blumauer's 'Glaubensbekenntniß' is built on antitheses. The main antithesis is between the intellect ('Verstand'), which enables man to think correctly, and the heart, which impels him to action on the basis of belief. The two are at odds because the heart desires so much and yet the intellect can know so little. Accordingly, the greater part of the poem consists of antithetical quatrains in which the first two lines formulate a belief and the latter two express knowledge that runs counter to it:

> Ich glaube, daß du uns in allen Zeiten
> Durch Wunder kund getan, wie stark du bist:
> Allein ich seh's, daß dieser Bau der weiten
> Und schönen Welt dein größtes Wunder ist. (B ɪɪ, 10)

> [I believe that in all ages Thou hast shown us by miracles how strong Thou art; yet I see that Thy greatest miracle is the construction of this vast and beautiful world.]

As this example shows, Blumauer is not even-handed in thus juxtaposing faith and knowledge. This stanza actually contrasts revelation with natural religion, implying that the latter is self-evident. Similarly, the poem throughout sets the official doctrine of the Church against a series of sceptical doubts. Blumauer professes to believe obediently that faith sustains man's feeble intellect; that Europeans are closer to God than the rest of humanity; that certain ceremonies are more pleasing to God than others; that God has given us the Bible for our guidance; that His nature is mysterious; that humanity is sinful and needed to be redeemed by Christ; and so forth. But these propositions are undermined by two methods. One method is by opposing to them the doctrines of natural religion: that man's intellect is there to save him from sole reliance on faith; that Europeans can claim no merit from the accident of their birth; that pious Brahmins are as pleasing to God as pious Christians; that the book of Nature reveals God's purposes as well as the Bible; that an individual's sins are too trivial to annoy God; and so forth. The other, less obvious method consists in subverting official doctrine by a dryly ironic formulation that makes it appear unfamiliar. The claim that Europeans have superior access to religious truth is exposed as absurd by Blumauer's wording:

> Ich glaube, daß der Mensch in einer Zone
> Dem Licht sich mehr als in der andern naht,
> Allein ich weiß, er hat kein Recht zum Lohne,
> Weil Rom, nicht Japan, ihn erzeuget hat. (B ɪɪ, 9)

> [I believe that humanity in one zone approaches the light more closely than in another, yet I know that he deserves no reward for having been engendered in Rome instead of Japan.]

---

9   Bärbel Becker-Cantarino, *Aloys Blumauer and the Literature of Austrian Enlightenment* (Bern and Frankfurt a.M.: Peter Lang, 1973), p. 85.

The doctrine to which Blumauer feigns assent is here expressed with a bald literalness that calls it into question. This technique of defamiliarization has a long history which has recently been surveyed by Carlo Ginzburg.[10] The criticism of institutions by describing them in bare, alienating language can be found in La Bruyère's famous description of French peasants as unfamiliar animals, and it was especially used in the Enlightenment in order to criticize European institutions by adopting the perplexed outlook of a visitor from overseas, whether from Persia (Montesquieu's *Lettres persanes*) or North America (Voltaire's *L'Ingénu*). Hence the dryness to which exception has been taken turns out to be an essential part of Blumauer's rhetorical purpose.

Blumauer's implicit standpoint is an enlightened theism which attaches more value to revelation through Nature than through scripture. Its main target is the authority arrogated by the Church. In addressing God, Blumauer asserts that God alone, and not the merely human Pope ('der Mensch in Rom'; B II, 7), is able to judge him. The irony at the expense of official doctrine is sustained throughout the poem and reinforced in the final quatrain:

> Und hast du denn von dieser meiner Bitte
> Dein gütig Ohr auf immer weggewandt,
> So nimm — ich fleh's, o Herr! zu deiner Güte —
> Nimm mir den Glauben oder den Verstand. (B II, 14)

[And if Thou hast forever turned Thy kindly ear away from this my plea, then take — Lord, I beseech this of Thy kindness — take my faith or my intellect from me.]

The conclusion is clear: intellect without faith is perfectly viable; faith without intellect amounts to insanity.

II

There are close links between Blumauer and Franz Grillparzer. Not only was Grillparzer, as he tells us in his autobiography, brought up in the Josephinist spirit by his father, who had a low opinion of devotional practices; indeed Grillparzer senior had written a dissertation on canon law which the Church had placed on the Index of Prohibited Books. Grillparzer also shared Blumauer's morose temperament and solitary lifestyle. He read Blumauer's satires as a boy, paying tribute to Blumauer's *Aeneis* in his poem 'Mein Traum' [My Dream] (*c.* 1806), and, in an essay on the nature of parody (1808), maintaining: 'dieses Mannes Werk ist vielleicht das Beste was je in dem Gebiete der Parodie emporgeblüht ist' [this man's work may well be the best thing that has ever flowered in the realm of parody].[11]

---

10   See 'Making it Strange: The Prehistory of a Literary Device', in Carlo Ginzburg, *Wooden Eyes: Nine Reflections on Distance*, trans. by Martin Ryle and Kate Soper (London and New York: Verso, 2002), pp. 1–23.

11   Franz Grillparzer, *Sämtliche Werke*, ed. by Peter Frank and Karl Pörnbacher, 4 vols (Munich: Hanser, 1960–65), I, 12–18; III, 298. This relatively accessible edition is quoted whenever possible, and cited as G.

Among Grillparzer's poems, a large body of work that has been surprisingly little studied, the major works tend to be reflective and melancholy.[12] Often the melancholy can be explained from his personal life, as with the 'Tristia ex Ponto' cycle (1833), which explores feelings of sadness and bitterness with fortitude and without false heroics. Some poems, however, work on a more abstract level. For example, 'Abschied von Gastein' (Taking leave of Gastein, 1818) dwells on the sufferings of the poet, comparing them to a succession of natural phenomena. The poet's work resembles the blaze from a tree that has been struck by lightning; the pearl produced by the sick oyster; and the glittering of the waterfall which (as Grillparzer too anthropomorphically supposes) feels constant pain as its water is dashed on the rocks. All these events occur in an indifferent universe to which the poet addresses his futile laments:

> Was ihr für Lieder haltet; es sind Klagen,
> Gesprochen in ein freudeloses All. (G 1, 98)

[What you take for songs are really laments, spoken into a joyless universe.]

Alongside the image of the poet as martyr, familiar from Goethe's *Torquato Tasso* and from Grillparzer's own *Sappho*, we have a picture of the universe, no longer guided even by an inscrutable providence, but condemned to blind suffering. As Grillparzer wrote the poem, Schopenhauer was at work on the first part of *Die Welt als Wille und Vorstellung* [*The World as Will and Idea*], which elaborates a broadly similar picture of life as doomed to perpetual suffering by its subjection to the blind force of the Will.

Although such poems go far beyond Blumauer's emotional range, Grillparzer returns to anti-clerical themes reminiscent of Blumauer in 'Campo vaccino', a poem first drafted during his visit to Rome at Easter 1819. The *campo vaccino* or field for cattle is the ruins of the Roman Forum, which Grillparzer, as his diary indicates, explored systematically. Rome made a mixed impression on him. Approaching it along the Via Flaminia, he was sharply aware how the Papal States had been ruined by clerical misgovernment:

> Beinahe schon hinter Viterbo kündigt sich die Nähe der Priesterstadt auf eine traurige Art an. Unfruchtbare, dürre Heiden, ohne Kultur, ohne Wohnungen, ohne Menschen sagen vernehmlich: hier ist ein Wahlreich, und der Gewählte ist ein Priester und dieser Priester ist gewöhnlich ein Greis. (G IV, 299)[13]

[As soon as you leave Viterbo the priestly city announces its proximity in a dismal manner. Barren, infertile heaths, without cultivation, without dwellings, without people, say audibly: here is an electoral realm, and the elected one is a priest and this priest is usually an old man.]

He noticed gallows along the road with the dried corpses of murderers and thieves hanging from them. The road itself, the Via Flaminia, reminded him 'wie reich

---

12   There appears to have been no comprehensive study since Erich Hock, *Das Schmerzerlebnis und sein Ausdruck in Grillparzers Lyrik* (Berlin: Ebering, 1937), which badly needs updating.

13   For other examples of this commonplace, see *Voyages de Montesquieu*, 2 vols (Paris: Picard, 1894), I. 193; J. G. Seume, *Spaziergang nach Syrakus im Jahre 1802*, in his *Prosaschriften*, ed. with intro. by Werner Kraft (Cologne: Melzer, 1962), pp. 486–87.

und glücklich einst Gegenden waren, wo man derlei Straßen bauen konnte' [how rich and happy regions once were, where such highways could be built] (ibid.), and he imagined Roman armies marching along the highway. Examining the Forum, however, he was struck by how small its buildings must originally have been, and by the higgledy-piggledy way in which they seemed to be arranged. Christian Rome could offer more magnificence. Although the exterior of St Peter's disappointed him, because it is impossible to get a clear view of the façade, the interior made up for it. He saw Pope Pius VII blessing the city and the world from the balcony of St Peter's, and wrote: 'er allein, ein Gott, thronend hoch über allen — ich werde den Augenblick nie vergessen' [he alone, the god, enthroned high above everyone — I shall never forget that moment] (G IV, 293). This passage should remind us that, despite his Josephinist upbringing, Grillparzer did not entirely lose his attachment to Catholicism, though it was an emotional tie which accompanied an abstention from devotional practice and a consistently critical attitude towards the institutional Church.[14] The only ancient counterpart to St Peter's was the Colosseum, on which some restoration work had recently been done on the Pope's orders:

> Ein lebhaftes Bild der römischen Größe, so, daß die Phantasie dadurch wirklich erweitert wird, gibt unter allen hiesigen Denkmäler[n] alter Zeit, beinahe allein das Kolosseum. Dieses wird besonders in Rom klar, wo man so viele vorzügliche Gebäude sieht und doch verschwinden alle in nichts vor diesem Koloß (G IV, 296).

> [Of all the monuments of antiquity here, the Colosseum is almost the only one that conveys a vivid image of Roman greatness, so that the imagination is truly enlarged by it. This is especially clear in Rome, where so many admirable buildings can be seen, yet all disappear into nothing beside this colossus.]

These experiences are recorded in 'Campo vaccino' (G I, 114–18), of which part was actually written in the Colosseum.[15] It belongs to an already familiar genre of poetic tourism which included Wilhelm von Humboldt's great elegy 'Rom', and whose best-known exemplar was Byron's *Childe Harold's Pilgrimage*. In his autobiography, Grillparzer is modest about the poem's claim to originality. It surveys the monuments in turn, commenting on the disparity between classical and Christian Rome. There are two major or structural antitheses: between the Emperors Titus (AD 39–81) and Constantine (AD 272–337), and between the Colosseum and the Cross. The Arch of Titus, built to commemorate his pacification of the eastern provinces after the conquest of Jerusalem, is contrasted with the claims of Constantine, the first Christian Emperor, to bring peace to the Empire. There is a Josephinian subtext here, for Joseph's admirers were fond of calling him a second Titus.[16] Although the Arch of Titus may be close to collapse, Titus does not need a physical building to ensure that he is remembered. His fragile monument is contrasted with the

---

14   See Eda Sagarra, 'Grillparzer the Catholic?', *Modern Language Review*, 97 (2002), 108–22.

15   The fullest study of this poem remains August Sauer, 'Proben eines Commentars zu Grillparzer's Gedichten', *Jahrbuch der Grillparzer-Gesellschaft*, 7 (1897), 1–170.

16   See Johann Pezzl, *Faustin oder das philosophische Jahrhundert* [1780], ed. by Wolfgang Griep (Hildesheim: Olms, 1982): 'Es lebe, der deutsche Titus, die Lust des Menschengeschlechts, unser theure Joseph!' (p. 325).

'Siegesdom', the cathedral of victory, attained by Constantine; the image may suggest St Peter's, but, since that was built twelve centuries after Constantine's conversion, it implies more generally the whole edifice of the Catholic Church, and in particular the papal throne:

> Über Romas Heldentrümmern
> Hobst du deiner Kirche Thron,
> In der Kirche magst du schimmern,
> Die Geschichte spricht dir Hohn. (ll. 85–88)

[Over Rome's heroic ruins you raised your Church's throne; you may shine in the Church, but history derides you.]

The other antithesis, between the Colosseum and the Cross, continues, yet more extravagantly, the theme of the defeat of ancient Rome by Catholic Rome. Since a cross has been planted on the summit of the Colosseum in memory of the Christian martyrs, the huge building is depicted as itself a martyr, dying at the hands of its persecutor:

> Kolosseum, Riesenschatten
> Von der Vorwelt Machtkoloß,
> Liegst du da in Todsermatten,
> Selber noch im Sterben groß?
> Und damit, verhöhnt, zerschlagen,
> Du den *Martertod* erwarbst,
> Mußtest du das Kreuz noch *tragen*,
> An dem, Herrlicher, du starbst!
>   (ll. 97–103; italics in original)

[Colosseum, giant shadow of the ancient world's mighty colossus, are you lying in your death-throes, great even in dying? And in order that, mocked and shattered, you might gain a martyr's death, you were compelled still to bear the Cross on which, splendid one, you died!]

The motif of carrying the Cross equates the Colosseum not only with the early martyrs but also with Christ on the way to the Crucifixion. The image amounts to a rather over-complicated conceit, elaborated further by (involuntarily?) recalling Byron's stanzas on the dying Gladiator.[17] But the immediately following line, 'Nehmt es weg, dies heilge Zeichen!' [Take it away, this sacred sign!], shows, as Heinz Politzer points out, that the poem is not anti-Christian, or at least that Grillparzer was not wholehearted in his opposition to Christianity; 'Er glaubte seinem eigenen Unglauben nicht ganz' [He did not quite believe his own unbelief].[18]

While the poem's genre may be easy to recognize, its mode is less so. Instead of the dignified style of Humboldt, or the elegiac mode of Schiller's 'Die Götter Griechenlands' [The Gods of Greece], which clearly helped to inspire the poem, we find a surprising number of puns. The monument to Septimius Severus should not

---

17   *Childe Harold's Pilgrimage*, Book IV, stanzas CXL–CXLI, in Byron, *Poetical Works*, ed. by Frederick Page, rev. by John Jump (Oxford: Oxford University Press, 1970), pp. 245–46.

18   Heinz Politzer, *Grillparzer oder Das abgründige Biedermeier* (Vienna, Munich and Zurich: Molden, 1972), p. 105.

be placed at the entrance ('Eingang') to the Forum, because Severus marked the end ('Ausgang') of Rome's military greatness (ll. 25–28). Tourist guides have displaced orators: 'Rom hat nur noch Ciceronen, | Aber keinen Cicero' [Rome has only cicerones, but no Cicero] (ll. 55–56). The culminating stanza about the martyred Colosseum turns on the pun whereby the building, bearing a cross, is likened to Christ carrying the Cross. These puns would be out of place in a Schillerian elegy, or in a poem expressing personal feelings such as Politzer would like 'Campo vaccino' to be. They indicate that the mode of the poem is not so much elegiac as satirical and polemical, and thus in the tradition of Blumauer.

If that is the right way to read the poem, it is less surprising that this polemic got Grillparzer into so much trouble. It was accepted for publication in the poetic yearbook ('Almanach') *Aglaja*, edited by his friend and mentor Joseph Schreyvogel. Since Schreyvogel, like Blumauer before him, held the office of censor, he should have been able to judge what was or was not acceptable. But the poem was denounced to the authorities, who insisted that it must be withdrawn from *Aglaja*, and Grillparzer had to explain it away in a letter to Count Sedlnitzky, the chief of police. For many years afterwards Grillparzer was haunted by what people called 'die Geschichte mit dem Papst' (G IV, 109).

Who denounced the poem is not known, but Grillparzer thought it was Zacharias Werner, and his twentieth-century editor Reinhold Backmann is inclined to agree.[19] Zacharias Werner (1768–1823) was a prominent figure in the Romantic Catholic setting of post-Enlightenment Vienna. His fate tragedy *Der 24. Februar* (written 1809, published 1815) inspired a whole genre, including Grillparzer's own *Die Ahnfrau*; his mythical dramas were widely read; and as a convert who entered the priesthood in 1814, he attained a high reputation as a preacher. Moreover, in the previous number of *Aglaja* he had published a poem, 'Italia', celebrating the triumph of Christianity in Italy, to which Grillparzer's poem may well be a deliberate rejoinder.

Grillparzer's anticlericalism finds ample expression in his occasional poems and epigrams. The dominant tone is set by his great commemoration of Joseph II, 'Des Kaisers Bildsäule' [The Emperor's Statue] (1837), a poem supposed to be spoken by the Emperor's statue outside the National Library. Among other betrayals of his legacy, Joseph here condemns the tendency of quarrelsome priests ('Streitsüchtge Pfaffen'; G I, 254) to place factional allegiance above national loyalty. As early as 1826 Grillparzer equates the clergy with such vermin as gnats and bats ('Mück und Fledermaus'), the latter, by their blindness, implying obscurantism ('Klerisei'; G I, 393). And as late as 1871, irritated by the proclamation of papal infallibility, he remarks that Christ undertook to found his Church on Peter but said nothing about Peter's successors ('Päpste'; G I, 591).

In the intervening period Grillparzer was provoked especially by three events. The first was the expulsion in 1837 of four hundred Protestants from the Tyrol,

---

19   See Grillparzer, *Sämtliche Werke*, Historisch-kritische Gesamtausgabe, ed. by August Sauer and Reinhold Backmann, 43 vols (Vienna: Gerlach & Wiedling, 1909–48), I/x: *Gedichte, Erster Teil* (1932), 277–79.

which recalled to his mind the mass expulsion of heretics conducted in the early seventeenth century by the Archduke Ferdinand, later the Holy Roman Emperor Ferdinand II, whose intolerance Grillparzer later castigated in *Ein Bruderzwist in Habsburg*.[20] In his epigram Grillparzer warns the present Austrian Emperor, Ferdinand I, not to confuse himself with his over-zealous namesake ('Die Tiroler Religionsgeschichte'; G 1, 423).

Still more provocative was the affair of the Holy Coat of Trier. According to a tradition dating back to the twelfth century, this is said to be Christ's seamless garment (John 19. 23). Between 18 August and 6 October 1844 at least half a million pilgrims, organized by the Church and conducted by their local priests, visited Trier to see the Coat displayed in the Cathedral. This was no spontaneous outburst, but a carefully orchestrated demonstration of popular piety and of the Church's organization. Every parish in the diocese was assigned a day when its members were to venerate the Coat, and they went to the Cathedral in strict order, led by their priests.[21] The Coat was said to have brought about a miraculous cure of the illness of Johanna von Droste zu Vischering, niece of the former Archbishop of Cologne. In protest, the Catholic priest Johannes Ronge denounced in print the spiritual darkness ('Geisternacht') in which the Church left its adherents and the financial contributions it demanded even from bitterly poor manual workers who visited the shrine. Excommunicated, Ronge founded the German Catholic movement which sought a free national Church independent of Rome. It held its first Council in Leipzig in 1845 and attracted many middle-class liberal Catholics, but after the failure of the 1848 Revolutions it was dissolved, and Ronge went into exile in England.[22] In the pithiest of several epigrams on this affair, Grillparzer, in an ironically enlightened spirit, recommended the Vatican to adopt a rational outlook and thus make the German Catholics superfluous:

> Um Ronges Spaltung zu erdrücken,
> Braucht ihr kein weiteres Mittel künftig,
> Wer fragt noch viel nach Deutsch-Katholiken,
> Sind erst die römischen vernünftig (G 1, 482).

[To crush Ronge's schism, you won't need anything extra: nobody will care about German Catholics once the Roman ones are rational.]

Grillparzer also shared the dismay of liberals at the Concordat concluded between the Austrian state and the Catholic Church in 1855. The Concordat restored and indeed extended the power of the Church over education, over all questions relating to the faith, including marriage law, over clerical appointments and discipline, and over the censorship of books that the Church judged objectionable.[23] For liberals

---

20 See Regina Pörtner, *The Counter-Reformation in Central Europe: Styria, 1580–1630* (Oxford: Clarendon Press, 2001).

21 See Jonathan Sperber, *Popular Catholicism in Nineteenth-Century Germany* (Princeton, NJ: Princeton University Press, 1984), pp. 70–71.

22 A brief account in Jutta Osinski, *Katholizismus und deutsche Literatur im 19. Jahrhundert* (Paderborn: Schöningh, 1993), pp. 157–60.

23 A convenient summary in C. A. Macartney, *The Habsburg Empire, 1790–1918* (London: Macmillan, 1969), p. 458.

in education, such as Adalbert Stifter, Inspector of Schools in Upper Austria, these provisions were a deeply demoralizing blow.[24] Grillparzer, more detached from their practical implications, responded with several scurrilous epigrams. One derides the Church's power of excommunication or cursing, contrasting it with the blessings that the restoration of ecclesiastical power is alleged to promise:

> Ob die frühere Macht der Kirche frommt,
> Will man von neuem versuchen;
> Bis nun der erwartete Segen kommt,
> Treibt vorderhand sie das Fluchen. (G I, 528)

[A new attempt is to be made to restore its former power to the Church, and till the awaited blessing arrives, it spends its time cursing.]

Another, tendentiously entitled 'Symbolik', notes scornfully and callously, as an early product of the Concordat, that the Archduke Ferdinand Max, who had formally thanked the Church on behalf of the Emperor for bringing the agreement about, had soon afterwards fallen from his carriage and suffered serious brain damage (G I, 535). A longer poem, 'Zeloten', mocks an 'Eifrer' or bigot who not only kneels before the image of the Virgin at Mariazell but also declares it an aesthetic masterpiece; this extravagant claim shakes the other believers out of their blind devotion, prompting them to discover that the image is a mere daub:

> Die Gläubigen sehen genauer hin
> Und jetzt erst belehrt sie der eigene Sinn,
> Als kritische Note zum gläubigen Text,
> Das Wunderbild sei nur eben geklext. (G I, 357)

[The faithful take a closer look, and now their own senses inform them, as a critical comment on a faithful text, that the miraculous image is merely a daub.]

Empirical observation and aesthetic judgement, Grillparzer suggests, are a surer guide to truth than religious devotion.

III

Grillparzer's slender reputation as a lyric poet was easily eclipsed by Nikolaus Lenau, some ten years his junior. Each man was critical of the other's work. Lenau thought Grillparzer's poetry too dryly intellectual ('Bei ihm ist der Verstand alles'); Grillparzer thought Lenau too much the victim of an emotional pessimism which he failed to master intellectually.[25] This was a clash of generations rather than of temperaments. Unlike the Josephinist Grillparzer, Lenau leaned towards a Romantic emotionality. But the pessimism they express is similar. We find the hints of cosmic

---

24   See Wolfgang Matz, *Adalbert Stifter oder Diese fürchterliche Wendung der Dinge* (Munich: Hanser, 1995), p. 341; *Documenta Paedagogica Austriaca: Adalbert Stifter*, ed. by Kurt Gerhard Fischer, 2 vols (Linz: Oberösterreichischer Landesverlag, 1961), I, p. lxxxvi.

25   See Michael Ritter, *Zeit des Herbstes: Nikolaus Lenau. Biografie* (Vienna: Deuticke, 2002), p. 168; the original passages are in G III 832–33 and *Lenau und die Familie Löwenthal*, ed. by Eduard Castle (Leipzig: M. Hesse, 1906), p. 79.

pessimism present in such poems as 'Abschied von Gastein' developed by Lenau into a full-blown expression of *Weltschmerz*, while the anti-clericalism of Blumauer and Grillparzer appears fitfully in Lenau's work alongside a pessimism that is sometimes varied by an apparent return to theism. Lenau has a reputation as the key poet of *Weltschmerz*. The cosmic pessimism found in Schopenhauer, Heine, Büchner, Grabbe, and further afield in Byron, Vigny and Musset, is generally thought to be the very basis of Lenau's large body of lyrical and semi-dramatic poetry. But a closer look will show that matters are more complicated.

Critics disagree about the extent to which Lenau's pessimism is predominantly personal, philosophical or rhetorical. His life was notoriously unsettled: his dissipated father died when he was four, and the smothering affection of his adoring mother no doubt hindered him from establishing relationships with women in adult life; he never completed a university course or adopted a career; his famous trip to America, where he hoped to invest in property, ended in disappointment; his love for Sophie von Löwenthal, an unhappily married woman who invested in Lenau emotionally but not sexually, was frustrating; and he may have had syphilis. But although he complains repeatedly of depression (variously called 'Melancholie', 'Schwermuth' or 'Hypochondrie'),[26] he was clearly a quite different type of personality from the confirmed bachelors Blumauer and Grillparzer, with their notorious moroseness. While his lyric poetry may be Byronic in its dismissal of the world, his part-narrative, part-dramatic *Faust* is brisk and pointed, even recalling the satirical Byron of *Don Juan*. Although he read energetically in philosophy — Spinoza, Herbart, Hegel and possibly Schelling — the pessimism of his poetry hardly needed a philosophical foundation and is unlikely to be the expression of previously acquired philosophical convictions. *Weltschmerz*, the public profession of cosmic despair, was by the time Lenau began writing in the late 1820s a readily available literary attitude. To understand what Lenau did with it, we should bear in mind his rhetorical training. Richard Dove, in an indispensable but too little noticed article, has reminded us that Lenau was a craftsman who, rather than aiming to express certain feelings, set out to produce certain effects in his readers.[27] His consciousness of his craftsmanship emerges clearly from such self-praising utterances as the following:

> Das, worin ich neu bin, worin ich Epoche mache in der deutschen Literatur, und worin mir keiner, wie viele Nachahmer auch schon aufgetreten sind, gleichkommt, ist meine Naturpoesie, meine poetische Durchdringung und Abspiegelung der Natur und ihres Verhältnisses zur Menschheit, ihres Ringens nach dem Geiste, meine Illustration der Natur. Meine effektvollsten Stellen sind jene, wo ich die Natur belauscht habe, die organische wie die menschliche. Diese meine Eigenschaft ist schon anerkannt und wird es noch mehr werden.[28]

26 Ritter, *Zeit des Herbstes*, pp. 92–93, 107, 152.
27 Richard Dove, 'The Rhetoric of Lament: A Reassessment of Nikolaus Lenau', *Orbis Litterarum*, 39 (1984), 230–65.
28 Castle (ed.), *Lenau und die Familie Löwenthal*, pp. 104–05.

[My originality, by which I mark an epoch in German literature, and in which nobody equals me, no matter how many imitators have appeared, is my nature poetry, my poetic grasp and depiction of Nature and her relation to humanity, her search for the spirit, my portrayal of Nature. My most effective passages are those where I have eavesdropped on Nature, both organic and human. This quality of mine has already received recognition, and will receive yet more.]

However, although Dove is certainly right to query simplistic accounts of Lenau's sincerity, it remains the case that he found images of death and destruction congenial, and that while he was doubtless following a contemporary fashion for Byronic world-rejection, his success in doing so implies a more than merely opportunistic adoption of the theme.

In Lenau's life and work we find, differently weighted, the conflict between religious faith and scepticism, between the desire to believe and the need to obey the authority of reason that we have seen in Blumauer and Grillparzer. Both an attraction to Christianity, and a destructive Voltairean scepticism, can be found in Lenau's childhood. According to the biography by his brother-in-law Anton Schurz, the young Lenau was extremely devout. He loved to say his morning and evening prayers, to read Mass from a chair that served as an altar, and to preach so fervently that his mother and his nurse were reduced to tears. In adult life he recalled this devotion vividly:

> Auch noch als Mann sprach Lenau mit Entzücken von der wahrhaft himm-
> lischen Seligkeit, die ihn durchströmte, als er das erstemal, rein wie ein Engel,
> von der Beichte gegangen war[29]

[Even as an adult Lenau would speak with delight about the truly heavenly bliss that filled him the first time he left confession, pure as an angel.]

This suggests not the rational religion of the Catholic Enlightenment but a more intense, emotional and above all theatrical form of religion, characteristic of the Romantic generation. But Schurz also tells us that in his late teens Lenau came under the influence of his uncle Sebastian Mihits (or Mihitsch), a lieutenant of hussars, with whom he stayed in Alt-Ofen (Buda). This uncle would read to him from Voltaire's correspondence with Frederick the Great and would tell him there was no God.[30]

The conflict between faith and reason is dramatized in Lenau's *Faust*. At least one contemporary, Anastasius Grün, recognized Faust as a portrait of the author: 'Lenau's Faust [ist] nur eine Individualität, allerdings eine große und bedeutende, Niembsch-Lenau selbst' [Lenau's Faust is only an individual, albeit a great and significant one, Niembsch-Lenau himself].[31] But if Faust represents one aspect of Lenau, his antagonist Mephistopheles represents another. Faust is an egotist who recalls that during his pious youth, when he served as an altar-boy, he really wished to be God:

---

29 Anton X. Schurz, *Lenau's Leben*, 2 vols (Stuttgart and Augsburg: Cotta, 1855), I, 16.
30 Ibid., p. 25.
31 Quoted in Ritter, *Zeit des Herbstes*, p. 167.

> Daß ich dem Gottesbild zu Füßen
> Hab' knien und opferrauchen müssen,
> Mir schien's an meinem Werthe Spott:
> Daß ich nicht lieber selbst ein Gott.[32]

[That I had to kneel before the image of God and offer it incense seemed to mock my own merit: that I was not myself a God.]

He fails in successive attempts to identify with greater realities, becoming estranged from religion when Mephistopheles makes him burn the Bible, and from Nature when, having committed murder, he feels that his 'Freundin' Nature is now alien (l. 2050). At last he finds himself trapped in the confines of the self, from which he can escape only by the idealist supposition that he was always one with God and that his experiences were mere dreams. Mephistopheles, however, undermines all Faust's philosophical positions. Not only do his closing words deride Faust's desperate idealism, but earlier he has cogently pointed out that both Faust's attachment to Nature, and his alienation from it, are mere anthropomorphism:

> [...] ob die Natur
> Dir freundlich scheint und wohlgewogen,
> Ob feindlich grollend, beides nur
> Hast du in sie hineingelogen. (L III, 196)

[Whether Nature was friendly and well disposed to you, or hostile and angry, both were lies that you projected onto it.]

He even undermines Faust's theatrical defiance of God by remarking that blasphemy is a sign of belief in God:

> Seht meinen Freund hier, Doctor Faust,
> Wie hat er doch im Schiffe neulich,
> Als da der tolle Sturm gehaust,
> Auf seinen Gott gezankt so gräulich!
> Das war, verlaßt euch drauf, mein Lieber,
> Noch immer was vom Glaubensfieber. (L III, 229)

[Look at my friend here, Dr Faust! A short time ago, aboard ship, when the wild gale was raging, how dreadfully he denounced his God! Take my word for it, my dear fellow, that was a lingering touch of the fever of faith.]

Lenau, however, could admit Mephistophelean irony only as a counterpoint to Faust's search for belief. Ironic and negative writing, such as he found in Heine and the Young Germans, was uncongenial to him.[33]

While Lenau rejected irony, however, it is not clear that he ever found refuge in a secure religious faith. He was not closely attached to the Catholicism in which he was brought up, being quite prepared, in 1844, to convert to Protestantism in order to marry Marie Behrends. Claims that he, at least temporarily, adopted definite Christian convictions are usually based on his epic poem *Savonarola* (1837).[34] This

---

32 Nikolaus Lenau, *Werke und Briefe*, Historisch-kritische Gesamtausgabe, ed. by Helmut Brandt et al., 7 vols (Vienna: Deuticke, 1995–), III, 236. This edition is henceforth cited as L.

33 Ritter, *Zeit des Herbstes*, p. 148.

34 See Boshidora Deliiwanowa, 'Religion und Religionskritik in den Epen von Nikolaus Lenau',

poem in 995 quatrains places the Dominican preacher Girolamo Savonarola (1452–98) in opposition to the corrupt Borgia papacy which had him excommunicated, tortured and burned. It was written under the influence of the Catholic mystic Franz von Baader (1765–1841), an opponent of papal absolutism, and of the Danish Protestant theologian Hans Lassen Martensen (1808–1884), a student of Hegel, Baader and the mystics.[35] But the theistic interpretation probably owes much to the study of Lenau's *Faust* published by Martensen, who, according to Hugo Schmidt, used Lenau's work as a pretext for presenting his own view that rationalism must now give way either to unconditional faith or to despair.[36] Lenau himself was not so sure that his work affirmed Christianity. He said of *Savonarola*: 'Die Zweifel meiner eigenen Seele klingen in den Versen' [My own soul's doubts resound in the lines].[37] The poem, moreover, has a strong political element. Much is made of Savonarola's attempt to persuade the dying Lorenzo de' Medici to grant freedom to the city of Florence. The poem is an intervention in politics rather than in theology. It was intended as the second of three epics, the first dealing with Jan Hus and the third with Ulrich von Hutten. The only other epic that Lenau completed, *Die Albigenser* (1842), which recounts the Church's brutal extermination of the Cathar heretics of Provence in the early thirteenth century, is still more political, seeing the Albigensian heretics as unwitting actors in a long struggle for freedom and unexpectedly interpreting them as precursors not only of Hus and the Protestant reformers but also of the revolutionaries who stormed the Bastille in 1789. These epic poems need to be understood as protests against the ultramontanism of the reactionary Popes Gregory XVI and Pius IX.[38]

Attempts have also been made to relate Lenau's work to the pantheism which Goethe and his contemporaries constructed in opposition to what seemed the arid theism of late Enlightenment theology. Herder wrote to the theist Friedrich Heinrich Jacobi: 'Gott ist freilich außer Dir und wirkt zu, in und durch alle Geschöpfe (den extramundanen Gott kenne ich nicht); aber was soll Dir der Gott, wenn er nicht in Dir ist und Du sein Dasein auf unendlich innige Art fühlest' [God is of course outside you, working on, in and through all creatures (I know no God outside the world); but what can God mean to you unless He is within you and you feel His existence with infinite emotion].[39] Goethe rejected the idea of an external God, operating mechanically on a lifeless Nature, in the famous lines: 'Was wär

in *Vergleichende Literaturforschung: Internationale Lenau-Gesellschaft 1964 bis 1984*, ed. by Antal Mádl and Anton Schwob (Vienna: Österreichischer Bundesverlag, 1984), pp. 329–46, who lists previous commentators who have held this view.

35   See Ritter, *Zeit des Herbstes*, pp. 169, 179.

36   Hugo Schmidt, *Nikolaus Lenau* (New York: Twayne, 1970), p. 120.

37   Letter to Emilie von Gleichen-Russwurm, 6 June 1838, in L VI/1 22–23.

38   See Norbert Altenhofer, 'Ketzerhistorie und revolutionäre Geschichtsphilosophie im Werk Lenaus', *Vergleichende Literaturforschung*, pp. 312–28, and Carl Gibson, *Lenau. Leben — Werk — Wirkung* (Heidelberg: Winter, 1989), who opposes theistic interpretations with a political reading of both poems.

39   Herder, letter of 20 December 1784, quoted in Walter Weiss, *Enttäuschter Pantheismus: Zur Weltgestaltung der Dichtung in der Restaurationszeit* (Dornbirn: Vorarlberger Verlagsanstalt, 1962), p. 25.

ein Gott, der nur von außen stieße, | Im Kreis das All am Finger laufen ließe!'
[What would a God be who merely pushed from outside, twirling the universe
round his finger!][40] Lenau is known to have read Spinoza, the source from which
many writers drew their pantheism, and probably also knew Schelling's pantheistic
philosophy of Nature, which was widely discussed in Vienna.[41] However, closer
examination of some of his shorter poems will show that disillusioned pantheism is
not the sole key to them, and that many passages that have often been considered
pantheistic are not so. God is always represented by the symbol of the Cross,
betokening the Incarnation, a concept difficult for pantheism to accommodate.
Lenau does not seem definable as either a pantheist or a theist, disappointed or
otherwise. His poetry gives the impression of seeking restlessly for something to
believe in. It should be seen not as expressing convictions but as exploring beliefs
that are only held provisionally. These explorations employ not so much theological
ideas but rather Christian symbols which retain their emotional power even after
the reality they point to has ceased to carry conviction.

The early poem 'Glauben. Wissen. Handeln' [Faith, Knowledge, Action]
(originally 'Fantasie', 1830) presents the basic situation of the poetry in an allegorical
narrative that moves from belief in God to disillusionment. The speaker recalls
his youthful wandering through 'des Glaubens Paradiese' [the paradises of faith],
accompanied by the figure of Life in the form of a veiled bride. Testimony to God's
presence came both from the whispering of the breezes and from the howling of
the gale. This lost paradise was not a pantheistic one. Natural forces spoke of God;
they did not convey the direct presence of God. The ultimate message of Paradise
refers to the Crucifixion, and is reported only as the speaker recalls his departure
from Paradise:

> Doch zogen fort wir aus dem Paradiese,
> Wo jedes Lüftchen uns von Gott erzählt,
> Wo uns von ihm jed' Blümchen auf der Wiese
> Ein Liebeszeichen froh entgegenhält;
> Wo eine Blum' aus allen Blumen ragend,
> Prangt, hold umstrahlt vom rothen Morgenlicht,
> Die schönste Liebesblüthe Gottes tragend,
> Des todten Heilands lächelnd Angesicht. (L 1, 8)

[Yet we departed from Paradise, where every breeze tells us about God, where
every flower in the meadow is glad to offer us a sign of His love; where
one magnificent flower, in the dawn's red beams, stands forth from all the
rest, bearing the fairest blossom of God's love, the smiling face of the dead
Saviour.]

The lost paradise of Christian faith, then, was not one where God was present in

---

40 Johann Wolfgang Goethe, *Sämtliche Werke: Briefe, Tagebücher und Gespräche*, Deutsche
Klassiker-Ausgabe, 40 vols (Frankfurt a.M.: Deutscher Klassiker Verlag, 1986–99), I/ii: *Gedichte
1800–1832*, ed. by Karl Eibl (1988), p. 379.

41 Lenau's intellectual sources are usefully surveyed in Astrid Pucharski, 'Weltanschauliche
Positionen in der späten Lyrik Nikolaus Lenaus', *Jahrbuch des Wiener Goethe-Vereins*, 97/98 (1993–94),
121–31.

Nature, but where Nature testified to the existence of God and to the sacrifice made by Christ for humanity.

The speaker leaves Paradise — voluntarily, it would seem — for 'der Forschung Wälder'. Instead of the cultivated flower-garden, he finds himself in the thickets of a labyrinthine forest through which light can hardly penetrate. Eventually, however, a confused path leads him to the Tree of Knowledge, but a whisper from its foliage warns him that the fruit he seeks is inaccessible, because it hangs from slender boughs that will not bear his weight. Disappointed, he turns back to his bride, and finds that she has lost her veil and with it all her charms, like a rose withered by the frost. In the allegorical bride we recognize an image of Nature, recalling the veiled statue in Schiller's poem 'Das verschleierte Bild zu Sais' [The Veiled Statue of Sais] (1795) and its adaptation by Novalis in *Die Lehrlinge zu Sais* [*The Apprentices at Sais*] (1802). Thus the speaker's attempt to understand the world by rational inquiry leads only to disillusionment, and when he and his bride turn back in the hope of regaining the 'Wunderblume' which may restore the bride to her former beauty, they are lost in a labyrinth with no prospect of finding the way back. The poem then introduces worshippers of a majestic lady called Germania, but on closer inspection she proves to be dead. Patriotism is no substitute for lost religious emotion. The speaker's companion assumes a second veil of grief ('Gram') which will remain with her until they both die:

> Erst wenn wir uns zu seligem Vergessen
> Hinlegen in das traute, liebe Grab,
> Löst er von Deinem Angesicht sich ab
> Und hängt sich an die säuselnden Cypressen. (L I, 11)

[Only when we lie down in the beloved grave to enjoy blissful oblivion will it
fall from your face and hang upon the murmuring cypresses.]

The vivid specificity of the final phrase stands out against the extreme generality with which the poem hitherto has been formulated. After the allegorical flowers and trees, the only scene imagined precisely is one which the speaker has not experienced and will not experience, since it will exist only after his death.

This poem contains many motifs familiar from Lenau's subsequent lyrics. Yearning for a lost paradise is developed in 'Doppelheimweh' (1837), where our homesickness goes in two directions: we mourn for the earth, knowing that we must die; and we long for heaven, though the poem expresses no confidence that our yearning will be fulfilled:

> Das Erdenheimweh läßt uns trauern, bangen,
> Daß Lust und Leid der Erde muß vergehn;
> Das Himmelsheimweh fühlt's herüberwehn
> Wie Morgenluft, daß wir uns fortverlangen. (L II, 101)

[Earthly homesickness makes us tremble and lament that earth's joy and grief
must pass away; it feels heavenly homesickness blowing past like morning air,
so that we long to be gone.]

The image of 'Morgenluft' combines two suggestions. One is that we long to abandon our earthly lives and breathe the richer air of heaven. But the morning air also warns ghosts that they must cease wandering and return to their graves (as in *Hamlet*, I. 4. 58, whence 'Ich wittere Morgenluft' has become a common German expression). It implies that our earthly life is that of a ghost. The poem then introduces the image of the song allegedly uttered by swans before they die: 'Dies Doppelheimweh tönt im Lied der Schwäne' [This double homesickness is heard in the song of the swans], implying that the exceptional beauty of this song comes from the moment of death at which both yearnings are felt most acutely. Part of this idea is present also in 'Heimathklang' (1835), where poetry is said to express yearning for the paradise from which every soul has been expelled; the myth of the Fall has now been combined with a Platonic myth of pre-existence (L II, 112). That the search for scientific truth is futile is another favourite theme. In 'An die Biologen' (1835; L II, 109) Lenau rebukes natural scientists for trying to discover the secret of life, which they can never hope to find, and similarly he represents Faust as an anatomist, indicating, as Friedrich Sengle says, 'daß die Wahrheit immer nur zur zersetzenden Analyse, zum toten Stoff und zum Anblick des Nichts führen kann' [that truth can only lead to reductive analysis, to dead matter and the sight of nothingness].[42]

Even for non-scientists, Nature is presented as alien without God. The famous double sonnet 'Einsamkeit' (Solitude, 1838) represents the desolation of Nature by a heath, where the wanderer vainly seeks emotional solace from the impalpable wind and the indifferent rocks, and even among his fellow-humans, who are described by the alienating term 'Geschöpfe' [creatures] (L II, 214). Worse than that, Nature may be hostile. 'Der Urwald' (1835?) describes the American primeval forest as a scene where life grapples with death in a struggle in which death will always win. It has been pointed out that someone used to the relatively well-managed European woodlands would be taken aback by an American forest, where fallen and dead trees were only removed by natural decay.[43] In 'Der Schiffsjunge' (1834) a boy who falls overboard is swallowed up by the murderous but indifferent ocean: 'Klar blickt der alte Mörder Ocean | Dem Himmel zu, als hätt' er nichts gethan' [Ocean, the old murderer, gazes as serenely at the sky as though he had done nothing] (L II, 24). Lenau's landscapes are populated by vultures and crows, which eye defeated and wounded soldiers, deciding which ones each will devour ('Die Drei' (1842); L II, 278). In 'Auf meinen ausgebälgten Geier' [On my Stuffed Vulture] (1838), the vulture and the snake represent emblematically the destructive effects of war and plague; the speaker asserts that their destruction is necessary for the furtherance of life: 'Doch wie der wilde Aar, mit seinen scharfen Fängen, | Will auch die Schlange nur das Leben vorwärts drängen' [But like the savage eagle with his sharp claws, the snake too only seeks to advance life] (L II, 24). In the second part of the poem, the scene shifts to India, where we are invited to imagine that large numbers of Hindus and Muslims (incongruously called 'Gentlemen') have died of cholera, and

42   Friedrich Sengle, *Biedermeierzeit*, 3 vols (Stuttgart: Metzler, 1971–80), III, 670.

43   See Mary C. Crichton, ' "And no birds sing": Lenau's Desolate *Urwald*', *Michigan Germanic Studies*, I (1975), 152–64.

that their unburied corpses are being devoured by ravens, vultures, wild dogs, jackals and storks. (If only there were a crocodile, we would have a neat anticipation of Kipling's story 'The Undertakers'.)[44] This gruesome description is presented as an affirmation of Nature's maternal love ('Mutterliebe'), but critics have generally found it unconvincing. 'Wer kann in dieser über alles Maß gewaltsamen, ja grotesken Umdeutung den falschen Ton überhören?' [Who can miss the false note in this monstrously violent, indeed grotesque reinterpretation?], asks Walter Weiss indignantly.[45] The grotesquerie of the scene, however, is not a false note but an intrinsic part of its presentation. Lenau is forcing upon us the ironic and grotesque paradox that bountiful Mother Nature feeds some of her children with the corpses of others. It is a change of perspective similar to the one Hamlet brings about when he describes the 'convocation of politic worms' feasting on Polonius (*Hamlet*, IV. 3. 20). The antithetical language of the conclusion underlines the paradox and introduces a series of puns:

> Fort wird das Bild des Tods vom Lebenssturm getragen,
> Der Siegesruf verschlingt mir alle Todesklagen.

> Und mit den Geiern dort, die um die Leichen schwanken,
> Lass' fliegen ich am Strom Unsterblichkeitsgedanken. (L ii, 26)

[The image of death is borne away by life's gale, the cry of victory swallows up all death-laments. And with the vultures there, that hover round the corpse, I let thoughts of immortality fly along the river.]

The word 'verschlingt' not only recalls what the vultures are doing to the corpses' flesh, but picks up an earlier couplet:

> Die Schlange Cholera mit mörderischer Tücke
> Verschlang sie rasch und spie sie schwarz und kalt zurücke. (L ii, 25)

[The serpent cholera, with murderous spite, quickly swallowed them and spewed them up again, black and cold.]

And the speaker indicates that he is discarding ideas of immortality by saying that he lets them fly away, along with the vultures. Given the undignified language, the puns, the jarring *Fremdwort* 'Gentlemen', we should take this not as first and foremost an affirmation of pantheism (as Weiss does), but as an exercise in the mixed poetic style.

None of these poems can be taken as expressions of pantheism. Rather, they depict the play of natural forces in a manner familiar from Goethe's *Die Leiden des jungen Werther*, especially from the famous passage that ends: 'Ich sehe nichts als ein ewig verschlingendes, ewig wiederkäuendes Ungeheuer' [I see nothing but a monster, eternally devouring and eternally chewing].[46] Lenau is preoccupied with transience and death. Nature is not just empty; it has been abandoned by God. In the late 'Waldlieder' (1843?), in which a strong sense of pantheism at times comes to

---

44   See Rudyard Kipling, *The Second Jungle Book* (London: Macmillan, 1895).
45   Weiss, *Enttäuschter Pantheismus*, p. 101.
46   Goethe, *Sämtliche Werke*, i/viii: *Die Leiden des jungen Werther, Die Wahlverwandtschaften, Kleine Prosa, Epen*, ed. by Waltraud Wiethölter (1994), p. 109.

the fore, life and death coexist, though less drastically than in 'Auf meinen ausge-
bälgten Geier' and more lyrically: 'Es blüht die Welt in Todesbanden' [The world
blooms in bonds of death]. A cemetery is overlooked by a crucifix, on which, in
turn, sits a bird:

> Dort lächelt auf die Gräber nieder
> Mit himmlisch duldender Gebärde
> Vom Kreuz das höchste Bild der Erde;
> Ein Vogel drauf, sang seine Lieder. (L II, 309)

[There, with a gesture of heavenly forbearance, the earth's supreme image smiles
down from the Cross upon the graves; a bird upon it was singing its songs.]

It is not the Cross, but the figure of Christ, that is 'das höchste Bild der Erde'. But
the word 'Bild' does not necessarily imply that the sign has any referent. It may be
merely an image devised by the human imagination. That is suggested by the bird,
a symbol of life, perched on the Cross, and by the speaker's turning to Nature for
'Heilung' [healing] (incorporating and thus relativizing the religious word 'Heil'
[salvation]).

Elsewhere Lenau imagines the Cross as damaged or broken. In 'Der trübe
Wanderer' [The Gloomy Wanderer] (also entitled 'Trüber Gang' [Gloomy Walk];
1830–31), the speaker sees the Cross, planted on the shore, broken by the waves in
a high tide:

> Das Christuskreuz, vor dem in schönen Tagen
> Ein Kind ich, selig weinend, oft gekniet,
> Es hängt hinab vom Strande nun, zerschlagen,
> Darüber hin die Todeswelle zieht. (L I, 113)

[The Cross of Christ, before which, as a boy, I would often kneel in happy
times, weeping with bliss, now hangs down from the shore, shattered, as the
wave of death passes over it.]

The Cross itself, without the figure of Christ, is the subject of the famous poem
'Das Kreuz' (1840 or 1841):

> Ich seh ein Kreuz dort ohne Heiland ragen,
> Als hätte dieses kalte Herbsteswetter,
> Das stürmend von den Bäumen weht die Blätter,
> Das Gottesbild vom Stamme fortgetragen.
>
> Soll ich dafür den Gram, in tausend Zügen
> Rings ausgebreitet, in ein Bildnis kleiden?
> Soll die Natur ich, und ihr Todesleiden
> Dort an des Kreuzes leere Stätte fügen? (L II, 250)

[I see a Cross there rise without a Saviour, as though this cold autumn storm
that blows the leaves from the trees had borne the divine image away from
the trunk. Shall I instead clothe in a metaphor the sorrow that is displayed in
a thousand places? Shall I set Nature and her deadly sorrow in the empty place
on the Cross?]

Nature, once again, is pervaded by death. Its destructive forces are typified by the autumn wind, which sweeps away not only the leaves but apparently also the image of Christ, and hence mankind's attempts to imagine a religious consolation. But Nature is here both the destroyer and the victim, showing the grief caused by its own ravages. Lenau imagines Nature suffering on the Cross instead of Christ.

The idea of Nature's suffering occurs in other poems, such as 'Meeresstille' (previously 'Atlantica'; 1833):

> Trägt Natur auf allen Wegen
> Einen großen, ew'gen Schmerz,
> Den sie mir als Muttersegen
> Heimlich strömet in das Herz? (L I, 269)

[Does Nature bear on all her journeys a great, eternal pain, which she secretly infuses into my heart as her maternal blessing?]

This idea is also embodied in the legendary tale, 'Der traurige Mönch' (1836?), where a knight takes refuge, one stormy evening, in a ruined tower in Sweden which is supposed to be haunted by a sorrowful monk. Although the knight does not take the legend seriously, the monk does appear to him, and undeterred by the sign of the cross, turns on him a look of unutterable woe:

> Der große und geheime Schmerz,
> Der die Natur durchzittert,
> Den ahnen mag ein blutend Herz,
> Den die Verzweiflung wittert,
> Doch nicht erreicht — *der* Schmerz erscheint
> Im Aug' des Mönchs, der Reiter weint. (L II, 35)

[The great and secret pain that quivers through all Nature, that a bleeding heart may sense, that despair apprehends but does not attain — that is the pain that appears in the monk's eye; the horseman weeps.]

The sorrow conveyed by the monk soon drives the knight to drown himself, together with his horse.

How are we to understand this topos of Nature's suffering? Commentators have tried to fit it into Lenau's supposed pantheism. Walter Weiss draws attention to a remarkable passage in Schelling about the sadness of Nature:

> Dieß ist die allem endlichen Leben anklebende Traurigkeit, und wenn auch in Gott eine wenigstens beziehungsweise unabhängige Bedingung ist, so ist in ihm selber ein Quell der Traurigkeit, die aber nie zur Wirklichkeit kommt, sondern nur zur ewigen Freude der Ueberwindung dient. Daher der Schleier der Schwermuth, der über die ganze Natur ausgebreitet ist, die tiefe unzerstörliche Melancholie alles Lebens. Freude muß Leid haben, Leid in Freude verklärt werden.[47]

[This is the sadness that adheres to all finite life, and even if God is at least

---

47 'Philosophische Untersuchungen über das Wesen der menschlichen Freiheit und die damit zusammenhängenden Gegenstände' (1809), in *Schellings Werke*, ed. by Manfred Schröter (Munich: Beck, 1927), Vierter Hauptband: Schriften zur Philosophie der Freiheit 1804–1815, p. 291. Weiss, *Enttäuschter Pantheismus*, pp. 74–75, quotes part of this passage (noting the dialectic that is absent from Lenau), misattributing it to a different work by Schelling.

relatively independent, yet He himself contains a source of sadness which is never realized but only serves the eternal joy of overcoming. Hence the veil of despondency which is spread over the whole of Nature, the deep, indestructible melancholy of all life. Joy needs sorrow, sorrow must be transfigured in joy.]

However, this passage is very different from Lenau, both in its argumentative context and in its immediate emotional content. Schelling is explaining how human freedom is not only possible but necessary within a pantheistic universe, in which man is not identical with God (as claimed by Spinozism) but dependent on Him. The acceptance of our finitude as natural beings arouses sorrow, but its compensatory opposite is the joy that comes from approaching God through activity. This latter notion is foreign to Lenau. The tone of the passage is also much milder than the language of 'Der traurige Mönch', which speaks not just of sorrow but of intense pain pervading all of Nature.

For this concept there is a biblical reference point that was formerly familiar to Catholics and Protestants alike, namely Chapter 8 of St Paul's Letter to the Romans, where the suffering of creation is acknowledged: 'For we know that the whole creation groaneth and travaileth together in pain until now' (Rom. 8. 22); 'Dann wir wissen, daß alle Creatur seufftzen, und sich ängstigen noch immerdar.'[48] They took comfort from St Paul's suggestion that such suffering resembled the pains of childbirth and would help ultimately to bring about the deliverance of Creation 'from the bondage of corruption into the liberty of the glory of the kingdom of God' (Rom. 8. 21), and that the conflict in Nature was a side-effect of Adam's fall.[49] Tieck audaciously borrows St Paul's language in order to place 'die Seufzer und Klagen, die allenthalben in der ganzen Natur vernehmbar sind' [the groans and laments that are audible throughout Nature] within a narrative derived from *Naturphilosophie*, in which the organic world is explained as the inferior and moribund residue of past inorganic splendours.[50] Often, however, they placed the greatest emphasis on the destructive energies of Nature. Thus Mörike's poem 'Die Elemente' (1824), which has Romans 8. 19 as its epigraph, evokes the turmoil of the elements in the person of an unruly giant, though it anticipates a future when the elements will be reconciled with God and at peace with one another.[51]

---

48 *Das Neue Testament unsers HERRN und Heylands JEsu Christi, Nach der uralten gemeinen Lateinischen und von der Heil. Katholischen Kirch bewährten, und in derselbigen bishero allzeit gebrauchten Übersetzung* (Nuremberg, 1763). Luther's translation is significantly different: 'Denn wir wissen, daß alle Kreatur sehnet sich mit uns, und ängstet sich noch immerdar.'

49 See N. P. Williams, *The Ideas of the Fall and of Original Sin* (London: Longmans, Green, 1927), pp. 77, 157–59. For this motif in German literature, see Wilhelm Kühlmann, 'Das Ende der "Verklärung": Bibel-Topik und prädarwinistische Naturreflexion in der Literatur des 19. Jahrhunderts', *Jahrbuch der Deutschen Schiller-Gesellschaft*, 30 (1986), 417–52, with extensive bibliographical references.

50 'Der Runenberg', in Ludwig Tieck, *Werke*, ed. by Marianne Thalmann, 4 vols (Munich: Hanser, 1964), II, 77. Wolfdietrich Rasch, 'Blume und Stein: Zur Deutung von Ludwig Tiecks Erzählung *Der Runenberg*', in *The Discontinuous Tradition: Studies in German Literature in honour of Ernest Ludwig Stahl*, ed. by P. F. Ganz (Oxford: Clarendon Press, 1971), pp. 113–28, elucidates this aspect of the story (see especially pp. 122–26) but misses the Pauline language.

51 Eduard Mörike, *Sämtliche Werke*, ed. by Jost Perfahl, 2 vols (Munich: Winkler, 1967), I, 775–77.

IV

The author who develops this topos most fully is another Catholic, Annette von Droste-Hülshoff. An extended comparison between Lenau and Droste-Hülshoff would be rewarding. Both were troubled souls who expressed much religious uncertainty, Droste from the side of faith, Lenau from that of scepticism. The topos of suffering Nature finds expression in a late poem by Droste, 'Die ächzende Kreatur' [The Groans of Creation]. She was pressed to write it by her friend Christoph Bernhard Schlüter, a lecturer in philosophy at the Catholic Academy in Münster; but Schlüter, who was strictly orthodox in his views and thought she should write nothing but devotional poetry, was taken aback by the poem's uncompromising statement of the suffering present in Creation, culminating in the last two stanzas:

> Und dennoch giebt es eine Last
> Die Keiner fühlt und Jeder trägt
> So dunkel wie die Sünde fast
> Und auch im gleichen Schoß gehegt
> Er trägt sie wie den Druck der Luft
> Gefühlt vom kranken Leibe nur
> Bewußtlos wie den Fels die Kluft
> Trägt er die Mord an der Natur
>
> Das ist die Schuld des Mordes an
> Der Erde Lieblichkeit und Huld,
> An des Gethieres dumpfem Bann
> Ist es die tiefe, schwere Schuld,
> Und an dem Grimm, der es beseelt,
> Und an der List, die es befleckt
> Und an dem Schmerze, der es quält
> Und an dem Moder, der es deckt[.][52]

[And yet there is a burden that no one feels and everyone bears, almost as dark as sin and sheltered in the same womb; he bears it like the pressure of the air, which only the sick body feels; unconsciously, as the abyss bears the rock, he bears the murder of Nature.

That is the guilt of murdering the charm and grace of earth; it is the deep, heavy guilt of the torpid spell cast upon the animal kingdom, and of the fury that animates it, and of the cunning that pollutes it, and of the pain that tortures it, and of the putrefaction that covers it.]

Droste moves onto something harder to envisage, the guilt for the suffering of Creation, which we do not feel consciously except in unusual states like that evoked early in the poem ('Gefühlt vom kranken Leibe nur'), yet which weighs on us like the pressure of the atmosphere. The verb 'tragen' moves between an abstract sense (as in 'die Schuld tragen') and a directly physical sense of bearing a burden, as in a variant, 'Trägt er der Schöpfung Todeswunden' [He bears creation's deadly

---

52 Annette von Droste-Hülshoff, *Werke und Briefwechsel*, Historisch-kritische Ausgabe, ed. by Winfried Woesler (Tübingen: Niemeyer, 1978–), IV/I, 207–09.

wounds].[53] This implies that we are ourselves wounded, as a result of the injury which we have ourselves inflicted on Creation. We are unwittingly injured by our guilt in bringing about the fall of the natural world, in placing animals under their 'dumpfem Bann', and infusing them with the emotions — fury, cunning and pain — that presumably dominate their consciousness. The last stanza hammers home this message, beginning with a strikingly clumsy enjambement ('Das ist die Schuld des Mordes *an* | Der Erde Lieblichkeit und Huld'; my emphasis) which nevertheless works poetically by conveying a sense of urgency.

By comparison, Lenau's poetry seems more casual, playing with theological ideas rather than imaging an existential commitment to them and their consequences. There is, nevertheless, a wide overlap between his and Droste's poetic subject matter. Both are sufficiently rooted in Catholicism to draw back before the fantasies of a godless universe that preoccupied poets of the *Weltschmerz* generation such as Heine, Büchner and Grabbe. Karl S. Guthke notes that on the few occasions when Lenau evokes ideas of an absent or evil God, he places them in the mouth of Mephistopheles, who in *Faust* refers to God as 'der ewige Despot' and 'der alte Zwingherr' [the everlasting despot; the old autocrat] (L III, 129, 139).[54] The commonality between Lenau and Droste extends even to the way they imagine the end of the world. Droste, a keen amateur geologist, drew on the latest scientific speculations to envisage the earth, in the remote future, as a burnt-out desert ('Die Mergelgrube'; 1842).[55] In Lenau's 'Die Zweifler' (1831?) one of the speakers imagines God ultimately destroying the world by freezing it, with as much satisfaction as He originally took in creating it:

> Dann brütet auf dem Ocean die Nacht,
> Dann ist des Todes großes Werk vollbracht;
> Dann stockt und starrt zu Eis die grause Flut,
> Worin der Wunsch des finstern Gottes ruht;
> Er wandelt auf der Fläche und ermißt,
> Wie alles nun so still, so dunkel ist;
> Er lächelt dann voll selbstzufriedner Freude
> In seine Welt, in seine Nacht hinein,
> Und es erglänzt des Eises stille Haide
> Nur noch von seines Lächelns Wiederschein. (L I, 19)

[Then night will brood upon the ocean; then death's great work will be accomplished; then the hideous flood, in which the desire of the dark God rests, will freeze into solid ice; He walks upon the surface and beholds how all is now so silent and dark; then He smiles, full of joyous self-satisfaction, into His world, into His night, and the silent wasteland of ice is lit only by the reflection of His smile.]

53   Ibid., p. 666.
54   Karl S. Guthke, *Die Mythologie der entgötterten Welt: Ein literarisches Thema von der Aufklärung bis zur Gegenwart* (Göttingen; Vandenhoeck und Ruprecht, 1971), p. 175.
55   See Ritchie Robertson, 'Faith and Fossils: Annette von Droste-Hülshoff's poem "Die Mergelgrube"', in *Das schwierige 19. Jahrhundert: Germanistische Tagung zum 65. Geburtstag von Eda Sagarra im August 1998*, ed. by Jürgen Barkhoff, Gilbert J. Carr and Roger Paulin (Tübingen: Niemeyer, 2000), pp. 345–54.

Hugo Schmidt wrongly identifies the dark God here with Death, overlooking the fact that Lenau's fantasy still operates within a Christian conception of the Creation which is here reversed.[56] The destruction of the world is the counterpart of its creation. By extinguishing the stars, God has undone the original act of creating light. He is now a dark god, whose spirit again rests upon the waters, enjoying the absence of anything that might threaten the divine egotism and pleased to find his own face reflected in the ice that covers the globe.

In conclusion, Blumauer, Grillparzer and Lenau show the profound influence of the Austrian Enlightenment. To understand and appreciate poems that are not immediately accessible to the modern reader, we need to read them with some awareness of their authors' rhetorical training. If we do, we find a range of satirical and elegiac devices which express two aspects in particular of the Josephinist heritage. One is a confirmed opposition to the pretensions of the clericalist Catholic Church to political and intellectual authority (especially once the humiliations suffered by the papacy during the Revolutionary period had been erased by a settled policy of ultramontanism). The other is an attachment to Christian assumptions and images which proved more durable for these writers than for their Protestant counterparts.

---

56 Schmidt, *Nikolaus Lenau*, p. 30.

CHAPTER 14

The Complexities of Caroline Pichler:
Die Schweden in Prag (1827)

Caroline Pichler (1769–1843), famous in her day as poet, dramatist, and above all as a historical novelist, has barely begun to benefit from the current revival of interest in women writers of the past. Yet in the early nineteenth century she was not only the pre-eminent woman writer in Austria, but also at the centre of its social and intellectual life. The Swedish poet Per Atterbom, who visited Vienna in the winter of 1818–19, wrote that she and St Stephen's Cathedral were the two landmarks that attracted every visitor to Vienna.[1] By then, Caroline Pichler was the hostess of Vienna's most important literary salon, frequented by Beethoven, Schubert, and Grillparzer among many others, from 1802 to 1824. Visitors to Vienna — Ludwig Tieck, Zacharias Werner, the Schlegel brothers, Madame de Staël, Ottilie von Goethe — always made her acquaintance. Many years earlier, her parents had held one of the city's main salons in the 1780s, and as a girl she had met Haydn, Mozart, and all the luminaries of the Austrian Enlightenment.[2] Her literary career began when her husband, the civil servant Andreas Pichler, encouraged her to publish a collection of poems (*Gleichnisse*, 1800). He then persuaded her, despite her initial reluctance, to write for the theatre, and she had several historical dramas performed at the Hoftheater (now the Burgtheater). She subsequently turned to novels, which did most to establish her fame. Of her copious literary works — the collected edition runs to sixty volumes — the bulk consists of historical fiction. Her novel about early Christianity, *Agathokles: Kulturgeschichtlicher Roman aus der Römerzeit*

---

1   Per Daniel Amadeus Atterbom, *Ein Schwede reist nach Deutschland und Italien: Jugenderinnerungen eines romantischen Dichters und Kunstgelehrten aus den Jahren 1817 bis 1819*, ed. by Elmar Jansen (Weimar: Kiepenheuer, n.d. [1967]), p. 261.

2   On her parents' salon, see Roswitha Strommer, 'Wiener literarische Salons zur Zeit Joseph Haydns', in *Joseph Haydn und die Literatur seiner Zeit*, Jahrbuch für österreichische Kulturgeschichte, 6, ed. by Herbert Zeman (Eisenstadt: Selbstverlag des Instituts für österreichische Kulturgeschichte, 1976), pp. 97–121. Caroline Pichler's own social activities are recounted in detail in her *Denkwürdigkeiten aus meinem Leben*, ed. by Emil Karl Blümml, 2 vols (Munich: Georg Müller, 1914), henceforth cited in the text as D with volume and page number. The copious notes to Blümml's edition are an invaluable source of information about Pichler and many contemporaries. For a recent introduction to her work, see Barbara Becker-Cantarino and Gregory Wolf, 'Caroline Pichler', in *Major Figures of Nineteenth-Century Austrian Literature*, ed. by Donald G. Daviau (Riverside, CA: Ariadne Press, 1998), pp. 417–34.

[*Agathocles: A Novel about the Cultural History of Roman Times*] (1808), intended as a Christian reply to the sceptical portrayal in Gibbon's *Decline and Fall of the Roman Empire* (D I, 255), won praise from Goethe (D I, 393).[3] Most of her novels, however, follow the example of Walter Scott by seeking to bring the history of her native country to life. After her husband's death in 1837, she occupied her widowhood by writing her memoirs, published posthumously in 1844 as *Denkwürdigkeiten aus meinem Leben* [*Memorable Events of my Life*].

Not only have Pichler's imaginative works been neglected by recent scholarship, but some important studies of women's autobiographies in German have strangely overlooked Pichler's memoirs, perhaps because of their extreme length (over 800 pages).[4] Yet they are not only an invaluable source for the cultural history of her time, but also express some intriguing tensions. These tensions suffice to disprove the bland account of Pichler given in the substantial but rarely cited monograph by André Robert, who represents her, in contrast to such contemporary women writers as Rahel Varnhagen, as too placid to be really interesting: 'Cet élément de mystère a totalement fait défaut à Caroline Pichler. Tout dans sa vie fut parfaitement clair, absolument raisonnable' [This element of mystery was totally lacking in Caroline Pichler. Everything in her life was perfectly clear, absolutely reasonable].[5]

The most obvious tension is between Pichler's strikingly conservative views about women's allotted role, and her adoption of a literary role, that of patriotic historical novelist, for which the obvious exemplars were male. Instead of writing domestic fiction, like her friend Therese Huber, Pichler devoted herself, alongside her male friends Heinrich von Collin and Josef von Hormayr, to strengthening Austrian national consciousness through literature.

Pichler's conservatism is expressed with particular strength late in her memoirs, when she deplores 'das unselige Geschwätz von der Emanzipation der Frauen, dieser schrecklichsten Abirrung vom Pfade der Natur' [the dreadful talk about women's emancipation, that most frightful of deviations from the path of nature] (D II, 307). Even in her youth, she tells us elsewhere, she was convinced that women were naturally subordinate to men: 'Ich fühlte mich überzeugt, daß der notwendige Geschlechtscharakter und die Einrichtungen in der physischen wie in der moralischen und bürgerlichen Welt uns die untergeordnete Rolle mit Recht angewiesen haben' [I felt convinced that the necessary character of our sex and the structure of the physical as of the moral and social worlds rightly directed us to the subordinate role] (D I, 132). Women should always run the household. After all, men who attempt domestic tasks like cooking and sewing are always much inferior to women. But women are equal to men, perhaps even superior, in emotion, tact, self-control, and courage (ib.).

3   See the letter of 30 August 1812 from Goethe to Eleonore von Flies (a Viennese friend of Pichler, whom Goethe had met on holiday in Karlsbad), in Goethe, *Sämtliche Werke*, XXXIV, 94–96.

4   Magdalene Heuser, *Autobiographien von Frauen: Beiträge zu ihrer Geschichte* (Tübingen: Niemeyer, 1996); Mererid Puw Davies, Beth Linklater and Gisela Shaw, *Autobiography by Women in German* (Bern: Peter Lang, 2000).

5   André Robert, *L'Idée nationale autrichienne et les guerres de Napoléon: L'Apostolat du baron de Hormayr et le salon de Caroline Pichler* (Paris: Alcan, 1933), p. 342.

In particular, Pichler professes to dislike and avoid intellectual women, of the type that Madame de Staël called 'femmes supérieures' [superior women] (D I, 259). She says that she disliked the prospect of meeting a female writer because such people are seldom true women ('wahre Frauen'), that is, they cannot fit into a domestic environment (D II, 27). Yet Pichler's only example of an uncongenial intellectual woman is Caroline von Humboldt, who snubbed her, and whom she criticizes mainly for having a reputation as a coquette (D II, 26). The female writer who causes her apprehension on the occasion just mentioned is Caroline von Wolzogen, Schiller's sister-in-law and author of the novel *Agnes von Lilien*, who turns out to be extremely likeable. Even the formidable Madame de Staël, though tyrannical towards her companion August Wilhelm Schlegel, is pleasant once Pichler gets to know her (D I, 314–22).

Pichler acknowledges the contradiction in her views:

> Es wird manchem, der dies liest, seltsam auffallen, eine Frau, welche selbst schreibt, so über ihre Kunstgefährtinnen reden zu hören; aber es war nun einmal meine individuelle Ansicht, und daß sie sich nicht auf alle erstreckte, denen die Musen ihre Gaben mitgeteilt, läßt sich daraus erkennen, daß Frau von Schlegel, von Weißenthurn, Fräulein Artner und andere schriftstellernde Frauen, die ich später kennen lernte, mir vom ersten Augenblicke an teuer waren und blieben. (D II, 28)

> [Many people who read this will find it strange to hear a woman who herself writes speaking thus about her female fellow-artists; but that was just my individual opinion, and that it did not extend to all women gifted by the Muses can be seen from the fact that Frau von Schlegel, Frau von Weissenthurn, Fräulein Artner and other writing women whom I later got to know were and remained dear to me from the very first moment.]

Despite the somewhat disparaging tone of the phrase 'schriftstellernde Frauen' ('writing ' or even 'scribbling women'), these friends were among the most notable writers of their day. Dorothea Schlegel was not only the wife of Friedrich Schlegel but the author of the novel *Florentin*. Johanna von Weissenthurn was a successful playwright.[6] The poet Therese von Artner, who published under the pseudonym 'Theone ', was a particularly close friend of Pichler, who recounts how at their very first meeting she recognized in her a kindred soul ('eine gleichgestimmte Seele'; D II, 18). Some of Pichler's friends even pursued science, such as Baroness von Matt, who studied astronomy (D I, 408). Female friendship was so important to her that she used to spend several weeks every summer with Therese von Artner, Maria von Zay, and other female friends on or near von Zay's Hungarian estate. She also had a long correspondence with the novelist Therese Huber, not only about literary but also about personal matters such as the progress of her daughter, even though she and Huber never met.[7] All this, as Susanne Kord has argued, shows a degree of independence that hardly fits the subordinate role assigned by the elderly and

6 See Ian F. Roe, 'The Comedies of Johanna von Weissenthurn', *Austrian Studies*, 9 (1998), 41–57.

7 *Schriftstellerinnen und Schwesterseelen: Der Briefwechsel zwischen Therese Huber (1764–1829) und Karoline Pichler (1769–1843)*, ed. by Brigitte Leuschner (Marburg: Tectum, 1995).

conservative Pichler to women.[8] Neither does the obvious fact that Pichler herself devoted her life, from the age of thirty onwards, to the prolific, even compulsive production of literature. Why does Pichler insist that most intellectual women are odious viragos, when her text makes it clear that the opposite is the case?

While Pichler's highly conservative view of women can in part be attributed to old age and low spirits, that does not explain its incongruity with her actual narrative. Susanne Kord has argued that Pichler's conservatism is simply a masquerade, but such a description makes it sound arbitrary and wilful. Pichler's insistence on her 'individual opinion' (D II, 28), however strange or indeed unfounded it may appear, sounds more like an effort at denial. What she is denying may come to light if we examine the portrayal of Pichler's mother, Charlotte Hieronymus, who married the distinguished civil servant Franz Sales von Greiner. Unlike her husband, whose tastes were literary and musical, Charlotte had a strong interest in the sciences, particularly in astronomy. She disliked poetry and history, because they could not provide definite truths. She did, however, study the religions and mythologies of various nations, and came to the conclusion (strangely anticipating the matriarchal theories of Bachofen and Engels) that women had been destined by nature and providence to rule society, but had had their position usurped by the superior physical strength of the male sex. She read feminist writings, insofar as such things existed: Caroline had to read aloud to her from a French translation of Mary Wollstonecraft's *A Vindication of the Rights of Women*.

Why then was Charlotte not a role model to her daughter? Why is Caroline so anxious to distance herself from her mother? She goes so far as to assert: 'selbst meiner Mutter Ansichten von dem unbilligen Verhältnis, worin wir gegen die Männer stehen, von den Anmaßungen, die sie sich im bürgerlichen und häuslichen Leben über uns erlaubt haben sollten, von den sogenannten Rechten des Weibes fanden keinen Anklang in meiner Seele' [even my mother's views about our unfair relation to men, about the dominance that they are supposed to have claimed over us in social and domestic life, found no echo in my soul] (D I, 131–32). This is the more surprising since Caroline, by her own account, was far from docile by nature. She was an extremely lively child who people said should have been a boy (D I, 34), and had such a vivid imagination that her parents had her taught mathematics in order to restrain it (D I, 38).

Something very important is not mentioned in the memoirs themselves. In contrast to Goethe, whose mixture of truth and fiction ('Dichtung und Wahrheit') she disapproves of, Pichler undertakes to tell only the truth, but also to pass over some matters in discreet silence (D I, 169–70). Thanks to the editor of the memoirs, Emil Karl Blümml, we know that the Greiners' marriage was troubled. Charlotte von Greiner had either a love affair, or a relationship close enough to cause scandal, with Lorenz Leopold Haschka, one of her daughter's tutors (and later famous for writing the text of the Austrian national anthem, 'Gott erhalte Franz den Kaiser'

---

8   Susanne Kord, '"Und drinnen waltet die züchtige Hausfrau"? Caroline Pichler's Fictional Auto/biographies', *Women in German Yearbook*, 8 (1993), 141–58.

[God save Emperor Franz] to music by Haydn).[9] Haschka actually moved into the Greiner household (along with an aunt, a tutor and a lady companion for young Caroline), and this enlargement of the household, we are told mysteriously, led to 'Verdrießlichkeiten' [irritations] and even 'manches Unglück' [much misfortune] (D I, 56). The only clue Pichler gives to the nature of these troubles and misfortunes is that she quotes from Goethe's *Die Wahlverwandtschaften* [*Elective Affinities*] — a novel which, in keeping with her conservatism, she claims to dislike — on the dangers that can follow when one adds members to a household, and we remember that in the novel the addition of Ottilie to the household breaks up the marriage between Eduard and Charlotte. Disapproval of her mother's affair perhaps also lies behind her regret that she should have been exposed in her youth to many literary works dealing with extra-marital relationships such as Wieland's *Oberon* (D I, 92). We can only speculate about the distressing effect these domestic troubles had on the young Caroline, though she recounts a series of disappointments in love, which may suggest her anxiety to leave home. But we can see why Charlotte von Greiner represented in some ways a negative model of the intellectual woman.

Fortunately, Pichler had another role model in the person of the Empress Maria Theresia. Her mother, an orphan, had as a child been taken into the Empress's service, and when her unusual intelligence was noticed, she was given the task of reading aloud to the Empress. For this purpose she was taught French, Italian and Latin. Hers was no easy service: it had to be performed kneeling, and it continued for hours on end, even after the Empress was in bed. In addition, Charlotte Hieronymus helped to do Maria Theresia's hair, another laborious task. The Empress could be irritable and inconsiderate. Physically robust, and fond of fresh air, she kept windows open even in the coldest weather, so that snow sometimes fell onto the page from which Charlotte was reading (D I, 18). Her daughter thinks that her prolonged reading, often by candle-light, was partly responsible for the bad eyesight and eventual blindness that afflicted Charlotte in later years (D I, 146). Nevertheless, Caroline is in no doubt that Maria Theresia was a truly great personality ('dieser wahrhaft großen Frau'; D I, 19), especially for her loyalty to the memory of her husband, even though he had made her unhappy by his various love affairs. She combined the virtues of a monarch and a woman: 'so steht Maria Theresia, welche als Regentin einen der ersten Plätze in der Reihe der großen Monarchen einnimmt, als Frau nicht minder groß und erhaben vor uns' [thus Maria Theresia, who as ruler assumes one of the first positions in the series of great monarchs, appears no less great and sublime as a woman] (D I, 28). Maria Theresia serves as a model for the practice of public duties along with femininity and morality. Moreover, Maria Theresia was seen during and after her lifetime as a maternal figure. She was often described as 'Mutter ihrer Völker' [mother of her peoples].[10] She herself had many children (listed by Pichler, D I, 54), and she used

9 The evidence is examined by Gustav Gugitz, 'Lorenz Leopold Haschka', *Jahrbuch der Grillparzer-Gesellschaft*, 17 (1907), 32–127.

10 See Wolfram Mauser, 'Maria Theresia: "Mutter der Völker". Legendenbildung als Legitimation der Macht', in his *Konzepte aufgeklärter Lebensführung: Literarische Kultur im frühmodernen Deutschland* (Würzburg: Königshausen & Neumann, 2000), pp. 137–48.

her motherhood to advantage on the famous occasion (mentioned also by Pichler, D I, 17) when she presented her six-month-old son Joseph to the Hungarian Diet in September 1741 in order to appeal for their support. When Charlotte von Greiner in later life made an annual visit to the court, accompanied by young Caroline, the Empress treated the little girl with maternal kindness (D I, 55–56). Maria Theresia thus serves in the autobiography as an ideal (though not idealized) mother, in contrast to Pichler's actual mother.

Not only did Maria Theresia fulfil an exemplary feminine role as loyal wife and mother; she also, of course, combined it with a public role as Empress. How a woman can play a public role is a key problem for Pichler. It is thematized in her writings, notably in the novel *Die Schweden in Prag* [*The Swedes in Prague*] (1827), which will be discussed later. It also underlies her career. She wrote not on domestic themes but on national topics drawn from Austrian history. Her Austrian patriotism is strongly apparent in her autobiography. She deplores the tendency to disparage Austria, shown by German visitors such as Clemens Brentano (D I, 424). (There is doubtless some subliminal recollection here of the annoyance caused in Vienna by the pejorative account of it given in the travel book by the Berlin Enlightener Friedrich Nicolai.)[11] After Napoleon's troops defeated an Austrian army at Ulm in 1805, Vienna was occupied and the Pichlers had to have French officers quartered on them. Pichler felt humiliated. She hated the French troops bitterly (D I, 279). After the Austrian campaign against France in the spring of 1809 had ended in a futile victory at Aspern and a decisive defeat at Wagram, Pichler saw Napoleon at Schönbrunn and wished that some Tyrolean sharpshooter would assassinate him, as Wilhelm Tell assassinated Gessler (D I, 345). She complicates her portrayal of femininity by telling us that she never cries on the occasions that usually produce tears in women, such as her wedding, but only when her patriotic feelings are aroused, as they were by the later Austrian victories of 1813 and 1814 (D I, 190).[12]

Pichler shared this intense patriotism particularly with her friends Therese von Artner, Heinrich von Collin and Josef von Hormayr.[13] Artner wrote a heroic poem, *Die Schlacht von Aspern* [*The Battle of Aspern*], but its publication was forbidden by Metternich; the manuscript is lost, and the poem is only known from the extracts which appeared in journals.[14] Collin was a distinguished dramatist, notable

11   Friedrich Nicolai, *Beschreibung einer Reise durch Deutschland und die Schweiz im Jahre 1781: Nebst Bemerkungen über Gelehrsamkeit, Industrie, Religion und Sitten*, 8 vols (Berlin and Stettin: no pub., 1783–87).

12   On Pichler's nationalism, see Malcolm Garrard, '"Der Herrscher geheiligtes Haus": Caroline Pichler and Austrian Identity', in *Women Writers of the Age of Goethe VIII*, ed. by Margaret Ives (Department of Modern Languages, Lancaster University, 1996), pp. 1–35; Anke Gilleir, 'Geschlecht, Religion und Nation: Caroline Pichlers *Agathokles* als Antwort auf den Nationalismus der Napoleonischen Ära in Österreich', *Colloquia Germanica*, 35 (2002), 125–44; Karin Baumgartner, 'Staging the German Nation: Caroline Pichler's *Heinrich von Hohenstaufen* and *Ferdinand II.*', *Modern Austrian Literature*, 37.1–2 (2004), 1–20.

13   See Robert; Carl Glossy, 'Hormayr und Karoline Pichler', *Jahrbuch der Grillparzer-Gesellschaft*, 12 (1902), 212–343.

14   See Wynfrid Kriegleder, 'Therese von Artner und ihr vaterländisches Heldengedicht *Die Schlacht von Aspern*', in *Deutsche Sprache und Kultur, Literatur und Presse in Westungarn/Burgenland*, ed. by Wynfrid Kriegleder and Andrea Seidler (Bremen: edition lumière, 2004), pp. 249–66.

especially for *Regulus* (1802), whose hero lays down his life for his fatherland Rome in an exalted discourse of sacrifice that anticipates the Prussian patriotism of Kleist's *Prinz Friedrich von Homburg*. Hormayr, a historian, compiled a series of seventy-six biographies of Austrian rulers, statesmen, generals and scholars entitled *Österreichischer Plutarch [Austrian Plutarch]* (1807–14) which was intended to awaken Austrian national consciousness and provide material for artists and poets. He wanted to include a biography of Pichler, but she refused permission (D I, 570). She testifies, however, to Hormayr's effectiveness in inducing people to write on national ('vaterländisch') subjects. Having herself begun, like Collin, by writing a play on a Roman topic (*Germanicus*), she turned to German history with *Heinrich von Hohenstauffen*. When the tide of events had turned against Napoleon, this play was performed in the presence of the entire Austrian Court for the benefit of those wounded at the battle of Leipzig in 1813, with the prologue spoken by Johanna von Weissenthurn; when the curtain rose, a portrait of the Emperor was displayed, and the national anthem was sung (D II, 4). Pichler had less success with her next effort, *Ferdinand der Zweite*, a play intended to rehabilitate the seventeenth-century Emperor Ferdinand II who was notorious for his intolerance. It fell foul of the censorship, for the same reason as Grillparzer's *König Ottokar* a few years later — because it was thought that the unflattering portrayal of the Bohemians would irritate their modern descendants.[15] After Austria's campaign against France had ended in a humiliating peace treaty, and Metternich had helped to reconcile the two countries by arranging Napoleon's marriage to the Archduchess Marie Louise, any interest in politics or history was suspect, and patriotism in particular suggested a dangerous interest in liberty. The unfortunate Hormayr was imprisoned for over a year for trying to stir up a popular insurrection in the Tyrol; after his release he found himself marginalized, and was eventually obliged to seek his fortune in Germany.

Pichler turned to novels, which could sustain interest in the past without seeking, like drama, to have any inflammatory effect. Her imagination had been stirred at an early age by the novels of chivalry such as *Herrmann von Unna, Elisabeth von Toggenburg*, and *Walter von Montbarry*, which were published anonymously but were later known to be the work of Benedikte Naubert (D I, 103). Around 1820 she read Walter Scott's poems and novels, and was impressed not only by their evocations of the past but by their psychological insight and the author's kindly and generous personality (D II, 68–69). She contrasts Scott with Byron, whose display of wild passions aroused in her both fascination and horror, later succeeded by pity for his inner turmoil ('Zerrissenheit'; D II, 70). But since she translated Byron's *The Corsair* into German, one can fairly surmise that the fascination she felt was very strong and that in her memoirs she is seeking to minimize it by playing off Byron against Scott.

Her reading of Scott led Pichler to write a series of historical novels, beginning with *Die Belagerung Wiens [The Siege of Vienna]*. She completed it in June 1824, and it was published the same summer (a rapidity that modern publishers and authors might

---

15   For a brief account of Pichler's plays, and full bibliographical details, see Susanne Kord, *Ein Blick hinter den Kulissen: Deutschsprachige Dramatikerinnen im 18. und 19. Jahrhundert* (Stuttgart: Metzler, 1992), pp. 155–56, 415–16.

well envy). There followed *Die Schweden in Prag* (1827), *Die Wiedereroberung von Ofen* [*The Reconquest of Buda*] (1829), and *Elisabeth von Guttenstein: Eine Familiengeschichte aus der Zeit des Österreichischen Erbfolgekrieges* [*Elisabeth von Guttenstein: A Family History from the Period of the Austrian War of Succession*] (1835). All these are based on the study of history (though of secondary rather than primary sources) and on close acquaintance with the topography. Thus *Die Schweden in Prag* was based on Pichler's extended visit to her daughter in Prague in 1825, and when planning *Die Wiedereroberung von Ofen* she paid a special visit to Budapest.

The contradictions and ambivalences traced hitherto in Pichler's autobiography find literary expression in *Die Schweden in Prag*. This was among her most successful novels. It was translated twice into English, once into French, and also adapted as a romantic opera. Set during the siege of Prague by Swedish troops in October 1648, immediately before the end of the Thirty Years' War, it turns on the question how a woman can intervene in historical events. Pichler's conception of the possibilities open to women is divided between the two main female characters, Johanna Vorritsch and Helene von Berka, who are both attracted to the hero Hynko von Waldstein (a fictitious nephew of the great Wallenstein). In some respects the contrast between them follows familiar stereotypes. Johanna is auburn-haired, gentle, quiet, middle-class. Helene is of noble descent, though poor, being the orphaned daughter of an officer, and is dark, intelligent, ambitious, passionate, and proud. Johanna, like her namesake in Schiller's *Die Jungfrau von Orleans*, takes a hand in history only when events draw her out of her domestic setting. By plying a Swedish commander with drink, she discovers the Swedes' plans for attacking the Old Town of Prague, and single-handed sends up a flare to warn the defenders when the attack is imminent.

Much more narrative space, however, is devoted to Helene, who can fairly claim to be the novel's central character. Already a secret Protestant, she forms a passionate relationship with a renegade Bohemian, now in Swedish service, called Odowalsky. The name, somewhat unlikely for a Bohemian, also comes from Schiller, being that of a conspirator in the unfinished play *Demetrius*. Pichler's Odowalsky is unscrupulous, amoral, and tortured by unsatisfied ambition; he betrays Prague to the Swedes, enabling them to gain possession of the Kleinseite (the area across the river from the Old Town), and is indifferent to the massacres which the Swedish troops inflict on the population. He is clearly a Byronic figure, reminiscent of the Corsair, whom Byron describes as follows:

> Fear'd, shunn'd, belied, ere youth had lost her force,
> He hated man too much to feel remorse,
> And thought the voice of wrath a sacred call,
> To pay the injuries of some on all.[16]

This reminds us of how Byron's poetry had both fascinated and horrified Pichler when she encountered it a few years earlier.

When we look more closely at Helene, we hear further echoes from Pichler's

16 Lord Byron, *Poetical Works*, ed. by Frederick Page, rev. by John D. Jump (Oxford: Oxford University Press, 1970), p. 281.

own life. Helene's uncle says to her in annoyance: 'von Jugend auf sagte ich, daß an dir ein Bube verdorben sey'.[17] Pichler tells us that in her childhood people said she should have been a boy (D I, 34). Rather than Pichler, however, Helene resembles Pichler's mother. Charlotte Hieronymus, like Helene, was a Protestant. She was likewise the daughter of an officer, and taken into a noble household when orphaned. Helene shares her fondness for the sciences, subjects deemed unsuitable for a woman, in which Helene is instructed by an Utraquist priest. And Helene's illicit and passionate affair with Odowalsky recalls the relationship with Haschka that Charlotte developed after her marriage to Greiner. In short, Helene embodies those aspects of femininity which did not fit into the conservative portrayal given by Pichler when she came to write her autobiography and which were disturbingly represented by her mother.

These overtones indicate that there is much more to the novel than an array of simple stereotypes.[18] A sympathetic critic, Barbara Becker-Cantarino, has praised the psychological subtlety of Pichler's novels.[19] That quality is amply apparent in the presentation of Helene. It is given more scope by the fact that whereas conventionally a male hero finds himself torn between two women, Hynko in fact loses interest in Helene quite early in the novel on discovering her relationship with Odowalsky, whereas Helene becomes more interested in him as her relationship with Odowalsky comes under strain. Thus Helene moves into the centre of the novel and becomes its psychologically most complex character.

One example of Pichler's subtlety is at the party given by the Governor of Bohemia in Volume I. Domestic novels often use social occasions, such as parties or dances, as the background to intense private relationships. Pichler imports this device into her historical novel in order to interweave private emotional tensions with political intrigue. Helene and Hynko are both present at the party, and Helene, who is still attracted to him despite her clandestine affair with Odowalsky, continually but unsuccessfully seeks an opportunity of urging him to escape from Prague before the impending Swedish attack, which only she knows about. Hynko meanwhile, having learned of her relationship with Odowalsky, is moody and reserved, and does his best to avoid her. Emotional tensions are conveyed even better in the dramatic confrontation between Helene and Odowalsky in Volume II. By now the Kleinseite has been occupied by the Swedes and the relationship between Helene and Odowalsky is public. Having believed that Hynko was killed in the attack, Helene has now been thrown into turmoil by learning that he is still alive. She confronts Odowalsky, who demands to know why she bought a cloak and brooch, and is angry on learning that they were mementos of Hynko. The background to their quarrel is that Helene wants to be an equal partner in Odowalsky's enterprises, while he, being in any case frustrated by what he considers insufficient recognition

17   Pichler, *Die Schweden in Prag*, 3 vols (Vienna: Anton Pichler, 1828), II, 89.

18   The recent discussion of the novel by Waltraud Maierhofer, *Hexen — Huren — Heldenweiber: Bilder des Weiblichen in Erzähltexten über den Dreißigjährigen Krieg* (Cologne: Böhlau, 2005), pp. 147–60, is confined to its use of stereotypes.

19   Becker-Cantarino, 'Caroline Pichler und die Frauendichtung', *Modern Austrian Literature*, 12.3–4 (1979), 1–23 (p. 19).

from the Swedish commander for his betrayal of Prague, wants her only to provide emotional support. He sums up their conflict in the words: 'Du willst herrschen, du willst die Vertraute, wohl gar die Lenkerinn meiner Handlungen und Absichten seyn; ich aber bedarf eines liebenden Weibes' [You want to dominate, you want to be the confidante, perhaps even the controller of my actions and plans, but what I need is a loving woman].[20] Thus Pichler indicates that Helene, whatever her ambitions, can play only a subordinate part in historical events, not because of some predestined natural law, but because of the actual behaviour of men and the conflict between men's and women's emotional needs.

The third volume becomes somewhat melodramatic. Odowalsky's violent temperament, which leads him to express his frustration in plans for revenge against Hynko and Johanna, estranges Helene from him and makes her encourage advances from the Rheingraf Carl Gustav, thereby giving Odowalsky grounds for jealousy and further violence. Johanna, in order to save the Governor of Bohemia from maltreatment by the Swedes, confesses that she lit the flare, and is threatened with execution, from which Hynko and Helene both independently try to rescue her; Hynko gets there first. Odowalsky is killed. Johanna, quite gratuitously, is revealed as not a middle-class girl at all but as the long-lost daughter of the Swedish commander Count Königsmark. When the siege of Prague is lifted and peace is restored by the signing of the Treaty of Westphalia, she and Hynko marry, while Helene disappears towards Dresden. Some years afterwards she turns up in Stockholm, married to an elderly Swedish nobleman but carrying on an intrigue with the Rheingraf. Even in this volume, however, the focus is on the complicated emotions of Helene, rather than on the firm but simple courage shown by Johanna.

As the intricacies of the plot (here reduced to the barest summary) suggest, the complex Helene, in contrast to the simple Johanna, fails to fit into a conventional narrative pattern. Johanna's story has a simple and predictable narrative shape. Torn by historical circumstances from her domestic role as her father's helper, she reveals her courage and resourcefulness, only to return to a domestic role as Hynko's wife and mother of his child. Thus her story ends in closure of a very familiar kind. Helene's story lacks any such clear shape. The oscillation of her emotions between Odowalsky and Hynko leads to indecision and inconsistency which are psychologically plausible but also incompatible with the simple pattern of a conventional narrative. While Johanna's actions — sending up the flare, and later releasing the Governor by confessing that she did so — are straightforward and successful, Helene's plans repeatedly go awry. Thus she buys Hynko's cloak and brooch, believing that he is dead, only to find that she is mistaken and has aroused Odowalsky's jealousy to no purpose; she tries to release Johanna from prison, only to find the cell already empty; and her relationship with Odowalsky founders on his violence, secrecy, and mistrust, even before his death. Instead of reaching closure, her story peters out into uncertainty: we know nothing about the husband she finds in Sweden, nor about the intrigues she is pursuing there. Narratively, this can be seen as a condemnation of her: the woman who rejects the proper limits

---

20 Pichler, *Die Schweden in Prag*, II, 103.

of female action is denied any coherent story. But it can also be claimed that by refusing to fit into a conventional narrative pattern, Helene's experiences gain yet more verisimilitude. A reality effect results which makes Helene appear living and unpredictable, precisely because, unlike Johanna, she is not confined within any predictable plot.

Caroline Pichler's choice of the historical novel as her preferred genre not only gave her something of a public role, but also helped to release her imagination. The tensions that find expression in the novel — between admiration and disapproval of the transgressive femininity represented by her mother and Helene; between the humanity of Scott and the emotional turbulence of Byron — might well have been harder to articulate if Pichler had written domestic novels set in her present.[21] Instead, by transferring her conflicts to a period two centuries in the past, she was able to explore them with greater freedom. While her autobiography expresses, not without some strain, the official anti-feminism with which the elderly Pichler chose to align herself, *Die Schweden in Prag* discloses the tensions that underlay Pichler's conservative stance.

Susanne Kord has argued that readers should not take at face value the conservative fictions by which women writers such as Pichler and her circle adjusted their image to suit conventional expectations. Nor should this self-presentation deter us from reading their work with as open a mind as possible. In Pichler's case, as I have tried to show, we find her venturing into a genre (the historical novel as developed by Scott) and a subject matter (patriotic activity) that were conventionally deemed to be masculine territory. Her contact with Maria Theresia, however, had taught her that a woman could under certain circumstances be a historical actor without violating accepted ideals of femininity. But her mother served to illustrate how easily a strong-willed woman with intellectual aspirations could be led into violating those ideals. Pichler resolved the tension between these two role models — the one positive, the other tempting but predominantly negative — by playing them off against each other within an elaborate historical novel, and thereby implicitly acknowledging also her own fascination with the turbulent Byronic character represented in different ways by Helene and Odowalsky. Her choice of genre simultaneously allowed Pichler to make a symbolic intervention in her nation's destiny and to explore the complexities surrounding women's participation in national history.

---

21   Kord, '"Und drinnen waltet"', pp. 151–52.

PART III

The Nineteenth Century

CHAPTER 15

Hoffmann's *Die Elixiere des Teufels* and the Lasting Appeal of Conspiracy Theories

Conspiracy Theories and Fiction

The legacies bequeathed by Romanticism to the present include a fascination with conspiracy theories. This term can refer both to the malign plots readily ascribed by the public to governments of every political shade, and also to the belief in an international, invisible conspiracy, organized from a hidden nerve-centre by a small group of plotters who control a network of cells and agents scattered across the world. The latter belief, which is my main concern in this paper, has usefully been called 'conspiracism'.[1] Conspiracist beliefs not only flourished in the eighteenth century but provided the foundation for a genre of fiction, the 'Geheimbundroman' or secret-society novel, which in turn was adopted and transformed by Romantic writers, notably E. T. A. Hoffmann. The purpose of this paper is to take a fresh look at Hoffmann's conspiratorial masterpiece, his novel *Die Elixiere des Teufels* (1815–16), by placing it in a perspective suggested by some recent discussions of conspiracy theories.

Conspiracism may be attached to real organizations, such as the Communist International, the Catholic Church, or al-Qaeda. It detects the hand of such organizations in events, often with little or no evidence, as when terrorist acts are promptly ascribed by the media to al-Qaeda or groups linked with al-Qaeda. Conspiracism can also conjure up conspiratorial organizations which are imaginary: thus the *Protocols of the Elders of Zion*, a fabrication forged by the Tsarist police, published in Western Europe immediately after the First World War, soon discredited, yet widely current even at the present day, claim to report the plans for world domination drawn up by a secret Jewish organization comprehending both right-wing capitalists and left-wing revolutionaries.

It is easy, and often right, to laugh at conspiracy theories. But our justified scepticism should not deter us from regarding conspiracism as a significant and durable cultural phenomenon. If we look back through the centuries, we find that strikingly similar fantasies have attached themselves to an astonishing variety of real and imaginary bodies. These include the Knights Templar, a military order

---

1 Daniel Pipes, *Conspiracy: how the paranoid style flourishes and where it comes from* (New York: Free Press, 1997), p. 22.

established in 1128 but broken up, charged with devil-worship and obscene practices, and dispossessed of their wealth by Philip the Fair of France early in the fourteenth century. The witch craze which claimed, not millions of victims as sometimes alleged, but certainly thousands, in many parts of early modern Europe, often charged its victims with forming an international society. In the aftermath of the Reformation, religious sects were often represented as an international conspiracy. Thus in Catholic polemics against Protestant sects, such as Antoine Varillas's *Histoire des révolutions arrivées dans l'Europe en matière de religion* (1686), Calvinists were described as a secret society meeting at night, with passwords, and the whole of Protestantism as 'une conjuration pour abolir tout ensemble la Religion Catholique et la Monarchie Françoise'.[2] Particular opprobrium attached to the Society of Jesus, which was established on the lines of military hierarchy and discipline and soon became an instrument of the Counter-Reformation, drawing its recruits from many countries and classes; it was said to be a monolithic organization, directly subservient to the Pope, ruled by iron rationality and operating with zombie-like obedience, devoted to gaining wealth through its members' influence over the well-to-do and political power by providing confessors to kings and princes, and responsible for many political assassinations.[3] Fear of Jesuits did not diminish when the Society was officially dissolved in 1773, for its members then became ex-Jesuits and doubly dangerous because invisible. The re-establishment of the Society in 1814 reanimated these fears, which remained powerful in many countries throughout the nineteenth century. These fears, particularly fear of Jesuits as an international conspiratorial society, provided a template for subsequent anxieties attached to Freemasons, Illuminati, international Jewry, Socialists, Communists, and many other targets.[4]

The persistence and adaptability of conspiracism suggest that we should not consider it simply a series of mistaken beliefs. Rather, these mistaken beliefs are the expression of an underlying mind-set or intellectual disposition; they have the imaginative appeal and carry the emotional conviction that is characteristic of myths. Hence one of the best-known historical studies of eighteenth-century conspiracism calls secret societies the subject of a 'mythology'. Mythologies, as Rachel Bowlby has recently said, are 'both inescapable and ubiquitous; they are the implicit explanatory stories through which we make sense of the world, and also the kinds of realistic or likely stories through which, at any one time or in any particular culture, we experience and narrate our own and others' lives'.[5]

Mythologies are thus extended fictions, and conspiracism provides the material for much literary fiction, especially popular fiction. Jesuit and Jewish conspirators

2   Quoted in Amos Hofman, 'The Origins of the Theory of the *philosophe* Conspiracy', *French History*, 2 (1988), 152–72 (pp. 164–65).

3   See Peter Burke, 'The Black Legend of the Jesuits: An Essay in the History of Social Stereotypes', in *Christianity and Community in the West: Essays for John Bossy*, ed. by Simon Ditchfield (Aldershot: Ashgate, 2001), pp. 165–82.

4   See Johannes Rogalla von Bieberstein, *Die These von der Verschwörung, 1776–1945: Philosophen, Freimaurer, Juden, Liberale und Sozialisten als Verschwörer gegen die Sozialordnung* (Bern: Peter Lang, 1976).

5   Rachel Bowlby, *Freudian Mythologies: Greek Tragedies and Modern Identities* (Oxford: Oxford University Press, 2007), p. 8.

have provided material for innumerable thrillers. One of the enduring bestsellers in Germany is Gustav Freytag's *Soll und Haben* (1855), in which the stolid German hero has an evil but much more interesting shadow-self in the villainous Jew Veitel Itzig. A comparable bestseller in nineteenth-century France is *Le Juif errant* (1844–45) by Eugène Sue, which, contrary to what one might expect, turns on the machinations of Jesuits. Its main character is the Jesuit Rodin whose ambition is to become Pope. By his indomitable will, power of dissimulation, and gift for psychological manipulation, he manages to induce all seven descendants of the Wandering Jew to commit suicide in the hope that the vast sum thus left without an heir will accrue to the Society of Jesus. From Victorian Britain one could mention a number of thrillers turning on Jesuits, perhaps the best being *Father Eustace: A Tale of the Jesuits* (1847) by Frances Trollope, mother of the more famous Anthony. Frances Trollope gets beyond the standard charges of villainy and gives a sympathetic psychological study of a young Jesuit's emotional condition. He falls in love with his charge, yet is obliged to persuade her to become a nun so that the Society may acquire her fortune.[6] At the present day, we may think of the popularity of Dan Brown's *The Da Vinci Code*, a page-turner which gives a highly distorted representation of the Catholic society Opus Dei as the vehicle for a millennia-old conspiracy. Beside it we may set a novel of infinitely greater sophistication and learning, Umberto Eco's *Foucault's Pendulum* (1988), which offers an enthralling tongue-in-cheek exploration of a range of conspiratorial fantasies, from the Templars to the *Protocols*; its central characters, fantasists who become obsessed with a conspiratorial fiction of their own making, eventually have to accept that what seemed a crucial document is nothing more than a medieval laundry-list. Hoffmann's *Die Elixiere des Teufels* is another, highly sophisticated conspiratorial narrative.

Conspiracism and the History of Mentalities

Given that conspiracy theories and conspiratorial fictions have had such a long life, what justification is there for associating either of them with Romanticism in particular? Romanticism followed a series of events which have plausibly been claimed as a watershed in the history of conspiracism. The Illuminati were a radical offshoot of Freemasonry, dedicated to spreading the atheism and materialism of such Enlightenment *philosophes* such as Helvétius, and to replacing the power of kings and aristocrats with some form of democratic government. Though these principles were indeed held by the founder of the Illuminati, Adam Weishaupt, there was no chance of their ever being put into practice: the Illuminati never had more than about 650 members, and attracted few of the prominent figures of the time. Concern about their activities led the Elector of Bavaria in 1785 to forbid Illuminism and Freemasonry on his territories and to order a raid on Weishaupt's premises, where some incriminating letters were found that confirmed suspicions

---

6   For these and more examples, see Ritchie Robertson, 'Jesuits, Jews, and Thugs: Myths of Conspiracy and Infiltration from Dickens to Thomas Mann', in *In the Embrace of the Swan: Anglo-German Mythologies in Literature, the Visual Arts and Cultural Theory*, ed. by Rüdiger Görner and Angus Nicholls (Berlin: de Gruyter, 2010), pp. 126–46 (in this volume).

of their subversive intentions. A widespread 'moral panic' about secret societies seemed to be confirmed soon afterwards by the outbreak of the French Revolution. It was known that a leading Illuminatus, J. J. C. Bode, had visited Freemasons in Paris in 1787, and though the purpose of his visit was harmless, it was conjectured that German Illuminati and French masons had laid an international plot which had led straight to the Revolution. The Revolution was unmasked as the product of a world conspiracy in a series of widely read books, of which the best-known was Augustin Barruel's five-volume *Mémoires pour servir à l'histoire du jacobinisme* (1797), which 'provided a remarkably clear and well-ordered historical account, heavily and plausibly documented, which wove together almost all the existing plot theories and all the well-known events of the Revolution into one great synthesis'.[7] According to Barruel, a conspiratorial organization had existed continuously since early in the Christian period; it went back to the heretic Mani, founder of the Manichaean religion, and had been carried on by the medieval Knights Templar, and then by the Freemasons; they in turn had provided the organizational basis for the Jacobins. This conspiracy theory is often claimed as the template for subsequent conspiracy theories involving Jews, Socialists, anarchists, and the like, though, as I have indicated, such theories have a much longer history, and the most striking example of an international conspiratorial organization seemed to be offered by the Jesuits.

Their interest in conspiracy theories lets us place the Romantics within the historical framework proposed by a far-reaching and deservedly influential study of conspiracy theories, published by Gordon S. Wood some thirty years ago.[8] Wood explains the rise of conspiracism by positing a sequence of explanatory models. Until the advent of modern scepticism with the Enlightenment, events could be explained by reference to divine providence. Admittedly, the notion of 'special providence', the belief that divine providence took a hand in individual lives and everyday events gradually came to be regarded as a self-important, possibly superstitious, certainly trivializing abuse of the concept.[9] Even if special providences were discarded, however, the concept of a general providence, governing the world on a large scale and ensuring that events would ultimately turn out for the best, remained an essential plank of natural religion. Without such a concept of providence, there could be no defence against scepticism, materialism, and naturalism, which instead posited a blind fate or a mere meaningless concatenation of natural causes. Defenders of providence, however, had to use considerable ingenuity to reconcile it with the evident existence and perhaps prevalence of evil, pain, and injustice in the world. One of the most sophisticated upholders of providence, Lessing, argued accordingly that providence was not a source of privileged insight into God's

---

7   J. M. Roberts, *The Mythology of the Secret Societies* (London: Secker & Warburg, 1972), p. 193. See also Ralf Klausnitzer, *Poesie und Konspiration: Beziehungssinn und Zeichenökonomie von Verschwörungsszenarien in Publizistik, Literatur und Wissenschaft, 1750–1850* (Berlin: de Gruyter, 2007).

8   Gordon S. Wood, 'Conspiracy and the Paranoid Style: Causality and Deceit in the Eighteenth Century', *William & Mary Quarterly*, 3rd ser., 39 (1982), 401–41.

9   For many examples, see Alexandra Walsham, *Providence in Early Modern England* (Oxford: Oxford University Press, 1999).

plans for the future, but could only reveal God's purposes in retrospect.[10] Thus a notorious problem in Old Testament history, God's apparent failure to inform Moses about the important doctrine of the immortality of the soul, could make sense in retrospect once enough time had passed for us to see that God doled out his revelation piecemeal, entrusting relatively simple information to the child-like ancient Hebrews and reserving a more complex message for the subsequent revelation made through Jesus. Hence one should continue to trust in Providence, even if its operations seemed to follow a circuitous or retrograde path:

> Geh deinen unmerklichen Schritt, ewige Vorsehung! Nur laß mich dieser Unmerklichkeit wegen an dir nicht verzweifeln. — Laß mich an dir nicht verzweifeln, wenn selbst deine Schritte mir scheinen sollen, zurückzugehen! — Es ist nicht wahr, daß die kürzeste Linie immer die gerade ist.[11]

While many Enlightenment thinkers questioned the concept of providence as part of their hostile critique of religion, others transferred their interests to the understanding of human nature and human society as a means of ameliorating human life. '[W]hat characterised the Enlightenment from the 1740s onwards', writes John Robertson, 'was a new focus on betterment in this world, without regard for the existence or non-existence of the next'; 'intellectual effort was now concentrated on understanding the means of progress in human society, not on demolishing belief in a divine counterpart.'[12] One of the intellectual tools available to the High Enlightenment was the nascent study of statistics. With its help, the social sciences which originated at this period could explain many events with reference to social forces and statistical regularities. The history of statistics goes back to the seventeenth-century London merchant John Graunt, who in his *Natural and Political Observations* (1662) drew demographic inferences from the bills of mortality.[13] In 1741 J. P. Süssmilch (who later had a controversy with Herder about the origins of language) published a detailed study of births, deaths and sex ratios, based on parish registers and following the example of Graunt. His work gained Süssmilch election to the Berlin Academy.[14] Graunt's work also provided the basis for Diderot's article 'Arithmétique politique' in the *Encyclopédie*.[15] Kant in 1784 points out that although individual actions, such as marriages, may be subject to free will, yet the annual statistics show regularities in marriages, births, and deaths which reveal underlying natural laws; similarly, the weather, though

10   On Lessing's conception of Providence, see now K. F. Hilliard, *Freethinkers, Libertines, and 'Schwärmer': Heterodoxy in German Literature, 1750–1800* (London: Institute of Germanic and Romance Studies, 2011), pp. 86–96.

11   Gotthold Ephraim Lessing, *Werke und Briefe*, ed. by Wilfried Barner et al., 12 vols (Frankfurt a.M.: Deutscher Klassiker Verlag, 1987–98), x: *Werke, 1778–1781*, ed. by Arno Schilson and Axel Schmitt (2001), pp. 97–98.

12   John Robertson, *The Case for the Enlightenment: Scotland and Naples, 1680–1760* (Cambridge: Cambridge University Press, 2005), p. 8.

13   Ian Hacking, *The Taming of Chance* (Cambridge: Cambridge University Press, 1990), p. 16.

14   Ibid., pp. 20–21. The title of Süssmilch's work was *Die göttliche Ordnung in der Veränderung des menschlichen Geschlechts, aus der Geburt, dem Tode und der Fortpflanzung desselben erwiesen* (Berlin, 1741).

15   See John Lough, *The 'Encyclopédie'* (London: Longman, 1971), p. 327.

unpredictable in detail, is subject to natural regularities, and it may eventually be possible to discover an analogous 'Naturabsicht' underlying human history.[16] Adam Smith, as is well known, argued that the operation of an 'invisible hand' ensured that the selfish pursuit of one's individual interest was compatible with the well-being of society as a whole, and indeed more likely to benefit society than consciously public-spirited action: 'By pursuing his own interest [a merchant] frequently promotes that of the society more effectually than when he really intends to promote it.'[17] Divine providence, imagined as a force external to human life, was now a superfluous concept. The internal workings of society — a term which itself signalled a new and secular focus on the study of humanity — themselves accounted for the patterns visible in human life.

Between the decline of providentialism and the rise of sociology, however, there was a period, broadly coterminous with the eighteenth century, in which political events seemed explicable only as resulting from the deliberate actions of individuals. The scientific revolution of the seventeenth century owed its success to a mechanistic logic of cause and effect. It seemed an obvious step, therefore, to apply this mechanistic logic to history, and to suppose that individual actions brought about the corresponding effects. This logic was challenged, however, by the French Revolution, which struck contemporaries as a monstrous, cataclysmic event. Writing at an early stage in the Revolution, before the execution of Louis XVI, but after the fall of the Bastille, the Declaration of the Rights of Man and the Citizen, the abolition of feudalism, and the expropriation of the Church, Edmund Burke already maintained: 'All circumstances taken together, the French revolution is the most astonishing that has hitherto happened in the world.'[18] It was hard to explain this cataclysm in terms of human agency. For the mechanistic model to hold, the Revolution must result from a monstrous international conspiracy, similar to, but far exceeding, the political plots which had given rise to successive panics, for example, in British history. 'But the scale and complexity of the Revolution now required conspiratorial interpretations of an unprecedented sort. No small group of particular plotters could account for its tumult and mass movements; only elaborately organized secret societies, like the Illuminati or the Freemasons, involving thousands of individuals linked by sinister designs, could be behind the Europe-wide upheaval.'[19]

Although the conspiracy theory of the French Revolution may not be quite such a novelty as Wood maintains,[20] his scheme of successive explanatory models — providential, conspiratorial, and sociological/statistical — has considerable appeal.

16   Immanuel Kant, 'Idee zu einer allgemeinen Geschichte in weltbürgerlicher Absicht', in his *Werke*, ed. by Wilhelm Weischedel, 6 vols (Darmstadt: Wissenschaftliche Buchgesellschaft, 1964), VI, 33.

17   Adam Smith, *An Inquiry into the Nature and Causes of the Wealth of Nations*, ed. by Kathryn Sutherland, World's Classics (Oxford: Oxford University Press, 1993), p. 292.

18   Edmund Burke, *Reflections on the Revolution in France*, ed. by L. G. Mitchell, World's Classics (Oxford: Oxford University Press, 1993), p. 10.

19   Wood, pp. 431–32.

20   Besides Hofman, see now Darren McMahon, *Enemies of the Enlightenment: The French Counter-Enlightenment and the Making of Modernity* (New York: Oxford University Press, 2001).

Less plausible is his hopeful assumption that the third model has triumphed, leaving conspiracism behind as the resource of dispossessed and simple-minded people who cannot cope with the modern world: 'In our post-industrial, scientifically saturated society, those who continue to attribute combinations of events to deliberate human design may well be peculiar sorts of persons — marginal people, perhaps, removed from the centres of power, unable to grasp the conceptions of complicated causal linkages offered by sophisticated social scientists, and unwilling to abandon the desire to make simple and clear moral judgments of events.'[21] A few minutes on the Internet will show that conspiracism is much too popular to be dismissed in this way. It is genuinely difficult to grasp the causes lying behind, for example, the international financial meltdown of 2008: hence people are ready to explain it in terms of human agency by blaming it on the greed and irresponsibility of bankers, an explanation which, though probably not false, is certainly inadequate. And, as we have seen, conspiracism has an imaginative appeal similar to that of fiction, which helps it to solidify into a mythology.

Accepting Wood's scheme, it would appear that Romanticism marks an intellectual step back from the Enlightenment. While thinkers of the Enlightenment abstract from social affairs in order to explore the underlying statistical patterns that the incipient social sciences could disclose, the Romantics objected to Enlightenment abstraction and sought to understand the world in vivid and concrete terms. Thus Novalis in 'Die Christenheit oder Europa' denounced the mathematical rationalism of the Enlightenment by contrast with the charm and colour of poetry: 'Reizender und farbiger steht die Poesie wie ein geschmücktes Indien dem kalten, toten Spitzbergen jenes Stubenverstandes gegenüber.'[22] This concrete representation of the world is the business of imaginative literature. So in Romantic fiction we find a hankering after Wood's first explanatory model, that of providentialism; but since providentialism no longer seems truly believable, it tends to be replaced by conspiracism, which can be represented by natural and supernatural agents. A large-scale conspiracism which attributes agency to supernatural powers is accompanied by a small-scale conspiracism which acknowledges human agency in the form of plots and intrigues.

Conspiracism in the 'Geheimbundroman'

Conspiracism is the theme of an entire genre of German fiction, the 'Geheim-bundroman' or secret-society novel, which was extremely popular in the late eighteenth century and served as a seedbed for much Romantic fiction. The authors of 'Geheimbundromane' were responding to the fascination with secret societies which pervaded the Germany of their time. After the establishment of the Grand Masonic Lodge in London in 1717, Freemasonry spread rapidly throughout France and Germany. By 1789 there were an estimated six hundred lodges in France, with between 50,000 and 100,000 members, while in Berlin alone forty-three lodges

---

21   Wood, p. 441.
22   Novalis, *Schriften*, ed. by Paul Kluckhohn and Richard Samuel, 5 vols (Stuttgart: Kohlhammer, 1960–88), III, 520.

were founded between 1740 and 1781. Its condemnation by the Catholic Church in 1738 strengthened its association with the Enlightenment. The Freemasons provided the template for the multitude of societies, clubs, academies and circles that sprang up in late eighteenth-century Germany to enable middle-class citizens, clerics and nobles to discuss enlightened aims and further Bildung. Adolph Freiherr von Knigge, briefly a leading Illuminatus, wrote in 1788: 'Man wird heutzutage in allen Ständen wenig Menschen treffen, die nicht [...] wenigstens eine Zeitlang Mitglieder einer solchen geheimen Verbrüderung gewesen wären.'[23] Some measure of secrecy was usually advisable. Even in Berlin in the 1780s, the society dedicated to enlightenment, the Mittwochgesellschaft, required its members to keep the matters discussed there in strict confidence and even to conceal the Society's existence.

The best-known example of the 'Geheimbundroman' is probably Carl Grosse's *Der Genius* (1791–95), which Hoffmann read enthusiastically at the age of nineteen.[24] In this and similar novels, secret societies admit their initiates with elaborate rituals usually held in sinister subterranean vaults and thereafter control their initiates' lives with a degree of power and omniscience that seems inexplicable. The 'Verbindung' which admits Grosse's protagonist, a young Spanish nobleman, has powers extending through the whole of Spain and even beyond. Its aims appear to be enlightened, the 'Vervollkommnung der ganzen Menschheit', but in pursuit of these aims the society is prepared to sacrifice human life and to assassinate monarchs if 'das Glück der Menschheit' requires such measures.[25] Any means are justified in pursuit of its exalted aims. Its initiation ceremony is particularly sinister, and apparently without parallel in its genre: an incision is made in the narrator's arm and all the assembled brothers drink his blood. This ritual of blood-drinking has no counterpart in Masonic ritual. It is in part a parody of the Eucharist, in which symbolic blood is replaced by the real thing. It can also be traced back to the ritual with which, according to the Roman historian Sallust, one of history's most notorious conspirators, Catiline, united his adherents: he made them take an oath and affirm its seriousness by drinking wine mixed with blood.[26]

The concept of providence features ambiguously in Grosse's novel. His conspirators describe themselves as 'gleichsam Unterbeamte der Vorsehung'.[27] This implies that, in their pursuit of human perfection, they are simply accelerating a process which is happening anyway, in accordance with the providential design of the world. But their apparent omnipotence also suggests that, despite presenting themselves as mere agents of providence, they have taken the place of providence. Such a metaphysical concept no longer has any validity or efficacy; it has been superseded by human agency.

23   Adolph Freiherr von Knigge, *Über den Umgang mit Menschen*, ed. by Gert Ueding (Frankfurt a.M.: Insel, 1977), p. 391.

24   Letter to Hippel, 19 February 1795, in Hoffmann, *Briefwechsel*, ed. by Friedrich Schnapp, 3 vols (Munich: Winkler, 1967–69), I, 53–54.

25   Carl Grosse, *Der Genius*, with afterword by Günter Dammann (Frankfurt a.M.: Zweitausendeins, 1982), pp. 87, 115.

26   *Sallust*, with an English translation by J. C. Rolfe, Loeb Classical Library, rev. edn (Cambridge, MA: Harvard University Press, 1931), pp. 38, 39 (*Bellum Catilinae*, XXII).

27   Grosse, p. 89.

At the same time, human agency appears to have expanded beyond human understanding. The conspirators appear to be in alliance with a supernatural being, the 'Genius' of the title. This, however, expresses the dilemma of enlightened rationalism. Confronted with complex and mysterious events which the logic of cause and effect seems inadequate to explain, the rationalist must either overcome his scepticism and acknowledge a supernatural agency, or else posit a human agency which takes the form of a barely credible conspiracy.[28] For much of the novel Grosse seems to be inviting the former solution, but when the 'Genius' is explained away, events are reduced to a human scale.

Der Genius begins with the narrator's declaration: 'Aus allen Verwickelungen von scheinbaren Zufällen blickt eine unsichtbare Hand hervor, welche vielleicht über *manchem* unter uns schwebt, ihn im Dunkeln beherrscht, und den Faden, den er in sorgloser Freiheit selbst zu weben vermeynt, oft schon lange diesem Gedanken vorausgesponnen haben mag'.[29] At first glance, this recalls Schiller's reference to the 'invisible hand of Providence' in the advertisement for *Die Räuber*, promising the lesson 'daß die unsichtbare Hand der Vorsicht auch den Bösewicht zu Werkzeugen ihrer Absichten und Gerichten brauchen und den verworrensten Knoten des Geschicks zum Erstaunen auflösen könne'.[30] Schiller is here upholding a relatively traditional conception of Providence while conceding that its workings are not readily apparent. Grosse's invisible hand, however, is not that of a supra-human Providence but of human agency. His 'invisible hand' is an agent, or rather a number of human agents who have joined together in a gigantic conspiracy. But since responsibility rests with a number of individuals, Grosse is also remote from Adam Smith's use of the metaphor of the 'invisible hand' to signify a hidden mechanism which ensures a balance among individual and general interests. Smith's 'invisible hand' has nothing to do with personal agency. The metaphor refers to a principle which can best be understood in the perspective of social science. To Grosse, however, that perspective is not yet available, and so he personalizes the occult machinations as the work of a highly organized conspiracy.

The 'Geheimbundroman' tends to represent such a conspiracy as a kind of mechanical contrivance. It has little to say about the psychological motives which animate the conspirators and secure the allegiance of the initiate. Grosse's protagonist is a highly sexed young man who has little acquaintance with deeper emotions and therefore easily falls into the honey-traps set for him by the secret society, which sends amorous women to seduce him. This example confirms Marianne Thalmann's contention that the psychology of the 'Geheimbundroman' is basically rationalist and mechanical.[31] Psychological complexity was introduced into the genre, however, by Schiller in his unfinished novel *Der Geisterseher*. Here Schiller

---

28   See Marion Beaujean, *Der Trivialroman in der zweiten Hälfte des 18. Jahrhunderts* (Bonn: Bouvier, 1964), pp. 124–25.

29   Grosse, p. 7.

30   Friedrich Schiller, *Sämtliche Werke*, ed. by Gerhard Fricke and Herbert G. Göpfert, 5 vols (Munich: Hanser, 1958), I, 490.

31   Marianne Thalmann, *Der Trivialroman des 18. Jahrhunderts und der romantische Roman: Ein Beitrag zur Entwicklungsgeschichte der Geheimbundmystik* (Berlin: Ebering, 1923), p. 70.

traces the psychological development of a Prince who, brought up as a Protestant to associate religion with gloom, adopts an emotionally unsatisfying materialism. From the resulting despair he escapes by entering the Catholic Church, to which he is also attracted by the allure of a beautiful woman. Hoffmann pays tribute to it by making the narrator of 'Das Majorat' call it 'das Buch [...], das ich, so wie damals jeder, der nur irgend dem Romantischen ergeben, in der Tasche trug'.[32]

Die Elixiere des Teufels as Conspiratorial Novel

Although Hoffmann's *Die Elixiere des Teufels* owes much to the 'Geheimbundroman' genre, it differs by placing the protagonist's psychology in the foreground. Unlike Schiller, however, Hoffmann does not give his protagonist a particularly complex set of motives. The monk Medardus, like his prototype in Matthew Gregory Lewis's novel *The Monk*, is motivated principally by pride, ambition, lust, and fear.[33] From his early success as a preacher, which he enhances by drinking the ancient wine known as the Devil's elixir, down to the extravagant public piety which he displays in Rome and his hopes of becoming confessor to the Pope, he shows an overweening vanity which is finally replaced by exemplary penitence. His story asks to be read as a psychological allegory about the splitting of the self when it is torn between contradictory impulses: for example, between Medardus's admiration for the heavenly purity embodied in Aurelie and his intense desire to enjoy her sexually. These contradictory impulses are externalized in figures — the mad monk, the Doppelgänger who fulfils Medardus's unconscious wish by stabbing Aurelie at the altar, the naked man who emerges from the floor of his prison cell and hands him a knife — for whose existence the novel offers only the most threadbare explanation, if any. Hence Horst Daemmrich is no doubt right to suggest that the novel should be seen 'as a precursor of the modern psychological novel or a dream sequence in which Hoffmann attempts to portray the hero's psychological state'.[34]

---

32   E. T. A. Hoffmann, *Sämtliche Werke*, ed. by Wulf Segebrecht and Hartmut Steinecke, 6 vols (Frankfurt a.M.: Deutscher Klassiker Verlag, 1985–2004), III: *Werke, 1816–1820*, ed. by Hartmut Steinecke (1895), p. 207.

33   Lewis's *The Monk* (1796) is mentioned in Hoffmann's text: see Hoffmann, *Sämtliche Werke*, II/2: *Die Elixiere des Teufels*, ed. by Hartmut Steinecke (1988), p. 241. On its relation to Hoffmann's novel, see Horst Meixner, *Romantischer Figuralismus: Kritische Studien zu Romanen von Arnim, Eichendorff und Hoffmann* (Frankfurt a.M.: Athenäum, 1971), pp. 155–72; Wolfgang Nehring, 'Gothic Novel und Schauerroman: Tradition und Innovation in Hoffmanns *Die Elixiere des Teufels*', *E. T. A. Hoffmann-Jahrbuch*, 1 (1992–93), 36–47 (pp. 36–44). Another model, which appears not to have been noticed by commentators, is the monk Medardus in Benedikte Naubert's 'Der Fischer' (1792), a criminal with the reputation of a saint. This Medardus is a painter who paints but then defaces a picture of the Virgin Mary; with the Devil's help he conducts an affair with a (willing) nun, and, when caught stealing Church treasures, is saved by the Devil, who replaces him with a double. See Naubert, *Neue Volksmärchen der Deutschen*, ed. by Marianne Henn, Paola Meyer and Anita Runge, 4 vols (Göttingen: Wallstein, 2001), III, 7–88. Karl S. Guthke in *Englische Vorromantik und deutscher Sturm und Drang: M. G . Lewis' Stellung in der Geschichte der deutsch-englischen Literaturbeziehungen* (Göttingen: Vandenhoeck & Ruprecht, 1958), p. 33, suggests that Naubert helped to inspire *The Monk*, but does not make a connection with Hoffmann.

34   Horst S. Daemmrich, *The Shattered Self: E. T. A. Hoffmann's Tragic Vision* (Detroit, MI: Wayne State University Press, 1973), p. 93. Cf. the similar formulation by Horst Meixner: 'Hoffmann

Not surprisingly, the novel has received psychoanalytical readings which easily detect a conflict between Medardus's incestuous desire for his mother (represented by the pure Aurelie) and the prohibitions and punishments imposed by the paternal super-ego.[35] Such readings can readily seem obvious and facile. Interpretations of Medardus's psychology need to take into account the psychological knowledge available to Hoffmann from his extensive reading in medical treatises; they also need to remember that Medardus's adventures all occur within a larger, cosmic, supernatural framework which, however we interpret it, is essential to the meaning of the novel.[36]

Medardus is the victim not only of his own impulses but of an overarching conspiracy, which proceeds not from mere human agency but from the scheme of sin and redemption that appears to govern the novel. It is revealed shortly before the end that Medardus is caught up in a fateful pattern of events that go back several centuries. His remote ancestor, Francesco, was a Renaissance painter who led a sinful life, worshipped the pagan goddess Venus, and, when commissioned to paint St Rosalia, painted her resembling Venus. For this sacrilegious confusion of the sacred with the profane (or rather, of the sacred and the sexual) he has been punished by having to remain on earth until his family becomes extinct. Medardus is the last of the line and must therefore, in order to satisfy Francesco, remain a monk and have no children. Hence his ancestor pursues him, appearing at intervals as a tall, gaunt man with a piercing gaze, and Medardus's many sexual misdemeanours are therefore, though he does not know it, attempts to defeat the will of his ancestor. Hence his marriage with Aurelie must be frustrated, and the double, in stabbing Aurelie, is not only acting out Medardus's innate violence but also fulfilling the demands of the family curse.

Die Elixiere thus presents itself as a religious novel in which sacrilege is punished, however many generations late, and a penitent sinner ultimately returns to the fold to die in the odour of sanctity. But how seriously is the element of Catholic religiosity to be taken? Neither Hoffmann's biography, nor the tone of the novel itself, suggests that he was writing for the edification of Catholic readers — in sharp contrast, say, to the exactly contemporary novel *Ahnung und Gegenwart* (1815), with its solemn and didactic tone, by the devout cradle Catholic Joseph von Eichendorff. Certainly the novel inquires into the relationship between human life and the supernatural world; but the latter seems to owe less to Christian theology than to the

---

verwischt die Grenzen zwischen Einbildung und Wirklichkeit in einem Maße, daß das Geschehen wie ein ungeheurer Alptraum erscheint' (Meixner, p. 195).

35   See e.g. the bald summary in *E. T. A. Hoffmann: Leben — Werk — Wirkung*, 2nd, enlarged edition, ed. by Detlef Kremer (Berlin: de Gruyter, 2010), p. 156, and for a searching psychoanalytical interpretation, Elizabeth Wright, *E. T. A. Hoffmann and the Rhetoric of Terror* (London: Institute of Germanic Studies, 1978), ch. 5.

36   For a recent reading in the light of Hoffmann's psychological knowledge, see Walter Hinderer, 'Die poetische Psychoanalyse in E. T. A. Hoffmanns Roman *Die Elixiere des Teufels*', in *'Hoffmanneske Geschichte': Zu einer Literaturwissenschaft als Kulturwissenschaft*, ed. by Gerhard Neumann (Würzburg: Königshausen & Neumann, 2005), pp. 43–76. A strong case for reading the novel in the light of the psychological information available to Hoffmann is made by Victoria Dutchman-Smith, *E. T. A. Hoffmann and Alcohol: Biography, Reception and Art* (London: Maney, 2010), p. 152.

theosophical fantasies of Jakob Böhme and Gotthilf Heinrich von Schubert.[37] The religious atmosphere is present, not as a matter of presumed belief by either author or reader, but as a framework which gives Medardus something to rebel against and enables him to display his conflicting impulses to the full. As Horst Meixner puts it: 'Die Figuren und Bilder des Christentums sind nur noch Hohlformen, die ihren Gehalt vom Ausdrucksverlangen des Subjekts empfangen.'[38]

On this reading, the novel's centre of gravity lies not in its alleged spiritual or moral theme but in the fascination of Medardus's anarchic rebellion and the mysterious forces which ultimately defeat him. Medardus gains the reader's covert sympathy in his frantic transgressing of all institutional and ethical boundaries. His defeat can be ascribed only superficially to the conventional moral and religious sanctions which he has overridden; his real antagonist is a supernatural power which leads him into sin and then arranges for his punishment.

Struggling in the clutches of this power, Medardus loses his moral autonomy. At several key points in the narrative, the supernatural power takes over Medardus's will. When he preaches on St Anthony's day, in the presence of the mysterious painter, he feels impelled by an alien force ('wie von einer fremden zauberischen Gewalt getrieben') to challenge the stranger and declare: 'ich bin es selbst! — ich bin der heilige Antonius!'[39] When, on arriving at the castle, he is recognized by Reinhold, he feels that an alien voice ('eine fremde Stimme im Innern') is putting the right words into his mouth.[40] When he has an extraordinary run of luck at the Prince's faro table, he feels he is the mere passive instrument of an alien force ('die fremde Macht, die in mein Wesen getreten').[41] These and many other occasions when Medardus's will is usurped by an alien force turn him into a mere puppet, an actor following a predetermined script from which, despite his desperate efforts, he is unable to deviate. He can thus be seen as the hapless victim of a supernatural plot. Christian providentialism has been replaced by a heterodox theosophy, and while Lessing conceived providence as wise and benevolent, the power that rules Medardus's life seems mainly concerned with hunting down its victim and forcing him into sanctity.

We have, then, a conspiratorial narrative, in which Medardus is entrapped both by a cosmic and by an earthly conspiracy. While the 'Geheimbundroman' ultimately reduced all apparent supernatural phenomena to mere human contrivances, Hoffmann restores the supernatural, but represents it as in many ways sinister and frightening, intent on punishment and revenge. On the earthly level, conspiracy is presented as the intrigues within the Catholic Church to which Medardus is exposed and which nearly bring about his premature death.

---

37 See Monika Fick, 'E. T. A. Hoffmanns Theosophie: Eine Interpretation des Romans *Die Elixiere des Teufels*', *Literaturwissenschaftliches Jahrbuch im Auftrag der Görres-Gesellschaft*, 36 (1995), 105–25.

38 Meixner, p. 192.

39 Hoffmann, *Die Elixiere*, p. 41.

40 Ibid., p. 64.

41 Ibid., p. 157.

Versions of Catholicism in *Die Elixiere*

Catholicism in *Die Elixiere* appears under three aspects: aesthetic, enlightened, and conspiratorial. In these three forms, it is presented as being of interest in its own right, and not as a mere backdrop or 'Kulisse'.[42]

Hoffmann, like many contemporaries, was alive to the aesthetic appeal of Catholic symbolism and ritual, though he appears never to have been tempted to follow his friend Zacharias Werner into conversion.[43] As a theatre director in Bamberg, he staged Calderón's religious drama *La devoción de la cruz* [*Die Andacht zum Kreuz*] on 13 June 1811, appealing with great success to the Catholic population.[44] Catholic imagery, in Hoffmann's view, served to provide spiritual things with a vivid sensory form: he asserts that 'es ganz in dem Geiste des Katholizism liegt, die Sinne bei der symbolischen Darstellung des Übersinnlichen in Anspruch zu nehmen'.[45] Early in the novel, Medardus describes enthusiastically the ceremonies, the High Mass and the procession, celebrated at the church 'zur heiligen Linde'. This church, now Święta Lipka, near Ketrzyn in northern Poland, centres on a chapel which, having been destroyed by Protestants in the Reformation, was rebuilt and consecrated in 1619 by the Jesuits after Catholicism was once again permitted in Prussia. The church itself, a magnificent Baroque structure, was built for the Jesuits between 1687 and 1730 by the mason Georg Ertly.[46] We may assume that Hoffmann knew it from his upbringing in nearby Königsberg. However, Medardus's devout enthusiasm may arouse scepticism in the reader. Hoffmann reported in a letter to his publisher Kunz, rather flippantly, that St Joseph and the Christ child would appear in the novel ('Joseph und das Christuskind erscheinen pp.') ,[47] and they are no doubt to be identified with the aged pilgrim and the beautiful child who figure in Medardus's earliest recollections, though Medardus himself attributes his memories mainly to his mother's subsequent account ('unerachtet ich gewiß glaube, daß nur aus der Beschreibung meiner Mutter sich im Innern sein lebhaftes Bild erzeugt hat').[48]

Alongside this religious enthusiasm, we find a more temperate devotion being encouraged by Leonardus, the prior of the Capuchin monastery where Medardus is educated. This is surprising, since the Capuchins were a militant missionary order who rose to prominence alongside the Jesuits in the Counter-Reformation. They were energetic missioners, worked among the poor, dressed in coarse robes and

---

42   Nicholas Saul, 'E. T. A. Hoffmanns erzählte Predigten', *Euphorion*, 83 (1989), 407–30 (pp. 408, 410).

43   Cf. Theodor's sceptical account of Werner's 'mystischer Schwärmerei' in *Die Serapions-Brüder*: Hoffmann, *Sämtliche Werke*, IV: *Die Serapions-Brüder*, ed. by Wulf Segebrecht (2001), p. 1032.

44   See Henry W. Sullivan, *Calderón in the German Lands and the Low Countries: His Reception and Influence, 1654–1980* (Cambridge: Cambridge University Press, 1983), pp. 251–53; Hartmut Steinecke, *Die Kunst der Fantasie: E. T. A. Hoffmanns Leben und Werk* (Frankfurt a.M.: Insel, 2004), pp. 83–85.

45   'Über die Aufführung der Schauspiele des Calderon de la Barca auf dem Theater in Bamberg' (1812), *Sämtliche Werke*, I: *Frühe Prosa*, ed. by Gerhard Allroggen et al. (2003), pp. 625–30 (p. 628).

46   See Thomas daCosta Kaufmann, *Court, Cloister and City: The Art and Culture of Central Europe, 1450–1800* (London: Weidenfeld & Nicolson, 1995), p. 378.

47   Letter to Kunz, 24 March 1814, in *Briefwechsel*, I, 454.

48   Hoffmann, *Die Elixiere*, p. 16.

went barefoot to display their own poverty, and had a reputation for ignorance, though their ranks included such famous preachers as Procopius of Templin and Marco d'Aviano. Counter-Reformation preaching tended, like that of Medardus, to describe the lives of the saints as exemplary; enlightened Catholics, however, thought that sermons should serve, as the Abbess says Medardus's should have done, 'die Gemeinde zu belehren und zu frommen Betrachtungen zu entzünden'.[49] The Catholic Enlightenment is represented by Leonardus. Besides being truly devout and an excellent theologian, he has more acquaintance with the secular world than is usual among monks; he speaks French and Italian, and has therefore been sent on many important missions. All the monks under his leadership are there because of a true spiritual vocation, and those who have sought refuge in the monastery from worldly disaster find comfort and ease after a light penance. Medardus tells us that these are 'ungewöhnliche[] Tendenzen des Klosterlebens'.[50] They stand in sharp contrast to the standard presentation of monastic life in Enlightenment treatises and satires, where the seclusion and routine of the monastery are said to generate discord, feuding, melancholy, and madness, and where monks are satirized for their laziness and self-indulgence.[51] Leonardus has abandoned the common Counter-Reformation practice of enforcing piety through spiritual terror, vivid descriptions of hell and purgatory, and warnings about God's inexorable justice.[52] Instead, he encourages people's aspiration towards heaven: 'Unerachtet der strengen Ordensregel, waren die Andachtsübungen dem Prior Leonardus mehr Bedürfnis des dem himmlischen zugewandten Geistes, als aszetische Buße für die der menschlichen anklebende Sünde.'[53] He shows his shrewdness by distrusting Medardus' sudden enthusiasm for entering the monastery, by questioning him discreetly about sex, and by doubting his visions of St Joseph and the Christ child. Similarly, Leonardus says little about the miracles and saints' legends which were so important in Counter-Reformation piety but played down by enlightened clerics; and he takes an equally enlightened view of religious relics, considering that, though seldom genuine, they serve to inspire the devotion of believers and sometimes do bring about remarkable physical cures, not through their intrinsic qualities, but through the spiritual strength they promote in worshippers.[54]

Leonardus' enlightened piety, however, is represented as untypical of the Catholic Church as a whole. The closer we get to Rome, the more the Church corresponds to the conspiratorial fantasies characteristic of the 'Geheimbundroman'. The Pope

---

49   Ibid., p. 50; cf. Saul, p. 104.

50   Ibid., p. 27.

51   See Hans-Wolf Jäger, 'Mönchskritik und Klostersatire in der deutschen Spätaufklärung', in *Katholische Aufklärung: Aufklärung im katholischen Deutschland*, ed. by Harm Klueting (Hamburg: Meiner, 1993), pp. 192–207.

52   See Jean Delumeau, *Le Péché et la Peur: La Culpabilisation en Occident, XIIIe–XVIIIe siècles* (Paris: Fayard, 1983), esp. part III, 'La Pastorale de la peur: En pays catholique', pp. 369–547. The Capuchin Procopius of Templin was famous for his hell-fire sermons: see R. J. W. Evans, *The Making of the Habsburg Monarchy, 1550–1700* (Oxford: Clarendon Press, 1979), p. 188.

53   Hoffmann, *Die Elixiere*, p. 25.

54   Ibid., pp. 33–34. On the Catholic Enlightenment, see now *A Companion to the Catholic Enlightenment*, ed. by Ulrich L. Lehner and Michael Printy (Leiden: Brill, 2010).

is described by Leonardus as a soft, impressionable, and credulous character who is easily manipulated by the intriguers around him.[55] Learning of Medardus's extravagant displays of devotion, the Pope summons him, hears his story, and half promises to make Medardus his personal confessor. However, the current confessor, a Dominican, forms an alliance with a Cardinal who has misappropriated revenues properly due to Medardus's convent, and between them they stage a conspiratorial intrigue modelled on those of the 'Geheimbundroman'. Such novels often feature reactionary secret societies, which are typically associated with the Catholic Church. Its agents are sometimes Jesuits, since the Society of Jesus was thought to offer the paradigmatic example of a tightly structured body intent on a single goal and united by obedience to their superior, the Pope. Elsewhere the agents may be monks, for monastic orders readily serve to represent dehumanized organizations dedicated to the suppression of liberty and the spread of obscurantism. Marianne Thalmann sums up the fictional image of the monk, with unconcealed disapproval, as follows:

> Der Mönch ist sozusagen die charakteristische Type des Mittelalters, das abergläubisch und beschränkt die finstere Vorstufe zur aufgeklärten Neuzeit ist. Es ist zu betonen: *Das Mittelalter ist für den Romanschriftsteller des 18. Jahrhunderts die Zeit der Finsternis, des Aberglaubens, der Menschenknechtung.* Diese aufgeklärte Ansicht entspricht der rationalen, begrenzten Meinung der Freigeister und Atheisten aller Zeiten. Er sieht nur die Schatten einer metaphysisch ringenden und vielfach chaotischen Zeit, das Sinnenabgewandte der Mystik, die Folter der Hexe, die Unduldsamkeit der Inquisition und nirgends das Licht, um das die Dunkelheit kämpft. Daher ist der Mönch der eigennützige Betrüger, der Seelenfänger, der gewissenlose Schlemmer, der Feind freigeistiger Bewegungen, das Prototyp der geistigen Beschränktheit.[56]

The Dominicans who plot against Medardus fully conform to this stereotype. One of them summons Medardus to the bedside of a dying man but takes him first to an underground vault where Dominicans are seated on benches; this subterranean assembly is a staple of the 'Geheimbundroman', and also recalls the secret court or 'Vehmgericht' which features regularly in historical works set in the Middle Ages (the court which pronounces sentence on Adelheid in Goethe's *Götz von Berlichingen* is a familiar example).[57] From there Medardus is led to a small chamber where he finds Cyrillus, a close associate of Leonardus and an exemplar of enlightened piety, who has come to Rome as the representative of their monastery. The Dominicans wish to dispose of Cyrillus so that their ally the Cardinal can continue to enjoy his revenues without dispute, and have persuaded the gullible Pope that Cyrillus is part of a plot to dethrone him. Cyrillus has evidently been tortured by the

---

55   Which Pope is meant? Hoffmann's editor, Hartmut Steinecke, assumes it is Clement XIV (reigned 1769–74), but since Clement at least had the strength of character to abolish the Jesuits, it is more likely to be his successor, Giovanni Angelo Braschi, who ruled as Pius VI from 1775–99 and who was worldly, spendthrift, and ineffectual; Eamon Duffy describes him as 'a particularly poor specimen'; Duffy, *Saints and Sinners: A History of the Popes* (New Haven, CT, and London: Yale University Press, 1997), p. 198.

56   Thalmann, p. 147.

57   The reappearance of 'Bundeszeremoniell' in this scene is noted by Thalmann, p. 260.

Dominicans, whom he describes as 'die entsetzlichen Diener der Hölle', and once Medardus has given him absolution, a Dominican takes a sword and beheads him.[58] Medardus himself narrowly escapes death, for his Dominican guide then offers him wine which Medardus, recognizing it as poison, surreptitiously pours into his sleeve; soon afterwards he finds that the flesh of his arm has been eaten away by acid. Prudently, he returns to his monastery, where he finds that Leonardus is fully informed about his experiences in Rome, thanks to a network of spies which has even recorded every word of his conversation with the Pope. The Catholic Church is represented as such a hotbed of conspiracy that even an honest and devout cleric is obliged to resort to some defensive counter-conspiracy.

Where, finally, is Hoffmann's novel to be located in the sequence of mentalities described earlier in this article? Hoffmann implicitly rejects the Christian providentialism which was already proving unsustainable, but does not seek social or sociological explanations for surprising events. Instead, he goes in two directions. He attributes some events to human agency, and to provide an agent commensurable with the events, he imagines a conspiracy within the Church, thus falling back on the conspiracism of the 'Geheimbundroman'. But unlike the authors of 'Geheimbundromane', such as Grosse, who generally ended up with a rationalist explanation of extraordinary events, Hoffmann resorts to the supernatural and makes Medardus the victim of a narrative of sin, suffering, and redemption, steeped in the atmosphere of Baroque Catholicism. When we penetrate this atmosphere, however, we find that the Catholicism is only aesthetic, and that Hoffmann, unlike such a contemporary as Eichendorff, is not really preaching a religious message. Rather, the novel is an exploration of mysterious but powerful forces both within the self and external to the self, and the latter can only be described in enigmatic terms which Hoffmann derived from such unorthodox and heterodox sources as the theosophies of Böhme and Schubert. These forces are ambivalent: they entrap the individual in wrong-doing and then compel him to undergo punishment and penance. Their relation to the individual in their power is that of a conspiracy to its victim. The victim is meanwhile being assailed not only by a supernatural but also by an earthly conspiracy, which in this novel is embodied in the agents of certain factions within the Catholic Church. Thus Hoffmann mobilizes the paranoid fantasies of his time (and later) to convey the power of human agency and confirm the status of *Die Elixiere* as a conspiratorial novel, in which a cosmic conspiracy finds a small-scale man-made counterpart in a sinister plot contrived by human agents.

---

58   Hoffmann, *Die Elixiere*, p. 308.

CHAPTER 16

Faith and Fossils: Annette von Droste-Hülshoff's Poem 'Die Mergelgrube'

Long ago, before Friedrich Sengle's epoch-making trilogy transformed our understanding of the Biedermeier period, Annette von Droste-Hülshoff seemed typical of the small-scale, provincial, quietist outlook that was then supposed to characterize early nineteenth-century German writers.[1] She herself, it must be said, often claimed to be content to inhabit a backwater. 'Gottlob ist unser gutes Westphalen noch um hundert Jahre zurück,' she wrote to Bishop Diepenbrock of Regensburg in 1845, ' — möge es nie nacheilen auf dem Wege des Verderbens! und mögen andre Länder auf ihrem Kreislaufe bald wieder bey ihm eintreffen!' (HKA x/i, 286).[2] The intellectual forces of the time, however, found their way into her provincial solitude. Her firm Christian faith was far removed from the simple belief that the nineteenth century called a 'Köhlerglaube': it was difficult and strenuous, shot through with doubt. While some commentators may have tried, as Sengle complains, to smooth away the tensions in her devotional verse, others have recognized that her poetry expresses a dialectic of faith and doubt, 'eine Dialektik von Geborgenheit und Ungeborgenheit, von Trost und Anfechtung'.[3] Droste's difficulties came not only from her own personality but from her awareness of the age she lived in. She makes this clear in a well-known stanza from 'Am zweiten Weihnachtstage (Stephanus)', written in 1840:

> War einst erhellt der schwanke Steg,
> Und klaffte klar der Abgrund auf,
> Wir müssen suchen unsern Weg
> Im Haiderauch ein armer Hauf.
> Des Glaubens köstlich theurer Preis
> Ward wie gestellt auf Gletschers Höhen;
> Wir müssen klimmen über Eis
> Und schwindelnd uns am Schlunde drehen.
>
> (HKA iv/i, 161)

1 For a defence of Droste against older detractors like Emil Staiger, see Friedrich Sengle, *Biedermeierzeit*, 3 vols (Stuttgart: Metzler, 1971–80), III, 592–95.

2 All quotations from Droste-Hülshoff are from: Annette von Droste-Hülshoff, *Werke und Briefwechsel*, Historisch-kritische Ausgabe, ed. by Winfried Woesler (Tübingen: Niemeyer, 1978–). References are given in the text as HKA with volume and page number.

3 Edgar Eilers, *Probleme religiöser Existenz im 'Geistlichen Jahr': Die Droste und Sören Kierkegaard* (Werl: Dietrich Coelde-Verlag, 1953), p. 3.

One difficulty for the nineteenth-century Christian writer was the integration into her world-view of the findings of science, particularly geology, which placed human life in an unfamiliar and alarming context of vast geological epochs. In English literature this challenge to faith was most famously expressed by Tennyson. In his elegy for Arthur Hallam, *In Memoriam*, he tries to accommodate a supernaturalist faith alongside an awareness that the ordered frame of the universe has given way to a world which is disturbingly fluid:

> There rolls the deep where grew the tree.
> O earth, what changes hast thou seen!
> There where the long street roars, hath been
> The stillness of the central sea.
>
> The hills are shadows, and they flow
> From form to form, and nothing stands;
> They melt like mist, the solid lands,
> Like clouds they shape themselves and go.[4]

Tennyson's knowledge of geology and palaeontology came from the English school of geologists, notably from Adam Sedgwick, whose lectures he and Hallam attended at Cambridge.[5] The sources of Droste's scientific knowledge have been explored in detail by Josefine Nettesheim.[6] In her studies of natural history, especially botany and geology, Droste drew on the science of her day via such compendia as Friedrich Justin Bertuch's popular books on natural history. She was in contact with Romantic 'Naturphilosophie' through her brother-in-law Lassberg, who was a friend of Lorenz Oken, and she met Oken himself several times.[7] Through Oken and Bertuch she was aware of the geological theories put forward by the French anatomist and palaeontologist Georges Cuvier. In exploring some of these links, I want to argue that while both Tennyson and Droste were aware of conflicts between geology and Genesis, they regarded these conflicts differently, in keeping with the differences in intellectual atmosphere between Britain and the Continent.[8]

Droste's poem 'Die Mergelgrube' shows how her interest in geology was based in her immediate experience. She was a passionate collector of fossils. Her enthusiasm for this hobby, and her awareness of the tension between geology and religion, find expression in a letter of 26 August 1839 to Wilhelm Junkmann:

> [...] ich muß jetzt, auf ärztlichen Befehl, fleißig Steine klopfen, was ich nicht halb so gern thue als früher freywillig, doch zuweilen klopfe ich mich wieder in den Eifer hinein, und habe meine Freude und Bewunderung an den Schalthieren

---

4   Alfred Tennyson, *In Memoriam*, ed. by Susan Shatto and Marion Shaw (Oxford: Clarendon Press, 1982), p. 136.

5   See Nicolaas A. Rupke, *The Great Chain of History: William Buckland and the English School of Geology, 1814–1849* (Oxford: Clarendon Press, 1983), pp. 225–30.

6   See Josefine Nettesheim, *Die geistige Welt der Dichterin Annette Droste zu Hulshoff* (Münster: Regensberg, 1967).

7   See Droste's letter to August von Haxthausen, 2 August 1844, HKA x/i, 203.

8   Droste has often been compared to the English Romantic poets. See Brigitte Peucker, *Lyric Descent in the German Romantic Tradition* (New Haven, CT, and London: Yale University Press, 1987), p. 77. More fruitful comparisons, I suspect, would be with Tennyson and Browning.

und Pflanzen, die, den Worten des Psalmisten zum Trotz (Der Mensch verdorrt wie eine Blume des Feldes) ihr zerbrechliches Daseyn durch Jahrhunderte erhalten haben, es wird mir zuweilen ganz wunderlich, wenn ich manche Stengel oder Muscheln, genau in der Form wie sie damals der Augenblick verbogen hat, wieder hervor treten sehe, gleichsam in der Todeskrümmung — ich wolte ich träfe einmahl auf ein lebendiges Thier im Stein! — was meinen Sie, wenn ein Mensch mahl so aus seiner viertausendjährigen Kruste hervor kriechen könnte? was müste der nicht fühlen! und was zu fühlen und denken geben! (HKA IX/i, 66)

The questions that Droste here touches on with whimsical humour are explored in her poem 'Die Mergelgrube', which I want here to explicate in detail. By doing so, I want to argue that while Droste does indeed articulate the tension between science and religion, it is a different and less painful conflict than the one explored by Tennyson. I want also to treat 'Die Mergelgrube' as a poem of science, a poem which helps us to imagine science and thus to bridge the regrettable and unnecessary gulf between the sciences and the humanities. Droste is unwittingly carrying out the programme formulated by Wordsworth in his 1800 preface to the *Lyrical Ballads*:

> If the labours of Men of science should ever create any material revolution, direct or indirect, in our condition, and in the impressions which we habitually receive, the Poet will sleep then no more than at present; he will be ready to follow the steps of the Man of science, not only in those general indirect effects, but he will be at his side, carrying sensation into the midst of the objects of the science itself. The remotest discoveries of the Chemist, the Botanist, or Mineralogist, will be as proper objects of the Poet's art as any upon which it can be employed, if the time should ever come when these things shall be familiar to us, and the relations under which they are contemplated by the followers of these respective sciences shall be manifestly and palpably material to us as enjoying and suffering beings. If the time should ever come when what is now called science, thus familiarized to men, shall be ready to put on, as it were, a form of flesh and blood, the Poet will lend his divine spirit to aid the transfiguration, and will welcome the Being thus produced, as a dear and genuine inmate of the household of man.[9]

'Die Mergelgrube' was written in 1842 and published in the 'Heidebilder' section of her poems in 1844 (HKA I/i, 50–53). Like its neighbour, 'Der Hünenstein', its first-person voice is clearly male, being addressed by another speaker as 'Herr'. This may prompt curiosity, but probably has a simple explanation: no doubt Droste did tramp across the heath and descend into marl-pits, but she may not have wanted to display herself to her readers doing such unconventional and un-ladylike things.[10] The poem begins with a realistically minute description of the different kinds of rock and mineral which Droste's interest in geology leads her to unearth: gneiss, spar, ochre-druse, mica, flint, porphyry. Soon afterwards the speaker discovers a slab of slate with fossil jellyfish on it. These jellyfish were called medusae because their tentacles recalled the snaky hair of Medusa. Droste thus introduces current

---

9   *Wordsworth's Literary Criticism*, ed. by Nowell C. Smith (London: Henry Frowde, 1905), p. 28.
10   See, however, some interesting reflections on gender in this poem in Peucker, pp. 111, 113.

controversies about how they got there, and hence the difficulty of reconciling the findings of geology with the Book of Genesis. She opens up dizzying temporal perspectives, looking back to the primeval ages of the earth and forward to its end.

One of the problems facing early nineteenth-century geology, and confronted in this poem, was to explain the presence of gravel beds and erratic boulders at a distance from the nearest outcrops of similar rock. Droste tells us that many of her rock samples come from far afield:

> Nur wenige hat dieser Grund gezeugt,
> *Der* sah den Strand, und *der* des Berges Kuppe —

She seems at first to accept the diluvial theory of their provenance, that they were attributed to a great flood that had swept them away from their origins in the recent geological past. This explanation was soon to be disproved when scientists came to understand how rocks were moved by glaciers, but the glaciation theory, put forward by Louis Agassiz in *Studies on Glaciers* (1840), was rejected by Alexander von Humboldt and other continental scientists and not widely accepted until the 1860s. The diluvial theory had the advantage of harmonizing with the Biblical narrative of the Flood. Droste distances herself from it, however, by reporting it with gentle humour. She imagines Leviathan, the sea monster celebrated in the Book of Job, swimming above the summit of Mount Sinai, and the mountain-ranges melting like icing-sugar ('Gebirge schmolzen ein wie Zuckerkand').

A different problem, however, was presented by the fossil remains of living creatures that were found preserved in rocks.[11] Fossils were important to geologists because rock strata could not be dated by their mineral content alone. The presence of similar fossils allowed rock formations of different mineral composition to be assigned to the same period. Thanks above all to the mineralogist Abraham Gottlob Werner, whose pupils at the Freiburg mining school included Friedrich von Hardenberg and Alexander von Humboldt, geologists were able by the 1840s to establish the stratigraphical column, showing the period in which every stratum of rock had been laid down. But this achievement made it even harder to accept the narrative presented in the Book of Genesis. The problem was not that Genesis represents the world as created in seven days: ever since St Augustine it had been clear that these could not be twenty-four-hour periods such as we know, and it was therefore permissible to interpret the seven days as a metaphorical designation for much longer periods.[12] But however long the past might be, the problem remained that large numbers of animals, preserved as fossils, were no longer to be found on earth. Ammonites and belemnites, for example, were known only in fossil form. The idea that creatures might have become extinct was resisted for a long time because it seemed to imply an imperfection in creation. Instead, it was argued that these creatures might still be living in the depths of the sea or unexplored parts of the globe. This was not as desperate an argument as it may sound: crinoids or sea-

---

11   For information about fossils and palaeontology I am comprehensively indebted to Martin J. S. Rudwick, *The Meaning of Fossils: Episodes in the History of Palaeontology*, 2nd edn (Chicago, IL: University of Chicago Press, 1976).

12   St Augustine, *Concerning the City of God against the Pagans*, trans. by Henry Bettenson (Harmondsworth: Penguin, 1972), pp. 435–37. Book XI, chapter 7.

lilies were known only in fossil form until the mid-eighteenth century, when living specimens were found in very deep water in the West Indies. Fossil mammals, however, were a different matter. By the late eighteenth century it was unlikely that any large mammals remained to be discovered, and so Cuvier could safely argue in 1796 that the megatherium or giant sloth, whose fossil bones had been discovered in Paraguay, must be an extinct animal, as were the mammoth and the mastodon.

Geology thus confirmed not only that the earth was very ancient but that animal life extended back through huge vistas of pre-Adamite life. In her already quoted letter to Junkmann of 26 August 1839, Droste wonders why we never come across any fossil humans:

> [...] seltsam bleibts immer, daß man nicht wenigstens <u>versteinerte</u> Menschen findet, auch niemals ein Zeichen menschlichen Fleißes, doch finden sich wohl hundert versteinerte Bäume, aber nie auch nur ein Stückchen Holz, was Spuren der Bearbeitung trüge — so scheint es wohl ausgemacht, daß Alles einer PRÆADAMITISCHEN Erdperiode angehört, die jedoch der späteren sehr ähnlich gewesen seyn muß — nur gewaltiger in allen Formen, und ohne die Krone der Schöpfung. (HKA ix/i, 66)

Droste's notion of finding fossil humans was less whimsical than it may sound. Some scientists had considered it a real possibility. In 1725 the Swiss naturalist Johann Scheuchzer thought he had found a fossil man, but it was later identified by Cuvier as a large amphibian, dating from the relatively recent period of geological time called the Cainozoic, hence no older than 70 million years.[13]

To explain the disappearance of pre-Adamite creatures, Droste has recourse to the theory of one or more primeval catastrophes. This had been suggested speculatively by Herder in his *Ideen zur Philosophie der Geschichte der Menschheit* (1783–91).[14] It was formally proposed by Cuvier in his *Discours sur les révolutions de la surface du globe* (1812). Cuvier pointed out that the fossilized bones of existing species were found mainly in recent rocks, while deeper strata contained the bones of creatures now extinct. Besides, the more ancient deposits were askew and fractured, thus bearing witness to some elemental violence which had hurled them there. Accordingly, he argued that the earth had undergone a series of violent upheavals involving floods:

> La vie a donc souvent été troublée sur cette terre par des événemens effroyables. Des êtres vivans sans nombres ont été victimes de ces catastrophes; les uns habitans de la terre sèche se sont vus engloutis par des déluges; les autres, qui peuplaient le sein des eaux, ont été mis à sec avec le fond des mers subitement relevé; leurs races mêmes ont fini pour jamais, et ne laissent dans le monde que quelques débris à peine reconnaissables pour le naturaliste.[15]

These theories, as Nettesheim has shown, reached Droste via Oken. The 'Geo-

13   Rudwick, pp. 87, 145.

14   See the section headed 'Unsre Erde ist vielerlei Revolutionen durchgegangen, bis sie das, was sie jetzt ist, worden' in Johann Gottfried Herder, *Werke*, ed. by Günter Arnold and others, 10 vols (Frankfurt a.M.: Deutscher Klassiker Verlag, 1985–2000), VI: *Ideen zur Philosophie der Geschichte der Menschheit*, ed. by Martin Bollacher (1989), pp. 29–32.

15   M. le Baron G. Cuvier, *Discours sur les révolutions de la surface du globe*, 5th edn (Paris: G. Dufour et Ed. d'Ocagne, 1828), pp. 17–18.

gnosie' section of his *Naturgeschichte für alle Stände* (1839) envisaged a dynamic process of perpetual destruction which perpetually brought forth new forms.[16] Droste summarizes the catastrophe theory with reference to fossils by saying of the fossil jellyfish:

> Noch schienen ihre Stralen sie zu zücken,
> Als sie geschleudert von des Meeres Busen,
> Und das Gebirge sank, sie zu zerdrücken.

By favouring Cuvier's catastrophism, Droste places herself in implicit opposition to a major current of scientific thought in Germany. Many German thinkers, including Werner, Novalis and Goethe, inclined to the diluvial theory, also known as Neptunism. They ascribed geological strata to chemical precipitation during the gradual retreat of the universal ocean. In the view of the Romantic physician Gotthilf Heinrich Schubert, the presence of fossils on mountain tops from the Alps to the Andes was compelling evidence for this theory.[17] Instead, Droste comes surprisingly close to some unlikely contemporaries. Byron prefaced his drama *Cain: A Mystery* (1821) with the following explanation:

> The reader will perceive that the author has partly adopted in this poem the notion of Cuvier, that the world had been destroyed several times before the creation of man. This speculation, derived from the different strata and the bones of enormous and unknown animals found in them, is not contrary to the Mosaic account, but rather confirms it; as no human bones have yet been discovered in those strata, although those of many known animals are found near the remains of the unknown.[18]

As if Byron were not strange enough company, Droste also rubs shoulders with Georg Büchner. In *Dantons Tod* (1835) Büchner puts into the mouth of his fanatical revolutionary Saint-Just an account of world history as a succession of catastrophes which make it foolish to worry about the further loss of life incurred in the Reign of Terror. By espousing this theory, Büchner aligns himself with one group of catastrophists, the Vulcanist school who ascribed changes in the earth's surface to volcanic upheavals.[19]

Droste's outlook contrasts not only with that of Werner and Goethe, but also with that of the English school of geology which was adopted by Tennyson. Contrary to what is often believed, catastrophe theory was not an attempt to shore up the Genesis narrative. Cuvier argued that the last catastrophe was a localized event, not a universal deluge. Like other Continental scientists, he was unconcerned about the compatibility of his findings with the text of the Scriptures. It was only in England that conflicts between Genesis and geology caused serious concern. Cuvier's English translator, Robert Jameson, added lengthy editorial notes to show

---

16   Nettesheim, p. 90.

17   G. H. Schubert, *Ansichten von der Nachtseite der Naturwissenschaft* (Dresden: Arnold, 1808), pp. 180–81.

18   Byron, *Poetical Works*, ed. by Frederick Page, rev. by John Jump (Oxford: Oxford University Press, 1970), p. 521.

19   See Dorothy James, *Georg Büchner's 'Dantons Tod': A Reappraisal*, MHRA Texts and Dissertations, 16 (London: Modern Humanities Research Association, 1982), p. 60.

that Cuvier's most recent revolution could be identified with the Biblical Flood, and the Oxford geologist William Buckland, though ostensibly following Cuvier, actually modified his theory to show that the Flood had covered the entire globe. Yet this meant ignoring the long-standing problem of where such a quantity of water could have come from and where it had afterwards gone. In his *Sacred Theory of the Earth* (1684) the English physico-theologian Thomas Burnet had tried to compute how much water would be needed for a flood that reached the mountain-tops, and found that on the most modest estimate it would require eight times the volume of water to be found in the world's oceans.[20]

Droste seems insouciant about the interpretation of Scripture. When she evokes the diluvial theory, compatible with Genesis, she does so humorously, evoking a topsy-turvy world in which Leviathan breasts the foam above Mount Sinai. We shall soon see, however, that she explores the imaginative implications of the catastrophe theory in a much more serious spirit.

The poem's tone changes after the speaker has descended into a clay-pit from which the surface of the earth is no longer visible. Geologists in Droste's time were fascinated by caves and other perforations in the earth's surface, imagining them 'as corridors to the deep recesses of our globe in which the archives of its history were stored, and where the secrets of its past could be discovered, including those of its antediluvian inhabitants'.[21] Hence the importance of caves and mines to Novalis, who sends Heinrich von Ofterdingen down a mine. Fossil bones were often found in caves, and while Leibniz had supposed that they belonged to creatures still living in unexplored parts of the globe, more recent naturalists assigned them to species which had either become extinct or had declined in size (so that the cave-bear, for example, was thought to have degenerated into the modern brown bear).

However, Droste's speaker descends into the clay-pit in a very different frame of mind from Novalis's Ofterdingen. Droste's imagination carries her forward from the creation of the earth to its demise. Her speaker imagines himself as the last man to survive in the burnt-out earth of the remote future:

> ein Bild erstand
> Von einer Erde, mürbe, ausgebrannt;

This conception distances Droste from the science of her day. A long-held view, bearing the authority of Descartes and Leibniz, maintained that the earth had originated as a fiery, star-like globe and was gradually cooling down, so that it would end in utter cold. Buffon in his book *Des Epoques de la nature* (1778) argued that the earth, originally incandescent, was gradually cooling. The cooling of its crust had produced mountains; the giant size of some fossils, such as ammonites, found in temperate climates, showed that these regions had formerly been much hotter. The geothermal gradient observed in mines provided further evidence for

20 Thomas Burnet, *The Sacred Theory of the Earth*, with an introduction by Basil Willey (London and Fontwell: Centaur Press, 1965), pp. 28–33.

21 Nicholas A. Rupke, 'Caves, Fossils and the History of the Earth', in *Romanticism and the Sciences*, ed. by Andrew Cunningham and Nicholas Jardine (Cambridge: Cambridge University Press, 1990), pp. 241–59 (p. 242).

the cooling of the globe. Nevertheless, Buffon's theory seemed based on doubtful observations, and dropped out of favour, until Adolphe Brongniart, in his *Prodrome d'une histoire des végétaux fossiles* (1828), argued that the history of plant life could be divided into four phases, the earliest consisting mainly of tropical plants such as giant tree ferns and club mosses which could nowadays only be found in tropical rain forests; hence the climate of the Carboniferous period must have been as hot as, or hotter than, the present tropics, and the earth had cooled down since then.[22] Tennyson adheres cautiously to this view: 'They say | The solid earth whereon we tread | In tracts of fluent heat began'.[23]

In assuming that the earth will ultimately be consumed by fire, Droste is harking back to a theological tradition, namely, that God would eventually destroy the earth in a conflagration. The Biblical authority is the second epistle ascribed to Peter: 'the day of the Lord will come as a thief; in the which the heavens shall pass away with a great noise, and the elements shall be dissolved with fervent heat, and the earth and the works that are therein shall be burned up' (II Peter 3. 10). John Donne alludes to this notion when, in his sonnet on the Last Judgement, he speaks of 'All whom the flood did, and fire shall o'erthrow'.[24] The seventeenth-century English philosopher Henry More suggested that the *novae* observed by astronomers represented conflagrations destroying other worlds.[25] His contemporary Thomas Burnet devoted one quarter of his *Sacred Theory of the Earth* to a scientific explanation of this conflagration.

Looking to the end, Droste asks the question:

> War ich der erste Mensch oder der letzte?

As Fiona Stafford has recently shown, the nineteenth-century imagination, with the huge temporal vistas opened up by science, was preoccupied by images of extinction.[26] The 1820s brought forth several literary works about the last man on earth, including Mary Shelley's novel entitled *The Last Man* (1826). In imagining the end of humanity, Droste also anticipates a vision from the end of the century, in H. G. Wells' *The Time Machine* (1895), where the traveller, having gone forward too rapidly, finds himself on the beach of a dying world, populated only by gigantic crustaceans and dimly lit by a sinister sun.

Not only the ultimate extinction of humanity, but the imminent extinction of human races is alluded to in the poem. Droste compares the varied rocks found on the Westphalian heath to the variety of human pigmentation:

> O welch' ein Waisenhaus ist diese Haide,
> Die Mohren, Blaßgesicht, und rote Haut
> Gleichförming hüllet mit dem braunen Kleide!

This recalls the conflict between palefaces and redskins recounted by Fenimore

22 Rudwick, pp. 146–47.
23 Tennyson, *In Memoriam*, p. 133.
24 Holy Sonnet 4, in John Donne, *The Divine Poems*, ed. by Helen Gardner, 2nd edn (Oxford: Clarendon Press, 1978), p. 8.
25 Rudwick, p. 77.
26 Fiona J. Stafford, *The Last of the Race: The Growth of a Myth from Milton to Darwin* (Oxford: Clarendon Press, 1994).

Cooper in *The Last of the Mohicans* (1826), a novel that was soon translated into German as *Der letzte Mohikaner*. Droste's speaker also moves to and fro in human history, feeling like one of the corpses buried in the Roman catacombs, or like one of the mummies discovered in Egyptian tombs.

We need to note also the emotional tone of the poem. The apprehension generated by these fantasies is focused in the recurring images of solitude and abandonment. Since erratic blocks and displaced geological specimens are called 'Findlinge' in German, Droste uses this term emphatically, extending it, as we have seen, to describe the whole landscape as an orphanage ('Waisenhaus'). The sense of being orphaned then afflicts the speaker as he imagines himself the last man left alive, or as the last spark flickering in the ashes of the burnt-out planet:

> Ich selber schien ein Funken mir, der doch
> Erzittert in der todten Asche noch,
> Ein Findling im zerfall'nen Weltenbau.

Terrified by these vast perspectives, the speaker no longer feels at home in the world, but rather stranded on a planet shaped by catastrophes and doomed to turn into the desolate wilderness prefigured by the clay-pit.

The poem ends with the encounter between the speaker and the shepherd. Here two mentalities are juxtaposed. Although he reads 'Bertuchs Naturgeschichte', presumably the compendium issued in 1801 by the Weimar publisher Bertuch under the title *Tafeln der allgemeinen Naturgeschichte nach ihren drey Reichen*, the shepherd does not take it seriously. He still believes firmly in the Biblical account of the Flood, and is convinced that since all the animals were drowned (except for those rescued in Noah's Ark) none of them can have been preserved as fossils. His undisturbed faith, his peace of soul, and his comfort amid his surroundings, are all conveyed with friendly humour:

> 'Ave Maria' hebt er an zu pfeifen,
> So sacht und schläfrig, wie die Lüfte streifen.
> Er schaut so seelengleich die Heerde an,
> Daß man nicht weiß, ob Schaf er oder Mann.

The speaker, on the other hand, is exposed to the perplexities suggested by modern scientific research. But what restores his mental balance is not explicit religious assurance; it is rather the solid reality of an object here and now. A piece of fabric falls down into the clay-pit; the speaker, dazed by his Egyptian fantasies, first thinks it is some linen from a mummy-cloth, then realizes: 'Nein, das ist Wolle, ehrlich Lämmerhaar.'

This turning point invites comparison with Heine's 'Seegespenst'. In the most famous example of 'Stimmungsbrechung', Heine's narrator, about to leap overboard in search of the sorrowful girl in the underwater city, is caught by the ship's captain and restored to mundane reality with a surly exclamation 'Doktor, sind Sie des Teufels?' Similarly, Droste's speaker is saved from increasingly morbid reflection by the shepherd's ball of yarn falling into the clay-pit. Heine juxtaposes an insubstantial world of fantasy with a banal reality, so that art and life are both unsatisfactory. In place of Heine's 'neither-nor', Droste supplies a 'both-and': her speaker's fantasies are founded on scientific knowledge, and the everyday reality he returns to is not banal, but firm and reassuring. It offers the solid presence of real material objects — 'ehrlich Lämmerhaar' — as a relief from the unbridled activity of the imagination. And the shepherd, despite his shortcomings, connects the speaker with a community of faith. He represents, as a perceptive commentator pointed out long ago, 'not the religious as such, but the religious as it manifests itself in custom and natural life'.[27]

Commentators have differed about how to interpret the relationship between the shepherd and the speaker. Josefine Nettesheim describes him, in a now antiquated idiom, as offering 'ein Bild aus dem Ewigen, aus der Ruhe des Spiegels, in dem das vollendete Sein als Ordnungs-Sein sich im Da-Sein offenbart'.[28] For her, the shepherd embodies the simple faith and the intimacy with nature that the speaker can only envy. Clemens Heselhaus, more soberly, maintains that the complacent ignorance with which the shepherd mocks the educated speaker rebounds on him by making him an ironic figure.[29] Although Droste's humour at the shepherd's expense is gentler than Heselhaus implies, it does establish an ironic distance between shepherd and speaker, and the irony is of a kind familiar from late Romanticism. The shepherd's love song is a Romantic 'Volkslied' embedded in an intellectually complex and ambitious text, just as songs are often inset in complex works of Romantic fiction. The speaker, a complex and troubled embodiment of modernity, cannot return to the pastoral simplicity of the shepherd. His situation resembles that of Heine's literary persona among the fisher-folk of Norderney (*Die Nordsee*) or among the miners of Clausthal (*Die Harzreise*). Simple, tradition-bound ways of living are not to be dismissed as backward in an arrogant spirit of progress; but neither can they be regarded with nostalgic envy. Like Schiller's 'sentimental' reader of 'naive' literature, the speaker appreciates the shepherd's simplicity and locates it within a complex understanding of the world.

If we apply this 'naive/sentimental' contrast to the religious implications of 'Die Mergelgrube', we can see more clearly the difference between Droste and Tennyson, and between their respective intellectual cultures. Neither poet finds a simple faith acceptable or attainable. Religious belief needs to be accommodated to the requirements of the modern intellect. For Tennyson, such adjustment runs the risk of watering religious affirmation down into a vague agnosticism that ventures, at most, to 'faintly trust the larger hope'.[30] Droste's poem, however, implies a dialectical conception in which the shepherd's simple faith remains valid as one moment within a complex religious outlook that permits faith to coexist with doubt.[31]

---

27   G[otthard] Guder, 'Annette von Droste-Hülshoff's Conception of Herself as a Poet', *German Life and Letters*, 11 (1957–58), 13–24 (p. 20).

28   Nettesheim, p. 99.

29   Clemens Heselhaus, *Annette von Droste-Hülshoff: Werk und Leben* (Düsseldorf: Bagel, 1971), p. 244.

30   Tennyson, *In Memoriam*, p. 79.

31   For an exploration of similar complexity in Heine's religious outlook, see Karl-Josef Kuschel, 'The Critical Spirit and the Will to Believe: Heinrich Heine. A Test Case', in *The Critical Spirit and the Will to Believe: Essays in Nineteenth-Century Literature and Religion*, ed. by David Jasper and T. R. Wright (London: Macmillan, 1989), pp. 158–90.

CHAPTER 17

Mörike and the Higher Criticism

It may be tempting to see Mörike as quintessentially a minor, provincial author, a representative of the Biedermeier period — at least as that was understood before the epoch-making work of Friedrich Sengle transformed our understanding of Biedermeier.[1] In such a spirit, T. J. Reed once neatly described Mörike as 'a great minor poet'.[2] Certainly, Mörike in his Swabian seclusion had a very different perspective on his age from, say, Heine, who after travels in Italy and England took up residence in Paris, already the capital of the modern world. But though Mörike was remote from the geographical centre of his age, he was still alert to many of its central intellectual and spiritual concerns. In his analysis of 'Mein Fluss' in *German Lyric Poetry*, Siegbert Prawer remarks on how Mörike 'has here evoked for us, through his intensely personal experience, the experience of the whole epoch to which he belonged': in that instance, the transition from Romanticism to Biedermeier.[3] The focus of this paper will be on a later poem, 'Auf eine Christblume', and my aim is to follow Prawer's example by linking the apparently marginal to the central. I want to argue that the apparently obscure experience of a provincial clergyman on an autumn afternoon is linked with the wider experience of his epoch — above all, with the problem of retaining Christian belief in an epoch of secularization.

Having studied theology at the Tübinger Stift and thus equipped himself for an unwelcome career as a clergyman, Mörike was well informed about the Higher Criticism and its impact on the understanding of the Bible.[4] Though the term 'Higher Criticism' came into use only in the late nineteenth century, the activity

---

1 Friedrich Sengle, *Biedermeierzeit*, 3 vols (Stuttgart: Metzler, 1971–80), esp. the section on Mörike in vol. III (1980), 691–753.

2 T. J. Reed, 'The Goethezeit and its Aftermath', in *Germany: A Companion to German Studies*, ed. by Malcolm Pasley (London: Methuen, 1972), 493–553 (p. 546).

3 S. S. Prawer, *German Lyric Poetry: A Critical Analysis of Selected Poems from Klopstock to Rilke* (London: Routledge & Kegan Paul, 1952), p. 173.

4 Mörike's reluctant acceptance of a clerical career, after failing to find a foothold in private tutoring, librarianship, publishing, or journalism, is typified by his letter to his friend Johannes Mährlen, 26 March 1829: 'Du hast keinen Begriff von meinem Zustand. Mit Knirschen und Weinen kau ich an der alten Speise, die mich aufreiben muß. Ich sage Dir, der allein begeht die Sünde wider den heiligen Geist, der mit einem Herzen wie ich der Kirche dient.' Eduard Mörike, *Werke und Briefe*, Historisch-kritische Ausgabe (henceforth HKA), ed. by Hans-Henrik Krummacher and others, 17 vols (Stuttgart: Klett, 1967–), XI: *Briefe, 1829–1832*, ed. by Hans-Ulrich Simon (1985), p. 21. For an introduction to the higher criticism and its impact on German and English literature, see E. S. Shaffer, *'Kubla Khan' and the Fall of Jerusalem* (Cambridge: Cambridge University Press, 1975).

to which it referred, the critical and historical study of the sources and methods used by the authors of the Old and New Testaments, had been under way since the Enlightenment. Its early landmarks included Johann Gottfried Eichhorn's *Einleitung ins Alte Testament* (1780–83), which first distinguished the 'Elohist' from the 'Yahwist' narratives composing the Book of Genesis; Lessing's *Neue Hypothese über die Evangelisten als bloße menschliche Geschichtsschreiber betrachtet* (published posthumously in 1788) which argued that the Gospel of Matthew was based on a lost Aramaic original; and, most scandalously of all, the anonymous *Wolfenbütteler Fragmente* by Hermann Samuel Reimarus, published after his death by Lessing. The importance of Reimarus should not be obscured by his pedantic literal-mindedness, as when he calculates how long it would have taken the Israelites to cross the Red Sea, or by his psychological obtuseness, as when he seeks to explain the Resurrection away as a successful fraud perpetrated by the disciples. His achievement was to examine closely the text of the Bible and to show how little evidence it provided for many of the claims made by the Churches. Jesus did not aim to institute a new religion, but to retain and purify the Judaism of his time. He did not found the sacrament of baptism; indeed he himself did not perform any baptisms. He did not institute a new ceremony called the Lord's Supper, but simply continued the Jewish practice of the Passover meal. His positive aim was to be recognized as the Messiah, to stir up a popular uprising, and to liberate his people from Roman rule, aims in which he was tragically disappointed.

This tradition of close historical study of the New Testament was carried on in the nineteenth century by David Friedrich Strauss, who was a personal friend of Mörike's. They got to know each other at the Tübinger Stift, which Strauss, along with another close friend, the aesthetician Friedrich Theodor Vischer, entered three years after Mörike, in 1825. Strauss's approach to the Bible, however, was significantly different from that of Reimarus. Reimarus belonged to the phase in Bible criticism known as rationalism, represented in Strauss's day especially by the theologian Heinrich Eberhard Gottlob Paulus (1761–1851) (whom we also encounter as an object of Heine's humour, 'Kirchenrat Prometheus').[5] The rationalists were no longer willing to accept the supernatural elements in the Old and New Testaments. Dealing with the Gospels, they particularly questioned the birth and childhood narratives, the miracles, and the Resurrection. They tried to retain the biblical text but to explain its events in everyday, common-sense, naturalistic terms. They thought that it was possible to strip away the legendary accretions and arrive at a core of 'what really happened'. But the explanations they offered were often shallow or trivial. A well-known example is Paulus' explanation of Jesus walking on the water (Matt. 14. 25). He supposes that Jesus was in fact standing on the shore, but that there was a low mist around his feet, so that to the disciples in the boat he appeared to be walking on the surface of the water.[6] Can we really suppose that the disciples

---

5   Heinrich Heine, *Werke*, Historisch-kritische Gesamtausgabe, ed. by Manfred Windfuhr, 16 vols (Hamburg: Hoffmann und Campe, 1973–97), II/i, ed. by Elisabeth Genton (1983), p. 124. The main target is Schelling, whose copyright Paulus was said to have infringed. The rationalist Paulus is a perverse modern Prometheus who wants to steal obscurity from heaven instead of fire.

6   I take this example from Albert Schweitzer, *The Quest of the Historical Jesus* (London: Adam & Charles Black, 1952), p. 52.

were so foolish? A more serious example, criticized by Strauss, is Eichhorn's attempt to make sense of the story of the Fall in Genesis by suggesting that the reason Adam and Eve were told not to eat of the fruit was that it was poisonous. This, as Strauss notes, takes all the profundity out of the story and makes the destiny of the human race turn on a mere silly mistake.[7] Strauss also refuses any truck with Reimarus's view (already expressed by the second-century pagan Celsus) that the disciples convinced people of the Resurrection by practising a deception: after Jesus' death, they did not want to give up their wandering lives and return to work, so they stole his body and pretended that he had risen again. On this, Strauss remarks:

> Dieser Verdacht ist schon durch die Bemerkung des Origenes niedergeschlagen, daß eine selbsterfundene Lüge die Jünger unmöglich zu einer so standhaften Verkündigung der Auferstehung Jesu unter den größten Gefahren hätte begeistern können, und mit Recht bestehen noch jezt die Apologeten darauf, daß der ungeheure Umschwung von der tiefen Niedergeschlagenheit und gänzlichen Hoffnungslosigkeit der Jünger bei dem Tode Jesu zu der Glaubenskraft und Begeisterung, mit welcher sie am folgenden Pfingstfest ihn als Messias verkündigten, sich nicht erklären ließe, wenn nicht in der Zwischenzeit etwas ganz ausserordentliches Ermuthigendes vorgefallen wäre, und zwar näher etwas, das sie von der Wiederbelebung des gekreuzigten Jesus überzeugte. Daß aber dieses Überzeugende gerade eine wirkliche Erscheinung des Auferstandenen, daß es überhaupt ein äusserer Vorgang gewesen sein müsse, ist damit noch keineswegs bewiesen. (Strauss, II, 654)

This gives some indication of the method Strauss practises in *Das Leben Jesu*. Dealing in turn with each of the controversial incidents in the Gospels, he first examines the conventional supernatural explanation and shows it to be incoherent even on its own terms, as well as being incompatible with the present state of knowledge. He then considers the rationalist or naturalist explanation, referring in detail to recent commentators, and shows it to be full of absurdities. Thus, discussing the birth narratives, Strauss considers side by side Luke's story of the shepherds and Matthew's of the Magi, and points out that they cannot both be true (I, 221). The story of the Magi is analysed in great detail and shown, on supernaturalist terms, to be incoherent. For example, the star moved from east to west, yet to guide the Magi from Jerusalem to Bethlehem it would have had to move southwards, and in any case it could not stand still over one house, or even seem to do so. As for the massacre of the Innocents, when all the children in Bethlehem were supposedly killed on Herod's orders in order to destroy the infant Jesus (Matt. 2. 16–18), this blood-bath is never mentioned by Josephus or the rabbis (I. 232), and anyway Herod could easily have found out that the child in question was no longer in Bethlehem. Strauss then examines the attempt at a naturalistic explanation given by Paulus. According to this, the Magi are Jews living abroad who, on a business trip to Jerusalem, hear rumours of a new-born king, connect them with a strange astronomical phenomenon (which may be a meteor, a comet, or a planetary conjunction), and are curious to see the king. Strauss shows that such an interpretation does violence to Matthew's text. In addition, none of the astronomical phenomena cited as possible

---

7   David Friedrich Strauss, *Das Leben Jesu, kritisch bearbeitet*, 2 vols (Tübingen: Osiander, 1835–36), I, 54.

naturalistic explanations of the star actually corresponds to its behaviour in the Gospel: it does not act like a comet or a meteor.

Having disposed of both the supernatural and the naturalist explanations, Strauss proposes that we are dealing with a legend. Legends naturally grow up around great figures. The Gospel writers were all the more likely to embroider their texts with legends because none of them was an eye-witness to the events described. Although it had previously often been thought that St John's Gospel was an eye-witness report, Strauss stresses that it is very different in character from the three Synoptic gospels, much more concerned to present a philosophical interpretation of Jesus' life and teachings. Moreover, the Gospel writers, in their presentation of Jesus, were all influenced by the conviction that he was the Messiah. Strauss makes much of this fact, thus bringing into the open a source of considerable embarrassment to orthodox Bible commentators. For the belief in his own messianic status, which Jesus seems gradually to have acquired, led him to expect that the messianic kingdom would be established quite soon, at least within the lifetime of his disciples, and that he would celebrate Passover with them in the kingdom, where they would sit on thrones and judge the twelve tribes of Israel. Since the Evangelists represent Jesus as the Messiah, they are not concerned to establish the empirical facts of his biography, but readily adjust these facts to match the expectations attached to the Messiah. For example, the Messiah was to be born in Bethlehem, so, although Jesus came from Nazareth, various incompatible pretexts are alleged to get his parents to Bethlehem in time for him to be born there. As for the star of Bethlehem, Strauss explains that the story of the star is modelled on Balaam's prophecy in Numbers 24. 17: 'there shall come a Star out of Jacob, and a Sceptre shall rise out of Israel', which was soon interpreted as being about a star heralding the birth of the Messiah. The journey of the Magi to Jerusalem is based on the prophecy that foreign kings will bring rich gifts to Jerusalem to honour the Messiah (Isaiah 60. 4: 'the Gentiles shall come to thy light, and kings to the brightness of thy rising'). The Massacre of the Innocents belongs with legends about how other great men narrowly escaped death, notably Moses (Exodus 1. 2). The flight into Egypt by Jesus' parents corresponds to stories of Abraham and Moses escaping death by fleeing abroad. Hence the birth narratives do not provide biographical data but show what a powerful messianic impression Jesus left.

Unlike the rationalist interpretations of the Bible put forward in the late eighteenth century, Strauss's is neither destructive nor reductive. He wants the Gospels to be understood as the kind of texts they are: not biographies, not historical texts in our sense, but religious texts full of legends, springing from a mentality very different from ours. He does not question the historical substance of Jesus' life — his baptism, preaching, trial and crucifixion. Nor does he question the essential truths of the Christian message. Indeed, his critical examination of the Gospels is intended to put these truths on a firmer foundation than before. For a supernaturalist interpretation is unacceptable to modern educated people, while naturalist explanations are incoherent, trivial, and frivolous:

> Den inneren Kern des christlichen Glaubens weiss der Verfasser von seinen kritischen Untersuchungen völlig unabhängig. Christi übernatürliche Geburt,

seine Wunder, seine Auferstehung und Himmelfahrt, bleiben ewige Wahrheiten, so sehr ihre Wirklichkeit als historische Fakta angezweifelt werden mag. Nur die Gewissheit davon kann unsrer Kritik Ruhe und Würde geben, und sie von der naturalistischen voriger Jahrhunderte unterscheiden, welche mit dem geschichtlichen Faktum auch die religiöse Wahrheit umzustürzen meinte, und daher nothwendig frivol sich verhalten musste (I, p. vii).

The effect of Strauss's book, however, is ambivalent. It is of inestimable value that Strauss takes seriously both the intelligence of his readers and the integrity of the Gospel text, and, instead of trying to explain away the innumerable puzzles and inconsistencies that strike the reader, confronts them and accounts for them historically. He takes away the dubious facts and gives them back as inspiring legends. But in recuperating all the problematic passages as legends, he also removes them from the modern reader. These legends belong to an earlier phase of humanity. For Strauss was a Hegelian, who thought that modern humanity was moving on from images to abstract ideas and should grasp religion as a set of philosophical truths which did not need a narrative embodiment. Hence the response of his first translator, Mary Ann Evans (better known as George Eliot), who, after working for two years to produce *The Life of Jesus, critically examined*, was described by a friend as 'Strauss-sick — it made her ill dissecting the beautiful story of the crucifixion, and only the sight of her Christ-image and picture [a cast of Thorwaldsen's figure of the risen Christ and an engraving] made her endure it'.[8]

This ambivalence is present in Mörike's response to Strauss. He may not have read the *Leben Jesu*, but he certainly knew what it contained, and he did read the polemics with which Strauss defended himself against his antagonists. The publication of the *Leben Jesu* cost Strauss his teaching post at the Tübinger Stift and obliged him to scrape a living as a freelance writer. Mörike writes to Vischer on 13 December 1837:

> Du schreibst auch von den Straußischen Bewegungen. Ich sehe ihnen mit dem größten Antheil zu. Dasjenige, was er gemeiner Christenheit durch die Kritik der EVANGELIEN nimmt, war freilich ihm und Dir und mir u. Tausenden auf einem andern primitivern Weg im Voraus weggenommen und es könnte sich nur fragen, wie denn bei einem so landkundig werdenden theol[ogischen] Bankerott zulezt der unvernünftige Haufe sich befinden u.beruhigen werde? In meiner öffentlichen Stellung als Geistlicher habe ich jederzeit geglaubt, gewisse Dinge hergebrachter Maßen als ausgemacht & faktisch voraussetzen zu dürfen, ja zu müssen, und zwar theils nach dem Grundsatz von der Unmündigkeit des Volks, teils weil doch selbst auch der Gebildete u. Wissende gern seine Andacht an die von Kindheit auf gewohnten Vorstellungen u. Formen knüpfen mag; obwohl ich Dir gestehe, daß mir bei dieser Auskunft niemals ganz wohl u. frei zu Muthe war. Inzwischen ist Straußens Maxime daß alle Forschung völlig unbekümmert um die Folgen ihre gerade Bahn fortschreiten müsse, auf keine Weise anzufechten. Er ist ein tapferer und feiner Geist & es ist eine Freude, ihn in den Streitschriften zu hören.[9]

8   Quoted in Rosemary Ashton, *George Eliot: A Life* (London: Hamish Hamilton, 1996), p. 52.

9   Mörike, letter to Vischer, 13 December 1837, HKA XII: *Briefe, 1836–1838*, ed. by Hans-Ulrich Simon (1986), 146–47.

From this letter it is clear that Mörike is thoroughly on Strauss's side. He admires his courage and his devotion to the truth. Strauss has simply pointed out what eventually everyone was bound to notice, that the Emperor has no clothes, i.e. that traditional full-scale supernaturalist Christianity cannot survive a close reading of the Gospel text, and that traditional theology is bankrupt. Thousands of educated people already know this, and eventually the uneducated masses will realize it too.

For the time being, however, the masses have not realized that much of the Gospel text is legendary, and as a practising clergyman Mörike cannot import Strauss's findings into his own work. He has to adjust his teaching to the popular understanding of the Bible, and to assume without discussion that certain things — presumably the supernatural events in the Gospels — are matters of fact. This makes his relation to his parishioners somewhat uncomfortable, for he knows that what is he teaching them is not quite what he believes to be true. Ten years earlier, Mörike had been put painfully on the spot by his sister Luise, who had often monitored his conduct with disapproval based on her pietistic religiosity.[10] Shortly before her death she questioned him about his beliefs: 'Einmal fragte sie mich: Hast Du auch einen Glauben an den Heiland E.? worauf ich leider nicht frischweg antwordten konnte.'[11] Evidently he did not share her strong faith. A few years later he acknowledged that the discrepancy between his personal Christianity, and the official version which he was obliged to present to his parishioners, was stronger than ever. He reports to Hartlaub a serious conversation with Strauss in which he explained to the latter 'daß ich bei meiner fortdauernden Neigung zum Christentum, die in den 3 lezten Jahren sich eher gestärkt u. näher bestimmt, als vermindert habe, gleichwohl den großen Unterschied zwischen dem Gebrauch, den ich davon für meine Person machen könne, und zwischen meiner Aufgabe als Prediger, so sehr es mich oft nach der Kanzel ziehe, fast lebhafter als ehmals empfinde.'[12]

But there is another element in Mörike's letter. If in one way he is on Strauss's side against his parishioners, in another way he is on their side against Strauss. When, in his letter to Vischer, he uses the phrase 'weil doch selbst auch der Gebildete u. Wissende gern seine Andacht an die von Kindheit auf gewohnten Vorstellungen u. Formen knüpfen mag', he implies that that is how he himself feels. He is not ready, either, to abandon the heart-warming Christian legends for a philosophical Hegelian religion. And this feeling, as we can see from the letter to Hartlaub just quoted, was to become stronger with the years.

Mörike's personal Christianity is not easy to explore. But it was connected with the legendary aspects of Christianity and particularly with the legends surrounding Jesus' birth and childhood. These images appear in his poetry, often linked with images from the classical world. We meet them as early as 1825, in 'An einem

10   See Mathias Mayer, *Mörike und Peregrina: Geheimnis einer Liebe* (Munich: Beck, 2004), *passim*, esp. p. 87; she disapproved, for example, of his relations with Maria Meyer ('Peregrina').

11   Mörike, letter to Charlotte Späth, 3 April 1827, HKA x: *Briefe, 1811–1828*, ed. by Bernhard Zeller and Anneliese Hoffmann (1982), p. 147.

12   Letter to Wilhelm Hartlaub, 20 March 1843, HKA xiv: *Briefe, 1842–1845*, ed. by Albrecht Bergold and Bernhard Zeller (1994), p. 91.

Wintermorgen, vor Sonnenaufgang':

> Ich höre bald der Hirtenflöten Klänge,
> Wie um die Krippe jener Wundernacht,
> Bald weinbekränzter Jugend Lustgesänge [...][13]

In *Maler Nolten*, the first version of which was completed in 1830 and published in 1832, a conversation between Nolten and Larkens introduces rather suddenly the problem of reconciling Christian feeling with the spirit of the classics, and Larkens tells Nolten that he has succeeded in doing so:

> Es frug sich, weißt du, über das Verhältnis des tief religiösen und namentlich des christlichen Künstlergemüths zum Geist der Antike und der poetischen Empfindungsweise des Altertums, über die Möglichkeit einer beinahe gleich liebevollen Ausbildung beider Richtungen in einem und demselben Subjekte. Ich gestand dir eine hohe und seltne Universalität zu, wie denn hierüber nur Eine Stimme sein kann. Ich überzeugte mich, es sei für deine Kunst von seiten deines christlichen Gefühlslebens, das immerhin doch überwiegend bleibt, nichts zu befürchten, selbst wenn zulezt der Argwohn gewisser Zeloten sich noch rechtfertigen sollte, die einen heimlichen Anhänger der katholischen Kirche und den künftigen Apostaten in dir wittern.[14]

The relation between the classics and Christianity is here presented as a tension, not between two philosophical outlooks or even two religious views, but between two sensibilities, and the 'Geist' and 'Empfindungsweise' of antiquity are contrasted with the more strongly emotional 'Gemüt' and 'Gefühlsleben' characteristic of the Christian artist. This sounds rather like Hegel's contrast between the external, sensuous character of Greek art and the inwardness of Christian art, and sure enough, in a later conversation Nolten himself draws a sharp contrast between the imagination of the plastic artist ('Vorstellungsart des bildenden Künstlers'), associating it especially with the Greeks, and the sensibility of the poet, who regards the external world with 'holde Befremdung' and, unlike the Greeks, can accommodate '[e]in Totes, Abgestorbenes, Fragmentarisches'. He concludes: 'Ich müßte mich sehr irren, oder man stößt hier wiederum auf den Unterschied von Antikem und Romantischem' (HKA III, 282).

Was Mörike a Hegelian in aesthetics, though not in religion? It would almost seem so. He is unlikely to have studied Hegel's posthumously published *Ästhetik*. In March 1843 Strauss read aloud to him 'ein schönes Capitel über MUSIK' from the *Ästhetik* (HKA XIV, 95). Mörike's report implies that he had no other knowledge of the work. But somebody educated at the Tübinger Stift in the 1820, and friendly with Strauss and Vischer, could not fail to know at second hand what Hegel was about. The important thing to note, however, is that Mörike differs in practice from Hegel as he does from Strauss. He could not quite agree with Strauss that the appreciation of Christian legends should be consigned to the past. And he does not quite agree

---

13 Eduard Mörike, *Sämtliche Werke*, 2 vols, ed. by Jost Perfahl (Munich: Winkler, 1976), I, 665. As the volumes of HKA containing the poetry are not yet complete, poems are quoted instead from this edition (henceforth SW).

14 Mörike, HKA III: *Maler Nolten*, ed. by Herbert Meyer (1967), 230–31.

with Hegel that the classical world is remote from modern sensibilities. He wants to retain the Christian legends along with the aesthetic principles of classicism. He wants, like Nolten, to reconcile classical form with Christian 'Gemüt'.

Mörike's absorption in classical poetry in the late 1830s, when he was preparing his anthology of Greek and Latin verse in translation, *Klassische Blumenlese*, had a marked effect on at least some of his poems in non-classical metres. The wayward, hesitant manner of such early poems as 'Im Frühling' largely disappears. Its reappearance in 'An eine Äolsharfe' (1837) is illusory, since the poem in fact consists of a selection of classical Greek verse-forms.[15] Mörike's songs and other strophic poems show a firm structure derived from his absorption in the classics. 'Auf eine Christblume' (1841), as we shall soon see, illustrates this development.

Larkens notes that Nolten's tendency might lead him to be suspected of Catholicism, and even to become a Catholic. There is indeed a Catholicizing tendency in Mörike's religious sensibility. It was not present in his intellectual convictions: he read Luther enthusiastically. But he clearly appreciated the prominence of sense-objects in Catholic religious practice, and he writes about Catholic services with great sympathy, as in 'Josephine', evoking the wedding of the schoolmaster's daughter in the Catholic village of Scheer.[16] He shows an ambivalent sympathy also in 'Katholischer Gottesdienst' (1845), where the emphasis is on what Protestants are missing. He owned and valued a picture of the Virgin Mary, copied after Sassoferrato.[17] His wife, Margarete Speeth, whom he married in 1851, was a Catholic. He also appreciated the simplicity of religious legends, such as the story recounted in *Maler Nolten* about the robber Jung Volker and his miraculous conversion by a deer with the sign of the cross on its back (HKA III, 298).

We have found so far in Mörike an attachment to the aspects of the Christian story that Strauss had criticized as legendary, particularly the narratives surrounding Jesus' birth; and a desire to reconcile classical form with modern, especially Christian, sensibility. But his attachment to Christian legend was in tension with another area of his imagination: the fascination with sinister supernatural forces that is so prominent in *Maler Nolten*. One of the paintings that impress Nolten's admirers shows a supernatural scene in which dead people in long robes are dancing or playing musical instruments around an organ, adorned with Gothic decoration, and played by a noble virgin with her head bowed (HKA III, 14–15). These dead people have escaped from the nearby graveyard and are defying the authority of the Church which is represented by the chapel partly visible at the edge of the picture. In the course of the novel we learn that the organist is the gipsy girl Elisabeth who exerts such a baneful influence over Nolten's life. She is the product of his uncle Friedrich's romance with a gipsy woman; she intervenes in Nolten's life in order to frustrate his attachments to Agnes and Constanze; and finally she is seen in a vision

---

15   Detailed in Walter Höllerer, *Zwischen Klassik und Moderne: Lachen und Weinen in der Dichtung einer Übergangszeit* (Stuttgart: Klett, 1958), pp. 321–56.

16   On the relation between this poem and the literary motif of the erotically charged encounter in a Catholic church, see Gerhard von Graevenitz, *Eduard Mörike: Die Kunst der Sünde* (Tübingen: Niemeyer, 1978), pp. 21–24.

17   Reproduced in Mayer, *Mörike und Peregrina*, p. 105.

as a shadowy figure embracing the dead Nolten and accompanying him arm in
arm to an unknown destination. But if she is the messenger of death to Nolten, she
also inspires his art. In addition, she is an erotic figure, contrasting sharply with the
girlish Agnes. She has a counterpart within the novel in the fairy Thereile, who, in
Larkens' shadow-play 'Der letzte König von Orplid', keeps the king Ulmon alive
under her erotic spell for a thousand years. She is linked to the real figure of Maria
Meyer, the mysterious vagrant who entered Mörike's life, briefly but fascinatingly,
in 1823–24, and to the fictional figure of Peregrina ('pilgrim') whom Mörike based
on Maria Meyer. Versions of the Peregrina poems appear in *Maler Nolten*, including
the one headed 'Warnung', which contains a powerful erotic temptation:

> Willst, ich soll kecklich mich und dich entzünden —
> Reichst lächelnd mir den Tod im Kelch der Sünden! (HKA III, 363)

The word 'Kelch', cup or chalice, jarringly combines sexual implications with a
strong suggestion of a blasphemous parody of Communion.[18]

Mörike was painfully aware of the attraction of what we may call the 'Peregrina'
dimension of life. In *Maler Nolten* he puts a harsh criticism of it into the mouth
of the Hofrat who, at the end of the novel, turns out to be Nolten's uncle: 'Was
malt er denn? Eine trübe Welt voll Gespenstern, Zauberern, Elfen und dergleichen
Fratzen, das ist's, was er kultiviert! Er ist recht verliebt in das Abgeschmackte, in
Dinge, bei denen keinem Menschen wohl wird. Die gesunde, lautere Milch des
Einfach-Schönen verschmäht er und braut einen Schwindeltrank auf Kreuzwegen
und unter'm Galgen' (HKA III, 28). This 'trübe Welt' has a position in *Maler Nolten*
comparable to that of Mignon and the Harper in *Wilhelm Meisters Lehrjahre*. Both
domains are associated with obsession, madness, vagrancy, and illicit sexuality.
Goethe invokes an oppressive atmosphere of Italian Catholicism which is also present
in some of the 'Peregrina' poetry, though Mörike links the 'Peregrina' domain with
Germanic folk-tales about elves and ghosts.[19] By writing *Maler Nolten*, that doom-
laden novel in which all the main characters go mad or die or both, Mörike at least
brought this side of his personality under control, but he did not lose contact with
the domain of Peregrina and Elisabeth, and I want to argue that in the poem 'Auf
eine Christblume' he returns to this domain and seeks to Christianize it.

First and foremost, however, 'Auf eine Christblume' goes back to an actual
experience of Mörike's. On 28 October 1841 he and his sister were looking at family
graves in the churchyard at Neuenstadt, near Cleversulzbach, when they came
across a flower, the 'Christblume' or Christmas rose. This is not really a rose, but
the black hellebore, also known prosaically as 'Nieswurz', which blooms in winter.
Mörike describes the flower in minute detail in a letter to Wilhelm Hartlaub. It has
five petals, white and coarse-textured, with a hint of pale green near the ends, and a

---

18   See von Graevenitz, p. 26, who relates this motif also to the occurrence of the word 'Kelch'
in Goethe's *Werther*; and Heinz Gockel, 'Venus-Libitina. Mythologische Anmerkungen zu Mörikes
Peregrina-Zyklus', *Wirkendes Wort*, 24 (1974), 46–56 (esp. p. 54).

19   See the discussion of the early version of a 'Peregrina' poem entitled 'Agnes, die Nonne' in von
Graevenitz, pp. 16–31, and for a comparison of Mörike's and Goethe's novels, S. S. Prawer, 'Mignon's
Revenge: A Comparative Study of *Maler Nolten* and *Wilhelm Meister*', *Publications of the English Goethe
Society*, 25 (1956), 63–85.

deeper green in the calyx. He compares it to a lily and a 'Wasserrose' or water lily. These descriptions are not botanically accurate. R. M. Browning tells us that the flower belongs to the Ranunculi family, so presumably it is a kind of buttercup.[20] But it is the emotional associations that count. As often with flowers, Mörike was moved by its fragile, vulnerable appearance. 'So reizend fremd sah sie mich an, sehnsucht-erregend!' he told Hartlaub.[21]

In the poem, an atmosphere of mystery surrounds the flower. Mörike addresses it in a tone of quiet awe and deference (SW I, 766). He says that he expected to find it growing in the wood beside the chapel; instead, he has at last discovered it on a grave in the wintry churchyard. The contrast between the two settings is only subtly intimated. The chapel and its surroundings are already steeped in holiness; even the deer grazing nearby is 'fromm' [pious].[22] Thus the flower is, as it were, sanctified by growing on consecrated soil.

Although Mörike in fact found the flower in late October, his poem makes the discovery occur later, in the depth of winter, in a setting which is 'öd und winterlich'. Later the phrase 'um die Weihnachtszeit' implies that it is actually Christmas. The image of a flower growing on a grave is a powerful and suggestive one in itself. But, more than that, the idea of birth in midwinter, in the dead season, is in Northern Europe an essential part of Christian imagery. The notion that Christ was born in the dead of winter has no historical basis, and does not need any. Its imaginative power is enough. One need only think of the well-known hymn by Christina Rossetti beginning 'In the bleak midwinter, | Frosty wind made moan'.[23] And the events of Christmas have long been imagined as taking place in winter: almost half a millennium ago, Pieter Breughel the Elder placed the Massacre of the Innocents in a snow-covered town. In this way, Mörike is subtly reclaiming the legendary aspect of Christianity from the scepticism (however respectful) of Strauss.

The flower in Mörike's evocation acquires many other Christian attributes. Again revealing his imaginative sympathy with Catholic symbolism, he associates it with the Virgin Mary, comparing its faint scent to that of her bridal dress. In calling the flower 'du Lilienverwandte', he is not providing a botanical classification but alluding to one of the symbolic attributes of the Virgin, generally shown in depictions of the Annunciation (a sacred event suggested also by the reference to the angel and Mary's bridal dress). And he wishes that the flower had five purple spots to commemorate the Passion of Christ:

> Dich würden, mahnend an das heil'ge Leiden,
> Fünf Purpurtropfen schön und einzig kleiden [...]

That would make the flower resemble the 'Blume der Passion' described in one of

20   R. M. Browning, 'Mörike's "Auf eine Christblume"', *Germanic Review*, 42 (1967), 197–214 (p. 200).

21   Mörike, HKA XIII: *Briefe, 1839–1841*, ed. by Hans-Ulrich Simon (1988), p. 218.

22   The comparison with the legend about the deer in *Maler Nolten* is developed by Browning, p. 203.

23   'A Christmas Carol' in *The Poetical Works of Christina Georgina Rossetti* (London: Macmillan, 1904), p. 246.

Heine's last and greatest poems, 'Es träumte mir von einer Sommernacht'.[24] Since, however, the flower does not in fact have such spots, Mörike is showing his imagination at work. He is not just describing the flower, he is actively interpreting it. And he has to do so, for the flower has a quite different set of associations which need to be interpreted in a Christian spirit. I agree with R. M. Browning that Mörike actively Christianizes natural phenomena, but I want to go further by arguing that Mörike is applying his Christianizing imagination to something recalcitrant, something that offers resistance, and that the resistance shows in the poem.

What is this recalcitrant element? The poem's opening words, the phrase 'Tochter des Walds', also occurs in *Maler Nolten*, 'Ein Tag aus Noltens Jugendleben', where the gipsy girl Elisabeth is called 'die seltsame Tochter des Waldes' (HKA III, 195). Later, her obsessed and disordered imagination is called a 'schlimme Zauberblume' (HKA III, 313). Elisabeth represents the pagan supernatural which in Mörike's imagination was connected with sexuality. Mörike was far from alone in making this association: Heine develops it at great length and in great variety in the first part of *Zur Geschichte der Religion und Philosophie in Deutschland* and in many other works, notably the Wild Hunt episode in *Atta Troll*. The gipsy Elisabeth occupies a place in Mörike's imagination analogous to that held in Heine's by the nymphomaniac wild huntress Diana and her two companions Abunde and Herodias, who, despite their incongruous names, come from medieval Germanic mythology.[25]

So we have here the dimension of experience which I earlier called the domain of Peregrina. There are some supporting hints of paganism. Previously, when searching for the flower, Mörike associated it with magic: 'deiner Heimat Zauberreich'. Accordingly, he did not expect to find it growing on consecrated ground, but rather in a grove, a 'Hain', a word which here, as in 'Die schöne Buche', has pagan implications. Not only might a Greek temple be surrounded by a 'Hain', as in the second line of *Iphigenie auf Tauris*, but, according to Tacitus, the ancient Germans worshipped their gods in groves. In Mörike's poem 'Die schöne Buche' the speaker feels the presence of a pagan divinity, 'des Hains auflauschende Gottheit'.[26]

However, the flower is reclaimed from paganism. It is not Elisabeth's 'schlimme Zauberblume' but a Christianized flower. But it is Christianized at a price. The price is that its beauty becomes almost incorporeal.

> Schön bist du, Kind des Mondes, nicht der Sonne;
> Dir wäre tödlich andrer Blumen Wonne,
> Dich nährt, den keuschen Leib voll Reif und Duft,
> Himmlischer Kälte balsamsüße Luft.

The beauty celebrated in this enchanting stanza is bought at the price of corporeal

---

24 Heine, *Werke*, III/i, ed. by Frauke Bartelt and Alberto Destro (1992), 391–96.

25 Heine relied especially on Friedrich Ludwig Ferdinand von Dobeneck's *Des deutschen Mittelalters Volkglauben und Heroensagen* (1815): see *Werke*, IV, ed. by Winfried Woesler (1985), p. 767. On these legends and their possible ethnographic significance, see now Carlo Ginzburg, *Ecstasies: Deciphering the Witches' Sabbath*, trans. by Raymond Rosenthal (London: Hutchinson, 1990), pp. 90–94.

26 SW I, 726. See Theodore Ziolkowski, 'Mörike's "Die schöne Buche": An Arboreal Meditation', *German Quarterly*, 56 (1983), 4–13.

existence. It is a beauty that can only exist in the cold light of the moon, not in the blaze of the sun. And it is 'keusch' [chaste], in extreme opposition to the demonic sexuality of the Peregrina domain. This beauty is the reward for renunciation. Only by renouncing gross bodily satisfaction can one enjoy the subtler pleasure of being nourished by the heavenly sweetness of the winter air. And the cost of renunciation is hinted at when Mörike meditates on the grave where the flower is growing:

> Von welcher Hand gepflegt du hier erblühtest,
> Ich weiß es nicht, noch wessen Grab du hütest;
> Ist es ein Jüngling, so geschah ihm Heil,
> Ist's eine Jungfrau, lieblich fiel ihr Teil.

Why should the grave be that of a young person — the only possibility Mörike considers? Such a person, whether male or female, will have died before experiencing adult sexuality, and before being tempted by the Peregrina domain. The flower, which itself is 'kindlich', beautifies their death, and perhaps signals their salvation ('Heil'). However bewitchingly it may be presented, the idea that it is better to die young and avoid sexual temptation is a deeply rebarbative one. It expresses the life-denying asceticism against which Nietzsche was later to campaign in *Zur Genealogie der Moral*.

This asceticism appears diffusely throughout the poem. Although in reality he found the Christmas rose on an October afternoon, Mörike has transferred the incident to a midwinter night. Everything suggests a cold translucence, a frozen delicacy. Light comes from the moon reflected on the snow, indicated by the evocative word 'Schneelicht'. The pond is frozen, and as clear as crystal ('am kristallnen Teich'). But this is not a dead landscape. It is one of refined, almost ethereal sensation. Mörike excels at evoking the feel of cold air — the 'flaumenleichte Zeit der dunklen Frühe' (SW I, 665), the 'klare Winterluft' on the Albaniturm in *Maler Nolten* (HKA III, 38), the 'Sternenlüfteschwall wie rein' in 'Der alte Turmhahn' (SW I, 790). Here the sensation of cold has a special significance. It is what you are left with if you succeed in banishing the Peregrina element, or in sublimating it out of existence. You are left with a mode of experience which is as nearly as possible incorporeal. It cannot be quite incorporeal, because the sensation of cold has to be felt by the body; rather, the body has been disciplined to appreciate sensations which are so close to the verge of corporeality as to convey some idea of what purely spiritual experience might be like. This experience has its own rewards and discoveries. The winter cold turns into 'balsamsüße Luft'. The calyx of the greenish-white flower turns out to contain 'goldne[] Fülle' and a delicate scent of supernatural, spiritual potency. Dieter Borchmeyer goes so far as to say: 'Metaphern wie diese bergen in sich mystische erotische Versprechen, die erst jenseitige Erfüllung finden'.[27] These erotic suggestions show that corporeal experience has not been transcended (how could it be?) but subtilized and sublimated to an extreme degree.

---

27 Dieter Borchmeyer, '"Auf eine Christblume"', in *Gedichte von Eduard Mörike: Interpretationen*, ed. by Mathias Mayer (Stuttgart: Reclam, 1999), pp. 144–53 (p. 51).

Suggestions of the spiritual are reinforced in the seventh stanza (which must be the conclusion of the poem, whatever the relation to it of stanzas eight and nine may be), where the humble whitish-green flower is enveloped in a mystical radiance, a 'Glorie', suggesting a halo. This is something purely spiritual; it has no counterpart in the empirical existence of the flower. By this stage in the poem we have passed through and beyond the world of the senses, into a domain of spiritual realities. In this domain, the dividing line between Christian and pagan at last becomes clear. The flower stands firmly on the Christian side, emitting a divine radiance. The elf, a pagan being, dares not come close to it, though it attracts him and arouses his curiosity. But the poem remains ambivalent about the two domains, the Christian and the pagan. On one side we have the spiritual radiance attributed to the flower. On the other, we have the elves dancing. Dancing is above all a bodily activity. Although the body is still subjected to discipline by following the steps of the dance, it moves more freely and vigorously than in everyday life. Dancing also has powerful erotic associations. For Heine, in his reflections on paganism, dancing typifies the transgressive energies of the body, and he makes a link between legends of medieval dancers and the dangerously subversive reputation of the cancan in nineteenth-century Paris. The elves may be shut out from the spiritual dimensions of the Christian imagination; but their existence is one of uncomplicated physical enjoyment.[28]

This reading of 'Auf eine Christblume' makes no claim to exhaustiveness. I have tried to present it not as a static, unproblematic poem, but as one in which several domains of Mörike's imagination, things that mattered deeply to him, are held together in suspension. I have followed the New Critical method of reading the poem as a structure of tensions which are, for aesthetic purposes, reconciled in the symbol, but which can be traced (in a way New Criticism preferred to avoid) to the biography and the historical setting of the author. With Mörike's literary and personal biography in mind, the poem can be linked to *Maler Nolten* and, beyond that, to the reverberations of his encounter with Maria Meyer. It can and should be associated also with Mörike's ambivalent response to the Biblical criticism of David Strauss, with the competing imaginative claims of the Christian and classical worlds and the world of Germanic myth and folk-tale, and thus with the tensions and conflicts of religious thought and experience in the mid-nineteenth century.

---

28   Or so one assumes. But in an impressive recent attempt to imagine fairies as embodying an alternative mode of existence to that of humans, Susanna Clarke portrays their continual dances and processions as an obsessive-compulsive activity which soon becomes wearisome, even tormenting, for the humans tricked into joining them: see *Jonathan Strange and Mr Norrell* (London: Bloomsbury, 2004).

CHAPTER 18

'Conversations with Jehovah': Heine's Quarrel with God

The last eight years of Heine's life were dominated by painful, scarcely endurable illness. His health had been uncertain for many years. From February to May 1848 he stayed in a sanatorium in Paris. In May he suffered a decisive physical collapse. He described it in a letter to his publisher, Julius Campe, on 7 June 1848:

> Meine Krankheit hat zugenommen in einem fürchterlichen Grade. Seit 8 Tagen bin ich ganz und gar gelähmt, so daß ich nur im Lehnsessel und auf dem Bette seyn kann; meine Beine wie Baumwolle und werde wie ein Kind getragen. Die schrecklichsten Krämpfe. Auch meine rechte Hand fängt an zu sterben und Gott weiß ob ich Ihnen noch schreiben kann. Diktiren peinigend wegen der gelähmten Kinnladen. Meine Blindheit ist noch mein gringstes Uebel.[1]

> [My illness has increased to a frightful degree. For a week I have been completely paralysed, so that I can only be in my armchair or in bed; my legs are like cotton and I am carried like a baby. The most horrible cramps. My right hand is also beginning to die, and God knows if I can still write to you. Dictation a torture because my jaws are paralysed. My blindness is the least of my afflictions.]

The paralysis was intermittent, but moved around his body. At times he had to hold his eyes open in order to see. Finally he became blind in one eye. Facial paralysis also meant that he had to be fed, as he put it, like a bird. Cramps caused him great pain, often making him roll up into a ball. Paralysis led to constipation (letter to Maximilian Heine, 9 Jan. 1850). The seat of his illness appeared to be the spinal cord, which was decaying. He was treated with morphine, which was inserted into open wounds on his back, and the wounds were then burned in order to cauterize them. One can only imagine what he suffered in bedsores. The exact nature of his illness is still not known. It has often been thought to be a form of syphilis which affected the spine instead of the brain, though now the consensus appears to be a form of tuberculosis.[2] For, though sometimes dazed by opiates, Heine retained his

---

1 Heine's letters are quoted from the *Säkularausgabe*, ed. by the Nationale Forschungs- und Gedenkstätten der klassischen deutschen Literatur in Weimar and the Centre National de la Recherche Scientifique, Paris (Berlin and Paris, 1970–).

2 See Hennig Montanus, *Der kranke Heine* (Stuttgart and Weimar: Metzler, 1995), p. 490; [Heinrich Tölle, 'Der kranke Heine', *Heine-Jahrbuch*, 37 (1998), 211–24].

mental clarity throughout his illness. 'Mein Kopf ist frey, geistesklar, sogar heiter', he wrote on 26 April 1848, '[...] und der Leib so gelähmt, so makulaturig. Bin wie lebendig begraben' [My head is free, my mind is clear [...] and my body so paralysed, like waste paper. As if buried alive].

Heine was looked after by his wife Mathilde (Crescence-Eugénie Mirat). She was an angel, he told his brother Gustav; 'Doch machen einem auch die Engel manchmal das Leben zur Hölle' (21 March 1851). Mathilde had a violent temper and gave her husband many rows. She drove away one of the best of his physicians, Dr Wertheim, to whom Heine excused her behaviour on grounds of insanity (5 April 1849). In fairness, though, Mathilde had much to drive her to occasional fury. Not only did she have to care for an invalid, but she was sometimes ill herself: once she hurt herself so badly falling off a ladder that she could not walk for two and a half months. They relied heavily on her companion, Pauline, who was herself at times very ill. After some moving about, they settled in a poky flat at 50 rue d'Amsterdam, where the sound of piano practice from neighbouring flats, and of hammering from a workshop, often tormented the sick man.

Worse still, Heine's financial position was insecure. The revolutionary upheavals of 1848 led to the loss of his savings, just when he had to pay for expensive medical treatment. It also came to light that for some years past he had been receiving a pension from the French government, which of course he now lost. This revelation severely embarrassed Heine, for it made it seem that he had not only supported the regime of Louis-Philippe, which he had so much criticized in print, but even rendered it unspecified services. Heine relied on regular support from his cousin Carl, with whom he was on bad terms, and on income from his books. He wanted his publisher Campe to bring out a collected edition of his works, but Campe failed to reply to Heine's letters for several years.

Besides the breakdown of his health, Heine also suffered from the disillusionment of his political hopes. The revolutions of 1848, beginning with the February Revolution in Paris, came just at a time when, having been devoted all his life to the cause of emancipation, he was too ill to take part or even to write about these events. His sole direct contact with the upheavals was on the evening of 23 February 1848, when, returning from dinner at home to his sanatorium, he met a crowd of insurrectionaries who commandeered his carriage in order to build barricades. The revolution struck him first as an occasion for posturing; then he was horrified by the bloodshed of the June days, when the national workshops were suppressed and the resulting workers' revolt was crushed by the Minister of War, Eugène Cavaignac, with some ten thousand people killed. In 1852 he opined that the foolish parliamentarians of the Second Republic had allowed Louis Napoléon's *coup d'état* to happen, not seeing that he possessed real power, but the result was that the political ideals of the Enlightenment had been shattered:

> Die schönen Ideale von politischer Sittlichkeit, Gesetzlichkeit, Bürgertugend, Freyheit und Gleichheit, die rosigen Morgenträume des achtzehnten Jahrhunderts, für die unsere Väter so heldenmüthig in den Tod gegangen, und die wir ihnen nicht minder martyrthumsüchtig nachträumten — da liegen sie nun zu unseren Füßen, zertrümmert, zerschlagen, wie die Scherben

von Porzellankannen, wie erschossene Schneider. (Letter to Gustav Kolb, 13 February 1852)

[The fine ideals of political morality, the rule of law, civic virtue, freedom and equality, the roseate dreams of the eighteenth century, for which our fathers went so heroically to their deaths, and which we too dreamed with no less desire for martyrdom — they lie now at our feet, broken, shattered, like shards of china jugs, like tailors who have been shot.]

Talking to Ludwig Kalisch, he recalled the violence of the June days and declared that in such times one could not do without religion:

Ich bin in Passy gelegen, als meine böse Krankheit anfing. Während ich mich krampfhaft auf dem Lager wälzte, wurde draußen der entsetzliche Junikampf gekämpft. Der Kanonendonner zerriß mein Ohr. Ich hörte das Geschrei der Sterbenden; ich sah den Tod mit seiner unbarmherzigen Sense die Pariser Jugend hinmähen. In solchen gräßlichen Augenblicken reicht der Pantheismus nicht aus; da muß man an einen persönlichen Gott, an eine Fortdauer jenseits des Grabes glauben.[3]

[I was lying in Passy [a suburb of Paris] when my terrible illness began. While I was writhing in cramps on my sick-bed, outside the dreadful July battle was being fought. The cannons' thunder lacerated my ears. I heard the cries of the dying; I saw death with his merciless scythe mowing down the young men of Paris. At such hideous moments pantheism is not enough; one must believe in a personal God, in a continued existence beyond the grave.]

By this time, rumours had long been circulating in the press that Heine had returned to religion, even become a convert to Catholicism. He assured his correspondents and visitors that these rumours were much exaggerated. He had not become a Bible-thumper or a pietist, a 'Frömmler' or a 'Betbruder'. '[G]lauben Sie nicht den umlaufenden Gerüchten, als sey ich ein frommes Lämmlein geworden', he warned Campe in a strongly worded letter of 1 June 1850:

Die religiöse Umwälzung, die in mir sich ereignete, ist eine bloß geistige, mehr ein Akt meines Denkens als des seligen Empfindelns, und das Krankenbett hat durchaus wenig Antheil daran, wie ich mir fest bewußt bin. Es sind große, erhabne, schauerliche Gedanken über mich gekommen, aber es waren Gedanken, Blitze des Lichtes und nicht die Phosphordünste der Glaubenspisse.

[Don't believe the rumours going around that I have become a meek little lamb. The religious upheaval that has taken place within me is merely an intellectual one, more an act of thought than of happy-clappy emotion, and my sickbed has very little to do with it, as I am well aware. Great, sublime, terrifying thoughts have come over me, but they were thoughts, flashes of light and not the phosphorescent vapours of pious piss.]

He told Heinrich Laube that a revolution had occurred in his mind, corresponding to the February Revolution in Paris:

---

3   *Begegnungen mit Heine: Berichte der Zeitgenossen*, ed. by Michael Werner, 2 vols (Hamburg: Hoffman and Campe, 1973), II, 155. Henceforth quoted in text as Werner followed by volume and page number.

> [I]ch habe nämlich, um Dir die Sache mit einem Worte zu verdeutlichen, den Hegelschen Gott oder vielmehr die Hegelsche Gottlosigkeit aufgegeben und an dessen Stelle das Dogma von einem wirklichen, persönlichen Gotte, der außerhalb der Natur und des Menschen Gemüthes ist, wieder hervorgezogen. (25 January 1850)

Indeed, he claims repeatedly to have written a book about Hegel which he destroyed for its impiety. He may be referring to this act of destruction when he tells Laube in the same letter: 'Ich habe ein schreckliches Auto-da-Fè gehalten, woran ich noch jetzt nicht ohne Erschütterung denken kann' [I have held a terrible auto-da-fé which I still cannot think of without a shudder]. In his *Geständnisse* [*Confessions*] (1854) he tells us that this act was provoked by a fear of damnation that he recognized as superstitious but was still a real fear, and that the pages gave out a strange chuckling crackle as they flew up the chimney (VI, 476–77).[4] That he did burn manuscripts is further confirmed by his conversation with Kalisch in January 1850 (Werner, II, 156).

The rejection of Hegel is a major motif in Heine's statements about his religion. In his *Geständnisse* he associates Hegel with the doctrine of the divinity of man:

> Ich war jung und stolz, und es tat meinem Hochmut wohl, als ich von Hegel erfuhr, daß nicht, wie meine Großmutter meinte, der liebe Gott, der im Himmel residiert, sondern ich selbst hier auf Erden der liebe Gott sei. (VI, 473–74)

> [I was young and proud, and it flattered my arrogance to learn from Hegel that it was not, as my grandmother supposed, the God who resides in heaven, but I myself, here on earth, who was God.]

That Heine really acquired this idea from Hegel is unlikely. It seems more like a synthesis of various ideas from Romantic philosophy and early utopian Socialism. It hangs together with many other ideas that were dear to Heine in the 1830s and earlier 1840s: the idea, for example, that Judaism and Christianity had degraded the body for the sake of the spirit, and that mankind needed sensual emancipation in the form of physical love and material well-being. Heine combined the radical Young German slogan of the emancipation of the flesh with the insistence of the French revolutionaries on material prosperity, summed up in Saint-Just's saying 'Le pain est le droit du peuple' [Bread is the people's right] (III, 23). But Heine imagined emancipation within a religious framework. He alters Saint-Just's formula to read 'le pain est le droit divin de l'homme' (III, 570). Instead of worshipping a divinity that was remote in the heavens, man should regard himself and his fellow humans as sacred. Rather than Hegel, his religious ideas were derived from Lessing, whom he described as his favourite writer, and who in *Die Erziehung des Menschengeschlechts* [*The Education of the Human Race*] (1777–80) surmised that God was educating mankind through progressive revelations, beginning with the rudimentary lessons delivered by Moses, graduating to the more refined teaching of Jesus, and moving towards the sublime doctrines which would some day be imparted by the Holy

---

4   Quotations in this form are from Heine, *Sämtliche Schriften*, ed. by Klaus Briegleb, 6 vols (Munich: Hanser, 1968–76), with volume and page number.

Spirit. In the poem 'Bergidylle' [Mountain Idyll], originally included in *Die Harz-reise* (1826) and subsequently printed in the *Buch der Lieder* [*Book of Songs*] (1827), the speaker professes himself a knight of the Holy Spirit with a mission to emancipate mankind.

Heine accordingly found uncongenial the militant atheism that was inspired by David Strauss's sceptical *Leben Jesu kritisch betrachtet* [*The Life of Jesus critically examined*] (1835–36) and propagated by the German radicals of the 1840s. Heine charges that the German atheists are 'Selbstgötter' [self-worshippers], especially Daumer, Bauer, and Feuerbach (*Geständnisse*, VI, 479; also letter to Campe, 7 June 1852). Georg Friedrich Daumer (1800–1875) was an eccentric opponent of Christianity who maintained that it was really based on the worship of Moloch which was also the basis of Judaism. Ironically, Daumer much later in life converted to become a Roman Catholic of the most extreme ultramontane variety. Ludwig Feuerbach (1804–72) was the author of *Das Wesen des Christentums* [The Essence of Christianity] (1841), which explained God as a mere projection of humanity's unsatisfied desires. Feuerbach was particularly disparaging about Judaism, claiming that the Jews were so base that they could imagine no higher act of worship than eating. Bruno Bauer (1809–1882) was a radical Young Hegelian who argued that the Gospels were mythical, that Judaism was a religion of egoism, that Christianity had a core of human love which needed to be freed from its mythical coverings by a 'reign of critical terror'.[5] It may be significant that all these three were antisemites. At all events, they formed part of a highly visible intellectual movement of radical atheism, which Heine associated also with political radicalism. '[I]ch sah nämlich,' he tells us in his *Geständnisse*, 'daß der Atheismus ein mehr oder minder geheimes Bündnis geschlossen mit dem schauderhaft nacktesten, ganz feigenblattlosen, kommunen Kommunismus' [I saw that atheism had formed a more or less secret alliance with the most horrifyingly naked common Communism, with not even a fig-leaf] (VI, 467). The people were bound to come to power. Heine thought the social revolution inevitable. But if guided by atheism, they would institute a tyranny. Left to themselves, the people would call for Barabbas to be freed and for Jesus to be crucified (VI, 469). Popular education was required, along with bread and butter to appease undeniable material needs.

Hegelian atheism is then Heine's shorthand for an outlook that was short-sighted and dangerous as well as mistaken. In its place he puts Moses. 'Hegel ist bey mir sehr heruntergekommen', he tells Laube on 25 January 1850, 'und der alte Moses steht in Floribus' [Hegel is lost all credit with me, and old Moses is flourishing]. In the poem 'Vitzliputzli', published in 1851 in the collection *Romanzero*, Moses is placed above Columbus: for while Columbus discovered a new world, and thus, without breaking people's chains, at least gave them more space for their servitude, Moses went further and gave humanity a God:

> Einer nur, ein einzger Held,
> Gab uns mehr und gab uns Beßres

---

5   Quoted in Paul Lawrence Rose, *Revolutionary Antisemitism from Kant to Wagner* (Princeton, NJ: Princeton University Press, 1990), p. 264.

> Als Kolumbus, das ist jener,
> Der uns einen Gott gegeben.
>
> Sein Herr Vater, der hieß Amram,
> Seine Mutter hieß Jochebeth,
> Und er selber, Moses heißt er,
> Und er ist mein bester Heros. (VI, 60)

[Only one, a single hero, gave us more and gave us better than Columbus — he who gave us a God. His father was called Amram, his mother was called Jochebeth, and he himself is called Moses, and he is my favourite hero.]

In his *Geständnisse* Heine dwells on the character of Moses, depicting him as an early Socialist because he instituted the year of jubilee in which property was redistributed: 'Freiheit war immer des großen Emanzipators letzter Gedanke, und dieser atmet und flammt in allen seinen Gesetzen, die den Pauperismus betreffen' (the last word is a deftly employed term of the 1840s; VI, 488). He also talks of Moses' gigantic greatness:

> Wie klein erscheint der Sinai, wenn der Moses darauf steht! Dieser Berg ist nur das Postament, worauf die Füße des Mannes stehen, dessen Haupt in den Himmel hineinragt, wo er mit Gott spricht — Gott verzeih mir die Sünde, manchmal wollte es mir bedünken, als sei dieser mosaische Gott nur der zurückgestrahlte Lichtglanz des Moses selbst, dem er so ähnlich sieht, ähnlich in Zorn und Liebe — Es wäre eine große Sünde, es wäre Anthropomorphismus, wenn man eine solche Identität des Gottes und seines Propheten annähme — aber die Ähnlichkeit ist frappant. (VI, 480)

[How small Mount Sinai seems when Moses is standing on it! This mountain is only the pedestal for the feet of the man whose head projects into heaven, where he speaks with God — God forgive me the sin, but sometimes I fancied that this Mosaic God was only the reflected glory of Moses himself, whom he so much resembles, similar in wrath and love — It would be a great sin, it would be anthropomorphism, to assume such an identity between God and his prophet — but the similarity is striking.]

This eulogy of Moses, with its hint that Moses created God in his own image (a precursor to Freud's study of Moses, *Der Mann Moses und die monotheistische Religion* [*Moses and Monotheism*], and to Thomas Mann's story 'Das Gesetz' [The Tables of the Law]) raises the question how far Heine's return to religion was a return to Judaism. It was certainly not a return to the practice of Judaism, something in any case impracticable for a bedridden man. However, he told a visitor, the novelist Fanny Lewald, about his 'sehr ernste Gespräche mit Jehovah in der Nacht' (Werner II, 112). Writing to his brother Maximilian, he says: 'der Gott unserer Väter erhalte dich' [May the God of our fathers preserve you], and adds this reflection:

> Unsere Väter waren wackere Leute: sie demüthigten sich vor Gott und waren deshalb so störrig und trotzig den Menschen, den irdischen Mächten, gegenüber; ich dagegen, ich bot dem Himmel frech die Stirne und war demüthig und kriechend vor den Menschen — und deßwegen liege ich jetzt am Boden wie ein zertretener Wurm. Ruhm und Ehre dem Gott in der Höhe!
> (3 May 1849)

[Our fathers were fine upstanding people: they humbled themselves before God, and that's why they were so obstinate and defiant towards men, mere earthly men; I, on the other hand, I brazenly challenged heaven and was humble and obsequious to men — and that's why I am lying on the ground like a crushed worm. Glory and honour to God on high!]

To another visitor, Ludwig Kalisch, Heine said:

Ich mache kein Hehl aus meinem Judenthume, zu dem ich nicht zurückgekehrt bin, da ich es niemals verlassen hatte. Ich habe mich nicht taufen lassen aus Haß gegen das Judenthum. Mit meinem Atheismus ist es mir niemals Ernst gewesen. Meine früheren Freunde, die Hegelianer, haben sich als Lumpen erwiesen. Das Elend der Menschen ist zu groß. Man *muß* glauben. (Werner II, 155)

[I make no secret of my Judaism, to which I have not returned, for I never left it. It was not because I hated Judaism that I had myself baptized. My atheism was never serious. My former friends, the Hegelians, have turned out to be scoundrels. The misery of humanity is too great. You *have* to believe.]

Heine's late work is rich in allusions to Jewish culture and history, notably in the section of *Romanzero* entitled 'Hebräische Melodien' [Hebrew Melodies], but also elsewhere. He finds an analogue for his own suffering, for instance, in that of the Babylonian king Nebuchadnezzar, who, as we learn from the Book of Daniel, 'was driven from men, and did eat grass as oxen' (Daniel 4. 33). Heine signs a letter 'Nebukadnezar II.' (to Elise Krinitz, undated). He reflects on him in *Geständnisse*:

Wie oft [...] denke ich an die Geschichte dieses babylonischen Königs, der sich selbst für den lieben Gott hielt, aber von der Höhe seines Dünkels erbärmlich herabstürzte, wie ein Tier am Boden kroch und Gras aß (es wird wohl Salat gewesen sein). (VI, 478–79)

[How often I recall the story of that King of Babylon, who thought he himself was God, but plunged from the height of his conceit into misery, crawled on the ground like a beast, and ate grass (I daresay it was salad).]

We should remember, however, that even in his late years Heine's actual knowledge of Judaism was very limited. His family were largely assimilated. He did not have a markedly Jewish upbringing, though he seems to have been encouraged to keep the Sabbath and he shows familiarity with the Passover Seder; but there is no evidence that he had a bar mitzvah, and in the first version of *Romanzero* he referred to the destruction of Jerusalem as taking place on the tenth instead of the ninth day of Ab, a mistake he corrected only at proof stage (to Campe, 7 September 1851). He was sent to Catholic schools, and was familiar with the Bible. Some four hundred Bible quotations occur in his works, about equal numbers from the Old and New Testaments.

Moreover, Heine's intellectual formation encouraged a tolerant and undogmatic approach to religion, well described in an essay by Hermann Lübbe.[6] His admired Lessing had urged toleration in his drama *Nathan der Weise*, and in *Die Erziehung*

---

6 Hermann Lübbe, 'Heinrich Heine und die Religion nach der Aufklärung', in *Der späte Heine, 1848–1856*, ed. by Wilhelm Gossmann and Joseph A. Kruse (Hamburg: Hoffman und Campe, 1982), pp. 205–318.

des Menschengeschlechts interpreted Judaism and Christianity as historical stages in the providential enlightenment of humanity. In the 1820s Heine explains how classical paganism had to be supplanted by Christianity, because the Greek gods were holiday gods whose eternal joy could appeal only to fortunate people but not to the mass of mankind whose life consisted of suffering. He also celebrates Jesus, less as the incarnation of God, but rather as a social reformer and democratic God, 'dem Wahlgotte, dem Gott meiner Wahl' [the elective God, the God of my choice] (II, 500). It was in keeping with his view of Christianity as a religion for the sick that he should perplex a visitor to his sickroom, the Prague poet Alfred Meissner, by breaking into a mock-religious chant:

> Wo die Gesundheit aufhört,
> Wo das Geld aufhört,
> Wo der gesunde Menschenverstand aufhört,
> Dort überall fängt das Christenthum an. (Werner II, 122)

> [Where health ends, where money ends, where common sense ends, that's always where Christianity begins.]

And in the late writings it is suffering that tends to be accentuated, occasionally with a Christian emphasis. This passage from *Geständnisse*, for example, reflects his knowledge of Harriet Beecher Stowe's contemporary bestseller, *Uncle Tom's Cabin* (1852):

> Sonderbar! Nachdem ich mein ganzes Leben hindurch mich auf allen Tanz-böden der Philosophie herumgetrieben, allen Orgien des Geistes mich hinge-geben, mit allen möglichen Systemen gebuhlt, ohne befriedigt worden zu sein, wie Messaline nach einer liederlichen Nacht — jetzt befinde ich mich plötzlich auf demselben Standpunkt, worauf auch der Onkel Tom steht, auf dem der Bibel, und ich knie neben dem schwarzen Betbruder nieder in derselben Andacht. (VI, 480)

> [Strange! After spending my whole life whirling about on all the dance-floors of philosophy, abandoning myself to all the orgies of the mind, whoring with all possible philosophical systems and remaining unsatisfied, like Messalina after a night of debauchery — now I find myself adopting the same standpoint as Uncle Tom, that of the Bible, and I kneel down beside my black brother with the same devotion.]

More often, however, his statements about his relation to God do not bear the impress of one particular religion. Rather, they explore the difficult questions to which religion hesitates to provide answers: questions about why people suffer, and why the good suffer in particular. As early as 19 October 1848 Heine asks in a letter to Gustav Kolb (editor of the *Augsburger Allgemeine Zeitung*, where Heine often published):

> Warum muß der Gerechte so viel auf Erden leiden? Das ist die Frage, mit der ich mich beständig auf meinem Marterbette herumwälze. Es ist wahr, daß der Schmerz ein seelenreinigendes Medicament ist, aber mich dünkt, ich hätte doch diese Kur entbehren können.

> [Why must the just man suffer so much on earth? That is the question with

which I constantly roll about on my bed of torment. Granted, pain is a medicine that purifies the soul, but I feel I could have done without this treatment.]

These thoughts found expression in the famous poem beginning 'Laß die heilgen Parabolen' [Drop those holy parables] (VI, 201), which conjectures that God may not be omnipotent, or may even be the author of evil, and concludes that such questions are unanswerable.[7] When Heine showed this poem to his friend Alfred Meissner, the latter exclaimed: 'Das nennen Sie religiös? Ich nenne es atheistisch.' 'Nein, nein, religiös,' replied Heine, 'blasphemisch-religiös' [You call that religious? I call it atheistical. — No, no, it is religious — blasphemously religious] (Werner II, 351).

Heine perplexed his visitors and correspondents by telling them that he had returned to God. He had not become a devotee of any religious denomination (he was of course formally a Lutheran), and he was able to make more scathing attacks than ever before on official Christianity. 'Vitzliputzli', for example, daringly suggests an equivalence between the Aztecs' human sacrifices, which were supposed to include cannibalism, and the Christian sacrament of the Eucharist, in which the believer is said to be consuming the flesh of Christ.

Whatever this return to God may have amounted to, it was as ambivalent as every previous attitude Heine had adopted. For the God he imagined was no merciful or loving God. It was the God who had struck him down with an agonizing illness, and about whom he told his fellow writer Heinrich Laube:

> Ich liege zusammengekrümmt, Tag und Nacht in Schmerzen, und wenn ich auch an einen Gott glaube, so glaube ich doch manchmal nicht an einen guten Gott. Die Hand dieses großen Thierquälers liegt schwer auf mir.[8]

> [I lie curled up, in pain day and night, and even if I believe in God, I often don't believe in a good God. The hand of this great vivisector lies heavy on me.]

Heine's God seems very close to the capricious despot we meet in the Old Testament. Such a God bestows his favour on some people who by no means seem to deserve it, while deliberately hardening the hearts of their antagonists and encouraging them to commit genocide against their enemies. Writing from a standpoint of professed belief in God, Heine strangely recalls the most extreme Enlightenment polemics. He takes up some of the darkest speculations of the radical Enlightenment. Much worse than the non-existence of God was the possibility that he might exist and be evil. Voltaire confronted this possibility in his early anti-Christian poem 'Epître à Uranie' (1722):

> Les Prêtres de ce Temple, avec un front sévère,
> M'offrent d'abord un Dieu que je devrais haïr;
> Un Dieu qui nous forma pour être misérables,
> Qui nous donna des cœurs coupables
> Pour avoir droit de nous punir,
> Nous fit à lui-même semblables
> Afin de nous mieux avilir,

---

7   See *The Complete Poems of Heinrich Heine*: a modern English version by Hal Draper (Oxford: Oxford University Press, 1982), p. 709.

8   Letter to Heinrich Laube, 12 October 1850, *Werke, Briefwechsel, Lebenszeugnisse*, vol. 23, p. 56.

Et nous faire à jamais sentir
Les maux les plus insupportables.[9]

[The priests of this temple, looking severe, first offer me a God whom I ought
to hate; a God who formed us to be miserable, who gave us guilty hearts so that
he could have the right to punish us, made us in his own image so as to degrade
us better, and to make us always feel the most unendurable evils.]

In 1755, in his poem on the destruction of Lisbon by an earthquake, Voltaire
cautiously tiptoes round the idea of an evil God. The destruction of a city with
sixty thousand inhabitants makes no sense with reference to divine justice, and
if it is simply a natural catastrophe, is God not powerful enough to prevent it
happening?

Others were forthright in asserting that the God of the Old Testament was
plainly evil:

Quant aux traits, sous lesquels Moyse a peint sa divinité, ni les Juifs, ni les
Chrétiens, n'ont point droit de s'en glorifier. Nous ne voyons en lui qu'un
despote bizarre, colere [sic], rempli de cruauté, d'injustice, de partialité, de
malignité, dont la conduite doit jetter tout homme, qui le médite, dans la plus
affreuse perplexité.[10]

[As for the features in which Moses paints his divinity, neither the Jews nor the
Christians have the slightest reason to glorify him. We can see in him nothing
but an eccentric and choleric despot, filled with cruelty, injustice, partiality,
malignity, one whose conduct must plunge anyone who reflects on it into the
most terrible perplexity.]

To Heine, God's actions seem sometimes arbitrary, sometimes openly unjust. In
1850 Heine learned that the husband of his cousin Therese, a man he had always
disliked, had gone mad: 'Daß Dr. Halle verrückt ist und wie ein Hahn kräht, wirst
Du wissen', Heine tells his brother Max. 'Wie witzig ist Gott!' [You will know that
Dr Halle has gone mad and crows like a cock. How witty God is!] (9 January 1850).
Sometimes God is the great humorist who plays unfunny practical jokes:

Ach! der Spott Gottes lastet schwer auf mir. Der große Autor des Weltalls,
der Aristophanes des Himmels, wollte dem kleinen irdischen, sogenannten
deutschen Aristophanes recht grell dartun, wie die witzigsten Sarkasmen desselben nur armselige Spöttereien gewesen im Vergleich mit den seinigen. (VI, 499)

[Alas! God's mockery weighs heavy on me. The great author of the universe,
the Aristophanes of heaven, wanted to show the little earthly German
Aristophanes, as they called him, in harsh terms, how his wittiest sarcasms were
only trifling jests in comparison to His.]

---

9   Les Œuvres complètes de Voltaire / The Complete Works of Voltaire, 135 vols (Geneva: Institut et
Musée Voltaire; Toronto: University of Toronto Press; later Oxford: Voltaire Foundation, 1968–):
1B: 1707–1722, ed. by Catriona Seth and others (Oxford: Voltaire Foundation, 2002), pp. 488–89.

10   [Nicolas Antoine Boulanger], Le Christianisme dévoilé, ou Examen des principes et des effets de la
religion chrétienne (London: n.pub., 1767), p. 87. Recent scholarship attributes this work to D'Holbach:
see Jonathan I. Israel, Democratic Enlightenment: Philosophy, Revolution, and Human Rights, 1750–1790
(Oxford: Oxford University Press, 2011), pp. 131–32.

But, Heine continues, though he humbly acknowledges God's superior power, his innate reason entitles him to subject God's actions to respectful criticism:

> Und da wage ich nun zunächst die untertänigste Andeutung auszusprechen, es wolle mich bedünken, als zöge sich jener grausame Spaß, womit der Meister den armen Schüler heimsucht, etwas zu sehr in die Länge; er dauert schon über sechs Jahre, was nachgerade langweilig wird (VI, 499)

> [And now I venture to make the very humble suggestions that I feel as though the cruel joke that the Master is inflicting on his poor pupil is going on rather too long; it has now lasted more than six years, which is positively boring.]

Elsewhere Heine draws on the classical myth of Prometheus to suggest that he is being punished for trying to enlighten humanity. Prometheus gave humanity the gift of fire, Heine gave them a few glimmerings of enlightenment:

> Ich leide außerordentlich viel, ich erdulde wahrhaft prometheische Schmerzen, durch Rancüne der Götter, die mir grollen, weil ich den Menschen einige Nachtlämpchen, einige Pfennigslichtchen mitgetheilt. Ich sage: die Götter, weil ich mich über den lieben Gott nicht äußern will. Ich kenne jetzt seine Geier und habe allen Respect vor ihnen. (Letter to Campe, 21 August 1851)

> [I suffer an extraordinary amount, and endure truly Promethean agonies through the ill-will of the gods, who are cross with me because I gave humanity a few tiny night-lights, a few penny candles. I say 'the gods', because I do not wish to say anything about God. I know his vultures by now and have every respect for them.]

Prometheus appears here not only as the mythical benefactor of humanity, who brought down the fire which the gods wanted to withhold from mankind; he is also the light-bringer, the bearer of enlightenment. The gods punished Prometheus (as we know from Shelley's *Prometheus Unbound*) by binding him to a mountain-peak in the Caucasus, where a vulture arrived every day to tear out his liver. The liver grew again so that the vulture could return and tear it out again the following day. Heine makes this a gruesome image of divine cruelty, sliding easily from the Greek gods to the Christian god, who is here said to be the master of the vultures. The image is also drastic in conveying that Heine's physical suffering is agonizing, and, like the vulture's repeated visits, unremitting.

It does not seem, then, that Heine's return to God can be understood within the confines of any one religion or denomination. It would seem rather that Heine acknowledged a reality for whom and for whose inexplicable actions there was a range of more or less symbolic expressions. As a poet, he was an expert on symbolism, as he explained in a letter to the radical poet Georg Weerth (a person Heine esteemed highly):

> Der Dichter versteht sehr gut das symbolische Idiom der Religion und das abstracte Verstandeskauderwelsch der Philosophie, aber weder die Herren der Religion noch die der Philosophie werden jemals den Dichter verstehen, dessen Sprache ihnen immer spanisch vorkommen wird. (5 November 1851)

> [The poet understands very well the symbolic idiom of religion and the abstract intellectual gobbledygook of philosophy, but neither the masters of religion nor

those of philosophy will ever understand the poet, whose language will always be double Dutch to them.]

The symbolic language of poetry in which Heine expressed his situation is best illustrated from the figure of Lazarus with whom he identified. Lazarus is a complex figure. He is a compound of two New Testament figures, the man whom Jesus brought back from the dead (John 11) and the beggar who lay at the rich man's gate where the dogs licked his sores (Luke 16). Heine associates him with Job, who is mentioned in the third section of *Romanzero*. After 'Historien' and 'Lamentationen', the latter recalling the lamentations of Jeremiah, we have a third entitled 'Hebräische Melodien' (incongruously borrowed from a group of poems, 'Hebrew Melodies', by Byron, one of Heine's literary heroes). The longest of the three poems in this section is called 'Jehuda ben Halevy', Heine's inaccurate name for the medieval Hebrew poet Jehuda Halevy. (As Heine gives him his correct name elsewhere, he may have introduced 'ben' only for the sake of the metre.) It is a loosely structured, ostensibly rambling poem, but with its own principle of unity through association. Every so often Heine returns to his own situation and relates it to that of the Biblical exiles:

> Bei den Wassern Babels saßen
> Wir und weinten, unsre Harfen
> Lehnten an den Trauerweiden –
> Kennst du noch das alte Lied?

> Kennst du noch die alte Weise,
> Die im Anfang so elegisch
> Greint und sumset, wie ein Kessel,
> Welcher auf der Herde kocht?

> Lange schon, jahrtausendlange
> Kochts in mir. Ein dunkles Wehe!
> Und die Zeit leckt meine Wunde,
> Wie der Hund die Schwären Hiobs. (VI, 135)

[By the waters of Babylon we sat and wept, we hung our harps on the weeping willows — do you still know the old song? Do you still know the old tune which begins by wailing and humming so elegiacally, like a kettle boiling on the stove? For long now, for thousands of years, it has been boiling in me. A dark sorrow! And time licks my wound as the dog licked Job's boils.]

Here Heine quotes from Psalm 137, suggesting a continuity from Biblical exile via Jehuda ben Halevy's situation as an unhappy poet to his own situation as a modern Job in Parisian exile; and his sores, which were all too real sores induced by his illness and its treatment, are equated not only with the boils of Job but with the sores of the beggar Lazarus which were licked by dogs. By evoking the passage of the millennia, moreover, Heine puts himself forward as representative and personification of the Jewish people. Alongside the patience of Job, however, he also has outbursts of rage, in one of which he quotes the last line of Psalm 137, originally addressed to a 'daughter of Babylon, that art to be destroyed':

> Heil dem Manne, dessen Hand
> Deine junge Brut ergreifet
> Und zerschmettert an der Felswand. (VI, 136)

[Hail to the man whose hand seizes thy brood and dashes them against a rock.]

'Happy shall he be, that taketh and dasheth thy little ones against a rock' (Ps. 137. 9). This shocking verse is here adapted to express the anger of the Jewish people against their persecutors, and also Heine's anger against the relatives whom he considered indifferent, against the injustice of the world, and, possibly, the sadistic humour of the divine Aristophanes. His anger finds expression also in the subsection of 'Lamentationen', a group of twenty poems, entitled 'Lazarus'. One of the poems is directed against the relatives who he thought had cheated him out of an inheritance. He bequeaths them his ailments:

> Meine Krämpfe sollt ihr haben,
> Speichelfluß und Gliederzucken,
> Knochendarre in dem Rücken,
> Lauter schöne Gottesgaben.
>
> Kodizill zu dem Vermächtnis:
> In Vergessenheit versenken
> Soll der Herr eur Angedenken,
> Er vertilge eur Gedächtnis. (VI, 120)

[You shall have my cramps, my floods of saliva and my twitching limbs, the desiccation of my spine, all beautiful gift of God. Codicil to the legacy: the Lord shall plunge your memory into oblivion, annihilate all recollection of you.]

The last line, as Heine knew, was an old Jewish curse, 'May his memory be forgotten', which he later makes the refrain of a poem that curiously mingles Jewish and Christian imagery of the apocalypse, as it ends:

> Selbst am Auferstehungstage,
> Wenn, geweckt von den Fanfaren
> Der Posaunen, schlotternd wallen
> Zum Gericht die Totenscharen,
>
> Und alldort der Engel abliest
> Vor den göttlichen Behörden
> Alle Namen der Geladnen —
> Nicht gedacht soll seiner werden! (VI, 324)

[Even on the Resurrection Day, when, woken by the trumpet fanfares, the hosts of the dead shall stagger to receive judgement, and the angel there shall read to the divine authorities all the names of those who have been summoned — his memory shall be forgotten!]

This is bitter, indeed savage. But there is an energy and honesty in the very bitterness. David Constantine has said of the Lazarus poems:

> Lazarus in one incarnation or another ghosts these poems. But their total effect is by no means ghastly. They come from a ground of horror and suffering, but,

without ever denying that truth, their total achievement is something we can be glad of and can live with.[11]

There is also something intriguing in the constant eclecticism of Heine's imagery, which both confirms the tolerant view of religion he had acquired from Lessing, and forbids us to identify his 'return' with the adoption of any specific religion, whether Christianity or Judaism. One last aspect of this eclecticism is the hint of an identification, not only with Job, the archetypal Jewish sufferer, but with Christ, the Christian example of suffering. Among the strangest of Heine's late poems is the untitled poem which begins 'Es träumte mir von einer Sommernacht', addressed to 'die Mouche', Elise Krinitz, the young woman whose visits lightened the last year of his life. In a dream-vision, the speaker discerns, amid classical ruins, an open marble sarcophagus, in which there lies 'Ein toter Mann mit leidend sanften Mienen'. The gentle sufferer recalls Christ, as pictures of the sick Heine bear some resemblance to the conventional iconography of the martyred Christ.[12] It also recalls another image that lingered in Heine's memory: that of King Charles I in his coffin as painted by Paul Delaroche and described by Heine, a quarter of a century earlier, in his report on the 1831 Paris Salon.[13] The identification is confirmed by the strange flower growing at his head, called the passion flower because its parts were popularly thought to resemble the implements — scourge, cross, crown of thorns, cup, nails and hammer — employed in the Crucifixion. But Heine, who for so many years upheld the emancipation of the senses, adds another twist by identifying the flower with Elise Krinitz, imagining a wordless communion between her and the dead man, and exploiting thus both senses of the word 'Passion': the suffering enacted by Christ and re-enacted by the sick Heine, and the unfulfilled passion, deflected from its obvious sexual consummation, that unites him with his woman friend. If in the person of Job Heine identifies himself with the archetype of Jewish suffering, in 'Es träumte mir...' he evokes the Christian atmosphere of Romanticism, confirming that his diverse heritage and his imaginative agility make it impossible to claim him finally for any one religious or cultural camp.

11   David Constantine, 'The Lazarus Poems', in *Heine und die Weltliteratur*, ed. by T. J. Reed and Alexander Stillmark (Oxford: Legenda, 2000), pp. 202–14 (p. 212).
12   See those reproduced in Montanus, esp. pp. 290 and 293.
13   Reproduced in *Paintings on the Move: Heinrich Heine and the Visual Arts*, ed. by Susanne Zantop (Lincoln and London: University of Nebraska Press, 1989), Plate 20.

CHAPTER 19

Nestroy's Dickensian Realism

In his massive and wide-ranging study *Ungleichzeitige/verspätete Moderne: Prosaformen in der österreichischen Literatur, 1820–1880*, Primus-Heinz Kucher addresses the question of realism in nineteenth-century Austrian literature.[1] Covering not only the German-speaking regions of the Austrian Empire but also including those in Hungary, Bohemia and Northern Italy, Kucher shows both that German-language literature is non-contemporaneous with the greater progress towards realism in Hungarian and to some extent Italian fiction, and that in German-language writing realism is to be found less in prose fiction than in travel writing — a genre whose possibilities had been explored in Germany in the 1820s by Heine, though in Austria realism in travel writing can be found already in the late eighteenth century: Franz Kratter's *Briefe über den itzigen Zustand von Galizien* (1786) would be a prime example.

A somewhat different picture might have emerged, however, if Kucher had not limited himself to prose. For a remarkable contribution to the development of realism can be found in drama, particularly in the comedies of Johann Nestroy. Geographically, Nestroy's work is of course centrally located in Vienna. But in a narrower sense, it is remote from the theatrical world of the Burgtheater at the centre of Vienna; Nestroy's comedies were staged in the suburban theatres, and the dyspeptic remarks by Viktor von Andrian-Werburg about the vulgar triviality of the 'Vorstadttheater', quoted by Kucher, illustrate their lowly status in the eyes of the cultural elite.[2] However, the realism developing in the Viennese suburbs differs markedly from the programmatic realism that developed in Germany after 1848 under the leadership of Julian Schmidt, Gustav Freytag, and other contributors to the liberal journal *Die Grenzboten*.[3] It is a kind of realism, or a succession of different realisms, which I call Dickensian.

1 Primus-Heinz Kucher, *Ungleichzeitige/verspätete Moderne: Prosaformen in der österreichischen Literatur, 1820–1880* (Tübingen und Basel: A. Francke, 2002).

2 Kucher, 'Legitimität und "trostlose Realität der Gegenwart..."': Österreich um 1840 aus dem Blick von Anastasius Grün und Viktor von Andrian-Werburg', *Oxford German Studies*, 40 (2011), 253–69 (p. 266).

3 For a useful sketch of this critical school, see Peter James Bowman, 'Fontane and the Programmatic Realists: Contrasting Theories of the Novel', *Modern Language Review*, 103 (2008), 129–42.

One way of putting this would be to say that Nestroy is a realist only in a Pickwickian sense. This is, or was, a proverbial expression in English. It will be recalled that at the meeting of the Pickwick Club solemnly recorded by Dickens in the first chapter of *The Pickwick Papers*, a member who has called Mr Pickwick a humbug, and refused to withdraw the expression, is asked by the chair whether he used the expression in a common sense, and replies that 'he had merely considered him a humbug in a Pickwickian point of view'.[4] But Nestroy is a realist in another Pickwickian sense: his realism, especially in his plays of the 1830s, resembles *The Pickwick Papers* (published serially from April 1836 to November 1837, and in book form in 1837) in combining realism with comedy and fairy-tale.

The comparison is not arbitrary. For one thing, Nestroy knew some of Dickens's work. Early in 1848 he adapted *Martin Chuzzlewit* as *Die lieben Anverwandten*, turning Pecksniff into Edelschein, and the loyal Tom Pinch into Lampl.[5] Edelschein was the role played by Nestroy himself, while his colleague Wenzel Scholz, who always played the stooge, had the part of Lampl. Nestroy also noted down some striking phrases from the novel in the notes he collected as his *Reserve*. Although his adaptation did not include the American chapters of *Chuzzlewit*, Nestroy noted some examples of American grandiloquence: thus the utterance by the Transcendentalist lady, 'Howls the sublime, and softly sleeps the calm Ideal, in the whispering chambers of Imagination', reappears in the *Reserve* as 'Während die Wirklichkeit heult wie Sturm, schlummert das stille Ideal in den flüsternden Kammern der Phantasie'.[6]

For another, Nestroy's contemporaries noticed the resemblance to Dickens — not specifically to *The Pickwick Papers*, though it was available in a German translation made by another Viennese dramatist, Eduard von Bauernfeld. In 1842 Ludwig August Frankl (not intending a compliment) called Nestroy 'der deutsche Boz auf den Brettern'.[7] In the same year, Moritz Saphir called him 'der "Boz" der *Volksdichter*'.[8] 'Boz', it will be remembered, was the pseudonym under which Dickens began writing in 1834 and published *Sketches by Boz* and the early numbers of *Pickwick*; his identity was not exposed until July 1836.[9] Saphir, too, meant this as a criticism. He continues by saying that Nestroy abuses his exceptional talent by depicting a world devoid of the ideal and the typical: 'Wie bei Boz ist bei Nestroy

4   Charles Dickens, *The Posthumous Papers of the Pickwick Club*, The Oxford Illustrated Dickens (Oxford: Oxford University Press, 1966), p. 5.

5   Nestroy's adaptation is examined by W. E. Yates, *Nestroy: Satire and Parody in Viennese Popular Comedy* (Cambridge: Cambridge University Press, 1972), pp. 126–32, and exhaustively by the editor of *Die lieben Anverwandten* in Johann Nestroy, *Stücke 25/II*, ed. by Friedrich Walla (Vienna: Deuticke, 2001), pp. 111–35; four German translations of *Chuzzlewit* were produced within five years, but Walla has established that Nestroy read the translation by E. A. Moriarty, published in 1844.

6   See *Martin Chuzzlewit*, The Oxford Illustrated Dickens, p. 542; *Reserve und andere Notizen*, ed. by W. E. Yates, Quodlibet, 2, 2nd revised edn (Vienna: Lehner, 2003), p. 103.

7   Quoted in Nestroy, *Stücke 22*, ed. by W. Edgar Yates (Vienna: Deuticke, 1996), p. 174.

8   Saphir in *Der Humorist*, 20 November 1843, quoted in *Stücke 25/II*, p. 111.

9   See Michael Slater, *Charles Dickens* (New Haven, CT, and London: Yale University Press, 2009), pp. 42, 75.

Alles und Jedes ein Individuum: Alles ist *materiell*, Alles rohes *Fleisch* und Blut.'[10]
He deplores the presence in their works of empirical reality reproduced for its own
sake and not for its symbolic significance:

> In was aber Nestroy am meisten Aehnlichkeit mit Boz hat, ist seine *Vorliebe
> zur Karrikatur*, seine *Herabziehung zum Gemeinen*, seine innige *Vorliebe für das
> Häßliche*, seine Leidenschaft für das Niedrige und Triviale im Leben, in der
> Gesellschaft, seine Anhänglichkeit an den moralischen Trotteln und Cretins
> in den Spelunken des Volkslebens! Bei Nestroy und bei Boz sind die Scheuß-
> lichkeit und die Gräulichkeit der Figuren und der Lokale nicht *symbolische
> Behelfe*, sondern sie sind um ihrer selbst willen da, sie sollen sich darstellen
> als absolut scheußlich, als die unausweichlichen lebendigen Wegweiser auf
> dem Wege der Gesammtmenschheit! Allein bei Nestroy fehlt, was an Boz so
> wundersam erquickend ist, das rückkehrende Gleichgewicht der Gestalten, die
> wiedererrungene Harmonie in der Dissonanz, die genügende Wiederkehr aller
> Formen in ihre gleiche Maße.[11]

This passage is interesting for the perplexity it evinces. Saphir seems still to
acknowledge a classical aesthetic of harmony in which the ugly should only serve
symbolic purposes and empirical reality should be idealized. When a play, story,
or sketch represents materials that disturb such harmony, Saphir resorts to such
strong language as 'caricature', 'meanness', 'ugliness' to indicate how discordant
they are with his expectations of art. He has no conception of the realism already
adumbrated by Büchner's Lenz: 'Ich verlange in allem — Leben, Möglichkeit des
Daseins, und dann ist's gut; wir haben dann nicht zu fragen, ob es schön, ob es
häßlich ist.'[12] He is responding to a literary phenomenon which he can perceive but
not yet categorize.

My concern here is not with Nestroy's possible debt to Dickens but with the
affinities and resemblances between the two. Both are popular writers dealing
in literary genres and modes — farce, broad comedy, fairy-tale and, in Dickens's
case, melodrama — which might seem incompatible with realism, but which do
in fact allow a great deal of realism to be smuggled in. The fairy-tale element is
familiar in the early plays by Nestroy which draw on the Viennese 'Zauberstück'
and 'Besserungsstück', such as *Der confuse Zauberer* (1832) and *Der böse Geist Lumpacivagabundus* (1833), while confronting magical spirits with such solid realities as the
incurable dissipation of the journeymen Knieriem and Zwirn. (Even in the printed
version of 1835, it requires the forceful intervention of the fairy king Stellaris to cure
Kniereim of his obsession with astronomy and turn Zwirn into a caring husband
and father.)[13] Dickens not only employs a supernatural apparatus in *A Christmas
Carol* (1843), where Scrooge is reformed by successive visits from his partner Marley's
ghost and by the Spirits of Christmas Past, Christmas Present and Christmas Yet to
Come, but also, more unobtrusively, makes the story of Mr Pickwick into a fable

---

10 *Stücke 25/II*, p. 111.

11 *Stücke 25/II*, pp. 111–12.

12 Georg Büchner, *Sämtliche Werke, Briefe und Dokumente*, ed. by Henri Poschmann, 2 vols
(Frankfurt a.M.: Deutsche Klassiker Verlag, 1992), I, 234.

13 *Stücke 5*, ed. by Friedrich Walla (Vienna: Jugend und Volk, 1993), pp. 185–87.

of innocence and experience. Underneath the clowning, *The Pickwick Papers* is the story of a truly good man who undergoes voluntary suffering (he chooses to serve a prison sentence rather than pay damages after losing a flagrantly unjust lawsuit brought against him for breach of promise of marriage) and in the end manages to forgive his enemies and live happily ever after.[14]

Comparing Nestroy and Dickens, we need to distance ourselves somewhat from the older tradition in Nestroy scholarship which saw him as a purely local product emerging from the Viennese popular theatre and downplayed his international aspect. While the internationalization of theatre is recognized in the later nineteenth century, W. E. Yates has recently noted that the process begins in the Viennese popular theatre in the 1830s and is unmistakable by the 1840s.[15] Much of Nestroy's drama is adapted mainly from French and in a few instances from English sources to which he has given a Viennese character.[16] Besides *Martin Chuzzlewit*, he adapted John Oxenford's *A Day Well Spent* (1835) as *Einen Jux will er sich machen* (1842), John Poole's *Patrician and Parvenu* (1835) as *Liebesgeschichten und Heurathssachen* (1843), and Dion Boucicault's *London Assurance* (1841) as *'Nur keck!'* (1855).[17] Nestroy drew, in other words, on an international repertoire of comic plots and characters which could be adapted to local circumstances, and which particularly favoured farce. Here we recognize the theatrical world familiar to the young Dickens, who attended the theatre almost every night, contemplated becoming an actor, and was recognized by his friends as having exceptional dramatic talent.[18] Many of the plays Dickens saw were translated from French; it has been estimated that such translations and adaptations accounted for at least half the repertoire of the early nineteenth-century London stage.[19] In the episodes of *Nicholas Nickleby* (1839) concerning the theatrical company of Mr Vincent Crummles, we have a satirical insight into how plays might get written. Mr Crummles has asked Nicholas, a new recruit to his company, to write a play over the weekend:

> 'Upon my word,' said Nicholas, taking the manager aside, 'I don't think I can be ready by Monday.'
> 'Pooh, pooh,' replied Mr Crummles.
> 'But really I can't,' returned Nicholas; 'my invention is not accustomed to these demands, or possibly I might produce — '
> 'Invention! what the devil's that got to do with it!' cried the manager, hastily.
> 'Everything, my dear sir.'

---

14   See W. H. Auden, 'Dingley Dell and the Fleet', in his *The Dyer's Hand and Other Essays* (London: Faber & Faber, 1963), pp. 407–28.

15   W. E. Yates, 'Internationalization of European Theatre: French Influence in Vienna between 1830 and 1860', *Austrian Studies*, 13 (2005), 37–54.

16   See Susan Doering, *Der wienerische Europäer: Johann Nestroy und die Vorlagen seiner Stücke* (Munich: Ludwig, 1992).

17   Nestroy's treatment of his English models is surveyed in Friedrich Walla, 'Von "Einem Jux will er sich machen" bis "Nur keck!": Johann Nestroy und seine englischen Quellen', *Nestroyana*, 3 (1981), 33–52.

18   Slater, pp. 30–32, 291.

19   Catherine Peters, *The King of Inventors: A Life of Wilkie Collins* (Princeton, NJ: Princeton University Press, 1991), p. 83.

'Nothing, my dear sir,' retorted the manager, with evident impatience. 'Do you understand French?'

'Perfectly well.'

'Very good,' said the manager, opening the table-drawer, and giving a roll of paper from it to Nicholas. 'There! Just turn that into English, and put your name on the title-page.'[20]

I will now explore three kinds of realism in Nestroy's work, suggesting some resemblances to Dickens as well as pointing out some differences.

1. Detailed Realism

Nestroy outstrips most of his German-language contemporaries in what C. S. Lewis called 'realism of presentation', that is, in making his material vivid by means of sharply observed detail.[21] The plots he takes over from his sources belong to the artificial universe of farce; Nestroy fleshes them out with details drawn from the world around him. A fine example is *Eine Wohnung ist zu vermiethen in der Stadt. Eine Wohnung ist zu verlassen in der Vorstadt. Eine Wohnung mit Garten ist zu haben in Hietzing* (1837). As W. E. Yates has pointed out, this play does not offer a comprehensive panorama of Viennese street life.[22] There are no beggars and no prostitutes. It builds on conventional images of the pleasure-loving Viennese with Herr von Wohlschmack and of surly Hausmeister with Cajetan Balsam. Within those limits, it provides an immense amount of detail about daily life, especially transport and housing. Herr von Gundlhuber goes house-hunting for various trivial reasons, such as his unwillingness to move into a bedroom painted green when his daughter marries, and drags his family, including his three ill-behaved little boys and the nursemaid carrying the two-year-old baby, round a succession of flats where he wreaks havoc. The high point is when he enters the Wohlschmack apartment, just as the guests are about to celebrate the betrothal of Eduard and Therese, bringing not only his family but a dripping wet umbrella, which he unfolds to dry on the dining-room floor. One of the little boys steals a biscuit from the sideboard and in doing so breaks a plate, whereupon Gundlhuber excuses the children on the grounds that this is their normal meal-time and gives each of the boys one of Herr von Wohlschmack's apples, and a biscuit to the baby. Soon afterwards we see on the stage Gundlhuber stuffing his entire family into a coach, and getting the door closed only with great difficulty; the coach actually comes onto the stage, and its departure is celebrated by a chorus of coachmen. Gundlhuber is also a connoisseur of urban life. In his introductory song he lists the banal sights he has seen as a 'stiller

20 *Nicholas Nickleby*, The Oxford Illustrated Dickens, pp. 295–96. On the pressure on English dramatists to adapt plays from French, see Michael R. Booth, *Theatre in the Victorian Age* (Cambridge: Cambridge University Press, 1991), pp. 143, 189. G. H. Lewes outdid Nicholas by taking only thirteen hours to adapt Balzac's *Mercadet* into his own, highly successful play *The Game of Speculation* (1851) (ibid., p. 180).

21 C. S. Lewis, *An Experiment in Criticism* (Cambridge: Cambridge University Press, 1961), p. 57.

22 W. E. Yates, 'Zur Wirklichkeitsbezogenheit der Satire in Nestroys Posse *Eine Wohnung ist zu vermiethen*', *Maske und Kothurn*, 27 (1981), 147–54 (esp. p. 152).

Beobachter' or *flâneur*, such as a milk-woman quarrelling with a beggar.[23] He is willing to hold forth at great length about the overcharging on various coach routes, comparing the journey to Hietzing with the journey to Obermeidling. The play is saturated in material detail, and much of this detail is made visible on stage.

The realities of transport are also visible in both earlier and later plays. The journeymen Leim, Knieriem and Zwirn in *Lumpacivagabundus* make their journeys on foot. Überall, the Scholz character in *Weder Lorbeerbaum noch Bettelstab* (1835), who is obsessed with trivial events in Fischamend (then a village south-east of Vienna), walks from there to Vienna and back at least two hundred times a year, and calculates that if he keeps going for twenty years, he will have walked round the equivalent of the Earth seven times, thus putting to shame such overpraised voyagers as Captain Cook.[24] More modern transport appears a few years later in *Eisenbahnheirathen* (1844). By that time Vienna, Neustadt and Brünn were connected by a railway network. Rail travel from Vienna to Brünn was possible from 1839 onwards, from Vienna to Wiener Neustadt from 1841.[25] The characters are enthusiastic about this new and accelerated means of transport, as were contemporaries: to the musical and poetic tributes to the railway listed by Jürgen Hein, we can add Karl Beck's once famous poem 'Die Eisenbahn' (1838), and Heine's assertion in a letter of 9 July 1848 that because of the railway, 'Der Raum existirt nicht mehr'.[26] At the beginning, Frau Zaschelhuberinn describes how she has come by train from Wiener Neustadt to Vienna in under two hours. The foolish Peter Stimmstock has come from Krems by coach, and set out the previous morning. As Peter is still bemused by the railway, the Nestroy figure Patzmann manages to take him to Neustadt under the impression that it is Brünn. The third act opens in the railway station at Brünn, and at the very end all the cast run to catch a train, only the slow Peter being characteristically left behind. The backdrop shows the viaduct near Brünn, and at the end, according to the stage direction, we see the train going over the viaduct.[27]

The novelty of train travel also enters Nestroy's imagery. When Peter tells Patzmann he cannot say how much he hates him, Patzmann replies with typical fertility: 'Als wie der Zimmermahler den Spaliermacher, wie der Wachsler den Milly, wie der Landkutscher die Eisenbahn, das werden so ziemlich die drey größten Häße auf Erden seyn.'[28] All three comparisons suggest the ambivalence of

23   Johann Nestroy, *Stücke 12*, ed. by W. E. Yates (Vienna: Jugend und Volk, 1982), pp. 13–14.

24   Nestroy, *Stücke 8/II*, ed. by Friedrich Walla (Vienna: Deuticke, 1998), pp. 54–55.

25   Nestroy, *Stücke 20*, ed. by Jürgen Hein (Vienna: Jugend und Volk, 1986), p. 338.

26   Ibid., p. 247; Karl Beck, *Nachts: Gepanzerte Lieder* (Leipzig: Wilhelm Engelmann, 1838), pp. 29–33; Heinrich Heine, *Werke, Briefwechsel, Lebenszeugnisse*, Säkularausgabe, 27 vols (Berlin: Akademie-Verlag; Paris: Éditions du CNRS, 1970–), XXII: *Briefe, 1842–1849*, ed. by Fritz H. Eisner (1972), p. 287. See also Wolfgang Häusler, '"Überhaupt hat der Fortschritt das an sich, daß er viel größer ausschaut, als er wirklich ist.": Stichworte für den Historiker aus Johann N. Nestroys vorrevolutionärer Posse *Der Schützling*', *Römische Historische Mitteilungen*, 31 (1989), 419–51 (pp. 427–30).

27   Nestroy has no counterpart to the tragic use of the railway made by Dickens in *Dombey and Son* (1848), 'the first English novel in which the villain meets his death under the wheels of a train' (Slater, p. 250).

28   *Stücke 20*, p. 148.

progress: the 'Spaliermacher' who papers walls supersedes the 'Zimmermahler' who merely paints them; Milly's stearin candles put the manufacturer of wax candles out of business; and the railways are putting paid to coach travel. This anticipates the famous monologue on progress delivered by the protagonist Gottlieb Herb in *Der Schützling* (1847):

> Und wir leben doch in der Zeit des Fortschritts. Der Fortschritt ist halt wie ein neuentdecktes Land: ein blühendes Kolonial-Sistem an der Küste, das Innere noch Wildniß, Steppe, Prairie. Ueberhaupt hat der Fortschritt das an sich, daß er viel größer ausschaut, als er wirklich ist.[29]

This comparison too has a basis in contemporary realities. It expresses scepticism about emigration to America, something Gottlieb Herb contemplates. Immigrants were often gullible, like Martin and his companion Mark Tapley in *Martin Chuzzlewit*, who are deluded into buying land somewhere in the American South which turns out to be an uncultivable and malarial swamp. Some years later, the Austrian journalist Ferdinand Kürnberger was to issue a savage warning to immigrants in his satirical portrayal of American life, *Der Amerika-Müde* (1855).

These examples must suffice to illustrate Nestroy's realism of detail. The subject is potentially a vast one, and has not been addressed systematically, as Wolfgang Häusler has repeatedly remarked.[30]

2. Reductive Realism

Realism, however, does not mean just an accumulation of items from the real world. It also implies an attitude to the world that we call realistic. In Nestroy's case this often means a negative and satirical outlook, typified by the famously cynical remark by Strick in *Die beiden Nachtwandler* (1836): 'Ich glaube von jeden [*sic*] Menschen das Schlechteste, selbst von mir, und ich hab mich noch selten getäuscht.'[31] It is often safer to take things at face value. In *Eine Wohnung...* both Frau Gundlhuber and Amalie put their partners' faithfulness to the test, and both Gundlhuber and August fail the test. Amalie draws the conclusion that one should not test people's love: 'mein ist die Schuld, ich hätte glauben sollen und nicht prüfen, denn selten gibt's ein Glück, das nicht in Schaum zerfließt, wenn man es genau ergründet.'[32]

This reductive realism is quite alien to Dickens, who notoriously inclines towards the sentimental. Yet it is the hallmark of the 'Nestroy-Rolle', along with the ambition to master one's unfortunate circumstances through intelligence and calculation. It is tempting to see Mr Pickwick's street-smart servant Sam Weller as

29   Nestroy, *Stücke 24/II*, ed. by John R. P. McKenzie (Vienna: Deuticke, 2000), p. 91.

30   'Die Entwicklung realistischer und kritischer Züge in der Gesellschaftschilderung des Wiener Volkstheaters bedarf freilich noch intensiver Erforschung', Häusler, '"Überhaupt hat der Fortschritt das an sich [...]"', p. 449; a similar remark with particular reference to Nestroy in Häusler, *Von der Massenarmut zur Arbeiterbewegung: Demokratie und soziale Frage in der Wiener Revolution von 1848* (Vienna and Munich: Jugend und Volk, 1979), p. 91.

31   Nestroy, *Stücke 11*, ed. by Jürgen Hein (Vienna: Deuticke, 1998), p. 21.

32   Nestroy, *Stucke 12*, ed. by W. E. Yates (Vienna: Jugend und Volk, 1982), p. 80.

a prototypical Nestroy character. If Mr Pickwick represents indomitable innocence, his servant Sam Weller embodies experience and resourcefulness. A comparison suggests itself with Titus Feuerfuchs in *Der Talisman* (1840), an ingenious rogue who thanks to his quasi-magical talisman, a series of wigs, manages to hide his red hair and rise through the social ranks to become the confidential secretary of Frau von Cypressenburg, before being plunged down again by the revelation of his hair colour; but he too finds a happy ending in renouncing his ambition and marrying Salome, the humble but loving and also red-haired goose-girl.

Titus resembles Sam Weller in his resourcefulness and in his verbal dexterity. The Nestroy character typically stands apart from the others by his ability to manipulate language. Conventional phrases are 'beim Wort genommen' (to quote Karl Kraus) and turned back against their users. When Titus' uncle, on meeting his long-lost nephew, exclaims 'Ist's möglich?', Titus replies 'Wirklichkeit ist immer das schönste Zeugniß für die Möglichkeit.'[33] Sam Weller, interrogated in court, replies to a barrister's sarcasm — 'Have you a pair of eyes, Mr Weller?' — with the famous speech:

> 'Yes, I have a pair of eyes,' replied Mr Weller, 'and that's just it. If they wos a pair o' patent double million magnifyin' gas microscopes of hextra power, p'raps I might be able to see through a flight o' stairs and a deal door; but bein' only eyes, you see, my wision's limited.'[34]

Ingenuity and verbal agility are the standard features of the 'Nestroy-Rolle' which Nestroy always provided for himself. However, the difference is that Sam Weller is selflessly loyal to his master, whereas the Nestroy character is generally out for himself, a self-centred survivor in a hostile world. The Nestroy character may be a confidence trickster, like Titus Feuerfuchs, who at least gains our sympathy because he is persecuted for having red hair, or the considerably less likeable fortune-hunter Nebel in *Liebesgeschichten und Heurathssachen* (1843). He may abuse his intelligence, as Schlankel does with his malicious mischief-making in *Das Haus der Temperamente* (1837). The nastiest character in Nestroy is probably the servant Johann in *Zu ebener Erde und erster Stock* (1835), who takes rational calculation to an extreme in working out that marriage to Fanny would be uneconomic: 'Weshalb soll ich s' denn heurathen, wenn es sich nicht rentiert? Der Ehstand, wenn er kinderlos is, is um 50 Prozent kostspieliger als der ledige; kommt Familie so steigt es auf 100 Prozent; Gall und Verdruß kann man auch auf a etliche Prozent anschlag'n; ergo muß die Frau immer etwas mehr Vermögen haben als der Mann, sonst schaut für unserein ein klares Deficit heraus.'[35] Johann's downfall occurs not because he miscalculates or because calculation is shown to be unsuitable in emotional matters, but simply because he is caught stealing a purse and carried off to prison.

Johann's calculating outlook on marriage is actually congruous with Nestroy's negative attitude to the Biedermeier ideal of domestic bliss. His own unhappy

---

33   Nestroy, *Stücke 17/I*, ed. by Jürgen Hein and Peter Haida (Vienna: Jugend und Volk, 1993), p. 79.
34   *The Posthumous Papers of the Pickwick Club*, p. 484.
35   Nestroy, *Stücke 9/II*, ed. by Johann Hüttner (Vienna: Deuticke, 2003), p. 63.

marriage to Wilhelmine von Nespiesni, which effectively ended in 1827 after four years and was dissolved in 1845, lies behind the famous description of marriage in *Der Färber und sein Zwillingsbruder* (1840) as 'die wechselseitige LebensverbitterungsAnstalt'.[36] It is reflected in an early play, *Der Tod am Hochzeitstag oder Mann, Frau, Kind* (1829), in which the supernatural world intervenes in domestic life for an ostensibly moral purpose. To show him how wrong he is to regret his wife's death on their wedding day, Dappschädl is admitted successively to three alternative realities: one in which he is unhappily married, then one in which he assumes the role of his unhappy wife, and finally one in which, swaddled in blankets, he inhabits the identity of a neglected child: so much unhappiness would have resulted from the marriage, in other words, that it is best that Frau Dappschädl died before anyone could experience it.[37] The three possibilities to which Dappschädl is exposed may seem to anticipate Scrooge's three visitations in *A Christmas Carol*, except that Nestroy is even bolder than Dickens: while the Spirits of Christmas Past and Christmas Present show Scrooge real events, the Ghost of Christmas Yet to Come shows him what *will* happen if he does not undergo a change of heart, whereas in the Nestroy play, all three fantasy-sequences are firmly counter-factual ('what *would* have happened if ...').

Nestroy's first major success, *Der böse Geist Lumpacivagabundus oder das liederliche Kleeblatt* (1833), satisfies both the official ideal of domesticity and the unofficial desire for self-indulgence. Thanks to supernatural intervention, the three ragged journeymen win the lottery; but while Leim the carpenter uses the money to establish himself in business and domestic bliss with his love Peppi, the cobbler Kneipp (in the later printed version Knieriem) and the tailor Zwirn, devoted respectively to drink and dancing, squander their money and return happily to the former life of dissipation supported by begging. Thus the assumptions of the Viennese 'Besserungsstück' are overturned. Two of the dissolute trio prove incorrigible. The audience's official values are confirmed by the solid domestic life of Leim and Peppi, while their secret anarchic desires are satisfied by the incorrigibility of Kneipp and Zwirn.

Comedies end with marriage, and there are seldom hints about how the characters will go on living. We are not invited to wonder how Kathi will manage as Frau von Lips after the end of *Der Zerrissene* (1844), or Weinberl as the second husband of Frau von Fischer after the end of *Einen Jux will er sich machen*. We do have a hint in *Der Talisman* that Titus and Salome will, no doubt with great enjoyment, produce a large number of red-haired children and thus undermine prejudice against redheads by increasing their number. However, Nestroy did return to the marriage of Leim and Peppi in a sequel, *Die Familien Zwirn, Knieriem und Leim* (1834), in which their happy marriage has turned, twenty years on, into a domestic hell where 'Madame

---

36   Nestroy, *Stücke 16/I*, ed. by Louise Adey Huish (Vienna: Deuticke, 1999), p. 18. On Nestroy's marriage, see Walter Schübler, *Nestroy: Eine Biographie in 30 Szenen* (Salzburg: Residenz, 2001), pp. 76–78.

37   See Friedrich Walla, 'Nestroys Spiel mit der Biographie: *Der Tod am Hochzeitstage oder Mann, Frau, Kind*', *Seminar*, 15 (1979), 97–113. The play is included in *Stücke 1*, ed. by Friedrich Walla (Vienna and Munich: Jugend und Volk, 1979).

Leim' is a shrew and 'Herr von Leim' a social climber. In *Weder Lorbeerbaum noch Bettelstab* Blasius dreams ominously before his wedding-day about stags, and twenty years later we see him severely henpecked, obliged on a trip to the country to carry all his wife's belongings including her two lapdogs, and constantly reprimanded.[38]

In fairness to Nestroy, he also satirizes bad husbands who abuse their wives. Pechberger und Kipfl in *Genius, Schuster und Marqueur* (1832) are punished for their marital faults by becoming the slaves of Amazons. They have to rock the cradle and wash glasses while Amazons with such warlike names as Bellona, Mordiana, Lanzina and Pfeilosa lounge and drink. In this servitude, the husbands long for their previous domestic lives:

> KIPFL.   [...] Ich hab der Meinigen oft d'Kleider versetzt daß sie nicht
>   ausgehn hat können, und hab 's Geld verspielt; sie hat sich
>   nicht gmuckst.
> PECHBERGER.   Wenn mir eine Speis nicht recht war, hab ich der meinigen 's
>   Hefen nachg'worffen; sie hat um Verzeihn gebethen, und hat
>   versprochen daß sie einandersmahl besser kocht.
> KIPFL.   Das waren Weiber. O meine Ehe war so glücklich.[39]

Nestroy is particularly interesting in his treatment of children. The naughty boys in *Eine Wohnung...* are only too lifelike. He satirizes parental sentimentality. In *Unverhofft* (1845), where the confirmed bachelor Herr von Ledig finds a baby in his bed, every potential father thinks the baby looks like him. In *Die verhängnißvolle Faschings-Nacht* (1839), the proud Helene and her henpecked husband Philipp are absurdly smitten with their 'Engel' of a baby. Philipp's father Tatlhuber complains: 'wie du und deine Frau immer ach du Engel, ach du Göttergesichterl, ach das Himmelslächeln, wie ihm der Suzel [Schnuller] ausn Mund gfallen is, das seyn halt verrückte Sachen, das muß selber dem klein Kind fad wer'n.'[40] But in his remarkable opening monologue in *Der Schützling*, Gottlieb Herb speaks up in defence of children:

> Den Kindern g'schieht ohnedem viel Unrecht. Is das nicht schon Unrecht genug,
> daß man sie für glücklich halt't,? und sie sind es so wenig als wir; sie haben in
> ihren Kinderseelen alle Affecte, eine Sehnsucht, die sie mit Täuschungen, eine
> Eitelkeit, die sie mit Kränkungen, eine Phantasie, die sie mit Wauwaubildern
> quält — und dabey haben sie nicht die Stütze der Vernunft, die uns wenigstens
> zu Geboth steht, wenn wir sie auch nicht gebrauchen.[41]

Here we have a glimpse of the inner world of children which Dickens presented so intimately, above all in *David Copperfield* (1850) and *Great Expectations* (1861); the obvious counterpart in German would be the early chapters of Gottfried Keller's *Der grüne Heinrich* (1854–55). However, while Dickens and Keller can recapture imaginatively the outlook of a child, Nestroy can only reconstruct it intellectually. Here Nestroy's imagination works very differently from Dickens's. It is very much

---

38 *Stücke 8/II*, pp. 47, 68.
39 Nestroy, *Stücke 4*, ed. by Hugo Aust (Vienna: Deuticke, 1999), pp. 153–54.
40 Nestroy, *Stücke 15*, ed. by Louise Adey Huish (Vienna: Jugend und Volk, 1995), p. 113.
41 *Stücke 24/II*, p. 13.

the imagination of an adult, inclined to see the world in a disillusioned and cynical way.

3. Critical Realism

In Nestroy's later plays, written in the hungry forties, social problems are more prominent and presented in a more sharply realist manner, with less possibility of fairy-tale intervention than before. There is a comparable change in Dickens from the humorous or melodramatic tone of the earlier novels to the sombre portrayals of society that we find from *Dombey and Son* (1848) onwards. Certainly, poverty features in Nestroy's earlier plays. In *Zu ebener Erde und erster Stock* (1835), there is a sharp contrast of poverty and wealth at the end of Act 1, where the Schlucker family have nothing to eat but dry bread, while upstairs Herr von Goldfuchs is preparing to host a grand dinner. But the play's transitions from poverty to wealth and from wealth to poverty are flagrantly absurd. The Schluckers first get three hundred Gulden as a reward because a coat Damian has bought has in its lining a thousand pounds belonging to an English lord; then they win the lottery; finally, their adopted son Adolf turns out to be the son of a millionaire from the East Indies who learns of Adolf's whereabouts by a far-fetched coincidence. Goldfuchs meanwhile loses his fortune when a ship is wrecked in which it was invested; but as Johann rightly points out, he ought to have insured it.[42] In real life Goldfuchs no doubt would have insured his ship. Its loss is an artificial, literary version of sudden impoverishment, recalling the loss of Antonio's ships in *The Merchant of Venice*. The quasi-magical character of the transformation is acknowledged by signs that the Schlucker family will not cope with their new wealth: Schlucker is 'aufgeblasen', Damian and Salerl are 'mit Überladung aufgeputzt'.[43]

In the later plays, however, we hear of the 'angeborne Feindschaft zwischen Arm und Reich' (Peter Spann in *Der Unbedeutende*, 1846).[44] A significant word of the period, 'Pauperismus', occurs in *Unverhofft*, where Ledig describes what he would do if he were in charge:

> Abgeschafft würde allenthalben der Pauperismus,
> Eingeführt allgemeiner Vielsauff- und Vielfrießmus.[45]

'Pauperismus' appears again in *Höllenangst* (1849), where Wendelin introduces himself with the words: 'Ich heiße Wendelin Pfrim. Ich bin ein Proletariatsbeflissener, der den ganzen practischen Curs vom Pauperismus durchgemacht hat.'[46] It was a newly current word expressing the state of irremediable immiseration which appeared to afflict a large part of the population: by the late 1840s, as many as eighty per cent of Austrians may have been living in poverty or at least in extremely precarious

42   *Stücke 9/II*, p. 87.
43   *Stücke 9/II*, pp. 116, 119.
44   Nestroy, *Stücke 23/II*, ed. by Jürgen Hein (Vienna: Jugend und Volk, 1995), p. 71.
45   Nestroy, *Stücke 23/I*, ed. by Jürgen Hein (Vienna: Jugend und Volk, 1994), p. 51.
46   Nestroy, *Stücke 27/II*, ed. by Jürgen Hein (Vienna: Deuticke, 1998), p. 45.

circumstances.[47] A contemporary reference book explained:

> Pauperismus ist ein neuerfundener Ausdruck für eine neue höchst bedeutsame
> und unheilvolle Erscheinung, den man im Deutschen durch die Worte
> Massenarmut oder Armentum wiederzugeben versucht hat. [...] Der Pauperismus
> ist da vorhanden, wo eine zahlreiche Volksklasse sich durch die angestrengteste
> Arbeit höchstens das notdürftigste Auskommen verdienen kann, [...] und dabei
> immer noch sich in reißender Schnelligkeit ergänzt und vermehrt.[48]

In using this neologism, Nestroy was drawing attention to what was considered
a new and destructive phenomenon and evoking the possibility that the mass of
the population was doomed to increasing poverty and eventual starvation. The
word and its implications tend to undermine the comic resolution of the plays by
reminding us of the irresolvable structural problems of the wider society.

This was a new note which contemporaries recognized. An obituary recalls the
'Gewitterschwüle, die vor der achtundvierziger Bewegung die Luft so drückend
machte', which found expression as 'ein Anflug politisch-sozialen Ernstes' in the
plays *Der Unbedeutende* und *Der Schützling*.[49] Well before 1848, Nestroy's democratic
sympathies are apparent, for example, through the character of Peter Spann in *Der
Unbedeutende* (1846). Spann, a carpenter, asserts his honour, and that of his sister,
who is defamed by the nobleman's secretary Puffmann in order to provide himself
with an alibi: 'was den Punkt der Familienehre betrifft, da steht der Unbedeutende
dem Größten gleich'.[50] In *Die lieben Anverwandten* (1848), a nobleman who boasts
of his ancestors is asked by Lampl (the 'Scholz-Rolle', here endowed with unusual
dignity) why it should be honourable to be descended from robbers: 'Meine
Vorältern waren Bandlkramer. Die Ritter haben vom Stegreif gelebt, den Krämern
Zoll abgenommen, auf deutsch, sie ausg'raubt, jetzt frag' ich also, warum is das
edler, wenn man von die Rauber, als wenn man von die Beraubten abstammt?'[51]

The darkening of tone is apparent if we compare two passages from plays written
early and late in the 1840s. In *Einen Jux will er sich machen* (1842) we have Weinberl's famous monologue, delivered soon after he has been singing the praises of
commerce:

> Glauben Sie mir junger Mann, der Commis hat auch Stunden, wo er sich auf ein
> Zuckerfaß lehnt und in süße Träumereien versinckt; da fallt ihm dann wie ein
> 25 Pfundgewicht aufs Herz, daß er von Jugend auf ans Gwölb' gefesselt war wie
> ein Blaßl an die Hütten. Wenn man nur aus uncompletten Makulaturbüchern

47   Ernst Bruckmüller, '"Unbedeutende" und "untere Stände" bei Nestroy', in *Hinter den Kulissen
von Vor- und Nachmärz: Soziale Umbruche und Theaterkultur bei Nestroy*, ed. by II. Christian Ehalt,
Jürgen Hein and W. Edgar Yates (Vienna: WUV Universitätsverlag, 2001), pp. 19–36 (p. 22).

48   The *Brockhaus Real-Encyklopädie* (1846), quoted in Wilhelm Abel, *Massenarmut und Hungerkrisen
im vorindustriellen Deutschland* (1972), Kleine Vandenhoeck-Reihe (Göttingen: Vandenhoeck &
Ruprecht, 1977), pp. 60–61. See the extended study of this concept and Austrian discussions of it in
Häusler, *Von der Massenarmut zur Arbeiterbewegung*, pp. 101–23.

49   Quoted in W. Edgar Yates, 'Johann Nestroy: Sein Leben — sein Werk — seine Zeit', in Birgit
Pargner and W. Edgar Yates, *Nestroy in München: Eine Ausstellung des Deutschen Theatermuseums 28.
September 2001 — 6. Januar 2002* (Vienna: Lehner, 2001), pp. 9–94 (p. 54).

50   *Stücke 23/II*, p. 24.

51   Nestroy, *Stücke 25/II*, ed. by Friedrich Walla (Vienna: Deuticke, 2001), p. 64.

etwas vom Weltleben weiß, wenn [man] den Sonnenaufgang nur vom Boden-
fensterl, die Abendröte nur aus Erzählungen der Kundschaften kennt, da bleibt
eine Leere im Innern die alle Öhlfässer des Südens, alle Haringfässer des
Nordens, nicht ausfüllen, eine Abgeschmacktheit die alle Muska[tblüth] Indiens
nicht würzen kann.[52]

This was written thirteen years before Freytag's *Soll und Haben* (1855), a novel whose
debt to Dickens was acknowledged by its author and recognized by contemporaries.[53]
Yet one is reminded of the eulogy of commerce uttered by Freytag's hero Anton
Wohlfart:

'Da widerspreche ich', erwiderte Anton eifrig, 'ich weiß mir gar nichts, was so
interessant ist, als das Geschäft. Wir leben mitten unter einem bunten Gewebe
von zahllosen Fäden, die sich von einem Menschen zu dem anderen, über Land
und Meer aus einem Weltteil in den anderen spinnen. [...] Wenn ich einen
Sack mit Kaffee auf die Waage setze, so knüpfe ich einen unsichtbaren Faden
zwischen der Kolonistentochter in Brasilien, welche die Bohnen abgepflückt
hat, und den jungen Bauernburchen, der sie zum Frühstück trinkt, und wenn
ich einen Zimtstengel in die Hand nehme, so sehe ich auf der einen Seite den
Malaien kauern, der ihn zubereitet und einpackt, und auf der anderen Seite ein
altes Mütterchen aus unserer Vorstadt, das ihn über den Reisbrei reibt.'[54]

Both Weinberl and Anton evoke the poetry of trade. But in Weinberl's speech, the
imaginative appeal of international commodities is used to bring out the tedium
and deprivation which forms the real day-to-day life of the commercial employee.
Anton's evocation of international links, by contrast, is an abstraction from the
everyday realities of office life and is a means of concealing or denying these
mundane facts. Nestroy's writing is thus richer and more honest than Freytag's.
Reading between the lines, we can see that Freytag's idealized firm T. O. Schröter
& Co. has a completely stultifying effect on its workforce. Nestroy foregrounds
the dehumanizing effect of regular work, in a way that anticipates characters
like Dickens's Wemmick, in *Great Expectations*, who is discreet to the point of
woodenness at work and human only at home.

In 1847, however, we have a more sombre tone in *Der Schützling*, the first act of
which is among the most astonishing things Nestroy ever wrote. Gottlieb Herb
is a man of education and talent, and also proud and sensitive. He feels acutely
the bitterness of poverty, saying: 'die Noth ist noch ein Genuß gegen die Noth-
wendigkeit die Noth zu verbergen'.[55] He complains of the misery of being a
copying-clerk: 'das Abschreiben ist ja leicht — (*mit Bitterkeit*) nur für den leicht, der
nichts als abschreiben kann; aber, weh' dem! der mehr kann und abschreiben muß,
für den ist es eine Marter, die nur durch den Hunger überboten wird, der ihn zum

52   Nestroy, *Stücke 18/I*, ed. by W. Edgar Yates (Vienna: Jugend und Volk, 1991), p. 27.
53   See Antje S. Anderson, 'Ein Kaufmann "von sehr englischem Aussehen": Die literarische und
soziokulturelle Funktion Englands in *Soll und Haben*', in *150 Jahre Soll und Haben: Studien zu Gustav
Freytags kontroversem Roman*, ed. by Florian Krobb (Würzburg: Königshausen & Neumann, 2005), pp.
209–24 (esp. p. 217).
54   Gustav Freytag, *Soll und Haben* (Munich: dtv, 1978), pp. 239–40.
55   *Stücke 24/II*, p. 41.

Copier-Tisch treibt.'[56] He pretends to a friend that he has commissioned someone else to copy out the friend's novel, though he is doing it himself. Accumulated humiliations bring Herb to the brink of suicide, and the first act of *Der Schützling* seems to be a parody of *Faust*: Herb is about to shoot himself, when he is distracted, not, like Faust, by the Easter bells, but by a barrel-organ playing an over-familiar tune from the then popular opera by the Irish composer Balfe, *Die vier Haimons-Kinder*.[57] Finally Herb achieves a compromise with reality. He abandons the 'fixe Idee' of rising entirely by his own merits, and accepts some measure of patronage. But in the course of the play Nestroy has vividly shown how painful it is for a sensitive and thin-skinned person to accept support from others.

Nestroy's radicalism again invites comparison with that of Dickens. The obvious difference this time is an external one: for most of his career, except for a three-month period in the early summer of 1848, Nestroy was obliged to submit his work to censorship, whereas Dickens in his later novels could write freely about the 'condition of England', its perceived political stagnation, its time-consuming legal and bureaucratic systems, and its subjection to small-minded religious authorities. Only in *Die lieben Anverwandten* and his comedy of revolution, *Freiheit in Krähwinkel* (both performed in 1848), could Nestroy speak without compromise. Even so, there are inevitably some thematic overlaps. Where Dickens in *Little Dorrit* castigates the Circumlocution Office, Nestroy includes in *Freiheit in Krähwinkel* a jibe against the slowness of Metternich's bureaucracy: we meet the official Reakzerl Edler von Zopfen, who instructs his subordinate to deal with documents thus: 'Was schon über drei Monate hier liegt, können Sie mir gelegentlich zur Unterschrift unterbreiten.'[58] Dickens's frequent satire on the joyless and often hypocritical puritanism of the dissenting clergy, from Stiggins in *The Pickwick Papers* to Chadband in *Bleak House*, finds a counterpart in Nestroy's anticlericalism, which, normally suppressed in his plays, bursts out in *Freiheit in Krähwinkel* with the expulsion of the Redemptorists and a warning about the resurgent power of the Jesuits.[59]

More broadly, the radicalism of both authors finds expression, as W. E. Yates points out with respect to Nestroy, in a sympathetic portrayal of the underprivileged — Salome in *Der Talisman*, Kathi in *Der Zerrissene*, Peter Spann in *Der Unbedeutende*, Bernhard Brunner (for once, an ordinary name that does not bespeak its bearer's profession or character) in *Kampl* (1852).[60] It does not imply a commitment to Socialism, a claim that has sometimes been confuted by the equally implausible ascription to Nestroy of a conservative outlook.[61] Neither Nestroy nor Dickens portrays any social or political group as the repository of unalloyed virtue: hence the

---

56 Ibid., p. 14.

57 Häusler, on different grounds, compares Herb to Faust: see '"Überhaupt hat der Fortschritt das an sich [...]', pp. 445–46.

58 Nestroy, *Stücke 26/I*, ed. by John R. P. McKenzie (Vienna: Jugend und Volk, 1995), p. 24.

59 See Colin Walker, 'Nestroy and the Redemptorists', in *Bristol Austrian Studies*, ed. by Brian Keith-Smith (Bristol: University of Bristol Press, 1990), pp. 73–116, and cf. Nestroy's letter of 2 August 1842 in his *Sämtliche Briefe*, ed. by Walter Obermaier (Vienna: Zsolnay, 2005), pp. 47–48.

60 Yates, *Nestroy: Satire and Parody in Viennese Popular Comedy*, p. 161.

61 A mistake made e.g. by Eva Reichmann, *Konservative Inhalte in den Theaterstücken Johann Nestroys* (Würzburg: Königshausen & Neumann, 1995).

poor family in *Zu ebener Erde und erster Stock* show signs of being corrupted by their new-found wealth, and the parlour-maid Lisette in *Eine Wohnung...* is keen to marry the odious, elderly, but rich Cajetan, observing: 'Hausherrn haben noch selten hoffnungslos geliebt.'[62] Among political figures, Ultra in *Freiheit in Krähwinkel* is a comic character by virtue of his rhetorical excesses but puts the resourcefulness of the 'Nestroy-Rolle' solidly in the service of the revolution; he thus differs widely from Heugeig'n in the post-revolutionary play *Lady und Schneider* (1849), a caricature of an unprincipled demagogue, who has a Dickensian counterpart in the trade unionist Slackbridge in *Hard Times* (1854). Nestroy's radical sympathies emerge clearly from the late plays *Kampl*, focusing on a doctor who has chosen to practise among the poor, and *Der alte Mann mit der jungen Frau* (1849), whose protagonist saves a revolutionary from the police. The latter play, which because of the restored censorship could not be performed or even published in Nestroy's lifetime, ends with the main characters emigrating, not to America as is common in nineteenth-century German fiction, but, much more unusually — and like a group of characters in *David Copperfield* — to Australia.

In broad outline, then, Nestroy's realism resembles that of Dickens in certain respects, while diverging from it in others. Both astonished their contemporaries by their realism of presentation, by representing reality often with satirical exaggeration but never with idealization. Dickens's love of sentiment differs markedly from the reductive cynicism which is part of the 'Nestroy-Rolle'. But the two authors again resemble each other in the darker atmosphere, and the increasing focus on social evils (so far as the censorship permitted Nestroy to do so), in their later works.

If, finally, we compare the realism of Nestroy and Dickens with the programmatic realism outlined from 1848 in *Die Grenzboten*, we shall find that programmatic realism, far from constituting a bold step forward, is actually rather conservative. The programmatic realists hold fast to the classical aesthetic principle of idealization, memorably formulated by Schiller in his harsh critique of G. A. Bürger's demotic poems.[63] According to *Die Grenzboten*,

> Der *Zweck* der Kunst, namentlich der Dichtkunst, ist, Ideale aufzustellen, d.h. Gestalten und Geschichten, deren Realität man wünschen muß, weil sie uns erheben, begeistern, ergötzen, belustigen usw.; das *Mittel* der Kunst ist der Realismus, d.h. eine der Natur abgelauschte Wahrheit, die uns überzeugt, so daß wir an die künstlerische Ideale glauben.[64]

Hence to the young Fontane, although he appreciated the realistic detail supplied by Dickens and Thackeray, Freytag's *Soll und Haben* seemed superior, because it subjected its representation of reality to 'ideelle Durchdringung'.[65] Satirical comedy was inferior to the quiet 'Humor', often present in Dickens, and in such English predecessors as Oliver Goldsmith, which helped to recreate the idyll for modern

---

62   *Stücke 12*, p. 24.

63   Friedrich Schiller, *Sämtliche Werke*, ed. by Gerhard Fricke and Herbert G. Göpfert, 5 vols (Munich: Hanser, 1958), v, 970–85 (esp. p. 979).

64   *Die Grenzboten* (1860), IV, 481, quoted in *Roman und Romantheorie des deutschen Realismus*, ed. by Hans-Joachim Rückhaberle and Helmuth Widhammer (Kronberg: Athenäum, 1977), p. 48.

65   Quoted ibid., p. 131.

times.[66] Such 'Humor' supported 'die Idealität des Kunstwerks'.[67] Satire also found an unacceptable expression in Dickens's comical descriptions of his characters — the 'sowohl moralisch als auch ästhetisch verderblich wirkenden steckbriefartigen Personalbeschreibungen' which Herman Marggraff, reviewing *Hard Times*, deplored as transgressing the 'Grenze der Schönheitslinie und des Schönheitsgefühls'.[68] The later Dickens, with his focus on specific social evils, illustrated 'die satirische Richtung der neuesten Poesie', which differed markedly from the more conciliatory realism practised by Freytag and praised by Schmidt:

> Der eigentliche Realist in seiner reinsten Erscheinung wird nur selten satirisch, das heißt, er geht nur selten von der Absicht aus, durch seine Darstellung auf bestimmte Schäden der Gesellschaft aufmerksam zu machen und zur Abhilfe derselben beizutragen, weil in diesem Vorhaben wieder etwas Dogmatisches, wieder eine Auflehnung gegen das Recht der Natur liegen würde.[69]

The problematic relation between centre and periphery undergoes, in this context, another twist. For the theorists of *Die Grenzboten* undoubtedly considered themselves to be supporting a literary programme which could claim to be central in that it adapted the long-established values of classicism to the selective portrayal of modern conditions of life. Dickens's reliance on comedy and satire made him, in their eyes, marginal to the development of modern literature. Yet, in retrospect, their programme now seems tame and restrictive. As such, it marks a decided retreat from the creative practice of Nestroy and Dickens.

66   Julian Schmidt, 'Charles Dickens', ibid., pp. 158–70 (p. 163).
67   Schmidt, ibid., p. 161.
68   Marggraff, 'Charles Dickens und der Materialismus', *Blätter für literarische Unterhaltung* (1854), repr. in *Quellen zur Rezeption des englischen und französischen Romans in Deutschland und Österreich im 19. Jahrhundert*, ed. by Norbert Bachleitner (Tübingen: Niemeyer, 1990), pp. 359–61 (p. 360).
69   Schmidt, 'Der neueste englische Roman und das Princip des Realismus', in *Roman und Romantheorie*, pp. 207–14 (p. 211).

CHAPTER 20

The Limits of Metaphor in Nietzsche's *Genealogy of Morals*

Nietzsche's *Genealogy of Morals* is a hugely, almost insanely ambitious treatise. It undertakes to explain the origins not only of morals but of society, custom, law, class differences, religion, priesthood and scholarship, all under the sign of the Will to Power. Being concerned with origins, it is also concerned with change and continuity. It asks, for example, how primitive man, who lived from day to day, was changed, over the millennia, into the modern autonomous subject capable of remembering the past and making promises about the future. But it also undertakes to reveal the continuity, for instance, between the early priest with his terrifying ascetic practices and the modern scholar whose asceticism takes the form of a devotion to truth. Nietzsche therefore needs models for change combined with continuity, and he finds two such models in the sciences of his own day. One is philology, which traces the transformation of words; the other is evolutionary biology, which examines the transformation of organisms. In addition, especially in the third essay, he appeals also to physiology and medicine. His constant reference to these sciences gives Nietzsche's late prose a rich metaphorical texture.

Where, though, does metaphor stop and literal meaning begin? Many of Nietzsche's recent interpreters ascribe to him a radical epistemological scepticism which would deny the possibility of knowledge and truth. Hence there could be no literal language, because there would be no solid reality for such language to refer to. And indeed *The Genealogy of Morals* ends by questioning the search for truth, describing it as the last remnant of Christian asceticism, and speaking admiringly of the Islamic sect whose secret doctrine was 'Nothing is true, everything is permitted' (III, 24).[1] Yet the Preface seems to announce a factual, scholarly, painstaking search for the truth about morality. Contrasting his own project with the Kantian concept

---

1 References to *The Genealogy of Morals* are by section and sub-section, which should enable orientation in both English and German texts. The German text is Friedrich Nietzsche, *Werke*, ed. by Giorgio Colli and Mazzino Montinari (Berlin and New York: de Gruyter, 1972–), division VI, vol. II. Translations, unless otherwise specified, are from *On the Genealogy of Morals*, trans. by Douglas Smith, World's Classics (Oxford and New York: Oxford University Press, 1996), but I have also consulted *On the Genealogy of Morality*, ed. by Keith Ansell-Pearson, trans. by Carol Diethe, Cambridge Studies in the History of Political Thought (Cambridge: Cambridge University Press, 1994), and *On the Genealogy of Morality*, trans. by Maudemarie Clark and Alan J. Swensen (Indianapolis: Hackett, 1998), the latter being the most fully annotated recent edition.

of an innate sense of right and wrong, Nietzsche explains his conviction that morality has a history. He found some provocation in the English philosophers who traced the 'moral sense' back to sociability or utility. In order to approach 'the real *history of morality*' (Preface 7; emphasis in original, here and elsewhere), however, his hypotheses needed a firmer basis. Instead of such speculation 'into the blue', his approach is 'grey': 'by that I mean what has been documented, what is really ascertainable, what has really existed, in short, the whole long hieroglyphic text, so difficult to decipher, of humanity's moral past!' (Preface 7). Astonishingly for postmodern interpreters of Nietzsche, this sounds very like a commitment to ascertainable data. And these data are to be found especially in two sciences which Nietzsche in another late work, *The Antichrist* (section 47), described as 'the two greatest opponents of all superstition, philology and medicine'. Nietzsche's genealogy of morals is then an account of morality from a scientific perspective. He was equipped to undertake it by his training in classical philology and by a keen amateur interest in the natural sciences which led him to read widely and to conduct arguments with scientists in his notebooks which occasionally spill over into his published texts.

Nietzsche's interest in science has recently been thoroughly explored in an invaluable book by Gregory Moore.[2] He sets Nietzsche's thought against a background of biologism, or broad assumptions that biology can ultimately explain many phenomena including social and intellectual ones, that can be traced back to German Romantic thought. Within this context, Moore asks how Nietzsche's biological language is to be understood. Is he redescribing human phenomena reductively in biological terms, as many early twentieth-century readers thought? Or, as later readers, anxious to dissociate Nietzsche from the Nazis' misuse of biologism, have contended, is he using biological language simply as an array of metaphors for metaphysical concerns? Moore proposes a flexible reading of Nietzsche that evades both these extremes. He refers to a body of recent work on the use of metaphor and analogy in science. If a metaphor is a single comparison, analogy is a sustained metaphor or prolonged comparison, always implying a narrative.[3] Thus when Nietzsche describes modern man as a domestic animal, a narrative is implied, analogous to the narrative of how wild animals came to be domesticated and in some cases kept as pets. It is suggested that human beings similarly moved from savagery to domestication. Although the analogy breaks down when pressed too far (if we are pets, who are our owners?), it serves as a powerful instrument for thinking about modern society and perhaps making discoveries about it. The analogy is illuminating because of a real affinity between humans and animals, and, for Nietzsche and his contemporaries, because analogies resting on biologism point towards the kind of biological explanation which science can be expected ultimately to supply. So the analogy with domestic animals is not just useful at one point in the exploration of human society. Whatever its limitations, it may be a rough sketch for an eventual scientific explanation.

---

2   Gregory Moore, *Nietzsche, Biology and Metaphor* (Cambridge: Cambridge University Press, 2002).

3   See Gillian Beer, *Darwin's Plots: Evolutionary Narratives in Darwin, George Eliot and Nineteenth-Century Fiction* (London: Routledge & Kegan Paul, 1983), p. 80.

In this way, much of Nietzsche's later thought is biologistic, but not reductionist. It does not seek to explain human phenomena away within the current state of scientific knowledge; instead, it finds biological metaphors and analogies for human phenomena, in the expectation that in future science will reveal these metaphors to have been anticipations of the literal truth. And, as Moore's work shows abundantly, Nietzsche's metaphors and analogies often turn out to depend on nineteenth-century science much more closely than commentators have hitherto recognized.

There remains, however, an apparent contradiction between Nietzsche's own reflections on language which describe all language as metaphorical, and the fact that, as Moore notes, 'in practice biology retains the status of a privileged discourse in Nietzsche's thinking, one that is exempt from his epistemological relativism' (p. 14).

This apparent contradiction needs to be resolved, and Nietzsche's intellectual tools 'genealogy' and 'perspective' need to be briefly elucidated, before we look in detail at how scientific models operate in Nietzsche's text.[4] Two kinds of truth can be distinguished in Nietzsche's arguments.[5] First, there are philosophical and religious claims to know the timelessly true nature of reality: Plato's theory of Forms, Christian conceptions of God, Kant's noumenal reality, all meet Nietzsche's scorn as being fraudulent constructions of a 'truly real' world which serves to disparage the real world in which we actually live. Second, there are the truths pragmatically available to us within our picture of the world. Even in his early lectures on rhetoric, and still more as he assimilates evolutionary thought, Nietzsche comes to regard cognition and language as adaptive: as devices whereby human beings cope with the world, and therefore as providing only the information that people happen to need and providing that information in a form that serves people's purposes. We know what our cognitive apparatus allows us to know, and our cognition provides us with a useful simplification of the external world.[6] The cognitive apparatus of a fly allows it a different kind of knowledge which is no less useful to it in the evolutionary struggle for survival. It would be pointless to ask whether a fly's knowledge of the world is truer than ours: both its knowledge and ours are true for its and our respective purposes, and there is no criterion by which the two can be compared.[7]

Although we cannot have absolute knowledge of the nature of things, we can have true knowledge within our own perspective. Nietzsche insists that, just as one can only see from the standpoint where one happens to be, one can only have knowledge from one's own perspective. The claim to objective, non-perspectival

---

4   For a firm rebuttal of some recent misreadings of these concepts, see Robert C. Holub, 'Reading Nietzsche as Postmodernist: Rhetoric, Genealogy, Perspectivism in Ahistorical Context', in *Why Literature Matters: Theories and Functions of Literature*, ed. by Rüdiger Ahrens and Laurenz Volkmann (Heidelberg: Winter, 1996), pp. 247–63.

5   See Mary Warnock, 'Nietzsche's Conception of Truth', in *Nietzsche: Imagery and Thought*, ed. by Malcolm Pasley (London: Methuen, 1978), pp. 33–63; Maudemarie Clark, *Nietzsche on Truth and Philosophy* (Cambridge: Cambridge University Press, 1990).

6   See *Beyond Good and Evil*, §24, and for elucidation, Moore, *Nietzsche*, pp. 96–102.

7   *Friedrich Nietzsche on Rhetoric and Language*, ed. and trans. by Sander L. Gilman, Carole Blair and David J. Parent (New York: Oxford University Press, 1989), p. 252.

knowledge is as fraudulent as the Platonic or Kantian claim to know the true nature of things. But that does not mean that all perspectives are equally valid, or that one is limited to one's own perspective. Knowledge is attained, not by finding a single absolutely correct perspective (for there is none to be found), but by comparing a number of different perspectives (III, 12). Thus the historian of morals has to examine numerous different perspectives on morality, several different moral outlooks. But he should not consider them all equally valid. Thus, Nietzsche says, the concept of 'sinfulness' only exists 'seen from the perspective of morality and religion, which is no longer binding for us' (III, 16). The post-religious, scientific perspective subsumes and corrects the religious one. Taking Nietzsche's thought further, one can imagine that in future the modern post-religious perspective will itself be superseded and subsumed by a different and as yet unforeseeable one, rather as, in Thomas Kuhn's account of scientific progress, each paradigm supersedes its predecessor, retaining much of what previously counted as scientific knowledge but reshaping it in a different form.[8] This model of intellectual advance has implications for the status of literal as opposed to metaphorical statement. If 'truth' is the truth available within the best available paradigm, then literal statement is the expression of that truth. But the paradigm, or perspective, can always be superseded, and when that happens, what now counts as literal statement will become metaphor, and a new set of statements, which we cannot foresee, will count as literal.

When Nietzsche talks about 'perspective', he is therefore not advocating relativism, but implying a model of intellectual progress through paradigm change which is familiar to present-day scholarly practice. The concept of 'genealogy' is likewise less startling than some interpreters claim. An influential essay by Foucault argues that genealogy is not the search for an origin but a record of the successive interpretations of a concept; and this record is not a punctilious chronicle but an account that is explicitly slanted by the genealogist's perspective.[9] At the beginning of his text, however, Nietzsche explicitly defines his task as a 'history of the genesis of morality' ('Entstehungsgeschichte der Moral', I, I), a history of the origins of morality. Alexander Nehamas accordingly corrects Foucault by pointing out that Nietzsche, despite Foucault's wayward reading of him, does not contrast genealogy with history, but 'insists that genealogy simply *is* history, correctly practised'.[10] Richard Schacht similarly understands genealogy as a form of historical inquiry supplemented by sociological, psychological, and physiological investigation.[11] It would seem misguided to credit Nietzsche with practising 'genealogy' as a new and specific method of interpretation, as Raymond Geuss does.[12] By genealogy, a word he uses only in the title of his book, Nietzsche means going back beyond recorded

8   See Thomas S. Kuhn, *The Structure of Scientific Revolutions*, 2nd edn (Chicago, IL: University of Chicago Press, 1970).

9   Michel Foucault, 'Nietzsche, Genealogy, History', in *The Foucault Reader*, ed. by Paul Rabinow (London: Penguin, 1991), pp. 76–100.

10   Alexander Nehamas, *Nietzsche: Life as Literature* (Cambridge, MA: Harvard University Press, 1985), p. 246.

11   Richard Schacht, *Nietzsche* (London: Routledge, 1983), p. 351.

12   'Nietzsche and Genealogy', in Raymond Geuss, *Morality, Culture, and History: Essays on German Philosophy* (Cambridge: Cambridge University Press, 1999), pp. 1–28.

history in the search for origins. He intends to trace morality back to the prehistory in which, according to *Human, All Too Human* (section 2), everything essential in human development must have taken place. This might seem a dubious strategy: Nietzsche is arguing from the unknown (prehistory) to the known (the present). But, to nineteenth-century thinkers who accepted evolutionary principles, it seemed clear that the evolution of modern society could be traced back to prehistoric beginnings, of which the still abundant 'primitive' peoples could provide many clues.[13] Edward Tylor (1832–1917), the first Professor of Anthropology at Oxford, argued that ceremonies and superstitions in modern society were the residual 'survivals' of features of primitive society. Sir John Lubbock (1803–1865) combined evolutionary biology and prehistoric archaeology in his inquiries into primitive religion and society. Nietzsche read both, but he seems to have carried the German translation of Lubbock's *The Origin of Civilization and the Primitive Condition of Man* (1870) around on his travels and drawn from it the arguments about primitive animism and hallucinations that appear especially in *Human, All Too Human* and *Daybreak*.[14]

Reading *The Genealogy of Morals* against this intellectual background will help us both to judge the balance between metaphor and literal statement in the text, and to understand the confidence with which Nietzsche speaks of the primeval past (the 'Vorzeit' or 'Urzeit'). He assumes that in the primeval past humanity lived in clans composed of blood relatives. When a smaller but more warlike clan conquered a larger but ill-organized and defenceless group of people, and imposed its tyranny on them, that was the origin of the state. He speaks also of a later 'mittlere Zeit' or intermediate period (II, 19) in which aristocratic dynasties developed, tracing their origins back to gods and heroes. This sounds like the ancient Greek civilization evoked in the Homeric epics.

But Nietzsche also complicates this picture of prehistory by blurring the division between man and animals, and between the primitive nomads and the later heroic dynasties. Thus the first state was founded by a 'horde [...] of blond predatory animals' ('Rudel blonder Raubtiere') who conquered a 'raw material of common people and half-animals' ('Rohstoff von Volk und Halbtier'; II, 17). Primitive men, 'half-animals who were happily adapted to a life of wilderness, war, nomadism, and adventure' (II, 16), were forced by their conquerors to lead a settled life. The famous passage about the 'blond beast' plays even more ambiguously with the term 'animal'. Ancient aristocrats might be vigilantly courteous towards their peers, but towards their inferiors they were 'not much better than predators on the rampage' (I, 11),[15] indeed they regressed to something of an animal level, 'to the innocence of

---

13   See J. W. Burrow, *Evolution and Society: A Study in Victorian Social Theory* (Cambridge: Cambridge University Press, 1966), esp. ch. 5, and *The Crisis of Reason: European Thought, 1848–1914* (New Haven, CT, and London: Yale University Press, 2000), ch. 2. This is also the context for Nietzsche's startling assertion that 'negroes' are the modern 'representatives of prehistoric man' (II, 7).

14   See David S. Thatcher, 'Nietzsche's Debt to Lubbock', *Journal of the History of Ideas*, 44 (1983), 293–309.

15   Nietzsche's phrase 'nicht viel besser als losgelassene Raubtiere' is translated by Diethe, and also by Clark and Swenson, as 'uncaged beasts of prey', which may be too specific, but does convey that the mutual restraint that the warriors observed among themselves was felt as a confinement which needed to be compensated for by bouts of violence.

the predator's conscience, as rejoicing monsters, capable of high spirits as they walk away without qualms from a horrific succession of murder, arson, violence, and torture, as if it were nothing more than a student prank'; 'the animal must emerge again' (I, 11). We are told that the blond beast, the lion prowling in search of its prey, is recognizable 'auf dem Grund aller dieser vornehmen Rassen', but the exact relationship between warriors and lions must remain a matter of suggestion. The language of evolution is here overlaid by the traditional associations of animality with savagery. But the savagery is not just that of beasts of prey, but of warriors existing well into historic, even quite recent times: Nietzsche briefly instances the Roman, Arab, Germanic and Japanese nobility (the Samurai), Homeric heroes, Scandinavian Vikings, as examples of this regression to bestial fury. Thus he implies that the animal within man does not belong just to a remote stage of evolution but still exists as a latent possibility.[16]

The trope of man as animal is one that Nietzsche plays with through *The Genealogy of Morals* and elsewhere. Evolutionary theory suggested that it was more than a trope. But a shock effect could still be gained from bold formulations of man's difference from other animals. Man is fluid, malleable, imperfectly adapted to his environment, and hence without the health that characterizes all other animals: 'For man is more sick, more uncertain, more mutable, less defined than any other animal, there is no doubt about that — he is *the* sick animal' ('*das* kranke Tier'; III, 13, emphasis in original). The social change resulting in the establishment of the state is compared to the evolutionary change in which sea-creatures first moved to the land, implying that it is not just *like* a stage in evolution but actually *is* a stage in evolution. Just as the sea-creatures, no longer borne by the water, were hampered in their movements by gravity and unable to rely on their instincts, so man in society, under the ruthless tyranny of the earliest rulers, was hindered in his actions and obliged to direct his energies inwards. He was 'this animal which is to be "tamed", which rubs himself raw on the bars of his cage' (II, 16).[17] But in turning inwards and acquiring an inner life, he moved further away from the other animals. This move happened most decisively, according to Nietzsche, in the primeval priest. Unlike the warriors, who discharge their impulses in action, the priest is restrained by weakness or disinclination from releasing his energies outwards and instead stores them up inside him in the form of malice, pride, vengefulness, cultivating his intellectual faculties meanwhile and thus perceiving new, indirect ways of exerting power: 'it is only on the basis of this *essentially dangerous* form of human existence, the priestly form, that man has at all developed into an *interesting animal*' (I, 6).

The priestly animal becomes 'böse', a word that joins animality with humanity in a way that cannot be easily rendered in English. 'Ein böses Tier' is a dangerous animal, not simply a wild one, but a vicious one that will bite you when you are not looking. 'Ein böser Mensch' is an evil person; otherwise, applied to people, 'böse'

---

16   What such a master race might be like is memorably imagined in S. M. Stirling, *The Domination* (New York: Baen Books, 1999), where the Draka, a slave-holding warrior society based in South Africa, combine utter ruthlessness with aesthetic taste and environmental concern.

17   Nietzsche's image of an animal futilely hurling itself against the bars is better conveyed by Diethe's version: 'this animal who battered himself raw on the bars of his cage'.

means 'angry' or vengeful'. Nietzsche first tells us that in the primeval priest man has become 'böse' (I, 6), then that priests are well known to be the worst enemies, 'die *bösesten Feinde*' (I, 7).[18] He thus suggests, without needing to argue, an animal origin for the concept of 'böse', evil, which appears both in the title of this treatise ('"Gut und böse", "gut und schlecht"') and in the title of the book he had published the previous year, *Jenseits von Gut und Böse* [*Beyond Good and Evil*]. Thus, simply by juxtaposing two uses of 'böse' in what are normally separate contexts, Nietzsche dismantles the concept of 'evil' by hinting that it is merely a term for animal behaviour that has been first applied to human beings that show animal-like malice and then projected onto the cosmos to imply a metaphysical principle of evil.

Here Nietzsche is suggesting an identity between two things — the vicious nature of an animal and the malicious nature of a priest — that are generally thought to be remote from each other. More often, however, he seeks to explain how two things that really are remote from each other are nevertheless related. For this purpose, he repeatedly asserts that the things we most value in modern society originated from very different sources and were made what they now are by a long and painful process that it is terrifying to contemplate. Thus the modern autonomous individual, mindful of the past, responsible towards the future, and governed by conscience, is the ultimate product of a millennial training of the memory through the infliction of pain. The same applies to the modern concepts of obligation and duty: 'its beginning, like the beginning of everything great on earth, has long been steeped in blood' (II, 6). Part II concludes with a powerful reminder that every ideal is set up only at the cost of violence, deceit, sacrifice, and pain, and of the destruction of earlier ideals: 'In order for a shrine to be set up, *another shrine must be broken into pieces*' (II, 24). These warnings make it clear that Nietzsche's models of change must accommodate conflict, and though philology and biology might seem peaceful disciplines, Nietzsche uses both to disclose or imply a past dominated by what Herbert Spencer (not Darwin) called the 'struggle for existence'.

Dealing with philology, Nietzsche draws both on his own classical training and on the relatively new discipline of Indo-European language history. He accepts the common assumption that the Indo-European languages were brought to Europe by fair-haired, warlike Aryans who imposed their rule on a darker-skinned, dark-haired native population.[19] He cites such evidence as the Celtic syllable *fin* (modern Gaelic *fionn*) meaning both noble and fair-haired. As a counterpart, he conjectures that the Latin *malus*, 'bad', is related to the Greek *melas*, 'black' (I, 5), though present-day philology considers this conjecture unfounded.[20] He also suggests a connection between the words 'good' and 'Goths' ('gut' and 'Goten'), which was also made in Felix Dahn's bestselling novel *Ein Kampf um Rom* (1876).[21]

18 All the translations I have consulted render this phrase as 'the most evil enemies', thus unavoidably losing Nietzsche's pun and the serious point that goes with it.

19 On the ubiquity of such notions in nineteenth-century European thought, see Léon Poliakov, *The Aryan Myth: A History of Racist and Nationalist Ideas in Europe*, trans. by Edmund Howard (London: Heinemann and Sussex University Press, 1974), esp. pp. 224–30.

20 I thank Dr Philomen Probert (Oxford) for this information.

21 See the quotations about 'die guten Goten' in Hans Rudolf Wahl, *Die Religion des deutschen*

These examples, however, serve to illustrate a linguistic tendency that Nietzsche is right to identify: the tendency for words initially denoting status to acquire ethical meanings. The English word 'noble' and its German equivalent 'edel' are obvious instances, and though Nietzsche's examples are mostly taken from Greek, one could add such English instances as 'churl' and 'villain', where servile status came to imply bad manners and morals, and 'generous' (originally meaning 'well-born'), 'gentle', and 'fair', the last example combining racial, moral, and aesthetic connotations. In linguistic history Nietzsche finds the traces of a past set of values, in which 'good' and 'bad' ('gut' and 'schlecht') did not have their modern ethical significance: instead, 'good' was the complacent description applied by the masters to themselves, and 'bad' was the term they applied to their slaves, with no more ethical implication than in such modern usages as 'bad luck', 'bad eggs', or 'bad breath'. Nietzsche is entirely serious in this argument. He is not using philology in any metaphorical sense, but as a means of learning about prehistoric society, and his method differs little from that of the reputable philologists who used linguistic evidence to discover the original home of the first Indo-European speakers or the tripartite structure thought to have been characteristic of early Indo-European society. As a model of change, however, philology serves Nietzsche's own purposes. For if, to the philologist, a word can disclose its past meanings, then those meanings are not wholly past. They may even survive alongside more recent meanings, as the status meaning of 'noble' still coexists with its ethical sense. But even if the earlier meaning is lost to everyone but the philologist (as the putative meaning 'warlike' which Nietzsche strives, implausibly, to discover in the Latin *bonus* 'good'), it is still latently there, just as the primitive savage, or the still more primitive beast of prey, is latent in the modern civilized man.

Biology is a more complex model. Metaphors derived from organic change are a familiar part of language, as in the use of 'grow' to mean 'become'. Nietzsche uses many familiar organic analogies, such as the growth of a tree or the emergence of a butterfly from a caterpillar, and the question is whether, in the context of his biologism, they are more than metaphorical. When he talks specifically about the development of an organism, such change seems to provide his master model for development in general. A crucial feature of this model is that it is not directed towards a purpose. The old teleological conception whereby the hand was created in order to grasp, or the eye in order to see, is as risible to Nietzsche as it was, fifty years earlier, to Georg Büchner, who dismissed the idea in his inaugural lecture 'On Cranial Nerves' and caricatured it in his play *Woyzeck*.[22] Teleological explanations for organic change are as naive as the utilitarian explanations for morality put forward by the English philosophers who are among Nietzsche's favourite targets. Instead of developing towards the perfect achievement of a purpose, an organism

Nationalismus. Eine mentalitätsgeschichtliche Studie zur Literatur des Kaiserreichs: Felix Dahn, Ernst von Wildenbruch, Walter Flex (Heidelberg: Winter, 2002), p. 70.

22   Both texts are available in George Büchner, *Complete Plays, 'Lenz' and Other Writings*, trans. by John Reddick (London: Penguin, 1993). Cf. also Heine's poem 'Zur Teleologie', translated as 'Contribution to Teleology', in *The Complete Poems of Heinrich Heine*, trans. by Hal Draper (Oxford: Oxford University Press, 1982), pp. 799–802.

changes unpredictably under the pressure of circumstances and guided by the will to power. Its component organs serve not purposes but functions, and an obsolete organ is liable to be forced into serving a new purpose (as the nose, normally used for smelling, has become in the elephant a trunk used for grasping). The will to power animating the organism exerts compulsion on the component organs, which in turn may offer resistance. Here Nietzsche was inspired by the arguments of the biologist Wilhelm Roux that the constituent cells within every organism, far from forming a harmonious whole, are constantly contending for dominance.[23] Change is therefore not a progression towards a goal but a series of opportunistic adaptations which result from conflict within the organism as well as the organism's struggle to adjust to a changing environment.

This model of change applies also to human institutions. Thus in the second treatise Nietzsche has much to say about punishment. While the set of actions involved in inflicting punishment has remained relatively constant over the centuries, the justifications given for punishing people are wholly diverse and mostly implausible: to prevent the guilty party from doing further harm, to deter him, to improve him morally, to bring him to repentance, to satisfy the injured party, to provide a public spectacle, and so forth. It is not the case that a purpose exists first and means of punishment are created to fulfil it; rather, punishment is a given, and different pretexts are invented to justify it. (Or one could go back even further and say that the given is man's desire to inflict cruelty on others, and that punishment provides a stable means of satisfying this desire, though the reason for it can never be admitted and hence innumerable pretexts for punishment have to be devised.) With a human institution Nietzsche finds it appropriate to speak not of functions but of meanings. The concept of punishment is the 'semiotic' summary of a long historical process (II, 13). And semiotic language, involving signs, meanings, and interpretations, can be applied to organic as well as social development:

> But all aims, all uses are merely *signs* indicating that a will to power has mastered something less powerful than itself and impressed the meaning of a function on it on accordance with its own interests. So the entire history of a 'thing', an organ, a custom may take the form of an extended chain of signs, of ever-new interpretations and manipulations. (II, 12)

A further analogy exists between the structure of an organism and the structure of society. Nietzsche applies a social metaphor to organic life when he says: 'our organism is structured as an oligarchy' (II, 1). That is, within the organism some components dominate the others, and are subject to displacement by their subordinate components. The metaphor moves the other way when Nietzsche applies organic language to the origin of the state. We must not imagine that the state originated 'as an organic growth into new conditions' (II, 17); rather, it was a sudden breach, or leap, when a defenceless population suddenly found itself subjected to the ruthless tyranny of a band of conquerors. Is this perhaps more than an analogy or a metaphor? Has Nietzsche identified processes of change which

---

23   See Wolfgang Müller-Lauter, 'Der Organismus als innerer Kampf: Der Einfluß von Wilhelm Roux auf Friedrich Nietzsche', *Nietzsche-Studien*, 7 (1978), 189–223.

differ only superficially when they occur in organisms or in societies? It would seem so, since Nietzsche, denying that any social occurrence can be intrinsically right or wrong, explains social phenomena as sharing in the non-moral, violent character of life itself:

> To talk of right and wrong *as such* is senseless; *in themselves*, injury, violation, exploitation, destruction can of course be nothing 'wrong', in so far as life operates *essentially* — that is, in terms of its basic functions — through injury, violation, exploitation, and destruction, and cannot be conceived in any other way. One is forced to admit something even more disturbing: that, from the highest biological point of view, legal conditions may be nothing more than *exceptional states of emergency*, partial restrictions which the will to life in its quest for power provisionally imposes on itself in order to serve its overall goal: the creation of *larger* units of power. (II, 11)

Alongside biology, Nietzsche draws heavily on the related science of physiology. He does so especially when he translates religious phenomena into medical terms, often with anticlerical sarcasm. Thus fasting, or the avoidance of certain foods, are explained as dietary measures. Eremitism, or the search for solitude as undertaken by the first monks in the Egyptian desert, is compared to the rest cure prescribed by the American doctor Silas Weir Mitchell. And practices of meditation, especially in Indian religion, are equated with hypnotism, which, as Nietzsche knew, was pioneered for medical purposes by Charcot (I, 6).[24] These analogies, introduced abruptly in the first treatise, are discussed at more length in the third, where the ideal-typical figure of the priest appears as a fraudulent physician (III, 17–21). Instead of curing his flock, the priest keeps it submissive, partly by imposing a quasi-medical regimen that avoids excitement, prescribing mechanical activity (such as regular prayers), and promoting the 'herd instinct' under the guise of brotherly love, but partly also by more dangerous and reprehensible measures such as encouraging the hysteria that found expression, for example, in the persecution of witches, in hallucinations, and in self-castigation. When Nietzsche describes such practices as medical treatment of the sick, he is not speaking metaphorically, nor is he implying that medical and religious languages have equal validity. Rather, religious language is evacuated of its own meaning and translated into the terms of a medical, scientific, and therefore superior perspective. Outbreaks of widespread pessimism and melancholy are explained not in spiritual but in explicitly physiological terms and ascribed to the mingling of races and classes, to unsuitable diet, or to the spread of diseases such as malaria and syphilis (III, 17). And in putting forward such arguments Nietzsche is drawing, as Moore has shown, on a large body of nineteenth-century anticlerical writing that reinterpreted religious phenomena as hysterical, neurasthenic and degenerate (Moore, p. 151).

Physiology yields an explanation of change when Nietzsche takes from it the concept of 'Ressentiment'. He found this term in a book by Eugen Dühring,

---

24   See Moore, *Nietzsche*, p. 146. Nietzsche also read the work of James Braid on hypnotism: see Marco Brusotti, 'Wille zur Macht, Ressentiment, Hypnose: "Aktiv" und "reaktiv" in Nietzsches *Genealogie der Moral*', *Nietzsche-Studien*, 30 (2001), 107–32 (pp. 121–22).

where it is a psychological version of a mechanical process.[25] In his account of slave morality, Nietzsche explains this process not by a mechanical but by a physiological analogy:

> In order to exist at all, slave morality from the outset always needs an opposing, outer world; in physiological terms, it needs external stimuli in order to act — its action is fundamentally reaction. (I, 10)

Yet it does not seem quite right to talk of analogies. Neither physiology nor psychology is here the literal discourse to which the other is related metaphorically. Rather, it seems that both share the same deep structure, or homology, in that the process of reaction is the same whether it occurs in physiology, in psychology, or in mechanics. The concept of a shared deep structure is implied also when Nietzsche talks about forgetting and digestion. To forget the past, he says, is as necessary as to digest one's food, and a person who cannot forget properly 'may be compared to a dyspeptic (and not only compared)' (II, 1). The parenthesis suggests that forgetting and digesting are not just analogous processes, but homologous ones which share the same deep structure. Such a suggestion is a standard move in scientific thought, as Gillian Beer writes: 'Analogies may turn out to be homologies. In such a case the parallel narrative patterns reveal actual identity, and the distance between the two patterns vanishes' (p. 80).

As a reaction, slave morality can define itself only by reference to the master-morality which it opposes, whereas the masters derive their morality only from satisfaction in their own strength, vitality and beauty. While the masters regard the slaves, at most, with tolerant disgust, the slaves regard the masters with all-consuming hatred. In slave-morality, the masters' self-satisfaction becomes sinful pride, their physical enjoyment is redefined as lust and greed, while the slaves' enforced servility is redefined as humility, obedience, and patience, and their inability to injure their masters is hypocritically explained as the desire not to injure anyone (I, 14). In thus generating a new moral system, 'Ressentiment' becomes creative. It has produced a new perspective or paradigm, that of Judaeo-Christian morality, which has redefined the pagan virtues as sins, and, despite such rare exponents of master-morality as Cesare Borgia and Napoleon, has dominated Europe for almost two millennia. So persistent is slave-morality that even in post-Christian Europe it has established a yet more secure dominance in the form of democracy, which enviously and maliciously seeks to pull down anyone who rises above the herd.

With this idea, one of the most powerful and compelling in the whole of *The Genealogy of Morals*, Nietzsche confronts his most intractable problem, for he needs to explain how hatred can change into love. Aristocratic warriors do not hate. If they notice their slaves at all, they despise them. Aristocratic priests do hate. Unable to discharge their energies in violent activity, they become as vicious as caged animals. Slaves also hate; their entire system of values is intended to justify their hatred for the aristocrats who carelessly command, control, and kill them. Christianity, according

---

25 See Aldo Venturelli, 'Asketismus und Wille zur Macht: Nietzsches Auseinandersetzung mit Eugen Dühring', *Nietzsche-Studien*, 15 (1986), 107–39 (p. 131).

to Nietzsche, is a religion of hatred, apparently based (though he does not make this connection explicit) on an alliance between aristocratic priests and plebeian slaves who provide a willing flock. To prove his point, he quotes alarming passages from the Church Father Tertullian and from St Thomas Aquinas about how the pleasures of the saved in heaven will be enhanced by watching the sufferings of the damned in hell (I, 15).[26] He also remarks that the Revelation of St John the Divine, in which the saints are elevated and their persecutors punished, is really a 'book of hatred' which, by a perfectly logical Christian instinct, was ascribed to St John, whose Gospel contains so much about love (I, 16).

But how did hatred turn into love? How is it that the Gospels do convey a spirit of love anticipated only occasionally in the Old Testament and very rarely in any pre-Christian text? Nietzsche confronts this difficulty, and deploys a range of metaphors in the attempt to resolve it. His main metaphor is the organic one of the growth of a tree:

> But *this* is indeed what happened: from the trunk of that tree of revenge and hatred, Jewish hatred — the deepest and most sublime hatred, that is, the kind of hatred which creates ideals and changes the meaning of values, a hatred the like of which has never been seen on earth — from this tree grew forth something equally incomparable, a *new love*, the deepest and most sublime of all the kinds of love — and from what other trunk could it have grown?... But let no one think that it somehow grew up as the genuine negation of that thirst for revenge, as the antithesis of Jewish hatred! No, the opposite is the case! Love grew forth from this hatred, as its crown, as its triumphant crown, spreading itself ever wider in the purest brightness and fullness of the sun, as a crown which pursued in the lofty realm of light the goals of hatred — victory, spoils, seduction — driven there by the same impulse with which the roots of that hatred sank down ever further and more lasciviously into everything deep and evil. (I, 8)

Not only is the arboreal image sustained ('grow', 'roots', 'crown'), but the image of the tree contains an allusion to the tree of Jesse (Isaiah 11. 1): the birth of Jesus from the family of Jesse, the father of David.[27] Above all, however, it is an organic image, conveying that though the flourishing outspread branches look very different from the bare trunk and the gnarled subterranean root, all are animated by the same impulse (*Drang*). Yet this image explains nothing, for the root and the branches of a tree, however dissimilar, are not antithetical, as hatred is antithetical to love. So Nietzsche slips in a word suggesting another kind of change, the word 'sublime', which comes from chemistry and suggests the purification of an element through transformation. Nietzsche uses the image of sublimation later to suggest that modern man, far from ceasing to enjoy cruelty, has subjected his cruel impulses to 'a certain sublimation and refinement' ('einer gewissen Sublimirung und Subtilisirung')

26   Nietzsche borrowed these quotations from the rationalist historian Lecky, whom he read in German translation. See W. E. H. Lecky, *History of the Rise and Influence of the Spirit of Rationalism in Europe* (1865), 5th edn, 2 vols (London: Longman, Green, & Co., 1872), I, 319 (Aquinas) and I, 325 (Tertullian).

27   Nietzsche's word 'Stamm' [trunk] is used in Luther's version of this passage: 'Und es wird eine Ruthe aufgehen von dem Stamm Isai, und ein Zweig aus seiner Wurzel Frucht bringen.'

translating them 'into the imagination and the psyche' ('ins Imaginative und Seelische', II, 7). This is a more promising image, since the change from a solid substance through chemical processes to a fine vapour conveys something of the difference between hatred and love, but it still does not explain how hatred can change into its opposite. Implicitly admitting defeat, despite his bluster, Nietzsche then resorts to a conspiracy theory, according to which Jesus with his gospel of love served simply as the bait whereby Israel satisfied its 'sublime Rachsucht' (I, 8), attracting a hapless population under the sway of a slave morality that was soon to triumph over the Roman Empire.

The passage just quoted is unusual in *The Genealogy of Morals* in the use it makes of specific organic metaphors. Elsewhere, as we have seen, Nietzsche takes the growth of an organism through conflict to illustrate a model of change which can also be applied to such human institutions as punishment. There he goes beyond metaphor to disclose the deep structure of change. In many other places, Nietzsche uses organic images more as local embellishment than as means of explanation. Thus the modern autonomous individual is described as the slow-ripening fruit on the tree of moral development (II, 2). To enforce his point that imprisonment does not produce remorse, Nietzsche takes literally the German word for remorse, *Gewissensbiss* ('bite of conscience'), and expands it into the image of a gnawing worm ('Nagewurm') that does not breed in prisons (II, 14). Bad conscience is 'this most sinister and most interesting plant of our earthly vegetation' (II, 14), 'this ugly weed' ('dieses häßliche Gewächs'; II, 17), or a kind of polyp, 'eating its way in, spreading down and out like a polyp' (II, 21). The frightening figure of the ascetic priest was the caterpillar ('Raupenform') from which the philosopher emerged (III, 10). Apart from reinforcing the diffuse biologism of the text, these images do not offer explanations of the processes they refer to; they simply enable us to imagine these processes in a vivid and often repugnant manner. When Christian love is described as the crown of a tree whose root is hatred, however, Nietzsche is trying to make a similar organic image do much more work by *explaining* a process that would otherwise be paradoxical. However, his image buckles under the strain, and the paradox remains unresolved.

It is necessary to mention one other important way in which Nietzsche uses organic language to explain, or to try to explain, processes of change. Such language helps him to account for agency. He is not content to describe evolutionary processes as simply happening, without agents to make them happen. If these processes are driven by the will to power, there must be agents that exercise their will and strive for power. At the lowest level, that of the organism, the component cells are imagined as actively contending for power, and at the highest level, that of human society, the origin of the state is imagined not as impersonal, nor as agreement on a social contract, but as the active conquest and oppression of a population by a primitive band of robbers. To remind us that there must always be an agent, Nietzsche often uses the image of breeding. Thus in discussing the origin of memory, Nietzsche repeatedly talks about the task of breeding an animal that is able to make promises (II, 1, 2). And in arguing that man's intellect was first employed on calculating the equivalence of injuries and compensations, Nietzsche maintains: 'it is here that the earliest form of astuteness was bred' (II, 8). The metaphor of breeding is, once again, more than a metaphor. Nietzsche was well read in contemporary discussions of racial degeneration and the possibility of counteracting it by eugenic breeding. In *Beyond Good and Evil* (section 203) he speaks of the need for new and terrible leaders to counteract degeneration by 'discipline and breeding' ('Zucht und Züchtung'). Although, like most reputable eugenicists, he did not contemplate trying to breed a super-race, he envisaged monitoring procreation and laying down rules of hygiene which would help to produce a ruling elite (Moore, p. 163).

When placed in the context of nineteenth-century science, many of Nietzsche's late texts, certainly *The Genealogy of Morals*, take on a different appearance. What may have looked like metaphors, images, or analogies, turn out to have quite literal status within the philology, biology and physiology of the time. When Nietzsche draws on these sciences to explain processes of change, his language often points to a deep structure underlying changes in areas so diverse as living organisms and social institutions. And even when his organic metaphors can be read simply as embellishments without explanatory ambitions, they serve to underline the biologism that governs so much of his and his contemporaries' thought. Instead of the single (misleading) perspective that has prevailed in much recent interpretation of Nietzsche, we need to follow his advice by reading him from several perspectives, including his own.

CHAPTER 21

Jesuits, Jews and Thugs:
Myths of Conspiracy and Infiltration
from Dickens to Thomas Mann

The age of nationalism is now yielding, let us hope, to an age of internationalization and globalization. As the owl of Minerva flies at dusk, the twilight of nationalism has revealed to us a great deal about how national communities constitute themselves through myths. Some of these myths are internal to the nation. These include national symbols such as Britannia, Germania, and Marianne; historical (or semi-historical) figures transformed into myth, such as Hermann the Cheruscan, Frederick Barbarossa, Joan of Arc, or Queen Elizabeth I; sites of memory; and the ceremonies and festivals that help to sustain social, collective and national memory.[1] Besides these internal myths, however, there are also external myths, including xenophobic stereotypes of foreign nations against which we define ourselves. Another way of defining ourselves against an enemy, however, and one characteristic of the age of nationalism, is the construction of myths about dangerous outsiders who can move easily between the nations. These may be people who have loosened or lost their contact with the nation to which they originally belonged: who have transferred their allegiance to a foreign power, who have moved overseas and 'gone native', or, worst of all, have joined an international movement without a national base. Examples of such international movements have included the Communist International, the supposed international network of Jews, the Freemasons, and the Catholic Church, particularly the Society of Jesus. Myths about dangerous outsiders do not provide such secure self-definition as do images of other nations which can be imagined as homogeneous and predictable blocks based on a limited territory. For the outsiders, bound together in conspiratorial organizations, disguise

---

1 See František Graus, *Lebendige Vergangenheit: Überlieferung im Mittelalter und in den Vorstellungen vom Mittelalter* (Cologne and Vienna: Böhlau, 1975); *Arminius und die Varusschlacht: Geschichte — Mythos — Literatur*, ed. by Rainer Wiegels and Winfried Woesler (Paderborn: Schöningh, 1995); Marina Warner, *Joan of Arc: The Image of Female Heroism* (London: Weidenfeld & Nicolson, 1981); Michael Dobson and Nicola J. Watson, *England's Elizabeth: An Afterlife in Fame and Fantasy* (Oxford: Oxford University Press, 2002); *Deutsche Erinnerungsorte*, ed. by Etienne François and Hagen Schulze, 3 vols (Munich: Beck, 2001), a very diverse collection of essays on everything that could possibly be considered a national symbol.

their foreignness by taking on the appearance of every nation they inhabit. Their lack of a territorial base paradoxically makes them stronger by forcing them to rely on a combination of powerful wills and rational planning. Their invisibility enables them to penetrate and infiltrate the nation, to work underground and undermine the national culture. Such myths accordingly reveal the insecurity that haunts national communities. Their controlling metaphors are those of conspiracy and infiltration. And the models by which we imagine conspiracies are closely connected with fiction. Consider the present popularity of *The Da Vinci Code,* a novel purporting to reveal an international organization whose grand masters include Leonardo da Vinci, dedicated to preserving the blood-line descending from the marriage between Jesus and Mary Magdalen. Though the novel is no more than a fast-moving page-turner, large numbers of people apparently believe that it refers to real historical events, or at least to events that cannot be proved not to have happened — and though one can never prove a negative, this impossibility is regarded as a positive proof by conspiracy theorists.

Let us start with a relatively familiar example of a conspiracy theory: *The Protocols of the Elders of Zion.* Originating in Tsarist Russia, this work first appeared in the West in a German translation in January 1920 as *Die Geheimnisse der Weisen von Zion.*[2] This crude fabrication purports to present the Jews' cynical scheme for taking over the world by violence and deceit. They have used the French Revolution and its slogans 'liberty, equality, fraternity' to replace the Gentile aristocracy with a plutocracy. They control finance and the press. They intend to come forward as Socialists, offering to lead the masses in order to enslave them; by fomenting revolution among unemployed workers, they will conduct a reign of terror and thus install their despotism. Alternatively, they will conduct a sudden *coup d'état* and thus install their world government. They will introduce a caste system, remove the word 'liberty' from the dictionary, and destroy all religions except Judaism. They have planned all this through their unrivalled powers of reasoning.

The *Protocols* were the most popular among several books which appeared in Germany just after the First World War, purporting to explain Germany's defeat by the machinations of Jews, Freemasons, and other such international conspiratorial bodies. They appealed not only to the exiled Kaiser, who blamed the Elders of Zion for his fall from power, and to Ludendorff, but to a vast, largely middle-class public including many professors and schoolteachers. The English translation, entitled *The Jewish Peril*, appeared in February 1920. It was soon seen through. In August 1921 *The Times* published the evidence that the Protocols were a forgery with literary origins. They were derived from a number of mostly fictional sources, notably the *Dialogue aux enfers entre Montesquieu et Machiavel*, by a French lawyer called Maurice Joly, published in 1864. Further back, they owed much to the five-volume denunciation of the French Revolution by the Abbé Barruel, *Mémoires pour servir à l'histoire du Jacobinisme* (1797), which argued that the Revolution was the work of a conspiracy

---

2   On the Protocols, their history and their reception, see Norman Cohn, *Warrant for Genocide: The Myth of the Jewish World-conspiracy and the Protocols of the Elders of Zion* (London: Eyre & Spottiswoode, 1967).

reaching back to the fourteenth century, founded by the Knights Templar and continued by the Freemasons. And the setting of the Protocols, the supposed secret meeting of Jewish leaders, was taken from a work of fiction entitled *Biarritz* (1868) by Hermann Goedsche, who wrote under the pseudonym Sir John Retcliffe; this novel includes a scene, 'In the Jewish Cemetery of Prague', where representatives of the twelve tribes of Israel gather in the presence of the Devil and report on the progress they are making in undermining Christian civilization. Given all these sources, the appeal of the *Protocols* was in part the appeal of imaginative fiction.

The *Protocols* powerfully influenced the outlook of National Socialism by offering apparent support for the myth of the Jewish world conspiracy and for denunciations of world Jewry. But their sources indicate that this myth was modelled on an earlier template, that of earlier alleged conspiracies aiming at world domination. An important one was the Jesuit myth.[3] The Jesuits were originally a group of students at the University of Paris centring on Ignatius de Loyola. As the Society of Jesus, dedicated to propagating the Catholic faith through education and missionary work, they were officially founded by a Papal bull in 1540. In the 1560s they assumed the additional task of combating Protestantism. Sinister stories about them soon sprang up. They were said to be organized on the lines of an absolute monarchy or military regiment, and to use their educational system to brainwash their members into a condition of blind obedience. Jesuits were thought to defend themselves under interrogation by equivocation, and under oath by mental reservations. They were also credited with encouraging tyrannicide. The Jesuit Juan de Mariana in *De Rege et regis institutione* (1599) argued that a legitimate ruler who persistently abused his power could be killed by an individual. This was a highly unpopular doctrine in the age of absolutism, when divinity was thought to hedge a king, and the Parlement de Paris had Mariana's book burned by the public hangman in 1610.[4] Jesuits were also credited with the doctrine that the end justifies the means. By putting forward these lax doctrines, it was argued, the Jesuits made themselves popular as confessors and gained positions of influence, for it was thought that a confessor could even direct the public policy of his charge. Voltaire wrote of the typical Jesuit confessor (noting that Jesuits were also popular because princes did not need to worry about rewarding them with bishoprics): 'C'est un ministère secret qui devient puissant à proportion de la faiblesse du prince.'[5] In the early modern period, the Jesuits were charged with plotting the assassination of many monarchs and even of two Popes and one cardinal. For a handy summary of these allegations, one need look no further than the article 'Jésuite' in that central Enlightenment text, the *Encyclopédie*.[6]

    3   See J. C. H. Aveling, *The Jesuits* (London: Blond & Briggs, 1981); Geoffrey Cubitt, *The Jesuit Myth: Conspiracy Theory and Politics in Nineteenth-Century France* (Oxford: Clarendon Press, 1993); Peter Burke, 'The Black Legend of the Jesuits: An Essay in the History of Social Stereotypes', in *Christianity and Community in the West: Essays for John Bossy*, ed. by Simon Ditchfield (Aldershot: Ashgate, 2001), pp. 165–82.

    4   The record is set straight by Harro Höpfl, *Jesuit Political Thought: The Society of Jesus and the State, c. 1540–1630* (Cambridge: Cambridge University Press, 2004).

    5   Voltaire, *Essai sur les mœurs*, ed. by René Pomeau, 2 vols (Paris: Garnier, 1963), II, 287.

    6   See the *Encyclopédie ou Dictionnaire raisonné des sciences, des arts et des métiers* (Neuchâtel:

There is even a Jesuit counterpart to the *Protocols*, a book purporting to reveal their secrets. The *Monita secreta Societatis Iesu* appeared in 1614, claiming to be a set of secret rules governing the Jesuits' pursuit of power, influence, and wealth.[7] It was in fact written by a renegade Polish Jesuit called Zaharowski as a satire, and its satirical intention is, or should be, obvious, though it was widely taken as serious. For example, it advises Jesuits to cultivate rich widows, who must be prevented from remarrying and induced to leave their property to the Order. If they have daughters, these must be encouraged to become nuns; it is recommended to make the mother embitter her daughter's life by scolding her and by telling her of the hardships of marriage. Sons, if at all suitable, should be encouraged to enter the Order, with the aid of a sympathetic tutor. Young men should not be admitted to the Order till they have received the inheritances which they can then give to the Order. Such allegations would later provide the plots — as we shall see — of several sensational novels.

One might have expected, however, that the Jesuits would vanish from people's minds after the dissolution of their order in 1773. Surely they were no longer of any interest except as characters in a historical drama? Far from it. To many writers of the Enlightenment, the Jesuits had become more dangerous, not less, since the dissolution of their order. They still existed as 'Exjesuiten', still formed an international network, and were still gathering influence in the hope of returning to power under some future Pope, as indeed did happen when the Society was restored by Pope Pius VII in 1814. When re-established, the Jesuits were in fact a more tightly knit body, loyal to a Church which was by now strictly ultramontane, seeking to impose its authority on all its members.

Fear of Jesuits in nineteenth-century Britain, Germany, and Switzerland rested on the view of them as spearheading the campaign by the Church to consolidate and extend its influence. Jesuits were held responsible for the Swiss Civil War. In 1844 the Grand Council of Lucerne invited them to take over the canton's seminary and theological institutions, two months after the Federal Diet had discussed but rejected a motion to expel Jesuits from the whole of Switzerland. There was an anti-Jesuit rising in Lucerne, which was suppressed; then volunteer Free Corps were organized against the Jesuits, and in Vaud the government was overthrown because it reacted inadequately to anti-Jesuit agitation. Gottfried Keller responded with his 'Jesuitenlieder', which include such verses as:

> Von Kreuz und Fahne angeführt,
> Den Giftsack hinten aufgeschnürt,
> Der Fanatismus als Profoß,
> Die Dummheit folgt als Betteltroß:
> Sie kommen, die Jesuiten![8]

Faulche, 1765), VIII, 512–16. The author of the article was Jean d'Alembert. These and other charges were systematically examined and rejected in Bernhard Duhr, SJ, *Jesuiten-Fabeln: Ein Beitrag zur Culturgeschichte* (Freiburg i.Br.: Herder, 1891).

7   There have been many editions; I have used *Geheime Vorschriften des Jesuiter-Ordens. Aus dem Lateinischen* (n.p. [Vienna], 1782).

8   Gottfried Keller, *Sämtliche Werke*, ed. by Clemens Heselhaus, 3 vols (Munich: Hanser, 1958),

Keller's imagery compares the Jesuits to an army under the strict discipline of the 'Profoß' and followed by beggars, thus combining authoritarian fanaticism with ignorance and poverty, while his additional image of the 'Giftsack' recalls associations of Jews with poison and perhaps suggests an inversion of the Eucharist in which the Jesuits will distribute poison instead of bread.[9] In the chapter 'Juden und Jesuiten' of his *Bilder aus der deutschen Vergangenheit* (1859–67), Gustav Freytag transcribes a Jesuit narrative about a Jewish boy in seventeenth-century Prague who was attracted by Christianity and visited the Jesuit College to receive baptism and instruction, but was forcibly restored to his father, who beat, starved, and finally killed him. Freytag observes that the Jesuits were at least as fanatical as the Jews, and concludes that by now assimilated Jews have become Germans, whereas Jesuits, now expelled for the second time, are forever aliens: 'Und die Enkel der asiatischen Wanderstämme sind unsere Landsleute und brüderliche Mitstreiter geworden. Die geistliche Genossenschaft der Gesellschaft Jesu aber, schon einmal beseitigt, dann wieder lebendig gemacht, ist bis heut geblieben, was sie am ersten Tag ihrer Einwanderung in Deutschland war, — fremd dem deutschen Leben.'[10] Eda Sagarra suggests that Freytag's story anticipated and perhaps inspired Thomas Mann's account in *Der Zauberberg* of Leo Naphta's adoption by the Jesuits.[11] Freytag must in turn have been aware of the Mortara affair, in which Pope Pius IX in 1858 authorized the removal from his parents of a Jewish boy, Edgardo Mortara, who had been baptized at the age of six by a Christian servant-girl; Edgardo was brought up in a Catholic seminary and eventually became a priest.[12] The Mortara affair no doubt helped to gain support for Bismarck's Kulturkampf, which began in 1872 with the expulsion of the Jesuits from Prussia by the so-called 'Jesuitengesetz' of May 1872. The Kulturkampf had the enthusiastic backing of most of the literary intelligentsia of Protestant Germany. Two examples will suffice. In Felix Dahn's much-read 'Professorenroman', *Ein Kampf um Rom* (1876), the villainous Empress Theodora is a Catholic bigot, bitterly hostile to the heretical Goths, and supported by the ascetic Roman prefect Cethegus, who strongly resembles the standard caricature of the Jesuit.[13] Wilhelm Busch's *Pater Filuzius* depicts a wily Jesuit who tries to ingratiate himself with the female relatives of the wealthy bachelor Gottlieb Michael, in order to obtain his money, but is foiled and thrown out of the house;

III, 144; I have substituted 'Sie' for a suspicious-looking 'So' in the line given as 'So kommen, die Jesuiten!'

9   On suspicion of Jesuits, see Michael B. Gross, *The War against Catholicism: Liberalism and the Anti-Catholic Imagination in Nineteenth-Century Germany* (Ann Arbor: University of Michigan Press, 2004), pp. 65–73.

10   Gustav Freytag, *Bilder aus der deutschen Vergangenheit*, 5 vols (Leipzig: Hirzel, 1886), III, 420.

11   Eda Sagarra, 'Intertextualität als Zeitkommentar. Theodor Fontane, Gustav Freytag und Thomas Mann oder: Juden und Jesuiten', in Eckhard Heftrich et al. (eds), *Theodor Fontane und Thomas Mann* (Frankfurt a.M.: Klostermann, 1998), pp. 25–47 (p. 25).

12   See David I. Kertzer, *The Kidnapping of Edgardo Mortara* (London: Picador, 1997).

13   See Hans Rudolf Wahl, *Die Religion des deutschen Nationalismus. Eine mentalitätsgeschichtliche Studie zur Literatur des Kaiserreichs: Felix Dahn, Ernst von Wildenbruch, Walter Flex* (Heidelberg: Winter, 2002), p. 77. On the wider literary response to the Kulturkampf, see Peter Sprengel, *Von Luther zu Bismarck: Kulturkampf und nationale Identität bei Theodor Fontane, Conrad Ferdinand Meyer und Gerhart Hauptmann* (Bielefeld: Aisthesis, 1999).

Gottlieb empties a dish of soup over his head, and when he gathers ruffians to take revenge, Gottlieb and three friends beat them up, and Gottlieb marries his cousin Angelika. Thus the Jesuits' intrigues serve merely to prompt the sleepy 'deutscher Michel' into asserting his manhood by violence, marriage, and (presumably) pro-creation.[14]

In Britain, indignation and fear were aroused when Pope Pius IX in 1850 restored the English Catholic hierarchy under Cardinal Nicholas Wiseman; this action was widely known as 'the Papal Aggression'. The Prime Minister, Lord John Russell, wrote a letter to the Bishop of Durham, which was published on *The Times* on 7 November 1850, agreeing with the Bishop's condemnation of 'the late aggression of the Pope upon our Protestantism', and denouncing the Catholic Church's 'mummeries of superstition' and its 'laborious endeavours which are now making to confine the intellect and enslave the soul'.[15] Two days earlier, on Guy Fawkes Day, the Pope, Cardinal Wiseman, and hundreds of Jesuits were burned in effigy around the country. These developments strengthened unease at the increase in the Catholic population caused by immigration, often under the pressure of famine, from Ireland, while the Oxford Movement, promoting ritual within the Church of England, was thought to be a kind of Roman fifth column.

In Victorian fiction 'Jesuit' is a standard term of abuse and the Jesuit a frequent villain. Thus in Wilkie Collins's novel *Armadale* a private detective is described as 'a regular Jesuit at a private inquiry — with this great advantage over all the Popish priests I have ever seen, that he has not got his slyness written in his face.'[16] Frances Trollope, mother of the more famous Anthony, in her novel *Father Eustace: A Tale of the Jesuits* (1847), shows a sincerely and devoutly obedient young priest being used by the ruthless General of the Jesuits to persuade an English heiress to convert and become a nun, so that her estate may pass to the Society. Alluding to Mrs Radcliffe's thriller *The Mysteries of Udolpho*, Trollope juxtaposes a Gothic atmosphere (the General has a piercing gaze, the heiress's castle is full of concealed passages, rooms, and dungeons) with English social comedy reminiscent of Jane Austen.[17] She goes beyond paranoid stereotyping by exploring the young priest's conflicts with considerable psychological insight. A much cruder approach is taken by Charles Kingsley, who in *Westward Ho!* (1855) gives his stalwart Elizabethan hero, Amyas Leigh, a kind of shadow-self, a physically weak and cowardly cousin, Eustace Leigh, who has been trained at the Jesuit seminary at Rheims, conspires with Jesuits who operate in England in disguise (the actual figures of Robert Persons and Edmund Campion), hands over Amyas's brother and the girl he unavailingly loved, Rose

---

14   Wilhelm Busch, *Sämtliche Werke und eine Auswahl der Skizzen und Gemälde in zwei Bänden*, ed. by Rolf Hochhuth (Gütersloh: Bertelsmann, n.d.), I, 686–715.

15   Quoted in E. R. Norman, *Anti-Catholicism in Victorian England* (London: Allen & Unwin, 1968), pp. 159–61.

16   Wilkie Collins, *Armadale*, ed. by Catherine Peters, World's Classics (Oxford: Oxford University Press, 1989), p. 195. This passage illustrates the paranoid assumption that enemies are both invisible, passing unseen amid the population, and also immediately recognizable.

17   Frances Trollope, *Father Eustace: A Tale of the Jesuits*, 3 vols (London: Henry Colburn, 1847); 'Udolpho', I, 336. See the excellent study of this novel in Susan Griffin, *Anti-Catholicism in Nineteenth-Century Fiction* (Cambridge: Cambridge University Press, 2004), pp. 78–90.

Salterne, to the tortures of the Spanish Inquisition, and finally enters the Society, becoming 'a thing, a tool, a Jesuit; which goes only where it is sent, and does good or evil indifferently, as it is bid; which, by an act of moral suicide, has lost its soul, in the hope of saving it; without a will, a conscience, a responsibility, (as it fancies) to God or man, but only to "The Society." '[18] Thus in Kingsley's view a Jesuit is emotionally burnt-out, miserable, and takes refuge in surrendering his moral autonomy to his Society. Elsewhere the Jesuits are seen less as a body of people than as an amorphous influence pervading a whole period of history. The historian John Addington Symonds wrote of the Counter-Reformation: 'over the Dead Sea of social putrefaction floated the sickening oil of Jesuit hypocrisy'.[19]

Even earlier, fiction played a large part in shaping and perpetuating the Jesuit myth. Eugene Sue's *Le Juif errant*, serialized in the Liberal paper *Le Constitutionnel* from June 1844 to June 1845, depicted the Society of Jesus as a secret society unscrupulously bent on world domination and intent on reducing people to servile submissiveness. Sue developed two memorable stereotypes, the asexual, reptilian Jesuit Rodin, whose magnetic personality transfers sexual energy into power-hunger (though he is only using the Society as a means to make himself Pope); and the handsome, elegant but sinister d'Aigrigny, an ex-soldier, who enjoys manipulating underlings. Both d'Aigrigny and Rodin are trying to destroy the seven descendants of the Wandering Jew so that the Jesuits may acquire the vast fortune that these descendants stand to inherit. In the first half of the book, d'Aigrigny tries to have them killed by all sorts of intrigues, which they survive. In the second half, Rodin takes over. With his powerful intellect and indomitable will (which enables him to undergo an agonizing operation during the cholera epidemic of 1832), and above all his power of psychological insight, Rodin succeeds where d'Aigrigny failed, by driving all seven descendants to suicide.

Sue also suggested powerful analogies between Jesuits and other conspiratorial movements. He equated the Jesuits with the Indian Thugs. His novel includes a Thug called Feringhea, apparently based on a real Thug who bore that name. The Indian Thugs were robbers and highwaymen whose speciality was making friends with travellers on lonely roads and, after lulling them into false security, suddenly strangling them and then robbing them. They were a real danger in early nineteenth-century India, and they were thought to be a tightly knit conspiratorial body spread across the subcontinent and united by religious fanaticism. Sue's description makes the Thugs sound like Jesuits by stressing their lack of national and familial allegiance: 'for them there is neither country nor family; they owe no allegiance save to a dark, invisible power, whose decrees they obey with blind submission'.[20] With Thuggee, a real phenomenon was blown up into a myth of conspiracy.[21] It was assisted by the sensational novel, *Confessions of a Thug* (1839), by

18   Charles Kingsley, *Westward Ho!*, Everyman's Library (London: Dent, 1906), p. 428.

19   Quoted in J. R. Hale, *England and the Italian Renaissance*, revised edn (London: Fontana, 1996), p. 197.

20   Eugène Sue, *The Wandering Jew*, The Modern Library, 2 vols in one (New York: Random House, n.d.), i, 166. On his depiction of Jesuits, see Cubitt, esp. p. 289.

21   On the 'creation of knowledge about the "thugs" ', see C. A. Bayly, *Empire and Information:*

Philip Meadows Taylor. Taylor presents the confessions made by his Thug, Ameer Ali, to a European narrator, as a true story. Stress is laid on the secrecy of the Thugs' operations and on their vast numbers: between 1831 and 1837, 3266 were arrested for Thuggee. Telling his story, Ameer Ali presents Thuggee as a 'brotherhood' (I, 39) spread all over India and uniting Hindus and Muslims.[22] It is said to be a religious movement. The Thugs' goddess is Bhowanee or Kalee (I, 66); at Ameer's initiation ceremony a prayer is uttered to her, and also at the beginning of an expedition (I, 70, 76). Much stress is laid on the dissimulation practised by the Thugs when they appear to befriend travellers (I, 83–84, 168–69). On learning to strangle, Ameer feels like an animal: 'Like a tiger, which, once having tasted human blood, will if possible take no other, and runs every risk to get it, so I feel it will be with me' (I, 124). The Thugs thus embody an alliance between religious fanaticism and animal savagery. Its antithesis in the novel is the rational and ultimately infallible system of British police investigation and judicial decision which reassuringly frames this peril: as Patrick Brantlinger notes, the novel reproduces in its structure 'the dominative relationship of its imagined context'.[23] Victorian anti-Catholic polemics use this analogy: in Catherine Sinclair's novel of counter-propaganda *Beatrice; Or, the Unknown Relatives* (1852) a Protestant bishop describes Jesuits as 'the Thugs of Christendom, who murder the soul by steeping it in crime as an act of devotion'.[24] In Sinclair's paranoid horror story, inspired by the Oxford Movement and confessedly influenced by Frances Trollope, Jesuits enter Britain via the partly Catholic West of Scotland, plotting with their tame accomplices to corrupt children's imaginations by tales of saints, to break up families, and to keep their flocks in ignorance, squalor and subjection.[25]

A further example of the tendency to map one imagined conspiracy onto another occurs in Louise Otto-Peters's novel *Schloß und Fabrik* (1846). Here a letter from a Jesuit in Germany to a colleague abroad reveals that the spread of Communism is being masterminded by the Jesuits, not only to defeat liberalism, but so that, once Communism has reduced everyone to a single obedient flock, the Jesuits will step in as the shepherds and keep the flock in submission.[26] This is just the fantasy — promoting equality in order to assume control — that the *Protocols* ascribed to the Jews.

Intelligence Gathering and Social Communication in India, 1780–1870 (Cambridge: Cambridge University Press, 1996), pp. 173–76; Mike Dash, *Thug: The True Story of India's Murderous Cult* (London: Granta, 2005).

22   Captain Meadows Taylor, *Confessions of a Thug*, 3 vols (London: Richard Bentley, 1839), I, 39. Future references in text.

23   Patrick Brantlinger, *Rule of Darkness: British Literature and Imperialism, 1830–1914* (Ithaca, NY, and London: Cornell University Press, 1988), p. 88.

24   Catherine Sinclair, *Beatrice; or, The Unknown Relatives*, 3 vols (London: Richard Bentley, 1852), II, 42–43; cf. III, 81. On this novel, see Griffin, pp. 132–47.

25   Contemporary British converts are mentioned in Sinclair, I, 100, and 'Mrs Trollope's Jesuit' at I, 221. One of her characters is called Father Eustace.

26   Louise Otto-Peters, *Schloß und Fabrik*, ed. by Johanna Ludwig (Leipzig: LKG, 1996), pp. 276–77.

One has the impression that fear of Jesuits was more powerful in mid-Victorian England than fear of Jews. Casual antisemitism, mockery of Jews' language and manners, and an automatic association of Jews with money-lending and selling old clothes, were of course widespread, and can be amply illustrated from Dickens, Thackeray, and many other writers. But we seldom find anxiety about an international Jewish network. Trollope perhaps comes closest with his presentation of Melmotte, the financier in in *The Way We Live Now* (1875), whose main associate is 'Samuel Cohenlupe, Esq., Member of Parliament for Staines, a gentleman of the Jewish persuasion'.[27] Melmotte's own origins, however, are tantalizingly uncertain.[28] His wife is a Frankfurt Jew; he has lived on the Continent and in New York, has arrived in London from Paris, and is at first known as M. Melmotte; after his suicide it emerges that his father was an Irish forger in New York by the name of Melmody. As an all-purpose foreigner, the antithesis of the English landowner Roger Carbury, Melmotte illustrates Trollope's suspicion that English society is being infiltrated by Continental and Jewish swindlers, American crooks like Hamilton K. Fisker, and unsettlingly independent women like Mrs Hurtle, another American. The important point about Melmotte is, as Bryan Cheyette says, his indeterminacy.[29] It is only in the Edwardian period, in the novels of 'the Chesterbelloc' — the ultra-patriotic Catholics G. K. Chesterton and Hilaire Belloc — that we find real paranoia about international Jewish finance and Jewish racial infiltration. Belloc's novels *Emmanuel Burden* (1904) and *Mr. Clutterbuck's Election* (1908) purport to reveal the machinations of 'the redoubtable and ubiquitous Abraham'.[30]

Myths of conspiracy easily pass into myths of infiltration. If the Jesuits can infiltrate Britain, so can other foreigners, including those from Britain's imperial possessions. The extension of British power over territories throughout the world also generated insecurity, especially the fear that the inhabitants of these territories would infiltrate Britain (note the imagery of infectious disease, explored by Laura Otis; note also how we stigmatize diseases as foreign — German measles, Spanish flu, French pox, Asiatic cholera, Asian flu) and take revenge over the British where they thought themselves most secure. Colonial subjects may be inspired by the desire for revenge. They embody the bad conscience of imperial power. An example is the three Brahmins in Collins's *The Moonstone* (1868) who come to Yorkshire in order to recover the diamond pillaged from the temple at Seringapatam. The repressed

27 Anthony Trollope, *The Way We Live Now*, ed. by John Sutherland, World's Classics (Oxford: Oxford University Press, 1982), p. 84.

28 See John Sutherland, 'Is Melmotte Jewish?' *Times Literary Supplement*, 4 August 1995, pp. 13–14, partially reprinted in id., *Is Heathcliff a Murderer?* (Oxford: Oxford University Press, 1996), pp. 156–62.

29 Bryan Cheyette, *Constructions of 'the Jew' in English Literature and Society: Racial Representations, 1875–1945* (Cambridge: Cambridge University Press, 1993), p. 39. I have explored this subject more widely in 'The Representation of Jews in British and German Literature: A Comparison', in *Two Nations: British and German Jews in Comparative Perspective*, ed. by Michael Brenner, Rainer Liedtke and David Rechter (Tübingen: Mohr Siebeck, 1999), pp. 411–41.

30 Hilaire Belloc, *Mr. Clutterbuck's Election* (London: Eveleigh Nash, 1908), p. 295. See David Lodge, 'The Chesterbelloc and the Jews', in his *The Novelist at the Crossroads and Other Essays on Fiction and Criticism* (London: Routledge & Kegan Paul, 1971), pp. 145–58.

returns also in the persons of the Andaman Islander in Arthur Conan Doyle's *The Sign of Four* (1890). Laura Otis, noting that Doyle visited Berlin in 1890 to report on Robert Koch's work on bacteriology, argues that the Holmes stories show the detective similarly warding off invaders by maintaining an Imperial immune system which enables him to detect even small threats: the Andaman Islander is the companion of the villain Jonathan Small and himself belongs to one of 'the smallest race[s] on earth'.[31]

Even if foreigners do not enter Britain in person, their occult power may extend there. In H. G. Wells's story 'Pollock and the Porroh Man', a disreputable Englishman in Sierra Leone shoots and wounds a 'Porroh man', a member of a secret society that practises magic. Attempts are made on his life, his bones ache, he is assailed by snakes and red ants. He pays an African to kill the Porroh man and is presented with the severed head, which mysteriously survives every attempt to destroy it. Even when Pollock returns to England, the hallucination of the head pursues him everywhere, till finally he cuts his own throat.[32]

Dickens, who admired Collins's *Moonstone*, may have sought to go one better in *The Mystery of Edwin Drood*, which turns on the contrast between an idyllic English cathedral town and the threats emanating from the East. Neville Landless, who is charged with the murder of Edwin Drood, was brought up in Ceylon, may be of mixed ancestry, and has wild passions associated with the foreign and the primitive. The most likely murderer, John Jasper, Edwin's nephew, leads a double life as a respectable choir-master in Cloisterham Cathedral and as an opium addict who frequents an opium den in the East End of London. He has a black scarf, and Dickens told his illustrator, Luke Fildes, that he was to strangle Edwin with it.[33] This has led to the conjecture that Jasper is himself a Thug, and while it is unlikely that he is a full-blown worshipper of Kali it certainly seems plausible that not only his opium habit but his method of murder should be derived from the East.[34] Jasper thus becomes a representative of that frightening fictional type, the renegade or 'Überläufer', who has in important respects 'gone native'.[35] He is both the agent and victim of Oriental infiltration. Opium, produced mainly in Turkey and later in Persia (the Indian crop was mainly for export to China), had already featured in the lives of such Romantic writers as Coleridge and De Quincey. De Quincey tells us that his opium-inspired nightmares were filled with terrifying imagery from 'the ancient, monumental, cruel, and elaborate religions of Indostan', and haunted

31   Quoted in Laura Otis, *Membranes: Metaphors of Invasion in Nineteenth-Century Literature, Science and Politics* (Baltimore, MD, and London: Johns Hopkins University Press, 1999), p. 95.

32   H. G. Wells, *The Plattner Story and Others* (London: Methuen, 1897), pp. 142–64.

33   Charles Dickens, *The Mystery of Edwin Drood*, ed. by Margaret Cardwell, The Clarendon Dickens (Oxford: Clarendon Press, 1972), p. xxvi.

34   This forms part of the solution to the mystery put forward — to my mind, convincingly — by Edmund Wilson in 'Dickens: The Two Scrooges', in *The Wound and the Bow* (London: W. H. Allen, 1941; repr. London: Methuen, 1961), pp. 1–93. The evidence is reviewed, perhaps too sceptically, by Wendy S. Jacobson, 'John Jasper and Thuggee', *MLR* 72 (1977), 526–37.

35   See Karl-Heinz Kohl, '"Travestie der Lebensformen" oder "kulturelle Konversion"? Zur Geschichte des kulturellen Überläufertums', in *Die andere Welt: Studien zum Exotismus*, ed. by Thomas Koebner and Gerhard Pickerodt (Frankfurt a.M.: Athenäum, 1987), pp. 88–120.

by the figure of 'the Malay'.[36] This imaginary Malay was apparently based on the actual person who called at his cottage in the Lake District, on his way to or from the port of Liverpool, seemed to the servant-girl to be 'a sort of demon' (p. 56), and, unable to communicate, received from De Quincey a dose of opium 'enough to kill three dragoons and their horses' (p. 57) but went off, apparently unaffected by it. As De Quincey was obsessively afraid of infection by Eastern diseases, John Barrell has argued that his use of opium was an attempt to inoculate himself against such terrors: an attempt which could only be self-defeating, since to inoculate himself *against* disease meant inoculating himself *with* it.[37]

Infiltration can be embodied not only in suspicious foreigners, but also in 'the return of the native'. A person returns home after long years abroad which have changed him and perhaps made him seem alien and suspicious. A mild example is Peter Brown in Elizabeth Gaskell's *Cranford* (1853): though entirely benevolent, he has acquired an ironic distance from his home, and cannot resist teasing the old ladies by claiming that in the Himalayas he shot a cherubim.[38] Friedrich Mergel in Annette von Droste-Hülshoff's *Die Judenbuche* (1842) and Leonhard Hagebucher in Wilhelm Raabe's *Abu Telfan* (1868) have both endured years of slavery in Africa. But while Mergel's Algerian captivity is a narrative blank about which we learn nothing, Hagebucher's twelve years as a slave in the town of Abu Telfan in 'Tumurkieland', a fictional region of Darfur, are mentioned in some detail. In particular we learn of his subjection to the cruel Madam Kulla Gulla: 'nie hatte die Madam Kulla Gulla ihren Gefangenen so weich und gebrochen unter ihren Händen gespürt [...]'.[39] This makes Kulla Gulla sound partly like a dominatrix, partly like a terrible mother disciplining a child, and in the latter role she is the antithesis of the idealized mother, Klaudine Fehleysen, whose long-lost son Viktor, an animal-dealer in Africa, under the name of Kornelius van der Mook, released Hagebucher from captivity. Thus Africa becomes a primitive place where the terrors of childhood are still rampant, alongside those of perverse sexuality. Hagebucher meanwhile is an object of suspicion to the citizens of his home town, and the narrator reminds us of their suspicion by referring to him frequently as 'der Afrikaner'. Real-life captives often encountered similar difficulties in finding acceptance at home. An English case is that of Thomas Pellow, captured by Moroccan corsairs at the age of eleven and kept in captivity from 1715 to 1738, during which time he converted to Islam. After escaping to Britain, he had to ward off the suspicion attaching to a 'renegade' by publishing an account of his experiences in which he demonstrated his hostility to the Moors.[40]

---

36   Thomas de Quincey, *Confessions of an English Opium Eater*, ed. by Grevel Lindop, World's Classics (Oxford: Oxford University Press, 1996), pp. 73, 72.

37   John Barrell, *The Infection of Thomas de Quincey: A Psychopathology of Imperialism* (New Haven, CT, and London: Yale University Press, 1991), p. 17.

38   Elizabeth Gaskell, *Cranford*, ed. by Elizabeth Porges Watson, World's Classics (Oxford: Oxford University Press, 1998), p. 159.

39   Wilhelm Raabe, *Abu Telfan oder die Heimkehr vom Mondgebirge*, ed. by Werner Röpke, in *Sämtliche Werke*, VII (Freiburg and Braunschweig: Klemm, 1951), p. 228.

40   Linda Colley, *Captives: Britain, Empire and the World, 1600–1850* (London: Cape, 2002), pp. 93–97.

Ports are of course the obvious means of entry for foreigners and foreign diseases. In *Wuthering Heights*, Heathcliff is found as a child at the port of Liverpool. Although Terry Eagleton has suggested that he is 'quite possibly Irish',[41] the text Orientalizes him, describing him first as gipsy-like, then, more exotically, as 'a little Lascar, or an American or Spanish castaway', or fantastically as the son of the Emperor of China and an Indian queen.[42] Bram Stoker's Count Dracula enters Britain by the port of Whitby, in a ship whose entire crew has died during the voyage. Dracula too carries an infection, because by sucking blood he makes his victims into 'the undead', vampires who in turn create yet more vampires, so that by the logic of the tale everybody ought to be a vampire. Dracula comes from Transylvania and the feudal past. Yet he has mastered not only English but English legal procedures, and thus shows how the undead feudal aristocracy can establish themselves in the modern world. Since he comes from Eastern Europe, it is not quite accurate to cite him, as Stephen D. Arata does, as an example of 'reverse colonization'; but he certainly embodies the fear that the Imperial centre may be undermined and overthrown by underestimated threats from its periphery.[43] Coming from the past, yet undead, he recalls earlier fears of Catholic infiltration by representatives of a Church which symbolized the terrifying return of Protestantism's past.[44] And in imagining him passing unseen amid the huge population of London, Jonathan Harker associates him with fears of immigration as well as infection: 'This was the being I was helping to transfer to London, where, perhaps for centuries to come, he might, amongst its teeming millions, satiate his lust for blood, and create a new and ever widening circle of semi-demons to batten on the helpless.'[45]

The German-speaking world has few ports, but Vienna has traditionally been called the *porta Orientis*, the interface between Europe and an Asia which has sometimes been claimed to stretch into the Balkans. 'Asien fängt auf der Landstraße an,' asserted Ferdinand Kürnberger, citing a saying of Metternich's and referring to the inner suburb immediately east of the centre of Vienna.[46] Evoking the Viennese atmosphere in his characteristically inflated style, the Berlin journalist Maximilian Harden in 1911 combined the familiar stereotype of Viennese hedonism with that of Oriental languor: 'Hier wird Wein getrunken; ist das Gebirg nah; mordet das Uebermaß hastiger Arbeit nicht die Freude am Leben. Hier ist schon Orient. Die Luft singt davon und dem Wanderer begegnet mancher Levantinertypus. Der Vorhof des Orients; eines gründlich gesäuberten, civilisirten, ohne träges Geräkel,

41   Terry Eagleton, *Heathcliff and the Great Hunger: Studies in Irish Culture* (London: Verso, 1995), p. 3.

42   Emily Brontë, *Wuthering Heights*, ed. by Ian Jack, World's Classics (Oxford: Oxford University Press, 1995), pp. 31, 44, 50.

43   Stephen D. Arata, 'The Occidental Tourist: *Dracula* and the Anxiety of Reverse Colonization', *Victorian Studies*, 33 (1990), 621–45.

44   Griffin makes this point about Catholicism, p. 75 and *passim*.

45   Bram Stoker, *Dracula*, ed. by Maud Ellmann, World's Classics (Oxford: Oxford University Press, 1996), p. 51.

46   Ferdinand Kürnberger, ' "Asiatisch und Selbstlos" (16. November 1871)', in *Gesammelte Werke*, ed. by O. E. Deutsch, 2 vols (Munich and Leipzig: Georg Müller, 1910), I, 193–99 (p. 196). I am grateful to Gilbert Carr for locating this quotation and to Karen Leeder for supplying me with a photocopy.

Fäulnißgestank, Pestilenz.'[47] Just beyond Vienna, it seems, the traditional bogeys of Orientalism, indolence and plague, lie in wait. In 1922, however, Hofmannsthal interpreted the term differently, transferring the Orient to the depths of the psyche. After informing American readers about the upsurge of psychoanalysis in Vienna, he concluded: '[Wien] ist die porta Orientis auch für jenen geheimnisvollen Orient, das Reich des Unbewußten.'[48]

A similar shift occurs in Thomas Mann's *Der Tod in Venedig* (1912). The cultural and symbolic geography of Mann's story has recently received much attention.[49] Here the East appears in Venice, gateway to the Orient; in the Polish provenance of Tadzio, and indeed in Aschenbach's origins in Silesia; in Asia, the source of the cholera which infests Venice and kills Aschenbach; and in the mythic figure of Dionysus, whose cult reached Greece from the East. But the Eastern threat is not just an external one. At the beginning of the story, the sight of a traveller who may be an avatar of Dionysus unleashes in Aschenbach's mind an almost palpably vivid hallucination of the Ganges delta. The Dionysian dream which marks his abandonment of reason and morality reveals that the orgiastic cults of ancient Greece are still present in his unconscious — and by extension in the unconscious of civilized Europe. Just as Venice is founded on a swamp, so European civilization is founded on a repressed but still latent primitive stratum. Anticipating Hofmannsthal, Mann discloses the Orient within. Aschenbach could not have succumbed to infection if he had not been already susceptible.

The imagery of infiltration by invisible germs combines easily with that of subversion by disguised and hence invisible aliens, while one supposed conspiracy, as we have seen, can readily be mapped onto another. A further example of a supposed conspiratorial organization is the Freemasons. In late eighteenth-century Germany semi-secret societies, especially Freemasonry, were a popular form of sociability. Knigge writes in his famous manual of social skills, *Über den Umgang mit Menschen*: 'Man wird heutzutage in allen Ständen wenig Menschen treffen, die nicht [...] wenigstens eine Zeitlang Mitglieder einer solchen geheimen Verbrüderung gewesen wären.'[50] The Freemasons were dedicated to Enlightenment goals of virtue, humanity and toleration, yet their structure, with grades of initiates, resembled that of mystical societies like the Rosicrucians. Their offshoot, the Illuminati, founded by the Ingolstadt jurist Adam Weishaupt in 1776, were devoted to radical republicanism and egalitarianism. Weishaupt, a professor of law at Ingolstadt, had been educated by Jesuits in Bavaria and was deeply influenced by Jesuit organization and discipline. When the secrets of the Illuminati leaked out, the resulting panic caused the Elector of Bavaria, by an edict of 2 March 1785, to ban all Freemasons and Illuminati in his dominions. They were readily, though implausibly, associated with the recently

47   Maximilian Harden, 'Lueger', in *Köpfe*, 3 vols (Berlin: Reiss, 1923), II, 441–59 (p. 442).

48   Hugo von Hofmannsthal, 'Wiener Brief' [II], in *Gesammelte Werke in Einzelbänden*, ed. by Bernd Schoeller, 10 vols (Frankfurt a.M.: Fischer, 1979), IX, 185–96 (p. 195).

49   Yahya Elsaghe, *Die imaginäre Nation: Thomas Mann und das 'Deutsche'* (Munich: Fink, 2000), pp. 27–60; Elizabeth Boa, 'Global Intimations: Cultural Geography in *Buddenbrooks, Tonio Kröger* and *Der Tod in Venedig*', *Oxford German Studies*, 35 (2006), 21–33.

50   Adolph Freiherr von Knigge, *Über den Umgang mit Menschen*, ed. by Gert Ueding (Frankfurt a.M.: Insel, 1977), p. 391.

dissolved Society of Jesus. J. M. Roberts reports that there were 'no fewer than six different theories of Jesuit complicity in masonry put forward in the 1780s'.[51] It was alleged that the Society persisted under the guise of Templar Masonry, that they had resuscitated the Rosicrucian Order, and even that they had infiltrated the Illuminati.[52] But even without Jesuit complicity, Freemasons were widely thought to be pulling the strings of politics, while the unprecedented upheaval of the French Revolution soon seemed to demand a single, simple, conspiratorial cause. In his famous denunciation, Edmund Burke wrote: 'All circumstances taken together, the French revolution is the most astonishing that has yet happened in the world'; he blamed it on a 'literary cabal [which] had some years ago formed something like a regular plan for the destruction of the Christian religion', and also issued a dark warning against the underground activities of the Illuminati.[53] These various sources of subversion were combined in the conspiracy theory put forward by the Abbé Barruel, who ascribed the Revolution to a plot hatched by Voltaire, D'Alembert and Frederick the Great with the assistance of Diderot, using the *Encyclopédie* to disseminate irreligion and Rousseauism to attack monarchy, while the Freemasons and Illuminati worked to undermine the social order.[54]

Conspiracy theories involving Freemasons, Jesuits and Jews come together in Mann's *Der Zauberberg*. During the First World War Mann read articles about the malign influence of Freemasonry, and in *Betrachtungen eines Unpolitischen* (1918) he charged it with responsibility for the war and harked back to the conspiracy theory which blamed it for the French Revolution:

> Die Geschichtsforschung wird lehren, welche Rolle das internationale Illumi-natentum, die Freimaurer-Weltloge, unter Ausschluß der ahnungslosen Deutschen natürlich, bei der geistigen Vorbereitung und wirklichen Entfesselung des Weltkrieges, des Krieges der 'Zivilisation' *gegen Deutschland*, gespielt hat. Was mich betrifft, so hatte ich, bevor irgendwelches Material vorlag, meine genauen und unumstößlichen Überzeugungen in dieser Hinsicht. [...] Nicht geahnt hatten wir, daß, unter der Decke des friedsam internationalen Verkehrs, in Gottes weiter Welt der Haß, der unauslöschliche Todhaß der politischen Demokratie, des freimaurerisch-republikanischen Rhetor-Bourgeois von 1789 gegen uns, gegen unsere Staatseinrichtung, unseren seelischen Militarismus, den Geist der Ordnung, Autorität und Pflicht am verfluchten Werk war...[55]

51 J. M. Roberts, *The Mythology of the Secret Societies* (London: Secker & Warburg, 1972), p. 139.

52 On the conspiracy theories associated with the Knights Templar, see Peter Partner, *The Murdered Magicians: The Templars and their Myth* (Oxford: Oxford University Press, 1982).

53 Edmund Burke, *Reflections on the Revolution in France*, ed. by L. G. Mitchell, World's Classics (Oxford: Oxford University Press, 1993), pp. 10, 111, 156. See Nigel Aston, 'Burke and the Conspiratorial Origins of the French Revolution: Some Anglo-French Resemblances', in *Conspiracies and Conspiracy Theories in Early Modern Europe*, ed. by Barry Coward and Julian Swann (Aldershot: Ashgate, 2004), pp. 213–33.

54 Abbé Barruel, *Memoirs Illustrating the History of Jacobinism*, trans. by Robert Clifford, 4 vols (London: T. Burton, 1798). On the prehistory of this theory, see Amos Hofman, 'The Origins of the Theory of the *philosophe* Conspiracy', *French History*, 2 (1988), 152–72 [and more generally Darrin McMahon, *Enemies of the Enlightenment: The French Counter-Enlightenment and the Making of Modernity* (New York: Oxford University Press, 2001)].

55 Thomas Mann, *Gesammelte Werke*, 13 vols (Frankfurt a.M.: Fischer, 1974), XII, 32, 36. Hence-forth cited in text as *GW* with volume and page number.

Der Zauberberg partially retracts such allegations. It includes Freemasonry among the many secret societies described to Hans Castorp, first by Naphta and then by Settembrini, in the chapter 'Als Soldat und brav'. Naphta tells Castorp that Settembrini is a Freemason, implying that this allegiance is a counterpart of Naphta's own association with the Society of Jesus. We already know that Settembrini's grandfather was a 'Carbonaro', a member of a secret society dedicated to the liberation of Italy from foreign rule (*GW* III, 215, 701). But the initial implication, that a liberal and a religious society are each the antithesis of the other, is complicated as we learn more about what they have in common. Naphta concedes that Freemasonry has something 'Militärisch-Jesuitisches' about it (*GW* III, 703). That seems to apply still more to the Illuminati, whose founder, according to Naphta, was himself a Jesuit and modelled his order on the Jesuits. Just as the Jesuits have a military character, governed by a General, so the Masons of the Strict Observance established lodges with military grades harking back to the medieval Templars. Moreover, the Strict Observance derived occult knowledge from the Rosicrucians, and drew on alchemy for images of transmutation, the chief such image being the grave. Their mysteries were an initiation into knowledge of death. In its origin, therefore, Freemasonry turns out to be a religion, concerned with the mysteries surrounding existence. Naphta further explains that the Strict Observance resembles the Catholic Church in its ritual centring on love-feasts which go back ultimately to the Egyptian mysteries of Isis. From this passage, strands of imagery run through the novel: the word 'Hermetik', on which Castorp eagerly seizes (*GW* III, 706), links up with the earlier playful allusions to the god Mercury and the mercury in the thermometer; while the mention of love-feasts anticipates the vegetarian Eucharist which Peeperkorn will later administer. Both the Freemasons and the Society of Jesus give embodiment to a religious urge rooted deeply in human nature.[56]

By comparison, the version of Freemasonry espoused by Settembrini seems rather dull and superficial. According to Naphta, people like Settembrini have purified Freemasonry of religious elements and reduced it to a socially benevolent institution, 'die bourgeoise Misere in Klubgestalt' (*GW* III, 708). Settembrini himself, when questioned by Castorp, says that Masons are helping to build a new social structure, 'die Vollendung der Menschheit, das neue Jerusalem' (*GW* III, 712). It appears to be an extension of the benevolent aims that Settembrini has professed earlier. In the chapter 'Enzyklopädie' Settembrini tells how he belongs to the Internationaler Bund für Organisierung des Fortschritts which is compiling a twenty-volume encyclopaedia, *Soziologie der Leiden* (III, 343). For this

---

56 Mann took much information, sometimes verbatim, from Marianne Thalmann, *Der Trivialroman des 18. Jahrhunderts und der romantische Roman* (Berlin: Emil Ehering, 1923). See especially Thalmann, p. 105, on the Strict Observance and its supposed descent from the medieval Templars. For further details, see Scott Abbott, *Fictions of Freemasonry: Freemasonry and the German Novel* (Detroit, MI: Wayne State University Press, 1991), ch. 6; Rainer Scheer and Andrea Seppi, 'Etikettenschwindel? Die Rolle der Freimaurerei in Thomas Manns *Zauberberg*', in '*Die Beleuchtung, die auf mich fällt, hat ... oft gewechselt*': *Neue Studien zum Werk Thomas Manns*, ed. by Hans Wisskirchen (Würzburg: Königshausen & Neumann, 1991), pp. 54–84.

project Mann drew heavily on a treatise with this title by F. C. Müller-Lyer. This treatise calls for an organization to combat suffering, but insists that this cannot be a 'Kampforganisation', like the army or the Society of Jesus, in which all submit themselves blindly to a commander, but a free 'Arbeitsorganisation' which puts minimal pressure on its members and is animated by a civilized spirit.[57] This Bund is a relatively open, relatively benign, perhaps somewhat absurd organization: an open conspiracy.

In suggesting resemblances between the Freemasons and the Jesuits, Mann extends the now familiar process of mapping one conspiracy onto another. He does the same in presenting Naphta as both a Jew (by origin) and a Jesuit (though illness has prevented him from taking his vows). This is at the expense of probability. Mann admitted that he had never met a Jewish Jesuit, but claimed that the combination was (psychologically) plausible: 'Der kommunistische Jesuit ist mir wirklich nie vorgekommen, aber daß die Mischung möglich und plausibel ist, scheint mir das geschlossene Weltbild des Herrn Naphta zu beweisen', he wrote in 1934.[58] Naphta's life-story is a curious mixture of wild fantasy and documentary information. A Jewish Jesuit is extremely unlikely. A reference book devoted to the Jesuits asserts that there has never been such a person, though Lainez, a sixteenth-century General of the Society, was wrongly suspected of being descended from Spanish Marranos or crypto-Jews.[59] From 1593 to 1946 the rules of the Society explicitly excluded any baptized Jew from membership.[60] Naphta's family flee from a pogrom in their Galician village, where Elia Naphta, charged with ritual murder, is crucified against a door — an improbable combination of events, even though ritual murder charges were not uncommon in Imperial Germany and Austria.[61] They arrive not in Prague, Berlin or Vienna, the obvious destinations for Galician refugees, but in the Austrian provincial town of Feldkirch in Vorarlberg, so that Naphta, having been identified as a promising lad by Father Unterpertinger, may attend the famous Jesuit college there. This college, the Stella Matutina, was founded as a Jesuit private school in 1868. It closed for lack of pupils in 1979. Its pupils included Kurt von Schuschnigg, Hans Urs von Balthasar, and Sir Arthur Conan Doyle, who spent the year 1875–76 there before studying medicine at Edinburgh. It was an exclusive school, with many pupils from the Catholic aristocracy of the Rhineland, Westphalia and Silesia, and many also from nearby Switzerland.

---

57   F. C. Müller-Lyer, *Soziologie der Leiden* (Munich: Langen, 1914), pp. 153–55. See I. A. and J. J. White, 'The Importance of F. C. Müller-Lyer's Ideas for *Der Zauberberg*', *MLR* 75 (1980), 333–48.

58   Thomas Mann, letter to Pierre-Paul Sagave, 30 January 1934, in *Briefe, 1889–1936*, ed. by Erika Mann (Frankfurt a.M.: Fischer, 1962), pp. 350–51. For a useful account of Naphta, see Metin Toprak, *Die deutsche Mitte: Politische Betrachtungen des 'Zauberbergs'* (Bern: Peter Lang, 1999).

59   Ludwig Koch, SJ, *Jesuiten-Lexikon* (Paderborn: Bonifacius, 1934), s.v. 'Juden'.

60   Franka Marquardt, 'Judentum und Jesuitenorden in Thomas Manns *Zauberberg*: Zur Funktion der "Fehler" in der Darstellung des jüdischen Jesuiten Leib-Leo Naphta', *DVjs* 81 (2007), 257–81 (p. 275). Marquardt's careful investigation into the many implausibilities in Mann's presentation of Naphta as Jew and Jesuit concludes persuasively that their purpose is to make Naphta appear as dangerous as possible.

61   See Helmut Walser Smith, *The Butcher's Tale: Murder and Anti-Semitism in a German Town* (New York: Norton, 2002).

By defying probability and having Naphta trained as a Jesuit, Mann represents the Society of Jesus as an order that takes people from various backgrounds, subjects them to a homogeneous training and puts them into the same mould. Thus he confirms the stereotypical view of the Jesuits as deracinated, detached from all familial and national loyalties, and dominated by a single purpose conceived in coldly intellectual terms. He found this stereotype confirmed in the book which gave him his information about the medieval Church, and which depicts the Jesuits as an international conspiracy dedicated to restoring the medieval theocracy and indifferent to all ties of affection for their blood-relatives and their native countries.[62] This stereotype overlaps with that of the Jewish revolutionary as similarly detached from national loyalties and hence able to pursue his goals with complete ruthlessness. Naphta's deracination is shown especially in his detachment from his family. We are told that when he joined the Stella Matutina: 'Er war dorthin übergesiedelt, indem er seine jüngeren Geschwister mit größter Gemütsruhe, mit der Unempfindlichkeit des Geistesaristokraten der Armenpflege und einem Schicksal überließ, wie es ihrer minderen Begabung gebührte' (GW III, 614). With his commitment to installing a Communist theocracy through terror, he represents the type of revolutionary which Mann identified in the person of Eugen Leviné, the leader of the Munich Soviet of April–May 1919. In his diaries, Mann calls Leviné the 'Typus des russischen Juden, des Führers der Weltbewegung', representing a kind of chiliasm which was to be included in Der Zauberberg.[63] He speaks also of 'den brutalen, die Wirklichkeit mißhandelnden Idealismus der Leviné', suggesting that since such people no longer have any affective ties to people and institutions, they try to reshape the real world with a cruelty which is purely cerebral and all the more remorseless.[64]

By presenting Naphta as a coldly rational internationalist, detached from family and country, Mann established a clear and somewhat surprising contrast with Settembrini. Although we might expect this man of the Enlightenment, with his cosmopolitan ideals and his international affiliations, to be even more detached from his origins, Settembrini is in fact warmly attached both to his family and his country. Like Hans Castorp, he has been strongly influenced by his grandfather. The resemblance is ironic, since Giuseppe Settembrini was a revolutionary and Hans Lorenz Castorp an ultra-conservative Hamburg patrician, but it gives both characters a humane attachment to the past. As for Settembrini's cosmopolitanism, it turns out to be only skin-deep. On the outbreak of the War it yields to his Italian nationalism. His last words to Hans Castorp are: 'Mir aber verzeih, wenn ich den Rest meiner Kräfte daransetze, um auch mein Land zum Kampfe hinzureißen, auf jener Seite, wohin der Geist und heiliger Eigennutz es weisen' (GW III, 989). The expression 'heiliger Eigennutz' is an allusion to the doctrine of sacro egoismo proclaimed by the Italian Prime Minister Antonio Salandra in October 1914; to

---

62 Heinrich v. Eicken, *Geschichte und System der mittelalterlichen Weltanschauung* (Stuttgart: Cotta, 1887), pp. 809–11. Mann's fascination with this book is attested by his diary: *Tagebücher, 1918–1921*, ed. by Peter de Mendelssohn (Frankfurt a.M.: Fischer, 1979), pp. 200, 213.

63 Mann, *Tagebücher, 1918–1921*, p. 223.

64 Ibid., p. 257.

foreign critics, it seemed a shameless expression of Italian selfishness.[65] A professed cosmopolitan, therefore, easily reverts to nationalism and to supporting national self-interest. Although this is hypocritical, it is also human, suggesting that Settembrini's life contradicts his principles and is in some ways better: his attachment to his revolutionary grandfather is, paradoxically, a kind of traditionalism and supports the moderate conservatism which is the main emphasis of *Der Zauberberg*.

---

65   See Christopher Seton-Watson, *Italy from Liberalism to Fascism, 1870–1925* (London: Methuen, 1967), p. 426.

PART IV

Modernism

CHAPTER 22

Schnitzler's Honesty

In recent decades the publication of Schnitzler's diaries has deepened our under-standing of him and brought him closer to us. Increasingly he seems an attractive figure, who, despite the frequent sadness of his life, maintained a humane and rational outlook in an age of competing ideologies, nationalisms and pseudo-religions. Few contemporaries matched the sanity and prescience of his response to the outbreak of the First World War: 'Der Weltkrieg. Der Weltruin. Ungeheuere und ungeheuerliche Nachrichten' (T 4.8.1914).[1] Although the diaries are not a liter-ary work, like those of Thomas Mann, or a writer's notebook like those of Musil or Kafka, their very brevity helps to convey the honesty which was part of Schnitzler's rationalist approach to life. But his personal writings, taken together with his drama and fiction, also illustrate the difficulty of being honest, and, more generally, the aporias to which his rationalism led.

While it is broadly correct to see Schnitzler, like Freud, as continuing the tradi-tion of the Enlightenment, both writers can be related more precisely to nineteenth-century rationalism.[2] To Franz Werfel, who was toying with mysticism, Schnitzler described himself as a rationalist (T 15.8.1917). Such rationalism is more negative and more pessimistic than the hopeful, expansive doctrines we find in Kant or Herder; it lacks the sheer confidence of Voltaire, Hume or Gibbon. Although Schnitzler is generally hostile to religion, in his autobiography he looks back patronizingly on his youthful atheism and materialism, assuming instead an agnostic standpoint (J 97).

---

1   Schnitzler's works, letters and diaries are referred to by the following abbreviations:

A = *Aphorismen und Betrachtungen*, ed. by Robert O. Weiss (Frankfurt a.M.: Fischer, 1967);
D = *Die Dramatischen Werke*, 2 vols (Frankfurt a.M.: Fischer, 1962);
E = *Die Erzählenden Schriften*, 2 vols (Frankfurt a.M.: Fischer, 1961);
J = *Jugend in Wien*, ed. by Therese Nickl and Heinrich Schnitzler (Vienna, 1968);
B i = *Briefe 1875–1912*, ed. by Therese Nickl and Heinrich Schnitzler (Frankfurt a.M.: Fischer, 1981);
B ii − *Briefe 1913–1931*, ed. by Peter Michael Braunwarth et al. (Frankfurt a.M.: Fischer, 1984);
T = *Tagebuch*, followed (as with letters cited) by date. The individual volumes published to date, all by the Österreichische Akademie der Wissenschaften, are:

Tagebuch 1909–1912 (Vienna, 1981)	*Tagebuch 1913–1916* (Vienna, 1983)
Tagebuch 1917–1919 (Vienna, 1985)	*Tagebuch 1879–1892* (Vienna, 1987)
Tagebuch 1893–1902 (Vienna, 1989)	*Tagebuch 1903–1908* (Vienna, 1991)
Tagebuch 1920–1922 (Vienna, 1993)	

2   For reservations, see Hartmut Scheible, *Arthur Schnitzler und die Aufklärung* (Munich: Fink, 1977), p. 17.

An early diary entry, however, is characteristic, despite its callowness, in deploring the effects of religion on education and in questioning humankind's capacity for rational thought:

> Wie wär' es, wenn man von aller Jugend auf den Menschen richtige Ansichten einpflanzte. Der Satz scheint so natürlich, und doch ist noch wenig daran gedacht worden. Man schickt die Kinder in die Normalschule und bringt ihnen dort unklare, mystische unnaturwissenschaftliche also unnatürliche, ja geistlose Anschauungen bei — und da im Grunde genommen nur wenige Menschen Selbständigkeit des Denkens und den Willen zum Denken mit auf die Welt bringen, so schleppen die Esel von Generation zu Generation die miserabelsten Irrtümer mit. (T 31.5.1880)

He foresees that a rational approach to education would produce a 'Kampf mit den Clericalen und ähnlichem Gesindel', but adds: 'Aber ist es nicht die Pflicht jedes guten Menschen und aufrichtigen Bürgers, aufzuklären?' (ib.). What, however, are the 'richtige Ansichten' that should be implanted? They are first and foremost the views of scientific materialism. Like Freud, Schnitzler was a pupil of Theodor Meynert and Ernst von Brücke. He acquired from them a materialist and determinist outlook, which he later had difficulty in reconciling with his desire to believe in a modest measure of free will.[3] Even as a young man he expresses not missionary enthusiasm but regret: 'Die Anschauung der Materialisten wird mir zu meinem eigenen Leidwesen immer plausibler, wahrscheinlicher' (T 28.4.1880).

This depressing view of the universe seemed to rule out ethical action; all one could do was to face the facts. Honesty became an ethical imperative. Intellectuals steeped in rationalism thought themselves morally obliged to sweep away lies and illusions, and to face the truth revealed, however dismal it might be. Thus Max Nordau undertook to dismantle bourgeois morality in *Die conventionellen Lügen der Kulturmenschheit* (1883), while Freud tried to do the same for religion in *Die Zukunft einer Illusion* (1927). The chief exemplars of this destructive honesty were Nietzsche and Ibsen. Their names were habitually joined in *fin-de-siècle* writing, whether as inspiring representatives of individualism or as degenerate representatives of egomania.[4] Schnitzler admired both: in a letter to an unknown correspondent he ranks them together with Goethe, Beethoven, and Maupassant (!; B 1, 21.6.1895). He denies being influenced by Nietzsche, and certainly lacks the latter's rhetorical pathos, though there may be an echo of Nietzsche's mountain imagery when Schnitzler describes himself as 'ein Dichter für Schwindelfreie' (T 23.12.1917).

Ibsen was clearly more important. His plays provided a model for Schnitzler's *Liebelei* (1894) and *Freiwild* (1896). Enthusiasm for Ibsen — who was seen as a thoroughly modern writer, opposed to mere conventions and demanding a break with the past — was general in Young Vienna. Hermann Bahr, who had published a major critical essay on Ibsen in 1887, later wrote that Ibsen had stood godfather

---

3 See Kenneth Segar, 'Determinism and Character: Arthur Schnitzler's *Traumnovelle* and his Unpublished Critique of Psychoanalysis', *Oxford German Studies*, 8 (1973–74), 114–27.

4 Contrast Otto Weininger, 'Über Henrik Ibsen und seine Dichtung "Peer Gynt"', in his *Über die letzten Dinge* (Munich: Matthes & Seitz, 1980), p. 19, with Max Nordau, *Degeneration* (London, 1895), p. 415.

to Young Vienna.[5] In April 1891 Ibsen arrived in Vienna for an 'Ibsen-Woche', including the Austrian première of *The Pretenders* in the Burgtheater, followed by a dinner in his honour, and performances of *The Wild Duck* at the Deutsches Volkstheater. Hofmannsthal called on Ibsen in his hotel, and later wrote an essay 'Die Menschen in Ibsens Dramen' (1893). In 1896 Schnitzler visited Ibsen in Christiania (now Oslo) and had an amicable conversation with him, in which Ibsen praised *Liebelei* (T 25–26.7.1896). In 1917 he dreamt that he was acting the part of Relling in *The Wild Duck* (T 22.5.1917). No Ibsen role could have been more suitable: Relling is the doctor who sees through the delusions and deceptions in which the Ekdal family are trapped, and who sustains the family, not by undeceiving them, but by encouraging their 'life-lies'. He is contrasted with Molvik, the drunken clergyman who can no longer help anyone (representing the perceived futility of religion) and needs his sense of self-esteem supported by the illusion that he is a demoniac; and with Werle, the inept idealist, whose attempts to enlighten the family merely lead to the death of its most vulnerable member, the child Hedvik. Relling thus embodies honesty, but the despairing honesty of a perceptive onlooker who cannot improve the world. Honesty as Ibsen conceives it must be directed first and foremost at oneself: efforts to force honesty upon society are likely to be as futile as those of another scientist Dr Stockmann, who discovers the plague infesting the town's sewers in *An Enemy of the People*. Ibsen's honesty was summed up in the much-quoted quatrain that runs in German:

> *Leben* heißt — dunkler Gewalten
> Spuk bekämpfen in sich.
> *Dichten* — Gerichtstag halten
> über sein eigenes Ich.[6]

When Schnitzler quotes the phrase 'Gerichtstag halten' (J 36, 126), he does so with a trace of irony. Honesty, he now feels, is unlikely to be an end in itself. After quoting some early introspective poetry, he describes it as 'komisch-rührende und etwas affektierte Verse, mit denen ich wohl nicht nur Gerichtstag über mich zu halten, sondern mir zugleich — der häufige, uneingestandene Nebenzweck solcher Gerichtstage — in irgendeiner vagen Weise Absolution zu erteilen gedachte' (J 126).

Nevertheless, the early Schnitzler at least has some hope of using honesty to overcome conventional shams. In 1900 he writes:

> Ganz bestimmt, wahrhaftiger sind die (in Betracht kommenden) Menschen seit 1880 geworden; eine große Flucht vor der Phrase und vor den feststehenden Sätzen überhaupt ist erfolgt; die Achtung vor dem Einzelfall hat sich eingestellt, und das macht das Leben im allgemeinen doch reicher und schöner als es zu unsrer Eltern Zeit war. Freilich ist nicht zu vergessen, daß für die große Masse — die 'ewigen Wahrheiten', mit anderm Wort die 'heilgen Banalitäten' noch immer gut genug sind. (to Olga Gussmann, B 1, 4.8.1900)

---

5 Bahr, *Selbstbildnis* (Berlin: Fischer, 1923), p. 278. See 'Ibsen in Wien', in *Das Junge Wien: Österreichische Literatur- und Kunstkritik, 1887–1904*, ed. by Gotthart Wunberg, 2 vols (Tübingen: Niemeyer, 1976), pp. lxii–lxvi.

6 'Ein Vers', in Henrik Ibsen, *Sämtliche Werke*, ed. by Julius Elias and Paul Schlenther, 5 vols (Berlin: Fischer, 1921), I, 117.

Even here, though, the second sentence shows his scepticism about bringing enlightenment to masses, whose ignorance and credulity he could see being exploited by politicians and journalists.

Schnitzler's honesty, like Ibsen's, is first and foremost relentless self-knowledge. His first notes on autobiography emphasize this. In 1901 he resolves to be as honest as his memory permits. 'Ich weiß nicht,' he continues, 'ob die Neigung, wahr gegen mich selbst zu sein, von Anfang an in mir lag. Sicher aber ist, daß sie sich im Laufe der Jahre gesteigert hat, ja, daß mir diese Neigung heute die lebhafteste und beständigste Regung meines Innern zu sein scheint' (J 324). He dislikes Bahr because the latter is too much of a poseur: 'Denn Menschenseelen, die nur mit Lampions beleuchtet sind, und in die kein Strahl Wahrheit und kein Strahl Größe fällt, eignen sich nicht zu längerm Aufenthalt; man geht gelegentlich drin spazieren' (letter to Rosa Freudenthal, B 1, 9.10.1897). Similarly, he finds Herzl too histrionic: although, according to Herzl's diary, he was enthusiastic about Herzl's plans for a Jewish state, he commented long after Herzl's death on 'Das "Unechte" seines Zionismus. Unechtheit auf hohem Niveau' (T 5.10.1919). He admires honesty in writers: thus in 1919 he describes Arnold Zweig, with sure judgement, as 'einer der weitaus begabtesten und überdies honettesten Leute der jüngern Generation' (T 17.12.1919), and castigates the dishonesty that lay behind the Expressionists' protestations of humanism: 'diese literatische [sic] Sentimentalität kalter harter Streber und Struggler' (T 17.6.1919).

In *Jugend in Wien* Schnitzler describes himself, rather complacently, as free from illusions. Recalling a teenage love-affair, he tells us that even at the time he knew that it was a perfectly ordinary attraction: 'Denn schon damals besaß ich keineswegs das, was man Illusionen zu nennen pflegt; ein Besitz, den man so oft als beneidenswert preisen hört und nach dem ich niemals die geringste Sehnsucht empfunden habe' (J 83). But in *Buch der Sprüche und Bedenken* (1927) he is more searching:

> Es ist eine ganz leichte Sache, in aller Aufrichtigkeit von seinen Schwächen, seinen Lastern, selbst von seinen Verbrechen zu reden. Aber *so* von ihnen reden, als wenn diese Schwächen nicht höchst liebenswürdiger Natur, diese Laster nicht ausnehmend interessant oder gar im Grunde geheime Tugenden, — und als ob diese Verbrechen nicht so verwegen und großartig wären, wie sie vorher kaum noch je verübt worden sind, — *das* ist die Kunst, und hier erst begänne die eigentliche Wahrhaftigkeit. In Autobiographien ist sie selten zu finden. (A 110)

In the diaries, honesty requires an effort. He adjures himself: 'Aufrichtig mein Lieber!' (p. 301). His awareness of transience is one example; he complains that it spoils his happiness (p. 292). Another example occurs when he is in love with Mizi Glümer and at last has, but does not take, the chance to sleep with Olga Waissnix: 'Ja, ich hätte kaum das deutliche Bewußtsein, an Mz. eine Untreue begangen zu haben, wenn Olga schon mein wäre — ja, heute ist mir so — ganz aufrichtig wieder hierhergeschrieben: wenn Olga heute stürbe — empfänd ich nicht die Aufregung, wie wenn Mz. mich bei einem Rendezvous sitzen ließe' (T 10.8.1890). A slight disagreement with a later lover, Marie Reinhard, causes Schnitzler to foresee the end of their relationship and to reflect: 'Denn wie die Menschen werden auch die Beziehungen mit ihrem Tod geboren' (T 24.3.1895). After a 'frank' conversation with Marie Reinhard, in which they agree that it would be absurd to swear undying love, Schnitzler remarks: 'Es liegt was trauriges in dieser Aufrichtigkeit' (T 13.5.1895). And after another: 'Unsre Liebe wird an der Aufrichtigkeit zu Grunde gehen' (T 12.9.1895). This recalls how Anatol, starting a new love affair, already anticipates its end; in the play, however, the role of Anatol, sustaining his life by keeping up the necessary minimum of self-deception, is complemented by that of Max, the *raisonneur* and onlooker who plays no active part in life but comments on Anatol's delusions. A similar disjunction between insight and delusion structures *The Wild Duck*: the Ekdal family lead their deluded life while Relling plays the inactive observer. In his diaries, however, Schnitzler has both to live and observe, and each of the two activities interferes with the other.

The ethic of honesty presents Schnitzler with problems which may be classified under five headings.

(1) *Dealing with emotions.* In 1893 Schnitzler records the agonizing break-up of his relationship with Mizi Glümer. He is clear-sighted about their feelings, including at various times his pity as well as disgust for her, his wish at some moments to find an excuse for resuming the relationship, and the pleasure he takes in tormenting her by denunciations. Eventually things become too appalling, for while this is going on Schnitzler's father dies, and grief for him and for the relationship cause Schnitzler's self-analysis language to collapse into incoherence and yield to religious language:

> Arme todte Mizi! — Freilich ist die Liebe weg, und der Ekel hat sie aufgefressen; aber dort, wo sie glühte und so wohlthat, diese unendliche innige Liebe — dort ist irgend was, und nagt zuweilen ganz grausam — die Stelle, wo sie war, die empfinde ich — Wahrhaftig, die abergläubische Phrase und Frage drängt sich mir auf die Lippen! Mein Gott, mein Gott, was hab ich denn gethan?! (T 16.5.1893)

Similar religious vocabulary is used in the diary when Schnitzler performs self-criticism during a nocturnal stroll with Hofmannsthal. Of him, Schnitzler says: 'Er holt doch meine ganze Ehrlichkeit herauf; ihm gegenüber hab ich am stärksten Bedürfnis und Fähigkeit zu beichten' (p. 184; 17.4.1896). Hofmannsthal was younger than Schnitzler; he led a considerably more sheltered life; Schnitzler usually felt some constraint towards him, as is evident from their correspondence; this constraint must be connected with his sense of Hofmannsthal's moral authority, and perhaps also with the fact that Hofmannsthal, who came from a wealthy banking family that had been Christian for several generations, was more obviously assimilated to Viennese society. Religious language appears also in the passage quoted above from *Jugend in Wien* where Schnitzler remarks that attempts at honesty are usually intended to give oneself a kind of absolution (J 126). Schnitzler's irony here shows his uneasy awareness that painful emotional material cannot be dealt with simply by intellectual analysis, but require some kind of catharsis, one version of which is the confession and absolution that were unavailable to him.

(2) *Psychoanalysis.* Since psychoanalysis has often been seen as a secular substitute for the confessional, one might have thought it suitable for Schnitzler. However, he conceives self-knowledge mainly as introspection in which one is oneself the final authority. He does not adopt the psychoanalytic model of self-knowledge, in which the self's true motives are occluded behind verbal and other parapraxes, and can be brought to light only through the drama of transference and counter-transference; though he comes close to it in the play *Paracelsus* (1899), where emotional truth is brought to the surface by hypnosis, displacement and confession. Generally, however, he thinks of personal truth as private and incommunicable: 'wie man ja überhaupt nur Halbwahres reden kann, außer zu sich selbst, und da wohl auch nur im Traum' (T 19.1.1905).

Schnitzler's acquaintance with Freud was cordial though rather distant.[7] He read Freud's *Traumdeutung* as soon as it came out (T 26.3.1900), but found much in Freud unacceptable, particularly the assumption of psychic determinism and the theory of infantile sexuality.[8] On 16 August 1922 Schnitzler spent a pleasant morning with Freud; they talked about Freud's analysis of Mahler, and Schnitzler confirmed that it had made Mahler much happier; when Freud began offering interpretations of the symbols in his plays, however, Schnitzler was both intrigued and repelled:

> In seinem gesammten Wesen zog er [Freud] mich wieder an, und ich verspüre eine gewisse Lust, über allerlei Untiefen meines Schaffens (und Daseins) mit ihm zu unterhalten — was ich aber lieber unterlassen will. (T 16.8.1922)

The previous night he had had a dream in which, having talked of meeting Freud, he saw Freud moving away from him. He received Theodor Reik's psychoanalytic study of his work with cautious praise, but added: 'nach dem Dunkel der Seele gehen mehr Wege, ich fühle es immer stärker, als die Psychoanalytiker sich träumen (und traumdeuten) lassen' (B II, 31.12.1913); to his ex-wife he wrote concerning Reik: 'er hat leider den Complexen-Complex wie alle Psychoanalytiker' (B II, 9.12.1923).

Although many psychic forces in Schnitzler's life seem to call for psychoanalysis, he can do no more than record them. For example, he got on badly with his father. Johann Schnitzler was disappointed that his elder son, instead of applying himself to medicine, spent much time on literature, gadding about town, running up debts and consorting with unsuitable women. The year after his father's death, Schnitzler experienced auditory hallucinations in which voices uttered meaningless sentences, the only distinct voice being that of his father (T 24.10.1894). Two years later, in November 1896, he began to suffer from tinnitus (T 24.11.1896), and it may not be extravagant to suspect a psychosomatic connection: having refused to listen to his father's voice during his lifetime, Schnitzler was condemned to hear it incessantly after his death. More generally, after the age of thirty the life recorded in his diaries

---

7 See Freud, 'Briefe an Arthur Schnitzler', *Neue Rundschau*, 66 (1955), 95–106; for a recent and thorough study of their relationship, Michael Worbs, *Nervenkunst: Literatur und Psychoanalyse im Wien der Jahrhundertwende* (Frankfurt a.M.: Europäische Verlagsanstalt, 1983).

8 Ernest Jones, *Sigmund Freud: Life and Work*, 3 vols (London: The Hogarth Press, 1953–57), III, 88–89.

becomes increasingly frustrated and unhappy. He suffers major bereavements: not only the death of his father, but the stillbirth of his and Marie Reinhard's child, and the unexpected death of Marie herself. Add to that the emotional wear and tear of the slow-dying (and never quite dead) relationship with Mizi Glümer; his hypochondria, nourished by medical knowledge, his anxiety attacks, his tinnitus, and his increasing weariness of other people's company; and we have a state of mind in which honesty is of little use.

Schnitzler was acutely aware of his own unconscious. His diaries record many disturbing dreams, often with indications of the 'Tagesreste' of which they were composed.[9] In a recurrent nightmare, he arrived too late for his own funeral and his mother persuaded him to be buried (T 30.7.1897). During the break-up of his marriage, he had a dream in which his wife complained that their marriage had gone wrong because they did not dare to have a third child; he woke up in tears, and records: 'Wie wir im Traum zu letzten Gefühlswahrheiten kommen, deren sich im Wachsein unsre Eitelkeit schämt — die für das Wachleben kaum wahr sind!' (T 23.7.1919). Schnitzler's literary explorations of the unconscious, however, may be thought rather cautious: even Fräulein Else is not assailed by such agonizingly unrecuperable memories as afflict, for example, the protagonist of Hofmannsthal's *Andreas*. The story *Traumnovelle*, to be discussed later in this paper, suggests that exploring the unconscious is almost as dangerous as ignoring it.

(3) *The double standard.* Another limitation on Schnitzler's ethic of honesty is the sexual double standard. Despite his high estimation of frankness, Schnitzler constantly found himself lying to women, since he often sustained two (or more) affairs at once. On one occasion he felt like a character in a farce, since he was simultaneously seeking lodgings in which to pursue his brief affair with 'Y.' (Rosa Freudenthal) and a home for Marie Reinhard's baby (T 31.8.1897). His awareness of the double standard is clear from the remarkable diary entries concerning the agonizing break-up of the love-affair with Mizi Glümer. From anonymous letters, Schnitzler learns that she has slept with at least two other men while employed at provincial theatres. He is angry and disgusted, yet during her absence he has himself been having an affair with 'Fifi' (Josefine von Weisswasser), and is aware that things could well have turned out differently, with Mizi discovering his infidelity while he remained ignorant of hers (T 13.4.1893). The experience confirms his cynical axiom that one should always deceive one's girlfriend so as not to be at a disadvantage when she deceives one (T 11.4.1893). But his cynicism misses the point. In true liberal fashion, he regards honesty as a quality belonging to a relationship between two isolated individuals. He does not see that both he and Mizi are caught in a social and sexual system which made dishonesty inevitable. Young men like Schnitzler needed to satisfy both their sexual and emotional needs without committing themselves to marriage and supporting a family. Relatively late marriages were in any case usual. Until marriage, men found satisfaction among petty-bourgeois girls and, especially, among actresses, who, as Stefan Zweig observes, had an ambiguous social position

9 See Michaela L. Perlmann, *Der Traum in der literarischen Moderne: Untersuchungen zum Werk Arthur Schnitzlers* (Munich: Fink, 1987), pp. 24–32.

and were the only emancipated women of that period.[10] They did not readily see things from the women's viewpoint. Actresses in late nineteenth-century Germany and Austria were poorly paid (30 to 80 Marks a month in Germany) and had to pay for their own costumes. After acting, and having dinner with male admirers, they would go back to their lodgings and stitch their costumes. Frequent changes of costume were expected: they were virtually models. They were also regarded as sexually charged; an actress who married was likely to be dismissed; and it was difficult for them to avoid part-time prostitution. Having a lover made their situation financially bearable and gave some sexual and emotional satisfaction.[11]

Dishonesty was built into such relationships. Schnitzler explains to Mizi Glümer at great length why she cannot expect him to marry her (B I, 18.11.1890), yet he was obliged to vow everlasting love. The need to be loved and the need for faithfulness conflicted with the (almost) inevitable transience of such relationships. Very occasionally such cross-class relationships did result in marriage: in 1898 Richard Beer-Hofmann married Paula Lissy, an assistant in a cake-shop, when she was already pregnant with their second child. Hence these relationships, after lasting a certain time, must have become highly insecure: the deeper they became, the more fragile and tense they must have been. For Mizi to remain faithful to Schnitzler while employed at the theatre in St Gallen would have been difficult in practical terms and required extreme self-sacrifice. So when Mizi deceives him, Schnitzler clearly suffers dreadfully, but he shows no understanding of the pressures on her; in his angry letters, he treats her as a free agent. Mizi, who spends months pleading with him to take her back, seems to suffer worse; for Schnitzler must have represented her best prospect of financial comfort and possibly even marriage. Schnitzler was well enough aware of this problem to dramatize it in *Freiwild* and to end *Frau Berta Garlan* (1900) with an explicit reflection on the double standard, yet he could not carry such knowledge into his relationships. But this discrepancy is one instance of a more general problem with Schnitzler's ethic of honesty. It is purely intellectual honesty which does not issue in action and can easily remain remote from the social world. Schnitzler describes himself, in an unsparing character-analysis, as 'ein Selbsterkenner ohne Tendenz zur Besserung' (T 19.2.1903).

(4) *Remoteness from society.* Schnitzler's political loyalties were to the Austrian Liberal era, and though he censures its naivety, he paints an unduly glowing picture of it in *Jugend in Wien*. In fact, the emancipatory energies of Austrian Liberalism, which included the extension of full civil rights to Jews, were largely exhausted by 1870: it treated workers' and women's movements with hostility; its claim that economic freedom would raise the general standard of living was shattered by the Stock Market crash of 1873; a series of corruption scandals in public life discredited it morally.[12]

---

10   Stefan Zweig, *Die Welt von Gestern* (Stockholm: Fischer, 1944), p. 104.

11   See Malte Möhrmann, 'Die Herren zahlen die Kostüme: Mädchen vom Theater am Rande der Prostitution', in *Die Schauspielerin: Zur Geschichte der weiblichen Bühnenkunst*, ed. by Renate Möhrmann (Frankfurt a.M.: Insel, 1989), pp. 261–80.

12   See Albert Fuchs, *Geistige Strömungen in Österreich, 1867–1918* (1948; repr. Vienna: Löcker, 1984); Karlheinz Rossbacher, *Literatur und Liberalismus: Zur Kultur der Ringstraßenzeit in Wien* (Vienna: Jugend und Volk, 1992), pp. 43–52.

Schnitzler's view of post-Liberal politics was naturally coloured by the dominance of Karl Lueger, the Christian-Social mayor of Vienna from 1897 to 1910. Though Lueger, building on the Liberals' foundations, had many municipal achievements to his credit, such as the improvement of gas and water supplies, the electrification of the tramway system, and the creation of parks, he was also an opportunist with a repulsive line in antisemitic rhetoric.[13] The alarm he caused among Viennese Jews is reflected in Schnitzler's *Der Weg ins Freie* (1908) and in Herzl's Paris diary: after dining with a Viennese couple during Lueger's campaign, Herzl recorded: 'Der Mann erwartet eine neue Bartholomäusnacht. Die Frau meint, daß es nicht mehr schlechter werden kann.'[14]

When Schnitzler discusses politics, he judges politicians by their personal integrity, an indispensable but incomplete criterion. The most important political figure he knew personally was Herzl, and as we have seen, he disliked the element of the charlatan in Herzl's character; but Herzl's inspired charlatanry, his sense of drama and occasion, was crucial in founding the Zionist movement. Schnitzler despises politics as such: 'Sie ist das niederste und hat mit *dem Wesen* der Menschen am wenigsten zu thun' (T 10.5.1896). He detests both sincere and insincere politicians: the former, in his opinion, are monomaniacs, the latter — like Flint in *Professor Bernhardi* (1912) — are self-seeking manipulators. In 1895 he had a conversation with the anarchist Stefan Grossmann, who defended assassinations on the grounds that they brought out people's heroism; Schnitzler replied that heroism could be better displayed in such activities as colonization, and that in any case heroism belonged to the past and the supposedly heroic terrorists showed signs of degeneracy. Grossmann's rather feeble reply was to reprehend Schnitzler's lack of conviction, to which Schnitzler answered: 'Ich sprach für Anschauungen, gegen Ueberzeugungen' (T 24.9.1895). Many years later, Schnitzler satirized 'convictions' in his underrated comedy *Fink und Fliederbusch* (1917), where Fliederbusch, committed to fighting a duel with his alter ego Fink, solemnly declares that he is doing so to defend his convictions (D II, 629); this illustrates how journalists defend opposed convictions with equal assurance.

Until the First World War, the only political issue that excited Schnitzler was antisemitism. He regarded it both as intrinsically detestable and as cynical, for he was sure that Lueger's antisemitism sprang from opportunism rather than conviction (J 146). In 1899 he wrote to Georg Brandes:

> Lesen Sie manchmal Wiener Zeitungen, Parlaments- und Gemeinderaths-berichte? Es ist staunenswerth unter was für Schweinen wir hier leben; — und ich denke immer, selbst Antisemiten müßte es doch auffallen, daß der Antisemitismus — von allem andern abgesehen — jedenfalls die sonderbare Kraft hat, die verlogensten Gemeinheiten der menschlichen Natur zu Tage zu fördern und sie aufs höchste auszubilden. (B I, 12.1.1899)

13 See Richard S. Geehr, *Karl Lueger, Mayor of Fin de Siècle Vienna* (Detroit, MI: Wayne State University Press, 1990), ch. 5. For a milder view of Lueger, see John W. Boyer, 'Karl Lueger and the Viennese Jews', *Leo Baeck Institute Yearbook*, 26 (1981), 125–41.

14 Theodor Herzl, *Gesammelte zionistische Werke*, 5 vols (Tel Aviv: Hazaah Ivrith Co., 1934–35), II, 52.

In *Professor Bernhardi* Schnitzler gives a wonderfully nuanced portrayal of how antisemitism bedevils institutional politics.[15] However, he contributes little to the understanding of antisemitism itself. The protagonists of both his novels, Georg von Wergenthin in *Der Weg ins Freie* and the governess in *Therese* (1928), are Gentiles, and Schnitzler takes it for granted that they will be prejudiced against Jews (E I, 667; II, 742). Despite her tinge of antisemitism, however, Therese does not mind working for Jewish families; indeed, she hopes to marry one of her employers, Siegmund Wohlschein, whose name clearly indicates that he is Jewish. Therese's antisemitism is thus shown to be a shallow prejudice which coexists easily with cynical self-interest; it is not further explored. One cannot get far with antisemitism by treating it as an intellectual error: it is at the same time bewildering mobile and protean, blaming Jews for opposite and incompatible qualities, and alarmingly conservative, firmly rooted in the European imagination (and readily exported outside Europe). The social mechanisms of identification and exclusion that sustain antisemitism are more searchingly explored by Kafka in *Das Schloß*. Similarly, Schnitzler's judgement of politicians by their personal integrity illuminates only part of politics.

(5) *The self-defeating character of honesty.* Honesty is bound eventually to be turned against the ideal of honesty, as in Nietzsche, where the search for truth is 'unmasked' as a mere disguise for the will to power. In 1901, having formulated his ideal of honesty, Schnitzler wonders if it is anything more than a pathological compulsion ('Zwangsvorstellung') that he has developed to compensate for his 'innerer Schlamperei' (J 324). Thus the ethical urge towards honesty leads Schnitzler to explore the psychological motives for honesty and thence to the reductionist fallacy that honesty has no motives other than psychological ones.

Schnitzler's ethic of honesty does not necessarily mean not lying; it means not being taken in by his own lies. He resolves to be honest with himself about even trivial basenesses, and so records the slight twinge of satisfaction he feels on telling the cabman to drive to the Catholic cemetery (where Marie Reinhard's grave is):

> Da ich beschlossen habe, keine meiner Gemeinheiten und Dummheiten vor mir selbst zu verschweigen, auch diese erwähnt. Das einzige, was sie vor mir selber entschuldigt, ist, daß ich alles erkenne. Aber die leichte Befriedigung über diese Selbsterkenntnis paralysirt wieder ihr gutes. (T 13.3.1900)

Here Schnitzler notes the self-defeating character of self-knowledge. It should make one improve one's conduct. But the satisfaction it gives renders it ineffectual, and one is no better than before. Indeed, Schnitzler's freedom from illusions, his ethic of honesty, seem to have no influence on his conduct, as he admits in *Jugend in Wien*: 'daß ich niemals versucht habe, mich über die Natur meiner Gefühle, über das Wesen der Menschen, denen ich nahestand, zu täuschen, hat mich weder davor bewahrt, Unrecht zu leiden, noch, Unrecht zu begehen' (J 83). Subtract the self-congratulation from this statement, and it becomes a confession of despair. Such merely intellectual honesty makes one a paralysed spectator, observing events but unable to alter them.

---

15 See W. E. Yates, *Schnitzler, Hofmannsthal, and the Austrian Theatre* (New Haven, CT, and London: Yale University Press, 1992), pp. 77–98.

The negative side of honesty is apparent in Schnitzler's plays and stories. Many of them deal with disillusionment. An obvious example is *Liebelei*, where Christine kills herself on learning that her lover has been unfaithful to her. Another is *Frau Berta Garlan*, where an innocent young widow learns of sordid affairs going on among her friends, and re-establishes contact with a former lover only to learn that he wants her as his mistress every four to six weeks. On the more positive side, *Die Toten schweigen* (1897) ends with the wife about to come clean to her husband about her relationship with another man, now dead; her husband, in perceiving that she has a secret, seems more observant than the story has hitherto suggested, and one can imagine that she would find great relief in confessing to him. The cynical observation that 'dead men tell no tales' is only part of the story's message. The value of confession is implied more strongly in *Paracelsus*, where Justina acts out her earlier attraction to Paracelsus by projecting it on to Junker Anselm and thus reaffirms her commitment to marriage with Cyprian, who himself learns from the experience. Paracelsus' affirmation that all human activity is play is not the drama's final message, and not even its last word.[16]

The futility of intellectual subtlety is best illustrated by Heinrich Bermann in *Der Weg ins Freie*. Understanding other people, Heinrich assures Georg, is merely a sport:

> Aber mit unsern Gefühlen hat das Verstehen nicht das allergeringste zu tun — beinahe so wenig wie mit unsern Handlungen. Es schützt uns nicht vor Leid, nicht vor Ekel, nicht vor Vernachtung. Es führt gar nirgends hin. Es ist eine Sackgasse gewissermaßen. Das Verstehen bedeutet immer ein Ende. (E I, 842)

This scepticism is hard to reconcile with his individualist view that liberation cannot come through joining a cause, like the Zionists and Socialists by whom he is surrounded, but only through self-exploration: 'Ich glaube überhaupt nicht, daß solche Wanderungen ins Freie sich gemeinsam unternehmen lassen [...] denn die Straßen dorthin laufen ja nicht im Lande draußen, sondern in uns selbst. Es kommt nur für jeden darauf an, seinen inneren Weg zu finden. Dazu ist es natürlich notwendig, möglichst klar in sich zu sehen, in seine verborgensten Winkel hineinzuleuchten!' (E I, 833). At the end of the novel Heinrich's ex-lover commits suicide and Heinrich is left analysing his feelings, which leads him merely into labyrinths of futile ingenuity and does not palliate his pain. It seems that honesty is futile when applied to psychology: 'Es kommt immer darauf an, wie tief wir in uns hineinschauen. Und wenn die Lichter in allen Stockwerken angezündet sind, sind wir doch alles auf einmal: schuldig und unschuldig, Feiglinge und Helden, Narren und Weise' (E I, 957). This shows how useless mere knowledge is when it cannot issue in action. Georg goes on living; Heinrich is left to confront his pain and guilt, but his very commitment to intellectual understanding denies him any means of absorbing and transmuting these feelings.

In this novel Schnitzler presents the problem of self-defeating honesty as a Jewish problem. The contrast between Heinrich and Georg is a contrast between Jew

---

16 See Martin Swales, *Arthur Schnitzler: A Critical Study* (Oxford: Clarendon Press, 1971), pp. 133–38; Scheible, *Schnitzler und die Aufklärung*, p. 56.

and Christian. Schnitzler presupposes the familiar association, established in the Enlightenment by Moses Mendelssohn, between Judaism and rationality; similarly, Freud wrote to his fellow-Jew Karl Abraham about the Gentile Jung: 'We Jews have an easier time, having no mystical element.'[17] Georg and Heinrich are similar, however, in that their emotional entanglements both end in somebody else's death. Georg has been uncertain whether or not to marry his lover Anna Rosner, who is pregnant with his child. When it is suggested that Georg should marry her, he prevaricates shamefully. It is intended that the child, despite Anna's reluctance, shall be given to foster-parents. Conveniently (as Georg's acquaintance Nürnberger hints, E I, 932) the child dies, and even better, Anna terminates the relationship. Georg is thus able to find a 'road to the open' by starting a career as an orchestral conductor in Germany. Psychologically, it is plain that Georg regards Anna as a mother-substitute (E I, 868, 901): a typical Don Juan figure, he is promiscuous because he is always seeking to recapture maternal love, the only satisfying kind. Narrative logic therefore requires the child to die (being as it were incestuous), and forbids Georg to marry Anna. But this psychological reading in turn points to a subtext in which Georg, the nominal Christian, is saved by his devotion to an inaccessible mother-figure and by another person's sacrificial death. A viewpoint is conceivable (I do not say justifiable) from which this could appear as a rather selfish and over-comfortable way of escaping from guilt; while Heinrich, the Jewish intellectual, has no access to absolution, but could be seen as tragically courageous in bearing his guilt unaided. Schnitzler juxtaposes both their fates without endorsing either.

The limits of honesty and the truth of dreams are explored in the story *Traumnovelle* (1926). Set in pre-War Vienna, it concerns a couple, Fridolin and Albertine, a doctor and a housewife. At the outset, they have just been to a masked ball at the end of the Carnival season, and, stimulated by meeting attractive but unknown partners, they have returned home and made love with more intensity than for a long time past. Later, they resolve to be fully honest with each other, and each tells the other about a powerful erotic temptation experienced during the previous summer's holiday at a Danish seaside resort. They agree always to tell each other such things in future. But this frankness has clearly left some resentment behind, at least in Fridolin (the story's centre of consciousness).

Summoned to a patient, Fridolin is reluctant to return home and wanders about vaguely in search of adventure. Possibilities abound: the daughter of a newly dead patient declares her love for him beside her father's death-bed; a nationalist student jostles him and makes him consider (and dismiss) a duel which might disable or kill him; he picks up a prostitute, but does nothing for fear of catching venereal disease. Then comes the real adventure. In a café he meets a disreputable musician of his acquaintance who gets him secretly admitted to a masked ball by means of the password 'Dänemark' (thus establishing a mysterious connection with the Danish holiday). The ball takes place at a suburban mansion; the dancers are dressed as monks and nuns; at a certain stage in the evening all the nuns take off their robes and dance naked, as though preparing for a sexual orgy. Before Fridolin can witness

---

17   Letter of 20 July 1908, quoted from Jones, *Sigmund Freud*, II, 55.

the orgy, though, he is discovered and escapes only narrowly; one of the women present offers to take upon herself the unspecified punishment which Fridolin as an interloper has incurred. Fridolin is forcibly removed from the mansion, ordered to make no inquiries, and dropped on the outskirts of Vienna.

When Fridolin returns home in the early hours of the morning, Albertine recounts an elaborate dream. It is too long to repeat in full, but one episode in it concerns her searching through a wardrobe, on the eve of her wedding, to find a wedding dress. Instead of a wedding dress, she finds a whole range of costumes, Oriental in style, like magnificent opera costumes. The significance is clear: her inability to find a wedding dress symbolizes her regret at having married Fridolin; the magnificent costumes represent the other possibilities available to her which her marriage has ruled out. After further episodes, she dreams that she is dressed as a princess and that Fridolin is being mercilessly flogged at her command; and later still she dreams that he is about to be crucified while her only response is mocking laughter.

Taking this dream as evidence that Albertine does not love him, Fridolin fantasizes about separating from her and starting an affair with his patient's daughter. On his visit, however, he behaves impeccably, to his own surprise; and soon afterwards he discovers how risky it is to try to realize one's fantasies. The day after the ball, the woman who procured his release is found poisoned in a Vienna hotel. She has indeed suffered on his behalf. The prostitute whom he picked up the day before is now in hospital: she does indeed have a venereal infection. Emotionally drained, he abandons his hostility towards Albertine and gives up his plans to separate from her. He tells her everything. Confession brings catharsis: the two re-establish their marriage, now aware of the disturbing and unfathomable feelings that cannot be banished from their unconscious lives.

The conclusion suggests that the desire for truth cannot and should not be fully satisfied. Fridolin and Albertine have glimpsed the hostile impulses underlying their affectionate relationship. Albertine's dream discloses the aggressive impulses which are among her feelings towards Fridolin. More disturbingly still, there is a deep callousness present when she looks on mockingly as he is about to be crucified. And Fridolin is almost as callous when he visits the hospital and inspects the corpse of the woman who apparently gave her life to let him escape from the masked ball. 'War es ihr Leib? — der wunderbare, blühende, gestern noch so qualvoll ersehnte? Er sah einen gelblichen, faltigen Hals, er sah zwei kleine und doch etwas schlaff gewordene Mädchenbrüste, zwischen denen, als wäre das Werk der Verwesung schon vorgebildet, das Brustbein mit grausamer Deutlichkeit sich unter der bleichen Haut absetzte' (E II, 500). This is the clinical view of the medical rationalist. But it is no longer a disinterested inquiry into truth. Its function is now to draw a boundary between the erotic temptations offered by the outside world and the home, the nuclear family, which is the only permissible setting for the erotic and emotional life of the liberal individualist.

Fridolin's nocturnal adventures serve a purpose resembling that of the Magic Theatre in Hesse's almost contemporary *Steppenwolf* (1927). They let him explore his fantasy-life and retreat just in time from its implications. The story confirms Freud's statement, in *Civilization and its Discontents* (1930), that 'civilization is built up on a renunciation of instinct' and 'presupposes precisely the non-satisfaction of powerful instincts'.[18] Fridolin is offered not only new experiences which he rejects, but also new identities which he renounces. The costume dealer from whom he hires a monk's habit has all sorts of costumes hanging up: 'auf der einen Seite Ritter, Knappen, Bauern, Jäger, Gelehrte, Orientalen, Narren, auf der anderen Hofdamen, Ritterfräulein, Bäuerinnen, Kammerzofen, Königinnen der Nacht' (p. 458). All these identities belong to a feudal era, whereas Fridolin and Albertine are clearly defined as a bourgeois couple for whom such pretences would be absurd. (One thinks here of Schnitzler's lifelong dislike of snobbery, in which he thought Hofmannsthal fatally enmeshed; he called snobbery 'die Weltkrankheit unserer Epoche', J 18.) These other identities can only be enjoyed in fantasy and fiction, like the tale from the *Arabian Nights* with which the story begins. But the return to reality is not presented as disappointing: the story is convincing in its understated presentation of the deep love between Fridolin and his wife.

The couple's fantasies take on further meaning if we note that both contain Christian motifs.[19] Fridolin's masked dancers dress as monks and nuns; Albertine dreams of watching her husband's crucifixion. Are we to assume that Fridolin and Albertine are Jews? A Viennese doctor might well be Jewish; the name Fridolin, however, is too unusual to permit conclusions; Fridolin's irritation with 'Couleurstudenten' (E II, 447) may, but need not, reflect Schnitzler's own enforced preoccupation with duelling;[20] and while we are told explicitly that certain other characters are Jews (E II, 452, 454), we are not told this about the couple. The ambiguity may suggest that they are primarily members of the liberal bourgeoisie, and that Fridolin's exploration of the secret society is a fantasy of entering feudal, aristocratic society. By dressing as monks and nuns, the dancers parody Christianity, while their rituals and pass-words, along with numerous allusions to *The Magic Flute*, suggest eighteenth-century Masonic practices.[21] But the agent who brings Fridolin there is a Galician Jew called Nachtigall, formerly a fellow student of medicine, now an itinerant pianist, with a wife and four children in Lemberg. Schnitzler emphasizes his Jewishness even to the extent of reproducing his accent. Nachtigall is emphatically a different kind of Jew from the quasi-assimilated Jews who populate *Der Weg ins Freie*. He is an eccentric, marginal figure, socially and geographically mobile. Eastern Jews in Vienna, who congregated in the Second

18   *The Standard Edition of the Complete Psychological Works of Sigmund Freud*, ed. by James Strachey, 24 vols (London: The Hogarth Press, 1953–74), XXI, 97.

19   Even detailed studies of *Traumnovelle* ignore, or mention only perfunctorily, the Christian and Jewish motifs: e.g. William H. Rey, *Arthur Schnitzler: Die späte Prosa als Gipfel seines Schaffens* (Berlin: Schmidt, 1968), p. 118; Hertha Krotkoff, 'Themen, Motive und Symbole in Arthur Schnitzlers *Traumnovelle*', *Modern Austrian Literature*, 5.1 (1972), 70–95; Perlmann, *Der Traum*, p. 196.

20   See J 155, and cf. the figure of Willy Eissler in *Der Weg ins Freie* and Siegfried Trebitsch, *Chronicle of a Life*, trans. by Eithne Wilkins and Ernst Kaiser (London: Heinemann, 1953), pp. 19–23. Trebitsch told Schnitzler about his duelling: T 6.1.1907.

21   See Scheible, *Schnitzler und die Aufklärung*; Marc A. Weiner, '*Die Zauberflöte* and the Rejection of Historicism in Schnitzler's *Traumnovelle*', *Modern Austrian Literature*, 22.3/4 (1989), 33–49.

District, were seen as isolated on their 'Mazzesinsel'; even when they became as assimilated as Freud, whose father came to Vienna from Galicia via Moravia, they often remained uneasy about their background.[22] His presence suggests that the secret society allows Jews to be present only as recognizable Jews, tolerated aliens, employed for a subordinate task, like the Jews in feudal Austria before emancipation. Fridolin's attempt at complete assimilation by assuming a disguise and joining in the masked ball is detected and leads to punishment. He escapes only because somebody else takes his punishment upon herself. The motif of vicarious punishment, hinted at in *Der Weg ins Freie*, now becomes unmistakable in the form of deliberate self-sacrifice. It is a Christian motif which Fridolin finds difficulty in accepting. And it is uneasily related to the motif of crucifixion in Albertine's dream. In undergoing crucifixion, the Fridolin of her dream enacts a specifically Christian form of suffering and is, in a sense, at the centre of the Christian world, but at the same time he is symbolically identified as a Jew. And Albertine's attraction to the Nordic figure of the Danish holiday-maker represents her own identification with 'Germanic' culture, corresponding to Fridolin's attempted identification with the aristocracy.

No wonder that Fridolin and Albertine draw back from any further exploration of their unconscious lives. The story does so likewise, offering no explicit elucidation of their fantasies and no explanation of the secret society and its activities. Here Schnitzler's ethic of honesty comes up against its limit: personal honesty cannot do justice to the frightening and alluring richness of the inner life revealed in dreams (and in psychoanalysis). This, however, may not matter, for the search for truth is not now a mere intellectual inquiry, as it was for the unfortunate Heinrich Bermann; it is pursued only so that it may feed back into the domestic life of Fridolin and Albertine. Their domestic idyll has to be defended by the self-knowledge acquired through Fridolin's conscious and Albertine's unconscious exploration of the surrounding dangers. In this story, therefore, Schnitzler has overcome his earlier aporia in which the ethic of honesty remained remote from practical action. Instead of pursuing the truth of dreams so far that it becomes destructive, Fridolin and Albertine remain conscious of it as a dim penumbra surrounding the life they share. Given the critical tendency to overvalue negation and subversion, one can agree gratefully with the verdict of a sensitive reader of Schnitzler: 'The affirmation is not facile; it is tentative because of the weight of threat and negation that precedes it.'[23] The story's closing sentence beautifully associates the imagery of Enlightenment with the routine of everyday life: '[...] bis es wie jeden Morgen um sieben Uhr an die Zimmertür klopfte, und, mit den gewohnten Geräuschen von der Straße her, einem sieghaften Lichtstrahl durch den Vorhangspalt und einem hellen Kinderlachen von nebenan der neue Tag begann' (E II, 504).

22   See Sander L. Gilman, *Freud, Race, and Gender* (Princeton, NJ: Princeton University Press, 1993), pp. 14–15.
23   Swales, *Arthur Schnitzler*, p. 149.

CHAPTER 23

Savonarola in Munich:
A Reappraisal of Thomas Mann's *Fiorenza*

Thomas Mann's single attempt at drama, *Fiorenza*, is generally reputed to be a failure. Mann himself referred to it ruefully in 1913 as 'dies Sorgenkind, das nicht leben und nicht sterben kann'.[1] Its first performance, at the Residenztheater in Munich on 17 December 1907, was received with respectful but unenthusiastic applause. 'Der Beifall im ausverkauften Hause steigerte sich von Akt zu Akt, ohne jedoch die Grenzen eines starken Achtungserfolges zu überschreiten', reported the *Leipziger Neueste Nachrichten*.[2] Reviewers were unanimous in complaining that the work was undramatic. The report in the Berlin newspaper *Der Tag* put it most charitably: 'Das Drama selbst steht hinter den Kulissen und steckt nur einmal am Schluß, in der großen Abrechnung zwischen Lorenzo de Medici und Savonarola, den Kopf heraus.'[3] They conceded that the closing confrontation was exciting, but deplored the two and a half acts of exposition that led up to it. Even before the performance, the play in its published form had received a gratuitously savage *Verriss* from the Viennese writer Richard Schaukal, dismissing it as a failure, unreadable even as a 'Buchdrama', lifeless, frosty, with declamation instead of characterization: 'Langwierige Expektorationen, Selbstbiographien, wie auf Bandstreifen aus automatisch sich öffnenden Lippen gleitend, ersetzen das Charakteristische, das Ausinnenherausgestalten.'[4] Later performances in Frankfurt and Berlin were no more successful than the Munich premiere.

At least three considerations, however, should make us hesitate to accept these negative judgements. First, Mann is an exceptionally dramatic novelist. Many of his most memorable scenes are explosive confrontations: between Thomas and Christian Buddenbrook, for example, or between Detlev Spinell and Herr Klöter-

---

1   Letter to Hugo von Hofmannsthal, 9 Jan. 1913, in *Briefe I: 1889–1913*, ed. by Thomas Sprecher, Hans R. Vaget and Cornelia Bernini, Große kommentierte Frankfurter Ausgabe, XXI (Frankfurt a.M.: Fischer, 2002), p. 504. This edition of Mann's works will be quoted whenever possible, abbreviated as GKFA.

2   *Leipziger Neueste Nachrichten*, 19 December 1907. This and other reviews are available in the Thomas-Mann-Archiv at Zürich. I am grateful to the staff of the archive for their help, and also to Professor T. J. Reed for kindly showing me his draft introduction and notes to 'Gladius Dei'.

3   Edgar Steiger, 'Thomas Mann: "Fiorenza", *Der Tag* [Berlin], 20 Dec. 1907.

4   Richard Schaukal, 'Thomas Mann und die Renaissance', *Der Zeitgeist: Beiblatt zum Berliner Tageblatt*, no. 10, Monday, 5 March 1906, p. 2.

jahn. When he addresses more abstract issues, his method of presenting the clash between irreconcilable outlooks is the dramatic one of attributing them to opposed protagonists, the best-known being Settembrini and Naphta. If *Fiorenza* came across as undramatic, therefore, apart from the final scene, the reason can hardly have been Mann's incapacity for drama; he may rather have been attempting a kind of drama for which his audience was unprepared.

Second, *Fiorenza* has additional interest when placed against the background of cultural life of early twentieth-century Munich. Munich was a city of sharp antitheses. It was the 'Kunst-Stadt', the city of aesthetic enjoyment, with its classical architecture, its galleries, and its Bohemian quarter in Schwabing; it was also, of all Germany's major cities, most firmly dominated by the Catholic Church and constantly exposed to clerical suspicion of the arts. Mann's later statement in *Betrachtungen eines Unpolitischen* that he lived in Munich 'zwanzig Jahre im stillen Protest' (XI, 141)[5] may be taken with a pinch of salt, since in that book he was presenting himself as the embodiment of Germany's ethically serious Protestant tradition, but his ambivalence towards Munich is evident during the writing of *Fiorenza* and in the text itself.

Third, the criticisms made of *Fiorenza* — lack of action, excessive display of learning — markedly resemble those directed against the best-known English work to present the figure of Savonarola, George Eliot's novel *Romola* (1863). Eliot's research on Renaissance Florence drew on some sources also used by Mann, notably the great biography of Savonarola by the nineteenth-century historian Pasquale Villari. Her sedulous research shows itself in the very detailed and leisurely portrayal of Florence in the 1490s, with a group of characters dispensing information and local colour in the manner of Walter Scott, which makes the first hundred or so pages of her novel heavy going. Yet if one persists, one finds oneself in the hands of a great novelist, who makes the opposition between Tito Melema and the heroine Romola into a subtle demonstration of the immense difference between being nice and being good. If we persevere with *Fiorenza*, we should expect to find that Mann also has something interesting and original to say about the personality of Savonarola.

The construction of *Fiorenza* can be clarified by looking briefly at each act in turn. Schaukal described its construction quite accurately by saying that the three acts 'um eine einzige Szene herumgeschrieben sind, besser: in breiten Stufen zu ihr hinaufführen'.[6] All three acts take place on the same afternoon, that of 8 April 1492, on which Lorenzo de' Medici died. The first shows us the humanists at the Medici court. Angelo Poliziano, and later Pico della Mirandola, are seen in conversation with the seventeen-year-old Giovanni de' Medici, who has been a cardinal since the age of thirteen, and who is intended to bring further honour on the family by eventually becoming Pope. (As indeed he did, becoming Pope Leo X in 1513 at the age of thirty-eight.) From the outset we learn both that Lorenzo is dying and that

5 References in this form are to Thomas Mann, *Gesammelte Werke*, 13 vols (Frankfurt a.M.: Fischer, 1974).

6 Schaukal, 'Thomas Mann und die Renaissance', p. 2.

Savonarola is causing a furore by his sermons denouncing Florence for its impiety. Act II brings on stage a group of eleven artists (the number, for some undisclosed reason, is emphasized), and also Fiore, the mistress of Lorenzo, who once rejected advances from the young Savonarola. Thus Lorenzo and Savonarola, the representatives respectively of life and the spirit, are linked by sexual rivalry. Fiore also rejects Lorenzo's elder son Piero, a conventional embodiment of Renaissance prowess in art, sport, and love, on the grounds that his heroism is far inferior to the kind of heroism born of physical weakness and spiritual strength, as typified by Savonarola. The third act at last shows us Lorenzo, on his deathbed, no longer satisfied with art, unable to accept the pallid humanist afterlife promised him by Poliziano, and tiring of his entourage of artists. Just as one of the artists is telling a bawdy story taken from Boccaccio, in comes Savonarola himself, summoned to Lorenzo's bedside. His solemn entrance recalls the appearance of the Grand Inquisitor at the end of *Don Carlos*, Mann's favourite play by Schiller. The remainder of the act consists of the confrontation between the two men, whose opposed values turn out to be related dialectically and to rest on a Nietzschean will to power. After Lorenzo's death, the other characters try to dissuade Savonarola from seeking power in Florence, but he is immovable, saying: 'Ich liebe das Feuer', and the final stage direction tells us: 'Und im Fackelschein schreitet er langsam hindurch, hinauf, hinweg, in sein Schicksal' (VIII, 1067).

Mann has chosen a single episode and milked it for its dramatic possibilities. Lorenzo did indeed summon Savonarola to his deathbed. He had earlier invited him to Florence, at the request of Pico della Mirandola, on the strength of his fame as a preacher and theologian. Savonarola's sermons are reported at second hand, with full justice done to their apocalyptic fervour. His future career is alluded to only by the imagery of fire. After the French invasion of Italy, which seemed to fulfil his warnings, and the expulsion of the Medici in 1494, Savonarola established a kind of theocracy in Florence. Bands of young men entered private houses to demand works of art and other 'vanities' which were publicly burnt in the famous bonfire of the vanities. Savonarola further denounced the corruption of the Church under the Borgia Pope Alexander VI. For this he was excommunicated, arrested, tortured, hanged, and burnt, and his ashes were thrown into the river Arno.

A general knowledge of Savonarola's life and times was something Mann could reasonably expect his audience to possess. What reviewers condemned as an over-long exposition is not so much a report on the characters' earlier lives but rather a panoramic depiction of Renaissance Florence, presenting both the humanists and the artists in opposition to the defiant asceticism of Savonarola, as a version of the conflict between life and the spirit. For this purpose Mann stages a series of leisurely conversations reminiscent less of stage plays than of the Socratic dialogues. While working on the play he was also reading Plato's *Symposium*, in which the conversation around the dinner table has room for long narratives such as Aristophanes' famous account of the origin of sexual identity. Peter de Mendelssohn notes that Mann's original plan for the play, consisting of twelve consecutive scenes, was very similar to the structure of Platonic dialogues, particularly the *Symposium*.[7] Mann himself wrote to Maximilian Harden on 29 December 1912, expressing his worries about the forthcoming Berlin production, which he thought relied on gesture rather than words: 'Man hat das Ding seiner Sphäre enthoben und aus platonischen Dialogen ein Theaterstück zu machen gesucht, was nicht gelingen konnte' (GKFA XXI, 503). The similarity is still apparent after Mann arranged the scenes into three acts. If one approaches *Fiorenza* as in part a philosophical conversation, one can adjust oneself to its leisurely pace and the frequent length of the characters' speeches. One can appreciate also how the focus widens as more characters appear on stage, then narrows to the final, long-awaited confrontation between the representatives of opposed values. One reviewer at least appreciated the play as a conversation-piece: 'So weiß dieses Stück, das kein Drama ist, doch stark und bis zum Ende zu fesseln. Nicht durch tragische Schicksale, wohl aber durch die schöne, kultivierte, geistreiche Sprache.'[8] Most of the original audience, of course, did not expect a kind of symposium, so it is not surprising that they sat there in frustration waiting for something to happen.

I now want to suggest some respects in which *Fiorenza* is a product of Munich and of Mann's ambivalence towards Munich. It is a pity that though there is an essay by Jim Reed on the subject, there is no book-length study of Mann in Munich, corresponding to Thomas Sprecher's book on Mann in Zurich;[9] nor do I know any study of Munich's cultural life at the turn of the century corresponding to the many which have been written about Vienna.[10] We need a counterpart to *Wittgenstein's Vienna*, perhaps entitled *Wedekind's Munich*.

'München ist ein Arkadien zugleich und ein Babylon', says Wedekind's confidence trickster, the Marquis von Keith.[11] Thomas Mann found there a rich, perhaps over-rich, artistic life. The 'Kunst-Stadt' was marked not only by the Gothic and baroque churches in the centre but, around them, the neoclassical buildings which Leo von Klenze and Friedrich von Gärtner had designed in the 1830s for 'Isar-Athen'. Successive rulers had sought to build up a secular, classical culture whose leading figures were Emanuel Geibel and Paul Heyse. By the time Mann arrived in Munich, however, these figures were hopelessly dated. They had been swept aside by the Naturalism pioneered in Munich by Michael Georg Conrad and publicized in his journal *Die Gesellschaft*. An extension of Naturalism was the Akademisch-dramatischer Verein, founded by Ernst von Wolzogen in 1892, which performed plays by Ibsen, Hauptmann, Halbe, Oscar Wilde, and the world premiere of

7   Peter de Mendelssohn, *Der Zauberer: Das Leben von Thomas Mann*, vol. 1 (Frankfurt a.M.: Fischer, 1975), p. 643; see also Karl Werner Böhm, *Zwischen Selbstzucht und Verlangen: Thomas Mann und das Stigma Homosexualität* (Würzburg: Königshausen & Neumann, 1991), pp. 266–78.

8   R. B., *Münchner Zeitung*, 18 Dec. 1907.

9   Thomas Sprecher, *Thomas Mann in Zürich* (Munich: Fink, 1992); T. J. Reed, 'Thomas Mann in München: München bei Thomas Mann', in Albrecht Weber (ed.), *Handbuch der Literatur in Bayern* (Regensburg: Pustet, 1987), pp. 413–22.

10   A sketch for such an account is Jens-Uwe Schade, *Voraussetzungen und Besonderheiten des literarischen Lebens in München um 1900: Studien zur Dialektik von lokaler Eigenart und innovativer Leistung literarischer Zentren* (Aachen: Shaker Verlag, 1997).

11   Frank Wedekind, *Werke*, ed. by Erhard Weidl, 2 vols (Munich: Winkler, 1990), II, 67.

Wedekind's *Der Marquis von Keith* and was described by M. G. Conrad as the Munich equivalent to Berlin's Freie Bühne.[12] Mann was a member of the Verein, acting the part of old Werle in its production of *The Wild Duck* on 15 June 1895. He also wrote for the satirical weekly *Simplicissimus*, founded by the publisher Albert Langen in 1896, and joined its editorial staff in 1898. The *Bürgerschreck* Wedekind, who contributed satirical poems to the journal, was also a prominent performer, singing his songs to the guitar, in the cabaret Die Elf Scharfrichter which opened on 12 April 1901. In August 1903 Mann was asked to contribute, more soberly, to one of the cabaret's programmes by reading aloud from his work.[13] The financial backers of the cabaret included his future father-in-law Alfred Pringsheim.

Wedekind's assault on sexual taboos linked him with the radical avant-garde of the Munich Bohemia based in Schwabing, where we find such remarkable figures as the Cosmic circle, centring on Alfred Schuler and Ludwig Klages, with its cult of vitalism and its devaluation of spirit, and the scholarly German-Jewish poet Karl Wolfskehl, who, with the Cosmics, belonged to the circle around Stefan George, himself often resident in Munich from 1893 onwards; and the self-styled prophet Ludwig Derleth, whose apocalyptic work Mann heard read aloud by a disciple one spring evening in 1904, an experience commemorated with brilliant irony in the story 'Beim Propheten'. We also find such opposites as the anti-feminist Franziska zu Reventlow, who claimed to live the life of a 'hetaera' as advocated both by the Cosmics and by Wedekind (not only through the figure of Lulu, but also through Ilse in the still unperformable *Frühlings Erwachen*); and a group of declared lesbians and feminists including the photographer Sophia Goudstikker (1865–1924). Reventlow appears briefly in 'Beim Propheten' as 'eine unverheiratete junge Mutter von adeliger Herkunft' (VIII, 366).[14] Goudstikker, who was Wolzogen's aunt, played the part of Gina Ekdal in the above-mentioned production of *The Wild Duck*, and Mann seems to have borrowed her name for *Buddenbrooks* (GKFA I/i, 244). Her photographic studio, the Foto-Atelier Elvira, a meeting-point of Munich feminists, may be the 'Kunstbau [...] mit bizarrer Ornamentik' mentioned in 'Gladius Dei' (VIII, 198).[15]

Despite his active participation in Munich's cultural life, Mann found its atmosphere uncongenial. He gave Munich an unflattering, semi-comic memorial in Herr Permaneder in *Buddenbrooks*. Beyond that, he planned a novel about Munich society, entitled first *Die Geliebten* and later *Maja*; it was never written (except by Aschenbach), unless one counts the Munich chapters of *Doktor Faustus*,

---

12 Quoted in R. J. V. Lenman, 'Censorship and Society in Munich, 1890–1914, with Special Reference to *Simplicissimus* and the Plays of Frank Wedekind' (unpublished D.Phil. thesis, Oxford, 1975), p. 231.

13 Unpublished letter to Franz Blei, 7 Aug. 1903, cited in de Mendelssohn, *Der Zauberer*, p. 540.

14 See Yahya Elsaghe, *Thomas Mann und die kleinen Unterschiede: Zur erzählerischen Imagination des Anderen* (Cologne, Weimar, Vienna: Böhlau, 2004), pp. 261–75: 'Das Portrait Franziska zu Reventlows im *Propheten*'.

15 Information on all these circles may be found in Brigitta Kubitschek, *Franziska Gräfin zu Reventlow: Leben und Werk. Eine Biographie und Auswahl zentraler Texte von und über Franziska Gräfin zu Reventlow* (Munich and Vienna: Profil, 1998).

which use some material from the early notebooks.[16] Novels set in Munich's Bohemia do exist: *Das dritte Geschlecht* (1899) by Ernst von Wolzogen, *Herrn Dames Aufzeichnungen* (1913) by Franziska zu Reventlow, and some chapters of Jakob Wassermann's *Die Juden von Zirndorf* (1897) and *Renate Fuchs* (1900) are of interest as *romans à clef*. Mann in his notebooks indicates that reading his sources showed him similarities between Renaissance Florence and modern Munich: 'Die "moderne" Litteratur. Die litterarische Zote. Lorenzos C[h]arnevalsgesänge werden über die Göttl. Com. gestellt. (Wedekinds geschlechtliche Poesie.)'[17] His irritation with the Bohemians is clear not only from the end of 'Beim Propheten', where the young man (based on Mann himself) regrets the absence of 'das Menschliche' (VIII, 370), but also, earlier still, from 'Tonio Kröger', whose protagonist declares that a true artist desires not 'das Raffinierte, Exzentrische und Satanische' but rather yearns for 'dem Harmlosen, Einfachen und Lebendigen' (VIII, 302–03). 'Das Satanische' may allude to the goings-on of the Cosmics, to whom Reventlow in *Herrn Dames Aufzeichnungen* attributes Satanic ceremonies. It was a relief for him, once *Buddenbrooks* had made him famous, to gain access to more elevated circles. From 1903 onwards he was friendly with the Bernsteins. Max Bernstein, a distinguished lawyer, also wrote comedies and was for ten years drama critic for the liberal *Münchener Neueste Nachrichten*. His Viennese wife Elsa, daughter of the Wagnerian conductor Heinrich Porges, wrote many dramas under the pseudonym 'Ernst Rosmer'. Their daughter Eva later married Klaus, the third son of Gerhart Hauptmann. And it was through Elsa Bernstein's intermediacy that Thomas Mann secured an introduction to the Pringsheim home in the Arcisstrasse. There he found a combination of art, elegance, and humanity that enraptured him (see his letter to Heinrich, 27 Feb. 1904, GKFA XXI, 270).[18]

From the Schwabing Bohemia to the Bildungsbürgertum of the Arcisstrasse, however, all this energetic pursuit of the arts was overshadowed by the suspicion and occasional repression emanating from the Bavarian government. In 1868, Bavarian Catholics, uneasy at the prospect of incorporation into a Protestant-dominated German Reich, had formed the Patriots' Party, renamed in 1877 the Bavarian Centre Party and affiliated to the national party of that name. From 1869 until the end of the monarchy the Catholic Centre Party held an absolute majority of seats in the Bavarian Landtag and found itself in frequent conflict with the liberal and often Protestant cabinets appointed first by Ludwig II (1864–86) and then by the Prince Regent Luitpold (1886–1912). The Landtag often debated cultural issues. Centre deputies complained that the work of Arnold Böcklin was publicly exhibited and attacked the display of nude statues, even of the Venus de Milo. They were annoyed by the performance of Naturalist works that questioned family values and encouraged proletarian militancy. They strongly supported the so-called Lex Heinze, a draft law, named after a criminal condemned in 1891 for murdering a

---

16   See Hans Wysling, 'Zu Thomas Manns "Maja"-Projekt', in Paul Scherrer and Hans Wysling, *Quellenkritische Studien zum Werk Thomas Manns* (Bern and Munich: Francke, 1967), pp. 23–47.

17   Thomas Mann, *Notizbücher*, ed. by Hans Wysling and Yvonne Schmidlin, 2 vols (Frankfurt a.M.: Fischer, 1991), I, 238. Henceforth cited as Nb. Cf. VIII, 1023.

18   The story is told by de Mendelssohn, *Der Zauberer*, p. 585.

Berlin nightwatchman, which was intended to strengthen public morality by out-lawing indecency in artistic representations and theatrical performance. One article prohibited the display of works of art with religious subjects in shop windows, while the draft's 'Theatre Paragraph' (184b), if it had become law, would have made most Naturalist plays unstageable. *Simplicissimus* was much harassed. Its publisher Langen complained to the Social Democratic leader Georg von Vollmar in January 1898 that no paper in Germany had ever been so bitterly persecuted by the Government.[19] Many trials for indecency took place. Max Bernstein often appeared for the defence; M. G. Conrad was in frequent demand as an expert witness. According to Robin Lenman's indispensable thesis on censorship in Munich, trial-going became a popular activity among Munich's intellectual community.

In the autumn of 1903, however, matters became more serious. The Centre Party secured a dominant position in the government when the liberal prime minister Krafft von Crailsheim was replaced by the conservative Clemens von Podewils, who made much greater concessions to the Catholic deputies. The Centre Party resolved to clamp down on theatrical immorality. The Akademisch-dramatischer Verein, which had put on three scenes from Schnitzler's *Reigen* in a closed performance on 25 June 1903, was disbanded by the university in November, though it promptly reconstituted itself as the Neuer Verein. In the same month, the Elf Scharfrichter came under attack when the four major items in its programme, including the first act of Heinrich Leopold Wagner's crassly realistic Sturm und Drang drama *Die Kindermörderin*, were banned by the police. Unable to continue performing with such harassment, the Scharfrichter closed down in December. Mann has given the Elf Scharfrichter a teasing memorial in *Fiorenza* with his group of eleven artists.

How did this atmosphere of censorship and anticlericalism affect Mann? While in practice he advocated artistic freedom, privately he acknowledged that censorship was sometimes justified. He wrote in his notebooks (probably in 1903): 'Die Dummheit hat Recht, der Staat — die Censur — hat recht (im Grunde) und nicht die Feinen, die nach Cultur rufen. Cultur, Kunst — und Verfall. Ein Volk, das für Wedekind reif ist, ist geliefert...' (Nb II, 84). This private utterance may be compared to Tonio Kröger's feeling that the police were in some sense right to identify him as a confidence trickster. In practice, Mann took a tolerant attitude to literary freedom of expression, advising that it should occasionally be tempered by discretion. In April 1912 he accepted an invitation to become an adviser to the Bavarian Commission of Censorship in 1912–13. Having earlier declared his complete opposition to theatrical censorship, Mann hoped to mediate between the straitlaced Bavarian authorities and the artistic avant-garde, recommending, for example, that Wedekind's *Lulu* should be performed without cuts. He was not wholly opposed to all censorship: he warned the Berlin authoress Leonor

---

19   Quoted in Lenman, 'Censorship and Society in Munich', p. 84. See also Lenman, 'Art, Society and the Law in Wilhelmine Germany: The Lex Heinze', *Oxford German Studies*, 8 (1973–74), 86–113; Peter Jelavich, *Munich and Theatrical Modernism* (Cambridge, MA: Harvard University Press, 1985); Wolfgang Frühwald, '"Der christliche Jüngling im Kunstladen": Milieu- und Stilparodie in Thomas Manns Erzählung *Gladius Dei*', in *Bild und Gedanke: Festschrift für Gerhart Baumann zum 60. Geburtstag*, ed. by Günter Schnitzler (Munich: Fink, 1980), pp. 324–42.

Goldschmidt (unfortunately addressing her as Herr Goldschmidt) that her work was suitable for private reading but not for reading aloud in public, just as, he added, his current project, *Der Tod in Venedig*, would have been (GKFA XXI, 490–501). He fell out with Wedekind, however, because the latter was furious over the omission of a single sentence from his drama *Franziska* (GKFA XXI, 816–17).

Mann's own writings of course contain nothing so gross or so anticlerical as, for example, the satirical poems published in *Simplicissimus* by Ludwig Thoma under the pseudonym 'Peter Schlemihl'. Even in his notes for *Fiorenza*, he observed while reading Burckhardt's *Die Cultur der Renaissance in Italien* the function of the Dominican Order as a 'geistliche Polizei-Amt' (Nb II, 28), but did not develop this theme in the play. He comes closer to anti-Catholic satire in the earlier story 'Gladius Dei', which is a 'Vorstudie' for *Fiorenza*, but this story is above all a satire on the aesthetic atmosphere of Munich and on the commercialization of art. Nevertheless, Mann first published it outside Germany, in the Viennese journal *Die Zeit*, perhaps to avoid attracting the attention of the Munich authorities. Its protagonist, named Hieronymus after Girolamo Savonarola, is both an absurd and an idealistic figure; he denounces the sale of religious images in an art-dealer's shop, and is thrown out by a packer embodying the raw energies of Life. Some of the jokes in this story are common in anti-Catholic satire. The Madonna in the shop-window is based on a milliner (presumably the artist's mistress) and further eroticized. The use of loose women as models for saints and the Virgin Mary is a long-standing source of irony, which motivates the plot of Hoffmann's *Die Elixiere des Teufels*; and the sexual attractiveness of sacred images is mentioned also in Heine's Italian travel sketches.[20] One of the artists in Mann's play says to another: 'Und dabei ist überall bekannt, daß dir deine niedliche Lauretta, die du als büßende Magdalena modellierst, pünktlich ein Kind geboren hat' (VIII, 989). In his biography, Pasquale Villari quotes Savonarola as denouncing this practice in the words: 'Da sagen denn die jungen Männer von diesem oder jenem Weibe: das ist die Magdalena, das ist St. Johannes, das ist die Jungfrau. Denn ihre Porträts sind es, die ihr in den Kirchen malt, und das untergräbt die Ehrfurcht vor den heiligen Dingen.'[21] Mann wrote a large exclamation mark opposite the list of figures, perhaps struck by the idea of a woman posing as St John, and copied the list into his notebook (Nb I, 267). Wedekind makes a similar joke in *Frühlings Erwachen*, when Ilse, who has left home to live among a colony of painters in Munich, tells Moritz how she has posed as the Virgin Mary: 'ich saß den Tag bei Isidor Landauer. Er braucht mich zur heiligen Maria, Mutter Gottes, mit dem Christuskind.'[22] There is a further joke: Ilse, who isn't a virgin, is being painted as the Virgin Mary by Isidor Landauer who, judging from his stereotypical name, is not a Christian.[23]

20   See Heine, *Sämtliche Schriften*, ed. by Klaus Briegleb, 6 vols (Munich: Hanser, 1968–76), II, 498.

21   Villari, *Geschichte Girolamo Savonarola's und seiner Zeit*, trans. by Moritz Berduschek, 2 vols (Leipzig: Brockhaus, 1868), II, 16. Mann's copy, with annotations in pencil, is preserved in the Thomas-Mann-Archiv.

22   Wedekind, *Werke*, I, 514.

23   On 'Isidor' as *the* stereotypical Jewish name, see Dietz Bering, *Der Name als Stigma: Antisemitismus im deutschen Alltag, 1812–1933* (Stuttgart: Klett-Cotta, 1987).

There is also a reference to a Jewish art dealer earlier in the play: Hänschen Rilow, about to flush one of his art postcards down the toilet, recalls how he first saw one of them in the shop window of 'Jonathan Schlesinger'.[24] And that brings us back to 'Gladius Dei', where the art dealer's name, 'M. Blüthenzweig', identifies him as Jewish, even by the abbreviation of the first name — a common means of masking one's Jewishness, as in Schnitzler's *Professor Bernhardi*, where Dr Samuel Wenger has his name written as 'S. Wenger'.[25]

There is, then, a link between 'Gladius Dei' and Wedekind, in that both draw on the same anti-religious jokes. There is a stronger link between *Fiorenza* and another Munich *Bürgerschreck*, Oskar Panizza, whom Mann had known personally in the Akademisch-dramatischer Verein. To publish and perform a play in Munich about the Catholic Church in the Renaissance inevitably brought to mind the scandal of a decade earlier surrounding Panizza's brilliant and polished play *Das Liebeskonzil* (published at Zürich in October 1894). The play presents a decrepit God flanked by an asthmatic Christ and a worldly, lubricious Virgin Mary. Incensed by the wickedness of Renaissance Italy, God employs the Devil to punish mortals. Choosing Salome as the wickedest woman in Hell, the Devil sires on her a daughter, a *femme* literally *fatale*, who spreads syphilis among humankind, starting with the Pope. On 30 April 1895 Panizza was tried in Munich, convicted, and sentenced to a year's imprisonment. Many writers and intellectuals supported him. M. G. Conrad, a veteran anticlerical, testified in court to the play's merits; Max Halbe, Detlev von Liliencron, and Theodor Fontane all expressed admiration for it.[26] The exception was the young Thomas Mann, who, in a note published over his initials in the conservative journal *Das Zwanzigste Jahrhundert*, then edited by Heinrich Mann, suggested that in view of the play's artistic flaws the sentence passed on its author was acceptable (GKFA xiv/i, 26). Mann's most recent editor is no doubt right in surmising: 'Am nächstliegenden ist die Annahme, es gehe ihm um eine Demonstration eigener intellektuellen Unabhängigkeit, in diesem Fall gegenüber der "political correctness" der übrigen Äußerungen von Schriftstellern' (GKFA xiv/ii, 36). But that is not the end of Mann's interest in Panizza. While he was working on *Fiorenza*, his notes include a reference to one of Panizza's anti-Catholic polemics, *Der teutsche Michel und der römische Papst* (Nb 1, 211).[27] Mann owned a copy of this book, which is also noteworthy because the book was not easy to obtain, having been banned throughout Germany soon after its appearance. It is a long polemic against the Catholic Church for its dogmas of Immaculate Conception and Papal Infallibility; it recommends that Germany should detach itself from Rome and set up a national Catholic Church. Many faults and vices of

---

24   Wedekind, *Werke*, I, 504.

25   Arthur Schnitzler, *Die Dramatischen Werke*, 2 vols (Frankfurt a.M.: Fischer, 1962), II, 392–93. See Yahya Elsaghe, *Die imaginäre Nation: Thomas Mann und das 'Deutsche'* (Munich: Fink, 2000), pp. 116–23 ('Zu Thomas Manns Konnotierung abgekurzter Vornamen').

26   See Peter D. G. Brown, *Oskar Panizza: His Life and Works* (New York: Peter Lang, 1983).

27   Panizza, *Der teutsche Michel und der römische Papst: Altes und Neues aus dem Kampfe des Teutschtums gegen römisch-wälsche Überlistung und Bevormundung in 666 Tesen und Zitaten. Mit Begleitwort von M.G. Conrad* (Leipzig: Friedrich, 1894).

the medieval and Renaissance Church are listed, including the vices of Alexander VI and the resistance offered by 'der fanatisch-visionäre Asket *Savonarola*'.[28] And Panizza's play seems to haunt Thomas Mann's later work. Above all, the motif of syphilis reappears in *Doktor Faustus*. So does the *femme fatale*. The Devil creates the fatal woman by copulating with Salome, the dancer whose performance was rewarded with the head of John the Baptist. Hans Vaget has detected a reminiscence of Panizza when Adrian Leverkühn attends the premiere of Strauss's *Salome* in Graz before revisiting Esmeralda and being infected by her.[29]

Fiore, the play's only female character, was compared by several reviewers to Salome.[30] Her sexual attraction to Savonarola resembled, and was no doubt based on, that of Oscar Wilde's Salome to the captive John the Baptist, which makes her perversely demand his head. Wilde's *Salome* was among the plays performed by the Akademisch-dramatischer Verein. The motif of the spiritual man proving fatally attractive to the sensual woman goes back via Flaubert to Heine's *Atta Troll*, where Herodias is said to have demanded John's head out of love. But Fiore is not only a literary reminiscence. As a courtesan, free from sexual taboos, she implies a satire on the wilder fringes of Munich Bohemia, particularly on people like Franziska zu Reventlow, who argued that instead of adopting professions to which men were better suited, as feminists urged, women should instead imitate the hetairas of the ancient world and develop their natural gifts for sex, child-bearing and pleasure.[31] Mann's satire implies that even the most resolute hetaira must bow to the power of the spirit.

I want now to look more closely at the opposition which, using a rough shorthand, I have called the conflict between life and the spirit. For his intellectual framework, Mann is strongly indebted to Heine's distinction between the senses and the spirit, the Hellenes and the Nazarenes. In particular, Mann recalls the passage from *Die Stadt Lucca* in which Heine first quotes an account from Homer of the gods feasting on Olympus and then introduces the Nazarene figure of Christ:

> Da plötzlich keuchte heran ein bleicher, bluttriefender Jude, mit einer Dornen-krone auf dem Haupte, und mit einem großen Holzkreuze auf der Schulter; und er warf das Kreuz auf den hohen Göttertisch, daß die goldnen Pokale zitterten, und die Götter verstummten und erblichen, und immer bleicher wurden, bis sie endlich ganz in Nebel zerrannen.[32]

As Poliziano describes him, Savonarola interrupted the Florentine cult of beauty

---

28   *Der teutsche Michel und der römische Papst*, p. 242.

29   See Vaget, 'Thomas Mann und Oskar Panizza: Zwei Splitter zu *Buddenbrooks* und *Doktor Faustus*', *Germanisch-Romanische Monatsschrift*, N.F. 25 (1975), 231–37.

30   R. B., *Münchner Zeitung*, 18 Dec. 1907: 'Fiore ist eine Schwester der Salome.' On Salome as decadent icon, see Mario Praz, *The Romantic Agony*, trans. by Angus Davidson, 2nd edn (London: Oxford University Press, 1970), pp. 312–18.

31   See 'Viragines oder Hetären', in Franziska zu Reventlow, *Autobiographisches*, ed. by Else Reventlow (Munich: Langen Müller, 1980), pp. 468–81; first published in 1899 in the *Zürcher Diskussionen* edited by Oskar Panizza.

32   Heine, *Sämtliche Schriften*, II, 492. On connections with Heine, particularly Savonarola as a 'Nazarener', see Volkmar Hansen, *Thomas Manns Heine-Rezeption* (Hamburg: Hoffmann und Campe, 1975), pp. 120–26.

in a similar way:

> Des Gottes voll, der den Rausch spendet, folgt die Menschheit im Festzuge der lächelnden Führerin, und ihr Jauchzen ist ein Kultus der Schönheit und des Lebens. Da — was geschieht? Was tritt ein? Ein Mensch, ein einzelner, zu häßlich und ungelenk, um an dem Reigen der Lust teilnehmen zu können, verkümmert, mißwollend, undankbar, steht auf und erhebt Einspruch gegen diesen göttlichen Zustand. (VIII, 985)

Savonarola is a medieval figure, as Heine understood the Middle Ages: like the monks who denounced the nightingale as an evil spirit, he turns away from the seductive charms of this world and fixes his eyes on a supersensory other world.

Within this framework derived from Heine, Mann interpreted Savonarola with the aid of Nietzsche, as typifying the ascetic priest. In his copy of *Zur Genealogie der Moral*, Mann underlined the passage beginning 'Denn ein asketisches Leben ist ein Selbstwiderspruch' and wrote beside it: 'Savonarola!'[33] The notes he took from his principal source, Villari's biography of Savonarola, repeatedly add Nietzschean interpretations. He describes Savonarola as a decadent genius, 'dieser *geniale Verfallstypus*' (Nb I, 212), who escapes from middle-class life into the monastery and there attains power. For the ascetic priest is one in whom *Ressentiment* becomes creative. Striving for power over life, he creates an alternative, life-denying set of values. Savonarola has a further motive. According to Villari, as a young man in Ferrara, Savonarola proposed marriage to a girl of the Strozzi family, who rejected him scornfully as beneath her station. Villari embellishes this episode, describing how Savonarola was attracted by the hope of happiness and the joys of life: 'Seine Augen begegneten denen der jungen Florentinerin, und eine erste geheime Regung seines Herzens sagte ihm, daß das Glück auf Erden möglich sei. Das Leben erglänzte ihm im neuen Licht, seine von tausend Hoffnungen entzündete Phantasie träumte glückliche Tage, und voll Glut und Vertrauen öffnete er sein Herz der jungen Geliebten.'[34] Mann comments: 'Tschandala-Haß.' (Nb I, 233). This episode reappears in *Fiorenza* as Savonarola's unsuccessful wooing of Fiore.

It might seem that Mann is out to debunk Savonarola by showing that his otherworldly mission is based merely on resentment at his being deprived of sensual enjoyment. This does seem to have been Mann's initial conception. The marginalia in his copy of Villari are of interest here. When Savonarola, on being arrested, is quoted as telling his followers: 'wenn wir auf Erden verflucht sind, so sind wir im Himmel gesegnet', Mann underlines this and adds in the margin: 'beinahe Piepsam'.[35] This refers to the figure of Lobgott Piepsam in the story 'Der Weg zum Friedhof' (1900). Piepsam is one of Nietzsche's 'Schlechtweggekommenen', drunken, bereaved, unhappy; on the way to the cemetery where his family lie buried, he clashes with 'das Leben', embodied in a carefree young cyclist, and works himself

---

33 Quoted in Friedhelm Marx, *'Ich aber sage Ihnen ...': Christusfigurationen im Werk Thomas Manns* (Frankfurt a.M.: Klostermann, 2002), p. 36. On the play's genesis, see also the short account in de Mendelssohn, *Der Zauberer*, pp. 641–47, and the detailed account in Egon Eilers, 'Perspektiven und Montage: Studien zu Thomas Manns Schauspiel *Fiorenza*', diss. Marburg, 1967.

34 Villari, *Geschichte Girolamo Savonarola's*, I, 13.

35 Villari, *Geschichte Girolamo Savonarola's*, II, 194.

up into apocalyptic denunciations: 'Es kommt der Tag, ihr nichtiges Geschmeiß, da Gott uns alle wägen wird ... Ach ... ach ... des Menschen Sohn wird kommen in den Wolken, ihr unschuldigen Kanaillen, und seine Gerechtigkeit ist nicht von dieser Welt! Er wird euch in die äußerste Finsternis werfen, euch munteres Gezücht, wo da ist Heulen und ...' (VIII, 195). Another note, further down the same page, runs: 'beinahe Harden', thus comparing Savonarola's denunciations of his enemies to the comminations issued by the journalist Maximilian Harden in the pages of *Die Zukunft*. Together, these two marginalia suggest a complex understanding of the 'Sklavenmoral' attributed to Savonarola. The impotent threats issued by Piepsam and the widely read leading articles by Harden both spring from *Ressentiment*. The eminent preacher, the insignificant Pietist, and the newspaper editor all enjoy a substitute for power, which, in the right circumstances, can become real power.

Mann also saw Savonarola's asceticism more positively. In converting weakness into strength through the power of his will, there was an element of heroism. In the play, Savonarola, rejected by Fiore, tortures himself in order to overcome his sensuality by knocking his forehead against the edge of an altar-step (VIII, 1044). Mann's Savonarola becomes one of those heroes of weakness celebrated in *Der Tod in Venedig* in the person of Aschenbach. He is contrasted in the play with the merely strong hero Piero de' Medici, who boasts to Fiore of his sporting and sexual prowess. Rejecting him, Fiore declares that a true hero is 'wer schwach ist, aber so glühenden Geistes, daß er sich dennoch den Kranz gewinnt' (VIII, 1018).

While Savonarola's heroism is genuine, that does not make it attractive. He remains a forbidding figure driven by inhuman certainty. But he gains something by contrast with his environment. Mann depicts the humanists and artists, and even their patron Lorenzo, as trivial. Lorenzo appears not primarily as a poet but rather as a connoisseur and collector. Above all, the cultivated circle around Lorenzo are unable to face the fact of death. On his death-bed, Lorenzo is not satisfied with the humanist heaven Poliziano promises him: 'Das ist Poesie, Poesie, mein Freund! Das ist Schönheit, Schönheit, aber nicht Wissen noch Trost!' (VIII, 1024).

This is part of Mann's polemic against the cult of the Renaissance which flourished at the end of the nineteenth century. 'Renaissance' suggested an age of unbridled individualism, aestheticism and immorality, typified by Cesare Borgia.[36] This image of the Renaissance was spread especially by Count Gobineau in his book *Die Renaissance*, first published in French in 1877, which consists of a large number of short dramatic scenes, featuring Savonarola, Cesare Borgia, Machiavelli, Michelangelo, and many others. Whether Nietzsche read it is still uncertain, but it is hard to believe that Gobineau's book did not affect his conception of the Renaissance. Mann's surviving library contains two copies, published in 1911 and 1912 respectively, but a marginal note in his copy of Villari, questioning the

36 On this cult, see Gerd Uekermann, *Renaissancismus und Fin de Siècle: Die italienische Renaissance in der deutschen Dramatik der letzten Jahrhundertwende* (Berlin: de Gruyter, 1985); Hanno-Walter Kruft, 'Renaissance und Renaissancismus bei Thomas Mann', in August Buck (ed.), *Renaissance und Renaissancismus von Jacob Burckhardt bis Thomas Mann* (Tübingen: Niemeyer, 1990), pp. 89–102; W. E. Yates, 'Hofmannsthal and the Renaissance; or, Once more unto "Ein Brief"', *Publications of the English Goethe Society*, 61 (1992), 99–118.

assertion that Michelangelo attended Savonarola's sermons on the grounds that Gobineau said otherwise, shows that he had read Gobineau earlier.[37] Alfred Kerr denounced *Fiorenza* as 'gobinotorisch'.[38] But he missed the point. By the early twentieth century, this view of the Renaissance was ripe for satire. Both Thomas and Heinrich Mann criticized it. Heinrich, in the story 'Pippo Spano', showed a feeble modern type vainly trying to emulate a Renaissance condottiere whose picture he keeps above his desk, and in the novel *Die Göttinnen* coined the derogatory phrase 'die hysterische Renaissance', which Thomas adopted in *Betrachtungen eines Unpolitischen* (XI, 540).[39] Earlier, Thomas Mann shows his distance from the cult of the Renaissance when he makes Tonio Kröger reject Italy in favour of Denmark, saying 'Er ist mir nichts, dieser Cesare Borgia, ich halte nicht das geringste auf ihn, und ich werde nie und nimmer begreifen, wie man das Außerordentliche und Dämonische als Ideal verehren mag' (VIII, 302). Mann's satire is at its broadest when Lorenzo de' Medici admits that he has no sense of smell (VIII, 1062). This is a historically attested fact, but why mention it? Renate Böschenstein has pointed out that one of the clichés associated with the Renaissance as portrayed by Gobineau was the immorality denoted by the word 'ruchlos', and therefore Lorenzo, by describing himself as 'geruchlos', reduces the cult of the immoral to absurdity.[40]

The great confrontation between Lorenzo and Savonarola gains some of its power from Mann's own feeling of being on both sides. Writing to Kurt Martens on 28 March 1906, Mann called himself an 'Asket', but said there was as much of him in Lorenzo as in Savonarola (GKFA XXI, 360). Insofar as the scene is an explicit juxtaposition of 'Geist' versus 'Leben', it is somewhat too ventriloquial: the characters talk not in their own language but in that of their creator, and Savonarola does so yet more egregiously when he declares: 'Ihr schaut das Wunder der wiedergeborenen Unbefangenheit' (VIII, 1064). The interest of the scene lies less in the play with abstractions than in its dramatic confrontation of two human types, and the one that interests me is embodied in Savonarola. As a moralist, preacher, and prophet he is related to several other well-known figures in Thomas Mann's work. The last quotation connects him with Aschenbach, another moralist, another hero of weakness, who in his fiction has earned the gratitude of a generation by preaching a moral resolution unimpeded by self-analysis. Granted, self-analysis may paralyse the will needed for moral action; if you want to change the world, you may be better without self-knowledge. But you also put yourself at risk by confusing

37   'Seltsam, wenn es so wäre! Bei Gobineau liest man's anders', in Villari, II, 113.

38   Alfred Kerr, 'Thomas Mann: Fiorenza', *Der Tag*, 5 Jan. 1913, repr. in *Thomas Mann im Urteil seiner Zeit: Dokumente 1891–1955*, ed. by Klaus Schröter (Hamburg: Wegner, 1969), pp. 61–63 (p. 62).

39   See Uekermann, *Renaissancismus*, pp. 100–01.

40   Renate Böschenstein, 'Lorenzos Wunde: Sprachgebung und psychologische Problematik in Thomas Manns Drama *Fiorenza*', in *Sprachkontakt, Sprachvergleich, Sprachvariation: Festschrift für Gottfried Kolde zum 65. Geburtstag*, ed. by Kirsten Adamzik and Helen Christen (Tübingen: Niemeyer, 2001), pp. 39–59. Böschenstein's attempt to disclose a homosexual subtext in *Fiorenza* misses one possible piece of evidence: the tulip, which lacks a smell, is used by one of Mann's favourite poets, Platen, as a cipher for homosexuality; see Platen's 'Die Tulpe', the appearance of the tulip in Heine's attack on Platen in *Die Bäder von Lucca* (Heine, *Sämtliche Schriften*, II, 398), and Jeffrey L. Sammons, *Heinrich Heine: A Modern Biography* (Princeton, NJ: Princeton University Press, 1979), p. 145.

your public image with your real self and by underestimating how vulnerable you may be to sexual temptation. As *Der Tod in Venedig* conveys, sexual temptation may be degrading, disgusting, and criminal, but it may at the same time make life uniquely worth living. Savonarola may believe that his ascetic practices have freed him from temptation, but his conviction is belied by the vehemence with which he denounces Fiore, whenever she disrupts his sermons by arriving late, as the Whore of Babylon in person.

Insofar as Savonarola, despite and through his weaknesses, is the hero of the play, who forces humanists and artists to realize the limitations of their aesthetic playground, the play has a curious place in the reception history of Savonarola. For while the Enlightenment, typified by Bayle and Voltaire, regarded him as a fanatic, a common nineteenth-century view of him was as a precursor of Protestantism, as 'John the Baptist to Luther's Christ'.[41] The biography by the Dano-German Lutheran theologian Andreas Gottlob Rudelbach (1792–1862) presented Savonarola as a spiritual descendant of the great medieval mystics and as 'einen *Propheten der Reformation* im edelsten und tiefsten Sinn'.[42] Rudelbach's biography was the main source used by Nikolaus Lenau for his epic poem *Savonarola* (which Mann mentions in his notebooks, but may never have read), where the preacher, in calling for a renewal of the Church, heralds the Reformation. A contemporary of Mann's, Joseph Schnitzer, who was a professor of theology at Munich, and proponent of Catholic Modernism, published extensive research on Savonarola from 1898 onwards, culminating in a biography in 1924. He portrayed Savonarola as a reformer who could have preserved the integrity of the Church. In 1908 Schnitzer was suspended from his professorial chair and, in February 1908, excommunicated. The official Catholic line in the nineteenth century was that Savonarola's main battle was not with the admittedly corrupt Church, but against the revival of paganism.[43] This is also the view Mann takes. A Catholic paper criticized the play as anti-Catholic, but Mann replied that his Savonarola was the play's hero, and the play should have appealed to Christian critics: 'denn obgleich ich nicht Katholik bin, hatte ich im stillen gehofft, daß mein Stück einer von christlichem Geist beseelten Kritik allerlei Sympathisches werde zu sagen haben' (XI, 561).

Yet Mann's Savonarola is a deeply unattractive figure — more so than one might think from Mann's generally positive notes. One critic says he is 'vollends auf die Dimensionen eines Psychopathen reduziert'.[44] His moralism has gained him many followers. Even Botticelli, we learn, has become a disciple, has destroyed a painting in order to save his soul, and henceforth will paint nothing but Madonnas (VIII, 1034). He is the uncompromising spokesman for the spirit, denouncing everything

41 J. B. Bullen, *The Myth of the Renaissance in Nineteenth-Century Writing* (Oxford: Clarendon Press, 1994), p. 223.

42 A. G. Rudelbach, *Hieronymus Savonarola und seine Zeit: Aus den Quellen dargestellt* (Hamburg: Perthes, 1835), p. 314. Emphasis in original.

43 On the historiography of Savonarola, see Bullen, *The Myth of the Renaissance*, pp. 223–27; Donald Weinstein, *Savonarola and Florence: Prophecy and Patriotism in the Renaissance* (Princeton, NJ: Princeton University Press, 1970), pp. 3–25.

44 Uekermann, *Renaissancismus*, p. 141.

opposed to the spirit as evil. But he himself is human, all too human. He has honed his will by solitude and suffering, and he is clearly proud of having done so. One of the first things we are told about him is that, in his view, preachers rank immediately after angels in the hierarchy of created beings (VIII, 962); Mann took this saying from Burckhardt (Nb II, 28).[45] And his denunciation of his enemies is inspired by a sadism that becomes sharply apparent when he quotes Thomas Aquinas on how the pleasures of the saved in heaven will include watching the sufferings of the damned. Mann found this in Nietzsche's *Genealogie der Moral* (Book I, section 15).[46]

Contemporary reviews of Mann's play repeatedly call Savonarola 'der Fanatiker'.[47] But we should be careful of labelling him a fanatic. Fanatics are people with strong beliefs that we don't share. The conjugation goes: I am dedicated, you are obsessed, he or she is fanatical. I would rather use the more neutral word 'single-minded' and say that in the figure of Savonarola Mann has given us an impressive portrait of the single-minded person, showing the frustration, power-lust, and self-assertion — all components of Nietzschean *Ressentiment* — that make up his personality, and also doing justice to the courage and determination with which he has shaped himself. In attributing a crucial role to Savonarola's sexual disappointment, however, Mann has been too reductive to do justice to the psychology of the spiritual leader. Such a person generally derives his authority from overcoming an inner crisis (typified by the Biblical image of forty days in the wilderness) and adopting his mission with a new and indomitable conviction which infects others.[48] George Eliot's portrayal of Savonarola avoids this pitfall. Her version of Savonarola exercises an authority over others, notably Romola, which springs both from generous passion, devotion to the general good, and also from an 'imperious need of ascendancy' essential to his 'power-loving and powerful nature'.[49] In him, power both matches his own psychological needs and presents itself as a means of animating his followers to assist him in his selfless aims. Hence it can have all the more corrupting an effect.

Nonetheless, Mann has given us a very perceptive sketch of a type — the single-minded person — with a long ancestry among idealists in earlier drama, from Schiller's Karl Moor to Ibsen's Brand. The play is also forward-looking, for the type represented by Savonarola was to dominate the twentieth century. He anticipates the figures of the committed leader and the committed intellectual, who were often combined in the same person. The psychology of commitment is disclosed in the confrontation between Savonarola and Lorenzo, in which they discover many

---

45   For Burckhardt's brief, largely negative account of Savonarola, see *Die Cultur der Renaissance in Italien: Ein Versuch*, ed. by Ludwig Geiger, 2 vols (Leipzig: Seemann, 1899), II, 197–203. This is the edition Mann owned.

46   Nietzsche borrowed his Aquinas quotation from the Irish rationalist historian Lecky, whom he read in German translation. See W. E. H. Lecky, *History of the Rise and Influence of the Spirit of Rationalism in Europe* (1865), 5th edn, 2 vols (London: Longman, Green, & Co., 1872), I, 319.

47   e.g. the Munich *Allgemeine Zeitung*, 19 Dec. 1907.

48   See Anthony Storr, *Feet of Clay: A Study of Gurus* (London: HarperCollins, 1996). The classic account of this process is William James, *The Varieties of Religious Experience* (London and New York: Longmans, Green & Co, 1902).

49   George Eliot, *Romola*, ed. by Andrew Brown, World's Classics (Oxford: Oxford University Press, 1994), pp. 222, 462.

similarities between them. Both consider themselves superior individuals, entitled to despise the masses and to shape them according to their own will. Both are in search of power. Savonarola agrees with Lorenzo's statement that one can take the world as an instrument on which to play (VIII, 1065): thus the aesthete and the ascetic agree in valuing power, ultimately for aesthetic purposes. When Villari writes, 'Savonarola urtheilte streng über den Charakter Lorenzo's', Mann underlines this sentence and adds in pencil: 'Er sieht in L. den Rivalen in der <u>Macht</u>'.[50]

An important difference emerges, however, when Lorenzo expresses his understanding and appreciation of Savonarola's character. He acknowledges that in an age of uncertainty it is a great achievement to carve out a distinct character for oneself, even if one has for that purpose to impose limits on oneself, cultivating only one aspect of one's personality. Savonarola rejects Lorenzo's tolerant understanding, 'dies lüsterne Verstehen, diese lasterhafte Duldung des Gegenteils' (VIII, 1063). And he does so in revealing language. Tolerance is 'lasterhaft' because it means tolerating things that you disapprove of and that you should oppose if you are true to your principles. Understanding is worse: it is 'lüstern' [lustful]; it seeks to penetrate the other in a quasi-sexual manner, to break down the other's defences. Savonarola cannot endure such an approach, for his personal myth consists in seeing himself as hard and impenetrable. To become single-minded, he has cordoned off areas of his personality, and he cannot afford to open up the armour-plating in which he has chosen to encase himself. At the same time, his hard shell is an intolerable confinement, and for that reason the single-minded person is also ultimately self-destructive. This is made unmistakably clear at the end of the play. Fiore warns Savonarola that the fire he has fanned will devour him, thus alluding proleptically both to the bonfire of the vanities that Savonarola will stage and to his own public burning by the Church. She urges him: 'Hör auf, zu wollen, statt das Nichts zu wollen!' (VIII, 1067), conveying that his will is directed towards nihilism, and advising him, in Schopenhauerian fashion, to abandon the will altogether.[51] But Savonarola confirms his nihilistic, self-destructive will in the last words he utters on stage: 'Ich liebe das Feuer'.

Finally, Mann also brings out the peculiar moral authority conferred by commitment. A person who proclaims a single clear purpose, sweeping aside all qualifications that might make it seem difficult to attain or undesirable to have, thus acquires an authority, almost a charisma, which impresses those who have a more complex vision and are therefore less decisive. Among innumerable possible examples of commitment in twentieth-century literature I shall cite by way of comparison only one, the figure of Gifford Maxim in Lionel Trilling's novel *The Middle of the Journey* (1947) — a novel inspired by Thomas Mann, on whom Trilling once intended to write a critical study for the Fontana Modern Masters series. The intention, unfortunately, was short-lived: the series editor, Sir Frank Kermode, tells

---

50   Villari, *Geschichte Girolamo Savonarola's*, I, 97.

51   Though the formulation is Nietzschean, quoting the last words of *Zur Genealogie der Moral*: 'Lieber will noch der Mensch *das Nichts* wollen, als *nicht* wollen ...'; Friedrich Nietzsche, *Werke*, ed. by Giorgio Colli and Mazzino Montinari, 8 divisions (Berlin and New York: de Gruyter, 1969–), VI/ii, 430.

me that presently the project 'dropped out of the conversation'.[52] Trilling's book on Mann may be one of the unwritten masterpieces of Thomas Mann literature. His fictional character Maxim, however, is clearly modelled on Mann's representatives of commitment, especially Naphta from *Der Zauberberg*. Maxim is a Communist and Russian spy who horrifies his left-liberal hosts by revealing his true commitment. Just as Naphta's name suggest an inflammatory liquid, Maxim's name connotes not only Russia (Maxim Gorky) but also a 'maxim' in the sense of an unquestionable axiom and a type of firearm, the Maxim gun. He has dehumanized himself, made himself into a weapon, in the service of his unforgiving cause.

Mann's analysis of political, artistic, and even religious commitment — in Naphta, Leverkühn, and the Gregorius of *Der Erwählte* — makes him among the most perceptive commentators on the events and the moral atmosphere of the earlier twentieth century. He began this analysis in *Fiorenza*. That itself suggests that the play deserves rescue from the neglect into which it has unjustly fallen.

---

52 Personal communication, 3 Feb. 2004.

CHAPTER 24

Sacrifice and Sacrament in
The Magic Mountain

Der Zauberberg is concerned especially with death. Hans Castorp is initiated into an understanding of death and gradually led through and out of an obsession with death which was also Mann's. Mann acknowledged this obsession with death and the riddle of existence in his contribution to a 1931 volume entitled *Dichterglaube: Stimmen religiösen Erlebens*: 'Keinen Tag, seitdem ich wach bin, habe ich nicht an den Tod und an das Rätsel gedacht' [Not a day has passed since I awoke when I have not thought about death and the riddle].[1] Earlier, in the novel, Mann goes so far as to emphasize typographically a sentence warning us not to allow death to dominate our ideas: '*Der Mensch soll um der Güte und Liebe willen dem Tode keine Herrschaft einräume*n'[*For the sake of goodness and love, man shall grant death no dominion over his thoughts*] (GKFA 748).[23] This sentence was for him, he admitted, 'eine wirkliche Überwindung' [a real victory] (GW XI, 424). Detached by cursive type from the surrounding text, the sentence looks like a word of wisdom which we can take away with us and reflect on independently of the novel. But of course it grows out of the portrayal of Hans Castorp's development in the novel. An obvious interpretation would relate it to the great scene in which Hans Castorp, seeing the interior of his hand through an X-ray, becomes aware in a new way of his own corporeality and hence of his mortality: 'und zum erstenmal in seinem Leben verstand er, daß er sterben werde' (333) [and for the first time in his life he understood that he would die (Woods, p. 260)]. In relation to this episode, the highlighted sentence warns us that although our death is the one certainty in our future, and although we have to lose our childish innocence and become aware of

1 'Fragment über das Religiöse', in Mann, *Gesammelte Werke*, 13 vols (Frankfurt a.M.: Fischer, 1974), XI, 424, quoted also in the important essay by Thomas Rütten, 'Sterben und Tod im Werk Thomas Manns', in Thomas Sprecher (ed.), *Lebenszauber und Todesmusik: Zum Spätwerk Thomas Manns* (Frankfurt a.M.: Klostermann, 2004), pp. 13–34 (p. 22). Future quotations from this edition will be given in the text as GW with volume and page number.

2 *Der Zauberberg*, ed. by Michael Neumann, in Thomas Mann, *Große kommentierte Frankfurter Ausgabe: Werke — Briefe — Tagebücher*, ed. by Heinrich Detering et al. (Frankfurt a.M.: Fischer, 2002–), Text, p. 748. Future references in text.

3 Thomas Mann, *The Magic Mountain*, trans. by John D. Woods, Everyman's Library (London: Knopf, 2005), p. 588. Future references in text as 'Woods' and page number. Other translations are mine.

our mortality, we should not let this knowledge dominate our lives and make them gloomy, morbid or self-centred. Thus the key sentence about 'Tod' implies only natural death, as do some of Mann's own utterances about death, as when in 1924 he talks about 'unser religiöser Instinkt, der dem Gedanken des Todes entspringt' [our religious instinct which arises from the thought of death].[4]

However, the immediate context of Hans Castorp's message makes it clear that Mann means not only natural death but much more besides. Lost in the snow, Hans has a delightful vision of young people disporting themselves on the seashore, talking with civilized restraint, or showing a special reverence for a young mother nursing a child. In contrast to their seriousness without gloom ('ein unaussprechlicher geistiger Einfluß undüsteren Ernstes'; 742), a handsome boy sitting near Castorp turns his head and reveals a stony gravity ('ein Ernst, ganz wie aus Stein'; 743) as he gazes at an ancient temple which evidently stands above and overshadows the sunlit scene. Castorp enters the temple, marches between its rows of pillars, and discovers that it contains something horrible: two old women are tearing apart a child and devouring the fragments. On seeing him, they curse him, but he suffers the paralysis often found in dreams, and escapes only by waking from his trance and finding himself once more in the snow.

What we are to make of this dream is explained by Castorp's subsequent reflections. He has had an insight, not into his personal unconscious, but into the unconscious life of humanity, the dreams of the collective soul. Although this may sound like Jung, the theory behind it probably comes from Schopenhauer's essay 'Versuch über Geistersehn und was damit zusammenhängt' [Essay on Spirit-Seeing and Related Matters], which argues that in dreams time and space are suspended, and that prophetic dreams can therefore very occasionally afford insight into the past or the future.[5] But whether Castorp's vision reveals the distant past, or timeless archetypes, it appears to disclose something fundamental about human nature:

> Die große Seele, von der du nur ein Teilchen, träumt wohl mal durch dich, auf deine Art, von Dingen, die sie heimlich immer träumt, — von ihrer Jugend, ihrer Hoffnung, ihrem Glück und Frieden ... und ihrem Blutmahl. (746)

> [The great soul, of which we are just a little piece, dreams through us so to speak, dreams in our many different ways its own eternal, secret dream — about its youth, its hope, its joy, its peace, and its bloody feast. (Woods, p. 586)]

The 'Blutmahl', or cannibal feast, recurs in Castorp's reflections, interwoven with the idea of death. Not natural death, but the horror of cannibalism, represents the antithesis to the healthy life of the 'Sonnenleute' or Sun People, and the two poles of the antithesis are interdependent. The Sun People treat each other with such courtesy precisely because they know what is going on in the temple: 'Waren sie so höflich und reizend zueinander, die Sonnenleute, im stillen Hinblick auf eben

---

4   'Tischrede in Amsterdam', GW X/i, 354. See also the important letter to Josef Ponten, 5 November 1925, in Mann, *Briefe 1889–1936*, ed. by Erika Mann (Frankfurt a.M.: Fischer, 1962), pp. 230–32; quoted and discussed in T. J. Reed, *Thomas Mann: The Uses of Tradition* (Oxford: Clarendon Press, 1974), p. 244n.

5   Arthur Schopenhauer, *Sämtliche Werke*, ed. by Arthur Hübscher: Parerga und Paralipomena, 2 vols (Wiesbaden: Brockhaus, 1946), I, 241–329.

dies Gräßliche?' (747) [Were they courteous and charming to one another, those sunny folk, out of silent regard for that horror? (Woods, p. 587)]. And this rhetorical question is firmly answered soon afterwards when Castorp reflects further on their kindliness, 'im stillen Hinblick auf das Blutmahl' (748) [out of silent regard for the bloody banquet (Woods, p. 588)]. The sentence about keeping death in its place follows a few lines later. By now, however, it seems clear that 'death' means far more than the natural death which lies ahead for each of us. It is supposed to connote also savagery, violence, murder, cannibalism, and perhaps a further range of gruesome horrors.

Mann's commentators, especially in Germany, have been remarkably accepting of all this. Few critics find it surprising that the Sun People should lead perfectly happy lives so long as they avoid looking at the temple, even though they know what is going on there. Martin Swales is the only critic I know who has asked the obvious question: if they know what is happening, why don't they try to stop it?[6] Critics often translate the goings-on in the temple into reassuringly philosophical terms derived from Schopenhauer and Nietzsche, drawing attention to classical parallels, even when these are actually not similar to the events Mann describes. Thus Manfred Dierks, interpreting the chapter as an allegory of a Schopenhauerian encounter with the 'Nichts' symbolized by the snow, says of the dream-vision: 'Es spricht die Sprache Nietzsches, die der *Geburt der Tragödie*. Thomas Manns unzugehörige Motivwahl (Eleusis; der zwiefache Aspekt des Demeter-Kultes) darf nicht irritieren: Schopenhauers Doppelperspektive wird hier nach Nietzsches übersetzenden Symbolbegriffen bildhaft, in der vertrauten Apoll-Dionysos-Konstellation' [It speaks the language of Nietzsche, that of *The Birth of Tragedy*. Thomas Mann's inappropriate choice of motifs (Eleusis; the dual aspect of the cult of Demeter) should not disturb us: Schopenhauer's double perspective is here given visual form through Nietzsche's translation into conceptual symbols, in the familiar relationship of Apollo and Dionysus].[7] A pity that Mann chose the wrong motifs, but fortunately the critic can see through the text to the familiar reassuringly philosophical dualism. Thus a horrific vision is translated into a philosophical thesis which has in turn lost all its power to shock through over-familiarity and has turned into a truism. What Castorp actually sees in the temple, however, is not the allegorical representation of a philosophical position: it is a child being murdered. The commentators' eagerness to translate this brute fact into philosophical allegory recalls Lionel Trilling's famous remarks on how the classics of modern literature lose their power to shock when treated as classroom fodder: 'I asked them [his students] to look into the Abyss, and, both dutifully and gladly, they have looked into the Abyss, and the Abyss has greeted them with the grave courtesy of all objects of serious study, saying: "Interesting, am I not? [...]"'[8]

6   Martin Swales, *Mann, 'Der Zauberberg'*, Critical Guides to German Texts, 19 (London: Grant & Cutler, 2000), p. 46.

7   Manfred Dierks, *Studien zu Mythos und Psychologie bei Thomas Mann* (Bern: Francke, 1972), p. 124. Similarly Børge Kristiansen, *Unform — Form — Überform: Thomas Manns 'Zauberberg' und Schopenhauers Metaphysik* (Copenhagen: Akademisk Forlag, 1978), pp. 224–25.

8   Lionel Trilling, *Beyond Culture* ([1965] Harmondsworth: Penguin, 1967), p. 38.

Dierks and Kristiansen also illustrate the tendency of commentators to relate the imagery of the temple episode exclusively to the classics. The consensus view is that the scene there owes something to the image of Dionysus being torn apart, and to Erwin Rohde's accounts of ghostly women in Greek mythology who stole and murdered children.[9] Dierks says that the anachronistic imagery anticipates the syncretism of the Joseph novels and includes motifs from the legend of Thyestes (Dierks, p. 253). However, the child Dionysus was dismembered by Titans (as Kristiansen notes), and the story of Thyestes, who was cooked and served up to his unwitting father, is quite unlike this scene. Nor does it resemble Erwin Rohde's description of the Maenads tearing animals apart and devouring their raw flesh, despite Erkme Joseph's claim that Rohde thus provided its model.[10] The temple itself sounds Greek, with its rows of pillars, but it was also suggested to Mann by Böcklin's painting 'Heiliger Hain' [Sacred Grove].[11] The figures in it suggest Northern Europe. The old women resemble witches, 'mit hängenden Hexenbrüsten und fingerlangen Zitzen' (745) [their drooping witches' breasts had tits as long as fingers (Woods, p. 585)]. They curse Hans Castorp in Hamburg dialect, and the child they are dismembering is blonde. Mann's images are not taken only from the safely remote classical world.

Some possible associations of Böcklin's painting are evoked in a passage from *Betrachtungen eines Unpolitischen* in which Mann describes it. The description there serves to introduce the argument that despite the secularist progressivism represented by the 'Zivilisationsliterat' there is still a need for sacred spaces, where the soul can recover from the bustle of modern life: 'daß es *heilige* Orte gibt, heute noch, gefriedete Freistätten der Seele, wo der Mensch, dem üblen Gebrodel irgendeiner Großstadtstraße entronnen, umgeben plötzlich von hallender Stille, farbigem Dämmer, angehaucht vom Duft der Jahrhunderte, dem Ewigen, Wesentlichen, kurz dem *Menschlichen* Aug in Aug gegenübersteht'[that there are *sacred* places, even today, enclosed zones where the soul is free, where man, having escaped from the odious hubbub of some city street, suddenly surrounded by resonant silence, gloom tinged with colour, sensing the breath of centuries, stands face to face with the eternal, the essential, in short, with the human] (GW XII, 479). But these are not the associations suggested by the scene in *Der Zauberberg*. The temple explored by Hans Castorp is hardly a place for peaceful contemplation. Commentators seem to have overlooked a passage from an earlier text, 'Gedanken im Krieg' (1914), in which Mann deploys imagery similar to that of the temple scene, with a wide range of cultural reference:

> Kultur ist Geschlossenheit, Stil, Form, Haltung, Geschmack, ist irgendeine
> gewisse geistige Organisation der Welt, und sei das alles auch noch so aben-
> teuerlich, skurril, wild, blutig und furchtbar. Kultur kann Orakel, Magie,
> Päderastie, Vitzliputzli, Menschenopfer, orgiastische Kultformen, Inquisition,
> Autodafés, Veitstanz, Hexenprozesse, Blüte des Giftmordes und die buntesten

---

9   See Neumann, *Der Zauberberg: Kommentar*, p. 316.

10   See Erkme Joseph, *Nietzsche im 'Zauberberg'* (Frankfurt a.M.: Klostermann, 1996), p. 208.

11   See Reed, *Thomas Mann*, p. 243, quoting from Mann's description of the painting in *Betrachtungen eines Unpolitischen*, in GW XII, 478–79.

Greuel umfassen. Zivilisation aber ist Vernunft, Aufklärung, Sänftigung, Sittigung, Skeptisierung, Auflösung, — Geist. (GW XIII, 528)

[Culture is self-containment, style, form, posture, taste, is some definite spiritual organization of the world, however eccentric, ludicrous, savage, bloody and frightful it may be. Culture can comprehend oracles, magic, pederasty, Huitzlipochtli, human sacrifice, orgiastic cults, Inquisitions, autos-da-fé, St Vitus' dance, witch-trials, the rampant poisoning and the most colourful horrors. Civilization, however, is reason, enlightenment, appeasement, morality, scepticism, dissolution — spirit.]

This passage was important to Mann. A version of it also occurs in his notes for the essay 'Geist und Kunst', and was published among other 'Notizen' in *Der Tag* (Berlin), 25 December 1909.[12] All versions include the word 'Vitzliputzli', which calls to mind not only Heine's poem about the Spanish conquest of Mexico, but also the Aztecs themselves. They provide Mann here with an example of culture remote from civilization, proving his contention that culture is perfectly compatible with barbarism and can be 'eine stilvolle Wildheit'. If we relate this passage to the snow vision of *Der Zauberberg*, the latter seems to be offering us an image of 'Kultur' at its best, but accompanied by barbarism at its worst. Instead of the over-rational dissolution of artistic form that Mann associates with 'Zivilisation', the Sun People do have 'Form', as Hans Castorp acknowledges, but form depends on an awareness of horror: 'Auch Form ist nur aus Liebe und Güte: Form und Gesittung verständig-freundlicher Gemeinschaft und schönen Menschenstaats — im stillen Hinblick auf das Blutmahl' (748) [Form, too, comes only from love and goodness: form and the cultivated manners of man's fair state, of a reasonable, genial community — out of silent regard for the bloody banquet (Woods, p. 588)]. Artistic form and courteous manners are compatible with every sort of organized cruelty.

Mann is certainly 'indicating', as T. J. Reed puts it, 'that there is a side to humanity which rationalism ignores' (Reed, p. 244). More than that, he may be putting forward a bold thesis about human nature. We have a propensity towards violence and another towards kindliness. Knowledge of the former should not deter us from practising the latter. The trouble is that any such thesis sounds pallid and banal when translated into ordinary generalizations. Its power resides in the imagery with which it is expressed. It is in any case not the business of a novel to propound a thesis, but rather to convey an imaginative vision. Feeling myself unqualified to comment on a broad anthropological thesis, I will concentrate on the imagery in which the vision is conveyed.

The women in the temple are described as witches. Moreover, they are practising cannibalism. And as their activity takes place in a temple, it is evidently a human sacrifice. These three images have a long history in post-classical European culture. One could even say that Mann is exploring the terrors of the European unconscious. We do not need to have recourse to the Greeks to find sources and analogues.

---

12 See Paul Scherrer and Hans Wysling, *Quellenkritische Studien zum Werk Thomas Manns* (Bern and Munich: Francke, 1967), pp. 225–26; adapted from note 118 in the 'Geist und Kunst' draft, ib., p. 215.

The witch-like women remind us that the witch is frequently imagined as an evil mother-figure, one who does not nourish children but threatens and destroys them. If a mother had difficulty in bearing children, or in producing milk to feed them, or if the children died, as was often the case in early modern Europe, it was tempting to attribute these misfortunes to the malevolence of a witch.[13] The familiars who were supposed to attend a witch in the guise of toads or cats were imagined as being suckled by her, like a parody of children. In Mann's scene, the old women devouring a child form the precise antithesis to the young nursing mother, and are contrasted also with the statue of Demeter and her daughter Persephone.[14]

Another feature of witchcraft accusations is that they are made not only against outsiders suspected of malevolence, but against out-groups more generally. Thus the origin of the European witch-craze in the fifteenth century coincides with the Church's campaign against heretics. Learned demonologists imagined a counter-society of witches practising rites of devil-worship which were a parody and inversion of the rituals of Christianity. The concept of the witch is a version of othering, of demonizing others because they are felt to be different.

The same applies to human sacrifice, which is what the witches appear to be doing in the temple. Sacrifice has been defined as 'the destruction of a victim for the purpose of maintaining a right relationship of man to the sacred order'.[15] Human sacrifice is the subject both of Old Testament narratives and Greek myths, but always as something which could not be allowed to happen: hence the substitution of a ram for Isaac and a doe for Iphigenia. Although it is attested from some cultures, such as the Aztecs whom Mann alludes to with the name 'Vitzliputzli', human sacrifice is probably more present in the imagination than in reality. Human sacrifice is what others do, in a parody of true religion.[16] In particular, human sacrifice is often wrongly identified with cannibalism. The Spanish soldiers who saw their captive companions being sacrificed on the famous *noche triste* imagined that they were also being eaten, and the chronicler Bernal Díaz describes in lurid detail how their hearts were cut out with stone knives, but his account moves with deceptive

13   For a global survey of witch beliefs, see Wolfgang Behringer, *Witches and Witch-Hunts* (Cambridge: Polity, 2004); for a sensitive study of the emotional and imaginative worlds of 'witches' and their persecutors, Lyndal Roper, *Witch Craze: Terror and Fantasy in Baroque Germany* (New Haven, CT, and London: Yale University Press, 2004); and for the transference to 'witches' of fears about heretics, Norman Cohn, *Europe's Inner Demons* (Brighton: Sussex University Press, 1975).

14   Michael Maar, *Geister und Kunst: Neues aus dem 'Zauberberg'* (Munich: Hanser, 1995), p. 174, relates the old women narrowly to the 'Räuberweib' in Hans Christian Andersen's story 'The Snow Queen', and, more usefully, to witches in fairy-tales. Frederick A. Lubich discusses mother-symbolism in 'Thomas Manns Der Zauberberg: Spukschloß der Magna Mater oder Die Männerdämmerung des Abendlandes', *Deutsche Vierteljahrsschrift*, 67 (1993), 729–63 (p. 741).

15   E. O. James, *Sacrifice and Sacrament* (London: Thames & Hudson, 1962), p. 13. On various theories of sacrifice, see the incisive summary in John Bossy, 'The Mass as a Social Institution, 1200–1700', *Past and Present*, 100 (1983), 29–61 (p. 53).

16   So, for example, the Greeks of Constantinople attributed human sacrifice to the Turks who were threatening them: the Byzantine chronicler Chalcocondylas claimed that Sultan Murad, after defeating the Greeks in the Morea, bought six hundred prisoners from his Janissaries and sacrificed them to the memory of his father. Franz Babinger, *Mehmed the Conqueror and his Time*, ed. by William C. Hickman, trans. by Ralph Manheim (Princeton, NJ: Princeton University Press, 1978), p. 49.

seamlessness from what he witnessed to what he conjectured.[17] In Mann's temple scene, too, human sacrifice and cannibalism are combined.

Whether cannibalism, as a social practice — in contrast to the behaviour of insane individuals, or the desperate measures adopted in conditions of famine or shipwreck — really exists, or has existed, is uncertain. Reports of cannibalism have generally been accepted without critical scrutiny. A sceptical inquiry by an American anthropologist failed to find any plausible eye-witness report of cannibalism.[18] Such stories usually seem to rest on hearsay. Columbus was told by the Arawaks that on an island to the south there was another race called the Caribs who ate men (though as Columbus did not understand the Arawak language, we may assume that he was projecting his own fantasies). The Spanish conquistadors and missionaries told gruesome tales of Aztec cannibalism, but none claimed to have seen it happening. Somewhat stronger evidence comes from New Zealand, where James Cook, Joseph Banks and Georg Forster not only acquired circumstantial evidence but on at least one occasion saw Maori warriors eating portions of the bodies of their defeated opponents; this suggests that cannibalism was sometimes practised within an exceptionally warlike society, though it should be noted that the Maoris' eating of human flesh was also an action staged for the benefit of European onlookers, who actually cooked the flesh and invited the Maoris to eat it, and allows no conclusions about how cannibalism was practised before the Europeans' advent.[19]

But cannibalism bulks far larger in the imagination, especially the European imagination, than in reality. As Anthony Pagden says, 'The European interest in man-eating amounts almost to an obsession.'[20] The taboo on eating members of our own species defines us as human, as beings who inhabit culture as opposed to nature. Hence cannibalism is always imagined as being practised by the other, the uncivilized, the non-human. The ancient geographer Strabo (born *c.* 64 BC) claimed that the Irish were man-eaters; St Jerome said the same about the Scots. Europeans have often believed Africans to be cannibals, and Africans have held the same belief about Europeans. Gibbon, after quoting St Jerome on the cannibal Scots, adds:

> If in the neighbourhood of the commercial and literary town of Glasgow a race of cannibals has really existed, we may contemplate in the period of the Scottish history the opposite extremes of savage and civilised life. Such reflections tend to enlarge the circle of ideas, and to encourage the pleasing

---

17 Bernal Díaz, *The Conquest of New Spain*, trans. by J. M. Cohen (Harmondsworth: Penguin, 1963), p. 387.

18 See W. Arens, *The Man-Eating Myth* (New York: Oxford University Press, 1979); these arguments are developed in Gananath Obeyesekere, '"British Cannibals": Contemplation of an Event in the Death and Resurrection of James Cook, Explorer', *Critical Inquiry*, 18 (1992), 630–54, and *Cannibalism and the Colonial World*, ed. by Francis Barker, Peter Hulme and Margaret Iversen (Cambridge: Cambridge University Press, 1998).

19 See Georg Forster, *A Voyage Round the World*, ed. by Robert L. Kahn (Berlin: Akademie-Verlag, 1968), pp. 294–95, followed by interesting reflections, pp. 295–98; Nicholas Thomas, *Discoveries: The Voyages of Captain Cook* (London: Allen Lane, 2003), pp.105–06, 209–11. I thank T. J. Reed for drawing my attention to Forster's testimony.

20 Anthony Pagden, *The Fall of Natural Man: The American Indian and the Origins of Comparative Ethnology* (Cambridge: Cambridge University Press, 1982), p. 80.

hope that New Zealand may produce in some future age the Hume of the
Southern Hemisphere.[21]

It is notable here how ready Gibbon is to generalize from a single report. From
the accounts of Cook's voyages which were available in the 1770s, and from
the unsubstantiated accounts of ancient geographers and theologians, Gibbon
immediately draws the wide conclusion that cannibalism is a common feature of an
early stage in human development.

But while cannibalism is the subject of the ultimate taboo, it is also, curiously,
a subject for children's stories and for humour. Ogres, from Polyphemus in the
Odyssey to the giant at the top of the bean-stalk, are constantly imagined as
cannibals. The missionary in the cooking-pot is a standing joke. You can find jokes
about cannibalism in Dickens, Thackeray, Nestroy, Kafka, and W. S. Gilbert. Even
in *Der Zauberberg* the subject is not entirely serious. Martin Swales has commented
on the 'fee-fi-fo-fum' atmosphere of the moment when the witches threaten
Castorp (p. 46). The episode is grim, but not completely serious.

A similarly shifting tone characterizes Heine's poem 'Vitzliputzli'. This poem
offers a condensed history of religion, focusing on sacrifice and its transformations. The Aztecs — who are treated with considerable sympathy as victims of the
Spaniards' imperialism — are about to celebrate their temporary victory by enacting a 'Mysterium':

> 'Menschenopfer' heißt das Stück.
> Uralt ist der Stoff, die Fabel;
> In der christlichen Behandlung
> Ist das Schauspiel nicht so gräßlich.
>
> Denn dem Blute wurde Rotwein,
> Und dem Leichnam, welcher vorkam,
> Wurde eine harmlos dünne
> Mehlbreispeis transsubstituieret —
>
> Diesmal aber, bei den Wilden,
> War der Spaß sehr roh und ernsthaft
> Aufgefaßt: man speiste Fleisch,
> Und das Blut war Menschenblut.[22]

[The play is entitled 'Human Sacrifice'; its material, its plot, are ancient.
The Christian treatment of the drama is less gruesome. For the blood was
transubstantiated into red wine, and the corpse into a harmless slice of bread —
but on this occasion, among the savages, the joke was handled in a very crude
and unfunny way: people ate flesh, and the blood was that of people.]

Heine's history of religion begins with cannibalism and leads up to Holy Communion — a daring and disconcerting association, but not an unprecedented one.
For of course the imagery of eating flesh and drinking blood is explicitly present

---

21   Edward Gibbon, *The Decline and Fall of the Roman Empire*, Everyman's Library, 6 vols (London:
Dent, 1910), II, 500. Gibbon alludes to Cook's voyages at ib., IV, 111–12, at the end of the excursus
headed 'General Observations on the Fall of the Roman Empire in the West'.
22   Heinrich Heine, *Sämtliche Schriften*, ed. by Klaus Briegleb, 6 vols (Munich: Hanser, 1968–76),
VI, 68.

in the Christian liturgy. It may be most familiar to many of us from the Prayer of Humble Access. It has of course been disputed over many centuries whether Jesus' words 'Hoc est corpus meum' and 'hic est sanguis meus' (Mark 14. 22, 24) were to be understood symbolically or literally.[23] An argument which carried great weight with medieval theologians trained in Aristotelian logic was that the grammatical subject and the predicate must be fully equal. If the subject ('hoc', the bread) were literal, the predicate ('corpus meum') must be so likewise. To explain this, the doctrine of substance and accidents was evolved. The Fourth Lateran Council in 1215 affirmed that Christ's body and blood are substantially present in the bread and wine of Communion, the bread being transubstantiated into Christ's body, and the wine into His blood, by divine power. 'Una vero est fidelium universalis *Ecclesia*, extra quam nullus omnino salvatur, in qua idem ipse sacerdos est sacrificium Iesus Christus, cuius corpus et sanguis in *sacramento altaris* sub speciebus panis et vini veraciter continentur, transsubstantiatis pane in corpus, et vino in sanguinem potestate divina.'[24] This literal interpretation meant that the central ritual of Christian culture was close, perhaps disturbingly close, to its central taboo, and it has been argued, speculatively but to my mind plausibly, that the consequent unease was displaced onto those out-groups — heretics, Jews, and alleged witches — who were charged with parodying Christian communion in the forms of black mass or ritual murder involving cannibalism.[25] During the Reformation this unease occasionally became explicit. Thus the Swiss Protestant reformer Zwingli, who did not believe in the real presence, taunted his opponents by asserting that 'to believe one truly ate the body of Christ in the Eucharist was to believe oneself a cannibal' (Roper, pp. 73–74). In the French Wars of Religion, Protestant polemicists described the Catholic Eucharist as the butchery and consumption of raw flesh and compared it to the cannibalism reported from Brazil.[26] And in anti-Christian polemic of the nineteenth century we find the charge that Communion is a remnant of barbarism. Nietzsche says in *Der Antichrist* that Christianity required barbaric words and ideas in order to be accepted among barbarians, among these being 'das Bluttrinken im Abendmahl', and that St Paul distorted the religion founded by Jesus, and at the same time ensured its worldwide success, by incorporating into it elements of pagan cults such as those of Osiris, the Magna Mater, and Mithras.[27] Now I do not claim that Mann knew this history, apart from what he could find in Heine and Nietzsche.

23   See Miri Rubin, *Corpus Christi: The Eucharist in Late Medieval Culture* (Cambridge: Cambridge University Press, 1991).

24   Heinrich Denzinger, *Enchiridion symbolorum definitionum de rebus fidei et morum / Kompendium der Glaubensbekenntnisse und kirchlichen Lehrentscheidungen*, ed. and trans. by Peter Hünermann, 37th impr. (Freiburg im Breisgau: Herder, 1991), p. 358.

25   Peter Hulme, *Colonial Encounters: Europe and the Native Caribbean, 1492–1797* (London: Methuen, 1986), p. 85.

26   See Frank Lestringant, 'Catholiques et Cannibales: Le Thème du cannibalisme dans le discours protestant au temps des guerres de religion', in *Pratiques et discours alimentaires à la Renaissance*, ed. by Jean-Claude Margolin and Robert Sauzet (Paris: G.-P. Maisonneuve et Larose, 1982), pp. 233–45 (esp. pp. 240–42).

27   Friedrich Nietzsche, *Werke*, ed. by Giorgio Colli and Mazzino Montinari, 8 divisions (Berlin and New York: de Gruyter, 1969–), VI/iii. 187, 245.

I do claim that by placing a cannibalistic human sacrifice at a crucial juncture in his novel, he is, wittingly or not, taking part in a centuries-long discourse about the meaning of sacrifice in Christianity and of its counterparts in other cultures, which were always understood in relation to the Christian sacrifice — usually as the inversion, parody, mockery or distortion of the Eucharist.

From this episode run threads connecting it to two others where Mann focuses on priesthood and rituals. One is the account we receive of Naphta's father. Elia Naphta, living at the extreme north-eastern border of the Austro-Hungarian Empire, is not a rabbi, but nevertheless a kind of cleric, full of spirituality ('von stiller Geistigkeit erfüllt'); he has been known to perform apparent miracles and has the reputation of a wonder-worker, 'von einem Gottesvertrauten, Baal-Schem oder Zaddik, das ist Wundermann' (664) [as if he were conversant with God, a *baalschem* or *zaddik*, a miracle man (Woods, p. 523)]. He is thus a kind of priest, but the office he holds is that of ritual slaughterer. The slaughter of animals must conform to the Jewish ritual laws. It is therefore a ceremonial action. And it is also a survival of a very ancient conception of priesthood, recalling 'daß in Urzeiten das Töten von Schlachttieren in der Tat eine Sache der Priester gewesen war' (663) [recalling ancient times when the slaughtering of animals had indeed been the duty of priests (Woods, p. 522)]. Thus Mann is forcing us to hold together two apparently incompatible ideas, that of spirituality and that of bloodshed. The bloodshed is made worse because the ritual laws forbid the slaughterer to stun an animal, as Christian butchers do, but require that it should be allowed to bleed slowly and painfully to death. Thus pain and suffering are here associated with spirituality and religion. The strong implication is that Elia Naphta performs a bloody sacrifice. His respect for his father is the foundation of Leo Naphta's Christianity: his religion focuses on suffering, as we can see from the late-medieval Pietà that he has in his room. Thus Mann suggests that the connection between Judaism and Christianity consists especially in a morbid focus on pain and suffering, a tendency even to add to the pain already present in the world, and to make pain the centre of their interpretation of the world.

The two religions are identified still more closely when Elia Naphta is accused of the ritual murder of a child. From the late nineteenth century onwards there were numerous cases of alleged ritual murder by Jews. The most notorious cases were those of Tiszaeszlár in Hungary (1883) and Polna in Bohemia (1899). Arnold Zweig made the former the subject of his play *Ritualmord in Ungarn* [*Ritual Murder in Hungary*] (1914). But such terrors arose even in the heart of Germany. In 1891, when a boy's corpse was discovered in a barn near Xanten in the Rhineland, the local Jewish butcher and ex-slaughterer was charged with ritual murder; and though he was able to prove his innocence, his neighbours wrecked his house and compelled him to move to another district. Thereafter, rumours of ritual murder arose somewhere in Germany almost annually. The practice of ritual slaughter often caused people to suspect Jews of ritual murder.[28] So it is not altogether surprising

---

28   See Sander L. Gilman, *Franz Kafka, the Jewish Patient* (London and New York: Routledge, 1995), which has much on the sick Jew Naphta; R. Po-chia Hsia, *The Myth of Ritual Murder: Jews and*

that in *Der Zauberberg* the unexplained death of two Gentile children give rise to a popular panic of which Elia becomes the victim. The populace — and this is not something with contemporary parallels — actually crucify him with nails on the door of his house, while his wife and children flee the country. The network of associations is here very dense. Elia, the unjustly crucified Jew, invites comparison to Christ. His son Leo, on the other hand, resembles St Paul, another Jew who became a Christian, or at least the St Paul evoked by Nietzsche in *Der Antichrist*, 'das Genie im Hass' [the genius of hatred], a descendant of the power-hungry Jewish priesthood, who distorted what was valuable in Jesus' message and reduced it to a formula with which to outdo pagan cults by incorporating elements of their own practices.[29]

The image of ritual slaughter leads us forward to the scene Hans Castorp witnesses in the temple. The two women are dismembering a child. The child's blonde hair suggests that he is German. This is ritual murder as the ignorant populace imagined it, combined with a hideous reversal of motherhood so that the life-giving and nourishing mother becomes distorted into her opposite. The strong suggestions of sacrifice in these episodes find a lighter counterpart in the sacramental overtones that play around the figure of Peeperkorn. A sacrament is a symbol which serves as a visible and effective sign of a spiritual grace. The bread and wine in Holy Communion are sacramental because they transmit divine grace to the communicants. That might sound incongruously solemn when applied to Peeperkorn. After playing cards and drinking wine with the Berghof patients, Peeperkorn insists on making a night of it by ordering what sounds a lavish cold meal, with many kinds of cold meat accompanied by butter, radishes and parsley. His meal with his followers is a kind of Last Supper, a jocular sacrament. As Oskar Seidlin has pointed out, Peeperkorn presides over twelve guests, of whom Hans Castorp occupies the position of St John, the beloved disciple.[30] He uses strangely religious language that recalls Jesus. Simple food, he says, is 'Das Heilige! [...] Eine Flasche Wein, ein dampfendes Eiergericht, ein Korn' (852) [Whatever is holy! [...] A bottle of wine, a steaming dish of eggs, pure grain spirits (Woods, p. 670)]. Through 'Korn', meaning spirits made from grain (and also present in Peeperkorn's name), we have bread, and hence an allusion to the Eucharist. Later, when the guests are sleepy, Peeperkorn adopts the language used by Christ in the garden of Gethsemane, reproaching them for being unable to watch with him. But he is also a Dionysian figure reminding Hans Castorp of Bacchus himself (854). The association of Christ and Dionysus has precedents, in Hölderlin ('Brot und Wein' and 'Der Einzige'), but also in Nietzsche, who, as Mann well knew, signed his last letters sometimes 'Dionysos' and sometimes 'der Gekreuzigte' [the Crucified One].

Magic in Reformation Germany (New Haven, CT, and London: Yale University Press, 1988).

29 Nietzsche, *Werke*, VI/iii. 213.

30 Oskar Seidlin, 'Das hohe Spiel der Zahlen: Die Peeperkorn-Episode in Thomas Manns *Zauberberg*', in his *Klassische und moderne Klassiker* (Göttingen: Vandenhoeck & Ruprecht, 1972), pp. 103–25; Michael Köhler, *Götterspeise: Mahlzeitmotivik in der Prosa Thomas Manns und Genealogie des alimentären Opfers* (Tübingen: Niemeyer, 1996), pp. 117–25. Despite his title, Köhler disappointingly ignores the scene in the temple.

Indeed Ernst Bertram's book on Nietzsche, which Mann admired, makes much of Nietzsche's own attempt at a synthesis of Christianity and Hellenism. A deeply Christian figure, in Bertram's interpretation, Nietzsche did not openly affirm suffering, in the Christian manner, but revealed his awareness of it from behind a mask of Hellenist perfection and hedonism: 'Seine Bejahung des Leidenden Menschen ist nicht christlich offen: der nietzschesche Mensch bekennt sich nicht als leidenden; gleich seinem Homer und Epikur erfindet er den ergreifenden Schein des Glücks, der Fülle, der Gesundheit, hüllt er sich in den Mantel einer hellenischen Vollkommenheit [His affirmation of the Suffering Man lacks the openness of Christianity: Nietzschean man no longer confesses to suffering; like his Homer and Epicurus, he invents the attractive illusion of happiness, plenitude, health, he swathes himself in the mantle of Hellenic perfection].[31] This would also be a good description of Peeperkorn.

Peeperkorn is inevitably an ambivalent figure. Like Elia Naphta, Peerperkorn is also a priest, but this time a priest of life. Elia Naphta's bloodstained ritual killings find their counterpart and antithesis in Peeperkorn's vegetarian sacrament. To demand further refinements beyond simple food, he claims, is the unforgivable sin, and by this he means an offence against life itself. 'Die Niederlage des Gefühls vor dem Leben, das ist die Unzulänglichkeit, für die es keine Gnade, kein Mitleid und keine Würde gibt, sondern die erbarmungslos und hohnlachend verworfen ist, — er-ledigt, junger Mann, und ausgespien ...' (855) [The defeat of feeling in the face of life, that is the inadequacy for which there is no pardon, no pity, no honor, but only merciless shame and scornful laughter, — *set*-tled, young man, and spewed out again (Woods, p. 672)]. When he holds up his ring, he arouses feelings like those evoked by 'der bejahrte Priester eines fremden Kults [...], der mit gerafften Gewändern und wunderlicher Grazie vor dem Opferaltar tanzte' (864) [an elderly priest of some alien cult [who would] hitch up his robes and dance with strange grace before the sacrificial altar (Woods, p. 679)]. So he too is a priest, but a sensual priest, entirely different from the spiritual, life-denying priest Elia Naphta. Yet there is something forced and feverish in his devotion to the senses, and he finally commits suicide, like Naphta. His suicide suggests that there was a deep pain concealed behind his hedonism, just as in Bertram's understanding of Nietzsche. We are not to think that he is an infallible pedagogue. Neither Peeperkorn nor Naphta gets things right as much as Settembrini does. Of the latter's speeches Mann said that, though not to be taken seriously, they were 'das sittlich einzig Positive und dem Todeslaster Entgegenstehende'.[32]

We seem then to have in *Der Zauberberg* two conceptions of religion, one more sacrificial, the other more sacramental. The religion of sacrifice goes back to such atrocities as the human sacrifice conducted in the temple and continues via the Jewish practice of ritual slaughter and the adaptation of pagan practices in Pauline Christianity, at least as interpreted by Nietzsche in *Der Antichrist*. The religion of

31 Ernst Bertram, *Nietzsche: Versuch einer Mythologie*, ed. by Hartmut Buchner (Bonn: Bouvier, 1965), p. 147.

32 Thomas Mann, *Tagebücher, 1918–1921*, ed. by Peter de Mendelsohn (Frankfurt a.M.: Fischer, 1979), p. 319.

the sacrament is harmlessly vegetarian, based on an appreciation of the blessings of nature, above all bread and wine, and the priest who presides over it, benignly but with an undercurrent of suffering, is a combination of Christ and Dionysus. Thus the novel anticipates the increasing interest in the history of religion which would find expression in *Joseph und seine Brüder*. In the short essay of 1931 from which I quoted at the beginning of this paper, Mann said that this development followed naturally from the concentration on 'das Rätsel des Menschen' in *Der Zauberberg*: 'Kein Wunder und Zufall also, daß seither das Religions- und Mythengeschichtliche — eine Welt von rührendster Intimität und Geschlossenheit, in der von Anfang an alles da ist — sich ganz und gar meines human Interesses bemächtigt hat' [No wonder and no accident, therefore, that since then the history of religions and myths — a world of touching intimacy and self-containedness, in which all things are present from the very beginning — has come entirely to dominate my interest in humanity] (GW XI, 425).

CHAPTER 25

Kafka as Anti-Christian: *The Judgement, The Metamorphosis*, and the Aphorisms

In 1971 Evelyn Torton Beck broke new ground in studies of Kafka by suggesting that his contact with the Yiddish actors awakened a wide-ranging interest in Judaism that could be traced throughout his life and career.[1] That insight has now become a commonplace. Kafka's interest in aspects of Judaism, religious and political, has been documented by Marthe Robert, Giuliano Baioni, Karl Erich Grözinger, Hans Dieter Zimmermann, Marina Cavarocchi, myself, and others; the Jewish character of his work has been sensitively studied by Robert Alter; and his personal writings have been assigned by Dieter Lamping to the 'Jewish discourse' that develops within twentieth-century literature in German.[2]

It is important, however, to remember how eclectic Kafka was in drawing on religious traditions. The story of Kafka's estrangement from the Judaism in which he had been nominally brought up, and his rediscovery at least of aspects of Judaism with the help of Max Brod, Georg Langer and other friends, is by now familiar. But he read Christian writers: Pascal, Augustine, Tolstoy, and of course Kierkegaard. Christian imagery enters his work more prominently than images drawn from Judaism. A crucial chapter of *The Trial* is set in a cathedral; both Kafka's other novels mention churches; yet a synagogue is mentioned only in a short fragment ('In the Thamühl Synagogue'). On the other hand, Jewish imagery sometimes appears more discreetly. A few months before beginning *The Trial*, Kafka visited Martin Buber in Berlin and asked him about the 'unjust judges' in Psalm 82.[3] And Karl

---

1 Evelyn Torton Beck, *Kafka and the Yiddish Theater* (Madison: University of Wisconsin Press, 1971).

2 Marthe Robert, *Seul, comme Franz Kafka* (Paris: Calmann-Lévy, 1979); Giuliano Baioni, *Kafka: Letteratura ed ebraismo* (Turin: Einaudi, 1984); *Franz Kafka und das Judentum*, ed. by Karl E. Grözinger, Karl E., Stéphane Mosès and Hans Dieter Zimmermann (Frankfurt a.M.: Athenäum, 1987); Hans Dieter Zimmermann, *Der babylonische Dolmetscher: Zu Franz Kafka und Robert Walser* (Frankfurt a.M.: Suhrkamp, 1985); Marina Cavarocchi, *La certezza che toglie la speranza: Contributi per l'approfondimento dell'aspetto ebraico in Kafka* (Florence: Giuntina, 1988); Ritchie Robertson, *Kafka: Judaism, Politics, and Literature* (Oxford: Clarendon Press, 1985); Robert Alter, *Necessary Angels: Tradition and Modernity in Kafka, Benjamin and Scholem* (Cambridge, MA: Harvard University Press, 1991); Dieter Lamping, *Von Kafka bis Celan: Jüdischer Diskurs in der deutschen Literatur des 20. Jahrhunderts* (Göttingen: Vandenhoeck & Ruprecht, 1998).

3 Ritchie Robertson, '"Von den ungerechten Richtern". Zum allegorischen Verfahren Kafkas im *Proceß*', in *Nach erneuter Lektüre: Franz Kafkas 'Der Proceß'*, ed. by Hans Dieter Zimmermann

Erich Grözinger has pointed out many intriguing similarities between the imagery of the novel and that of the Kabbalah, with its judges and door-keepers, though he has not explained how Kafka knew about the Kabbalah at this stage in his life.[4] It seems that Kafka borrowed images eclectically to express religious concerns that are not esoteric but find many echoes in the religious experience of humankind. He himself wrote, distancing himself both from Christians like Kierkegaard and from inheritors of Judaism like the Zionists, 'Ich bin Ende oder Anfang,' 'I am the end or the beginning' (NS II, 98).[5] He drew not only on Jewish and Christian traditions but on philosophy: a key term he frequently uses, 'das Unzerstörbare,' 'the indestructible,' comes from Schopenhauer.[6]

The purpose of this paper is to define some features of Kafka's religious outlook a little more sharply than before, and to continue an investigation of his contact with Christianity by examining some signs in his work of a hostile critique of Christianity.[7] For a distinct component in Kafka's religious thought is a scepticism that was nourished by his early reading of Nietzsche. He and his friend Max Brod first met in 1902, at a meeting of a student society where Brod gave a paper on his idol Schopenhauer in which he attacked Nietzsche; Kafka, already a devoted reader of Nietzsche, sprang to the latter's defence, and they walked home in enthusiastic conversation.[8] In Nietzsche, Kafka found a searching critique of religion in general and Christianity in particular. Nietzsche denied that the moral and theological claims of Christianity had any divine origin. There was no single morality, but rather diverse systems of morals, whose origin could be explained historically and psychologically, and whose dominance was due not to their intrinsic excellence but to the power attained by their adherents. Christian morality represented the creative resentment felt by the physically weak against their masters, and was shot through with vengefulness and hatred. The priestly type, best realized in Judaism and Christianity, was a damaged person, lacking in vitality, maintaining power over his sick flock by psychological manipulation. Though Jesus had a valuable message, only a natural aristocracy could have understood it, whereas his disciples were mediocre individuals and St Paul a fanatical nihilist who distorted the message to satisfy his power-hunger. Nietzsche claimed to prefer the Old Testament, with its heroic figures, to the New. And yet he also acknowledged that the slave revolt

(Würzburg: Königshausen & Neumann, 1992), pp. 201–09.

    4   Karl E. Grözinger, *Kafka und die Kabbala* (Frankfurt a.M.: Eichborn, 1992).

    5   Kafka's works are quoted from the following editions: *Briefe an Felice und andere Korrespondenz aus der Verlobungszeit*, ed. by Erich Heller and Jürgen Born (Frankfurt a.M.: Fischer, 1967) (F); *Briefe an Milena*, ed. by Jürgen Born and Michael Müller (Frankfurt a.M.: Fischer, 1983) (M); *Drucke zu Lebzeiten*, ed. by Wolf Kittler, Hans-Gerd Koch und Gerhard Neumann (Frankfurt a.M.: Fischer, 1994) (D); *Nachgelassene Schriften und Fragmente II*, ed. by Jost Schillemeit (Frankfurt a.M.: Fischer, 1992) (NS II); *Der Proceß*, ed. by Malcolm Pasley (Frankfurt a.M.: Fischer, 1990) (P); *Das Schloß*, ed. by Malcolm Pasley (Frankfurt a.M.: Fischer, 1982) (S); *Tagebücher*, ed. by Hans-Gerd Koch, Michael Müller and Malcolm Pasley (Frankfurt a.M.: Fischer, 1990) (T). All translations are my own.

    6   John Zilcosky, 'Kafka Approaches Schopenhauer's Castle', *German Life and Letters*, 44 (1990–91), 353–69.

    7   Ritchie Robertson, 'Kafka und das Christentum', *Der Deutschunterricht*, 50 (1998), v. 60–69.

    8   Max Brod, *Streitbares Leben: Autobiographie* (Munich: Kindler, 1960), p. 234.

in morals which produced Christianity had also made humanity more inward, more complex, more interesting, and that the asceticism exemplified by the priest was shared by the artist and the scholar in whom it was the precondition for achievement.

Kafka's religious outlook, moreover, is not a static system. It is continually developing. The problem from which Kafka starts may be defined in personal terms as follows. He wished to belong to a physical community, based on the small community of the family. He wished to found a family of his own, feeling that otherwise his life would be incomplete, indeed a failure. He quotes the Talmud: 'Auch im Talmud heißt es: ein Mann ohne Weib ist kein Mensch'; 'The Talmud also says: A man without a wife is not a man' (T 266). But he also felt disgust for his own body, dislike of sexuality, and a desire for an ascetic form of existence. It has been argued that this aporia in Kafka's personal life reflected an aporia within Judaism.[9] For on the one hand, the Old Testament urges man to be fruitful and multiply, and to serve God through everyday life. But procreation means acknowledging that one is part of nature, and man is also enjoined to stand aloof from nature, to abstain from the nature worship of the surrounding heathen, and to fix his devotion upon a God who has no physical embodiment. Hence a discomfort with sexuality can be found throughout the history of Judaism, from Old Testament times down to Zionist experiments with communal living.[10] In Kafka's case, this conflict finds expression in the clash between two incompatible moralities. Characters like Georg Bendemann, Josef K. and the country doctor follow a worldly morality of hard work and professional devotion, expecting it to be rewarded by material and perhaps sexual success. But their lives are broken apart by the intervention of another morality — the anger of Bendemann senior, the Court, the horses that emerge from a pig-sty — in the light of which their material goals and their orderly lives are worthless, indeed reprehensible. The enigmatic, ungrammatical sentence passed by Bendemann senior — 'Ein unschuldiges Kind warst du ja eigentlich, aber noch eigentlicher warst du ein teuflischer Mensch!' [You were really an innocent child, but yet more really you were a devilish human being!'] (D 60) — contrasts the worldly, ultimately natural morality of the innocent child with the absolute morality, sharply dividing good from evil, that intervenes and annihilates the other. In the ten years that separate *The Judgement* from *The Castle*, Kafka explores the implications of this dualist outlook, and in the latter text he wins through, as I have argued elsewhere, to a more tolerant morality that finds value in the mundane details of everyday life and even in bodily love, and questions the desire for contact with the transcendent as a dangerous, Faustian temptation.[11] Instead of trying to link the village with the Castle, Kafka leaves the latter in its ambiguity,

9   Walter H. Sokel, 'Zwischen Gnosis und Jehovah: Zur Religions-Problematik Franz Kafkas', in *Franz Kafka Symposium, 1983*, ed. by Wilhelm Emrich and Bernd Goldmann (Mainz: v. Hase & Koehler, 1985), pp. 37–79 (pp. 41–42).

10   See David Biale, *Eros and the Jews: From Biblical Israel to Contemporary America* (New York: Basic Books, 1992).

11   Robertson, *Kafka*, p. 235; Richard Sheppard, *On Kafka's Castle* (London: Croom Helm, 1973).

and explores instead what Stephen Dowden calls an 'anthropological absolute', the possibility of sublime moments that illuminate from within an otherwise frozen and painful existence.[12]

Here I shall look briefly at two intermediate stages. One is represented by *The Judgement* and *The Metamorphosis*, which explore respectively questions of guilt and judgement, and the fate of humanity as an immaterial consciousness trapped in an animal body and a material world. The other is represented by the aphorisms which Kafka wrote in the winter of 1917–18 while trying to convalesce from tuberculosis in the Bohemian countryside.

Kafka's breakthrough story, *The Judgement*, can obviously be read as an oedipal narrative of family conflict, but such a reading leaves many questions unanswered. Why is Georg's friendship with the man in Russia incompatible with his engagement? Why does his father charge him with violating his mother's memory (or rather, as he mysteriously puts it, 'our' mother's memory ('unserer Mutter Andenken geschändet'; D 57)? Why is Georg so helpless when faced with his angry father? And why does the father condemn his son to death? These questions seem to invite a recourse to allegory, provided we do not understand allegory as the fixed symbolic expression of eternal verities. Rather, Kafka's kind of allegory responds to our desire for meaning, teases it, and never completely satisfies it. A meaning is always just out of reach. As John Zilcosky has recently put it: 'By withdrawing a traditional superstructure of meaning from above allegorical language, yet continuing to imply the negative allegory, Kafka creates texts in which more evident than their meaninglessness is their constant pointing toward a meaning'.[13]

In an attempt to answer questions like those just listed, and to account for the persistence with which the story seems to point to a dimension beyond the realistic or the symbolic, Wolf-Daniel Hartwich has turned to Jewish theology.[14] Hartwich recalls the well-known fact that Kafka wrote the story during the night following Yom Kippur, when he had failed to attend synagogue, and after a year of absorption in the full-blooded Jewish life represented by the Yiddish actors from Warsaw who were visiting Prague. Hartwich finds a contrast between Jewish assimilation, embodied by Georg with his plans to marry an apparent Gentile ('Brandenfeld' — burnt field — heath — heathen), and the friend in Russia, loyal to the home of the Eastern Jews. The father represents the authority of the Law; his back room is the Holy of Holies in the Temple; the wall visible outside is the Wailing Wall; the dead mother is both the Shekhinah (the divine wisdom, imagined in the Kabbalah as feminine) and the Virgin Mary; the father's wound recalls that of Jacob, gained by wrestling with the angel; the sick friend recalls the suffering servant in Isaiah 53, 'despised and rejected of men [...] stricken, smitten of God, and afflicted'; Georg himself is the scapegoat, typologically represented both by Isaac and Jesus. Though Hartwich's interpretation seems often far-fetched, it does respond to the details in

---

12   Stephen C. Dowden, *Kafka's Castle and the Critical Imagination* (Columbia, SC: Camden House, 1995), p. 125.

13   Zilcosky, p. 360.

14   Wolf-Daniel Hartwich, 'Böser Trieb, Märtyrer und Sündenbock: Religiöse Metaphorik in Kafkas Urteil', *Deutsche Vierteljahresschrift*, 67 (1993), 521–40.

the story that fail to fit into a realistic or a psychoanalytic interpretation. It imputes to Kafka, however, a degree of conscious planning which is hardly compatible with the way he wrote the story or with the perplexity he himself expressed (T 491–92) and a thorough knowledge of Jewish theology and tradition which is not attested in any contemporary biographical documents.

Parts of Hartwich's interpretation, however, do make sense of the enigmatic overtones in the story. The 'Schreckbild seine Vaters' [dreadful image of his father] (D 56) does indeed suggest an angry Jehovah, a reminder of the authority of tradition, who punishes Georg for his apostasy into worldly pursuits. Georg and his friend, implicitly made into brothers when the father says of the friend: 'Er wäre ein Sohn nach meinem Herzen'; D 56), faintly recall such contrasting Old Testament pairs as Jacob and Esau, or Ephraim and Manasseh (Gen. 48). More problematic is the interpretation of the Christian allusions in the story.[15] Most directly of all, Georg and his friend suggest the Prodigal Son and his stay-at-home brother. 'Petersburg', the city of Peter, recalls St Peter and possibly Rome. We have the striking and at first sight unmotivated image of the priest in Russia who stands up before a crowd and cuts a cross into the palm of his hand. After sentence has been pronounced, the maidservant cries 'Jesus!' as Georg dashes downstairs to his fate, and hides her face as though the sight of him were forbidden. Hanging from the bridge, Georg may call to mind the crucified Christ.

How are we to interpret these overtones? An obvious temptation is to discern in them a systematic key to the story, as Hartwich does when he reads the figure of the priest and the allusion to Jesus typologically: the priest's self-mutilation alludes to the alleged connection between circumcision and crucifixion; Georg, as scapegoat, represents Jesus (but also Judas, having betrayed his friend!). The trouble is that such interpretations seem over-specific, while leaving the story as open as it was before. A more perceptive, and, above all, more literary interpretation was suggested many years ago in an essay by John M. Ellis that has found too little resonance in Kafka studies. Having listed the Christian motifs, Ellis remarks that 'in *Das Urteil* the values of Christianity are thrown up in the air, and come down in an unfamiliar shape'.[16] He points out that the main characters keep changing their positions within the Christian scheme. Georg may resemble Jesus in his loving concern for his father, and in the manner of his death, but the friend resembles Christ in having been 'denied' by Georg, as Peter did Christ ('Wenigstens zweimal habe ich ihn vor dir verleugnet'; D 54), and the father, as the representative ('Vertreter') of the friend, stands to him in the position of Christ towards his divine father.

Kafka deploys Christian imagery to question the values of Christianity, particularly through the figures of the Russian priest and Georg himself. We may notice the resemblance between the priest standing on a balcony before a crowd and the father, a little later in the story, standing on the bed and towering over Georg. Both are figures of paternal authority. Both, moreover, owe their power in

---

15 See Gerhard Kurz, *Traum-Schrecken: Kafkas literarische Existenzanalyse* (Stuttgart: Metzler, 1980), p. 171.

16 John M. Ellis, 'Kafka: *Das Urteil*', in his *Narration in the German Novelle* (Cambridge: Cambridge University Press, 1974), pp. 188–211.

part to their injury. The father bears the scar obtained during military service; the priest mutilates himself. We may get closer to the implications of Kafka's Christian imagery if we remember that as a reader of Nietzsche he would have understood Christianity, in part at least, in the sceptical light of anti-Christian texts like *The Genealogy of Morals* and *The Antichrist*. The priest who wounds his own hand is then a version of the sick priest in *The Genealogy of Morals*, who owes his power over his flock to his sharing their illness.

As for Georg, his expression of concern for his father comes late, after he and his fiancée have been planning to move away and leave the old man alone. It is formulated in suspiciously saccharine and hyperbolic language ('Tausend Freunde ersetzen mir nicht meinen Vater' [A thousand friends can't replace my father]; D 52). He is clearly a determined, ambitious person with powerful material and sexual appetites. This does not correspond to the character of Christ in the Gospels. But there is something in Ellis's strongly phrased argument that 'the story explores the ambiguous and dark side of the Christian ethic. Christ was crucified because his humility was felt to be arrogance, his meekness to be aggressive and his advocacy of childlike innocence to be devious and insidious',[17] and Georg really does have the duplicity that Christ was supposed to have. We may recall too that Christ rejected his own family, denying that his mother and brothers were more important to him than anyone else (Matt. 12. 46–50), enjoining his followers to leave their families and follow him (Luke 14. 26), and upbraiding one potential disciple for waiting till he had buried his father (Luke 9. 59–60). The reader of Nietzsche would readily suspect that ostensible Christian values concealed a will to power.

Scepticism towards Christianity is also prominent in *The Metamorphosis*, written two to three months after *The Judgement*. Gregor is throughout the victim of his family. A devoted, selfless son who wears himself out in supporting his family, he learns that they do not need him, since they have secretly saved some money and can in any case earn their own living. Later, when his presence in their flat risks driving away the lodgers on whom they think they depend financially, they resolve, with self-serving illogicality, that it is his duty to disappear; the self-sacrificing Gregor agrees, and on his death the family cross themselves, show some shallow grief, and then re-immerse themselves in the mundane world of work and enjoyment. Neither sacrifice was necessary. For just as the family were better off than they allowed the hard-working Gregor to realize, after his death they discover that their jobs are really quite lucrative; there is evidently no need for them to take in lodgers any more, and therefore the economic objection to Gregor's presence vanishes.

The Metamorphosis also depicts a consciousness trapped in matter. Gregor's transformation raises questions about the relation between consciousness and the material world. Kafka shows that one not only inhabits a body, but to a disturbing extent one is that body. Gregor's body eludes his control; he devours his disgusting food without any conscious decision to do so. Kafka is here raising another question which will bulk large, especially, in the short stories collected under the title *A Country Doctor*. Is there any difference between human beings and animals? Is man

17 Ellis, p. 209.

just another animal? Kafka was well aware of Darwin, who argued that man had developed from animals by evolution.[18] There was no discontinuity between man and the animal kingdom. Nietzsche pursued the implications of this idea, repeatedly suggesting different ways in which man differed from other animals. While other animals are healthy, man is 'the sick animal'; but his inner life, which estranges him from nature, also makes him 'the most interesting animal'.[19] Kafka constantly elides the boundaries between man and animals. In *The Trial*, for example, the dog figures as an image of human degradation. Josef K. passes off the shrieks of the guard who is being whipped as the cry of a dog; he sees Block degraded into 'der Hund des Advokaten' [the Advocate's dog] (P 265); and by poetic justice, he himself dies 'wie ein Hund' [like a dog] (P 312). In the *Country Doctor* stories this metaphor becomes literal. In a kind of parody of Darwinism, an ape becomes human through an accelerated process of evolution, and Bucephalus, the warhorse of Alexander the Great, adjusts to an unheroic modern age by becoming a lawyer. In both cases the transformation is uncertain: the ape Rotpeter is not accepted as a human being but as an ape who imitates human beings, and his sensual desires are satisfied at night by a half-trained female chimpanzee; while in the case of Dr Bucephalus, his equine origins are still discernible to the practised eye of a frequenter of race-courses. Other stories contain human beings who are on the level of animals: the nomads who invade a Chinese-sounding city and sleep and eat alongside their carnivorous horses; the groom in 'A Country Doctor' who emerges from a pigsty along with two horses whom he addresses as brother and sister. In the latter instance, animality is not simply negative. The groom, whom the doctor addresses as 'Du Vieh' [you brute] (D 254), is possessed by a brutal sexuality which makes him assault the doctor's maid-servant Rosa; but the doctor, living alongside her for years, has barely noticed her, and has not treated her as an individual. Her name first occurs in the story when the groom uses it: before that, the doctor refers to her simply as 'the maidservant'. Here we have a split between the unbridled sensuality of the groom and the over-intellectuality of the professional man trapped in his narrow routine. The animal and intellectual sides of humanity have fallen asunder.

We might also be tempted towards a gnostic reading. Walter H. Sokel has written judiciously on the 'gnostic sensibility' which produces remarkable correspondences between Kafka's writing and the doctrines, current in the early centuries of the Christian era, which are grouped under the name of Gnosticism.[20] Gnostics broadly agreed in believing in two gods, a good deity who existed beyond the world, and a bad deity or demiurge who, having created the world, kept the soul a prisoner in it. The soul contained a portion of the divine essence, trapped in the world and desiring reunion with its extramundane source. Contact with the good, infinitely remote god could come only in the form of knowledge, conceived

18 See Leena Eilittä, *Approaches to Personal Identity in Kafka's Short Fiction: Freud, Darwin, Kierkegaard* (Helsinki: Academia Scientiarum Fennica, 1999), p. 119.

19 Friedrich Nietzsche, *Werke*, ed. by Karl Schlechta, 3 vols (Munich: Hanser, 1966), II, 862, 1174.

20 Sokel, 'Zwischen Gnosis und Jehova'; see Hans Jonas, *The Gnostic Religion: The Message of the Alien God and the Beginnings of Christianity*, 2nd edn (Boston, MA: Beacon Press, 1963).

less as intellectual apprehension than as mystical union. Many Gnostics thought that such knowledge (gnosis) required a severely ascetic way of life, abstaining so far as possible from food and certainly from sex and procreation. Whether Kafka actually encountered Gnostic ideas is unknown; he owned a small book, *Die Gnosis*, published in a series of short introductions to religious topics, but probably acquired it only towards the end of his life.[21] Sokel is doubtless right in identifying in Kafka a gnostic sensibility, an emotional affinity to Gnostic dualism, which, however, was in severe conflict with his ideal of founding a family. In *The Metamorphosis* we can see this gnostic sensibility at work. For while Gregor's animal body does affect him, enabling him (initially at least) to enjoy food that humans would consider disgusting and to amuse himself by walking on the walls and ceiling of his room, it does not engulf his humanity. In one respect it enhances his humanity. Before his transformation, Gregor took little interest in music, but when he peeps out of his bedroom and listens to his sister playing the violin to the inattentive lodgers, he appreciates music as never before, and wonders whether he can be an animal after all: 'War er ein Tier, da ihn Musik so ergriff? Ihm war, als zeige sich ihm der Weg zu der ersehnten unbekannten Nahrung' [Was he an animal, since music moved him so? He felt as though he were being shown the way to the unknown food he longed for] (D 185). If Gregor's loss of appetite expresses an unconscious wish to die to this world, his desire for something outside the world is figured as an unknown food. But what seems to offer satisfaction is music. And here another element enters the story. Although Kafka may have read Schopenhauer seriously only in 1917, he would have known a good deal about Schopenhauer from reading Nietzsche, who quotes Schopenhauer especially in *The Birth of Tragedy*, and from conversations with his friend the Schopenhauer devotee Max Brod. He would have known, therefore, about Schopenhauer's portrayal of the world as a prison from which one can only escape by renouncing the will; it is even possible, as has recently been suggested, that the name Samsa was suggested by *Samsara*, the term denoting enslavement to the world which Schopenhauer took from the Hindu Upanishads.[22] Kafka would certainly have known also that Schopenhauer assigns a special status to music as the direct utterance of the Will, and hence as the closest we can ever come to penetrating the veil of illusion which holds us captive. As the most impalpable art form, without any material embodiment, music offers Gregor a release from his imprisonment in the body. We may say, therefore, that Kafka's imaginative affinity with Gnosticism leads him to represent the body as a prison, in which humanity is held captive by an increasing animality. His knowledge of Schopenhauer encouraged him to use music as an image for what might lie outside the corporeal prison. He is remote from any Christian acceptance of the body as the divinely created temple of the spirit. Rather, he shares the ascetic impulse which also bulks large in the history of Christianity and has been traced back in part to Gnostic influence.

Kafka's religious preoccupations crystallized in a new way in the winter of 1917–

21 Klaus Wagenbach, *Franz Kafka: Eine Biographie seiner Jugend* (Berne: Francke, 1958), p. 263.
22 Michael P. Ryan, 'Samsa and *Samsara*: Suffering, Death and Rebirth in *The Metamorphosis*', *German Quarterly*, 72 (1999), 113–52.

18. Having been diagnosed with tuberculosis, he went to stay in the countryside with his sister Ottla, who was working on a farm at Zürau. Deep in rural Bohemia, Kafka was officially supposed to rest and recuperate, but his real mission was to confront the prospect of death, which from being remote and ignorable had suddenly become an imminent likelihood. His task, he told Max Brod just before he left, was to get clear about the last things: 'Über die letzten Dinge klar werden'.[23] That winter he put down his thoughts in a number of cheap school notebooks which are now preserved, fragile and frequently blurred, in the Bodleian Library, and have been reliably edited by Jost Schillemeit for the Critical Edition of Kafka's works.

These aphorisms are first and foremost the expression of a spiritual crisis. One finds oneself in a situation that cannot be resolved, not just because the solution is impossibly difficult, but because the solution is unimaginable: 'Du bist die Aufgabe. Kein Schüler weit und breit' [You are the problem. No scholar far and wide] (NS II, 46). In an impossible act of self-reflexivity, one is required to solve a puzzle, to do a piece of homework, that is nothing other than oneself. In this situation, one feels driven to make the crisis more desperate, to reach the point of no return. 'Von einem gewissen Punkt an gibt es keine Rückkehr mehr. Dieser Punkt ist zu erreichen' [From a certain point there is no longer any return. This point must be reached] (NS II, 34). When the crisis is at its most extreme, hope may emerge, as another aphorism suggests: 'Vom wahren Gegner fährt grenzenloser Mut in dich' [The true antagonist fills you with boundless courage] (NS II, 46).

The situation that Kafka is writing about, in general rather than personal terms, is first of all one of self-estrangement. When writing about Kafka's thought in the past, I found it convenient to distinguish between 'being' and 'consciousness'.[24] Consciousness is deceptive. It does not inform one about one's true being. The problem is not that one cannot know the truth; it is that one cannot know the truth and be the truth: 'Es gibt nur zweierlei: Wahrheit und Lüge. Die Wahrheit ist unteilbar, kann sich also selbst nicht erkennen. Wer sie erkennen will muß Lüge sein' [There are only two things: the truth and the lie. The truth is indivisible, so cannot know itself. Anyone who seeks to know it must be [a] lie'] (NS II, 69). If we wonder what it would mean to be the truth, we may be helped by a sentence from Flaubert which Kafka would often repeat. Referring to a family with many children, Flaubert said gravely: 'Ils sont dans le vrai' ('They are right', literally 'They are in the truth').[25] The family, absorbed in daily tasks, seemed to inhabit the truth, compared to the writer contemplating life from outside.

For Kafka, the contemplation of life is bound to be deceptive. This is partly because the signs of the world are ambiguous: 'Der Verzückte und der Ertrinkende — beide heben die Arme' [The man in ecstasy and the man drowning: both raise their arms] (NS II, 53); the same gesture can have opposite meanings. Similarly, in The Trial the all-powerful court is incongruously located in slum tenements and

---

23 Max Brod, Über Franz Kafka (Frankfurt a.M.: Fischer, 1966), p. 147.
24 Robertson, Kafka, p. 190.
25 Brod, Über Franz Kafka, p. 89.

neglected lumber rooms. Even photographic reproduction of reality is unreliable, as we know from *The Castle*, where a photograph shows a Castle messenger in a horizontal position, either lying on a board or vaulting over a rope (S 124–25): 'Alles ist Betrug' [All is deception] (NS ii, 59). But that is also because our powers of perception are inadequate. Estranged from one's true self, one perceives everything unreliably. One cannot know oneself: 'Selbsterkenntnis hat nur das Böse' [Only evil has self-knowledge] (NS ii, 48). One cannot know anything else, because either one is involved and hence biased, or else one is neutral and hence ignorant: 'Wirklich urteilen kann nur die Partei, als Partei aber kann sie nicht urteilen. Demnach gibt es in der Welt keine Urteilsmöglichkeit, sondern nur deren Schimmer' [Only the party concerned can really judge, but as a party concerned s/he cannot judge. Hence the world contains no possibility of judgement, only its semblance] (NS ii, 52).

The task of the individual, as Kafka sees it, is to resist the world. But how is one to do that if one cannot know anything for certain about the world? Worse still, since one is estranged from oneself, it may be that the self from which one is estranged is in league with the world. And that is bound to be the case insofar as estrangement divides the mind from the body. For with our bodies we are enmeshed in the world of the senses, which Kafka considers at best illusory, at worst evil. 'Es gibt nichts anderes als eine geistige Welt; was wir sinnliche Welt nennen, ist das Böse in der geistigen' [There is nothing but a spiritual world; what we call the sensory world is the evil in the spiritual [world]] (NS ii, 59). To fight against the sensory world is futile, because one's senses, and especially one's sexuality, are complicit with it. 'Eine der wirksamsten Verführungen des Teuflischen ist die Aufforderung zum Kampf. Er ist wie der Kampf mit Frauen, die im Bett endet' [One of the most effective temptations practised by the devilish [element] is the invitation to a fight. It is like the fight with women, which ends up in bed] (NS ii, 34–35). The sensual appeal of the world is represented by the Sirens in the story, written apparently on 24 October 1917, to which Max Brod later gave the resonant title 'Das Schweigen der Sirenen' [The Silence of the Sirens]. Instead of singing, the Sirens give every sign of sexual desire — 'die Wendungen ihrer Hälse, das Tiefatmen, die tränenvollen Augen, den halb geöffneten Mund' [the twistings of their necks, their panting, their tear-filled eyes, their half-open mouths] (NS ii, 41) — but since Odysseus thinks these are the gestures that accompany singing, he does not succumb to their sexual appeal.

The struggle against the world is especially a struggle against sexuality.

> Die Frau, noch schärfer ausgedrückt vielleicht die Ehe, ist der Repräsentant des Lebens mit dem Du Dich auseinandersetzen sollst. Das Verführungsmittel dieser Welt sowie das Zeichen der Bürgschaft dafür, daß diese Welt nur ein Übergang ist, ist das gleiche. Mit Recht, denn nur so könnte uns die Welt verführen und entspricht der Wahrheit. Das Schlimme ist nur daß wir nach geglückter Verführung die Bürgschaft vergessen und so eigentlich das Gute uns ins Böse, der Blick der Frau in ihr Bett uns gelockt hat. (NS ii, 95–96)

> [Woman — to put it more pointedly, perhaps, marriage — is the representative of life with which you are to struggle. The means by which this world tempts you, and the sign guaranteeing that this world is only transitional, are the same. Rightly so, for it is only thus that the world could tempt us, corresponding

to the truth. The bad thing is only that after the temptation has worked, we forget the guarantee, and so it is really the good that has lured us into evil, the woman's gaze has lured us into her bed.]

More generally, Kafka represents life, the physical world, in the image of a dog that has borne many puppies but is now dying and already decaying. The paragraph is headed 'Ein Leben' [A Life]:

> Eine stinkende Hündin, reichliche Kindergebärerin, stellenweise schon faulend, die aber in meiner Kindheit mir alles war, die in Treue unaufhörlich mir folgt, die ich zu schlagen mich nicht überwinden kann und vor der ich, ihren Athem scheuend, schrittweise rückwärts weiche und die mich doch, wenn ich mich nicht anders entscheide, in den schon sichtbaren Mauerwinkel drängen wird, um dort auf mir und mit mir gänzlich zu verwesen, bis zum Ende — ehrt es mich? — das Eiter- und Wurmfleisch ihrer Zunge an meiner Hand. (NS II, 37)

> [A stinking bitch, bearer of many children, already rotting in places, but which was everything to me in my childhood, which incessantly follows me faithfully, which I cannot bring myself to strike and before which, avoiding her breath, I move back step by step, and which, if I don't make a different decision, will force me into the already visible angle of the wall, so that there she may completely decay on me and with me, to the last — does it honour me? — the pus- and worm-filled flesh of her tongue on my hand.]

This is a drastically negative portrayal of physical life, involving fertility and its counterpart, decay. The dog is an embodiment of femininity, with its many puppies, its association with the speaker's childhood, and its overpowering affection which the speaker can hardly bear to resist, even though it seeks to drag him down into its own physical corruption. The speaker is tied to it, and thus to the world, by residual affection, by what used to be love. It is ultimately love that enslaves us to the sensual world: 'Die sinnliche Liebe täuscht über die himmlische hinweg, allein könnte sie es nicht, aber da sie das Element der himmlischen Liebe unbewußt in sich hat, kann sie es' [Sensual love deceives one into ignoring heavenly love; it could not do so by itself, but as it unconsciously contains the element of heavenly love, it can] (NS II, 68). Sensual love is a version of heavenly love; it contains enough that is genuine to distract us effectively from seeking after heavenly love. For Kafka, the soul is something eternal, temporarily confined within the physical world. 'Es ist mir zu eng in allem, was ich bedeute, selbst die Ewigkeit, die ich bin, ist mir zu eng' [I am too confined in everything I signify; even the eternity that I am confines me too much] (NS II, 84–85). The soul, it seems, is conceived as disembodied, almost abstract. We recognize here Kafka's gnostic sensibility: the immaterial soul is trapped in a disgusting and decaying mortal body.

How is one to escape from this confinement? First, one must become aware of one's condition. This leads to despair. 'Ein erstes Zeichen beginnender Erkenntnis ist der Wunsch zu sterben. Dieses Leben scheint unerträglich, ein anderes unerreichbar' [A first sign of the beginning of knowledge is the wish to die. This life seems unendurable, another [life] unattainable] (NS II, 43). But becoming aware of one's condition is not enough, for mere self-knowledge is a distraction from the necessary task of overcoming the world. Instead, one's motto must be: '"Verkenne Dich! Zerstöre Dich!" [...] und nur wenn man sich sehr tief hinabbeugt, hört man auch sein Gutes, welches lautet: "um Dich zu dem zu machen, der Du bist"' ['Fail to know yourself! Destroy yourself!' — and only when one bends very far down can one hear the good part, which runs: 'in order to make yourself into that which you are'] (NS II, 42). Kafka demands active self-destruction. One must die, but not a physical death: 'Unsere Rettung ist der Tod, aber nicht dieser' [Our salvation is death, but not this one] (NS II, 101). Rather, one must undergo a spiritual death, and the only development Kafka sees in human history is the development of this spiritual power: 'Die Menschheitsentwicklung — ein Wachsen der Sterbenskraft' [Human development — a growth of the power to die] (NS II, 101). He represents spiritual death by the image of the burning bush in which the Lord appeared to Moses in Exodus 3. 2: 'Der Dornbusch ist der alte Weg-Versperrer. Er muß Feuer fangen, wenn Du weiter willst' [The thorn bush is the ancient barrier in the road. It must catch fire if you want to go any further] (NS II, 48). Spiritual progress must be through the fire, an image recalling Purgatory. Kafka, however, adopts the Jewish image of the Holy of Holies:

> Vor dem Betreten des Allerheiligsten mußt Du die Schuhe ausziehn, aber nicht nur die Schuhe, sondern alles, Reisekleid und Gepäck, und darunter die Nacktheit, und alles, was unter der Nacktheit ist, und alles, was sich unter diesem verbirgt, und dann den Kern und den Kern des Kerns, dann das Übrige und dann der Rest und dann noch den Schein des unvergänglichen Feuers. (NS II, 77)

> [Before entering the Holy of Holies you must take off your shoes, and not only your shoes but everything, your travelling-clothes and your baggage, and beneath that your nakedness, and everything that is beneath your nakedness, and everything hidden beneath that, and then the core and the core of the core, then what is left and then the rest and then the light from the imperishable fire.]

Having undergone such self-destruction, such purgation, what new reality may the purified self enter? Kafka talks mysteriously of our life as being merely transitional. We need to enter the spiritual world, which is the only reality. 'Es gibt nur eine geistige Welt, was wir sinnliche nennen ist das Böse in der geistigen' [There is nothing but a spiritual world; what we call the sensuous world is the evil in the spiritual [world]] (NS II, 59); when arranging a selection of aphorisms in sequence, Kafka added to this one: 'und was wir böse nennen ist nur eine Notwendigkeit eines Augenblicks unserer ewigen Entwicklung' [and what we call evil is only a requirement of a moment in our everlasting development] (NS II, 124). Our mission is 'Aufsteigen in ein höheres Leben' [ascent into a higher life] (NS II, 81), indeed to attain eternal life. 'Wirst Du nach gewonnener Erkenntnis zum ewigen Leben gelangen wollen — und Du wirst nicht anders können als es wollen, denn Erkenntnis ist dieser Wille — so wirst Du Dich, das Hindernis, zerstören müssen' [If, having gained knowledge, you want to attain eternal life — and you cannot do other than want to, for knowledge is this desire — then you will have to destroy yourself, the obstacle] (NS II, 78).

It is tempting to relate these speculations about life after death to the Kabbalistic concept of tsimtsum or rebirth;[26] but they may also be related to the eighteenth-century concept of palingenesis (reincarnation), which some Christian theologians thought necessary so that people whose virtues were unrewarded, or vices unpunished, in this life should receive justice in another, and to conceptions of metempsychosis which the Enlightenment derived from Platonic and Pythagorean sources.[27] A preoccupation with previous and continued existence runs through Goethe's literary work from *Werther* and 'Warum gabst du uns die tiefen Blicke' down to the *West-östlicher Divan* (particularly the poems 'Selige Sehnsucht' and 'Wiederfinden') and *Faust II*. More importantly for Kafka, who often read writers' personal documents more eagerly than their published works, these concerns often found expression in Goethe's recorded conversations. In a strange conversation recorded by Falk on the day of Wieland's funeral (25 January 1813) Goethe maintained that the simple essence of the individual, for which he borrowed the Leibnizian term 'monad', must survive death, but its subsequent development would depend on its strength; powerful monads might become stars and draw weaker monads into their circle, transforming them into something appropriate. Goethe justified this idea by analogy with processes of metamorphoses in nature which produced a flower from a seed and a caterpillar and then a butterfly from an egg. Kafka would have known this conversation from its inclusion in Biedermann's edition of Goethe's *Gespräche*, which he was reading in 1913, for he quotes another passage in a letter to Felice (F 347).

So far we have a sharp division between the world of the senses, which one's body inhabits, and the 'geistige' world of eternity to which one is connected by one's bodiless inner or mental self. Some passages remind us strongly of Kafka's personal revulsion from sexuality which makes him in his notebooks equate marriage with martyrdom (NS II, 53). This revulsion underlay his curious relationships with Felice Bauer and Milena Jesenská which were carried on largely by correspondence. The letters to Milena, especially, convey Kafka's sense of being trapped in a sexuality which is irremediably filthy: in one he compares himself to the Wandering Jew, 'sinnlos wandernd durch eine sinnlos schmutzige Welt' (M 198), 'senselessly wandering through a senselessly filthy world'.

There is, however, a counter-current in Kafka's thought: the idea that possibly the world of the senses can after all be made acceptable. He contemplates this possibility at first with something approaching horror:

> Was an der Vorstellung des Ewigen bedrückend ist: die uns unbegreifliche Rechtfertigung welche die Zeit in der Ewigkeit erfahren muß und die daraus folgende Rechtfertigung unserer selbst, so wie wir sind. (NS II, 88–89)

> [What is depressing about the notion of eternity: the justification, incomprehensible to us, that time must receive in eternity, and the consequent justification of ourselves just as we are.]

---

26 Robertson, *Kafka*, pp. 195–96.
27 See Lieselotte E. Kurth-Voigt, *Continued Existence, Reincarnation, and the Power of Sympathy in Classical Weimar* (Rochester, NY: Camden House, 1999).

Supposing our destiny were not to escape from embodied existence into a higher, non-physical reality, but to see our limited, temporal reality as part of the eternal order and having its rightful place in the eternal order? Granted that the sensory world is the evil element in the spiritual world, perhaps even it can be reclaimed. A Christian would say 'redeemed'; Kafka's word is 'justification' ('Rechtfertigung'), and as this is an important word in the notebooks the concept deserves some attention. In the Old Testament, this word expresses a relationship between human beings and God. The man who is justified is acquitted or vindicated before a judge's tribunal, as in Psalm 119. 7: 'I will praise thee with uprightness of heart, when I shall have learned thy righteous judgements'. St Paul transfers this concept to the effect of Christ, thanks to whom, not to any merits or actions of our own, we are justified, found righteous, before God: while Abraham was justified by his faith ('And therefore it was imputed to him for righteousness' Rom. 4. 22), Christians are justified both by faith in Christ and by the death of Christ for their sake: 'Therefore being justified by faith, we have peace with God through our Lord Jesus Christ' (Rom. 5.1).

As Kafka develops the concept, however, justification does not come from an external source. It comes from man's own work in the world. Man does not consciously seek justification:

> daß es den Anschein hat, als arbeite er für seine Ernährung, Kleidung, u.s.w. ist nebensächlich, es wird ihm eben mit jedem sichtbaren Bissen ein unsichtbarer, mit jedem sichtbaren Kleid auch ein unsichtbares Kleid u.s.f. gereicht. Das ist jedes Menschen Rechtfertigung. (NS II, 99)

> [That it appears as though he were working to feed and clothe himself, etc., does not matter; for with every visible mouthful he also receives an invisible one, with every visible dress he also receives an invisible dress. That is everybody's justification.]

A person who concentrates on working to support himself and his family is already justified without consciously knowing it. In such a person, being and consciousness are reconciled. Such a person, like the family Flaubert envied, is 'dans le vrai'. We can relate this conception to *The Castle*. There K. seeks a justification for his presence in the village. He wants the authorities to confirm his position as land-surveyor. In his search for authorization, he becomes obsessed with the Castle and with his need to speak to an official competent to deal with his case. Early in this process, he takes up with Frieda, the girlfriend of the official Klamm, and they stumble into a relationship which both want to be lasting. K. finds work as a school janitor, and maintains a grotesquely impractical household in the schoolroom. It is not the difficulties of daily life, but the lure of the Castle, which ends his domestic life.

A further aphorism explores the bases of this justification. It is based on faith, not in the sense of conscious belief, but in the sense of trust, an unconscious assurance, which pervades one's whole being.

> Der Mensch kann nicht leben ohne ein dauerndes Vertrauen zu etwas Unzerstörbarem, wobei sowohl das Unzerstörbare als auch das Vertrauen ihm

dauernd unbekannt bleiben können. Eine der Ausdrucksmöglichkeiten dieses Verborgen-Bleibens ist der Glaube an einen persönlichen Gott. (NS II, 58)

[Man cannot live without lasting trust in something indestructible, even if in lasting ignorance both of his trust and of the indestructible. One possible expression of this concealment is the belief in a personal God.]

Here Kafka affirms that life needs to be based on a relationship to something outside oneself. He is sceptical about whether that something should be conceived as a personal God. In 1913 he asked Felice about her belief in God and enlarged on what conception he thought desirable:

Fühlst Du — was die Hauptsache ist — ununterbrochene Beziehungen zwischen Dir und einer beruhigend fernen, womöglich unendlichen Höhe oder Tiefe? Wer das immer fühlt, der muß nicht wie ein verlorener Hund herumlaufen und bittend aber stumm herumschaun, der muß nicht das Verlangen haben, in das Grab zu schlüpfen, als sei es ein warmer Schlafsack und das Leben eine kalte Winternacht, der muß nicht, wenn er die Treppe in sein Bureau hinaufgeht, zu sehen glauben, daß er gleichzeitig von oben, flimmernd im unsichern Licht, sich drehend in der Eile der Bewegung, kopfschüttelnd vor Ungeduld, durch das ganze Treppenhaus hinunterfällt. (F 289)

[Do you feel — this is the main thing — unbroken connections between yourself and some reassuringly remote, possibly infinite, height or depth? Anyone who constantly feels that does not have to run around like a lost dog, looking around beseechingly but mutely, he need not feel the desire to slip into the grave as though it were a warm sleeping-bag and life a cold winter night, and when he climbs the stairs to his office, he does not have to think he sees himself simultaneously falling from above down the entire staircase, shimmering in the uncertain light, revolving with the rapidity of his motion, shaking his head with impatience.]

This is a brilliant description of the existential insecurity that Kafka attributes to lack of faith. But we have already seen how between 1913 and 1917 Kafka's insecurity had reached the point of desperation. He worked through his crisis in the Zürau notebooks. There he formulates the concept of 'the indestructible,' derived from Schopenhauer's famous meditation on death in Book II of *The World as Will and Representation*.

Belief in 'the indestructible' is not intellectual. It is expressed in action. 'Glauben heißt: das Unzerstörbare in sich befreien oder richtiger: sich befreien oder richtiger: unzerstörbar sein oder richtiger: sein' [Belief means freeing the indestructible in oneself, or rather: freeing oneself, or rather: being indestructible, or rather: being] (NS II, 55). It bridges the gulf between consciousness and being. And it enables Kafka effortlessly to surmount a problem that worries many people who reflect on religion, namely the fact that the majority of people feel no need to reflect on religion. William James borrows from a Catholic writer the division of humanity into the once-born and the twice-born. The latter are the minority who feel anxiety about their relation to something beyond themselves. The former are unreflective, uncomplicated, and largely content to get on with their lives.[28] For Kafka, both

28   William James, *The Varieties of Religious Experience* (London: Longmans, Green, and Co., 1902).

classes of people arrive by different routes at the same goal, that of being; the twice-born like himself have a very much longer and more arduous journey, the others can be 'dans le vrai' already. Kafka also wrote: 'Der Weg zum Nebenmenschen ist für mich sehr lang' [The way to my neighbour is for me very long] (NS II, 112).

Kafka's concept of 'the indestructible' has further consequences. It frees the believer from isolation, for it is by definition something shared with other people. 'Das Unzerstörbare ist eines, jeder einzelne Mensch ist es und gleichzeitig ist es allen gemeinsam. Daher die beispiellos untrennbare Verbindung der Menschen' [The indestructible is one; every individual is it, and simultaneously it is common to all. Hence the extraordinarily firm unity of humanity] (NS II, 66). At this point Kafka again defines his difference from Christianity:

> Alles Leiden um uns werden auch wir leiden müssen. Christus hat für die Menschheit gelitten, aber die Menschheit muß für Christus leiden. Wir alle haben nicht einen Leib aber ein Wachstum und das führt uns durch alle Schmerzen, ob in dieser oder jener Form. So wie das Kind durch alle Lebensstadien bis zum Greis und zum Tod sich entwickelt — und jedes Stadium im Grunde dem vorigen Stadium im Verlangen oder in Furcht unerreichbar scheint — ebenso entwickeln wir uns — nicht weniger tief mit der Menschheit verbunden als mit uns selbst — durch alle Leiden dieser Welt gemeinsam mit allen Mitmenschen. Für Gerechtigkeit ist in diesem Zusammenhang kein Platz, aber auch nicht für Furcht vor den Leiden oder für die Auslegung des Leidens als eines Verdienstes. (NS II, 93–94)

> [We too shall have to suffer all the suffering around us. Christ suffered for mankind, but mankind must suffer for Christ. We all have, not one body, but one growth, and it leads us through all pains, whether in this or that form. As the child develops through all the stages of life to old age and death — and each stage basically seems unattainable to the preceding stage, whether in desire or fear — similarly we develop — no less deeply connected with mankind than with ourselves — through all the sufferings of this world, together with all our fellow-humans. In this context there is no place for justice, but nor is there one for fear of suffering, or for the interpretation of suffering as merit.]

Here Kafka relativizes the suffering of Christ. It is the task of each human being to assume Christ's role and share the suffering of the rest of humanity. And this ethical individualism, as it has been called, is realized in common with the rest of humanity.[29] Kafka implicitly denies St Paul's claim that all are members of the one body (Rom. 12.5). Instead, a shared process of development overcomes the isolation of the individual and brings about the messianic age. But Kafka undermines the various significances assigned by Judaism and Christianity to the figure of the Messiah, showing that the Messiah thus becomes superfluous:

> Der Messias wird kommen, bis der zügelloseste Individualismus des Glaubens möglich ist, niemand diese Möglichkeit vernichtet, niemand die Vernichtung duldet, also die Gräber sich öffnen. Das ist vielleicht auch die christliche Lehre, sowohl in der tatsächlichen Aufzeigung des Beispiels, als auch in

---

29 See Arnold Heidsieck, *The Intellectual Contexts of Kafka's Fiction: Philosophy, Law, Religion* (Columbia, SC: Camden House, 1994), pp. 132–39.

der symbolischen Aufzeigung der Auferstehung des Mittlers im einzelnen Menschen. (NS II, 55)

[The Messiah will come once the most unbridled individualism of faith is possible, nobody destroys this possibility, nobody tolerates its destruction, and thus the graves are opened. That is perhaps also the Christian doctrine, both in the actual displaying of the example and in the symbolic displaying of the resurrection of the mediator in the individual.]

There is, then, no need for a mediator like Christ to reconcile God with man. Kafka's impersonal divinity, the indestructible, is latent in every human being. To make contact with this imperishable essence is humanity's task, and when everyone does so human life will be transfigured. As a means to this goal, suffering is necessary and valuable:

Das Leiden ist das positive Element dieser Welt, ja es ist die einzige Verbindung zwischen dieser Welt und dem Positiven. Nur hier ist Leiden — Leiden. Nicht so als ob die welche hier leiden, anderswo wegen dieses Leidens erhöht werden sollen, sondern so, daß das was in dieser Welt Leiden heißt, in einer andern Welt, unverändert und nur befreit von seinem Gegensatz, Seligkeit ist. (NS II, 83)

[Suffering is the positive element in this world, indeed it is the only link between this world and the positive. Only here is suffering suffering. Not as though those who suffer here are elsewhere to be elevated because of this suffering; but what in this world is called suffering, in another world, unchanged and merely freed from its opposite, is bliss.]

In this hateful, prison-like world of pain, suffering connects us with higher reality. For we suffer because we are thrust down into this world. Our discomfort here reminds us that we belong to eternity. It is not the case that, as some Christians think, we shall be rewarded for our suffering here by corresponding happiness in the next world. Rather, in the next world the spiritual potential which makes us suffer here will be freed from confinement and make us happy.

Kafka is a highly individual and challenging religious thinker. His thought does not proceed within the framework of any one religion, but defines itself against a number of theologies and philosophies. That makes the historical understanding of Kafka a necessary but paradoxical exercise. For one simplifies Kafka and denies his originality and his eclecticism if one locates his thought within any religious system. Rewarding though it has been to see Kafka through lenses provided by Judaism, we need to see it only as one of the sources on which he drew for his highly personal intellectual and spiritual exploration.

CHAPTER 26

Alfred Döblin's Feeling for Snow: The Poetry of Fact in *Berge Meere und Giganten*

Some thirty-five years ago Klaus Müller-Salget said of *Berge Meere und Giganten* [*Mountains Seas and Giants*]: 'Es gehört heutzutage schon fast zum guten Ton, dieses (meist mit einem unterschobenen Komma zitierte) Buch mit abfälligen Bemerkungen zu bedenken' [Today it is almost a matter of propriety to make disparaging remarks about this book, usually citing it with an additional comma].[1] That has changed, thanks not only to the enthusiastic appreciation given by Müller-Salget in his chapter on this novel, but also to the minute and laborious research carried out by Gabriele Sander on its sources, its genesis and its imagery. Her book-length study of the novel and her recent edition, with extensive notes documenting the sources of Döblin's geographical and scientific information, are altogether invaluable.[2]

Döblin sets out to write the history of the future. It was not a unique endeavour. Two other attempts in English followed within a decade — Olaf Stapledon, *Last and First Men* (1930), and H. G. Wells, *The Shape of Things to Come* (1933). Wells's future history ends with the establishment of world government in 2106. Stapledon on the other hand follows the human race through a series of evolutionary and planned mutations which produce successive species, the last being the Eighteenth Men who live on the planet Neptune two thousand million years hence. By comparison, Döblin's undertaking is relatively unambitious. His novel begins at a point when the First World War has passed beyond living memory — 'Es lebte niemand mehr von denen, die den Krieg überstanden hatte, den man den Weltkrieg nannte' [None of the people who had survived the war called the World War was any longer alive] (BMG 13) — and the bulk of its action is set in the twenty-seventh century.

As Müller-Salget rightly points out, *Berge Meere und Giganten* is not an attempt to foretell likely events, and it would therefore be absurd to criticize it for making

1 Klaus Müller-Salget, *Alfred Döblin: Werk und Entwicklung* (Bonn: Bouvier, 1972), p. 201.
2 See Gabriele Sander, '*An die Grenzen des Wirklichen und Möglichen...*': Studien zu Alfred Döblins Roman 'Berge Meere und Giganten' (Frankfurt a.M.: Peter Lang, 1988); Alfred Döblin, *Berge Meere und Giganten: Roman*, ed. by Gabriele Sander (Düsseldorf: Walter, 2006). Unless otherwise indicated, all references to Döblin's novel (BMG) are to this edition.

inaccurate prophecies.[3] Nor is it, like some classic works about the future, a didactic exhortation to its readers to work for an ideal society which the text shows to be possible. Such works include William Morris's *News from Nowhere* (1890) and Theodor Herzl's *Altneuland* (1902) with its motto 'Wenn ihr wollt, ist es kein Märchen' [If you will it, it is not a fairy-tale]. Unlike Wells's rational World State, Morris's pastoral Socialist utopia or Herzl's tolerant Zionist state, Döblin's future world is more of a dystopia. Müller-Salget argues further that rather than a prophecy, it is partly at least an allegory, pointing to 'die ganz allegorische Struktur zumindest der letzten Bücher' [the entirely allegorical structure of at least the last books].[4] The concept of allegory, however, might be taken to imply that Döblin allows himself complete freedom of invention. Yet his central theme — man's urge to control nature, and nature's energetic, resourceful, and unpredictable resistance to human control — requires him to pay attention to the likely limits of technology and the actual behaviour of natural forces. As Gabriele Sander has shown, the knowledge of physical geography and geology that Döblin deploys in this novel is carefully researched and largely accurate. In his 'An Romanutoren und ihre Kritiker. Berliner Programm' (1913), attacking the concentration on psychology that he found characteristic of the contemporary novel, he called for 'Tatsachenphantasie', the factual imagination.[5] In *Berge Meere und Giganten* he deploys the factual imagination on a grand scale.

Döblin's respect for fact is important because it allows him to compensate for some of the difficulties involved in writing a novel about the future. The obvious difficulty — that we know nothing about the future — will not deter a writer with any imagination. But such a writer then falls prey to the real problem, namely, that the future is a blank screen onto which we can project what we like. The writer can imagine whatever he pleases. He lacks the imaginative constraints which are a precondition of fictional achievement. He risks playing a game in which there no rules and in which you therefore cannot lose, but you cannot win either.

Another difficulty is that Döblin, unlike Wells, sees no pattern in history and therefore cannot readily find any narrative structure for his events. The narrator of *Berge Meere und Giganten* declares that there is no meaning in history, merely 'das bekannte ganz ziellose Schaukeln der Weltgeschichte' [the well-known completely aimless to-and-fro of world history] (BMG 77), hence a succession of ebbs and flows in which individual motives count for little and there is only an unending struggle between man, technology, and nature. Technology appears as what Spengler in *Der Untergang des Abendlandes* called 'die faustische Technik, die mit dem vollen Pathos der dritten Dimension, und zwar von den frühesten Tagen der Gotik an auf die Natur eindringt, um sie zu beherrschen' [Faustian technology, which since the earliest Gothic period has imposed itself on nature with the full rhetorical force of the third dimension, in order to control it].[6] Both Spengler and

---

3 Müller-Salget, p. 210.
4 Müller-Salget, p. 210.
5 Döblin, *Schriften zu Ästhetik, Poetik und Literatur*, ed. by Erich Kleinschmidt (Olten: Walter, 1989), p. 123.
6 Oswald Spengler, *Der Untergang des Abendlandes: Umrisse einer Morphologie der Weltgeschichte*

Döblin see a self-destructive pattern within technical development. In Spengler's view, such development must eventually reduce man to the slave of the machine, leaving power in the hands of high finance. His *magnum opus* ends by foretelling that civilization will end in a conflict between the abstract power of money and the vital power of blood, in which the latter is bound to be the victor. Döblin formulates the destructive advance of technical progress in the sentence: 'Wilder als je erhob sich das Gespenst der neuen Erfindung, des vernichtenden Fortschritts' [More wildly than ever there arose the spectre of new invention, of destructive progress] (BMG 80). In the future he envisages, humanity congregates in vast cities called 'Stadtschaften'. After the invention of synthetic food by the scientist Meki in the twenty-sixth century, agriculture is abandoned and the zones between the cities become wildernesses. Synthetic food, however, symbolizes weariness with civilization. People do not like it, finding it too bland. Large numbers of settlers move to the land between the cities. It is to combat this 'Auslaufen der Städte' (BMG 283) that the London senator Francis Delvil proposes the creation of a new continent in the Arctic. Thus disgust with civilization leads to ever more grandiose applications of technology. Eventually cities are moved underground to avoid dangers on the surface of the earth: 'Ruhig gewaltig dehnten sich abgrundtief unter der Erde die neuen Städte mit den Menschen, das Lebendige von London Oxford Reading Colchester Hastings Ramsgate Luton Hertford Aldershot' [With quiet power the new cities with their people extended far below the earth, the life of London Reading Colchester Hastings Ramsgate Luton Hertford Aldershot] (BMG 522–23). Although the inhabitants regard this move underground as a technical miracle, feeling 'das Wunder des menschlichen Könnens' (BMG 523), it leads to outbreaks of mass hysteria ('Tanzwut und Liebesraserei'; BMG 530), even to a collective intoxication ('Rausch'; BMG 532) which induces people to offer themselves up as slaves. Mass violence has to be controlled by the police using electric prods or injections which often prove fatal. Döblin makes abundantly clear how destructive this dialectic of progress is.

Another difficulty in writing about the future, which Döblin does not entirely avoid, is that of parochialism. Novels ostensibly set in the future tend to be really about the present. Thus Anthony Burgess's *The Wanting Seed* (1962), set several centuries in the future when Greater London is bounded by the sea to south and east, is obviously about Britain in the early 1960s with high-rise flats and Commonwealth immigration. This need not matter if the novelist intends only to provide a satirical reflection on his own times; but since the future offers such a challenge to the imagination, it is a pity if a novel set in the future expresses only the parochial concerns of the decade in which it was written. Leo Kreutzer, in a hostile account of *Berge Meere und Giganten*, charges the novel with precisely this shortcoming: 'Durch seine hintergründig-politische Problematik erweist sich dieser "Zukunftsroman" als ebenso eng mit seiner Entstehungszeit verbunden wie Döblins gleichzeitiges naturphilosophisches Spekulieren' [Its obscure political

---

(Munich: dtv, 1972), p. 1186. Spengler's impact is mentioned by Winfried Georg Sebald, *Der Mythus der Zerstörung im Werk Döblins* (Stuttgart: Klett, 1980), p. 53.

problematic reveals this novel to be just as closely bound to the period of its composition as the speculations on the philosophy of nature that Döblin was engaging it at the same time].[7] To some extent, Döblin's future is indeed a distorted reflection of his present. David Midgley has summed up how much Döblin's future resembles Western Europe around 1920.[8] The 'Uralischer Krieg' [Ural War], in which large tracts of Russia are devastated by flames shot from mines, and huge numbers of troops are swept away, suggests the destruction wrought in the First World War, which Döblin observed as a doctor in a military hospital in Alsace. So does the war which later breaks out between Berlin under the consul Marduk and the 'Imperium' governed from London and New York. As in the First World War, Marduk is defending Berlin against 'England und Amerika' (BMG 261). Food shortages, crowds of refugees, atrocities, paramilitary forces ('Horden'), all suggest post-war Germany; the 'Völkerkreis' (BMG 291) suggests the Völkerbund or League of Nations. The invention of synthetic food recalls that of substitute foods during the wartime blockade of Germany. And the growth of cities into 'Stadtschaften' reflects the enormous expansion of German cities in Döblin's lifetime. In the novel, the 'ungeheure Stadtschaft' Hamburg in the twenty-seventh century incorporates Lübeck and Bremen (BMG 229), while Hannover has grown to include Braunschweig, Wolfenbüttel, Hildesheim and Celle (BMG 213).

In all these developments, Döblin extrapolates from his present with enough imagination to reduce the danger of parochialism. Where the novel appears dated is in its concentration on Western Europe. America features only seldom, though the Uralic War includes a naval campaign focusing on the Panama Canal. Disappointingly little is heard of the Indian-Chinese-Japanese civilization, described as one of the two world powers (BMG 49), but rarely in contact with the West, except as its antagonist in the Uralic War. However, much is said about Africa, in a strangely ambivalent way. As Gabriele Sander shows, Africa appears as a source of artistic creativity, almost as the unconscious counterpart of the hyper-conscious, over-technical Europe. Yet Africans are also presented in a manner that invites the epithet 'racist'. As Western fertility declines, perhaps through contact with radiation, that of African immigrants increases (BMG 20). They provide an underclass of industrial labourers, referred to as 'Plattgesichter' [flat-faces] (BMG 30). They are sexually attractive to women: Marion Divoise, one of the superwomen of the future, wants sex with a mulatto, yet feels disgust and self-contempt at her 'Schändung' by this 'Tier' [her violation by this animal] (BMG 169). Interbreeding ('Die afrikanische Durchflutung des europäischen Blutes' [The inundation of European blood by Africans]; p. 233) gives the Europeans a taste for cannibalism, so that in the war between Hamburg and Berlin, captives are devoured. The suggestion that cannibalism is an acquired and heritable genetic predisposition comes strangely from the trained medical scientist Döblin. His judgement in these passages may have been distorted by resentment against the French deployment

7 Leo Kreutzer, *Alfred Döblin: Sein Werk bis 1933* (Stuttgart, Berlin, Cologne, Mainz: Kohl-hammer, 1970), p. 95.
8 David Midgley, *Writing Weimar: Critical Realism in German Literature, 1918–1933* (Oxford: Oxford University Press, 2000), pp. 322–23.

of African troops in the War and in the post-war occupation of the Rhineland. Such racism occurs elsewhere in Döblin's writing. In February 1918 he wrote in the *Neue Rundschau*: 'Wir versprechen, wir werden selbst in unseren Reihen, in den Häusern, auf den Straßen diejenigen massakrieren, die nur einen Hauch von Friedensgesinnung dann äußern. Uns wird kein Hunger schlapp machen; das triumphierende Gesicht der Welschen, das Gejauchz der Senegalneger, die man gegen uns aufbietet, die heiseren Rufe der Briten halten uns bei Besinnung' [We promise that in our ranks, in houses, on the streets, we shall massacre those who so much as breathe of a peaceable disposition; the triumphant face of the Italians, the whooping of the Senegal negroes who are marshalled against us, the hoarse cries of the British will keep us alert].[9]

Another difficulty in writing about the future, which again Döblin does not entirely solve, is the lack of individual human interest. Opinions differ about the success with which Döblin has woven individual lives into his narrative. There is certainly some interest in the male bond between Marduk and Jonathan Hatton, and in the erotic contest of wills between Marduk and the powerful Marion Divoise, 'diesen Kampf des Mannstieres und Weibstieres' [this struggle between the man-beast and the woman-beast] as Döblin called it in a letter of 25 August 1922 to Efraim Frisch.[10] Reading about the volcanic passions of these supermen and superwomen, however, I must confess to feeling like the young man in Thomas Mann's 'Beim Propheten' who attends a reading from the apocalyptic tirades of the prophet Daniel and afterwards wonders: 'Was fehlt? Vielleicht das Menschliche? Ein wenig Gefühl, Sehnsucht, Liebe? Aber das ist eine vollständig improvisierte Hypothese' [What is missing? Perhaps humanity? A little emotion, yearning, love? But that's a hypothesis I've made up on the spur of the moment ...].[11]

If these episodes fail to command entire interest, however, it is not just because of the difficulty we may have in relating to the raging passions of Döblin's characters; there is also a problem of genre. Fiction that invites us to contemplate the remote

9 Döblin, *Schriften zur Politik und Gesellschaft*, ed. by Heinz Graber (Olten: Walter, 1972), p. 44. Note also the obsessive use of the word 'Nigger' in Döblin's review of Eugene O'Neill's play *The Emperor Jones*, '"Kaiser Jones"', in *Kleine Schriften*, ed. by Anthony Riley, 4 vols (Olten: Walter, 1985–2005), II, 352–56, published on 13 January 1924. The hypersexuality ascribed to the Africans recalls their portrayal in Filippo Marinetti's Futurist novel *Mafarka le futuriste*, to which Döblin refers in 'Reform des Romans' (1919): *Schriften zu Ästhetik, Poetik und Literatur*, p. 137. These racist slurs are notably absent from the science-fiction thriller by Hans Dominik, *Atlantis* (Leipzig: Scherl, 1925), which in other respects resembles *Berge Meere und Giganten* so closely as to arouse the suspicion of instant plagiarism. In 2002, the Emperor of Central Africa has discovered an inexhaustible supply of carbide deep under the Sahara; this source of energy will enable him to end the dominance of the white race, so a heroic German engineer forestalls such a catastrophe by blowing up the mine. Though presented as a danger to Europe, the Emperor is treated with respect as a 'black Napoleon', and the villain of the story is an American entrepreneur who, by setting off explosions along the Panama Canal, intends to fuse the Atlantic with the Pacific, thus diverting the Gulf Stream and causing Northern Europe to freeze over. Döblin's and Dominik's novels are compared by Volker Klotz in his 'Nachwort' to *Berge Meere und Giganten* (Olten and Freiburg i.Br.: Walter, 1977), pp. 515–39 (pp. 525–32).

10 Döblin, *Briefe*, ed. by Heinz Graber (Olten: Walter, 1970), p. 122.

11 Thomas Mann, 'Beim Propheten', in *Gesammelte Werke*, 13 vols (Frankfurt a.M.: Fischer, 1974), VIII, p. 370.

past or the remote future cannot accommodate the actions of plausible characters without undoing the effect of temporal distance that it strives to create. If we look down the vistas of the future, and discover at the end of them individuals like ourselves, we feel cheated; while if we discover individuals unlike ourselves, we cannot relate to them. There are two ways round this. One is to make individuals symbolic, as Döblin successfully does with Kylin, Venaska and Diuwa in the last section of the novel, where a symbolic reconciliation between humanity and nature is adumbrated. The other is to avoid individuals altogether. This is the choice generally made in science fiction, where characters, even if they have names, are merely instruments to present us with a hypothesis concerning the effects of technical change. The unnamed narrator in Wells's *The War of the Worlds*, for example, is of no interest in his own right; he merely typifies a civilized man who returns to savagery when the civilization that has supported him collapses. When Döblin imagines the sociological developments of the future, he has no need to anchor them to individual experiences. For example, we are told briefly and in general terms how a few centuries hence the family declines and woman, who are stronger and more brutal than men, form 'Frauenbünde',[12] and regulate the production and upbringing of children (BMG 79). They are intent on changing women's capacity for child-bearing from a weakness into a strength, and they realize that their control of childbirth, and hence of the population, is a powerful weapon against men. Indeed they are considering the possibility of exterminating the male sex, apart from the small number required for breeding purposes, when a flood of new inventions puts an end to their plans by bringing about the Uralic War and its consequences. All this is fascinating, and has no need to be embodied in a story about individuals. Döblin was anxious to avoid the merely personal concerns which in his view had no place in epic: 'Ich bin ein Feind des Persönlichen. Es ist nichts als Schwindel und Lyrik damit. Zum Epischen taugen Einzelpersonen und ihre sogenannten Schicksale nicht' [I am hostile to the personal. There's nothing to it but dishonesty and poetry. Individuals and their so-called destinies are not fit for epic].[13]

The central achievement of this book, I would want to argue, is its relegation of human life to the sidelines and its concentration on the poetry of fact. This is consistent with Döblin's attacks on an outworn, merely bookish humanism, his disapproval of psychology, and his desire to escape from merely human concerns: 'Die Erde muß wieder dampfen. Los vom Menschen!' [The earth must steam again. Away from man!].[14] The factual imagination and the poetry of science abound in the two central chapters, the first that Döblin wrote, recounting how the technocrats of the future harness the volcanic fires of Iceland to melt the ice of

---

12   No English translation ('women's groups', 'women's organizations') quite conveys the force of this word. It is modelled on 'Männerbünde', a heavily charged term in the gender discussions of early twentieth-century Germany, implying a tight-knit, all-male organization. See Bernd Widdig, *Männerbünde und Massen: Zur Krise männlicher Identität in der Literatur der Moderne* (Opladen: Westdeutscher Verlag, 1992).

13   Döblin, *Schriften zu Leben und Werk*, ed. by Erich Kleinschmidt (Olten: Walter, 1986), p. 56.

14   Döblin, *Schriften zu Ästhetik, Poetik und Literatur*, p. 123.

Greenland and thus create a new continent for humanity to inhabit — an enterprise which of course goes horribly wrong.

As a sample of Döblin's poetry of scientific fact, we may consider this passage from early in the chapter about Iceland. The volcanologists' fleet is assembling at the Shetland Islands. Döblin begins with an evocation of geology by describing the North Atlantic seabed:

> Das atlantische Wasser schwemmte zwischen den langgezogenen Küsten Amerikas und denen der östlichen Kontinente. In die ungeheure Spalte zwischen den auseinandergezerrten Erden warf es seine flüssigen Massen. Die Gneisgebirge von Kanada und Labrador jenseits waren gelöst von den schottischen Bergen. Zerfetzt zerbröckelt standen die Inseln an der schottischen Spitze, Shetland und Orkney. Hundert Inseln die Shetlands. Sie stiegen aus dem bleiernen rollenden Wasser auf der unterirdischen Scholle auf, die die irische Erde, das gebirgebestandene englische Hochland, die Ebenen des Südens trug. Nach den Shetlands nahmen die Schiffe der westlichen Stadtreiche ihren Kurs. (BMG 365)

> [The water of the Atlantic flooded between the long coasts of America and those of the eastern continents. It threw its fluid masses into the huge crack between the earths that had been dragged asunder. The gneiss mountains of Canada and Labrador were separated from the Scottish mountains. Tattered, shattered, stood the islands at the tip of Scotland: Shetland and Orkney. A hundred islands the Shetlands. They rose out of the leaden rolling water upon the subterranean soil that bore the earth of Ireland, the mountain-rimmed English uplands, the plains of the south. It was to the Shetlands that the ships of the western city-kingdoms took their course.]

This piece of writing shows its anti-humanist or post-humanist character by its remoteness from any imaginable human viewpoint. Nobody is actually looking at the North Atlantic; we are not invited to share the standpoint of any conceivable spectator. The sheer expanse that Döblin evokes between the continents is too vast for the eye to command. Instead, agency is transferred from humanity to natural forces: the water of the Atlantic, actively pouring through its channels, is itself the subject of the first two sentences. The third collapses the present into the remote past by evoking the process of continental drift in which Canada separated from Scotland. The Shetlands are then seen, not in relation to a human observer, but in relation to the geological substrate on which they stand, along with the rest of the British Isles. Only then does Döblin give us a more manageable perspective by guiding our gaze over Ireland and Northern and Southern England, though he still asks us to imagine them in geological, not human terms. Physical geography, rather than human geography, governs the factual imagination of these chapters. Finally we home in on the volcanologists' fleet as it heads for the Shetlands, though Döblin retains a sense of huge dimensions by reminding us that the fleet comes from all the city-states of the West.

The poetry of geology is again evoked in the descriptions of the basalt bed of the Atlantic, the Icelandic volcanoes, and also, near the beginning of the book, the Tibesti plateau in the Sahara and, at the start of the last book, the landscape of south-western France. By celebrating the poetry of geology, Döblin places himself at the furthest possible remove from the humanism he repudiated. In annexing geology for the imagination, he has such unlikely predecessors as Annette von Droste-Hülshoff in her poem 'Die Mergelgrube' and Alfred Tennyson in *In Memoriam*: both responded with a mixture of excitement and apprehension to the new geology and its drastically revised estimate of the age of the earth.[15] And he joins hands unwittingly with a near-contemporary, the Scottish poet Hugh MacDiarmid (the pseudonym of C. M. Grieve). Grieve was persuaded in the 1930s to move to the Shetlands by friends who hoped that isolation would help him to overcome his drink problem. It did at least produce two remarkable geological poems, 'On a Raised Beach' and 'Stony Limits', which seek to extend the range of the imagination by including technical scientific vocabulary. The former begins:

> All is lithogenesis — or lochia,
> Carpolite fruit of the forbidden tree,
> Stones blacker than any in the Caaba,
> Cream-coloured caen-stone, chatoyant pieces,
> Celadon and corbeau, bistre and beige
> Glaucous, hoar, enfouldered, cyathiform,
> Making mere faculae of the sun and moon [...][16]

This is less formidable than it looks. A little work with the *Shorter Oxford Dictionary* will explain the technical terms. But as one assimilates them, one comes to appreciate a form of writing with the minimum of familiar emotional associations. This again is post-humanist writing. It invites us to apprehend the world in a neutral, factual manner, and to accept that 'all is lithogenesis', i.e. that the emergence of stone is the primal event from which everything else follows and which relativizes everything else. The second and third lines convey economically that central symbols of Christianity, Judaism and Islam are mere by-products of geology. Human life, as we experience it, comes to seem a mere insignificant disturbance on the unimaginably ancient bedrock of the world.

The masterpiece of Döblin's scientific imagination is the virtuoso passage, published separately in 1925 as 'Der Erdball' [The Globe], which describes the magma at the earth's core and then the layout of the landmasses:

> Breit besetzt der Leib Asiens die nördliche Hälfte der Erde, mit einhundertvierundsechzig Längengraden und siebenundachtzig Breitengraden. Mit Gondwana, Angara, der Scholle Chinas hat es sich über den Spiegel der großen Ozeane erhoben, seine Seen ließ es versickern. Sein Rückgrat ist der Altai, das Massiv des Himalaya vom Chingan nach Pamir, vom Karakorum bis Bhutan und zur Krümmung des Dihong. Die kaspische und uralische Senkung hat das Meer verlassen; sie saugt den Ural und die Wolga an, schlammt sich mit ihnen voll. Gletscher bedecken den Kuenlun. Umrandet von den

15 See Ritchie Robertson, 'Faith and Fossils: Annette von Droste-Hülshoff's Poem "Die Mergelgrube"', in *Das schwierige 19. Jahrhundert: Germanistische Tagung zum 65. Geburtstag von Eda Sagarra im August 1998*, ed. by Jürgen Barkhoff, Gilbert J. Carr and Roger Paulin (Tübingen: Niemeyer, 2000), pp. 345–54 (now in this volume).

16 Hugh MacDiarmid, *Complete Poems, 1920–1976*, ed. by Michael Grieve and W. R. Aitken, 2 vols (London: Martin Brian & O'Keeffe, 1978), I, 422.

Schneegebirgen sind die östlichen Sandwüsten, das Tibet der Jaks, die grünen Hugel und Lößflächen Chinas, mandschurische Wiesen. (BMG 369)

[The broad body of Asia occupies the northern half of the Earth with a hundred and sixty-four degrees of longitude and eighty-seven of latitude. With Gondwana, Angara, the soil of China, it rose above the level of the great oceans and let its lakes trickle away. Its backbone is the Altai, the massif of the Himalayas from Chingan to Pamir, from the Karakorum to Bhutan and the bend of the Dihong. The sea has left the Caspian and Ural depression; it sucks the Ural and the Volga and fills itself with their mud. Glaciers cover the Kunlun. Snowy mountains border the eastern sandy desert, the Tibet of yaks, the green hills and loess plains of China, Manchurian meadows.]

This evocation of the vastness of Asia, of which I have quoted only part, challenges comparison with the epic tradition which Döblin wanted to rejoin. It may, for example, recall the geographical digressions of which Milton is so fond in *Paradise Lost*, and which continually remind us that the fate of the entire human race, eventually to be scattered over the terrestrial globe, is at stake. But a closer parallel would be with Melville's epic novel *Moby Dick*. Captain Ahab's quest for the white whale — itself a combat between Promethean humanity and nature — takes his ship, the Pequod, over much of the world's oceans. Setting out from Nantucket, the whalers sail down the Atlantic and spend some time south of the Cape of Good Hope before crossing the Indian Ocean, where they pass a great armada of sperm-whales at the straits separating Sumatra from Java. Ahab intends to head past the Philippines to the coast of Japan, where sperm whales gather, and then to descend to the equatorial zone of the Pacific, where he does indeed encounter Moby Dick.[17] Melville evokes the vastness of the world's oceans with a global sweep surpassed only by Döblin.

Moreover, Döblin goes beyond the human in evoking an epic conflict between the elements of fire and water, when the heat released from the Icelandic volcanoes meets the North Atlantic (BMG 479–83). Here again he recalls Melville, where Ahab is associated with fire, not only by the repeated references to Prometheus but also by the presence aboard the Pequod of the Parsee fire-worshipper Fedallah, and is in conflict with the element of water whose greatest inhabitant is the white whale.

All these passages in Döblin are based on careful study of topographical and geological works, mostly done with great intensity in a four-week period early in 1922 which Döblin took off from his medical practice in order to press on with the Iceland and Greenland chapters of his opus. 'Ich zeichnete Spezialkarten von Island, trieb Vulkan- und Erdbebenkunde. Es ging rasch ins Geologische und Mineralogisch-petrographische' [I drew technical maps of Iceland, studied volcanology and seismology. This rapidly led me into geology, mineralogy and petrography].[18] The geography of Iceland is handled with particular care. Döblin's scientists concentrate their efforts on the desolate north-east of the island,

17 Herman Melville, *Redburn, White-Jacket, Moby-Dick*, Library of America (New York: Viking, 1983), p. 1200.
18 Döblin, *Schriften zu Leben und Werk*, p. 53.

beginning with the volcanoes Krabla and Leirhukr, then moving down to the central wasteland called Odadahraun which Döblin correctly translates as 'Wüste der Missetaten', desert of crimes (so named because outlaws used to hide out there), and finally attacking the major volcano Hekla. If, as I did while reading it, you have a map of Iceland beside you, you can follow their movements with precision. What Döblin called 'Tatsachenphantasie' is remarkably faithful to fact.

There are, nevertheless, a few curious deviations. As the volcanologists sail northwards from the Shetlands, Döblin revels in what must seem the islands' exotic names:

> Da ließen die zweihundert ersten Fahrzeuge den sechzigsten Meridian, die steilen Abhänge des Sumburgh Head. Nach einer Stunde verschwand der Gipfel des Ronas auf Mainland. Das Surren und Schwirren der letzten Vogelberge verklang. Hinter ihnen lagen Muckle Roe und Foula, die zackigen Inseln Yell Haskosea Samphrey Fetlar Uyea Unst. (BMG 366)

> [The first two hundred vessels then left the sixtieth meridian, the steep slopes of Sumburgh Head. After an hour the peak of Rona on Mainland disappeared. The noise and fluttering of the last bird-cliffs died away. Behind them lay Muckle Roe and Foula, the jagged islands of Yell Haskosea Samphrey Fetlar Uyea Unst.]

These names are correct, but in the first edition they were travestied. Sumburgh Head was 'Simburg Haad', Muckle Roe and Foula became 'Munkle Roon und Toul', and the last three names were changed to 'Fellar Uya Umst'.[19] The faulty versions survived in the edition published in 1977 by the Walter-Verlag, which admitted to following the first edition, except that another mistake was introduced: Yell, originally spelt correctly, acquired an intrusive h ('Yhell'). In Gabriele Sander's edition these mistakes, and a few others, have been silently corrected. Presumably the original mistakes can be attributed to a mixture of inaccurate transcription, faulty printing, and careless proofreading. It has sometimes been a matter of controversy whether factual mistakes in fiction should be silently amended by editors. Max Brod, for example, corrected Kafka's spelling 'Oklahama' to 'Oklahoma'. By doing so he obscured the intriguing link with a picture in one of Kafka's sources showing a black being lynched and captioned 'Idyll in Oklahama'.[20] Generally, therefore, one should be cautious. But in Döblin's case, given his acknowledged respect for fact and the extreme ease with which unfamiliar names can be mangled by printers, it was right to amend the toponymic errors. The value Döblin placed on accuracy is apparent from the letter he wrote on 1 September 1923 to the nature poet Wilhelm Lehmann about his book:

> Und ich glaube, daß Sie, der Naturfreund, an diesem 'Sang' an die große Natur Freude haben werden. In mir habe ich diesen Hang zu der ausgebreiteten stummen organischen und anorganischen Natur erst seit ein paar Jahren bemerkt, entdeckt; der Hang führt mich stark in mystische Gefilde, aber man bändigt es immer wieder mit der Exaktheit.[21]

19 See Döblin, *Berge Meere und Giganten: Roman* (Berlin: Fischer, 1924), p. 342.
20 See Hartmut Binder, *Kafka-Kommentar zu den Romanen, Rezensionen, Aphorismen und zum Brief an den Vater* (Munich: Winkler, 1976), p. 156.
21 Döblin, *Briefe*, pp. 123–24.

[And I think that you, a lover of nature, will take pleasure in this 'hymn' to great nature. It's only in the last couple of years that I've noticed — discovered — in myself this leaning towards extensive, silent, organic and inorganic nature; the leaning is leading me into mystical territories, but one always keeps it under control by means of precision.]

Here Döblin is extending to the non-human world the ideal of factual precision imported into fiction by Naturalism.

Not all the novel, of course, is controlled by scientific precision. There does seem to be some scientific basis to the method by which Döblin imagines his volcano-logists extracting the volcanic fires of Iceland: they store the energy in tourmaline veils, and, as Gabriele Sander notes (BMG 744–45), Döblin knew about the electro-magnetic properties of tourmaline, a mineral compound containing aluminium, which when heated divides into positive and negative electric poles. When they have surrounded Greenland with a ring of ships and cast the tourmaline over the icecap in nets, however, the novel moves from science fiction to science fantasy. Not only does Greenland split in two, but the heat rapidly transforms it into a prehistoric, Cretaceous or Jurassic landscape with a population of dinosaurs, among which we can recognize the triceratops and the pterodactyl. These monsters then attack northern Europe, and in defence the ruling elites turn some of their members into giants which, placed strategically on various Scottish mountains, attract and destroy the dinosaurs. The scientists' experiments apparently enable them to change their shape at will, so that one of them, Kuraggara (formerly Mrs Macfarlane), turns herself first into a bat and then into a kangaroo. Here Döblin's imagination risks declining into whimsy.

At its best, Döblin's 'Tatsachenphantasie' breaks with the narrowly bookish classical humanism that he deplored and succeeds in making the truths of natural science available to the imagination. His achievement can be placed alongside Thomas Mann's presentation of medical and biological data in *Der Zauberberg* and Robert Musil's attempt to combine precision and soul ('Genauigkeit und Seele') in *Der Mann ohne Eigenschaften*.[22] But with Mann we have to differentiate. Although Mann integrates scientific knowledge into *Der Zauberberg*, he is relatively conservative in the kind of aesthetic response he seeks from the reader. He does take Hans Castorp to the verge of the non-human world. The situation of the Berghof, 6000 feet above the 'Flachland', permits detachment from ordinary human concerns, as does the seven-year holiday from life that Castorp takes as a presumed invalid. The chapter 'Schnee' takes him into a non-human landscape in which he cannot orient himself. His illness also gives him a new, medical perspective on his body. But the information about physiology and biology that Castorp absorbs on his balcony is presented in an aesthetically enjoyable style and thus drawn back into a traditional humanism that assigns primacy to words over things. *Doktor Faustus* marks a step forward: the humanism professed by Zeitblom is narrowly bookish and pedantic, with an explicit distaste for the revelations of modern science, whereas the

22   Robert Musil, *Gesammelte Werke*, ed. by Adolf Frisé, 9 vols (Reinbek: Rowohlt, 1978), II, 583.

post-humanist Leverkühn teases Zeitblom by claiming to have made journeys into space and to the depths of the sea, and expresses his response to the vast non-human cosmos in his composition 'Die Wunder des Alls'.[23] The novel holds the balance between Zeitblom's timorous adherence to an arguably outworn humanism and Leverkühn's attraction to the non-human which suggests a disturbing affinity with the sheer inhumanity espoused by the Nazis and by their fellow-travellers such as the intellectuals of the Kridwiss circle.

As a more recent example of post-humanist fiction, Peter Høeg's *Miss Smilla's Feeling for Snow* offers itself, especially as, like Döblin's novel, it centres on an expedition to Greenland.[24] Its protagonist and narrator. Smilla Jaspersen, is the daughter of a Dane and a Greenlander (Eskimo or Inuit), who lives in Copenhagen and has a scientific training; she has written among other things a compendium for students entitled *Main Characteristics of the Glacial Morphology of North Greenland*. Suspicious about the activities of the Danish Cryolite Corporation, she manages to smuggle herself aboard a ship that it is sending to Greenland. The purpose of the voyage, it turns out, is to retrieve a meteorite that landed some 65 million years ago on an island off the west coast of Greenland. Why this meteorite is so valuable, and so dangerous, emerges only at the end of the novel. Along the way we learn much about the history and sociology of the Greenlanders, about neo-catastrophe theory which postulates that major changes in the biology of the earth may be due to catastrophes such as meteor contact, about glaciation, pack-ice, and much else to do with the Arctic.

The novel is not anti-humanist in the sense of being hostile or indifferent to emotion. Smilla Jaspersen is angry at the hardships suffered by Greenlanders in Danish society, and it is the unexplained death of a Greenlander child that sets her on the investigation which ultimately leads her to the mystery concealed on the coast of Greenland. But she is also a person who fits uneasily into society; she has been expelled from many institutions; and though she has a lover, she usually refers to him simply as 'the mechanic' rather than by name. This detachment from conventional human concerns goes with Smilla's dedication to science. The novel is remarkable because it incorporates scientific information so smoothly into its narrative and because it admits us to a consciousness which is certainly not unemotional but for which things are important and interesting alongside people. Thus it marks a move away from humanism, not towards inhumanity, but towards a cooler, more detached view of the world.

Such detachment implies a reassessment of man's place in the world. The novels by Döblin and Høeg remind us that man is not the centre of a divine cosmos but simply a phenomenon, an unruly and destructive one, within the unimaginably larger system of nature. Both evoke the possibility that human life may be destroyed, either by man's damaging effect on his environment, or as the by-product of a cosmic accident. Döblin's novel about man's technological assault on the Arctic

---

23   On Mann's use of science, see Malte Herwig, *Bildungsbürger auf Abwegen: Naturwissenschaft im Werk Thomas Manns* (Frankfurt a.M.: Klostermann, 2004).

24   Peter Høeg, *Miss Smilla's Feeling for Snow*, trans. by F. David (London: Harvill, 1993); first published as *Frøken Smillas Fornemmelse for Sne* (Copenhagen: Rosinante/Munksgaard, 1993).

inevitably reminds us of the present-day effects of technical civilization on the polar ice-caps and on the natural environment generally.[25] It prompts the reflection that although we sometimes talk casually or saving or destroying the planet, we cannot destroy the planet, though we can destroy the prospects of a viable life for our grandchildren. Even, or especially, if humanity should be swept away, the planet itself will be regenerated. A fine passage describes how the Russian steppe, twenty-five years after the devastation of the Uralic War, is being regenerated by the forces of nature:

> Zerstreute Menschenherden schoben sich über die öden Flächen der Kontinente. Ein besonderes trübes Verlangen trieb Massen aus gestopft vollen Stadtschaften nach Osten in die russische verwüstete Ebene. [...] Die weite Tiefebene hauchte nicht mehr Gas. Regen Wind Schnee Sonne hatten lange Jahre gearbeitet. Über einem abenteuerlich dünn übergrünten Friedhof fuhren und gingen sie. Gerste Roggen wuchs in wilden Halmen. In das verstümmelte Riesengebiet, das von Wassern sprudelte, über das der Wolgastrom der Don Dnjepr ausgekentert war, waren Pflanzenkeime, leicht schlafende Wesen, den Menschen und Tieren vorausgeeilt. Pilze, kurze stämmige Boviste und Erdsterne hatten sich an den südlichen Flußmündungen, an den Meeren und Sümpfen geöffnet, Herbststürme trugen die leichten Kugeln in das wüste nördliche Land, streuten ihr Sporenpulver auf den losen nackten Boden. (BMG 227–28)

> [Scattered human herds trailed across the waste spaces of the continents. A particular sombre urge drove masses out of the crammed city-states eastwards into the devastated Russian plain [...]. The broad plain no longer smelt of gas. Rain wind snow sun had been at work for long years. They passed over a cemetery covered with an astonishingly thin layer of green. Barley rye grew in wild stalks. Plant seeds, lightly sleeping, had hastened ahead of men and animals into the huge mutilated territory, full of fountains, over which the Volga river the Don Dnieper had spilled their waters. Mushrooms, short stocky puffballs and earthstars, had opened at the southern river delta, at the seas and marshes, autumn gales carried the light globules into the desolate northern land, strewed the powder of their spores on the loose naked soil.]

This passage stands out by its quietness. Avoiding the Expressionist violence Döblin usually favours, it focuses on the tiny details, the seeds and spores, that are bringing the devastated steppe back to life. Instead of clashes among the elements, we have here the steady processes of growth and renewal which appeal equally to the factual imagination and are equally outside the limits of human control.

25   As I write, news comes that the melting of the Greenland ice sheet has produced a new island, previously connected by ice to the east coast of Greenland, but now a distinct piece of land: *Independent*, 24 April 2007.

CHAPTER 27

'My True Enemy':
Freud and the Catholic Church, 1927–1939

In 1937, a few months before the absorption of Austria into Greater Germany, Freud told a visitor, René Laforgue, that he was not afraid of the Nazis. 'Help me rather,' he said, 'to combat my true enemy.' When Laforgue asked who this 'enemy' was, Freud astonished him by replying: 'Religion, the Roman Catholic Church.'[1]

Moreover, Freud believed himself to have a dangerous enemy in the person of one Father Wilhelm Schmidt, who is mentioned in the correspondence with Arnold Zweig, once as Freud's enemy and once as a person of great power in the Austrian corporate state (*Ständestaat*). This paper is intended to suggest Schmidt's importance in the culture and politics of Austria in the 1930s and earlier; to account for Freud's antipathy to him; and to argue that Freud's last major work, *Moses and Monotheism*, is a covert and complex response to Schmidt's own theory of monotheism.

Freud's antipathy to religion in general is well known. Growing up as a Jew in a largely Catholic country, he absorbed many secular and anticlerical ideas. Some of these influences have recently been mentioned by Peter Gay, who points out how much Freud was pursuing the ideals of the Enlightenment through his scientific career.[2] His youthful heroes were scientists like Darwin, Huxley and Tyndall. He read the anticlerical historians Lecky and Buckle. He first declared his open opposition to religion in *Totem and Taboo*, where it is explained as originating, along with all other cultural achievements, in the Oedipus complex. He explored the topic further in *The Future of an Illusion*, proposing an evolutionary view of religion as a primitive survival to be replaced by science, and ending his peroration with a quotation from Heine:

> Den Himmel überlassen wir
> Den Engeln und den Spatzen.[3]

1   René Laforgue, 'Personal Memories of Freud', in *Freud as we knew him*, ed. by Hendrik M. Ruitenbeek (Detroit, MI: Wayne State University Press, 1973), pp. 341–49 (p. 344).

2   See Peter Gay, *A Godless Jew: Freud, Atheism, and the Making of Psychoanalysis* (New Haven, CT, and London: Yale University Press, 1987). Schmidt's importance to Freud is acknowledged by several references in Ernest Jones, *Sigmund Freud: Life and Work*, 3 vols (London: Hogarth Press, 1953–57), III, but goes unmentioned Gay's biography *Freud: A Life for our Time* (London: Dent, 1988).

3   'Heaven we'll leave to the angels and the sparrows' (from Heine, *Deutschland: Ein Wintermärchen*, Caput I); *The Standard Edition of the Complete Psychological Works of Sigmund Freud*, trans. by James Strachey et al., 24 vols (London: The Hogarth Press, 1953–74), XXI, 50.

The delusions of religion were once more set against the concrete achievements of science in 1932, in the last of Freud's second series of *Introductory Lectures on Psychoanalysis*. Here he notes that psychoanalysis is not just a technique of research and therapy. It presupposes a *Weltanschauung*, namely that of science. Freud sums up the scientific world-view as a programme of rigorous scepticism which dismisses revelation or intuition as sources of knowledge. He acknowledges that science most often has no answer to suffering. But then neither has religion, except a delusory one which must always be contradicted by harsh experience. Freud hopes that mankind will mature enough to discard religion and submit to the dictatorship of reason: 'Our best hope for the future is that the intellect — the scientific spirit, reason — will in time establish a dictatorship in man's psychic life.'[4]

Given these views Freud could hardly be at ease in the actual dictatorship ruled by Dollfuss. The Austrian corporate state represented an extreme reaction against the period of Liberalism in which Freud had grown up. It was dominated by the Catholic Church and drew on long-established conservative and antisemitic traditions. Its corporatist programme was an amalgam of traditions of Catholic and conservative political thought, opposed to what was seen as the atomizing and secularizing influence of liberal capitalism. One such tradition was 'social policy' (*Sozialpolitik*), represented by the Papal Encyclical 'Rerum novarum', which accepted the existing social order but wished to modify it by legislation to remove its harshness. The other was 'social reform' (*Sozialreform*), represented by the reactionary thinker Karl von Vogelsang and his successor Othmar Spann, who wanted society to be reorganized on feudal lines, all economic activity to be brought under state control, and the state to be closely linked with the Church.[5] At the first mass rally of the Fatherland Front (*Vaterländische Front*) on 11 September 1933, Dollfuss proclaimed the corporatist reorganization of the state and contributed to a conservative and Catholic definition of Austrian identity that implicitly excluded Jews. After glancing over the glories of Austrian history, he deplored the decline of feudal society and the rise of liberalism, soulless materialism, and unrestrained capitalism. He promised to roll back liberal democracy, replacing the ineffectual hegemony of political parties with the mass movement represented by the Vaterländische Front. He concluded: 'We want the social, Christian, German state of Austria on a corporate basis and under strong, authoritarian leadership!'[6]

The *Ständestaat*, however, avoided explicitly endorsing antisemitism, partly in order to distance itself from National Socialism. Moreover, the antisemitism current in Austria was not of the National Socialist variety, based on pseudo-scientific theories of race. It was primarily a Christian abhorrence of Jews as the people responsible for Christ's death, overlaid with the hostility of peasants and urban petty-bourgeois to the Jew seen as the embodiment of capitalism, and combined,

---

4   Ibid., XXII, 171.

5   See Alfred Diamant, *Austrian Catholics and the First Republic: Democracy, Capitalism, and the Social Order, 1918–1934* (Princeton, NJ: Princeton University Press, 1960).

6   'Wir wollen das neue Österreich', in *Dollfuß an Österreich: Eines Mannes Wort und Ziel*, ed. by Hofrat Edmund Weber (Vienna: Reinhold, 1935), p. 31.

at a higher social level, with resentment against Jewish competition for professional appointments.[7]

The Catholic and anti-capitalist version of antisemitism was formulated on 21 January 1933 in a pastoral letter from the Bishop of Linz. He condemned the racial doctrines of the National Socialists as well as all pogroms and other manifestations of antisemitism and disrespect for the Jewish religion. But he was also roused to anger by 'the international Jewish spirit', which, he said, dominated modern cultural and commercial life. 'Degenerate Jewry in alliance with world Freemasonry,' he proclaimed, 'is also the principal bearer of mammonistic capitalism and the principal founder and apostle of Socialism and Communism, the harbingers and pacemakers of Bolshevism.' To destroy the harmful influence of the Jews was the duty of every Christian. The Bishop referred with evident approval to the ghettos which had been set up in Italian cities during the Counter-Reformation and recommended that his contemporaries should 'erect a strong legislative and administrative barrier against all the spiritual filth and the immoral slimy flood, emanating principally from Jewry, which threatens to overwhelm the world'.[8]

Such public utterances help to explain why Freud was reluctant to publish his essay in Biblical criticism, *Moses and Monotheism*, for fear of arousing Catholic enmity. He gives his reasons in a letter to Arnold Zweig on 30 October 1934:

> We live here in an atmosphere of Catholic orthodoxy. They say that the politics of our country are determined by one Pater Schmidt, who lives in St Gabriel near Mödling. He is a confidant of the Pope, and unfortunately he is himself an ethnologist and student of comparative religion, whose books make no secret of his abhorrence of analysis and especially of my totem theory.[9]

Freud added that the journal of psychoanalysis recently founded in Rome had suddenly been banned, and that the ban was thought to have come direct from the Vatican and to have been instigated by Father Schmidt. If Freud were to irritate this person further, his influence in Austria might be used to outlaw psychoanalysis on its home ground. Later, in the prefatory note to part III of *Der Mann Moses*, Freud explained hat he had withheld the work from publication because the Catholicism of the Austrian corporate state was the last bulwark against the various barbarisms of Germany, Italy and Russia, and since Catholicism already viewed psychoanalysis with distrust he could not risk strengthening its suspicion.[10] In a later letter to Zweig he again referred to Schmidt: 'And I count it to my credit that our archenemy P.

---

7 See John Bunzl and Bernd Marin, *Antisemitismus in Österreich: Sozialhistorische und soziologische Studien* (Innsbruck: Inn-Verlag, 1983); Ivar Oxaal, Michael Pollak and Gerhard Botz (eds.), *Jews, Antisemitism and Culture in Vienna* (London: Routledge & Kegan Paul, 1987).

8 'Hirtenbrief des Bischofs Gföllner', in Emmerich Czermak and Oskar Karbach, *Ordnung in der Judenfrage* (4. Sonderheft der *Berichte zur Kultur- und Zeitgeschichte*, ed. by Nikolaus Hovorka (Vienna: Reinhold, 1934)), pp. 138–39. On Catholic antisemitism, I have found the following indispensable: Hermann Greive, *Theologie und Ideologie: Katholizismus und Judentum in Deutschland und Österreich, 1918–1935* (Heidelberg: Schneider, 1969); Erika Weinzierl-Fischer, 'Österreichs Katholiken und der Nationalsozialismus', *Wort und Wahrheit*, 18 (1963), 417–39, 493–526.

9 *The Letters of Sigmund Freud and Arnold Zweig*, ed. by Ernst L. Freud, trans. by W. and E. Robson-Scott (London: Hogarth Press, 1970), p. 92.

10 *Standard Edition*, XXIII, 57.

Schmidt has just been awarded the Austrian decoration of honour for his pious lies in the field of ethnology. Clearly this is meant to console him for the fact that providence has allowed me to achieve the age of 80.'[11]

Although Father Schmidt's name will be familiar to many Austrians, few people in the English-speaking world are likely to have heard of him. Yet in his time he was an anthropologist of world-wide reputation, and the few available glimpses of his political career suggest that he wielded considerable backstairs influence as early as the last years of the Habsburg Empire.[12]

Wilhelm Schmidt was not an Austrian, but a German. He was born at Hörde, in industrial Westphalia, in 1868, the son of a factory worker. While still in his teens he joined the missionary society called the Societas Verbi Divini, and much of his life was spent studying and later teaching at its seminary in St Gabriel on the edge of Mödling, near Vienna. From 1925 to 1938 he was also professor of anthropology at Vienna University. He founded the Anthropos Institute for anthropology, and was also involved in establishing the Museum für Völkerkunde in Vienna. In 1925 he helped to organize an exhibition of missionary work in Rome, and was appointed by the Pope as Director of the Museo missionario etnologico. In 1928 he was honoured by a huge Festschrift composed by an international array of authors, including the eminent American anthropologists A. L. Kroeber and Robert Lowie, and also the social reformer Othmar Spann.[13]

Despite his training, Schmidt seems not to have done any missionary work or anthropological fieldwork. Although he organized many expeditions, he himself never left Europe until 1935, when he went on a lecture tour of the United States, China, Japan, Korea, and the Philippines. His researches into Australian languages, on which he was an authority, were based on published accounts and on information sent him by missionaries. His productivity was awe-inspiring. Besides his linguistic publications, his main work was *Der Ursprung der Gottesidee* [The Origin of the Idea of God], in twelve massive volumes which cannot contain less than five million words. A bibliography of his works (not quite complete) lists 647 items, besides over sixty pieces of sacred music. His biographer tells us that Schmidt used neither a typewriter nor a card-index, and describes his working methods in a manner reminiscent of Kafka's Castle officials: 'His great ideas forced him to keep writing furiously. Thus in the course of his long life he wrote tens of thousands of pages in his own hand; as his works appeared in print, their manuscripts gradually

---

11   *The Letters of Freud and Zweig*, pp. 130–31.

12   [There is now a brief account of Schmidt in Yosef Hayim Yerushalmi, *Freud's Moses: Judaism Terminable and Interminable* (New Haven, CT, and London: Yale University Press, 1991), pp. 27–29.]

13   Biographical data on Schmidt are taken from Joseph Henninger, *P. Wilhelm Schmidt S.V.D., 1868–1954: Eine biographische Skizze* (Fribourg: Paulusdruckerei, 1956), and the obituary by Wilhelm Koppers in *Mitteilungen der Anthropologischen Gesellschaft in Wien*, 83 (1954), 87–96. Koppers also edited *Festschrift P. W. Schmidt: 76 sprachwissenschaftliche, ethnologische, religionswissenschaftliche, prähistorische und andere Studien* (Vienna: Mechitharisten-Congregations-Buchdruckerei, 1928). For Schmidt's bibliography see Fritz Bornemann, 'Verzeichnis der Schriften von P. W. Schmidt S.V.D. (1868–1954)', *Anthropos*, 49 (1954), 385–432. For his place in the history of anthropology, see the detailed account in Marvin Harris, *The Rise of Anthropological Theory* (London: Routledge & Kegan Paul, 1969), pp. 382–92.

grew into stacks a yard high beside his desk, and their blank sides served to draft new works.'[14]

Before giving some account of his anthropological theories contained in his voluminous works, I want to glance at Schmidt's political activities, hard though they are to make out. In 1916 Schmidt was appointed chaplain to the Imperial headquarters, which brought him close to the Imperial family. In 1918 he was active in the International Catholic Union, which organized conferences to discuss the social reconstruction of post-war Europe and forestall the influence of international Socialism on the peace settlement. He figures in the diary of Ignaz Seipel, who was soon to become leader of the Christian Social Party in the First Republic. On 11 January 1918 Seipel was summoned by telephone to see Schmidt at Mödling. When Seipel arrived, Schmidt gave him instructions from the Emperor, to attend a conference which the Catholic Union was planning at Zürich.[15] This suggests that Schmidt was already a grey eminence of considerable standing. Seipel's diaries contain some tantalizing entries mentioning heated discussions with Schmidt, who was visiting him at the time of the Emperor's abdication. On 7 November 1918 Seipel warned Schmidt against 'imprudent actions'. The Emperor abdicated on 11 November, and on the following day Seipel and Schmidt had a 'violent dispute' about Schmidt's politics.[16] Clearly Schmidt, like many of the Austrian clergy, was a loyal monarchist who found the prospect of a republic difficult to accept.

Schmidt's conservatism is made plain in his publications and sermons. In 1920 he issued a book, *Der deutschen Seele Not und Heil* [The Plight of the German Soul and its Salvation], in which he maintained that the War had revealed the bankruptcy of modern secular civilization and that mankind's only hope was to return to the Church. On 26 September 1920 Schmidt delivered an address to the Vienna Catholic Congress, which was published in the conservative Catholic weekly *Das Neue Reich* [The New Empire]. Schmidt's address referred to the elections which were scheduled for 17 October. The previous elections, in February 1919, had left the Social Democrats the largest party in Parliament, with just over forty per cent of the vote. Hence the title of Schmidt's speech: 'Befreiung Wiens vom jüdischen Bolschewismus!' [The Liberation of Vienna from Jewish Bolshevism!]. In this speech he denounced Social Democracy as 'a regime alien to our people and imposed by force', dominated by Jews who were plotting to destroy religion. By the end of his speech he had come to equate Socialism with Bolshevism, speaking of 'the shameful alien rule of the Jewish Bolsheviks'. The Jews are described in bold type as 'inferior members of an alien race'.[17]

At the same time Schmidt believed in social reform in the sense defined above.

---

14   Henninger, pp. 41–42.

15   Friedrich Rennhofer, *Ignaz Seipel, Mensch und Staatsmann* (Vienna, Cologne, Graz: Hermann Böhlaus Nachf., 1978), p. 115.

16   Ibid., pp. 727, 155.

17   'Befreiung Wiens vom jüdischen Bolschewismus! Eine Katholikentagsrede von Professor Dr Wilhelm Schmidt S.V.D.', *Das Neue Reich*, 3, 10 October 1920, pp. 42–43 (p. 43); Schmidt's words are 'der schmachvollen Fremdherrschaft des jüdischen Bolschewikentums' and 'minderwertige Fremdstämmlinge'. This item is not listed in Bornemann's bibliography.

He agreed with the Christian Social Party in opposing liberalism, deploring its atomizing effect on society, and urging that capitalism should be controlled. Accordingly, Schmidt was among the founder members of the Catholic Bund Neuland, which aimed to bring Christianity to the modern urban masses and thus remove them from the temptations of atheism and Socialism.[18] Resting on conservative anti-capitalism, the Bund Neuland identified capitalism with the Jews, and its periodical, *Neuland*, contains several articles denouncing Jews as a 'race of Cain' ('Kainsvolk')[19] and warning Austrian Catholics to practise 'racial conservation' ('Rassepflege') and combat 'Judaization' ('Verjudung').[20]

Since Schmidt was an anthropologist, it was easy for him to put forward theories of race. He was concerned first of all to condemn the racial theories of National Socialism. He rejected the National Socialists' genetic determinism, on the grounds that in Catholic doctrine the soul was an integral entity which could not be affected by the genes. Instead, Schmidt's mentor was his colleague at Vienna University, the prehistorian and racial theorist Oswald Menghin. Menghin criticized the National Socialists for confusing the materialistic concept of race with the cultural concept of 'Volkstum'.[21] But his book *Geist und Blut* [Spirit and Blood] shows Menghin himself to be confused: he maintains that the Jews are culturally unassimilable because they have become an urban people while the Germans are basically a peasant people; but he also wants to deny on racial grounds that a Jew, however thoroughly he may have absorbed German culture, can ever be accepted as a German.[22]

Schmidt follows Menghin in both these ways. For him, 'Volkstum' is primary, while race is secondary; the German 'Volkstum', a cultural entity, comprises a number of races, such as the Nordic and Ostic races. Along with the National Socialists' racial materialism, Schmidt rejects their programme of 'Nordification' ('Aufnordung') on the grounds that it may discriminate against one of Germany's racial minorities, the Westphalians, who according to Schmidt belong to the 'Dalic' race. And, like Menghin, he wants to fuse or confuse racial and religious categories in order to keep the Jews separate from the Germans.[23] The crucial difference between Jews and Aryans, he explained in an article in the Catholic journal *Schönere Zukunft* [A Brighter Future], lies in the 'psychic structure' of the Jews. Since rejecting the Messiah they have been 'a people who, in the deepest

18 See F. M. Kapfhammer, 'Die katholische Jugendbewegung', in Erika Weinzierl et al. (eds.), *Kirche in Österreich, 1918– 1965*, 2 vols (Vienna: Herold, 1967), II, 23–53. Schmidt contributed 'Der Neulandtechniker in seiner sozialen Stellung', *Neuland: Blätter jungkatholischer Erneuerungsbewegung*, I, iii (Christmond 1923), 49–55, setting out his anti-Socialist view of industrial relations.

19 Alfred Missong, 'Was sollen wir zum deutschen Faszismus sagen?', *Neuland*, I, viii (May 1924), 173–79 (p. 178).

20 Hans Dibold, 'Die Juden', ibid., 4, i (Hartung [*sic*] 1927), 9–15 (pp. 11–12).

21 Oswald Menghin, *Geist und Blut: Grundsätzliches um Rasse, Sprache, Kultur und Volkstum* (Vienna: Schroll, 1934), p. 53.

22 Ibid., pp. 171–72.

23 Wilhelm Schmidt, *Rasse und Volk: Ihre allgemeine Bedeutung; Ihre Geltung im deutschen Raum*, 2nd edn (Salzburg: Pustet, 1935). Menghin is quoted on p. 51; the races composing the German people are listed on p. 99.

region of their souls, have lost contact with their national roots'.[24] The Jews are not mentioned in his treatise 'Rasse und Volk', which is an essay on German 'Volkstum' and its need to be rooted in the soil of Germany. Schmidt's insistently organicist imagery strongly recalls the influential book by Julius Langbehn, *Rembrandt als Erzieher* [Rembrandt as Educator] (1890), which provided an influential definition of 'German-ness'.[25]

It is not surprising that Schmidt enthusiastically supported the corporate state. In 1934 he commended it for upholding the family and demanded that it should introduce further measures. Any defamation of the family in the media should be punished. People should be legally forbidden to live together outside wedlock. Girls should be educated for motherhood. Education should include eugenics. Religious intermarriage should be severely prohibited. The employment of women in offices and factories should be reduced to a minimum. And the tax laws should favour the fathers of large families, who should also be given jobs in preference to childless men.[26] He was the chairman of a commission set up in 1936 by the Austrian episcopate to establish a Catholic university at Salzburg, a project to which he was intensely committed.

Although Austria under Dollfuss largely avoided antisemitism, we have already seen that there were exceptions. The Bishop of Linz was one; Schmidt was another. In December 1933 Schmidt gave an address to the Catholic Congress in the First District of Vienna under the title 'Zur Judenfrage' [On the Jewish Problem]. He condemned the over-representation of Jews in the professions and the media, and deplored the corruption which had overtaken the Jews since their failure to accept Christ:

> As punishment for this crime, this people, as Christ himself prophesied, was expelled from its native soil and has wandered about ever since as a rootless people deprived of the soil of the homeland in which it was rooted. The distortion of its character and its severance from its roots, which have lasted for almost two millennia, have also affected its physical race, secondarily, but none the less effectively. If a Jew whole-heartedly and sincerely enters the Catholic Church, he has removed the strongest reason separating him from us and surmounted the true and deepest cause of his otherness. But the racial effects of this cause which have made themselves apparent in the course of these two millennia cannot be removed all at once, even by baptism; that requires much time and inward labour, so that he is indeed one of us, but not in the same way as our German kinsfolk.[27]

As this passage, combined with his publications on the racial question, may demonstrate, Schmidt came closer than perhaps anyone else in Austria to grafting

---

24 'Das Rassenprinzip des Nationalsozialismus', *Schönere Zukunft*, 7, 24 July 1932, 999–1000 (p. 999). Schmidt's words are 'ein im tiefsten Seelengrunde ihrer Nation entwurzeltes Volk'.

25 *Rasse und Volk*, p. 216.

26 'Die Familie im katholischen Staate', in *Der katholische Staatsgedanke: Bericht über die katholisch-soziale Tagung der Zentralstelle des Volksbundes der Katholiken Österreichs am 29. und 30. April 1934 in Wien* (Vienna: Volksbundverlag, 1934), pp. 41–51. See also his 'Freiheit und Bindung des Christen in der Gesellschaft', *Allgemeiner Deutscher Katholikentag Wien 1933* (Vienna, 1934), pp. 91–96.

27 'Zur Judenfrage', *Schönere Zukunft*, 9, 21 January 1934, 408–09.

a new racial antisemitism onto the traditional religious and anti-capitalist anti-semitism. The social implications of his views are indicated by his approving reference to a recent book by Emmerich Czermak and Oskar Karbach, *Ordnung in der Judenfrage* [Dealing with the Jewish Problem], which begins by declaring: 'Nowadays we can see with absolute clarity that liberal, socialist, Bolshevist Jewry is a degenerate Jewry.'[28] They do not propose to exclude the Jews from economic and cultural life, but rather to confer upon them the status of a recognized minority. Yet, since the authors also reject the possibility of Jewish assimilation, it is difficult to see what this would have achieved except singling the Jews out as targets for discrimination.

All this gives ample reason for Freud to dislike Schmidt. They had already crossed swords, however, as a result of Freud's venture into anthropology in *Totem und Tabu*. Schmidt himself held strong views on anthropological questions. He belonged to the diffusionist school, which attempted to explain cultural similarities (in institutions and material products) as resulting not from independent invention but from diffusion from an original centre. The German school of diffusionists tried to identify a number of 'Kulturkreise' [cultural circles], areas within which such diffusion had taken place.

Schmidt was particularly interested in the most primitive peoples, such as the Congolese Pygmies, the Andaman Islanders, the Australian Aborigines, and the inhabitants of Tierra del Fuego. Using data collected by explorers, mainly mission-aries, Schmidt began by studying these peoples' languages and then passed to their religions. He established to his own satisfaction that all these peoples shared a primeval monotheism. All believed in a Supreme Being who was the author of good. In addition, they led peaceful lives, were monogamous, cared altruistically for children, old people and fertile mothers, and had a clear concept of private property. So perfect was their social order, in fact, that Schmidt found himself driven to conclude that these peoples must have received a direct revelation from God. To have made such an impression on them, God must have appeared in person, in physical form. This conclusion forms the climax of the first six volumes of *Der Ursprung der Gottesidee*, and Schmidt leaves the reader in no doubt that his supernaturalism is absolutely literal:

> It was the really existing Supreme Being, the actual Creator of heaven and earth and, in particular, of mankind, who appeared before His most excellent creatures, mankind, and revealed Himself, His own being and workings, disclosed Himself to their minds, wills and emotions immediately after Creation, when He dwelt familiarly together with mankind.[29]

Hence myths about the primeval paradise must be true, and so must the creation myths of the most ancient peoples. After all, as Schmidt observes, they derived their information from God, the most reliable witness to an event which was still recent. Subsequently, however, this happy state was disrupted by sin. Schmidt considers it

28 Czermak and Karbach, p. 9. Schmidt refers to this book in 'Zur Judenfrage', p. 408.
29 *Der Ursprung der Gottesidee*, 12 vols (Münster: Aschendorffsche Verlagsbuchhandlung, 1926–55), VI, 493. This passage is also quoted, but misattributed, by Harris, p. 391.

most probable that the Fall resulted from the excessive pride of the tribal leader who communicated with God on behalf of his followers. Thereafter the male-dominated society of primeval mankind gave way to a matrilocal and matrilineal society, and all the troubles of history followed. Only in remote spots like the Andamans and Tierra del Fuego did remnants survive of man's original paradisal state.

It hardly needs to be said that Schmidt's anthropology has not worn well. For one thing, it is based on methods and assumptions which, however respectable in their time, have since been decisively rejected. Like the almost equally prolific British armchair anthropologist Sir James Frazer, Schmidt reached his conclusions by comparing multifarious data. This 'scrap-book treatment, which was dignified by being labelled the "comparative method"', as Sir Edward Evans-Pritchard later described it, risks misunderstanding ethnographic facts by considering them in isolation from their social context.[30] Data can thus easily be marshalled to support the anthropologist's pet theory. Another method employed by anthropologists who were unable to make field trips was to draw up detailed questionnaires for travellers. This was a well-tried method, going back to the ethnography of the late Enlightenment. It was used at the beginning of the twentieth century as a means of collecting information about peoples under German colonial rule, and Schmidt was among the anthropologists employed by the Imperial Colonial Office to draw up the questionnaire. But, as the unorthodox anthropologist and missionary Bruno Gutmann pointed out, the questionnaire method tends to force the ethnographic data into a rigid set of preconceived concepts which cannot be modified by first-hand experience in the field.[31] Diffusionism, long an anthropological orthodoxy, is now out of favour: cultural similarities are now thought to be adequately explained by independent invention in response to similar material environments. Schmidt's theory of primeval monotheism has antecedents going back to the eighteenth-century Jesuit missionary Lafitau, whose *Mœurs des sauvages américains comparés aux mœurs des premiers temps* (1724) was a path-breaking exercise in ethnographic comparison and diffusionist theory.[32]

Schmidt was patently biased in his use even of the data available to him. For example, in crediting the Andaman Islanders with a highly ethical monotheism, he was following a late nineteenth-century study which had been contradicted by the British anthropologist Radcliffe-Brown. After prolonged and careful enquiries, Radcliffe-Brown found that the Andamaners believed in several divinities and that their principal divinity was thought to be indifferent to moral offences, even murder and adultery, and to be angered only by such actions as melting wax, killing a cicada, and digging up yams. In *Der Ursprung der Gottesidee* Schmidt compares Radcliffe-Brown's account of the Andaman Islanders with earlier accounts at considerable length, but his criticism is directed exclusively at Radcliffe-Brown,

30   E. E. Evans-Pritchard, *Theories of Primitive Religion* (Oxford: Clarendon Press, 1965), p. 10.

31   J. C. Winter, *Bruno Gutmann, 1876–1966: A German Approach to Social Anthropology* (Oxford: Clarendon Press, 1979), pp. 52, 62–65.

32   See W. E. Mühlmann, *Geschichte der Anthropologie*, 2nd edn (Wiesbaden: AULA-Verlag, 1984), pp. 44–45, 206.

and his show of impartiality is unconvincing.[33] Schmidt's supernaturalism makes it clear that despite his pretence of objective research he was guided by his own fantasies. In particular, his account of primitive society sounds much too good to be true. Schmidt's primitives (whom he had never seen in the flesh) seem already to have attained the social harmony which the Austrian corporate state was striving to restore. And by blaming women for the loss of this primeval harmony, Schmidt has translated the myth of the Fall into terms that are anthropological, yet no less mythical.

Ironically, Schmidt's work is now held by anthropologists in even lower esteem than Freud's. Yet in their time Schmidt was in the scientific mainstream, while Freud was regarded as an impertinent amateur. Accordingly, the manual of anthropology for students, *Ursprung und Werden der Religion*, that Schmidt published in 1930, contains sharp attacks on Freud and Durkheim — both amateurs and, not coincidentally, both Jews. Schmidt opposes the argument by Freud that totemism is the basis of religion. He maintains that among the most primitive peoples such practices as parricide and cannibalism are unknown, and defends primitive men against Freud's slanders: 'To bring such men into connexion with modern sex-ridden neurotics, as he [Freud] would have us do, and from this connexion to deduce the alleged fact that all thought and feeling, especially subliminal, is founded on and saturated with sex, must remain lost labour. Thus Freud's hypothesis loses its last shadow of hope ever to corroborate or establish any single part of itself, for every part collapses in ruin.'[34] Durkheim's *Les Formes élémentaires de la vie religieuse* is likewise condemned as 'purely speculative'.[35] That antisemitism was among Schmidt's motives is clear from his attack elsewhere on the Jewish anthropologist Salomon Reinach, whom he accuses of adopting the theory of totemism from Robertson Smith's *Religion of the Semites* solely in order to undermine the pre-eminence of Christianity in the history of religions.[36]

The enmity between Freud and Schmidt was no mere scholarly disagreement. Each man held to his convictions the more strongly for their lack of scholarly foundation. Their beliefs were founded, rather, on incompatible ideologies — progressive liberalism versus Catholic conservatism — and on opposed historical myths. Freud sees human history as a slow and painful struggle from primitive animism through theology and philosophy up to the highest stage of consciousness, science, which can at last begin to confer some real instead of illusory benefits upon mankind. For Schmidt, on the other hand, history is a process of loss and decline: a primeval revelation by God himself showed the earliest men the essence of religion and the ideal social life. There could be no compromise between Freud's belief in progress and Schmidt's belief in decline.[37]

33 See Schmidt, *Der Ursprung der Gottesidee*, 2nd, enlarged edn, 12 vols (Münster: Aschendorffsche Verlagsbuchhandlung, 1926–55), III, esp. pp. 53–60; A. R. Brown [*sic*], *The Andaman Islanders: A Study in Social Anthropology* (Cambridge: Cambridge University Press, 1922).

34 Schmidt, *The Origin and Growth of Religion*, trans. by H. J. Rose (London: Methuen, 1931), p. 115. (The original was not available to me.)

35 Ibid., p. 117.

36 *Der Ursprung der Gottesidee*, I, 39–40.

37 A brief comparison between Freud and Schmidt is drawn by Walter Burkert, *Homo Necans:*

But this of course is an incomplete account of Freud's social thought. In his late works his belief in progress is counterpointed and indeed contradicted by an increasing cultural pessimism which brings him closer to Schmidt. His doubts about the value of civilization are clearly stated in *Civilization and its Discontents*. It also appears, more obliquely, in *Moses and Monotheism*. Though hardly to be taken seriously as Biblical criticism, this book is fascinating if seen as an exercise in myth-making.[38]

Very obviously, *Moses and Monotheism* opposes all that Schmidt stood for by describing Christianity as a neurosis and contrasting it with both Judaism and the modern scientific spirit. But in another way it resembles Schmidt's work. Both Schmidt and Freud are concerned with the transmission of a doctrine. In both cases the doctrine is monotheism. It is transmitted, in Schmidt's account, by diffusion; in Freud's, by repression. Schmidt asserts that God appeared in person to primitive man and taught him a monotheism which was diffused over the globe and, in the process, corrupted and forgotten, except in the refuges of primitive humanity. Freud maintains that the monotheism of the Pharaoh Akhenaten was transmitted by Moses to his followers the Jews, and, though repeatedly forgotten, it survived securely in the unconscious. Thus both Schmidt and Freud were constructing myths of decline, and both were concerned with how doctrines survive — a very understandable concern at a time when civilization seemed likely to be defeated by either Nazism or Communism. And Schmidt's work needs to be seen as the context in and against which Freud's last major book was written.

The end of the story is quickly told and establishes a strange parallel between the two men. After the *Anschluß* both went into exile. Because of his forthright and outspoken condemnation of National Socialism, Schmidt was arrested on 13 March 1938, the day after the *Anschluß*, kept under guard for several days, then released after Mussolini, prompted by the Pope, had intervened on his behalf. In April he was forbidden to teach. He went to Rome and arranged for the Anthropos Institute to be transferred to Fribourg in Switzerland, where he continued his anthropological work until his death in 1954. Freud meanwhile remained in Vienna till June 1938, then managed to leave with his immediate family for Britain. There he completed and published *Moses and Monotheism*, an exploration of religion which is, among many other things, a covert and ambiguous reply to Schmidt.

The Anthropology of Ancient Greek Sacrificial Ritual and Myth, trans. by Peter Bing (Berkeley and Los Angeles: University of California Press, 1983), p. 73.

38 For a fuller interpretation of *Moses and Monotheism* see Ritchie Robertson, 'Freud's Testament: *Moses and Monotheism*', in *Freud in Exile: Psychoanalysis and its Vicissitudes*, ed. by Edward Timms and Naomi Segal (New Haven, CT; and London: Yale University Press, 1988), pp. 80–89.

LIST OF PUBLICATIONS

excluding reviews and short articles

Books

Kafka: Judaism, Politics, and Literature (Oxford: Clarendon Press, 1985)

Kafka: Judentum, Gesellschaft, Literatur, trans. by Josef Billen (Stuttgart: Metzler, 1988)

Heine (London: Peter Halban, 1988)

Heinrich Heine, trans. by Andrea Marenzeller (Vienna: Eichbauer, 1997)

The 'Jewish Question' in German Literature, 1749–1939: Emancipation and its Discontents (Oxford: Oxford University Press, 1999)

Kafka: A Very Short Introduction (Oxford: Oxford University Press, 2004)

Japanese edition of *Kafka: A Very Short Introduction*, trans. by Kiyoko Myojo (Tokyo: Iwanami Shoten, 2008)

Chinese edition of *Kafka: A Very Short Introduction* (Yilin Press, 2008)

Franz Kafka: Leben und Schreiben, trans. by Josef Billen (Darmstadt: Wissenschaftliche Buchgesellschaft, 2009)

Mock-Epic Poetry from Pope to Heine (Oxford: Oxford University Press, 2009)

Goethe: A Very Short Introduction (Oxford: Oxford University Press, 2016)

Translations

Urs Bitterli, *Cultures in Conflict: Encounters between European and non-European Cultures, 1492–1800* (Cambridge: Polity Press, 1989). 'Introduction', pp. 1–19

E. T. A. Hoffmann, *The Golden Pot and other tales*, World's Classics (Oxford: Oxford University Press, 1992). 'Introduction', pp. vii–xxxii

Heinrich Heine, *Selected Prose* (London: Penguin, 1993). 'Introduction', pp. 1–24

Karl Philipp Moritz, *Anton Reiser*, Penguin Classics (London: Penguin, 1997). 'Introduction', pp. vii–xxx

The German-Jewish Dialogue: An Anthology of Literary Texts, 1749–1993, World's Classics (Oxford: Oxford University Press, 1999). 'Introduction', pp. vii–xxviii

Franz Kafka, *The Man who Disappeared (America)*, World's Classics (Oxford: Oxford University Press, 2012). 'Introduction', pp. xi–xxvii

Editions

Heinrich Heine, *Poems* (Bristol: Bristol Classical Press, 1993). 'Introduction', pp. 1–23

Sigmund Freud, *The Interpretation of Dreams*, trans. by Joyce Crick, World's Classics (Oxford: Oxford University Press, 1999). 'Introduction', pp. vii–xxxvii; notes, pp. 417–40

The Cambridge Companion to Thomas Mann (Cambridge: Cambridge University Press, 2002)

(With Katrin Kohl) *Words, Texts, Images: Selected Papers from the Conference of University Teachers of German, University of Oxford, April 2001* (Bern: Peter Lang, 2002)

Arthur Schnitzler, *Round Dance and Other Plays*, trans. by J. M. Q. Davies, World's Classics (Oxford: Oxford University Press, 2004). 'Introduction', pp. vii–xxx; notes, pp. 401–06

(With Joseph Sherman) *The Yiddish Presence in European Literature* (Oxford: Legenda, 2005)

(With Katrin Kohl) *A History of Austrian Literature, 1918–2000* (Rochester, NY: Camden House, 2006)

(With Judith Beniston and Robert Vilain) *Austrian Satire and Other Essays: Studies in Honour of Edward Timms*, Austrian Studies, 15 (Leeds: Maney, 2007)

Introductions and notes, Franz Kafka, *The Metamorphosis and Other Stories*, trans. by Joyce Crick; *The Trial*, trans. by Michael Mitchell; *The Castle*, trans. by Anthea Bell, World's Classics (Oxford: Oxford University Press, 2009)

(With Catriona Seth) Évariste-Désiré de Parny, *Le Paradis perdu*, French Critical Texts (London: Maney, 2009)

(With Manfred Engel) *Kafka und die kleine Prosa der Moderne* (Würzburg: Königshausen & Neumann, 2010 [actually March 2011])

Introduction and notes, Franz Kafka, *A Hunger Artist and Other Stories*, trans. by Joyce Crick, World's Classics (Oxford: Oxford University Press, 2012)

(With Manfred Engel) *Kafka, Prag und der Erste Weltkrieg* (Würzburg: Königshausen & Neumann, 2012)

Lessing and the German Enlightenment (Oxford: Voltaire Foundation, 2013)

Introduction and notes, Sigmund Freud, *A Case of Hysteria (Dora)*, trans. by Anthea Bell, World's Classics (Oxford: Oxford University Press, 2013)

(With Manfred Engel) *Kafka und die Religion in der Moderne* (Würzburg: Königshausen & Neumann, 2014)

Introduction and notes, Robert Musil, *The Confusions of Young Törless*, trans. by Mike Mitchell, World's Classics (Oxford: Oxford University Press, 2014)

(With Michael White) *Fontane and Cultural Mediation: Translation and Reception in the Nineteenth Century*, Festschrift for Helen Chambers (London: Legenda, 2015)

Introduction and notes, Theodor Fontane, *Effi Briest*, trans. by Mike Mitchell, World's Classics (Oxford: Oxford University Press, 2015)

(Ed. with Laurence Brockliss) *Isaiah Berlin and the Enlightenment* (Oxford: Oxford University Press, 2016)

Published Lectures

Scandinavian Modernism and the Battle of the Sexes: Kafka, Strindberg and 'The Castle', the Spring 2003 Rodig Maxwell Lecture (Dept of German Studies, Rutgers University, 2004)

Every Man a Murderer? Violent Death in German Modernism, the Bernays Lecture 2003 (King's College London, 2004)

Anticlericalism in Austrian Literature from Joseph II to Thomas Bernhard, the Ingeborg Bachmann Centre Lecture 2005, Occasions, 9 (London: Austrian Cultural Forum, 2007)

Zur Theorie und Praxis des Erhabenen bei Schiller, Lichtblicke, 1 (Jena: Garamond-Verlag, 2014)

Articles

'The Dual Structure of Hofmannsthal's *Reitergeschichte*', *Forum for Modern Language Studies*, 14 (1978), 316–31

'Some Revisions and Variants in the Poetry of Edwin Muir', *The Bibliotheck*, 10.1 (1980), 20–26

'"Our Generation"': Edwin Muir as Social Critic, 1920–22', *Scottish Literary Journal*, 9.2 (1982), 45–65

'Kafka's Zürau Aphorisms', *Oxford German Studies*, 14 (1983), 73–91

'Science and Myth in John Davidson's *Testaments*', *Studies in Scottish Literature*, 18 (1983), 85–109

'Goethe, Broch, and the Novels of Edwin Muir', *Forum for Modern Language Studies*, 19 (1983), 142–57

'Edwin Muir and Rilke', *German Life and Letters*, n.s. 36 (1983), 317–28

'Edwin Muir as Critic of Kafka', *Modern Language Review*, 79 (1984), 638–52

'"Antizionismus, Zionismus": Kafka's Responses to Jewish Nationalism', in *Paths and Labyrinths: Nine Papers from a Kafka Symposium*, ed. by J. P. Stern and J. J. White (London: Institute of Germanic Studies, 1985), pp. 25–42

'The Problem of "Jewish Self-hatred" in Herzl, Kraus and Kafka', *Oxford German Studies*, 16 (1985), 81–108

'Kafka und Don Quixote', *Neophilologus*, 69 (1985), 17–24

'Shakespearean Comedy and Romantic Psychology in Hoffmann's *Kater Murr*', *Studies in Romanticism*, 24 (1985), 201–22

'"Ich habe ihm das Beil nicht geben können": The Heroine's Failure in Hofmannsthal's *Elektra*', *Orbis Litterarum*, 41 (1986), 312–31

'Three Poems by Goethe', *Treffpunkt*, 18.3 (1986), 5–10

'Edwin Muir', in *The History of Scottish Literature*, vol. IV: *The Twentieth Century*, ed. by Cairns Craig (Aberdeen: Aberdeen University Press, 1987), pp. 135–46

'Nationalism and Modernity: German-Jewish Writers and the Zionist movement', in *Visions and Blueprints: Avant-garde Culture and Radical Politics in Early Twentieth-Century Europe*, ed. by Edward Timms and Peter Collier (Manchester: Manchester University Press, 1988), pp. 208–20

'Freud's Testament: *Moses and Monotheism*', in *Freud in Exile: Psychoanalysis and its Vicissitudes*, ed. by Edward Timms and Naomi Segal (New Haven, CT, and London: Yale University Press, 1988), pp. 80–89

'Western Observers and Eastern Jews: Kafka, Buber, Franzos', *Modern Language Review*, 83 (1988), 87–105

'National Stereotypes in Prague German Fiction', *Colloquia Germanica*, 22 (1989), 116–36

'Primitivism and Psychology: Nietzsche, Freud, Thomas Mann', in *Modernism and the European Unconscious*, ed. by Peter Collier and Judy Davies (Cambridge: Polity Press, 1990), pp. 79–93

'Edwin Muir as European Poet', in *Edwin Muir Centenary Assessments*, ed. by C. J. M. MacLachlan and D. S. Robb (Aberdeen: Association for Scottish Literary Studies, 1990), pp. 102–18

'The Theme of Sacrifice in Hofmannsthal's *Das Gespräch über Gedichte* and *Andreas*', *Modern Austrian Literature*, 23.1 (1990), 19–33

'Zydzi w kulturze europejskiej: Swoi czy obcy?', *Przeglad Historyczny*, 81 (1990), 179–87

'"My true enemy": Freud and the Catholic Church, 1927–1939', in *Austria in the Thirties: Culture and Politics*, ed. by Kenneth Segar and John Warren (Riverside, CA: Ariadne Press, 1991), pp. 328–44

'Musil and the "Primitive Mentality"', in *Robert Musil and the Literary Landscape of his Time*, ed. by Hannah Hickman (Salford: University of Salford, 1991), pp. 13–33

'Roth's *Hiob* and the Traditions of Ghetto Fiction', in *Co-Existent Contradictions: Joseph Roth in Retrospect*, ed. by Helen Chambers (Riverside, CA: Ariadne Press, 1991), pp. 185–200

'Canetti as Anthropologist', in *Elias Canetti: Londoner Symposium*, ed. by Adrian Stevens and Fred Wagner (Stuttgart: Heinz, 1991), pp. 131–45

'Heines orientalische Masken', *Akten des VIII. Internationalen Germanisten-Kongresses Tokyo 1990* (Munich: iudicium, 1991), x. 126–33

'Joseph Rohrer and the Bureaucratic Enlightenment', *Austrian Studies*, 2 (1991), 22–42

'Leadership and Community in Werfel's *Die vierzig Tage des Musa Dagh*', in *Unser Fahrplan geht von Stern zu Stern: Zu Franz Werfels Stellung und Werk*, ed. by Joseph P. Strelka and Robert Weigel (Bern: Peter Lang, 1992), pp. 249–69

' "Jewish Self-Hatred"? The Cases of Schnitzler and Canetti', in *Austrians and Jews in the Twentieth Century*, ed. by Robert S. Wistrich (London: Macmillan, 1992), pp. 82–96

' "Von den ungerechten Richtern": Zum allegorischen Verfahren Kafkas im *Proceß*', in *Nach erneuter Lektüre: Franz Kafkas 'Der Proceß'*, ed. by Hans Dieter Zimmermann (Würzburg: Königshausen & Neumann, 1992), pp. 201–09

'Between Freud and Nietzsche: Canetti's *Crowds and Power*', *Austrian Studies*, 3 (1992), 109–24

'From the Ghetto to Modern Culture: The Autobiographies of Salomon Maimon and Jakob Fromer', *Polin: A Yearbook of Polish-Jewish Studies*, 7 (1992), 12–30

'Reading the Clues: Franz Kafka, *Der Proceß*', in *The German Novel in the Twentieth Century*, ed. by David Midgley (Edinburgh: Edinburgh University Press, 1993), pp. 59–79

'Accounting for History: Thomas Mann, *Doktor Faustus*', ibid., pp. 128–48

'On the Sources of *Moses and Monotheism*', in *Reading Freud's Reading*, ed. by Sander L. Gilman et al. (New York and London: New York University Press, 1993), pp. 266–85

'Freud und Pater Wilhelm Schmidt', in *Die Wiener Jahrhundertwende: Einflüsse, Umwelt, Wirkungen*, ed. by Jürgen Nautz and Richard Vahrenkamp (Vienna, Cologne, Graz: Böhlau, 1993), pp. 349–59

'On the Threshold of Patriarchy: Brentano, Grillparzer, and the Bohemian Amazons', *German Life and Letters*, 46 (1993), 203–19

'Hofmannsthal sociologue: *Die Briefe des Zurückgekehrten*', *Austriaca*, 37 (Dec. 1993), 275–86

'*Der Proceß*', in *Interpretationen: Franz Kafka, Romane und Erzählungen*, ed. by Michael Müller (Stuttgart: Reclam, 1994), pp. 98–145

' "Herr Peregrinus": Persona, Race and Gender in Heinrich Heine's *Die Harzreise*', in *Bridging the Abyss: Reflections on Jewish Suffering, Anti-Semitism, and Exile: Essays in Honor of Harry Zohn*, ed. by Amy Colin and Elisabeth Strenger (Munich: Fink, 1994), pp. 145–57

'Der Künstler und das Volk: Kafkas "Ein Hungerkünstler. Vier Geschichten" ', trans. by Christa Krüger, *Text + Kritik*, Sonderband (1994), 180–91

'In Search of the Historical Kafka: A Selective Review of Research, 1980–92', *Modern Language Review*, 89 (1994), 107–37

'Difficult Truths: An Essay Review of J. P. Stern, *The Heart of Europe*', *Comparative Criticism*, 16 (1994), 247–61

'The Failure of Enlightenment in Grillparzer's *Ein Bruderzwist in Habsburg* and Goethe's *Die natürliche Tochter*', in *Für all, was Menschen je erfahren ... Beiträge zu Franz Grillparzers Werk*, ed. by Joseph P. Strelka (Bern: Peter Lang, 1995), pp. 165–85

'Schnitzler's Honesty', in *Order from Confusion: Essays presented to Edward McInnes on the Occasion of his Sixtieth Birthday*, ed. by Alan Deighton (Hull: New German Studies, 1995), pp. 162–85

'German Idealists and American Rowdies: Ferdinand Kürnberger's Novel *Der Amerika-Müde*', *Austrian Studies*, 7 (1996), 17–35

' "Urheimat Asien": The Re-orientation of German and Austrian Jews, 1900–1925', *German Life and Letters*, 49 (1996), 182–92

'From Naturalism to National Socialism (1890–1945)', in *The Cambridge History of German Literature*, ed. by Helen Watanabe-O'Kelly (Cambridge: Cambridge University Press, 1997), pp. 327–92

'1918 ... Joseph Roth', in *The Yale Companion to Jewish Writing and Thought in German Culture, 1096–1996*, ed. by Sander Gilman and Jack Zipes (New Haven, CT, and London: Yale University Press, 1997), pp. 355–62

'Reinventing the Jews: From Moses Mendelssohn to Theodor Herzl', *Austrian Studies*, 8 (1997), 3–11

'Mothers and Lovers in Some Novels by Kafka and Brod', *German Life and Letters*, 50 (1997), 475–90

'Historicizing Weininger: The Nineteenth-Century German Image of the Feminized Jew', in *Modernity, Culture and 'the Jew'*, ed. by Bryan Cheyette and Laura Marcus (Cambridge: Polity Press, 1998), pp. 23–39

'Die Erneuerung des Judentums aus dem Geist der Assimilation, 1900 bis 1922', in *Ästhetische und religiöse Erfahrungen der Jahrhundertwenden, II: Um 1900*, ed. by Wolfgang Braungart, Gotthard Fuchs and Manfred Koch (Paderborn: Schöningh, 1998), pp. 171–93

'Heroes in Their Underclothes: Aloys Blumauer's Travesty of Virgil's *Aeneid*', *Austrian Studies*, 9 (1998), 24–40

'"Dies hohe Lied der Duldung"? The Ambiguities of Toleration in Lessing's *Die Juden* and *Nathan der Weise*', *Modern Language Review*, 93 (1998), 105–20

'Freedom and Pragmatism: Aspects of Religious Toleration in Eighteenth-Century Germany', *Patterns of Prejudice*, 32.3 (1998), 69–80

'Kafka und das Christentum', *Der Deutschunterricht*, 50.5 (1998), 60–69

'Enlightened and Romantic Views of the Ghetto: David Friedländer vs. Heinrich Heine', in *Ghetto Writing: Traditional and Eastern Jewry in German-Jewish Prose*, ed. by Anne Fuchs and Florian Krobb (Columbia, SC: Camden House, 1999), pp. 25–40

'Varieties of Antisemitism from Herder to Fassbinder', in *The German-Jewish Dilemma: From the Enlightenment to the Holocaust*, ed. by Andrea Hammel and Edward Timms (Lampeter: Mellen, 1999), pp. 107–21

'The Representation of Jews in British and German Literature: A Comparison', in *Two Nations: British and German Jews in Comparative Perspective*, ed. by Michael Brenner, Rainer Liedtke and David Rechter (Tübingen: Mohr Siebeck, 1999), pp. 411–41

'*The New Ghetto* and the Perplexities of Assimilation', in *Theodor Herzl: Visionary of the Jewish State*, ed. by Gideon Shimoni and Robert Wistrich (Jerusalem: Magnes Press, 1999), pp. 39–51

'Faith and Fossils: Annette von Droste-Hülshoff's Poem "Die Mergelgrube"', in *Das schwierige 19. Jahrhundert: Germanistische Tagung zum 65. Geburtstag von Eda Sagarra im August 1998*, ed. by Jürgen Barkhoff, Gilbert J. Carr and Roger Paulin (Tübingen: Niemeyer, 2000), pp. 345–54

'Zum deutschen Slawenbild von Herder bis Musil', in *Das Eigene und das Fremde: Festschrift Urs Bitterli*, ed. by Urs Faes and Béatrice Ziegler (Zürich: NZZ-Verlag, 2000), pp. 116–44

'"A world of fine fabling": Epic Traditions in Heine's *Atta Troll*', in *Heine und die Weltliteratur*, ed. by Alexander Stillmark and T. J. Reed (Oxford: Legenda, 2000), pp. 64–76

'Rafael Seligmann's *Rubinsteins Versteigerung*: The German-Jewish Family Novel before and after the Holocaust', *Germanic Review*, 75 (2000), 179–93

'Literary Techniques and Aesthetic Texture in *Faust*', in *Goethe's Faust I and II: A Companion*, ed. by Paul Bishop (Rochester, NY: Camden House, 2001), pp. 1–27

'Britische Intellektuelle und Dichter über die Revolutionen in Österreich und Ungarn 1848–1849', in *Bewegung im Reich der Immobilität: Revolutionen in der Habsburgermonarchie 1848–49*, ed. by Hubert Lengauer and Primus-Heinz Kucher (Vienna: Böhlau, 2001), pp. 415–26

'Karl Beck: From Radicalism to Monarchism', *Leo Baeck Institute Year Book*, 46 (2001), 81–91

'Schopenhauer, Heine, Freud: Dreams and Dream-Theories in Nineteenth-Century Germany', *Psychoanalysis and History*, 3 (2001), 28–38

'Classicism and its Pitfalls: *Death in Venice*', in *The Cambridge Companion to Thomas Mann*, ed. by Ritchie Robertson (Cambridge: Cambridge University Press, 2002), pp. 95–106

'Kafka als religiöser Denker', in *Franz Kafka: Zur ethischen und ästhetischen Rechtfertigung*, ed. by Jakob Lothe and Beatrice Sandberg (Freiburg: Rombach, 2002), pp. 135–49

'Kafka as Anti-Christian: "Das Urteil", "Die Verwandlung" and the Aphorisms', in *A Companion to the Works of Franz Kafka*, ed. by James Rolleston (Rochester, NY: Camden House, 2002), pp. 101–22

'Modernism and the Self, 1890–1924', in *Philosophy and German Literature 1700–1990*, ed. by Nicholas Saul (Cambridge: Cambridge University Press, 2002), pp. 150–96

'An Appreciation of the Work of Siegbert Prawer, J. P. Stern and George Steiner', in *German Literature, Jewish Critics: The Brandeis Symposium*, ed. by Stephen D. Dowden and Meike G. Werner (Rochester, NY: Camden House, 2002), pp. 237–61

'Häusliche Gewalt in der Wiener Moderne: Zu Veza Canettis Erzählung "Der Oger" ', *Text + Kritik*, 156 (Oct. 2002), 48–64

'Eichendorff: *Aus dem Leben eines Taugenichts*', in *Landmarks in German Short Fiction*, ed. by Peter Hutchinson (Bern: Peter Lang, 2003), pp. 45–60

'Antisemitismus und Ambivalenz: Zu Achim von Arnims Erzählung *Die Majoratsherren*', in *Romantische Identitätskonstruktionen: Nation, Geschichte und (Auto)-Biographie*, ed. by Sheila Dickson and Walter Pape (Tübingen: Niemeyer, 2003), pp. 51–63

'Joseph II in Cultural Memory', in *Cultural Memory and Historical Consciousness in the German-Speaking World since 1500*, ed. by David Midgley and Christian Emden (Bern: Peter Lang, 2004), pp. 209–28

'The Limits of Toleration in Enlightenment Germany: Lessing, Goethe, and the Jews', in *Philosemitism, Antisemitism and 'the Jews': Perspectives from the Middle Ages to the Twentieth Century*, ed. by Tony Kushner and Nadia Valman (Aldershot: Ashgate, 2004), pp. 194–214

' "Conversations with Jehovah": Heine's Return to God', in *Denkbilder: Festschrift für Eoin Bourke*, ed. by Hermann Rasche and Christiane Schönfeld (Würzburg: Königshausen & Neumann, 2004), pp. 126–37

'Fritz Mauthner, the Myth of Prague German, and the Hidden Language of the Jew', in *Brückenschlag zwischen den Disziplinen: Fritz Mauthner als Schriftsteller, Kritiker und Kulturtheoretiker*, ed. by Jörg Thunecke and Elisabeth Leinfellner (Wuppertal: Arco, 2004), pp. 63–77

'Cultural Stereotypes and Social Anxiety in Georg Hermann's *Jettchen Gebert*', in *Georg Hermann: Deutsch-jüdischer Schriftsteller und Journalist, 1871–1943*, ed. by Godela Weiss-Sussex (Tübingen: Niemeyer, 2004), pp. 5–21

'Schnitzler and Wassermann', in *Confrontations/Accommodations: German-Jewish Literary and Cultural Relations from Heine to Wassermann: Essays in Honor of Jeffrey L. Sammons*, ed. by Mark H. Gelber (Tübingen: Niemeyer, 2004), pp. 249–62

'The Creative Dialogue between Brod and Kafka', in *Kafka, Zionism, and Beyond*, ed. by Mark H. Gelber (Tübingen: Niemeyer, 2004), pp. 283–96

'Gender Anxiety and the Shaping of the Self in Some Modernist Writers: Musil, Hesse, Hofmannsthal, Jahnn', in *The Cambridge Companion to the Modern German Novel*, ed. by Graham Bartram (Cambridge: Cambridge University Press, 2004), pp. 46–61

'Canetti and Nietzsche: An Introduction to *Masse und Macht*', in *A Companion to the Works of Elias Canetti*, ed. by Dagmar C. G. Lorenz (Rochester, NY: Camden House, 2004), pp. 201–16

'Poetry and Scepticism in the Wake of the Austrian Enlightenment: Blumauer, Grillparzer, Lenau', *Austrian Studies*, 12 (2004), 17–43

'Theodor Herzl et l'antisémitisme', *Austriaca*, 57 (June 2004), 61–71

'George, Nietzsche, and Nazism', in *A Companion to the Works of Stefan George*, ed. by Jens Rieckmann (Rochester, NY: Camden House, 2005), pp. 189–205

'"Der ungeheure Strindberg". Zu Kafkas Strindberg-Rezeption', in *Erfahrung der Fremde: Beiträge auf der 12. Internationalen Arbeitstagung 'Germanistische Forschungen zum literarischen Text', Vaasa 8.-10.5.2003*, ed. by Christoph Parry (Vaasa: Vaasan Yliopisto, 2005), pp. 85–99

'Kafka's Encounter with the Yiddish Theatre', in *The Yiddish Presence in European Literature*, ed. by Joseph Sherman and Ritchie Robertson (Oxford: Legenda, 2005), pp. 34–44

'The Limits of Metaphor in Nietzsche's *Genealogy of Morals*', *Nineteenth-Century Prose*, 32 (2005), 75–96

'Savonarola in Munich: A Reappraisal of Thomas Mann's *Fiorenza*', *Publications of the English Goethe Society*, 74 (2005), 51–66

'"Die Menschen zu ihrem Glück zwingen": Polemical and Judicial Violence in the Austrian Enlightenment', in *Violence, Culture and Identity: Essays on German and Austrian Literature, Politics and Society*, ed. by Helen Chambers (Bern: Peter Lang, 2006), pp. 86–99

'Schiller and the Jesuits', in *Schiller: National Poet, Poet of Nations*, ed. by Nicholas Martin (Amsterdam: Rodopi, 2006), pp. 179–200

'Kafka und die skandinavische Moderne', in *Franz Kafka und die Weltliteratur*, ed. by Manfred Engel and Dieter Lamping (Göttingen: Vandenhoeck & Ruprecht, 2006), pp. 144–65

'Narrative and Violence in George Saiko's *Der Mann im Schilf* (1955) and Hans Lebert's *Die Wolfshaut* (1960)', in *Schreiben gegen Krieg und Gewalt: Ingeborg Bachmann und die deutschsprachige Literatur 1945–1980*, ed. by Dirk Göttsche et al. (Göttingen: V & R unipress, 2006), pp. 131–43

'Poetry, Power, and Peter Huchel', in Mireille Gansel and Reiner Kunze, *'In Time of Need': A Conversation about Poetry, Resistance and Exile* (London: Libris, 2006), pp. 63–90

'Austrian Prose Fiction, 1918–1945', in *A History of Austrian Literature, 1918–2000*, ed. by Katrin Kohl and Ritchie Robertson (Rochester, NY: Camden House, 2006), pp. 53–74

'Sacrifice and Sacrament in *Der Zauberberg*', *Oxford German Studies*, 35 (2006), 55–65

'Canetti and British Anthropology', *Cultura Tedesca*, 30 (Jan.–June 2006), 31–38

'Goethe: *Wilhelm Meisters Lehrjahre*', in *Landmarks in the German Novel*, ed. by Peter Hutchinson (Bern: Peter Lang, 2007), pp. 31–48

'*Wallenstein*', in *Friedrich Schiller: Playwright, Poet, Philosopher, Historian*, ed. by Paul Kerry (Bern: Peter Lang, 2007), pp. 251–72

'Freud's Literary Imagination', in *The Academic Face of Psychoanalysis*, ed. by Louise Braddock and Michael Lacewing (London: Routledge, 2007), pp. 196–207

'Hofmannsthal as Sociologist: "Die Briefe des Zurückgekehrten"', in *Moderne begreifen: Zur Paradoxie eines sozio-ästhetischen Deutungsmusters*, ed. by Christine Magerski, Robert Savage and Christiane Weller (Wiesbaden: Deutscher Universitäts-Verlag, 2007), pp. 231–39

'Puritans into Revolutionaries: Butler's *Hudibras* and Ratschky's *Melchior Striegel*', *Austrian Studies*, 15 (2007), 17–40

'The Complexities of Caroline Pichler: Conflicting Role Models, Patriotic Commitment, and *The Swedes in Prague* (1827)', *Women in German Yearbook*, 23 (2007), 34–48

'Canetti, Freud, Lorenz, et le problème de la violence', *Austriaca*, 61 (2007), 67–77

'Mörike and the Higher Criticism', *Oxford German Studies*, 36 (2007), 47–59

'Religion and the Enlightenment: A Review Essay' (on Jonathan Sheehan, *The Enlightenment Bible*, and Jonathan Israel, *Enlightenment Contested*), *German History*, 25 (2007), 422–32

'Der Götterkrieg: Ein episches Motiv von Milton bis Heine', in *Harry ... Heinrich ... Henri Heine*, ed. by Dietmar Goltschnigg, Charlotte Grollegg-Edler and Peter Revers (Berlin: Schmidt, 2008), pp. 131–40

'Canetti and Violence', in *The Worlds of Elias Canetti*, ed. by Julian Preece and William C. Donahue (Newcastle: Cambridge Scholars Publishing, 2008), pp. 11–24

'Robert Hamerling and the Survival of Epic', *Austrian Studies*, 16 (2008), 142–53

'Women Warriors and the Origin of the State: Werner's *Wanda* and Kleist's *Penthesilea*', in *Women and Death: Warlike Women in the German Literary and Cultural Imagination since 1500*, ed. by Sarah Colvin and Helen Watanabe-O'Kelly (Rochester, NY: Camden House, 2009), pp. 61–85

'Alfred Döblin's Feeling for Snow: The Poetry of Fact in *Berge Meere und Giganten*', in *Alfred Döblin: Paradigms of Modernism*, ed. by Steffan Davies and Ernest Schonfield (Berlin: de Gruyter, 2009), pp. 215–28

'Virtue versus "Schwärmerei" in Lessing's *Emilia Galotti*', *German Life and Letters*, 62 (2009), 39–52

'Affinités épiques et libération sexuelle dans *La Pucelle* de Voltaire', *Revue Voltaire*, 9 (2009), 29–44

'Curiosity in the Austrian Enlightenment', *Oxford German Studies*, 38 (2009), 129–42

'Recent Work on Nietzsche' (review-article), *Nineteenth-Century Prose*, 36 (2009), 211–32

'Aufklärung, Kulturkampf und Antiklerikalismus als Themen der österreichischen Literaturgeschichte', in *Kanon und Literaturgeschichte: Beiträge zu den Jahrestagungen 2005 und 2006 der ehemaligen Werfel-StipendiatInnen*, ed. by Arnulf Knafl (Vienna: Praesens, 2010), pp. 187–201

'Jesuits, Jews, and Thugs: Myths of Conspiracy and Infiltration from Dickens to Thomas Mann', in *In the Embrace of the Swan: Anglo-German Mythologies in Literature, the Visual Arts and Cultural Theory*, ed. by Rüdiger Görner and Angus Nicholls (Berlin: de Gruyter, 2010), pp. 126–46

'"Ich" and "wir": Singular and Collective Narrators in Kafka's Short Prose', in *Kafka und die kleine Prosa der Moderne*, ed. by Manfred Engel and Ritchie Robertson (Würzburg: Königshausen & Neumann, 2010 [actually 2011]), pp. 67–77

'Der patriotische Minister in Grillparzers *Ein treuer Diener seines Herrn* und Hebbels *Agnes Bernauer*', *Hebbel-Jahrbuch* 2010, pp. 95–119

'Cosmopolitanism, Patriotism and Nationalism in the German and Austrian Enlightenment', in *Enlightenment Cosmopolitanism*, ed. by David Adams and Galin Tihanov (London: Legenda, 2011), pp. 12–30

'Wielands *Hexameron von Rosenhain* und die Anfänge der deutschen Novellistik', in *Kleine anthropologische Prosaformen der Goethezeit (1750–1830)*, ed. by Alexander Košenina and Carsten Zelle, Bochumer Quellen und Forschungen zum achtzehnten Jahrhundert, 4 (Hannover: Wehrhahn, 2011), pp. 301–17

'From Martyr to Vampire: The Figure of Mary Stuart in Drama from Vondel to Swinburne', in *Who is this Schiller now? Essays on his Reception and Significance*, ed. by Jeffrey High, Nicholas Martin and Norbert Oellers (Rochester, NY: Camden House, 2011), pp. 321–39

'Kafka, Goffman, and the Total Institution', in *Kafka for the Twenty-First Century*, ed. by Stanley Corngold and Ruth V. Gross (Rochester, NY: Camden House, 2011), pp. 136–50

'German Literature and Thought, 1810–1890', in *The Oxford Companion to German History*, ed. by Helmut Walser Smith (Oxford: Oxford University Press, 2011), pp. 260–77

'Edwin Muir, Kafka, and German Modernism', in *Scottish and International Modernisms*, ed. by Emma Dymock and Margery Palmer McCulloch (Glasgow: Association for Scottish Literary Studies, 2011), pp. 20–33

'Wieland's Nude Bathers: Visual Pleasure and the Female Gaze', *German Life and Letters*, 64 (2011), 31–42

'Nestroy's Dickensian Realism', *Oxford German Studies*, 40 (2011), 270–84

'Keller and Ariosto: The Seductive Imagination in *Der grüne Heinrich*', *Publications of the English Goethe Society*, 80 (2011), 127–42

'Myth versus Enlightenment in Kafka's *Das Schloss*', *Monatshefte*, 103 (2011), 385–95

'W. G. Sebald as a Critic of Austrian Literature', *Journal of European Studies*, 41 (2011), 305–22

'"Das ist nun einmahl slawische Sitte!" Die Bewohner Galiziens in Reiseberichten und Statistiken des späten 18. Jahrhunderts', in *Galizien im Diskurs: Inklusion, Exklusion, Repräsentation*, ed. by Paula Giersch, Florian Krobb and Franziska Schössler (Frankfurt a.M.: Peter Lang, 2012), pp. 42–56

'Nietzsche in Glasgow: Alexander Tille, John Davidson and Edwin Muir', in *Scotland and the 19th-Century World*, ed. by Gerard Carruthers, David Goldie and Alastair Renfrew (Amsterdam: Rodopi, 2012), pp. 213–30

'Max Brod's Novel *Tycho Brahes Weg zu Gott*: A Tale of Two Astronomers', in *Kafka, Prag und der Erste Weltkrieg*, ed. by Manfred Engel and Ritchie Robertson (Würzburg: Königshausen & Neumann, 2012), pp. 143–58

'Thomas Mann (1875–1955): Modernism and Ideas', in *The Cambridge Companion to European Novelists*, ed. by Michael Bell (Cambridge: Cambridge University Press, 2012), pp. 343–60

'Polymorphous Eroticism in the Early Plays of Hans Henny Jahnn', in *Modernist Eroticisms*, ed. by Anna Katharina Schaffner and Shane Weller (Basingstoke: Palgrave Macmillan, 2012), pp. 105–22

'Hoffmann's *Die Elixiere des Teufels* and the Lasting Appeal of Conspiracy Theories', *Limbus: Australian Yearbook of German Literary and Cultural Studies*, 5 (2012), 11–31

'Kafka's Writings: Private Confessions or Public Property?', *Bodleian Library Record*, 25.2 (2012), 84–93

'Freemasons vs Jesuits: Conspiracy Theories in Enlightenment Germany', *Times Literary Supplement*, 12 Oct. 2012, pp. 13–15

'Childhood's End: The Early Poetry of Franz Werfel', *Oxford German Studies*, 41 (2012), 348–62

(With Alexander Košenina) 'Lessing as Journalist and Controversialist', in *Lessing and the German Enlightenment*, ed. by Ritchie Robertson (Oxford: Voltaire Foundation, 2013), pp. 39–63

'Goethe and Machiavelli', in *The Present Word. Culture, Society and the Site of Literature: Essays in Honour of Nicholas Boyle*, ed. by John Walker (London: Legenda, 2013), pp. 126–37

'*On the Sublime* and Schiller's Theory of Tragedy', in *Philosophical Readings: Online Yearbook of Philosophy*, 5 (2013), 194–212 (special issue: *Reading Schiller. Ethics, Aesthetics, and Religion*, ed. Laura Anna Macor; <http://philosophicalreadings.files.wordpress.com/2013/09/pr2013.pdf>)

'Schiller, Kant, Machiavelli, and the Ethics of Betrayal', in *Playing False: Representations of Betrayal*, ed. by Kristina Mendicino and Betiel Wasihun (Oxford: Peter Lang, 2013), pp. 121–45

'Raabe und Shakespeare: Zum Spiel mit Zitaten in *Kloster Lugau, Die Akten des Vogelsangs* und anderen Texten', *Jahrbuch der Raabe-Gesellschaft*, 2013, pp. 1–22

'Introduction', Wilhelm Raabe, *The Birdsong Papers*, trans. by Michael Ritterson (London: MHRA, 2013), pp. vii–xvii

'Johann Pezzl (1756–1823): Enlightenment in the Satirical Mode', in *Enlightenment and Catholicism in Europe: A Transnational History*, ed. by Jeffrey D. Burson and Ulrich L. Lehner (Notre Dame, IN: University of Notre Dame Press, 2014), pp. 227–45

'Sex as Sin or Salvation: Max Brod's *Heidentum Christentum Judentum* and Kafka's *Das Schloß*', in *Kafka und die Religion in der Moderne*, ed. by Manfred Engel and Ritchie Robertson (Würzburg: Königshausen & Neumann, 2014), pp. 119–34

'Children and Childhood in Kafka's Work', in *Kafkas 'Betrachtung': Neue Lektüren*, ed. by Carolin Duttlinger (Freiburg: Rombach, 2014), pp. 179–99

'Das Bild des Kindes bei Kafka im Lichte von Ellen Keys *Das Jahrhundert des Kindes*', in *Influx: Der deutsch-skandinavische Kulturaustausch um 1900*, ed. by Søren Fauth and Gísli Magnússon (Würzburg: Königshausen & Neumann, 2014), pp. 217–30

'Kafka et le contexte historique: L'Exemple de *La Colonie pénitentiaire*', *Cahier de l'Herne: Kafka 2014*, ed. by Jean-Pierre Morel and Wolfgang Asholt, pp. 35–41

'"Le Chemin de retour au pays de l'enfance": Karl Kraus, la psychanalyse et l'ambivalence de l'enfance', *Europe: revue mensuelle littéraire*, 91 (May 2014), 91–103

'*Humanität, Bildung, Kultur*: Germany's Civilising Values', in *The Routledge Handbook of German Politics and Culture*, ed. by Sarah Colvin (London: Routledge, 2015), pp. 20–33

'Nietzsche and the Scottish Enlightenment', in *Fontane and Cultural Mediation: Translation and Reception in the Nineteenth Century*, ed. by Ritchie Robertson and Michael White (London: Legenda, 2015), pp. 120–33

'"The past is a foreign country": Constructions of History in Novels by Lion Feuchtwanger, Alfred Döblin and Arnold Zweig', in *Recasting the 'Other': Readings in German-Jewish Interwar Culture* (*Yearbook of European Jewish Literature Studies*, 2), ed. by Karin Neuburger (Berlin: de Gruyter, 2015), pp. 253–69

'Modernist Style and the "inward turn" in German-language Fiction', in *A History of the Modernist Novel*, ed. by Gregory Castle (Cambridge: Cambridge University Press, 2015), pp. 293–310

'*Weltliteratur* from Voltaire to Goethe', *Comparative Critical Studies*, 12 (2015), 163–81

'Émancipation et ambivalence' (on Heine), *Europe: revue mensuelle littéraire*, 93 (Aug–Sep 2015), 41–53

'The Rediscovery of Machiavelli in Napoleon's Germany: Heinrich von Kleist and his Contemporaries', *Ethics and Politics*, 17 (2015), iii. 58-77

'Berlin, Machiavelli and the Enlightenment', in *Isaiah Berlin and the Enlightenment*, ed. by Laurence Brockliss and Ritchie Robertson (Oxford: Oxford University Press, 2016)

'Ancients, Moderns, and the Future: The Querelle in Germany from Winckelmann to Schiller', in *Ancients and Moderns in Europe: Comparative Perspectives*, ed. by Paddy Bullard and Alexis Tadié (Oxford: Voltaire Foundation, 2016), pp. 257-75

'Felicitas Hoppe als letzte deutsche Weltreisende', in *Ehrliche Erfindungen: Felicitas Hoppe zwischen Tradition und Transmoderne*, ed. by Svenja Frank and Julia Ilgner (Bielefeld: transcript verlag, 2016), pp. 45-52

'Dreams as Literature: Heine, Dora, Freud', in *Writing the Dream / Écrire le rêve*, ed. by Bernard Dieterle and Manfred Engel (Würzburg: Königshausen & Neumann, 2017 [actually 2016]), pp. 57-69

'The Catholic Enlightenment: Some Reflections on Recent Research', *German History*, 34 (2016), 630-45

'Style' and 'Kafka as Reader'. forthcoming in *Kafka in Context*, ed. by Carolin Duttlinger (Cambridge: Cambridge University Press)

'Suffering in art: Laocoon between Lessing and Goethe', in *Re-thinking Lessing's 'Laocoon'*, ed. by Avi Lifschitz and Michael Squire (Oxford: Oxford University Press, 2017)

'The Reformation of Catholic Festival Culture in Eighteenth-Century Austria', forthcoming in *Austrian Studies*, 25 (2017)

'Frederick's Anti-Machiavel: Principles and Practice', forthcoming in *Frederick the Great and the Republic of Letters*, ed. by Katrin Kohl (Oxford: Voltaire Foundation)

'Everyday Transcendence? Robert Musil, William James, and Mysticism', forthcoming in *History of European Ideas*

INDEX

Lightning Source UK Ltd.
Milton Keynes UK
UKHW031354301018

331465UK00002B/60/P